SRI RAMAKRISHNA
THE GREAT MASTER

Vol. I

By

SWAMI SARADANANDA
(A Direct Disciple of Sri Ramakrishna)

Original in Bengali

TRANSLATION

BY

SWAMI JAGADANANDA

SRI RAMAKRISHNA MATH
MYLAPORE, MADRAS-600 004
INDIA

Published by :
© The President,
Sri Ramakrishna Math,
Mylapore, Madras 600 004.

3/98

Printed in India at
Sri Ramakrishna Math Printing Press,
Mylapore, Madras 600 004.

gift

PUBLISHER'S NOTE TO THE FIRST EDITION

WE have much pleasure in presenting to the public "*Sri Rama-krishna the Great Master*"—the most comprehensive, authentic and critical estimate of the life, Sadhana and teachings of Bhagavan Sri Ramakrishna. Sixty-six years have rolled down the stream of time since Sri Ramakrishna left the mortal coil. But the wave of spirituality raised by his life, has touched even the distant shores of both the hemispheres and is resurgent still in all its native potency in the thought-life of the different countries of the civilized world of today. In India his name has become a household world, a symbol of hope and solace and a sacred Mantra to conjure with. His inspired utterances have brought light where utter darkness prevailed before, solace to many a suffering soul and peace to many a distracted mind. The life which could have such a marvellous influence within such a short period, it is needless to say, is of unprecedented potency, whose full depth and significance it will take ages to get revealed to humanity.

Descriptions of this wonderful life were given to the world by his various disciples and admirers from time to time in different languages since his disappearance from earth. But none of them embodied a detailed account of this unique personality. Srimat Swami Saradanandaji Maharaj, a direct disciple of Sri Ramakrishna and the General Secretary of the Ramakrishna Math and Mission from its very beginning to his passing away in 1927, feeling the necessity of such a biography, brought out five volumes in Bengali under the title Sri *Sri Ramakrishna Lila-prasanga* which contain many unpublished details of the life of the Master and can fairly be called an exhaustive treatment of the subject. The Swami wanted to write an English version of his Bengali work, and in fact, he translated a few chapters which appeared in the two periodicals of the Mission, the *Vedanta Kesari* and the *Prabuddha Bharata* but owing to his illness and various other causes, he could not complete the work. The eager-ness of the general public outside Bengal to know more details of the wonderful life of the Master came to our notice , and we thought we would be doing some service to our eager readers, if not to humanity at large, if we could present them with a faithful English translation of the beautiful Bengali biography.

Srimat Swami Jagadanandaji, a very senior and learned monk of our Order, acceded to our request to undertake this Herculean task of translating the whole work of five volumes into English and has left us under a deep debt of gratitude. It is a matter of great regret that he passed away last December before this remarkable work of his devotion could see the light of day. He took up this translation when he was verging on seventy, but finished the work in an incredibly short time and passed it on to the Editors. A disciple of the Holy Mother, one who knew the revered Swami Saradanandaji Maharaj and several other direct disciples of Sri Ramakrishna intimately, the Swami is known to many readers of our literature and students of Vedanta as a very good teacher of the Scriptures, as the anonymous editor of many religious books and as the translator of some Vedantic Text-books like Sri San-karacharya's *Upadesha Sahasri*. His illuminating classes were a treat to all, young and old, lay and monastic students in the Uttarakhand. One would always notice in him a happy but rare combination of Jnana and Bhakti. Untiring in work and uncompro-mising in his adherence to the Siddhantas (conclusions) of Vedanta, he was throughout conspicuous by his great devotion to the Master and the Holy Mother.

Swami Nirvedananda, the learned writer of " Sri Rama-krishna and Spiritual Renaissance" (in the Cultural Heritage of India, Vol. II) and other books, has written a short but beautiful life of Srimat Swami Saradanandaji Maharaj.[1] This will give the reader an inkling of the real personality of the author of the book and will partly serve the purpose of an introduction to it. We are much beholden to him for this valuable addition to this work.

Prof. K. Subramanyam, M.A., L.T., Vice-Principal, Viveka-nanda College, Madras, has kindly gone through the entire manuscript and has ably edited it for us . He deserves our hearty thanks for this noble act.

Dr. Nandalal Bose, the famous artist of Santiniketan (Visva-bharati), has very kindiy drawn the Dust cover (Pancha-vati at Dakshineswar) as a labour of love. We are indeed grateful to him.

---

[1] This has been shifted to the second volume.

In bringing out such a big volume, we have received substantial help in various ways from many lay and monastic friends, who prefer to remain unknown soldiers. We offer our sincere thanks to them.

Diacritical marks, have not been used in the body of the book, but they have been explained and the pronunciation of important Indian words has been shown with diacritics in the Index.

A word about the book itself: *Sri Sri Ramakrishna Lila-prasanga* holds a unique place in hagiography. The life-story of a divine personality worshipped by millions as an Incarnation of God has never been written in this wise by any one of his apostles. Yet the reader will notice how the author has made the book so reliable and interesting by giving it a modern touch and using the scientific method all through. The book is not simply a biography of the latest Incarnation of the modern age; it combines the biography with a lucid study of the various cults of religion, mysticism and philosophy obtaining in India and elsewhere from the prehistoric times down to the modern era. The subject-matter, the life of Sri Ramakrishna, is nothing short of an encyclopaedia of religion and philosophy.

It will not be out of place to make some mention of the Tantras, the sacred literature of the Shaktas of Bengal and else-where. Sri John Woodroffe *alias* Arthur Avalon, and his Indian collaborators have made the Tantras partly available to the English-reading public. As they have used the scientific method, their studies of the Tantras have much appeal to the modern mind. Sri Ramakrishna practised all the disciplines enjoined in the sixty-four principal Tantras under the guidance of a good teacher. Some practices of the Tantras known as "left" which were not entirely ruled out by Sri Ramakrishna have been actually re-oriented by him. Much of modern scientific teaching is consonant with the fundamental teaching of the Tantras. Things or practices which *seem* repulsive to the modern mind are not actually so. Readers, endowed with an exalted vision and the modern spirit of enquiry into truth, will be able to understand that the Tantric aspirants' practices involving contacts with what are termed as lowly, bad, ugly and vulgar, helped them sublimate such feelings and sentiments to the extent of making them realize the divine power which is always high, true, good and beautiful. We crave the indulgence of the readers for the detailed description of Sri Ramakrishna's Tantric Sadhana as we have not sacrificed the beauty and the substance of that episode to satisfy the claims of "modern" taste.

A right attitude is also necessary to enter into the spirit of Sri Ramakrishna's Sadhana according to the Madhura Bhava of the Vaishnava school. We trust our readers will not lack it. "Where you cannot unriddle, learn to trust" is an adage that may be very helpful here. There is nothing queer or strange in the flights of the genius of one of the greatest master-mystics of the world like Sri Ramakrishna.

May a serious perusal of this new book inspire humanity to take a step forward on its march to Truth!

Sri Ramakrishna Math   PUBLISHER
Mylapore, Madras-4
October, 1952.

PUBLISHER'S NOTE TO THE FIFTH EDITION

The fifth edition of *Sri Ramakrishna the Great Master* is appearing in two parts. Both the reader and the buyer will find this division convenient. The Index and the Life of the author, Swami Saradananda, are shifted to the second part, in order to facilitate the division of the book into two equal parts. The new edition has also been carefully revised so as to make it more readable.

PUBLISHER

October 1978

CONTENTS

Part One

HISTORIC BACKGROUND AND EARLY LIFE

Part Two

AS THE SPIRITUAL ASPIRANT

Part Three

AS THE SPIRITUAL TEACHER (1)

Bhagavan Sri Ramakrishna

Swami Saradananda

Sri Ramakrishna The Great Master

PART ONE

BĀLYABHĀVA

OR

HISTORIC BACKGROUND AND EARLY LIFE

PREFACE BY THE AUTHOR

BY the grace of God, the First Part of *Sri Ramakrishna The Great Master* is now published. It contains a detailed account of the early life of Sri Ramakrishna and the purpose of his advent. An attempt is made herein to present to the reader the mental picture we have formed by hearing from various people a number of unrelated incidents of the Master's life at that time. Although persons like Hridayram Mukhopadhyaya, Ramlal Chattopadhyaya and others gave as much help as they could for ascertaining the correct dates of certain events, there still remains, in places, some doubt on such points. They could not produce the horoscopes of Sri Ramakrishna's father, his elder brother and other near relatives; but they gave instead, the approximate dates of certain events connected with the Master's life, saying, for example: "At the time of Sri Ramakrishna's birth his father was about sixty-one or sixty-two years old", "Ramkumar, his eldest brother, was his senior by about thirty-one or thirty-two years", and so on.

Nevertheless, the reader will be convinced, when he reads the fifth chapter of this part, viz., "A Great Soul Is Born", that there is no doubt regarding the correctness of the date of birth of Sri Ramakrishna as recorded therein. We have been reassured about this and many other events recorded in this book by the Master's own words, some of which were heard by the author himself. It is to the Master, therefore, that we are beholden for such information. When we first set about describing certain periods of his life, it seemed impossible for us to narrate the events of his childhood and youth in such a detailed and connected way. Realizing, therefore, that it is by the grace of the Lord, who "makes the dumb wax eloquent and the lame nimble enough to cross a mountain", that this has become possible, we bow down to Him again and again.

It may also be said, in conclusion, that if the reader, after finishing this part of the book, goes through the other parts, namely, "As the Spiritual Aspirant" and "As the Spiritual Teacher (I & II)", he will find the history of the Master's life recorded chronologically from the date of his birth to the year 1881.*

---

*Later, another volume, "The Master in the Divine Mood, and Narendra Nath" was added to bring the Life up to 1886.—Tr.

INTRODUCTION

(TOPICS; 1. Spirituality as pivot of life in India. 2. Birth of great souls is its cause. 3. Religion in India founded on realisation. 4. Development of the idea of the divine incarnation. 5. Personal God during the age of devotion. 6. Worship of the spiritual teacher (Guru). 7. Doctrine of divine incarnation based on the Vedas and Samadhi experience. 8. God's compassion and the idea of God incarnate. 9. Sastras on the divine nature of incarnations. 10. Incarnation's unbroken memory. 11. Incarnations give new shape to religion. 12. When do incarnations come? 13. Advent of the incarnation in the modern age.)

1. When we make a comparative study of the ideals and traditions of India in spiritual matters with those obtaining in other countries of the world, we find a vast difference between them. From time immemorial, India has accepted the supersensuous spiritual entities like God, soul and the hereafter as absolute facts, whose existence could be realised and verified even here in our earthly life, and has, as a consequence, formulated ways of life for man, both individual and collective, that are conducive to the attainment of this goal. The national life of the country has therefore been characterised by an intense spirituality all through the ages.

2. When we seek for the cause of this absorbing interest of the Indian mind in matters spiritual, we find it in the frequent appearance in this country of divine personages possessed of a direct knowledge of these spiritual entities. Because of the frequent opportunities to witness the lives and experiences of such personages and make a systematic study of them, there developed in the Indian mind a deep interest and faith in supersensuous spiritual experiences, visions and manifestations of spiritual power. India's national life was thus established from very ancient times on a solid foundation of spirituality. Keeping a firm hold on these spiritual ideals, this country developed a society based on a unique set of customs and practices which enabled its members to attain to the ultimate object of God-realisation in a most natural manner through the performance of their daily duties according to their special tastes and qualities. As these rules and regulations have

been followed from generation to generation, the spiritual ideals of India have remained alive and vigorous. Consequently men and women here have, even today, a strong conviction that with the help of austerity, self-control, and intense aspiration, everyone can have a direct experience of God, the source of this world of becoming, and gain union with Him.

3. That the religion of India is founded in God-vision becomes clear, when we reflect upon the significance of words and expressions such as Rishi (seer), Apta (one who has attained the goal of life), Adhikarika (one possessed of authority), Prakriti-lina Purusha (a person merged in the cause of the universe), and the like. These names have been used since Vedic times to describe the teachers who came to re-establish religion. It is beyond doubt that such men were designated by these names because they had given proof of their unique powers, acquired as a result of direct knowledge of the reality beyond the senses. This statement holds good in the case of every one of them, from the Rishis of the Vedic period to the divine incarnations of the Puranic (Epic) Age.

4. It is evident that certain Rishis of the Vedic period came to be recognised during the Puranic period as incarnations. In the Vedic period it was understood that certain persons had the power to perceive the reality beyond the senses, but the fact that the intensity of this power had variations in individuals, was not recognised. People were content to call all of them "Rishis" as a class. In course of time, however, with the growth of refinement in thought and philosophic insight, it was realized that not all the Rishis were endowed with the same degree of power or capacity for spiritual enlightenment. In this respect, some of them shone like the sun, some like the moon, some again like bright stars, and still others like ordinary fire-flies. So the philosophers began to classify the Rishis according to the spiritual capacities they evinced. Thus in the Philosophic Age, some Rishis came to be known as Adhikarika-Purushas (persons of special authority). Even Kapila, the founder of the Sankhya philosophy, who was sceptical regarding the existence of God, had to accept the existence of these Rishis; for he could not doubt what he actually saw. Accordingly, in his system of philosophy these Adhikarika-Purushas were included in the class of emancipated beings known as "those merged in Prakriti". Searching for the cause of the advent of these uniquely powerful persons, the Sankhya philosophers came to the conclusion

that, endowed with good qualities such as purity, self-control, etc., they had acquired infinite knowledge, but that an intense desire to do good to the people had prevented them, for a time, from being merged in the real nature of the Self of infinite glory. Identifying themselves with the all-powerful Prakriti, they came to look upon themselves as endowed with these powers. and became the centres of their manifestation. Equipped thus with special powers, they did good to men in an infinite number of ways for one cycle, and, at the end of it became completely identified with the Self.

5. The Sankhya teachers have again divided the " persons merged in Prakriti", according to the differences in their powers, into two classes: "Kalpaniyamaka Isvara" (or ruler for one cycle) and "Isvarakotis" (or those who are satellites of the former).

After the Philosophic Age, came a period when love for the Divine was especially developed. At that time, through the overwhelming influence of Vedanta, people came to believe in an Isvara, the all-pervading Person, the aggregate of all beings. They acquired also the strong faith that Knowledge and Yoga could be had to the fullest degree by meditation on Him with single-minded devotion. And they soon came to believe that the Isvara described in the Sankhya system as the ruler of a cycle, was either a partial or a full manifestation of the all-pervading Personal Isvara, who is by nature eternally pure, eternally awake and eternally free. Thus the belief in the doctrine of God-incarnate arose in the Puranic Age, and those Rishis of the Vedic Age who possessed unique and extraordinary qualities began to be known as incarnations. It was the advent of persons endowed with such qualities that made people gradually believe in the existence of incarnations. Founded on the supersensuous visions and experiences of these persons, the unshakable edifice of religion gradually rose, like the snow-capped Himalayas, to reach the sky. Because these persons had achieved the highest goal of life, they were also called "Aptas", and their words, expressing the highest knowledge, came to be known as the Vedas.

6. Another reason for accepting certain Rishis as incarnations was the practice of worshipping the spiritual teacher (Guru). In India, from the time of the Vedas and the Upanishads, men and women worshipped the teacher, the giver of spiritual knowledge, with great reverence. This worship, combined with meditation,

convinced them in course of time that no man could occupy the
position of a spiritual teacher till the divine, superconscious power
manifested itself in him.   At first they looked upon, and worshipped,
the Guru as belonging to a different and higher type of humanity,
because they found that, in contrast with the selfishness of the
ordinary human being, the pure teacher did good to the people out
of pure compassion and without any selfish motive. Later, through
faith, reverence and devotion, they perceived directly in the Guru
the manifestation of the divine power, and this convinced them
more and more of his divine attributes. They had prayed for so
long a time to the gracious Lord, imploring Him to " protect them
with His compassionate face" (*Rudra yat te dakshinam mukham,
tena mam pahi nityam*)*, and their prayer was granted at last.   The
compassion of the Lord stood revealed before them in the person
of the Guru.

7.   When men had proceeded thus far in the worship of the
Guru, it did not take them long to identify him—through whom
the special Lila (play) of the divine power was being manifested—
with the knowledge-giving, and benign aspect of the divine Lord.
Thus it seems that the continued worship of the Guru strengthened
the idea of God-incarnate. As already mentioned, the doctrine of
incarnation actually dates from the Puranic Age, but the idea itself
originated in the Vedic Age.   The varied experiences of the attributes, functions and nature of Isvara during the ages of the Vedas,
Upanishads and Darsanas (philosophical systems) appear to have
gradually assumed a definite shape and given rise to the belief in
the doctrine of God-incarnate.   It may also be that in the age of the
Upanishads, Rishis, coming down by the reverse process from the
state of Samadhi, which they had achieved by the path of "not this",
"not this" and through self-control, austerity, etc., realized that
the whole universe was actually the manifestation of the unqualified
(Nirguna) Brahman.   It was only then, perhaps, that they acquired
devotion to the all-pervading Brahman with attributes (Saguna),
called Isvara and began to worship Him. Having thus obtained a
clear idea of Isvara's qualities, actions, nature, etc., they might have
become convinced of the possibility of His being manifested in a
special way.

---

*Svetāśvatara Upaniṣad, 4.21.

8. It was in the Puranic Age, then, that belief in the existence of incarnations was especially developed. Notwithstanding various defects in the development of spirituality in that age, it was faith in the glory of the God-incarnate that made it really great. This belief in the existence of the incarnation also enabled men to comprehend the eternal play of the Saguna Brahman. As a consequence they realized that God, the Cause of the universe, was their only guide in the spiritual world; and they were convinced that the infinite compassion of the divine Lord would never let them be doomed, however reprobate they might be, but that He would in every age take form as an incarnation, discover new paths suited to man's nature and make Self-realization easy for him.

9. It will not be out of place to give here a brief summary of the essential ideas recorded in the Smritis and Puranas about the birth, action, etc. of the divine incarnation, who is by nature eternally pure, awake and free. Unlike a Jiva (mortal being), he never gets entangled in, or bound by, actions. For, established in the bliss of the Atman from his very birth, no selfish idea of worldly enjoyment arises in his mind as it does in the case of a Jiva. His whole life is dedicated to the good of others. Being always free from the meshes of Maya, he retains the memory of his previous lives.

10. It may be asked: Does he have that unbroken memory from childhood? The Puranas reply: Although latent within him, it is not always manifest during his childhood. But as soon as his body and mind mature, he becomes aware of it with little or no effort. This applies to all his actions. Since he assumes a human body, he has to behave in all respects like a human being.

11. As soon as the body and mind of the incarnation fully develop, the aim of his life is revealed to him. He then realizes that the sole purpose of his coming is to re-establish religion. Whatever aids are needed to fulfil that purpose, they come of themselves to him in unexpected ways. He walks in light where others grope in darkness. Fearless himself, he attains his goal and beckons to men to follow in his footsteps. Untrodden paths leading to the realization of Brahman beyond Maya and of Isvara, the cause of the universe, are discovered by him again and again, from age to age.

12. The authors of the Puranas did not confine their study of incarnations to a mere analysis of their actions and characteristics; they also came to definite conclusions regarding the occasion of their appearance in the world. It is the verdict of history that

with the passage of time the Sanatana Dharma (Religion Eternal) has a tendency to enter periodically into ages of decay and decline. In such periods men, deluded by the inscrutable power of Maya, begin to look upon the world and its pleasures as the sole concern of their lives. Eternal verities like the Self, Isvara, liberation etc, are looked upon as imaginings of dreamers and poets of a bygone age steeped in delusion and darkness. But when men at last discover that no amount of wealth and worldly enjoyment, obtained by fair means or foul, can fill the void in their hearts, and when they find themselves overwhelmed by the waves of the shoreless sea of despair, they cry out in the anguish of their hearts for deliverance. It is then that, out of His innate compassion for weak humanity, God incarnates Himself and frees the Religion Eternal from the encrustations of ages, thus restoring it to the pristine state of luminous purity like the moon freed from the mouth of Rahu* after an eclipse. Man is then brought back to the path of Dharma by the divine power. Every happening in this world has a cause, and accordingly the Lord, too, assumes a body in His Lila only when a universal need demands it. When such a want becomes overwhelmingly felt in every part of society, the infinite mercy of the Lord becomes, as it were crystallized, and He appears as the spiritual teacher of the world. This is the conclusion that the authors of the Puranas have arrived at after witnessing the repeated appearance of incarnations.

13. It is then the necessity of an age that calls forth an incarnation of God, the all-knowing teacher of the world, to shed a new light on religion. The land of India, which has always been the cradle of religion and spirituality, has become holy and sanctified by the footprints of incarnations again and again throughout the ages. Incarnations of transcendent greatness have appeared in India, even up to the present time, whenever the necessity for them has arisen. It is well known how, a little more than four hundred years ago, the shining example of Bhagavan Sri Chaitanya made people lose themselves in ecstasy in singing the name of Hari. Has such a time recurred? Has India, shorn of its glory and reduced to an object of contempt to foreigners, once again aroused the compassion of the Lord to incarnate Himself? That this has

---

* A demon in Hindu mythology, said to cause the eclipse by swallowing the sun and the moon.

happened, will become clear on a perusal of the life-story of the great soul, possessed of an infinite urge to do good, which is recorded herein. India has once more been blessed by the coming, in response to the need of the present age, of the One who, incarnating Himself as Sri Rama, as Sri Krishna and as other incarnations in the past, renewed the eternal religion again and again through the ages.

CHAPTER 1

THE NEED OF THE AGE

(TOPICS: 1. Power and progress of man in modern times.
2. Their spread from the West to the East. 3. Consequently the
Western ways of life became the standard of progress. 4. The
cause and the course of progress in the West. 5. Unspiritual
outlook results in dissatisfaction. 6. Selfishness and sensuality
the consequence of 'progress' in the Western sense. 7. Religion
the foundation of the ancient national life of India. 8. India
never made worldly enjoyments its ideal. 9. Occupation of
India by the West and its result. 10. Dangers of revitalising
India in imitation of the West. 11. National life of India; its
merits and demerits. 12. Western thought the cause of present
decline of religion. 13. God incarnates once again to stop
decline of religion.)

1. Even an ordinary person can see how, with the help of knowledge, wealth and self-effort, man is progressing at present in every
field. It seems as if he refuses to set a limit to his advance in any
department of life. Not satisfied with travelling on land and water,
he has invented a new machine to fly in the sky; his curiosity has
goaded him to go down to the bottom of the sea and to explore
seething volcanoes; he has scaled mountains covered with perpetual
snow, crossed the seas and observed accurately the mysteries of the
various regions of the world; he has discovered signs of life, common
with his own, pulsating in creepers, plants and trees. He has
extended his knowledge by subjecting all beings to his observation
and experimentation. Achieving control over the five elements—
earth, water, fire, air and ether—he has become acquainted with
innumerable facts relating to this earth of ours. Still unsatisfied,
he is eager to discover the secrets of distant stars and planets and
is already successful to some extent in his quest. Nor is there any
lack of effort on his part to investigate the laws of the inner life.
By experiment and research he is continually discovering new
truths in that domain. He has reached the conclusion that one
species of beings evolves into another and that the mind consists
merely of subtle matter, and therefore has a beginning and an end.
He is now assured that, as in the external, so also in the internal

world, every event is regulated by an inviolable law; and he is now familiar with the subtle laws governing irrational mental impulses, like the urge to commit suicide. Again although he has no positive evidence regarding the survival of the individual, the study of history has convinced him that the national life not only continues but also evolves. Thus, finding the fulfilment of the individual life in that of the nation, he wages perpetual war against ignorance with the aid of science and co-operative undertakings in order to achieve success in this regard. Imagining that through perpetual struggle, he can discover the most hidden regions of the external and internal worlds and can achieve eternal progress, he has launched the boat of his life on the current of endless desires.

2. This materialistic conception of life, based on the multiplication of wants, originated chiefly in the West. But a good deal of its influence is noticeable in India and other Eastern countries also. As science daily brings the East and the West closer to each other, the Eastern outlook on life is gradually undergoing a change and conforming more and more to the Western pattern. This becomes clear from a study of the history of Persia, China, Japan, India and other Oriental countries. For better or for worse, Western thought is, beyond any doubt, exercising a great influence on the East. It appears as if the whole world will, in course of time, be pervaded by Western ideas.

3. For an answer to the question whether such a conception of life has brought about good or bad results, we must go particularly to the West, where we shall also discover its source and its nature. Such an investigation will show us how far the early ideas of the West have resulted in progress or deterioration, and whether there has been loss or gain in the quantum of happiness available for man. When this has once been ascertained from the point of view of the individual and the nation in the West, the same process can, without difficulty, be extended to other countries, taking also into account the length of time they have been under these modern influences.

4. History has recorded in very clear terms, that from ancient times the severe cold in the dominant Western countries made men intensely body-conscious. This made them selfish. At the same time they realized that their selfish interests were best served by united effort, which in turn made them patriotic. The pursuit of self-interest and patriotism led them, in course of time, to wage

war against neighbouring nations and appropriate their land and wealth. With the improvement of living conditions and consequent lessening of the keenness of struggle for existence, men gradually acquired the capacity to look into themselves and seek learning and cultivate virtues. They felt more and more drawn towards these higher pursuits instead of being satisfied with the mere struggle for existence. But now they encountered other obstacles. Religious beliefs and a bigoted priesthood stood in the way of further progress in the investigation of the secrets of Nature. The priests did not merely utter threats, condemning men to hell if they acquired such learning. They went further, and actually employed fraud, force and stratagem to prevent them from proceeding along that path. But the Westerners, being accustomed to pursuing their own self-interest, did not take long to find out how to overcome the priests' opposition. They pressed forward, forcibly removing the priests from their path. Rejecting the scriptures and denouncing religion as well as the priests, they began to guide their life along a new channel, and made it a principle not to believe or accept anything that could not be perceived by the senses.

Holding that truth can be ascertained only by the direct evidence of the senses backed by reasoning, inference, etc., the West henceforward began to worship the objective world of matter. Thinking that the subject, perceived as the "I-consciousness", belonged likewise to the category of matter, scientists in the West proceeded to investigate the nature of that consciousness also by the methods of objective investigation adopted in the study of material phenomena. Thus, for the last four hundred years, men in the West have accepted the reality of only those things which could be investigated through the five senses. Within that period, physical science outgrew the mistakes and limitations of its infancy and entered upon its youth, characterised by a sense of confidence in its methods and pride in its achievements.

5. Although capable of achieving great progress in physical science, the procedure just mentioned could not lead men to the knowledge of the Atman. For, the only way to attain that knowledge is through self-control, selflessness and introspection, and the only instrument for attaining it is the mind with all its functions brought under absolute control. It is therefore not surprising that, being attracted only by external objects, the West has missed the path of Self-knowledge and got bogged in materialism based on the

identification of man with the body. That is why they regard worldly enjoyment as all-important and make special efforts to obtain the maximum of it.   Their knowledge of material pheno- mena, acquired through science , has been applied chiefly to that end, and that has made them more and more selfish and conceited, and brought into existence a social system based on wealth.   The manufacture of death-dealing weapons, deep-rooted discontent due to the existence of abject poverty side by side with abounding prosperity, an unquenchable thirst for wealth, and the occupation and oppression of other countries—these are some of the conse- quences of this materialistic philosophy of life.   The pursuit of such sordid values only brings restlessness and dissatisfaction to the human spirit.   Even the facile theory that though the individual perishes, the nation lives on and benefits by his sacrifices, can bring no solace to the living generation.   After careful thought, certain people in the West have at last come to realize that the knowledge obtained through the senses will not enable them to discover the reality beyond time and space.   Science may give them a fleeting indication of its existence, but nothing more;   for that reality is beyond its reach and understanding.   A feeling of utter helplessness has come over men, and there is a growing fear in their hearts over the collapse of the belief in God, the source of all strength, joy and prosperity of man.

6.   Thus a study of history shows that Western civilization is founded on self-love, desire for worldly possessions and absence of faith in religion.   Other peoples too, who base their life on these materialistic values, will reap the same fruits as the peoples of the West.   An example of this is found in Japan and some other Oriental countries that have modelled their national life entirely after the West.   We find that in spite of all their great virtues like patriotism, they have become subject to the evils of a materialistic civilisation.   This is the unfortunate result of being inspired by Western ideals, as will become clear also by a study of Indian life after it came in contact with the West.

7.   It may be asked if India ever had any national life before it came in contact with the West.   The answer is that, although it was not there in theory, it did undoubtedly exist in fact. For, even in those days the people of India as a whole venerated the Guru, the Ganga, the Gayatri and the Gita; and "Go" (the cow) evoked the tenderest and most reverential feelings of the people of India

everywhere. Ideas from the *Ramayana*, the *Mahabharata* and other religious books inspired and guided the life of every man, woman and child; and Sanskrit, the "language of the gods," was the common medium of expression for the learned. There were many more similar factors of unity, and there is no doubt that religious ideas and religious practices constituted the bed-rock of that unity.

8. Religion, the basis of the national life of India, has made her civilization unique. The chief characteristic of this civilization is self-control, which regulates both individual and national conduct. " Through pleasure beyond pleasure" is the maxim of every Hindu, and the life here in this world is looked upon only as a preparation for the life to come. Reminded of this high ideal at every stage of the individual or national life, a Hindu could not lose sight of it. He is forced, so to say, to keep himself always oriented towards this grand goal. It is for this reason that the caste or class system did not for a long time create any conflict of interests, nor lead to discontent in society; for when anyone could achieve supreme knowledge or liberation by the unselfish performance of his own caste or class duties, irrespective of his birth, high or low, what could possibly be the cause for discontent ? Contrary to what happened in Western society, which is based on the right to equal opportunities for enjoyment, there was no dissatisfaction among social groups in ancient Indian society based as it was on the equal right and opportunity for all to achieve the highest ideal, namely, supreme knowledge or liberation. The changes that have occurred in the national life of India since then, as a result of its contact with the West are discussed below.

9. It was natural and inevitable that the occupation of India by the West should bring about many changes in the distribution of the national wealth in the country. But the influence of the West went farther. It produced a radical change in the deep-rooted convictions which had guided men and women from time immemorial. As a result, the impression grew that the doctrine, "Enjoy to renounce," inculcating that the aim of enjoyment is only to renounce it ultimately, was an empty tale invented by self-seeking priests; that the idea of survival after death was but a poet's fancy; and that no rule could be more unjust and unreasonable than that a man should be condemned to remain all his life in the stratum of society where he was born. Coming more and more

2

under the spell of the West, India rejected the ideal of renunciation and self-control, and began to run after worldly pleasures. This attitude brought with it the decay of the ancient system of education and training, and there arose atheism, love of imitation, and lack of self-confidence. Thus the nation lost its backbone. People came to believe that their long-cherished beliefs and practices were erroneous, and they felt that perhaps their traditions were crude and semi-civilized, as the West with its wonderful knowledge of science declared them to be. Blinded by the desire for enjoyment, India forgot her ancient culture and glory. The loss of that memory confused her understanding, and the national existence itself was at stake. Finding that, even for worldly enjoyment, she had to depend on others, India was overcome by a sense of frustration. Having thus lost the way both to enjoyment and to liberation, and yet being bent on imitating others, the nation was now buffeted by waves of modern materialism, and resembled a boat drifting in the high seas without a helmsman.

10. There arose now a clamour on all sides that there never had been a national life in India; that although, thanks to the West, there was at last some sign of it now, there were still many obstacles to its full growth. Deep-rooted religious beliefs were said to have smothered it. Image worship—the adoration of the Supreme Being in many aspects as gods and goddesses—was also blamed for keeping it submerged so long. "Away with idolatry!", people shouted. "Root it out. Only then will the men and the women of the country have a new life instilled into them." Christianity began to be preached, and in imitation of it, the Western brand of monotheism. Prostrate India was made to listen to lectures—delivered at public meetings held in the Western manner—on politics, sociology, the freedom of women and widow-remarriage. But the feeling of frustration and despair, instead of lessening, only grew stronger. The railways, the telegraph and the other products of Western civilization came into use; but these did not mend matters, because all such innovations could neither touch nor stimulate the ideals on which the life of the land depended. Since the proper remedy was not applied, the disease could not be cured. How could India, whose soul was religion, be brought to life if her religion was not resuscitated? The influence of the West had brought about its fall. Would it not be futile, then, to look to the atheistic West for its resurrection?

Being itself imperfect, how could the West make another part of the world perfect?

11. It cannot be said that there were no defects at all in the national life of India before the coming of the Westerners. But the nation being then full of life and vigour, there was a constant endeavour on its part to remedy these defects. Now that the nation and the society were lacking in such effort, the spread of Western ideas and ideals, instead of curing the disease, was on the point of killing the patient.

12. It is thus clear that the decline of religion in the West has affected India also. One is surprised to find how far this decay of religion has spread all over the world at the present time. Religion as a body of truths to be realized in life by the grace of God, has totally disappeared in this modern age, steeped as men at present are in the pursuit of sensual pleasures. Science, too, though it has enriched life by providing men with new means of enjoyment, has failed to bring them peace. Who will give a helping hand to man in this tragic situation? Is there no spiritual power behind the universe that could be moved by this agony and restlessness of the soul of man for a religion suited to the age and capable of rescuing him from the snares of sense pleasures? What force can reverse the downward course of spiritual values, both in the East and the West, and teach man once again to follow the path of peace?

The Lord has promised in the Gita that He will assume a human body through His Maya and manifest Himself in the world whenever religion declines, and will help men to attain peace. Will not the need of the age rouse His compassion? Will not man's helplessness and despair urge God to assume a body?

13. The demand of the times has, O reader, actually brought this about; for the Lord has, in truth, once again been born as the spiritual Teacher of the world. Listen with faith to His gracious message: 'As many faiths, so many paths' and 'You will realize the Lord through any spiritual practice performed with a sincere heart.' Let us dwell in admiration on the unheard-of renunciation and austerities practised by Him in order to bring back that transcendent awareness of the Supreme Spirit into the mind of man. Come, let us discuss and meditate on that holy life, free from the slightest taint of lust, and thus purify ourselves!

CHAPTER II

SRI RAMAKRISHNA'S BIRTHPLACE (KAMARPUKUR) AND ANCESTRY

(TOPICS: 1. Why an incarnation is born in a poor family. 2. Kamarpukur, the birthplace of Sri Ramakrishna. 3. Kamarpukur then and at present. 4. The worship of Dharma. 5. The Haldar tank of Uchalan. 9. Ramananda Roy, the village landlord of Dere. 10. Manikram Chattopadhyaya of Dere. 11. Manikram's son Kshudiram. 12. Chandradevi, wife of Kshudiram. 13. Kshudiram's dispute with the landlord. 14. His being forced to leave Dere. 15. His migration to Kamarpukur.)

1. With the exception of Sri Ramachandra and Lord Buddha, all the divine incarnations were born in poverty and hardship. Consider, for example, the life of Bhagavan Sri Krishna, the glory of the race of Kshatriya princes. He was born in a prison and spent his childhood away from his kith and kin in a community of humble cowherds; or that of Lord Jesus, who was born in a stable with a manger for his cradle, but brought glory to his humble parents; or that of Bhagavan Sankara who was born posthumously as the son of a poor widow*; or that of Bhagavan Sri Chaitanya who was of common parentage; or finally, that of the Prophet Mohammed, the founder of Islam, who was born in a poor family. But despite this fact, none of them was born in a family where contentment did not reign supreme in the midst of want and poverty; or where the warmth of love and selflessness did not prevail over the chill of penury; or where the hearts of the parents were not adorned with renunciation and purity together with adamantine firmness and austerity, well balanced with sentiments of charity and kindliness.

If we think deeply, we find that there is a subtle connection between the condition of poverty and the future course of the lives of the incarnations. For unless, from their early years, they had known and sympathized with the lot of the poor, the oppressed and the miserable, how could they, in later years, have wiped away the tears of such people and brought them solace? That, however, is not all that the incarnations aimed to accomplish. We have

---

*This is according to the Calcutta edition of Anantanandagiri's *Sankara-dig-vijaya*. But according to the *Sankara-dig-vijaya* of Madhava, Sankara's father Sivaguru lived upto the third year of his śon.—Tr.

already seen that they came into the world mainly to arrest the decline of religion.   To fulfil that object they had to acquire intimate knowledge of the principles of religion as reflected in the lives of the people in the past, understand the causes of its decline, and formulate new and perfected forms of it suited to changing times and places.   It is in the huts of the lowly and not in the palaces of the rich that this intimate knowledge can be gained; for it is the poor man, deprived of the enjoyment of worldly pleasures, who clings to God and His dispensation as his main support.   Although, therefore, religion declines everywhere, a little gleam of the old teaching still brightens the poor man's hut.   That perhaps is the reason for these great souls, the world-teachers, taking their birth in the huts of the poor.   It was even so in regard to the great Master whose life-story we are about to relate.

2.   In the Province of Bengal, not far from the place where the north-western part of the district of Hooghly joinst the districts of Bankura and Medinipur, there is a cluster of three villages forming a triangle.   Although known to the local people as three separate villages with their distinct names of Sripur, Kamarpukur and Mukundapur, they nestle so close that they appear to the traveller as different parts of the same village.   The people of the surrounding villages called all the three together as Kamarpukur, probably because the local landlords had lived in that village for many generations.   At the   time   we   are   speaking   of,   Kamarpukur formed a part of the rent-free estate belonging to the family of the spiritual teacher of the Maharaja of Burdwan.   The descendants of this family, Gopilal Goswami, Sukhlal   Goswami and others* were living there.

The town of Burdwan is situated about thirty-two miles north of Kamarpukur.   A metalled road, skirting Kamarpukur, leads from there to Puri to the south-west.   Many poor pilgrims and Sadhus

---

*Hridayram Mukhopadhyaya spoke of one Anupama Goswami instead of Sukhlal; but his statement is not credible , because the landlords of the village, the Lahas, told us that the said Goswami's name was Sukhlal and that they had purchased   about fifty-five years ago most of the land of Kamarpukur from his son Krishnalal Goswami. There is also a tradition in the village that   Gopilal Goswami installed the large Sivalinga named Gopesvara. The said Gopilal Goswami may, therefore, have been an ancestor of Sukhlal; or it may be that another name of Sukhlal was Gopilal.

walk along this road to Puri to pay obeisance to Sri Jagannath, the Lord of the universe, and return the same way. The famous temple of Tarakeswar Mahadeva also is situated about nineteen or twenty miles north of Kamarpukur. A road, passing through Jahanabad also known as Arambag and situated on the bank of the river Dwarakeswar, connects that place with Kamarpukur. Moreover two highways—one from Ghata, eighteen miles to the south, and the other from Vanavishnupur, twenty-six miles to the west—enter Kamarpukur.

3. No words can express the atmosphere of peace that pervaded the mainly agricultural villages of Bengal before they were devastated by malaria in 1867. Surrounded by extensive fields, these small villages of the Hooghly district looked like islands floating in a vast green sea. The people were physically strong and healthy, and mentally happy and contented, since they led an outdoor life and had plenty to eat, the soil being extremely fertile. The villages were densely populated, and the villagers, besides cultivating the fields, engaged themselves in various small industries. Thus Kamarpukur is still famous in that part of the country for Jilepi and Nabat (sweets), and its people even now make a decent living by manufacturing hookah pipes of ebony and selling them in Calcutta. At one time it was famous for producing yarn, Dhotis (wearing cloth), towels and such other handicrafts. Well-known cloth merchants, Vishnu Chapdi and others, lived in this village and carried on a good business with Calcutta. A market is held in the village, even now, every Tuesday and Saturday, and people from the surrounding villages (Tarahat, Badanganj, Sihar, Desra etc.,) bring to it for sale articles of daily use, such as yarn, Dhotis, towels, cooking-pots, pitchers, baskets, fine and coarse mats etc., along with the produces of the fields. Numerous ceremonial festivals are still observed. To this day, in the month of Chaitra, Kamarpukur reverberates with songs in praise of the goddess Manasa, as well as with the Gajan (*garjana*) song in praise of Siva; and in the month of Vaisakha or Jyaishtha, with songs about Hari continuing uninterruptedly for a period of three days. Moreover, all kinds of ceremonies pertaining to special occasions (Pal Parvana)* are performed throughout the year in the house of the landlord, while daily and special worships take place in the established temples.

---

*Connected with lunar days —especially the eighth, the fourteenth, the full moon and the new moon days.—Tr.

The poverty of the village has now put a stop to many other similar festivities.

4. At one time the worship of Dharma, which was originally one of the three principal 'gems' of the Buddhists, was celebrated annually with great pomp and splendour. But this practice has now disappeared. Sri Dharma is now looked upon as Kurma (the second of the ten important incarnations of Vishnu), and receives only ordinary worship here and in the surrounding villages. Even Brahmanas are sometimes seen worshipping the image of this deity. One hears different names for Sri Dharma in different villages. Thus, the Dharma of Kamarpukur is called Rajadhiraja; the Dharma installed at Sripur is named Yatrasiddhiraja; and the one at the village called Madhuvati, near Mukundapur, is known as Sannyasiraja. The chariot procession (Ratha Yatra) of the Dharma of Kamarpukur used to be celebrated formerly with much pomp. The god's big chariot with its nine pinnacles could be seen near the temple; but after it broke down it was never rebuilt. The temple is also falling to pieces for want of repairs, and its priest, Yajnesvara, has now removed the deity to his own house.

5. People of various castes, high and low, such as the Brahmana, Kayastha, weaver, milkman, blacksmith, potter, fisherman and Dom (a low caste), live at Kamarpukur. There are three or four tanks in the village, the biggest being called the Haldarpukur. There are also many small ponds, some of them with large numbers of hundred-petalled lotuses and white water-lilies. There are still many brick houses and tombs in the village, though in earlier days there was a larger number of them. The broken temple of Ramananda Sankhari, the dilapidated Rasa-platform of Fakir Datta, heaps of bricks overgrown with jungle, and deserted shrines in various places are evidences of the former prosperity of the village. There are two burning ghats, called Budhui Moral and Bhutir Khal, one to the north-west, the other to the north-east. To the west of the Bhutir Khal are the common grazing ground, the public mango grove planted by Manikraja, and the Amodar river. The Bhuti stream flows south and joins this river not far from the village.

6. A mile north of Kamarpukur there is a village called Bhursubo. A very rich man named Manik Chandra Bandyopadhyaya, commonly known as Manikraja to the people of the surrounding villages, lived there. Besides the mango grove just mentioned, certain tanks named Sukhasayar and Hatisayar still

remind us of him. It is said that on several occasions, about a lakh of Brahmanas* were invited and fed at his place.

7. In the village of Mandaran, south-east of Kamarpukur, there used to be an impregnable fort built to protect the people of the surrounding villages from the attacks of enemies. The course of the neighbouring rivulet, Amodar, was skilfully diverted to serve as a moat for this fort.

8. The ruins of the gateway, the tower and the moat of the fort, and the temple of Siva named Saileswar, not far from it, exist to this day. They indicate the importance of this part of the country during the time of the Pathan rule. It is by the Mandaran fort that the road leading to Burdwan passes. On both sides of this road are many large tanks, the largest being the one at a place called Uchalan, eighteen miles north of the fort. There is also an elephant stable in ruins at a place along this road. This shows clearly that the road was constructed for use during wars and disturbances The existence of the battlefield of Mogalmari near this road also attests the same fact.

9. Two miles west of Kamarpukur there are three villages— called Satbere, Narayanpur and Dere—situated side by side. The former prosperity of these villages can be inferred from various signs, such as the tank in the village of Dere and the temple nearby. At the time of which we are speaking, the three villages were included in different estates, and Ramananda Roy, the landlord of Dere, lived in the village Satbere. This landlord, though not very rich, was a great village tyrant. When annoyed with any of his tenants, he did not hesitate to deprive him of all his possessions. None of his sons or daughters survived him. It is said that he could leave behind no progeny on account of the sin of oppressing the tenants. After his death all his estate and all properties fell into the hands of others.

10. About one hundred and fifty years ago, there lived a religious-minded Brahmana family of moderate means in the village of Dere. They were of noble descent, observed the customs of the pious Hindus, and worshipped Sri Ramachandra. The temple of Siva and the adjoining tank known as the Chaturjee tank still commemorate their memory. Sri Manikram Chattopadhyaya, the head of this family at the time we are speaking of, had three

---

*The feeding of a lakh of Brahmanas, the repositories of learning and holiness, was considered a rare and unique act of piety.—Tr.

sons and a daughter. Of these, the eldest, Kshudiram, was born probably in 1775 A.D. After him came Ramsila, the daughter, and the two other sons, Nidhiram and Kanairam.

11. It is doubtful if Kshudiram ever became proficient in any branch of learning making him eligible for any remunerative employment. But the Lord had blessed him with truthfulness, contentment, forgiveness, renunciation and other noble qualities, the possession of which is considered by the Sastras as the mark of a good Brahmana. He was tall and stalwart and had a fair complexion and pleasing looks. Kshudiram showed deep devotion to Sri Ramachandra, who was being worshipped in his family generation after generation. He was in the habit of performing Sandhya, along with his other daily observances, after which he would collect flowers for the worship of Raghuvir (Ramachandra). Not until he had finished his worship would he eat anything. He never accepted gifts from his inferiors, and would refuse invitations even from Brahmanas who officiated at religious rites for them. Nor would he drink water touched by Brahmanas who demanded bridal money while giving their daughters in marriage. He was greatly loved and respected by the villagers for his faithful observance of pious customs.

12. Kshudiram took up the management of the ancestral property on the death of his father. He performed this duty as best as he could, remaining at the same time steadfast in the path of religion. Some time earlier he had married, but his wife had died young. When he was about twenty-five years of age, he married a second time. The bride's name was Chandramani, but in the family she was called simply 'Chandra'. Her father's house was in the village of Saratimayapur. She was simple-hearted, good-looking and devoted to the service of the gods and holy men. But her outstanding qualities were her deep religious faith and her loving and affectionate nature. It was these that made her dear to all. Born probably in the year 1791, she must have been only about eight years old at the time of her marriage in 1799. Her first son, Ramkumar, is said to have been born in 1805. A daughter, Katyayani, was born five years later. She rejoiced again at the birth of a second son, Rameswar, in 1826.

13. It did not take Kshudiram long to discover how difficult it was to manage worldly affairs without deviating from the path of righteousness. Probably a short time after his daughter Katya-

yani was born, he had to undergo a very hard test.   We have already
spoken of Ramananda Roy, the oppressive landlord of the village.
Annoyed with a certain man of Derepur, Ramananda instituted a
false case against him, and since someone of good reputation was
needed as a witness, he requested Kshudiram to give evidence in
his favour.   The strictly upright Kshudiram always dreaded litigation, courts and the like, and never had recourse to them against
anyone, even when he had a just cause.   The request, therefore,
came to him as a shock.   Though he knew for certain that he would
incur Ramananda's bitter enmity if he did not give false evidence,
he never agreed to such a course.   The inevitable happened.   The
landlord filed a false petition in the court against him as well, won
the case, and got possession of the whole of Kshudiram's paternal
property through auction.   In consequence Kshudiram had not
even a square inch of land left in Derepur.   Although all the people
of the village felt great sympathy for him in his trouble, they did
not dare help him in any way out of fear of the landlord.

14.   At the time when this calamity befell him, Kshudiram
was about forty years old.   The property* inherited from his
ancestors, together with that acquired by him over many years,
had vanished like a cloud dispersed by the wind.   But this calamity
did not affect his upright conduct in the least.   He took absolute
refuge at the holy feet of Raghuvir, calmly reflected on what he
should do in order to escape the wicked landlord, and finally bade
goodbye for ever to his paternal homestead and village.

15.   We have already mentioned the name of Sukhlal Goswami
of Kamarpukur.   He and Kshudiram were of a like temperament,
and were old and intimate friends.   Sukhlal was much moved on
hearing of Kshudiram's misfortune, and vacating a few thatched
huts in a part of his homestead, invited him to come and live there
permanently.   Kshudiram thus found a haven of refuge.   He
accepted the invitation, regarding it as the incomprehensible play
(Lila) of the divine Lord, and with his heart filled with gratitude,
went to Kamarpukur, where he lived ever after.   Sukhlal, who
loved his friend dearly, felt very happy at his coming, and made a
permanent gift to the virtuous Kshudiram, of one Bigha and ten
Chataks** of land for his maintenance.

---

* We were told by Hridayram Mukhopadhyaya that Kshudiram had
about 150 *bighas* of land at Derepur.   (3½ Bighas = 1 acre)—Tr.

** 16 Chataks = 1 Katha, 20 Kathas = 1 Bigha.—Tr.

CHAPTER III

THE PIOUS FAMILY AT KAMARPUKUR

(TOPICS: 1. Kshudiram's austere life at Kamarpukur. 2. His mysterious acquisition of the Salagrama of Raghuvir. 3. His dependence on God. 4. Paddy field at Lakshmijala. 5. Progress of Kshudiram's devotion. 6. How the neighbours respected Chandradevi. 7. Kshudiram's sister Ramsila. 8. His two brothers. 9. His nephew Ramchand. 10. An incident showing Kshudiram's devotion to God. 11. Marriages of Ramkumar and Katyayani. 12. Death of Sukhlal Goswami and other events. 13. Kshudiram's pilgrimage to Setubandha and the birth of his son Rameswar. 14. Ramkumar's supernatural power. 15. An illustration of that power. 16. An incident concerning Ramkumar's wife. 17. The distinguishing feature of Kshudiram's family. 18. Chandradevi's spiritual vision. 19. Kshudiram's desire to make a pilgrimage to Gaya. 20. Hriday's story regarding it. 21. Kshudiram's divine dream at Gaya. 22. Kshudiram's return to Kamarpukur.)

1. It is difficult to imagine the thoughts that arose in the minds of Kshudiram and his wife the day they came to Kamarpukur with the ten-year-old Ramkumar and Katyayani, their daughter of four, and settled in the cottage given to them. The world, filled with jealousy and hatred, must have seemed to them a hideous place of the dead, shrouded in dismal darkness. Thoughts of affection, love, kindness and justice no doubt occasionally shed there a dim light, raising in quivering hearts some hope of happiness, but it is blasted the next moment, leaving behind deep depression. It is natural that many such thoughts should have arisen in the minds of Kshudiram and his wife when they compared their previous condition with the present one. Only when misery and calamity come, do men realize the transitoriness and worthlessness of this world. It is therefore not at all surprising that Kshudiram now felt detached from the world and that his profoundly religious mind was full of devotion to God and reliance on Him. For he could not forget how unexpected and unasked for was the shelter given to them. Is it then strange that, being indifferent to worldly prospects, he once more devoted his time to the service and worship of the divine Lord and surrendered himself completely to Raghuvir?

From now on he was living, no doubt, in the world, but like the
Vanaprasthas of ancient times, he was not of it.

2. An incident which happened at this time still further intensified Kshudiram's faith in God. One day he went to another
village on business. On his way back he became tired and rested
under a tree. The vast, lonely field and a soft, pure breeze brought
repose to his troubled mind and tired body. He felt a strong desire
to lie down, and no sooner had he done so than he was overcome
by sleep. He then had a dream in which he saw standing before
him his chosen Ideal, Bhagavan Sri Ramachandra, in the guise of
a divine Boy, His body green like the tender blades of Durva grass.
Pointing to a particular spot, the Boy said, "I have been staying
here for a long time without food and without anyone to take care of
me. Take me to your house. I have a very strong desire that you
should serve me." Kshudiram was overcome with emotion and
said, paying homage to the Lord again and again: "O Lord, I
am without devotion and am very poor. Service befitting you is
not possible in my hut, and I shall incur sin, should there be any
flaw in it. So why do you make such a difficult request to me?"
At this, the Boy Ramachandra comforted him and said graciously,
"Do not be afraid. I shall not take offence at any shortcoming.
Take me with you." Unable to control his feelings at the Lord's
unexpected grace, Kshudiram burst into tears. Just then his dream
came to an end. When he woke up, Kshudiram wondered at the
strangeness of his dream and thought, "Ah! If only such a good
fortune would be mine!" Then suddenly his eyes fell upon the
paddy field close by, and at once he recognized it as the very place
he had seen in the dream. Out of curiosity he approached the
spot, where he saw a beautiful Salagrama stone and a snake with
expanded hood guarding it. Eager to possess the stone, he hastened
towards it. On reaching it, he found that the snake had disappeared
and that the Salagrama was lying at the entrance to its hole. Seeing
that the dream had come true, his heart leaped with joy, and he felt
no fear of the snake, convinced as he was that he had received
God's command. Crying out, "Glory to Raghuvir!" Kshudiram
took the stone in his hands. He carefully examined the marks on
it and, with his knowledge of the Sastras, found it to be a Raghuvir
Sila (Salagrama). Beside himself with joy and wonder, he returned
home, performed the purificatory ceremony of the Salagrama
according to the Sastras, and installing it as the family deity, began

to worship it daily. Even before he came upon the Salagrama in this strange manner, Kshudiram had been worshipping Sri Ramachandra, his chosen Deity, every day. He also worshipped daily the goddess Sitala, invoking her in a consecrated pot filled with water.

3. His difficulties continued, but Kshudiram cheerfully bore all kinds of misfortunes, strictly observing as ever the religious injunctions. On some days, when there was nothing in the house to eat, his devoted wife, Chandradevi, would grow anxious and tell him about it. But, unperturbed, Kshudiram would comfort her, saying, "Never mind. If Raghuvir chooses to fast, why shouldn't we also?" At this the simple-hearted Chandra also, like her husband, would resign herself to Raghuvir and go on with her household duties. But somehow food sufficient for the day would come.

4. But Kshudiram did not suffer long from this uncertainty about food. For, by the grace of Raghuvir, the one Bigha and ten Chataks of land at Lakshmijala given to him by his friend Sukhlal Goswami, began by now to produce so much paddy that there was not only enough for the little family's annual needs, but something was even left over to feed guests and strangers. Kshudiram hired men to plough the field, and when the rice seedlings were ready, he would transplant a few himself, taking the name of Raghuvir, and then let the men finish the work.

5. Two or three years went by in this manner. Kshudiram depended entirely on Raghuvir and what chance brought him, but he did not lack plain food and clothing. Therefore the hard trials of these two or three years, instead of discouraging him, filled his heart with a sense of reliance on God and a continuous flow of peace and contentment such as few experience. Henceforth it was natural for him to be always indrawn, and in consequence he had from time to time various divine visions. Every morning and evening, during his prayers, he would repeat the meditation Mantra describing the Gayatri with such deep devotion and concentration of mind that his chest became flushed and tears of love flowed down from his closed eyes. Early in the morning he would go, basket in hand, to pick flowers for the worship, and at such times the goddess Sitala, who received his daily adoration, would appear before him as an eight-year-old girl dressed in red and wearing many ornaments. She would accompany him smiling, and help him pluck flowers by bending the branches in blossom. These visions filled his heart

with joy. His staunch faith and deep devotion, which were reflected
in his countenance, kept him always on a high spiritual plane. Seeing his calm and peaceful face, the villagers instinctively recognized
his spirituality and began to venerate him with the love and devotion
due to a Rishi. Whenever they saw him coming, they stopped all
idle talk, stood up and greeted him respectfully. They hesitated to
enter the tank when they saw him bathing, and waited in reverence
till he had finished. With complete faith in him, they came for
his blessings in weal and woe.

6. Chandradevi's loving and guileless nature also captivated
her neighbours and made them look upon her as their mother
From no one else did they receive such heartfelt sympathy in their
joys and sorrows. The poor knew that whenever they went to
Chandradevi, they would receive not only food but also such a
genuine welcome and affection as would fill their hearts with inexpressible joy. To holy men living on alms, her door was always
open. There was nothing that the children could not coax out of
Chandradevi. Thus everyone, young and old, was welcome at
any time at Kshudiram's cottage, which, in spite of poverty and
suffering, always radiated a wonderful peace and joy.

7. As already mentioned, Kshudiram had a sister named
Ramsila, and two younger brothers, Nidhiram and Kanairam, the
latter being also called Ramkanai. At the time of his loss of all
his property on account of the dispute with the landlord of Derepur,
his sister was thirty-five and his brothers thirty and twenty-five
respectively. By then all the three had married and set up their
own homes. Ramsila was married to Bhagavat Bandyopadhyaya
who lived at Silimpur, a village about twelve miles west of Kamarpukur. She had a son, Ramchand, and a daughter, Hemangini.
At the time of Kshudiram's misfortune, Hemangini was sixteen,
and Ramchand, who had then begun to practise as a Muktiar
(pleader), was about twenty one. Born in the home of her maternal
uncles at Derepur, Hemangini was a greater favourite with them
than her brother. Kshudiram brought her up like his own daughter,
and when she reached the proper age, he himself gave her away in
marriage to Krishnachandra Mukhopadhyaya of Sihar, a village
five miles north-west of Kamarpukur. In course of time she became
the mother of four sons: Raghava, Ramaratan, Hridayram and
Rajaram.

8. We could not find out whether Nidhiram had any children, but Kanairam had two sons, Ramtarak (otherwise known as Haladhari) and Kalidas. Kanairam was of a devotional and contemplative nature. Once he went to a drama (Yatra) which portrayed the banishment of Sri Ramachandra to the forest. The performance became so realistic to him that he took Kaikeyi's secret plotting and scheming to be real and was on the point of striking the actor who played the part. On the loss of the ancestral property, Nidhiram and Kanairam, it appears, settled in the villages of their fathers-in-law.

9. We have already said that Ramachandra Bandyopadhyaya, Ramsila's son, was a pleader. His practice in the town of Medinipur brought him a good income. Considering the straitened circumstances of his maternal uncles, he now sent fifteen rupees a month to help Kshudiram and ten rupees each to Nidhiram and Kanairam. If Kshudiram did not hear from his nephew for some time, he would become anxious and hasten to Medinipur to see him. We were told of a strange incident which occurred when Kshudiram was once going to Medinipur. We relate it here as an example of his deep devotion to God.

10. Medinipur is situated about forty miles south-west of Kamarpukur. Having had no news of Ramachandra and his family for a long time, Kshudiram set out one day to see him. It was probably during the month of Magh or Phalgun (January—March), when the Vilva trees shed their leaves, making the worship of Siva * difficult until new leaves appear. Kshudiram had been experiencing this difficulty for some time.

He started very early and walked steadily on till he reached a certain village at about ten o'clock in the morning. Finding that the Vilva trees there were already in leaf, his heart leaped with joy and all thought of proceeding to Medinipur left his mind. He bought a new basket and a piece of cloth and washed them thoroughly in a pond close by. Then he filled the basket with new Vilva leaves, covered it with the wet cloth and returned home, reaching there about three in the afternoon. Immediately on his arrival he bathed and then for a long time joyfully worshipped with these fresh leaves the great God Siva and Sitala, the Divine Mother. Not until he had finished the worship did he sit down for his meal. Chandradevi

---

*Leaves of the Vilva tree are necessary for the worship of Siva.—Tr.

thought this to be the right moment to ask him why he had not gone to Medinipur. When he told her everything, she was amazed to learn that he had come back all that distance solely on account of his eagerness to worship Siva with the leaves. Kshudiram started again for Medinipur very early the next morning.

11. Thus Kshudiram spent six years at Kamarpukur. His son Ramkumar was now sixteen years old, and his daughter Katyayani, eleven. His daughter being of the right age, he gave her in marriage to Kenaram Bandyopadhyaya, who lived at Anur, a village two miles north-west of Kamarpukur, while Ramkumar was married to Kenaram's sister. Ramkumar had by then finished his study of Vyakarana (Grammar) and Sahitya (Literature) in a Sanskrit school near the village and was now studying Smriti (the laws governing the Hindu society and religion).

12. Another three or four years passed. By the grace of Sri Raghuvir, Kshudiram was now considerably more prosperous than before, and, free from anxiety, he could give all his time to God. During this period Ramkumar finished his study of Smriti, and applied his mind to the best of his ability to the improvement of the family's economic condition. It was about this time that Sukhlal Goswami, Kshudiram's great friend, passed away. His death caused Kshudiram deep sorrow.

13. After finishing his studies, Ramkumar, now a young man, took upon himself the responsibility of maintaining the family. Kshudiram was thus free to apply himself to other things. He now had a great yearning to go on a pilgrimage, and before long, probably in A.D. 1824, he started on foot for Setubandha-Rameswar. His visit to the places of pilgrimage in South India took him a year after which he returned home. With him he brought a Banalinga (a symbol of Siva) from Setubandha, which he began to worship daily. This Banalinga, named Rameswar, can be seen even today near the Salagrama stone of Raghuvir and the water-jar symbolizing the goddess Sitala. A long time after the birth of her second child, Chandradevi gave birth to another son in A.D. 1826. In memory of his recent pilgrimage, Kshudiram named this son Rameswar.

14. The next eight years showed little change in the tenor of life of the poor family at Kamarpukur. Ramkumar now earned money by advising people on religious matters on the authority

of the Smritis and by performing various religious ceremonies. In consequence, the family was more affluent than before. He became an expert in the performance of those rites and is said to have obtained a supernatural power to make them effective. Study of the scriptures had given him faith in the worship of Sakti, the primordial Divine Power personified. He had also received initiation in the Mantra of Sakti from a competent teacher. He had a wonderful vision one day while worshipping this Goddess, his chosen Deity. He felt as if She was marking the letters of some Mantra with Her own finger on the tip of his tongue. This experience made him perfect in astrology. Henceforward whatever he predicted would come true. Simply by looking at a patient, he could know whether he would be cured or not. He acquired some fame in those parts for correct prediction of future events. It is said that on seeing a person suffering from a severe disease, he would start performing propitiatory rites for his recovery and would say emphatically, "As soon as the grains I am now sprinkling over the place of worship begin to sprout, this person will recover". And , as a matter of fact, what he said would actually come true. His nephew, Sivaram Chattopadhyaya, told us the following story as an illustration of this power :

15. Being in Calcutta on business, Ramkumar was bathing in the Ganga one morning, when a rich man and his family also came for a bath. The man's wife was seated in a palanquin, which was taken to the river so that she could take her bath inside it. Coming, as he did, from the village, Ramkumar had never seen a woman bathing in this way protected from public gaze. Looking at the palanquin with wonder, he happened to catch sight of the woman's face for a moment. He instantly knew through his supernatural power that she would die the next day, and was so overcome by the thought that he could not help muttering sadly to himself: "Alas, the body which today is being bathed with such propriety will tomorrow be immersed as a corpse in the Ganga and disposed of in the sight of all!" The rich man overheard this and, in order to test the truth of his words, pressed Ramkumar to come to his house. His real intention was to teach him a good lesson in case his prediction proved false. The young woman was in perfect health and there was no indication whatever at that time of such a mishap. But since what Ramkumar had predicted actually came to pass, the man finally could not but let him go in peace.

3

16. Once, looking into his wife's future, Ramkumar made a sad prediction, which unfortunately proved true afterwards. She is said to have had auspicious marks. From the very day he married her and brought her to his home, the wheel of fortune took a favourable turn for the family. She was then seven years old and the marriage took place probably in A.D. 1820. It was from this time that the improvement in his father's circumstances began; for it was just then that the monthly help from his nephew, Rama-chandra of Medinipur, began to come in. Naturally, any daughter-in-law who thus brings good luck to a family on becoming its member, is looked upon with love and respect. Moreover, since Ramkumar's child-wife was then the only daughter-in-law of the family, it is not surprising that everyone made much of her. We were told that, in spite of her good qualities, too much of indulgence and attention made her touchy and obstinate. But although these defects were noticed by all, no one ventured either to mention them or to correct her; for everyone overlooked her little defects, remembering that she had brought prosperity to the family since the day of her coming. But when she was grown up, Ramkumar one day looked at her and predicted that, although she had auspicious marks, she would die if she should ever conceive. When he found, however, that she did not conceive for several years, he thought that she was barren and felt relieved. But at the age of thirty-five she did conceive, and the following year, A.D. 1849, she passed away after giving birth to a very beautiful male child. The boy was named Akshay. Chronologically, this incident comes much later, but we have narrated it here for the sake of convenience.

17. A peculiar characteristic of a divine and subtle kind was shared by every one of Kshudiram's pious household. It is prob-ably because of the dominance of this characteristic in Kshudiram and his wife that it was inherited by their children. Since we have already mentioned several instances of it relating to Kshudiram, it will not be out of place if we relate here a similar event regarding Chandramani. This will show how Chandramani also, like her husband, saw divine visions from time to time. The event took place shortly before Ramkumar was married. The fifteen-year-old boy was then studying in a Sanskrit school and at the same time trying to help the family by performing worship in various houses.

18. Once in the month of Asvin, Ramkumar had gone to a house at Bhursubo to perform the evening worship of the goddess Lakshmi. When her son did not return home, though it was past midnight, Chandra became very restless, and coming out of the house, waited for him anxiously. While looking in the direction from which he was to come, she saw a lone figure approaching by the field-path leading from Bhursubo to Kamarpukur. Thinking that it was her son, she went a few steps forward in great joy to meet him. When the person drew nearer, she found that it was not Ramkumar but a very beautiful girl, bedecked with various ornaments. As Chandra was full of anxiety for the safety of her son, the sight of a respectable girl walking thus at dead of night did not strike her as something strange. She just went up to her and called out: "Where do you come from, my child?" The girl answered, "From Bhursubo." Chandra then asked her anxiously, "Did you meet my son, Ramkumar? Is he coming back?" It did not strike her mind even for a moment how an absolute stranger like this girl could possibly know her son. The girl replied, comforting, " I come from the very house where your son went to perform the worship. Do not worry; he will return soon." Hearing this, Chandra felt relieved and became more observant. Then noticing the girl's remarkable beauty, her melodious voice, her attractive dress and her exotic ornaments, she said, "You are so young! Where are you going at this time of the night, wearing such fine ornaments and dress? And what is this strange ornament on your ears?" With a smile the girl said, "It is called Kundala," and added, "I have yet to go a long distance." Thinking that she was in trouble, Chandra said affectionately, " Come, my child, rest for the night at our house. Tomorrow you may go at your leisure." "No, mother," replied the girl, " I must go just now. I will come to your house some other time." Taking leave of her, she went in the direction of the larger paddy stacks of the Lahas nearby. Surprised to see her going towards the house of the Lahas instead of following the regular path, Chandra thought that she had missed the way. She went after her, but could not find her, though she searched in all directions. Then, recalling what the girl had said, it suddenly dawned upon her that she might have seen the goddess Lakshmi! She hastened to her husband and, in great excitement, told him everything from beginning to end, in great detail. After hearing

the whole account, Kshudiram assured her that there was no doubt
that the divine goddess Lakshmi had graciously revealed Herself
to her. Soon after this Ramkumar returned home, and hearing
what had happened, was filled with wonder.

19. Time passed on, and it was now A.D. 1835. Feeling
once again a strong urge to go on a pilgrimage, Kshudiram decided
to go to Gaya to perform rites for the redemption of the spirits of
his forefathers. He was now sixty. Still he had no hesitation to
proceed on foot to the holy abode of Vishnu. Hriday, the son of
Kshudiram's niece Hemangini, told us of a strange event which
made him undertake this journey to Gaya.

20. Once, on receiving news that his daughter Katyayani
was seriously ill, Kshudiram went to Anur to see her. She was
then about twenty-five years old. Watching her gestures and manner of talk, he felt convinced that she was possessed by a spirit
Then, concentrating his mind on God, he thus addressed that spirit,
"Whatever you be, whether a deity or a demi-god, why do you harass
my daughter? Leave her at once and go your way." At this, the spirit
got frightened and said in a pleading voice through Katyayani, "I
shall leave your daughter's body immediately if you promise to offer
worship on my behalf at Gaya and thus bring to an end my present
miserable condition. I make a solemn promise that the moment you
leave your home to do this, she will be free from all troubles."

Moved by the suffering of the spirit, Kshudiram at once said,
"I shall go to Gaya, the abode of Vishnu, as soon as I can and
fulfil your wish. But it will make me very happy if I get some proof
that you have actually obtained deliverance after the worship has
been offered." The spirit replied: " I assure you that as a proof
of my deliverance, I shall break down the largest branch of yonder
Neem tree, while going away." According to Hriday, it was this
incident that made Kshudiram go to Gaya. As some time afterwards, the branch of the Neem tree suddenly broke, there was no
longer any doubt that the spirit had obtained deliverance. The
affliction also left Katyayani. We cannot vouch for the truth of
Hriday's story; but there is no doubt that it was about this time
that Kshudiram went to Gaya.

21. Some time during the winter of 1835, Kshudiram visited
Varanasi* (Banaras) and Gaya. It was the beginning of Chaitra

* Some say that Kshudiram visited Varanasi much earlier, when he
started from Derepur on pilgrimage to Vrindavan and Ayodhya. When

(middle of March) when he reached Gaya after paying obeisance to Visvanatha (the Lord of the Universe) at Varanasi. He came to Gaya at this time of the year probably because he knew that the spirits of his ancestors would have immense satisfaction if worship was offered at that holy place during spring in the month of Chaitra. He lived there for about a month, performed all the ceremonies according to the scriptures, and at last offered worship at the lotus feet of Gadadhara (Vishnu). Because of his great faith, Kshudiram experienced unspeakable peace and satisfaction on thus performing the prescribed obsequial rites in honour of his ancestors. Having fulfilled to the best of his capacity his obligations to his forefathers, he was now free from all anxiety. Then the thought came to him that the divine Lord had made it possible for an unworthy person like himself to accomplish all this, and his grateful heart overflowed with such a feeling of humility and love as he had never experienced before. Peace and joy were with him all that day and at night also. Scarcely had he fallen asleep when he had a dream. He saw himself in the holy temple, in the act of offering worship to his forefathers, at the divine feet of Gadadhara. He even saw his ancestors in luminous celestial bodies, joyfully accepting the Pindas and blessing him. He could not control his emotion at seeing them after what seemed a very long time. With tears in his eyes, and a heart overflowing with devotion, he bowed down to them and touched their feet. The very next moment he found that the temple was filled with a divine light as was never seen by him before. His forefathers were standing in the temple on both sides in a reverential, attitude with their hands folded, worshipping a wonderful Divine Being seated happily on a beautiful throne. He had a luminous body, green like the colour of new Durva grass. Looking at Kshudiram with benign, affectionate eyes, He beckoned him. Hardly conscious of what he was doing, Kshudiram drew near, and. full of devotion, prostrated himself at His feet in worship, and uttered hymns in praise. Pleased by his worship, that Divine Being addressed him thus in a sweet voice, " Kshudiram, your extraordinary devotion has made me very happy. I bless you. I shall be born as your son and be the object of your loving care." On hearing these words, strange even for a dream, Kshudiram's

shortly afterwards a son was born and then a daughter, he remembered this pilgrimage and named them Ramkumar and Katyayani. During the pilgrimage mentioned, some maintain, he visited only Gaya.

joy knew no bounds. But the very next moment the thought struck him how, being so poor, he could possibly feed and give proper shelter to such an exalted Being. This made him exceedingly sad and in a voice choked with emotion, he said, " No, no, Lord, I am not worthy of such a blessing. Is it not enough that Thou hast blessed me by graciously revealing Thyself to me and wishing to be born as my son? If Thou wert really to be born as my son, what service can a poor man like me render?" Hearing these words full of pathos, that celestial Being seemed to become even more gracious than before, and said, " Do not fear, Kshudiram, I shall relish whatever you give me to eat. Let my desire be fulfilled." Kshudiram had not the heart to say "No." Conflicting emotions like joy and sorrow assailed him with so much force that he could hardly contain himself, and he lost consciousness. This broke his dream.

22. For quite a while after waking up, Kshudiram did not know where he was. The reality of the dream overwhelmed him. Gradually regaining consciousness of the outside world, he rose from his bed, and recalling the details of the strange dream, thought over it from different points of view. His believing heart was at last convinced that since a divine dream must come true, some great soul would soon be born in his house. He was destined, even at that advanced age, to see again the face of a new child. He then decided not to speak of that remarkable dream to anyone till it had actually come to pass. A few days later he bade farewell to Gaya, the abode of Vishnu, and returned to Kamarpukur. It was then the month of April A.D. 1835.

CHAPTER IV

STRANGE EXPERIENCES
OF CHANDRADEVI

(TOPICS: 1. Pre-natal spiritual experiences of parents of incarnations. 2. Reason underlying that statement. 3. Value and relevance of such visions. 4. Kshudiram observing a change in Chandradevi's mental condition. 5. Her motherly affection finding a wider range. 6. Kshudiram's anxiety for her. 7. Chandradevi's strange dream. 8. Her experience at the Siva temple. 9. Kshudiram cautioning Chandradevi. 10. Chandradevi's visions in her pregnancy.)

1. The unique spiritual experiences and visions of the parents of great souls who sanctify the earth by their birth, are recorded in the religious books of all races. For example, this has been the case with the parents of divine personages like the glorious Sri Ramachandra, Bhagavan Sri Krishna, Buddha the son of Mayadevi, Jesus the son of Mary, Bhagavan Sri Sankara, Sri Chaitanya the great Lord, and others who, ever since their birth, have been receiving the adoration and reverence of devout human beings. It will be sufficient if we tell the reader a few instances.

It is well known that, according to the *Ramayana,* the mothers of Sri Ramachandra and his three half-brothers conceived on eating the milk-pudding left over in the sacrificial vessel. It is also recorded there that they came to know, more than once, before and after the birth of the sons, that these children were endowed with spiritual powers and were actually parts of Vishnu, the divine Lord and Preserver of the Universe. The parents of Sri Krishna knew, both at the time of his entering the mother's womb and also immediately after he was born, that he was God incarnate endowed with the six divine powers. Besides this, the Puranas like the *Bhagavata* recount strange incidents in their daily lives from the moment Krishna was born. When the Buddha came, Mayadevi saw in a vision an exalted Being entering her womb in the form of an effulgent white elephant and all the gods including Indra paying homage to her because of her great good fortune. Before Lord Jesus was born, his mother Mary felt that she had become pregnant without knowing her husband, Joseph. Filled with a spiritual radiance never seen before, she knew that she had conceived. The mother of Bhagavan Sankara knew that she had conceived when the God of gods, Mahadeva, came to her in a vision and granted her a boon. We read in *Sri Chaitanya Charitamrita* and other books that Sachidevi, the mother of Bhagavan Sri Chaitanya, also had similar spiritual experiences.

All the religions—Hinduism, Buddhism, Christianity, etc.,— have shown that the worship of God with intense love is the easiest way to obtain His grace. Since they all assert this, the question that naturally arises in the mind of an impartial investigator is, whether there is any truth underlying this statement; and if so, what part of the experiences narrated above should be accepted and what rejected.

2. Even reason suggests that, after all, there must be some truth in what has been said; for modern science accepts that only parents possessing great virtues can beget children of lofty character. So it cannot be denied that the parents of Krishna, Buddha, Jesus and those like them were endowed with the noblest qualities. And, again, it is clear that when those remarkable children were born, the parents dwelt in exalted planes of consciousness beyond the reach of ordinary human beings. It was this that made them fit for such unique visions and experiences.

3. Although the Puranas record many examples of such experiences, and though they are not opposed to reason, the human mind cannot accept them fully. Putting its trust only in knowledge gained by the senses, modern man cannot fully believe in the existence of entities such as the Self and God, and in states like liberation, and the hereafter on the ground that they are not directly cognised. But an impartial investigator cannot discard any experience only because it is rare or uncommon. He has to be patient enough to collect objective data for and against it and suspend his judgement until he has done so.

In any case, we have come to know through reliable sources that the parents of the great personage whose life we are writing had, at the time of his birth, various spiritual visions and experiences. We have, therefore, no alternative but to record those facts. In the previous chapter, we told the reader a few such instances about Kshudiram, and we shall now do the same in respect of Chandradevi.

4. On his return home, Kshudiram did not tell anyone about the strange dream he had had at Gaya, but waited to see what would

happen. The first thing he observed was the wonderful change that had come over Chandradevi. In his eyes, she was no longer an ordinary woman, but indeed a goddess. An all-embracing love, springing from some unknown source, filled her heart and raised her to a lofty plane beyond all worldly desires. She was now more concerned about the wants of her neighbours than about her own affairs. In the midst of her household duties she would now and then go to attend to their needs. Unobserved, she would take provisions and other daily necessaries from her store, and give them to the needy. After finishing the service of Raghuvir, she would serve food to her husband and children. Then, though already late, she would go, before taking food herself, to find out if her neighbours had taken theirs. If some day she happened to meet anyone who for any reason had gone without food, she would insist on taking him home and feeding him with her own share of cooked food. Then she would herself take what little was left and pass the day quite contented.

5. Kshudiram found that Chandra, who always loved the children of the neighbourhood as her own, now felt a motherly love for the gods also. She actually looked upon Raghuvir, the family deity, as her own son, and also regarded the goddess Sitala and the deity Rameswar represented by the Salagrama emblem as her very children. Formerly her heart always used to be filled with awe at the time of the service and worship of these deities; but now the powerful sentiment of love completely replaced that feeling. Any idea of fear or hesitation in her approach to the gods vanished, and she had now nothing to hide from them or ask of them. Instead, she felt the assurance that the gods were even closer to her than her own children, and in her were born an intense desire to sacrifice her all to make them happy, and an ecstatic sense of being bound to them in an eternal relation of love.

6. Kshudiram noticed that, as a result of her unreserved devotion to the gods and the joy born of her intimate relationship with them, the simple-hearted Chandra became more trusting than ever. She could no longer suspect any one, nor look upon another as a stranger. He thought, "The selfish world will never appreciate such guilelessness. On the contrary, she will be called silly or mad or something like that." Therefore, he looked for an opportunity to warn her.

7. It was not long before this opportunity came. The simple Chandra could not keep back a single thought from her husband. She often confided her thoughts even to her friends. How then could she keep them from one whom God had placed nearer to her than anyone else in the world? Therefore after Kshudiram returned home from Gaya, Chandradevi, for days together, took every opportunity to relate to him all that she had seen or experienced during his absence. One day she told him: "When you were away, I had a strange dream in which I saw a luminous Being lying on my bed. At first I thought it was you, but soon realized that no human being could be like that. Then I woke up, but the thought persisted that the luminous Being was still in the bed. The next moment, another thought came: 'Does a god ever appear to a human being in this way?' Then it occurred to me that some wicked person might have entered the room for an evil purpose and that perhaps the sound of his footsteps had caused my dream. A great fear then seized me. I got up hurriedly and lighted a lamp, but found that there was no one in the room and that the door was still bolted from within. But fear kept me awake the rest of that night. Then I thought, 'Is it possible that a person had entered the room somehow by removing the bolt, but seeing me awake, ran away after replacing it in a mysterious way?' As soon as it was morning, I sent for Dhani and Prasanna, and after telling them everything, asked: 'Do you think a man really entered my room? I have no quarrel with any one in the village. Only I had some words with Madhu Jugi, the other day, over a trifling matter. Is it possible that he entered my room because of some grudge against me?' Both of them laughed and chid me, saying, 'You silly woman! Has old age affected your brain? Why do you talk that way about your dream? Think what other people will say when they hear about it! It will give rise to a scandal and you will be ridiculed if you mention it to anybody again.' Hearing this, I thought, 'Oh, then it was really a dream! I would not tell it to anyone except to you on your return.'

8. "On another occasion when I was speaking with Dhani in front of the temple of the Jugis, I suddenly saw a divine Effulgence come from the holy image of the great God Siva, fill the temple and rush towards me in waves. Taken by surprise, I was on the point of telling Dhani about it, when all of a sudden the Light engulfed me and swiftly entered into my body. Stunned with wonder

and fear, I fell down unconscious. Afterwards, when Dhani had
helped me to recover, I told her everything. At first she was much
surprised; then she said, 'You had an epileptic fit.' But I have
the feeling that the Light has been in my womb ever since, and that
I am pregnant. I told this also to Dhani and Prasanna, but they
rebuked me and called me silly, mad and what not. According
to them what I had experienced was caused by some delusion or
bodily affliction. Trying in various ways to make me understand
this, they warned me not to speak of the occurrence to anyone else.
Determined not to divulge it to anyone except you, I have so far
kept silent. Well, what do you think? Was it the grace of God
that did it, or could it have been due only to ill health? Even now
I have the feeling that I am pregnant."

9. As he listened to everything that Chandra said, Kshudiram
remembered his own dream at Gaya. Then reassuring her in
various ways, he said: "Do not henceforth speak about such
visions and experiences to anybody except me. Be free from
all anxiety and know for certain that whatever Raghuvir shows by
His grace is for our good. During my stay at Gaya, Gadadhara
revealed to me in a supernatural way that a son would be born
to us." These words of her godlike husband set Chandradevi's
mind at rest; and obeying him, she henceforward depended entirely
on Raghuvir. Three or four months had passed after this conversation between Kshudiram and his wife, when it became clear to
everyone that Chandradevi, although past forty-five, had become
pregnant again. Women are said to gain in loveliness and grace
when they are in the family way. This was noticed in Chandradevi
also, and Dhani and other women of the village used to remark that
she appeared lovelier this time than on previous occasions. As
the news spread, some of them began to whisper among themselves:
"Imagine a woman conceiving at her age and looking so sweet!
She may even die at the time of delivery."

10. Day by day, after she had conceived, Chandradevi's
spiritual visions and experiences became more numerous. It is
said that at this time visions of gods and goddesses occurred to
her almost daily. At times, she was aware of a purifying fragrance
coming from the bodies of those holy beings and spreading over the
whole house; or, again, she would hear celestial voices and be
struck with wonder. It is also said that at this time her heart
overflowed with motherly love for all the gods and goddesses.

Almost every day she would tell her husband about these visions and experiences and ask why they should come to her. Kshudiram comforted her in various ways and told her not to be perturbed· We shall now relate an incident of this period. We were told that Chandra described it thus to her husband with a feeling of awe: "O revered one, there is no end to the number of gods and goddesses who have shown themselves to me from time to time ever since the day I saw the Light, standing in front of the Siva temple. Many of them I have never seen before, not even in pictures. Today, I saw a god come on the back of a swan. At first I was startled; but then feeling sorry for·him as his face was red with the heat of the sun, I called him and said, 'O dear little god riding a swan, your face looks burnt by the sun. There is in the house some cold rice, prepared yesterday. Come, eat a little and get refreshed before you go.' He heard me and smiled, but then faded away and I could see him no more. I see many such forms. I do not worship or meditate on them and yet I see them at any time of the day or night. Sometimes they come before me in human shapes, and then dissolve into thin air. Can you tell me why I see all this? Is it some disease? At times I wonder if I am possessed by the spirit of Gosain."* Then Kshudiram reminded her again of the dream he had had at Gaya and pointed out how fortunate she was to be actually carrying in her womb the Supreme Lord whose purifying influence alone gave rise to her spiritual visions. Because of her absolute faith in her husband's words, his explanation of the situation filled Chandra's heart with supreme devotion. Fortified by a new strength, she became free from anxiety.

Time rolled on. Completely surrendering themselves to Raghuvir, Kshudiram and his virtuous wife spent their days in the expectation of beholding, as their son, the Divine Being whose auspicious presence had already filled their lives with deep devotion·

---

* After the death of Sukhlal Goswami, various supernatural portents' had occurred and this gave the villagers the idea that either he or some other dead person of his family had become a ghost and was living in the Bakul tree in front of his house. Under the influence of that belief the villagers used to say, whenever anyone had a supernatural experience, that the person was possessed by Gosain (Goswami). The simple-hearted Chandradevi also thought so at the time.

CHAPTER V

A GREAT SOUL IS BORN

(TOPICS: 1. Chandradevi's apprehension removed by her husband. 2. Birth of Gadadhar. 3. Astrological signs at his birth. 4. His naming.)

1.   Autumn was succeeded by the 'season of dew' and winter. Spring, the 'king of the seasons', arrived. There was a pleasant softness in the air, and all creation was pulsating with a new life. The lovely month of Phalgun—neither hot nor cold—was only six days old. There was a great surge of love in Nature which manifested in its beauty—as the scriptures say—a particle of the bliss of Brahman latent in all things. Of all the seasons, spring has received just a little more of that divine effulgent bliss, since it showers such great joy on the world.

Chandradevi   was   near   her   time   and   her   heart was filled with a celestial joy as she prepared the daily food-offering for Raghuvir. But in her body   there   was a feeling of great lassitude. Then suddenly the thought came that something might happen at any moment, and that, if she should be delivered just then, there would be nobody in the house to prepare the offerings. What was she to do? Alarmed, she communicated her thoughts to her husband. Kshudiram put her mind at rest saying, "Fear not. Surely He who is now in your womb will not, by His birth, become a hindrance to the worship and service of Raghuvir. Don't be anxious; certainly you will be able to manage the service of Raghuvir today.   I have already arranged for the service from tomorrow, and Dhani has been asked to sleep here from tonight." At this Chandra felt a new strength in her body and cheerfully went on with her household duties. It happened exactly as Kshudiram had said. The midday and evening offerings to Raghuvir and the other services to Him were finished without any hitch. Kshudiram and Ramkumar went to bed after taking their night meals; and Dhani came and lay in the same room with Chandradevi. Besides the shrine-room of Raghuvir, there were two bedrooms with a thatched roof, and a kitchen. In another small room there was a

husking machine on one side, and a fire-place for boiling paddy
on the other. For want of a better place, this room, which also
had a thatched roof, was kept ready for Chandra's confinement.

2. It was some ten minutes before dawn that Chandradevi
felt the first pangs of labour. Dhani helped her to the lying-in
room, and there, almost immediately, she gave birth to a male
child. After rendering the necessary help to the mother, when
Dhani turned her attention to the baby, she was surprised to find
that it had disappeared from the place where she had kept it.
In alarm she took the lamp to look for the child and found that it
had rolled down the ground covered with blood and slime into the
hollow fireplace and was lying there, with its little body adorned
with ashes, and still not crying! Dhani tenderly picked up the
child, washed it, and looking at it in the light, wondered at its beauty
and its size. It looked like a six-month-old infant! Chandramani's friends, Prasanna and other women of the Laha family,
were sent for. As soon as they arrived. Dhani told them what
had happened. At the sacred solemn hour before sunrise, the
sound of the conch filled that humble cottage where Kshudiram
spent his pious and austere life, and proclaimed to the world the
advent of a great soul. Ascertaining the signs of the zodiac under
which the child was born, Kshudiram, well versed in astrology,
found that the boy had come into the world at an especially auspicious moment.

3. According to the Hindu calendar, which reckons the day
from sunrise to sunrise, it was Wednesday the sixth day of Phalgun
in B.E. 1242, or 1757 of the Saka year, or Thursday, February 18,
A.D. 1836 according to Gregorian calendar. The child was born
just twelve minutes before sunrise. The auspicious second lunar
day of the bright fortnight and the twentyfifth of the lunar constella-
tions (Purvabhadrapada) had combined to bring about the happy
astrological conjunction called the Siddhiyoga. Sun, Moon and
Mercury had come together in the sign of the zodiac under which
the boy was born. Saturn had then reached the highest point
of the zodiac, indicating that the boy would have a unique life.
Calculations according to the method of the great sage Parasara
showed that the 'planets' Rahu and Ketu occupied the highest point
of the zodiac and were in the ascendant. Finally, Jupiter which
was then beginning to rise, also exerted a strong and auspicious
influence on the child's destiny.

4. Later, well-known astrologers also said that the time * of birth came under a very auspicious sign of the zodiac (Lagna or Rasi), which indicated, beyond all doubt, that the person concerned "would be virtuous and respected and would always perform good deeds. Surrounded by many disciples, he would live in a temple; would found a new institution for teaching religion generation after generation; and would be universally revered as a great soul born of an aspect of Narayana." On hearing this, Kshudiram's mind was filled with wonder,and his grateful heart felt that his divine dream at Gaya had actually come true. He then performed the birth-ceremony and named the boy Sambhuchandra after the sign of the zodiac under which he was born; but in memory of his remark-able dream, he decided to call him Gadadhar, by which name he was afterwards known.

Looking at the face of their beautiful child, and assured of his unique destiny, Kshudiram and Chandramani thought themselves blessed. They performed the ceremony of taking the child out for the first time and naming him, and resolved to bring him up with great attention.

---

* The detailed description of Sri Ramakrishna's horoscope appearing in this chapter has been transferred to the appendix at the end of the volume.—Tr.

CHAPTER VI

GADADHAR'S CHILDHOOD AND THE DEATH OF HIS FATHER

(TOPICS; 1. Gift of a cow by Ramachandra. 2. Gadadhar's charms. 3. Chandradevi's divine visions. 4. Gadadhar looking much bigger. 5. Sarvamangala, the younger sister of Gadadhar. 6. Gadadhar's preparation for going to school. 7. School of the Lahas. 8. Gadadhar's peculiar temperament. 9. An incident indicating it. 10. Progress and range of Gadadhar's education. 11. His courage. 12. His aptitude for making friends. 13. His power of imagination. 14. Durga festival at Ramachandra's house. 15. Kshudiram attends the festival. 16. Kshudiram's illness and death.)

1. According to the scriptures, the parents of incarnations like Rama, Krishna and others knew that their sons were under the special protection of Providence, through the visions they had had, before and after their birth. Yet parental affection often made them oblivious of this fact and filled their minds with anxious thoughts about the welfare of their sons. This applies to Kshudiram and his wife Chandradevi also. For, the lotus face of their loving child made them often forget the divine dream at Gaya and the celestial vision near the Siva temple, and they began to devise various means for his proper care and nourishment. The news of the birth was sent to Ramachandra, Kshudiram's prosperous nephew, at Medinipur. Fearing that there might not be sufficient milk available in his uncle's poor family, he sent them a milch cow, thereby removing Kshudiram's anxiety on that score. But though all that was wanted for the new-born child came in unexpected ways from different quarters, there was no end to the anxiety of the parents. Time thus rolled on.

2. As days went by, the charming features of the baby began to attract people more and more. He captivated the hearts not only of his parents and every other member of the family, but also of the villge women. Whenever the village women had some leisure, they would hasten to Chandra, and if asked why they came, would answer, "What are we to do? Our longing to see your baby every day brings us here." From now on, women relatives

from the neighbouring villages also began to come to Kshudiram's humble cottage oftener than before. Growing up without want, and surrounded by love and care, the new-comer gradually passed his fifth month, and the time for his first rice-feeding ceremony was at hand.

At first Kshudiram decided to perform this ceremony in a simple way in keeping with his means. His idea was to limit all ceremonies to the minimum requirements of scriptural injunctions, confine invitations to a few close relatives and end the function with feeding the child with the usual rice offering of Raghuvir. But actually, things took a different course. At the secret prompting of Kshudiram's great friend, Dharmadas Laha, the village landlord, the foremost Brahmanas and other leading men of the village came to Kshudiram and, to his utter surprise, insisted that he should feed them all on that auspicious day. Kshudiram was in a great fix; for since all the villagers respected and loved him, he could not make up his mind as to whom to invite and whom to leave out. And, to invite all was out of the question because of his slender resources. Convinced in his heart that Raghuvir would show him the way out, he sought the advice of his friend Dharmadas. As soon as he came to know that Dharmadas desired to take on himself the responsibility of conducting the ceremony, Kshudiram left the whole matter to him and returned home. Dharmadas cheerfully made all arrangements for the ceremony, almost entirely at his own expense, and the function went off smoothly. We are told that people of all castes in the village came to Kshudiram's cottage for the ceremony and enjoyed taking the food offered to Raghuvir. Many poor beggars also had their fill that day, and all left, pronouncing blessings on Kshudiram's son.

3. Every little action of Gadadhar appeared sweeter with the passing of time, and filled Chandradevi's heart with joy. But she was not quite free from fear also. Before the birth of this child she had never asked the gods for any favour. But now, urged by maternal love, her heart poured forth prayers for her son a thousand times a day, consciously or unconsciously. And yet she could not shake off her anxiety altogether. The thought of her son's care and well-being filled her mind so completely that it obstructed even her spiritual visions. Still they came to her from time to time, and filled her with amazement, and at times with an

4

apprehension of evil. We shall now relate an example of this, as heard from a reliable source.

4. One morning, when Gadadhar was seven or eight months old, he fell asleep at his mother's breast. Chandra put him to rest under a mosquito-net and went out of the room to attend to her household duties. Shortly afterwards, when she happened to come back to the room for something, she found that, instead of the child, a strange tall person was lying under the net, filling the whole bed. In great alarm Chandra rushed out of the room and called out to her husband. As soon as he came, she told him what she had seen, but on examination they found none except the child sleeping on the bed as before. Even then Chandra's fears did not abate. She went on repeating, "I am certain that it was a mischievous spirit who did it. I distinctly saw a tall person lying in the bed where our son lies. It was certainly not a delusion. How could it be? Do call immediately an experienced exorcist to examine the child. Otherwise, some harm may befall him." Kshudiram consoled her, saying, "There is nothing strange in your getting visions even now about our son; for we were blessed with them even before his birth. So drive away the idea that it was the doing of a spirit. With Raghuvir in the house, is it ever possible for spirits to come here to harm the boy? Therefore be at rest and do not speak to anyone about it. Rest assured that Raghuvir always protects him." Although for the time being Chandra was pacified by her husband's words, the fear of harm befalling the child still haunted her mind like a shadow. For a long time that day, with folded hands, she poured out to Raghuvir the anguish of her heart.

5. Years thus went by, bringing to Gadadhar's parents joy and sorrow, exultation and anxiety. The joyous attraction that the little boy exerted over them and over others from the very beginning, increased day by day. Four or five years gradually passed. During this period, Kshudiram's last child, a daughter named Sarvamangala, was also born.

6. As Gadadhar grew up, Kshudiram was filled with wonder and delight at noticing the development of the boy's remarkable memory and intelligence. Sometimes he would take the lively boy on his lap and repeat to him a long list of names of his ancestors, or short hymns to gods and goddesses and the various ways of paying homage to them, or wonderful stories from the *Ramayana* and the *Mahabharata*. He found that Gadadhar could grasp and

remember, hearing only once, most of what he was told, and that, when asked to repeat them, he could do so without faltering. At the same time, he discovered that, just as the boy learnt and remembered some things with great eagerness, he also remained indifferent to certain other things which did not appeal to him, in spite of all efforts to rouse his interest in them. He noticed this when trying to teach him arithmetic, especially the multiplication table, and thought it unnecessary to force the impatient lad, still so young, to learn those lessons. But finding that the boy was becoming more and more restless, he sent him to a school after the usual ceremony. Gadadhar was then five years old. He was very happy to meet boys of his own age, and his loving ways endeared him to them and to the teacher.

7. The school was held in the spacious theatre-hall in front of the house of the Lahas, the landlords of the village. A teacher, paid mainly by them, taught their own children and those of the neighbourhood. In fact, it was the Lahas who were chiefly responsible for starting the school. It was not far from Kshudiram's cottage, and was held in two sessions daily, both morning and evening. The children attended the classes for two or three hours in the morning and then returned home for bath and food. They came again at three or four in the afternoon and remained till sunset. Very young boys like Gadadhar had not, of course, to study for so long a period, but they too had nevertheless to remain in the school. After finishing their lessons, the little boys stayed in their places or sometimes went to play. The older boys helped the new-comers with their lessons and also saw to it that they went through their old lessons every day. Thus, although the school had only one teacher, the work went on smoothly. One Jadunath Sarkar was in charge when Gadadhar first entered the school, but he retired shortly afterwards for various reasons, and one Rajendranath Sarkar was appointed in his place.

8. The wonderful dreams and visions, which foretold Gadadhar's great spiritual destiny even before his birth, had made a lasting impression on Kshudiram's mind. And so, whenever he found the boy doing something naughty, like all lively children, he would never be harsh with him. Instead, he would gently ask the boy not to do it again. He now and then noticed signs of wilfulness in Gadadhar, but he was not sure whether this was due to the excessive attention everybody bestowed on him or to the boy's

inherent nature. Instead of going to school, the self-willed boy
would go and play with his companions outside the village; or,
without caring to tell anybody, go to an open-air performance
called *Yatra,* at some place in the neighbourhood. Kshudiram
did not scold him for this wilfulness, as other parents would have
done; for he now felt convinced that it was this that would ultimately
help the boy to become great. And there was good reason for him
to think so, since he invariably found that Gadadhar would not
rest till he accomplished what he had undertaken; that he would
never try to hide any act of his by telling a lie; and that above all,
he would never think of doing harm to anybody. But there was
one thing that really worried Kshudiram. When the boy was
asked or forbidden to do anything, he would deliberately go counter
to the instruction until it was put to him in a way that appealed
to his heart and understanding. Kshudiram understood that this
really showed the boy's desire to know the 'why' and 'wherefore'
of everything. But he realized also that people would not normally
tolerate such behaviour, nor take the trouble to satisfy the boy's
curiosity by telling him the reason for everything. As a result,
he thought it was possible that the boy might occasionally be led
to ignore the conventional rules of good conduct. It was the
occurrence, at that time, of a small incident which gave rise to
this apprehension of Kshudiram. It also made him understand
the working of the boy's mind, and he began carefully to guide
him accordingly.

9. There is a big tank known as Haldarpukur, by the side of
Kshudiram's house. All the villagers used its clear pure water for
bathing, drinking, cooking, etc. It had two bathing ghats, one for
men and the other for women. Young boys like Gadadhar would
very often use the ghat reserved for women. Coming one day for
a bath to that ghat with a few boys of his own age, Gadadhar
started jumping and swimming in the water and made himself a
nuisance to the women who had come there to bathe. Elderly
women who were occupied with their daily prayers and other devo-
tions found that, now and then, a little water was being splashed
over them. They therefore asked the boys to stop, but they would
not listen. Annoyed at this, one of the women scolded them
saying, "Why do you come here? Can't you go to the men's
ghat? Here women wash their clothes after their bath. You
should know that women must not be seen undressed." Gadadhar

asked, "Why not?" Instead of making him understand, she began to scold him all the more. Seeing that the women were annoyed and fearing that they would complain to their parents, the boys behaved better. But Gadadhar hit upon a plan. For two or three days, he hid himself behind a tree near the tank and peeped at the women while they were taking their bath. When, later, he met the elderly woman who had scolded him, he told her, "Day before yesterday I saw four women bathing, yesterday six and today eight. But I find that nothing has happened to me!" She thereupon came to Chandra and told her laughingly what the boy had said. At an opportune moment, Chandra spoke to Gadadhar gently, but in a convincing manner, "It is true nothing will happen to you when you do that; but women will feel insulted. They are in no way different from me; and so, if you insult them, it is the same as insulting me. In future don't do anything that would hurt their sense of honour. Is it right to wound their feelings, which is the same as wounding mine?" This the boy could understand, and he never again behaved that way.

10. To resume the story, Gadadhar's progress at school was not bad. Within a short time he could read and write simple words and sentences. But his aversion for arithmetic continued. On the other hand, he became more and more adroit in imitating others and showed his originality in various ways. Seeing the village potters making images of gods and goddesses, he began to visit them, and learning their art, started practising it at home. It became one of his hobbies. Similarly he mixed with those who painted pictures and himself began to paint. Whenever he was told that someone was reading and expounding the Puranas in the village, or that a religious drama was being enacted, he would go there and thus come to know the stories contained in the scriptures. He would, at the same time, observe very minutely the manner of presentation that appealed most to the audience. His wonderful memory and keen insight were of great help in these matters. From that early age his remarkable power of imitation and an inherent sense of fun helped the lively lad to mimic the peculiar gestures of men and women. At the same time the daily example of his parents helped to bring out his innate guilelessness and love of God. In his more mature years he remembered this and used to acknowledge with a grateful heart his indebtedness to his parents in this respect. The following words of his, addressed to us in

later days at Dakshineswar, will help the reader understand this point better: "My mother was the very embodiment of simplicity. She did not understand anything of worldly matters and could not count money. Not realizing the danger of saying all things to all persons, she would give out whatever came to her mind to anybody and everybody. For this, people called her, 'silly'. She also liked to feed one and all. My father never accepted gift from inferior persons. He spent the greater part of the day in worship, Japa and meditation. At the time of his daily prayer, as he recited the invocation to Gayatri, saying, 'O Shining One, O giver of boons, come,' etc., his chest would expand, become flushed and be bathed in tears. When not engaged in worship or other religious practices, he spent his time making flower garlands with thread and needle, to adorn Raghuvir. His reluctance to give false evidence made him give up his parental homestead. The villagers paid him the respect and reverence due to a sage."

11. As days went by, the boy's remarkable courage also began to show itself in various ways. Without the least hesitation he went to places where even elderly persons dared not go for fear of ghosts, ghouls and the like. His father's sister Ramsila would sometimes be possessed by the spirit of the goddess Sitala. She then became, as it were, a different person. Once about this time, when she was staying with her brother at Kamarpukur, one of those periodic transformations came over her and everyone in the house regarded her with awe and devotion. But Gadadhar watched his aunt in that state, no doubt with reverence, but without the slightest fear. He stayed near her and observed very minutely the change that had come over her. Afterwards, he said: "It would be splendid if the spirit which possessed my aunt would possess me."

12. The reader is already acquainted with Manikraja, the landlord of the village of Bhursubo, who was known for his charity and devotion. Attracted by Kshudiram's pious nature, he became his intimate friend. One day Gadadhar, then a boy of six, was taken by his father to Manikraja's house. He behaved towards everybody in that house as if they were his old friends; he seemed so natural and sweet to them that he became dear to them all from that very day. Manikraja's brother Ramjay was so charmed that he said to Kshudiram, "Friend, this son of yours is not an ordinary child. It seems to me that he possesses godly qualities in a marked

degree. Whenever you come this way, please bring him along.
I feel so happy to see him." For various reasons, Kshudiram
could not go again to Manikraja's place for some time. So Manikraja sent one of the women of his family to find out the reason
and to bring Gadadhar, if possible, on a short visit to Bhursubo.
When his father asked him whether he would like to go, the boy
was happy and went with the woman. He returned to Kamarpukur before dusk with presents of various kinds of sweets and
ornaments. Gadadhar became such a pet of that Brahmana family
that they used to send for him whenever Kshudiram could not go to
Bhursubo for some days.

13.   Gradually a year went by and Gadadhar was now seven.
As the child's sweet nature developed, everybody loved him more
and more. Whenever the women of the village prepared any
delicacies in their homes, their first thought was to feed the boy
with a portion of it. His playmates never felt happy till they had
shared their food with him. He had such charming ways and spoke
and sang so sweetly that the neighbours cheerfully put up with his
childish pranks. About this time an incident occurred which made
Gadadhar's parents and friends very anxious about the boy. By
the grace of God, Gadadhar was born with a strong and robust
constitution, and until now he had not suffered from any disease.
As a result, he was wonderfully buoyant and cheerful like a free bird.
Well-known physicians say that it is the absence of body consciousness that is the sign of health. It was this kind of health
that the boy enjoyed from his birth. Endowed, as he was by
nature, with great powers of concentration, he became so identified
with an object on which he set his mind that he seemed to lose his
outer consciousness entirely. The enchanting view of the vast
green fields fanned by the gentle breeze, the incessant flow of the
river, the melodious songs of birds, and, above all, the magic
of ever-changing clouds in the deep blue sky would, at times,
unfold their mystery and glory to the boy's inner vision and hold
him spell-bound. He would then lose himself completely and
enter the unknown, distant, and solitary domain of the spirit. The
experience we now relate also had its origin in the boy's tendency
towards the spiritual contemplation of beauty. One day, while
roaming carefree in the fields, Gadadhar looked up towards the
sky and saw a newly formed dark cloud, and against it the orderly
movement of a flock of cranes in full flight, with their snow-white

wings outspread. The boy became so completely absorbed in the beauty of it all, that awareness of his own body and of all other earthly surroundings vanished altogether, and he fell down unconscious (vide II:2). His friends, finding him in that condition, were alarmed and distressed. They sent word to his parents, and the boy was carried home from the field. As soon as he regained consciousness, he was his old self again. Naturally, this incident caused a lot of worry to Kshudiram and Chandradevi, and they thought of various means to prevent its happening again. In fact they thought it to be the beginning of fainting fits and wanted to arrange for remedies like propitiatory rites. But Gadadhar told them again and again that what had happened to him was really due to his being merged in a feeling he had never experienced before; and that, although he was found outwardly unconscious, he was conscious inwardly and had experienced a unique bliss. However, as it did not recur. the boy's health was considered satisfactory, although Kshudiram felt he was subject to fits, and Chandra was convinced that he had come under evil eyes. Owing to these uncertainties, his attendance at school was stopped for some time. So, free as he was to go wherever he liked in the village, the boy gave himself up to play and fun even more than before.

14. Gadadhar was about seven years and a half at the time of the great autumn festival of Bengal in 1843. The reader already knows Ramchandra Bandyopadhyaya, Kshudiram's prosperous nephew. He used to spend most of his time at Medinipur in the interest of his profession as a pleader, until his family came to live at his parental home in the village of Selampur. Every year, Ramchandra celebrated the grand autumn festival at great expense at his village home. We have heard from Hriday that during the eight days of worship, the Selampur house used to ring with music and song. The family experienced a continuous flow of joy in feeding Brahmanas, offering parting gifts to Pandits, feeding the poor and giving them clothes. On those occasions Ramchandra would bring his revered uncle to his house and spend some happy days with him. That year, also, Kshudiram and his family were cordially invited when the time came.

15. Kshudiram had almost completed his sixty-eighth year, and had now lost his former vigour on account of dyspepsia and dysentery, from which he had been often suffering during the previous few years. So in spite of his desire to go, he hesitated

to accept his dear nephew's loving invitation. He began to feel
an unaccountable but strong disinclination to leave his humble
cottage, his family, and especially Gadadhar, even for a few days.
Then he thought: "If I do not go this year, who knows whether,
with my increasing weakness, I shall be able to go there again?"
He at first intended to take Gadadhar with him; but then he remembered that this would make Chandra very anxious. As he
could not take Gadadhar, he finally decided to go with his eldest
son Ramkumar, spend the few days of worship with Ramchandra,
and then return. He paid homage to Raghuvir, bade goodbye
to all, kissed Gadadhar and started for Selampur a few days before
the commencement of the festival. Ramchandra was very happy
at the arrival of his revered uncle and his cousin Ramkumar.

16.   Kshudiram had a relapse of his old complaint, dysentery,
immediately after reaching Selampur and was placed under treatment. But that did not interfere with the happy mood in which
the sixth, seventh, and eighth days of the bright fortnight were
spent. On the ninth day, however, Kshudiram's illness suddenly
took a serious turn and caused great anxiety in that mart of joy.
Ramchandra called in efficient doctors and started nursing his
uncle with the help of his sister Hemangini and cousin Ramkumar.
But Kshudiram's condition did not improve.   The ninth day
passed somehow; and now came the tenth day (Vijaya), especially
sacred to the Hindus as the time of re-union.   That day Kshudiram
became so weak that it was difficult for him to speak at all. As
soon as the immersion ceremony of the image of Durga was over
in the afternoon, Ramchandra hastened back to his uncle's bedside.
He found that the last moment was drawing near. On inquiry he
learnt that Kshudiram had been lying silent in the same condition
for a long time. Then Ramchandra said to him in tears: "Uncle, you
always take the name of Raghuvir; why don't you do so now?" The
sound of that name at once roused Kshudiram, and in a trembling,
halting voice he said: "Is that you, Ramchandra? Have you
come after immersing the image? Then make me sit up." When
Ramchandra, Hemangini and Ramkumar had helped him with
great care to sit up on the bed, Kshudiram in a solemn tone uttered
the name of Raghuvir thrice and left his body. The drop of water
thus mingled with the ocean. Lord Raghuvir merged the breath
of life of the devotee in His infinite life and thus blessed him with
immortality and peace everlasting. At the dead of night, the village

rang with the loud singing of the praises of the divine Lord.   Kshudiram's body was then brought to the river bank and was cremated
by consecrating it in fire.   The news reached Kamarpukur the
next day and filled Kshudiram's hitherto happy home with sorrow.
When the period of mourning was over, Ramkumar performed the
Sraddha ceremony as prescribed by the scriptures and fed many
Brahmanas, thus completing his father's last rites.   It is said that
Ramchandra gave a large sum towards the expenses of the ceremony performed in honour of his departed uncle.

CHAPTER VII

GADADHAR'S BOYHOOD

(TOPICS: 1. The impact of Kshudiram's death on his family. 2. Its effect on Gadadhar's mind. 3. Gadadhar's behaviour towards his mother. 4. Gadadhar's keeping company with holy men. 5. Gadadhar's Bhavasamadhi. 6. 7. His bosom friend Gayavishnu. 8. His Upanayana. 9. His solving a disputed point at a meeting of scholars. 10. His Bhavasamadhi for the third time. 11. Repeated Bhavasamadhis. 12. Causes of Gadadhar's aversion to attend school. 13. Progress of Gadadhar's education. 14. Marriage of Rameswar and of Sarvamangala. 15. Change in the behaviour of Ramkumar's wife. 16. Change in Ramkumar's financial condition. 17. Death of Ramkumar's wife.)

1. Kshudiram's death affected the life of the family in many ways. He had been Chandra's companion in weal and woe for forty-four long years. It was therefore natural that she found the world now empty without him and felt his loss every moment. She had been accustomed for long to take refuge at the lotus feet of Raghuvir, and now that the world had no more attraction for her, her whole mind was always drawn in that direction. But the world would not release her till the time was ripe. It gradually drew her back to the joys and sorrows of daily life through her concern for her seven-year-old son Gadadhar and her four-year-old daughter Sarvamangala. Thus the sorrow-stricken Chandra somehow passed her days in the service of Raghuvir and in bringing up her youngest son and daughter. After Kshudiram's demise, the entire responsibility of maintaining the family fell on the shoulders of his eldest and devoted son Ramkumar. Now, as he could not afford to waste any time in grief, his whole mind and energy were employed in seeing that his bereaved mother and little brother and sister did not lack anything. The younger brother Rameswar, now eighteen years old, was expected to help the family be earning money as soon as he had finished the study of Smriti and Jyotisha; and Ramkumar himself had to try to better the condition of the family by adding to his own income. His capable wife, finding that Chandradevi was no longer able to cope with all the work, took upon herself most of the cooking and other household duties.

2. It is a common experience that nothing makes life so empty as the loss of a mother in one's infancy, the death of a father in childhood, and the loss of a wife in youth. Being entirely dependent on the mother's care and love, the infant does not miss its father even if he dies. But when it grows up and there is an awakening of its intelligence, it becomes aware of the father's special affection. The child's heart begins to be drawn towards the father as soon as it finds that he alone can satisfy certain desires which even its fond mother cannot. Its feeling of loss is therefore very acute, if the father dies at that time. Gadadhar too felt likewise when Kshudiram died. Many little things reminded him daily of his father, and a deep sorrow lingered in his heart. But being more thoughtful and disciplined than other boys of his age, Gadadhar never openly gave way to his sorrow, out of regard for his mother's feelings. To all appearances, the boy was as full of mirth and merriment as ever. Although he was seen sometimes wandering alone in the Bhutir Khal cremation-ground or in Manikraja's mango grove and other solitary spots, nobody thought that there was any other reason for this than a boy's natural restlessness. But actually, Gadadhar was becoming more thoughtful and fond of solitude. He also studied the ways of various persons and observed everyone very minutely.

3. Those who have suffered and feel the same loss equally come close to one another. That is perhaps the reason why Gadadhar now felt especially drawn towards his mother. He stayed near her much longer than before, and took delight in helping her as far as he could in the service of the gods and in her household duties. It did not take him long to notice that when he was with her, his mother almost forgot the loss she had suffered. The boy's attitude towards his mother also showed some change. After his father's death, he never asked her for anything with the same insistence as before, for he realized that the feeling of sorrow would again well up in her heart and that she would be most unhappy if she could not fulfil any of his desires. In short, a strange desire to protect his mother in every way now arose in Gadadhar's heart.

4. Gadadhar now started going to school once again. Though he was expected to attend to regular lessons at the school, his real interest now turned towards listening to the recital of narratives from the Puranas and to making images of gods and goddesses in clay.

He perhaps felt that his absorption in these occupations helped
him to forget the loss of his father. He also found at this time a
new interest suited to his temperament. The Lahas had set aside
for the convenience of pilgrims a house situated at the south-east
corner of the village, on the road to Puri. Religious men,
unattached to worldly things, often took shelter in that house on
their way to Puri to pay obeisance to Lord Jagannath, and also
on their way back home. While staying there, they came to the
village to collect alms from different houses. Gadadhar knew
from the Puranas that monks, after acquiring detachment, renounce
this transitory world and devote themselves entirely to the realisation of the Lord. The boy's own feeling about the transitoriness
of the world had been strengthened since his father's demise. He
had also heard that association with holy men leads to the blessedness of ultimate peace. And so he now began to visit that pilgrim-
house, whenever he could, to become acquainted with the monks.
There he observed how morning and evening they blazed up the
Dhuni (sacred fire) and sat round it absorbed in meditation; how
they offered the simple food obtained as alms to their chosen
Deities and then partook of it themselves with relish; how, with
absolute dependence on God, they tried to bear even severe illness
patiently; and how they refrained from disturbing anybody for
securing even their urgent needs. But he also discovered how
their ranks consisted also of some hypocrites dressed as monks
but living only for selfish ends in disregard of all essentials of right
conduct. Gradually he began to mix intimately with genuine
monks by helping them in little things like collecting fire wood or
fetching drinking water. They, in turn, developed a liking for this
good-looking lad on account of his sweet ways, and taught him
how to pray to, and sing the praises of, the divine Lord. They
also instructed him in other religious matters and felt happy in
sharing with him the food they had collected as alms. Of course,
Gadadhar could mix this way only with those monks who, for
one reason or another, spent a considerable time at the pilgrim-
house.

5. When the boy was eight years old, a few monks stayed at
the pilgrim-house for many days to take some rest after a long and
fatiguing journey or for some other similar reason. Gadadhar mixed
with them in his usual way and soon became dear to them. At
first, no one knew about this; but when the boy's relations with

the monks became intimate and he began to spend much time with them, many came to notice it.   On some days he ate so much with them that when he returned home, he had no appetite for any food. When Chandradevi asked him the reason, he told her everything. At first the mother was not perturbed.   On the contrary, the fact that he had won the hearts of the mendicants appeared to her a blessing, and she began sending with the boy food-stuffs and other articles necessary for them.   But it so happened afterwards that the boy came home sometimes with sacred ashes covering his body or with emblems marked on his forehead, and at others wearing like monks a 'Kaupina' or a loin-cloth made by tearing his own wearing cloth. He would then say, "Look mother, how the holy men have adorned me!" This development made Chandra very uneasy, for she was afraid that one day the mendicants might tempt her son to go away with them. She expressed her fear to Gadadhar and began to weep. In spite of all efforts to remove her fear, he could not pacify her. He then made a resolve not to go to the monks any more, and told her about it. This at least relieved her anxiety. And so, Gadadhar went to the monks to bid them farewell once for all. When they asked him the reason, he told them of his mother's misgivings. On hearing this, they went with him to Chandradevi and assured her that the thought of taking away Gadadhar with them had never even crossed their minds; for, to take away a boy of that tender age, without the permission of his parents, they said, would be stealing, an offence unworthy of any religious man. At this, every shadow of her apprehension left Chandradevi, and she readily agreed to let the boy visit them as before.

    6. Another event of this period caused Chandra a great deal of anxiety about Gadadhar. Although everyone thought it a casual occurrence, it was actually the result of the boy's growing propensity for spiritual contemplation and deep thought. One day, on his way to the well-known temple of the goddess Visalakshi at Anur, a village about two miles north of Kamarpukur, he suddenly lost all external consciousness. Prasannamayi, the pious sister of Dharmadas Laha, who was one of his companions, realized that it was the boy's spiritual awareness that had brought about this unconsciousness (vide II. 2). But when Chandradevi heard of it, she became anxious, thinking it was due to some physical malady. But on this occasion also, Gadadhar insisted that he was in that

condition only because his mind had become merged in the goddess, as he was contemplating on her.

7. More than two years went by, and gradually the ups and downs of life made the boy almost forget the loss of his father. We have already mentioned Kshudiram's friend Dharmadas Laha. At this time Gadadhar became an intimate friend of Dharmadas's son, Gayavishnu. The two boys were drawn to each other while at school and during walks. They began to address each other as 'pal' and would daily spend much time together. Gadadhar always took his friend along with him when he was invited and fed by the village women. He would not take any of the sweets and other delicacies prepared by his old nurse Dhani, till he had given a share to Gayavishnu. It is needless to say that Dharmadas and the guardians of Gadadhar were happy to see this friendship between the two boys.

8. When Ramkumar found that Gadadhar would soon complete his ninth year, he started making arrangements for his investiture with the sacred thread (*Upanayana*). Long before this, Dhani, who belonged to the blacksmith caste, had told the boy one day that she would consider herself blessed, if at the time of his investiture, he would accept alms from her and call her 'mother'. The boy was so touched by her sincere affection for him that he promised to fulfil her desire. Putting her trust in the boy's promise, the poor woman started accumulating money and requisites as best as she could, and eagerly awaited that happy event. At the proper time Gadadhar mentioned his promise to his eldest brother. But Ramkumar objected, because such a departure from the usual custom was against the family tradition. The boy, on his part, insisted on keeping his promise, and argued that if he yielded to the objection, he would be guilty of breaking his promise and that an untruthful person was not fit to put on the sacred thread. As the time for the investiture ceremony approached, everything was made ready. But it was feared that there would be a hitch in the completion of the ceremony because of Gadadhar's insistence. When the news reached his ears, Dharmadas tried to reconcile the difference. He said to Ramkumar, "Although this has never so far happened in your family, it has been done in many good Brahmana families elsewhere. Therefore no blame attaches to those who permit. it. You must also consider the question of satisfying Gadadhar's conscience and his peace of

mind." At these words of their father's friend, the wise old Dharmadas, Ramkumar and others refrained from raising further objections. Gadadhar then, with a cheerful heart, put on the sacred thread in accordance with the scriptural injunctions and applied his mind to performing Sandhya, worship etc., as befits a Brahmana. From now onwards, Dhani also considered her life to be blessed on account of her new relationship with the boy, who had called her 'mother' and accepted Bhiksha from her. A little after this, the boy entered upon his tenth year.

9. About this time the villagers were wonderstruck at an event which showed Gadadhar's unique, heaven-born genius (vide III:4). A big meeting of scholars had been convened at the house of the Lahas during the performance of a Sraddha ceremony. At this meeting there arose a controversy regarding a complicated theological question and the scholars could not arrive at a correct solution of the disputed point. Gadadhar, who was present, solved the problem in such a way that, after hearing what he said, the scholars praised and blessed him heartily.

10. After he had put on the sacred thread, Gadadhar, with his innate spiritual tendency, was delighted to get an opportunity to do something after his own heart. The boy had heard how the living symbol of Raghuvir had shown itself to his father in a dream and was brought by him to their house; and also how, from the auspicious day of the god's coming, their little bit of land had begun to yield an abundance of paddy that was sufficient not only to meet the requirements of the family but also to leave a surplus for kind-hearted Chandradevi to entertain the poor that went to her. Since then the boy had looked upon that family deity with great devotion and reverence. Now that he had the privilege of touching and worshipping that deity, his heart was filled with a new fervour of devotion. Much time was now spent by him daily in worship and meditation, after concluding the customary daily prayers and other duties. He served Raghuvir with especial steadfastness and devotion, so that the god might bestow his grace on him, as he had bestowed on his father, by blessing him with his visions and giving him commands from time to time. The god Rameswar Siva and the goddess Sitala also received his service. It was not long before his intense devotion bore fruit. The pure heart of the boy became so absorbed in the worship that he experienced the state of Bhava-samadhi also known as Savikalpa-

The mango tree planted by Sri Ramakrishna

Family Deities: Sitala, Raghuvir and Rameswar Siva

The Temple where Gadadhar entered
Bhava Samadhi on a Sivaratri night

Sri Ramakrishna Temple
constructed on the very spot of his birth

samadhi. And after this experience, various spiritual visions came to him from time to time. He had this kind of Samadhi and vision on the Sivaratri of that year (vide II.2).

The boy had fasted that day and worshipped with intense devotion the great God Siva, the origin of all the gods. His friend Gayavishnu and some other boys of his age were also fasting and had decided to keep a vigil that night, witnessing a drama depicting the glory of Siva. That drama was to be staged in the house of their neighbour Sitanath Pyne. After finishing the worship of the first quarter, Gadadhar was sitting merged in the contemplation of Siva, when his friends suddenly came and told him that he would have to act the part of Siva and speak a few words in the play at the house of the Pynes; for, they explained, the person who usually played that role had suddenly taken ill and was unable to appear. Gadadhar at first declined on the ground that it would interfere with his ॒worship; but they brushed aside the objection, arguing that, if he acted the part of Siva, he would have to think of Him all the time, and that was as good as worship. Moreover, they said, his refusal would deprive very many people of the entertainment; they also were fasting and had decided to keep a vigil the whole night, witnessing the drama. Won over by such arguments, Gadadhar agreed finally and appeared on the stage in the role of Siva. With his make-up of matted hair, rudraksha beads and ashes, he became so merged in the thought of Siva, that he lost all external consciousness. As he continued to be in that state for a long time, the play had to be stopped for the night.

11. From now onwards, Gadadhar was in this kind of ecstasy from time to time. He would forget himself and his surroundings when meditating, or listening to songs, music, etc., in praise of gods and goddesses. Then his mind would remain indrawn for a time— short or long—during which it would not respond to any external stimulus. On occasions, when his absorption became very deep, he would appear like a lifeless statue.

On emerging from such states, he would say, if questioned, that he then experienced a marvellous joy accompanied by divine visions while meditating on some god or goddess or listening to songs glorifying them. All this caused much alarm to Chandra and the other members of the family for a long time. But their anxieties were laid at rest when they found that the boy's health was not affected in any way, and that he was always cheerful, active and efficient. Gadadhar was now so often in this condition that he gradually got accustomed to it and could almost control it as he wished. It helped him also to understand subtle matters and various truths about gods and goddesses. This made him very happy and he was never afraid of experiencing that state. His spiritual tendencies became especially strong and he began to join heartily in various religious functions of the village, whether in honour of Hari or Siva or Manasa or Dharma. His broad-mindedness not only made him entirely free from any ill-feeling against devotees of different gods and goddesses, but kept him in positive friendship with them all. The established tradition of the village no doubt helped him in this matter. For, in contrast to other villages, people of all denominations in Kamarpukur—whether worshippers of Vishnu, or devotees of Siva, or votaries of Dharma—bore no ill-will towards one another, but lived in peace and amity.

12. Although, as we have seen, there was considerable progress so far as Gadadhar's religious aptitudes were concerned, he never developed a liking for book-learning. When he saw the longing of learned scholars for wealth and worldly enjoyments, he became averse to acquiring knowledge like them. For, his keen insight made him first ascertain the motives underlying all actions and then judge their value by the standard of his father's good qualities like detachment from the world, devotion to God, truthfulness righteous conduct, etc. Such a comparison revealed, to his surprise, that the goal of most of these scholars was entirely different from that of his father. But he felt more sad than surprised to find that such people always suffered from delusion, because they looked upon this transitory world as permanent. Is it then to be wondered at, that, as a result of this discovery, there arose in his mind a desire to conduct his own life differently? After hearing all this, the reader may perhaps ask: " Is it possible for a boy of eleven or twelve to have such profound insight and discrimination?" The answer is that Gadadhar was not an ordinary boy. He was born with extraordinary genius, memory and spiritual tendencies. Therefore the possession of such powers was not surprising in his case, though he was so young. But this apart, we must, for the sake of truth, narrate all facts that our investigation has brought to light, irrespective of what others may think of them.

13. Although Gadadhar's dislike for the prevailing type of education gradually increased, he nevertheless continued going to

the school. He became proficient in reading books written in his
mother tongue and in writing in that language. He now read the
Ramayana, the *Mahabharata* and other religious books with such
devotion and in such a sweet voice that people were charmed to
listen. The simple-hearted, unlettered villagers showed great
eagerness to hear him read those books, and Gadadhar was always
happy to please them. Sitanath Pyne, Madhu Jugi, and others
invited him to their houses, and men and women, full of devotion,
heard him read the life of Prahlada, the story of Dhruva, or other
narratives from the *Ramayana*, the *Mahabharata*, and similar
other texts.

Besides the *Ramayana*, the *Mahabharata,* etc., there still exist
in Kamarpukur records containing the stories of gods and goddesses
written in simple verses by the village poets well known in those
parts. Narratives on the revelations of the great god Tarakesvar;
the musical composition relating to Yogadya; and songs of Madan-
mohan of Vanavishnupur, describing gods and goddesses revealing
their true nature to holy men and devotees and performing supernatural deeds—these reached Gadadhar's ears from time to time.
With the help of his extraordinary memory, the boy learnt by heart
many of these poetical compositions by merely listening to their recital and would sometimes himself copy any available manuscript or
printed book containing them. We came to know of this when we
found, on investigation at the Kamarpukur house, a manuscript of
Ramakrishnayana, the musical compositions on Yogadya and
Subahu, copied by Gadadhar himself. It is also beyond doubt
that many a time the boy read or recited these narratives to the
simple-hearted men and women of the village, whenever they
requested him to do so.

We have already spoken of Gadadhar's indifference to
arithmetic. But after he had been at school for some time, he
made a little progress in that subject also. We are told that he
committed to memory tables even up to that of land-measurement
called Katha in the Book of Tables, and that he progressed from
simple addition to simple multiplication and division. But when
he reached his tenth year and began to experience ecstasy, his
eldest brother Ramkumar left him free to go to school whenever
he wanted and to learn whatever subjects he liked. For, he was
afraid that Gadadhar had a tendency to some ailments. His
teacher also did not press him when he found he was not making

progress in the study of a particular subject. It is therefore needless to add that there was little general progress in Gadadhar's studies at school.

14. Two years passed, and Gadadhar reached his twelfth year. His second elder brother Rameswar and his younger sister Sarvamangala were now twenty-two and nine years old respectively. Finding that Rameswar had reached the proper age, Ramkumar arranged for his marriage with the sister of Ramsaday Bandyopadhyaya of the village of Gaurhati near Kamarpukur. It was also agreed that Ramsaday himself would marry Rameswar's sister. As both the marriages were arranged in this manner, Ramkumar had no anxiety about the payment of any bridal money to the other party. Another important event concerning Ramkumar's family took place at this time. As his wife did not conceive, even though she was no longer young, everyone felt certain that she was barren. But now, when they found that she was in the family way, all felt happy but also apprehensive at the same time, because some of them had heard Ramkumar predict that she would die if she ever conceived.

15. A radical change came over Ramkumar's affairs from the time his wife conceived. His income now dwindled. His health broke down and he was not able to keep up his former active habits. His wife's behaviour also underwent a complete change. There was a rule in the family, from the time of his revered father, that no one (except boys not yet invested with the sacred thread, and those who were ill) should eat anything or even drink water before the worship of Raghuvir was finished. Now Ramkumar's wife broke this rule and turned a deaf ear to the objections raised by the other members of the family, who were afraid that evil might befall them. She picked up quarrels with everyone in the family over trifles, thereby creating ill-feeling, and persisted in her perverse conduct in spite of the protests of her husband and Chandradevi. But remembering that a change often comes over women during their pregnancy, they let her alone. Yet, instead of the usual peace in that pious household at Kamarpukur, there was now continual disharmony.

16. Ramkumar's brother, Rameswar, was not good at earning money, though he had sufficient learning. So, while the number of persons in the family increased, there was a decrease in its income, thus threatening its former comfortable existence. Ramkumar

became anxious but could not find a remedy in spite of all his efforts. It seemed as if some unseen power obstructed all his plans and brought them to nothing. A succession of anxieties made his very life a burden. As days and months passed, and the time of his wife's delivery approached, he became more and more dejected, remembering his previous reading of her fate.

17. At last she gave birth to a very beautiful male child some time in the year 1849, and while looking at its face, passed away in the lying-in room. A pall of grief again fell over the poor family.

CHAPTER VIII

AT THE THRESHOLD OF YOUTH

(TOPICS: 1. Ramkumar started a Sanskrit school (Tol) in Calcutta. 2. Effect of the death of Ramkumar's wife on the family. 3. The story of Rameswar. 4. Rameswar's thoughts about Gadadhar. 5. Gadadhar's attitude and behaviour at this time. 6. Gadadhar's devotional reading and singing. 7. Devotion of the village women to him. 8. Gadadhar in a woman's dress. 9. Gadadhar and the family of Sitanath Pyne. 10. A blow to Durgadas Pyne's pride. 11. The women of the traders' quarter. 12. Rukmini on Gadadhar. 13. All villagers loved Gadadhar. 14. Gadadhar's aversion to a bread-winning education. 15. The natural urge of Gadadhar's heart. 16. Gadadhar leaving school and enacting dramas. 17. His progress in fine arts. 18. Ramkumar takes him to Calcutta.)

1. Ramkumar's misfortune continued even after the death of his wife, and he became poorer day by day. His income from gifts given by persons who invited him on ceremonial occasions, dwindled. Although paddy sufficient for their own use grew in the piece of land at Lakshmijala, it became more and more difficult to get clothes and other daily necessaries. Milk was also needed every day for his old mother and Akshay, his motherless baby; but it had to be obtained, along with other necessaries, only by borrowing money. Thus Ramkumar got into debts which began to accumulate day by day. He could not avoid this, try as he would. Thinking he might be able to earn more money elsewhere, he made preparations to leave Kamarpukur on the advice of his friends. His recent bereavement made it easy for him to take this step; for he thought that he might get some peace of mind if he left the house crowded with memories of his companion in life for thirty years. There was much discussion as to whether Calcutta or Burdwan offered better prospects of earning. Finally it was decided that he should go to Calcutta, because his friends pointed out that Maheshchandra Chattopadhyaya of Sihar, Ramdhan Ghosh of Desra and others whom he knew had gone there and found good opportunities to earn money and improve their condition in spite of their being much inferior to him in learning, intelligence and strength of character. Therefore Ramkumar handed over the charge of the family affairs to Rameswar and went to

Calcutta soon after his wife's death. He started a Sanskrit school in the quarter of the city called Jhamapukur and began to teach a few boys.

2. There came many changes in the life of the family at Kamarpukur on the death of Ramkumar's wife. Chandradevi was now compelled to take upon herself the burden of all the household duties, including the care of Ramkumar's little child, Akshay. Rameswar's wife tried, as far as possible, to assist her; but being still very young, she was not of much help. So Chandradevi had to do practically everything herself—the service of Raghuvir, the bringing up of Akshay, the cooking, and other household work· It took her all the day to do this and she had not a minute's rest. It was very difficult for her, a woman of fifty-eight,* to manage all those household affairs. But knowing that such was the will of Raghuvir, she carried on without a word of complaint.

3. Rameswar had now to look after the income and expenses of the family, and was thinking how he could make both ends meet and keep the family in comfort. But his learning never helped him to make a good living. On the other hand, he spent much time in talking to the wandering monks and religious men, whenever he met them, and even did not hesitate to supply all their wants. So, although he now earned a little more than before, he could not pay off the family debt, his income being sufficient only to meet the bare needs of his people. He could therefore save nothing and was always in need. He sometimes spent even more than what he earned and lived a care-free life, consoling himself with the thought that ' Raghuvir will provide for the family somehow.'

4. No doubt, Rameswar dearly loved his younger brother Gadadhar, but he never bothered to find out whether he made any progress in his studies. Apart from being temperamentally incapable of giving such attention, he had no time for it, since he had to go to various places in search of remunerative work. He had thus neither the inclination nor the leisure to keep an eye on his brother's education. He had also the firm conviction that Gadadhar's highly disciplined mind would always prevent him from going astray; for he had seen in him a remarkable development of religious tendencies even at that early age. This conviction became stronger

---

* Chandradevi was born in 1791 and passed away in 1876 at the age of eighty-five. It is said that she died on a birthday of Sri Ramakrishna.

when he saw how men and women of the village reposed full confidence in the boy and loved him dearly.   Nobody, he felt sure,
could win all hearts and be praised by everyone unless He had
inherent worth and nobility of character.   So Rameswar looked
forward with joy to his young brother's glorious future and had no
anxiety on his account.   Gadadhar was thirteen years old when
Ramkumar went to Calcutta.   He had henceforth no regular
guardian, and was therefore his own master, free to conduct himself
in whatever way he liked.

5. As already mentioned, Gadadhar's keen insight enabled
him, even at that young age, to see through the motives of the actions
of others.   Therefore it did not take him long to realize that their
only object of studying at school or of gaining distinction in studies
was to enable themselves to make money, or as he himself would
put it, " to bundle up rice and plantain."   He also came to understand that no one who spent all his energy in that pursuit for the
sake of worldly enjoyment could, like his father, be devoted to
truth, or acquire strength of character and realise God.   Blinded
by selfish interest, some families in the village quarrelled over land
and other property and took to litigation.   They then divided their
houses, lands, etc., with measuring tapes, declaring, "This side is
mine and that side is his."   But scarcely had they enjoyed their shares
for a few days when death was found to carry them away ! Gadadhar
sometimes saw these things actually happening before his eyes and
came to the conclusion that money and the desire for enjoyment
were the root cause of much of misery in human life.   Therefore it
is not surprising that he became more and more averse to the kind
of learning that was acquired with the object of making money.
On the other hand he looked upon the attainment of love of God
as the primary aim of life and was content, like his father, with the
bare necessaries of life, namely 'coarse food and coarse clothing'.
He, however, went to school for a while almost every day, but
this was due to his attraction for the company of boys of his own age.
He now spent most of his time in the worship of Raghuvir and in
lightening his mother's burden by assisting her in household work.
On account of all these activities, he had to remain at home for the
greater part of the day.

6. Since Gadadhar now spent much time at home, the women
of the village had good opportunities of seeing him there.   When
they were free from their household duties, many of them would

come to Chandradevi and if they found the boy at home, would
sometimes ask him to sing for them or read religious narratives.
Gadadhar obliged them accordingly, whenever he could. If they
found him busy helping his mother, they would themselves finish
up the work to afford him time to read out to them from the Puranas
or to sing. This became almost a daily routine. The women
enjoyed it so much that they tried to finish their own daily duties
as early as they could, so that they might listen to his songs and
readings for a longer time.

Besides reading the Puranas, Gadadhar entertained the women
in various other ways. There were then in the village three parties
of Yatra players, one of minstrels (Bauls) and one or two of versifiers
(Kavis). Again, as many of the villagers were Vaishnavas, there
used to be in their houses reading every evening from the *Bhagavata*,
or singing of the praises of the divine Lord. His gift of memory
enabled Gadadhar to remember many of those muiscal compositions, plays, songs and hymns to God, which he had heard from his
childhood. As a special entertainment, one day he would begin a
drama ; on another sing the songs of Bauls or Kavis ; or again
sing the praises of the divine Lord. When he enacted a play,
he would himself play the various parts, changing his voice to suit
each character. If on any occasion he found his mother or any
of the women dejected, he would start playing a farce from the
plays; or would imitate so well the peculiar manner and gestures
of some one in the village known to all of them that they would roar
with laughter.

7. Thus Gadadhar exercised an immense influence over the
village women. They had already heard of the strange dream and
spiritual visions that the boy's parents had had at the time of his
birth. And they had also seen with their own eyes the extraordinary
change that came over his mind and body whenever he came in
touch with the spirit of gods and goddesses. Therefore it was
quite natural that his intense devotion to God, his absorption when
reading the Puranas, his sweet singing and his unconventional
simple-hearted behaviour towards them all, aroused in those women
a unique devotion and affection for him. We are told that
Prasannamayi and other elderly women saw in Gadadhar the manifestation of the divine Boy (Gopala) and loved him even more than
their own sons. And younger women, believing that he was born as
a part of Bhagavan Sri Krishna, looked upon him as their spiritual

lover and friend. Many of these women were born in Vaishnava families and a simple poetic faith was the basis of their religion. Therefore it is not incredible that they actually believed this boy of noble mien and character to be God Himself. Because of this faith they would come and tell him, without any reserve, their innermost thoughts and would seek his advice and try to follow it. On such occasions, Gadadhar also behaved with these young women as if he were one of them.*

8. He would sometimes act the parts of well-known female characters and put on women's dress and ornaments. He did this when, at the request of his women friends, he acted the part of Radharani or of her intimate companion, Vrinda. He would then be exactly like a woman in his gestures, voice and movements. The village women would say that nobody could recognize him then. This shows how minutely the boy had observed the various ways of women. With his love of fun, he would often pass in that disguise in front of men with a pitcher under his arm to fetch water from the Haldarpukur ; and no one would ever suspect that he was not a woman!

9. We have already spoken of Sitanath Pyne, a rich man of the village. He had seven sons and eight daughters, who lived as a joint family in Sitanath's house even after marriage. It is said that such a huge quantity of spices was necessary for cooking their food that ten stone-slabs were required to grind these spices and make a paste of them every day. Many distant relatives of Sitanath had also built their houses near his, and lived there. Therefore that part of Kamarpukur was known as the traders' quarter. Being situated near Kshudiram's house, many women of that quarter— especially Sitanath's wife and daughters — used to come to Chandra-devi during their leisure, and thus they came to know Gadadhar intimately. They would often take him to their own houses and ask him to play the part of dramatic personalities or impersonate certain women characters in women's dress. Many of Sitanath's women relatives were forbidden to go to any place outside the family house. Therefore they had not the good fortune to listen to Gadadhar's readings and songs at Chandradevi's place. Perhaps that was why Sitanath's wife and daughters invited him to their

---

* It will be seen from the facts recorded in II. 14 what a strong desire Gadadhar had, at the time referred to there, to be completely like a woman.

house. There it was that many women of the traders' quarter, who could not go to Chandradevi, saw Gadadhar and became fond of him. Whenever they heard that he was at Sitanath's house, they went there and enjoyed listening to his readings or seeing his acting and impersonations. The master of the house, Sitanath, loved Gadadhar very much and the other men of that quarter knew what a fine character the boy possessed. Therefore they did not raise any objection to their womenfolk listening to the boy singing the praises of God.

The only person from the traders' quarter who raised any objection was Durgadas Pyne. He too had a high opinion of Gadadhar and liked him, but he would, under no circumstance, allow any relaxation of the strict purdah system observed by his women. He boasted to Sitanath and other relatives that nobody had ever seen the women of his house, or could know anything about the inner apartments where they lived. He even looked down upon Sitanath and others who did not, like him, enforce purdah.

10. One day Durgadas was bragging thus before a relative, when Gadadhar came there. On hearing him, the boy said, " Can women be protected by purdah ? They can be protected only through good moral training and devotion to God. I can see everyone and know everything of the inner apartments of your house, if I want to." At this, Durgadas became even more boastful and said: "Well, let me see how you do it." "Very well, we shall see," said Gadadhar accepting the challenge and went away.

Some time later, one afternoon, without a word to anyone, the boy disguised himself as a poor weaver woman, putting on a coarse dirty sari and, among other ornaments, a bangle of silver beads on his wrist. Then he came just before dusk to the house of Durgadas from the direction of the market with a basket under his arm and a veil covering his face. Durgadas was then sitting with some friends in the parlour of his house. Gadadhar introduced himself as a weaver woman who had come to the market for selling yarn, but had the misfortune to be left behind by her companions. She therefore begged for shelter for the night. Durgadas made enquiries about her, and satisfied with her replies, said: "Very well, go to the women in the inner apartment and ask them to take you in." Gadadhar bowed in gratitude and went to the inner apartment. He repeated his story to the women and amused them with his gossip. Seeing her so young, and pleased

with her sweet words, the women allowed her to stay with them.
Then they pointed out a place for her to rest and gave her some
refreshments consisting of parched rice and parched paddy husked
and sweetened. Gadadhar sat in the allotted place and, while eating,
observed very minutely every room and each of the women. Not
only did he hear the conversation they were having but took part
in it, and sometimes even put questions. The whole evening was
spent in this way. As Gadadhar had not returned home, though
it was very late, Chandradevi sent Rameswar in search of him to
the traders' quarter where, she knew, he often went. Rameswar
went first to Sitanath's house, but was told that the boy was not there.
Then coming near the house of Durgadas, he loudly called him by
his name. When Gadadhar heard his brother's voice, he knew it
was very late. he shouted back from the inner apartment, " I am
coming, brother," and ran out to meet Rameswar. It was then
that the truth dawned on Durgadas. .At first he was a little embarrassed and felt annoyed at the thought that Gadadhar should
have befooled him and his family; but the next moment he began
to laugh, seeing how well the boy had played his part. When they
heard of the incident the next day, Sitanath and the other relatives
of Durgadas were glad that Gadadhar had dealt a blow to his
conceit. Henceforward the women of Durgadas's family also
began to go to Sitanath's house whenever Gadadhar was there.

11. The women of Sitanath's family and of the traders'
quarter became so fond of Gadadhar that they would send for him
if they did not see him for some days. The boy sometimes went
into ecstasy while reading or singing at Sitanath's house; and when
they saw this, the women's devotion for him knew no bounds.
Many of them, we are told, worshipped the boy when he was in
ecstasy, as an embodiment of Sri Gauranga or Sri Krishna. They
had a gold flute and various costumes of male and female characters made for his use during impersonations.

12. From time to time we had the opportunity of hearing
some of these women speak of the influence that the many-sided
Gadadhar exerted over them. When some of us, including Swami
Ramakrishnananda, went to Kamarpukur in 1893, we met Sitanath
Pyne's daughter, Rukmini, who was then about sixty years old.
The reader will have a good idea of Gadadhar's influence when
we relate what she told us. Pointing to the north, Rukmini said:
"Our old house stands yonder. · It is now in a dilapidated condi-

tion since there is hardly any one of us left. But when I was
seventeen or eighteen, it was the home of a prosperous family. Sitanath Pyne was my father and we were seventeen or eighteen sisters
and cousins, including the daughters of my father's elder and younger
brothers. Although there were slight differences in our ages, we
were all grown-up girls at that time. Gadadhar used to play with
us from his childhood and we were great friends. Though he
was a big boy then, he continued coming to our house even when
we were no longer children. He had free access to our inner apartments. Father loved him very much. He looked upon him as
his chosen Deity and had great devotion and respect for him.
But some of our neighbours objected to this, saying, 'There are
so many grown-up girls in your house and Gadadhar is now a big
boy. Why do you allow him still to enter your inner apartments?'
He would then reply: 'Don't worry, I know Gadadhar very well.'
And they would not dare to say anything more. Ah, how many
stories from the Puranas Gadadhar used to tell us, and what fun
we had ! We used to attend to our household work while
listening to those stories almost every day. How can I with one
tongue express the great joy we all felt when he was with us ? If
sometimes he did not come, we would be in great anxiety, thinking
he was ill. We had no peace till one of us went to the 'Brahmani'
(Chandra) on the pretext of bringing water or doing something else,
and brought news about Gadadhar. Every word of Gadadhar
was like nectar to us. When he did not come to our house, we
would spend the whole day talking about him."

13. Gadadhar's popularity was not confined to the circle of
village women. His many-sided genius and winsome ways brought
him to the notice of all the people of the village, whether men,
women or children. He frequented all the places where the villagers,
young and old, gathered to hear readings from the Puranas or songs
in praise of God. There was great joy whenever and wherever
the boy was present; for none but he could read so well, or expound
religious truths with such earnestness. He had no equal in spiritual
fervour at the time of singing the glory of God and in the power
of arousing the spiritual sentiments. No one had a sweet voice
like his, nor could anyone dance like him. On occasions of merriment, he surpassed everyone in his ability to play farcical roles
and to imitate all kinds of affectations of men and women. Again,
no one could narrate so well new stories or sing new songs

befitting an occasion. So everyone, young and old, became fond of him and eagerly awaited his coming each evening. Gadadhar too was happy to meet and entertain the villagers, sometimes in one place, sometimes in another.

As even at that age the boy had a sound judgement, many of the villagers took his advice in the solution of their worldly problems. Attracted by his pure character and seeing that he went into ecstasy while uttering God's name or singing His praises, religious-minded persons sought his advice in following their own chosen paths of spiritual discipline.* Only hypocrites and knaves tried to avoid him, since Gadadhar's keen insight pierced through their deceptive exteriors and detected their secret designs. The truthful and outspoken boy sometimes put these persons out of countenance by exposing them before others. Gadadhar's love of fun would also occasionally make him imitate their hypocritical ways in the presence of others. Although this made them angry, they could not do anything about it, since everybody took his side. Their only safeguard was to appeal to his kind nature, because they knew the boy was always generous to those who appealed to his good sense.

14. As mentioned before, Gadadhar continued going to school for some time every day, because of his love for boys of his own age. But on his reaching the age of fourteen, his devotion and desire for spiritual contemplation increased to such an extent that he became convinced that he had no use for any bread-winning education of the type imparted at school. Even from that time, he felt that his life was meant for a higher purpose and that he would have to direct all his energies towards the realization of God. A faint picture of that goal often arose before his mental vision ; but as the details were not then clear to his mind, he was unable to grasp its meaning or understand its purpose. Whenever he was faced with the problem of taking a decision on the future trend of his life, the ideal of renunciation and total dependence on God came up before his discriminating mind. His imagination pictured to itself the various symbols and paraphernalia of a life of renunciation — the ochre robe, the sacred fire, alms-gathering, and wandering from place to place without any attachment. But the very next moment, his loving heart reminded him of the condition of his mother, brother and others of the family, and made him

---

* It is said that at that time Srinivas Sankhari and a few other young men worshipped him as an especial manifestation of God.

give up the desire to tread that path.   Instead, it urged him to help
them, as best as he could, by remaining in the world trusting God,
even as his father had done.   Since his head and his heart thus
pointed ·in opposite directions, he waited for God's guidance,
depending entirely on what Raghuvir might ordain; for with his
heart full of love for that Deity, the boy had always looked upon
Him as absolutely his own. Confident, therefore, that Raghuvir
would solve his problems at the proper time, he set his mind at rest.
Whenever there was a conflict between his head and heart, it was
his heart that always won, and he now did everything under its
influence.

15.   At this time a new feeling welled up now and then in
Gadadhar's pure heart, so full of a rare sympathy.   There existed such
an intimate relationship between him and the people of the village
that he looked upon them as his dear friends and shared fully
their joys and sorrows.   Therefore, as soon as the idea of renouncing the world arose in his mind, his heart reminded him of those
simple-hearted and loving villagers and of their implicit trust in
him.   He knew his path was to conduct his own life in such a way
that by following him as a model, they might realize high ideals
and transform their present relationship into one of spiritual kinship.
The boy's heart, free from the slightest taint of selfishness, spoke
to him: "It is selfish to renounce the world only for your own
salvation.   Do something that will be for the good of others also."

16.   But so far as his study at the school and later at the
Sanskrit school was concerned, Gadadhar's head and heart were in
full agreement.   Even then he did not leave the school altogether,
because he knew his friends would miss him badly.   For, all the
boys of his own age, Gayavishnu and others, loved him dearly and
looked upon him as their leader because of his great intelligence
and courage.   Gadadhar, however, found at last a favourable
opportunity to leave the school.   One day some friends who knew
his dramatic talent proposed that they should form a party of
Yatra players and requested him to take charge of their training.
Gadadhar agreed ; but knowing that their guardians would raise
objections, the boys were at first worried about a suitable place
where they could undergo that training.   Clever Gadadhar finally
selected Manikraja's mango grove, and it was settled that every
day some of them should absent themselves from school to meet
there at the appointed time.

This plan was immediately put into effect. Under Gadadhar's training the boys learnt by heart their own parts and songs, and the mango grove became the happy scene of the performance of the plays depicting the lives of Sri Ramachandra and Sri Krishna. All the details of each performance had to be arranged by Gadadhar with the aid of his own imagination, and he himself had to act the parts of the principal characters. The boys, however, were very happy to find their little group working in perfect harmony. It is said that, from time to time, Gadadhar went into ecstasy during these performances.

17. The boy's skill in painting could not now find much opportunity for improvement, since most of his time was spent either in religious singing or in enacting plays. But one day, on a visit to his youngest sister Sarvamangala at Gaurhati, he saw her cheerfully serving her husband. Shortly afterwards, he painted a picture showing the couple in that happy mood, and all the members of the family were surprised to see how lifelike the painting was.

Gadadhar, however, became very competent in modelling images of gods and goddesses. His religious leanings led him to do this often, and he and his friends would then worship those images in the manner prescribed in the scriptures.

After he left school, Gadadhar followed the dictates of his heart by engaging himself in these activities, besides helping Chandradevi in her household work.

He became very fond of Akshay, his brother's motherless child, who very often kept him busy. In order to allow Chandradevi time for her household duties, it now became a part of his daily routine to take the child on his lap and keep it amused in various ways.

Three years went by in this way and Gadadhar approached his seventeenth year. Through Ramkumar's exertions, the number of students in his Calcutta school had increased during this period, and he was now earning more than before.

18. Although he spent most of his time in Calcutta, Ramkumar used to come once a year to Kamarpukur for a few weeks, to see how things were going on with his mother and brothers. This time, when he came, he was particularly worried to notice Gadadhar's indifference to any kind of regular study. He made careful enquiries as to how he spent his time, and after consulting his mother and Rameswar, decided to take Gadadhar with him to Calcutta

and keep him there.   He thought it advisable to do so, because with
the increase in the number of students, the management of his
school had become difficult and he felt the need for an assistant.   So
it was settled that Gadadhar should go to Calcutta to assist him a
little, and, at the same time, study under him along with his other
pupils.   When this was put to Gadadhar, he did not raise the
slightest objection, because he knew that it meant helping his eldest
brother, whom he respected like his father.   Then, at an auspicious
time on a permitted day, Ramkumar and Gadadhar paid homage
to Raghuvir, took the dust of their mother's feet and started for
Calcutta.   There was an end to the mart of joy at Kamarpukur.
Chandra and the other women devoted to Gadadhar somehow
spent their days with his sweet memory and the thought of his
future welfare to sustain them.

Sri Ramakrishna The Great Master

PART TWO

AS THE SPIRITUAL ASPIRANT

PREFACE

WHAT THIS PART CONTAINS

BY the grace of God the discussion on the unique spiritual practices of Sri Ramakrishna as a spiritual aspirant is now presented to the public. We have attempted in this section not only to describe the nature of the Sadhanas he undertook and the philosophical principles underlying them, but also to take a historical view of this period of his life extending from his seventeenth to his fortieth year and set forth the events in a chronological order. Therefore this part of the book " As The Spiritual Aspirant" may be regarded as the history of his life as an aspirant down to the time when his boy disciples, including Swami Vivekananda, came to his holy feet.

We entertained great doubts at the time of writing the present part of the book, whether it would be possible to ascertain the dates of all the important events of the Master's life. Although he had told many of us the facts of his life as a spiritual aspirant, never did he chronologically narrate them to anyone. Consequently, the events of this period of his life have remained confused and complicated in the minds of his devotees. But as a result of investigations we have now been able to ascertain by his grace the dates of many of those events.

There has continued till now a controversy about the year of the Master's birth; for he himself told us that his original horoscope was lost and the one that was cast afterwards was full of errors. We have been able to solve that dispute by consulting a number of almanacs more than a hundred years old. Therefore, it has become easy for us to ascertain the dates of the events of the Master's life. The facts about the Master's worship of Shodasi were not so far known to anyone. It will be easy for the reader to understand that event when he reads this part of the book.

In conclusion, our humble prayer is that the book may receive the Master's blessings and be a source of good to all.

AUTHOR

INTRODUCTION

THE DIVINE INCARNATION AS A SADHAKA

(TOPICS: 1. Lack of records on the subject. 2. Devotees' misconceptions. 3. Unreasonableness of this. 4. Intimate spiritual love and awareness of Divine power. 5. Destruction of the spiritual attitude; an example at Cossipore Garden. 6 In the incarnate, God behaves as man. 7. Conversation between Vishnu and Narada on this topic. 8. Incarnations discover paths to liberation. 9. Without accepting the humanity of incarnations, the concept loses significance. 10. Unenlightened souls' view of incarnations. 11. Incarnation and God's compassion for humanity.)

1. The study of the religious history of the world reveals that, except in the case of Lord Buddha and Sri Chaitanya, no detailed account is available of the spiritual disciplines and practices of the incarnations of God as aspirants. In the history of their lives we do not meet with any detailed description of the indomitable zeal and unbounded love which they nurtured in their hearts and with which they proceeded to realize their spiritual goal. Nor do we get any clear picture of the alternating waves of awe and admiration, of pang and pleasure, of hope and despair, gripped by which they now felt elated and then dejected, without however allowing the vision of the goal to grow dim even for a moment. Further, we are not able to trace the connection between their wonderful actions and behaviour during the later parts of their lives on the one hand, and the education, actions and aspirations of their childhood, youth etc., on the other. For example, how Lord Sri Krishna, the darling of the Gopis of Vrindavan, became transformed into Sri Krishna, the Lord of Dwaraka and the Resuscitator of religion, is not clearly indicated. Only a fact or two of the wonderfully catholic life of Jesus the Christ before his thirtieth year are known to us. The all-conquering preaching peregrinations alone of Acharya Sankara are recorded. And so it is with all others.

2. The reason for this is difficult to envisage. Perhaps those details have not been recorded on account of the excessive devotion on the part of the devotees. Perhaps they were hesitant to attribute

human imperfections to divine characters, and therefore thought it reasonable to shut them out from people's gaze. Or it may be, the devotees thought that they would be doing more good to men by holding before their eyes as an ideal, the fully developed noble ideas and sentiments of these great ones, than by tracing the history of their superhuman efforts to arrive at them. So they deemed it useless to place on record those endeavours. The devotees like to see their beloved Masters ever perfect. They refuse to admit that even on assuming human forms, any kind of human weakness or any lack of insight or power could ever creep into their character. They are anxious to see an image of perfection in them from their very childhood. Not only are they ever eager to read the experience and intelligence of an adult into the meaningless acts of their childhood, but strive to see them as the perfect embodiments of omniscience and omnipotence and of universal love and tolerance. It is no wonder, then, that they look upon all the efforts of the incarnations in the practice of spiritual Sadhanas, as also their bodily experiences like hunger, fatigue, sleep, disease and death, as mere simulations to elude the notice of unworthy men. Even in our own times we have known many eminent devotees of our Master having the firm conviction that his disease was a feigning of this kind.

3. It is due to mere weakness of faith and understanding that these devotees arrive at such a conclusion. They do not like to attribute human efforts, aims etc., to the incarnations of God, only because they feel that such human failings contradict, and therefore obstruct, their cultivation of whole-hearted devotion to these divine personalities. Therefore we have nothing to say against them; but such a weakness, it is certain, is seen in a devotee only when his devotion is not sufficiently mature. At that stage of development he can think of God only as Power, and attribution of any kind of human weakness to him inhibits his devotional sense. In course of time when devotion matures and deepens into genuine love of God, he finds the position reversed. He feels that the thought of God as Power is an obstacle to the experience of Him as pure Love, and he ceases to attach any importance to the former aspect. All the devotional scriptures say this over and over again. We see that although Sri Krishna's foster mother Yasoda daily experienced his divine powers, she looked upon him as just a boy only and fondled or chastised him accordingly. The Gopis similarly could not attribute any relation to Sri Krishna other than

that of the beloved, in spite of their knowledge that he is the very source of the universe. Instances can easily be multiplied.

4. When the devotees of the Master expressed to him their great eagerness to have some kind of vision indicative of the majesty and power of God, he would tell them endearingly, "Ah, it is not good to have such visions; fear will intervene when you experience His powers. Feeding and dressing Him, and the deep loving relation of 'Thou' and 'I' will all cease." Alas, how often did we not feel piqued on such occasions and think that he was only evading our request! If, however, at that time any devotee took courage and said feelingly with a firm faith, "Your grace can make the impossible possible. Please be compassionate and grant me the vision," the Master would reply in an endearing tone, "Can I bring about anything, my child? What the Mother wills, happens." On being so answered, if one would still insist and say, "Your will is the Mother's too," the Master's usual reply was "My child, I do wish that all of you have all kinds of spiritual states and visions; but is it fulfilled?" Instead of desisting even then, if the devotee persisted in his faith, the Master only expressed his love for him by a gentle smile and an affectionate look, or would sometimes say, "What shall I say? Let the Mother's will be done." But the Master, although pressed so persistently, never tried to break that firm belief of the devotee and destroy his spiritual attitude. Many a time did we see such a behaviour on the part of the Master and hear him say "Ah! The spiritual attitude of no one should be destroyed."

5. Although not directly connected with the subject matter of this Introduction, this topic, once raised, has to be clarified by explaining it in the light of a certain incident. The power of transmitting to others, by a mere touch or by an act of will, the capacity to realize spiritual truths, falls to the lot of very few aspirants. The Master told us time and again that Swami Vivekananda in course of time would have such a power with which he would be able to do much good to the people. Such a highly qualified person as the Swami is indeed rare in the world. The Master knew it well from the very beginning of their meeting, and started moulding his character and religious life in a special way by imparting to him the knowledge of the unity of existence spoken of in the Vedanta. Accustomed to the dualistic mode of worship of the Brahmo Samaj, the Swami regarded the non-dualistic mode taught in the Vedanta as blasphemy. But the Master tried in various ways to make him

practise it.   The Swami said: "As soon as I went to Dakshineswar, the Master gave me those books which he forbade others to read. Among other books, a copy of the *Ashtavakra Samhita* was in his room.   When the Master found anyone reading that book, he would forbid him and would give him instead such books as 'Mukti and How to Attain it', the *Bhagavad Gita* or some Purana.   But, scarcely had I gone to him, when he took out that book and asked me to read it.   Or, he would ask me to read some part of the *Adhyatma Rama-yana* which is full of non-dualistic ideas.   I would reply, sometimes bluntly, 'What is the use of reading this book?   It is a sin even to think "I am God".   The book · teaches this blasphemy.   It should be burnt.'   The Master would smile and say, 'Do I ask you to read it for yourself?   I ask you to read a little to me.   Please do it. In that case, you will not have to think that you are God.'   So I had to read a little for him at his request."

Again, although he was training the Swami that way, the Master was guiding Swami Brahmananda and his other boy devotees in their spiritual lives in various other ways—some through the worship of God with forms, some through that of God with attributes but without forms, others through pure unalloyed devotion, and still others through devotion mingled with the discipline of dis-crimination between the real and the unreal.   Thus although Swami Vivekananda and other boy devotees sat, slept, ate, walked about, and discussed religious theories together in the company of the Master at Dakshineswar, the latter was training them all in diverse ways according to their peculiar tastes and tendencies.

It was March 1886.   The Master, then at the Cossipore garden, was daily becoming weaker on account of his disease in the throat. But he engaged himself with an enthusiasm far greater and more whole-hearted than before, in moulding the spiritual lives of his devotees, particularly the life of Swami Vivekananda.   He did not stop merely with teaching the Swami the path of Sadhana and helping him to carry the teaching into practice.   He was also training him up in something else, namely, how to prevent the other boy devotees from returning to worldly life and how to guide them and hold them together.   Every evening after dusk he would ask all others to move away, call the Swami to himself, and teach him all these for two or three hours continuously, sometimes drawing him into a discussion.   From the words and actions of the Master, it seemed to most of the devotees that he was feigning the throat disease in order to establish his Order firmly, and that he would be all right as soon as that purpose was fulfilled. As days rolled on, Swami Vivekananda alone felt in his heart of hearts that the Master was arranging everything and preparing, as it were, to take a long, long leave of the devotees. It is doubtful, however, whether even he was always conscious of it.

At this time there was a slight awakening in the Swami of the power of transmitting spirituality to others by a touch. No doubt, he had felt that power arise within him from time to time, but he had not yet tested the truth or falsity of it by touching anyone that way. He also got convinced of the truth of the doctrine of non-duality taught in the Vedanta, and he tried to introduce that doctrine among the devotees, young or old, married or unmarried, with the help of reason and arguments. There arose then a keen controversy over it, leading to sharp differences of opinion, nay, agitation, among the devotees. For, it was the peculiar nature of the Swami to assert vehemently whatever he understood to be true and to compel its acceptance from others by means of logical arguments. Immature as he was, the Swami did not then realize that the truth of these doctrines in the practical world assumed different forms according to different conditions and capabilities of the aspirants. It was the night of Sivaratri in the month of Phalgun. Three or four of the boy devotees were observing fast with the Swami. They had a mind to spend the night in worship and in keeping vigil. Lest the noise should disturb the Master's rest, the worship was arranged in a small room built for the kitchen, situated a little away to the east of the residential quarters. There was a fair shower of rain after dusk. The devotees were delighted to see in the masses of newly formed clouds, flashes of lightning ever and anon, simulating the matted hair of Siva.

After finishing the worship, Japa and meditation pertaining to the first quarter of the night, the Swami was taking rest and conversing with others, sitting on the worshipper's seat. One of his companions went out to prepare a smoke for him and another went towards the residential quarters on an important work. Just at that time, a keen awareness of that divine power arose suddenly in the Swami. He wanted to observe its effect by putting it to test that night and said to Swami A., who was sitting in front of him. "Do touch me for a while." In the meantime the boy, who had gone to prepare tobacco, entered the room and saw the Swami sitting motionless in meditation, and A., with his eyes shut, touching the Swami's right knee with his right hand, which, he noticed, was rapidly trembling. A minute or two elapsed thus when the Swami opened his eyes and said, "That is enough. How did you feel?"

A. "Exactly like something entering into one when one holds an electric battery, one's hand trembling all the while."

The other person asked A., "Was your hand trembling of itself when you touched Naren?"

A. "Yes, I could not keep it steady, though I tried to."

There was then no more talk about it. The Swami smoked. All of them then applied their minds to the worship and meditation pertaining to the second quarter of the night. A. entered into deep meditation at that time. We had never seen him enter into such a deep meditation before. The whole of his body became stiff, with his neck and head slightly bent; and the consciousnes of the outer world appeared to have completely disappeared from him for some time. Everyone present thought that he had such meditation as a result of having touched the Swami a little while before. The Swami also noticed that state of his, and indicated it to a companion by a sign.

After the worship of the last quarter was over at four in the morning, Swami Ramakrishnananda came to the worship-room and said to the Swami, "The Master wants you." As soon as he was told, the Swami went up to the Master in his room on the first floor of the residential quarters. Ramakrishnananda also accompanied him to attend to the service of the Master.

No sooner had the Master seen the Swami than he said, "What is this? Expenditure before any accumulation! Allow it first to accumulate well in yourself; then you will know where and how to spend it. Mother Herself will teach. Don't you see what harm you have done to him by injecting your attitude of mind into him? He has been progressing till now with a particular mental attitude, the whole of which has now been destroyed, like a miscarriage during the sixth month of pregnancy. What's done is done. Don't act so thoughtlessly from now on. The boy, however, is lucky." The Swami said afterwards, "I became completely flabbergasted. The Master had come to know whatever we did at the time of the worship! What else could I do but remain silent when he scolded me like that?"

As a result of this, not only was the old spiritual attitude of A. completely destroyed but the new attitude of non-dualism, being difficult to grasp and assimilate quickly, was also misunderstood; and in the name of non-dualism he would behave like an atheist, sometimes acting contrary to scriptural injunctions. Although the Master from then on taught him the truth of non-duality and affectionately pointed out the mistake he was committing in the day-to-day acts of his life, it was long after the passing away of the Master that A., guided by that attitude, could rightly adjust his daily actions to that ideal.

6. To the class of devotees who think that the efforts of the incarnations of God for the attainment of truth or the fullest manifestation thereof in life are mere simulation, our answer is that we never heard the Master express such a view. Rather, we have heard him say often, "When the Divine sports as a human being, He behaves exactly like an ordinary man and experiences weal and woe and attains perfection by dint of personal effort, endeavour and austerity." The history of the religions of the world bears witness to this. Besides, it is clear that otherwise the very purpose of the Divinity incarnating will itself be defeated.

The Master's teachings on the question of free will and self-surrender can be classified into two categories. On the one hand we find him saying to his devotees: "I have cooked the food, just sit down to partake of it"; "The mould is prepared, now cast your own minds in it and get the form"; "If you cannot do anything a all, give me your power of attorney". On the other hand, we find him also instructing: "Give up all desires one by one, that is the way to success" ; "Be like a cast-off leaf blown by the wind"; "Give up lust and greed and call on God"; "I have done all the sixteen parts, do at least one part yourselves." It seems that our progress in life is often retarded because we very often fail to understand the significance of these two sets of teachings of the Master and strike a balance between free will and pre-destination, self-effort and self-surrender.

One day at Dakshineswar we had a long discussion with one of our friends, Swami Niranjanananda, on free will and pre-destination, and not being able to arrive at any conclusion, went to the Master for a solution of our difficulty. The Master was amused at our boyish discussion at first, but then added seriously, "Is there any one who has free will or anything like that? It is by God's will alone that everything has always happened and shall happen. Man understands it in the long run. But then something has to be added. Just as, when a cow is tied to a post with a long tether, it can stand at a distance of one cubit from the post, or it can go up to the whole length of the tether according to its choice, so too it is with the free will of man. A man ties a cow with the idea, 'Let her lie down, stand or move about as she likes within that area.' Similarly God has given man some power. And He has also given him freedom to utilise it as he likes. That is why man feels himself free. But the rope is fastened to the post. And mark this: If anyone prays to Him in all humility, He may remove him to another place and tie him there; or He may lengthen the tether or even remove it compltely from his neck."

Thus instructed, we asked, "Is it then that man has no duty or responsibility in the matter of practising spiritual disciplines? Can he say, 'Whatever I do, is according to His will'?" The Master replied: "Of what avail is it merely to say so? They are empty words. Is there any use telling, 'There is no thorn; it is not pricking', when you actually cry out 'ugh', startled on touching the thorn. If men were free to practise Sadhana, all would have undertaken it. But how is it that they can't? There is, however, one thing: He does not give one more power, if the little that is given is not properly used. This is why individual effort and perseverance are necessary. Don't you see, everyone has to make some effort, however small, before he gets God's grace? When one does so, the experiences due to be undergone in ten lives will come to fruition in one, and man will attain to spiritual realisation immediately. But one has to make some effort. Listen to a story:

7. "Vishnu, who eternally sports in Goloka, for some reason, cursed Narada that he should go to hell. Narada's anxiety knew no bounds. He sang hymns in His praise and pleased Him. Then he said, 'O Lord, I wish to know what and where hell is and how many kinds of hell there are. Please be gracious to tell me all about it.' Vishnu then drew on the ground with a piece of chalk, heaven, earth and hell as they were situated, and said, 'This is heaven and this is hell.' Narada said, 'Is that so? My experience of the suffering of hell can then be undergone here as well.' So

saying, he rolled on the hell drawn on the ground, got up and bowed down to the Lord. Vishnu smiled and said, 'What's that? Can that be suffering hell?' Narada replied, 'Why not, Lord? Are not heaven and hell your creations? When you drew hell and called it such, the spot really became hell. And when I rolled on it, it was a real suffering of hell for me.' Narada said so with deep faith. That was why Vishnu said, 'Be it so'. But Narada had to roll on that hell drawn on the ground with true devotion and faith. It was by making that little effort that his suffering was annulled." The Master explained to us from time to time with the help of this story, how there was room for perseverance and individual effort in the realm of grace too.

8. The incarnations of God have to experience to a great extent the spiritual blindness and circumscribed knowledge experienced by us, when they assume human bodies and play their parts as human beings. They have to make efforts like us to discover the way out of spiritual darkness and ignorance. And although an awareness of their real divine nature arises in their minds now and then for a short time, that awareness becomes veiled again until it gets steadied by their discovery of it thorough the practice of Sadhanas. Thus, for the good of the many they have to assume a veil of Maya and grope their way like us all in this realm of light and darkness. But as they are free from even an iota of self-centred desires, they get a more vivid perception of the spiritual path and the goal. And then concentrating all the tremendous energies inherent in them, they solve life's problems very quickly and afterwards engage themselves in working for the good of the world.

9. Inasmuch as our Master, the god-man, had actually accepted human imperfections, much good will accrue to us from the study of those human feelings of his. And that is why we advise our readers to study his divine nature while keeping at the same time before their eyes his human characteristics also. If we do not take him as one of us, we shall not be able to discover any purpose behind his superhuman effort, perseverance, etc., at the time of his Sadhana. For then the question will naturally arise, why he was required to exert so much, if he were already perfect. We cannot also escape the idea that these great exertions threatening his very life, were but a sham. That is not all. It will for this reason offer no lesson or consolation for ordinary man in his spiritual struggle. For we feel the struggle against the oppressive

forces of ignorance real, and only the example of the victory of a real, and not a sham, struggle can serve us as a model and bring us hope and cheer in our predicament.

10. Dependent as we are on the Master's grace, we must accept him as being endowed with human feelings like ourselves. For, is it not his sympathy with our sorrows, that leads him to come forward to remove them? Therefore, from whatever angle we see, we have no other course than to think of him as having human feelings. In fact, until we ourselves are free from all kinds of bondage and are established in the nature of the attributeless Brahman, we shall have to think of, and accept, God and His incarnations as being endowed with human feelings. The saying, "Becoming God, one should worship Him", is indeed true. If you have reached the Nirvikalpa plane of consciousness by virtue of Samadhi, then alone will you be able to realize the real nature of God, have a correct conception of Him and truly worship Him. But if you have not been able to do so, your worship will be but an attempt at ascending to that divine plane and making yourselves fit for the true worship of God. Till then, you have to consider God, the cause of the universe, to be a being endowed with human sentiments coupled with extraordinary powers.

11. Persons who can really put into practice the dictum "Becoming God, one should worship Him", are therefore very few. Weak aspirants like ourselves are very very far from that state. Thus, feeling compassion for ordinary mortals like ourselves, and desiring to accept our heartfelt worship, God descends to the plane of human beings, putting on the appearance of a god-man by assuming a human body and human feelings. We are in an advantageous position to study the history of the Master's spiritual striving in comparison with that of the god-men of the past; for the Master himself delineatd in detail from time to time the facts of the Sadhana period of his life in such glowing colours that they have remained firmly imprinted in our minds. Again, the wonderful play of his life as an aspirant had been acted before all the people of the Kali temple just before we went to him. And, many of those people were still there. So we had also the opportunity of hearing from them some of those events. That apart, before we begin to study the history of these events, it is good to recapitulate once in a general way the fundamental principles of Sadhana. So we shall have a brief discussion on it.

CHAPTER I

SADHAKA AND SADHANA

(THE SPIRITUAL ASPIRANT AND SPIRITUAL DISCIPLINE)

(TOPICS; 1. Erroneous conceptions about Sadhana. 2.Sadhana is the means for realization of Brahman in all beings. 3. Delusion hides Truth ; The cause of delusion a mystery. 4. Wise men's realisation is the Truth : why ? 5. Delusion, although shared by many, is not right knowledge. 6. Why all have the same delusion. 7. The Universe is beyond time and space; Prakriti is beginningless. 8. Sadhana is the effort to know the universal cause. 9. Two paths of Sadhana. 10. The goal of the path of 'not this, not this', is to know 'What am I?' 11. Nirvikalpa Samadhi. 12. Nirvikalpa Samadhi and the path of "this, this". 13. Incarnations a combination of the divine and the human.)

To become truly acquainted with the state of the Master's mind as a Sadhaka, we must, first of all, know what Sadhana is. An objection may be raised: why do you increase the bulk of the book by introducing this topic, so familiar to the people of India, who have all along been engaged in Sadhana in some form or other? Which other nation of the world has applied and is still applying its powers to realize directly the truths of the spiritual realm as this country has done since the very dawn of time? In which other country have so many incarnations of God and knowers of Brahman been born? Therefore, it is superfluous to recount the fundamental principles of spiritual discipline to us, who are already acquainted with them.

1. Although what is said above is true, a real need will be served by this recounting; for people generally have fantastic ideas about Sadhana in many places. Having lost touch with authentic traditions, they generally identify Sadhana with the practice of extra-ordinary physical hardship, with rituals performed in out-of-the-way places, using rare objects gathered from far and wide, with the holding of the breath, and even with the fantastic doings of deranged minds. Again, they regard those peculiar practices, which were originally prescribed by some great souls for bringing

to normality certain minds obsessed with evil impressions and habits, as Sadhana, and these are being preached as suitable for all. There are still others, who, lacking in dispassion and wistfully craving for the enjoyment of the fleeting objects of the senses such as beautiful forms and delicious dishes, spend their lives in vain efforts under a delusion that the Lord, the cause of the universe, could be constrained by means of certain Mantras and practices, as snakes are. Therefore, it will not be out of place here to make a brief survey of the truths about Sadhana, discovered by the effort and perseverance of the sages and seers of India through millennia.

2. The Master used to say: "Seeing Brahman or God in all beings is the last word of Sadhana." This is the ultimate goal of spiritual disciplines, and the Vedas and the Upanishads, the most authoritative scriptures of the Hindus, support this idea. Whatever you see in the world, gross or subtle, sentient or insentient— bricks and beams, mud and stone, plants and trees, men and animals, gods and demigods—are all, they say, the non-dual Brahman. It is the reality of Brahman alone that you see, hear, touch, smell and taste in various forms. Although all your day-to-day dealings throughout your life are with It, you are not conscious of It, and you think you are dealing with different things and persons. This will probably be easily understood if we describe here, by way of questions and answers, the gist of the doubts entertained about these doctrines as also the answers to the same given in the scriptures.

Question: Why is this fact (that we are experiencing the non-dual Brahman and not individual objects and persons), not directly felt by us?

Answer: You are in delusion. How can you detect it till it is removed? It is only by comparison with real things and states that we detect external and internal delusions. Similarly, you must have that kind of comparative knowledge if you want to detect that delusion.

3. *Question:* Well, what is the cause of that delusion? And when did it arise in us?

Answer: The cause of delusion here is the same as it is everywhere. It is ignorance. How can you know when that ignorance arose? As long as you are in ignorance, your efforts to know its origin are in vain. As long as one dreams a dream one remains convinced that it is real. When sleep breaks, the dream is compared with the waking state and is known as unreal. You may raise the objection that certain persons have sometimes the feeling that they are dreaming when they are actually in the dream state itself. But there also they get that knowledge from the memory of the waking state. Similarly some people are seen to have the memory of the reality of the non-dual Brahman when they are conscious of the world in the waking state.

Question: Then what is the way out?

Answer: The way out is to remove that ignorance. I can tell you with certainty that this ignorance and delusion can be removed. The ancient seers were able to remove them and have left us instructions about the method.

4. *Question:* Very well. But before we proceed to know those means, we want to put one or two more questions. You assert *that* to be unreal which we and so many others see and feel to be real; and you call *that* alone to be real, which a few sages have seen and experienced. May it not be that their perception was wrong?

Answer: There is no such rule that what many believe is always true. I say that the direct knowledge of the seers is true, because with that knowledge they attained freedom from fear in all respects and enjoyed eternal peace devoid of every form of misery. Moreover this knowledge brought them to the awareness of a great purpose behind the otherwise meaningless struggles and sufferings of life ending with inevitable death. Besides, right knowledge always unfolds in the human mind forbearance, contentment, compassion, humility and other noble qualities, and endows it with a wonderful magnanimity. We know from the scriptures that the seers possessed those uncommon qualities and powers, and we shall come across them in people who, following in their footsteps, have achieved perfection.

5. *Question:* Well, how is it that all of us have the same delusion? What I identify as a beast is also known by you as a beast and not as a man; and so it is with everything else. It is unbelievable that all people are in the same delusion about all things at the same time. It is everywhere seen that if a few people have a wrong knowledge of a certain thing, there are many others who have the right perception. But here this truth seems to be contradicted. Therefore, what you say does not seem to be probable.

6. *Answer:* You find here an exception to the rule, because you do not include the few seers with correct knowledge among the people. Otherwise the reply is there in the answer to the previous question itself. (That is to say, the admission that a set of people see a phenomenon differently from what others perceive, is sufficient to disprove the universality assumed in the question about those ignorant men's perception). Further, in reply to your question, how all people are under the same delusion, the scriptures say: In the limitless infinite cosmic mind the universe has arisen by way of ideation (creative imagination). And as the individual minds of yours, of mine and of all people form parts of, and are comprised in that cosmic mind, we all are bound to experience the ideations of the cosmic mind in the same way. This is why we cannot, by our individual efforts, see a beast as anything else. It is for the same reason that while one of us attains right knowledge and becomes free from that delusion, all others still continue in it as before. (For that one, the illumined seer, goes out of that universal spell of delusion by realising his identity with, or sharing the knowledge of that cosmic mind or Divine Person Himself, while the others continue in the same state of delusion.) To grasp this idea one more point about the cosmic mind of the Divine Person has to be understood: Although the universe arises in the all-pervading mind of the omnipresent Person by ideation, He does not get entangled in the bondage of ignoranc, unlike us, centres of consciousness involved in it. For He, the all-knowing Person, sees the non-dual reality of Brahman interpenetrating the ideation, both within and without the universe born of ignorance. It is because we cannot do so that our case is different. (And the illumined sage, unlike ourselves, is one who gets the knowledge or insight of the all-knowing Divine Person through identification in being or consciousness with Him. He therefore becomes free from the illusion of cosmic ignorance to which we are subject). The Master has further elucidated the nature of the unaffectedness of the Divine Person in the following saying: "A snake has poison in its mouth. It takes its food daily through it, still it remains unaffected by the poison. But anyone whom it bites, meets with instantaneous death."

7. Therefore, from the standpoint of the scriptures it is seen that the universe, which is an idea in the universal mind is , in a way, an ideation of our minds also. For our limited individual

minds have an eternal, inseparable relation with the aggregate universal mind, like that between the limbs and the body. Again, it cannot be said that there was a time when the aforesaid ideation was not in existence in the universal mind and that it came into existence afterwards. For, the two categories, name and form or space and time, without which there could be no diversity, are included in the idea of the universe; or in other words, they have an eternal and inseparable coherence with the said idea. By a little calm thinking the reader will be able to understand it and know why the Vedas and other scriptures teach that Prakriti or Maya, the ultimate material of creation, is beginningless and beyond time. If the universe is an idea of the mind and if that idea is not within what we understand by "time", it comes to this that simultaneously with the idea of "time", the idea of the " universe" too exists in the cosmic mind, the support of that idea. As our limited individual minds have been experiencing that idea (i.e. the universe) for an infinitely long time, we have a firm belief in the real existence of the universe. And having been debarred from the immediate knowledge of the reality of the non-dual Brahman for a long time, we do not recognise that the universe is a mere idea and are unable to detect our error. For, as has been already stated, it is only by a comparison with real things and states that we can detect external and internal errors.

8.   Now it is clear that our conception, experience etc. of the universe have assumed their present forms as the result of our habits accumulated over an almost infinitely long time. So, if we want to have the right knowledge of the universe, we shall have to be acquainted with the entity beyond name and form, time and space, mind and intellect and all other things comprised in the universe. The striving to have that acquaintance has been described as Sadhana by the Vedas and other scriptures ; and men and women who are striving in this direction, knowingly or unknowingly, are called Sadhakas.

9.   Generally speaking the aforesaid effort in search of the reality beyond the universe, has taken its course along two main channels: One is what has been called in the Sastras as Neti, Neti, (not this, not this*) or the path of knowledge; and the other as Iti, Iti,

---

* *Brihadaranyaka Upanishad* 2, 3, 6 and in fact, all the Uapanishads advocate it. The rest of the Hindu scriptures, based on the "work" portion of the Vedas, emphasize the path of 'this', 'this'.—Tr.

(this, this), or the path of devotion. The aspirant following the path of knowledge has from the beginning a conception of the ultimate ideal; and always remembering it, goes forward consciously towards that ideal. The traveller on the path of devotion remains very often ignorant of where he will go ultimately. He accepts higher and higher ideals one after another ,as he goes forward and at last becomes directly acquainted with the non-dual reality beyond the universe. This is the only point of difference between the two ; for, the travellers on both the paths have to renounce the conception about the universe held by the common man. The man on the path of knowledge tries to renounce it in all respects from the beginning; and although the devotee proceeds by partly renouncing and partly retaining it, he too at long last renounces it wholly and arrives at the truth, "One without a second". The renunciation of that common conception of the universe coloured by our self-centredness, which has made enjoyment the only goal of life, has been called by the scriptures, detachment or dispassion (Vairagya).

As human life is ever changing and is sure to end in death, the knowledge of the transitoriness of the world comes naturally to the human mind. Therefore it is probable that, in the past, the search for the ultimate cause of the universe at first took the path of "not this", "not this", together with the complete renunciation of the common conception of the universe. And that is why the complete development of the path of knowledge is seen to have taken place in the Upanishads before the path of devotion became complete in all respects, though both were simultaneously in vogue.

10. The Upanishads bear witness to the fact that man advanced along this path of negation and became introspective in a short time. He found that, of all the entities of the world, his own body and mind are the most intimate and immediate objects of knowledge. Hence it seems to him that he would get the knowledge of the cause of the universe sooner if he proceeded to search for it through his body and mind than through the external world. Again, "just as by pressing with the fingers one grain of rice in the cooking pot one can know whether all the grains in the pot have been well boiled or not", so also as soon as one knows in oneself the eternal universal cause, one is able to know it in other things and persons too. That is why the investigation and understanding of "What am I?" becomes the only aim of the aspirant on the path of knowledge.

11. We have said before that the notion about the universe held by the generality of people has to be renounced both by men on the path of knowledge and by those on that of devotion. By the complete renunciation of it man becomes free from all mental modifications and is thereby fit for Samadhi. This kind of Samadhi is called in the scriptures Nirvikalpa Samadhi. We shall tell the reader elsewhere (cf. III. 3) how the aspirant on the path of knowledge makes the effort to know "What am I?", how he attains the Nirvikalpa Samadhi and what kind of experience he has at that time. Now, the reader should be told a little of how the aspirant on the path of devotion arrives at the realization of that superconscious state.

We have designated the path of devotion as the path of "this", "this". For, although the traveller on this path has the actual knowledge of the transience of the world, he believes in God, its creator, and has the conviction of the reality and existence of the world created by Him. The devotee looks upon the world ·and all things and persons in it as related with God and makes them His own. He shuns whatever he believes to be an obstacle on the path leading to the realization of that relation. It becomes the devotee's immediate ideal to become absorbed in Him through the love of and meditation on one of His forms* and also to perform all actions out of love for Him.

12. We shall now discuss how one can, forgetting the existence of the universe, reach the Nirvikalpa state of consciousness by being absorbed in the meditation on forms of God. We have said before that the devotee accepts as his chosen Ideal some particular form of God and continues to think of, and meditate on that form. He cannot in the beginning bring before his mind's eye, at the time of meditation, the complete picture of the person of his chosen Ideal. Sometimes the hands of that mental picture, sometimes the feet and sometimes only the face appears before him. These again, dissolve, as it were, as soon as they are seen; they do not continue to stand before him. As a result of practice, when meditation becomes deep, the complete picture of that form appears before his mind's eye. When meditation gradually becomes deeper, the

---

* We look upon the worship of the Brahmo Samaj as a meditation on a form of God; for when anyone meditates on a personality possessed of noble qualities but no form, he is bound to think of one or other of such things as ether, water, air, fire, etc.

picture presents itself to him in vivid and unbroken continuity as long as the mind remains steady and unswerving. Afterwards, according to the progress in the intensity of meditation, the devotee becomes conscious of the movement, the smile, the speech, and ultimately the touch of that living form. Then the devotee sees, with his eyes open or shut, the benign and living presence of the Lord and His graceful movements everywhere and in all conditions. The devout aspirant gradually comes to have also the visions of various divine forms springing from his own chosen Ideal as the result of his faith that "his chosen Ideal has, out of His own accord, assumed all forms." The Master used to say, "A person who has the vision of one such form as a living presence, gets easily the vision of all other forms."

One thing is clear from what has been said before. One who has the good fortune to have the vision of such living forms feels that these forms pertaining to the realm of ideas and experience during meditation, have as real an existence as things and persons of the waking state. Thus, as the feeling deepens that these experiences of the world of ideas are as real as those of the external world, the conviction that the latter also are a projection of the mind is intensified. Again, during deep meditation, the experiences of the realm of ideas become so powerful in the mind of the devotee that he does not have the slightest knowledge of the external world for the time being. This condition of the devotee has been designated by the scriptures as Savikalpa Samadhi. Although, owing to the strength of his mental power, the external world vanishes from the mind of the devotee at the time of such Samadhi, the realm of ideas still persists. His experience of the chosen Ideal in that world of ideas and the joy he derives from it are in no way less intense and real to him than that of the waking world and his contacts with men and things in that world. All the ideas, without any exception, that arise at that time in his mind have only his chosen Ideal for their object. The scriptures have called that condition of the devotee's mind as Savikalpa Samadhi, because at that time the series of the mental modifications of the devotee have only one thing as their main object.

Thus the gross external world vanishes from the mind of the devotee owing to the meditation on a particular object of the realm of the ideal world. For when one idea becomes dominant, all other ideas disappear. The attainment of the Nirvikalpa Samadhi is not

very remote from this devout aspirant who has been able to advance
so far.   Thus the mind of the person, who gets rid of the belief in the
existence of the external world to which he has been accustomed
for an infinitely long time, becomes endowed with much power
and determination.   The whole of his mind goes forward with
enthusiasm in the direction of the enjoyment of divine bliss, when
once there arises the conviction that the enjoyment of that bliss
becomes more intense if the mind can be made completely free from
modifications.   He then ascends to the highest plane in the realm
of ideas by the grace of the teacher and God, and establishes himself
firmly in the non-dual knowledge and attains eternal peace.   Or,
it may be said that the very intense love for his chosen Ideal shows
him that plane, and urged by it, he realizes his identity with that
Ideal, like the Gopis of Vraja.

13.   These are the ways laid down by the scriptures for persons
treading the paths of knowledge and of devotion to arrive at their
ultimate goal.   But as the divine incarnations are endowed with
the human and divine natures simultaneously all through their
lives, they are sometimes, seen to manifest the knowledge
and power of the perfect person even in their Sadhana period.
This happens because they naturally have the power of abiding in
both the planes, the divine and the human.   Or, because their
divine nature is inborn and spontaneous, sometimes it pierces the
external veil of their human nature and manifests itself from time
to time.   Whatever may be our conclusion, these facts have made
the lives of the incarnations of God impenetrably mysterious to the
human intellect.   It does not seem probable that this intricate
mystery will ever be solved completely.   But it is very certain that
endless good accrues to man if he studies these lives with reverence.
In the past Pauranic age the human nature of the incarnations of
God was kept hidden and the divine aspect alone discussed.   In
this sceptical modern age, the divine nature of those characters is
being completely disregarded while the human side is being high-
lighted.   In the present instance, we shall make an effort to explain
to the reader, by a discussion of these two aspects, that both the
natures co-exist in them.   It is needless to add here that we would
not have been able to look upon the character of the incarnations
of God in that way, had it not been for the privilege we had of
meeting the great Master and observing his life and doings.

CHAPTER II

THE ATTITUDE OF A SADHAKA IN THE LIFE OF AN INCARNATION OF GOD

(TOPICS; 1. Co-existence of the divine and the human in the Master. 2. The same with all incarnations. 3. Incarnations have no selfish desires. 4. Their compassion; they undertake Sadhana for the welfare of others. 5. The illustration of the 'Grove of Bliss'. 6. Incarnations and self-control. 7. Innumerable desires of the mind. 8. The Master gives up desires. 9. Instruction to women devotees about it.10. Struggle of incarnations with subtle desires 11. Refutation of objection about human feelings in incarnations. 12. The same viewed from another standpoint. 13. Differences of view from different planes of consciousness. 14. Incarnations viewed from an exalted plane of consciousness. 15. Evolution of the minds of incarnations. 16. Their all-embracing consciousness. 17. Natural sciences cannot reveal the cause of the universe. 18. Spiritual absorption of incarnations in childhood. 19. The Master's ecstasy at the age of six. 20. Ecstasy on pilgrimage to Visalakshi. 21. Ecstasy on Sivaratri.)

1.   Blessed by the opportunity of being in the holy company of the divine Master, we have been charmed to notice the wonderful co-existence of both the aspects of divinity and humanity in him. The more we have contemplated his life and character, the more have we been convinced of this fact. If we had not seen him, we could never have understood how such contrary aspects could co-exist in such sweet congruence and harmony in the same person. It is because we observed it in him that this conviction has grown in us that he was God and man in one, that he was exactly what the infinite being of God and His power are when manifested behind the veil of a human body and human feelings. It is because of our direct experience of this that we have come to understand that he feigned neither aspect, but actually assumed human nature for the good of humanity and showed us the path leading to divinity. Again, it is because we saw him that we have become convinced that there were certainly such wonderful manifestations of both these aspects in the lives of the incarnations of past ages also.

2.   We shall meet with the same truth if we study with reverence the life of any one of the incarnations of God. We shall find

that, impelled by a wonderful unknown power, they are sometimes in the same plane of consciousness as other human beings are and behave like ourselves with all the objects and persons of the world. But, at other times, we find them ascending to higher planes and bringing to us information about the unknown. Even without their awareness, some Power makes these arrangements and adjustments, and their actions seem to be guided by it. And it is so from their childhood. But getting, as they do sometimes, an indication of that Power in themselves in their childhood, they cannot at first understand that it is their own or that it lies deep within themselves. Also, they cannot draw upon that Power at will in order to ascend to higher spiritual planes and see all things and persons of the world in the light of the divine consciousness and behave with them accordingly. But as they go on getting more frequent experiences of that Power in their lives day after day, a strong desire to be fully acquainted with it arises in their minds. It is this desire that endows them with a unique ardour and enthusiasm and induces them to undertake spiritual discipline.

3. However, there does not exist the slightest tinge of selfishness in that desire of the incarnations of God. Not to speak of their not having any desire for the enjoyment of the petty pleasures of the senses here or hereafter, even the idea that they themselves might become liberated and enjoy the infinite bliss, irrespective of others' fate, does not exist in them. The sole motive behind their quest is the urge to know for certain whether that unknown, extraordinary Power really exists in the background of the universe or whether it is a mere fabrication of their own imagination — that extraordinary Power, under whose guidance and direction they experience from their birth unique ideas unintelligible to man, and by whose will they feel everything in the realm of ideas to have an existence as real as that of the things and persons known in the gross world. For, by comparing their knowledge and experiences with those of ordinary people, they become convinced in a very short time that these people do not have the same knowledge about the nature of the things and persons of the world as they themselves have always been having, and that they lack almost completely the power to see the world from a higher plane of consciousness.

4. That is not all. They become convinced simultaneously of another fact through that comparison. Because they

see the world in two different ways, from two planes of consciousness — the ideal and the material — the fleeting enjoyments offered by the senses like sight, taste etc. cannot allure them as they do human beings in general, and the dense shadows of despondency and anguish that arise from the reverses of fortune cannot cloud their intellect. Therefore, their compassionate minds become completely absorbed in the struggle to gain complete control over that power. Thereby they ascend to higher and higher planes of consciousness and remain there as long as they like, in order to teach the people of all classes and conditions, from the highest to the lowest, how to attain to those higher states of realisation and become endowed with peace. So, two mighty streams, those of Sadhana and of compassion, are always seen to flow side by side in their lives. The compassion of these incarnations increases a hundredfold by a comparison of their own condition with that of ordinary human beings. No one, however, knows the source of this infinite compassion of theirs. It must be inborn. Nothing further can be added to this. Let us quote an illustration cited by the Master:

5. "Three friends went for a walk through a field. In the middle of the field they saw an area enclosed by a high wall. Sweet sounds of music, both vocal and instrumental, were coming out of it. Attracted by the music, they wished to know what was going on within. They went round the wall and found that there was not a single entrance in it. What could they do? One of them somehow procured a ladder and climbed up the wall, while the other two stood below. The first man got up on the wall and was beside himself with joy on seeing what was happening within. He laughed loudly and jumped into the enclosure. He could not wait even to tell the other two standing below, what he saw within. They thought, ' Ah, our friend is a fine man ! He did not even tell us once what he saw! However that may be, we have to see what is inside.' Then the second of them climbed up that ladder. The moment he got to the top, he also, like the first, burst out laughing and jumped within. What was the third man to do then? He climbed up that ladder and saw the mart of bliss within. When he saw it, his first thought was to jump within and join it. But he checked himself, thinking, 'If I now join it, the public outside cannot know that there is a place here for the enjoyment of such bliss. Should I enjoy it alone?' Thinking so, he turned back and

came down to the field. Then he began to proclaim to one and all, to whomsoever he happened to see,'Listen, there is a mart of bliss here. Come, let us enjoy it together.' He thus took all the people with him to join the mart of bliss. You see now, just as we cannot find out the cause of the third friend's inclination to share the enjoyment with the many, so also we cannot point out why the desire to do good to humanity is present in the incarnations from their very childhood."

6. From what has been said, some perhaps may come to the conclusion that the incarnations of God have never to fight like ourselves with the unruly senses. They may conclude that the senses are naturally submissive like children to these divine personages all through their lives, and that it is therefore very easy for them to direct their minds from sense objects to spiritual verities. But we have to say that it is not so. Having assumed the human role, they too are like other men and have to come out victorious in a struggle with their lower nature before they could proceed to the spiritual goal.

7. Anyone who has tried to know even a little of the nature of the human mind can see that, beginning from the gross, there exist in it many strata of desires—subtle, subtler, and still more subtle. If you are somehow able to go beyond one, another comes and obstructs your path; and when you conquer the latter, still another takes its place. When you have left the gross ones behind, the subtle ones come and oppose you. If you give up the allurement of sex, that of gold arises in its stead; if you refrain from indulging in both in a gross way, attachment to outward beauty, desire for name and fame, and the like come to you. Or if by force you circumvent all attachments, they once again manifest surreptitiously as pseudo-retirement from activities or as pseudo-sympathy for others.

8. The Master spoke of this treacherous nature of the mind and always warned us to shun the net of desires. In order to carry conviction to us he would sometimes cite examples from his own life of how he thought and acted under similar circumstances. And he narrated them repeatedly to all the women devotees too as he did to the men and kindled the love of God in their hearts. The following incident will make this clear:

Man or woman, whoever went to the Master felt so much attracted in their heart of hearts by his amiability, courtesy and his extraordinary love without the slightest contamination of selfish motives that they became impelled to seek his blessed company again and again, whenever there was an opportunity. Not only did they themselves visit him again and again but they also took with them all their acquaintances, so that they too might enjoy pure bliss in his company. One afternoon, one of our acquaintances went to the Master at Dakshineswar with her step-sister and a sister of the latter's husband. They saluted him and took their seats. The Master then inquired about their welfare and started a conversation, which brought them to the topic that the only aim of human life is the practice of loving devotion to God. "Can one," he continued, "easily take refuge in the divine Lord? Inscrutable are the ways of Mahamaya! Does She allow this to happen? She makes one, who has no relative in the world, rear a cat and live a worldly life. One then goes round to procure milk for the cat and say, 'What can I do? The cat does not take anything but fish and milk.'

9. "Perhaps one comes of a rich and noble family. The husband and children have all died. Those who are left behind are so many widows, lingering as if there is to be no death for them. Some parts of the house are falling to pieces, others have already given way. Saplings of banyan tree and some greens like spinach have grown on the roof. The widows gather the spinach for curry and go on with their worldly life! But why? Why do they not take refuge in the divine Lord? It is, indeed, the time for them to do so. But they will not!

"Again, perhaps one loses one's husband soon after one's marriage and becomes a child-widow. She is now a childless grown-up widow. Why does she not call on God? But that she will not do. She becomes the guardian of her brother's household. With her hair tied up in a knot and her key bunch hanging from the end of her cloth, she moves about with arrogance, commanding all. At the sight of her the neighbours run away to avoid her malevolent presence. And she goes about saying, 'My brother cannot have even a meal if I am not there.' Ah, that wretch of a woman! Why does she not look at what has happened to her — what, after all, has she gained for herself!"

Well, there was a peculiar coincidence here. The third lady of the party, who was meeting the Master that day for the first time, was one of this type of woman-guardians of their brothers'

household. Nobody had told the Master of it before. But in the
course of conversation the Master referred to that example, and
began to explain the powerful influence of desires and about the
existence of endless strata of desires in human minds. Needless
to say, these words entered deep into the heart of that lady. Hearing
of the examples, the sister of the lady of our acquaintance nudged
her and whispered, "Sister, just fancy, that such words should
come out of the Master's lips today of all days! How will my
sister-in-law take these words?" To this our acquaintance replied,
"What can we do about it? It is his pleasure. Nobody tutored
him."

10. It becomes very clear from a study of human nature that
the higher a man's mind ascends, the more intensely do the subtle
desires pain him. One who has committed thefts, uttered false-
hoods or indulged in licentiousness innumerable times, is not much
pained by repeating those actions; but an honest and high-
minded man considers himself guilty and becomes distressed even
at the thought of such things. Although incarnations of God
are often seen to refrain from gross worldly enjoyments all their
lives, they too have to fight with the subtle desires of their minds
but with one difference. Unlike our hardened minds, their pure
and sensitive minds feel, as testified by themselves, a terrible anguish
a hundredfold more intense than ours, at the slightest awakening
of these subtle desires within. How can we, therefore, regard
their struggles to withdraw their senses from sights, tastes, and other
sense faculties as feigned ?

11. Perhaps, even now some reader acquainted with the
scripture may say: "But how can I accept what you say?
Don't you see what Sankara, the paragon of monists, says in the
beginning of his commentary on the *Gita* regarding the birth and
the assumption of a human body on the part of Sri Krishna ?
He says there, 'God, eternally free, eternally awake and eternally
pure in nature, the controller of all living beings, devoid of birth
etc., is born, as it were, is possessed of a body, as it were, through
Maya, His own power, in order to do good to humanity.' When
Sankara himself says so, how does your statement hold good?"
Without contradicting Sankara, we say that we still have sufficient
reason to support us. In order to understand Sankara, we must
remember one thing. Just as he regards God's possession of name
and form as apparent, so does he consider our possession of them

as equally false.   He regards the whole universe as a false superim-
position on the reality of Brahman, and does not admit its real
existence.*   Therefore, his conclusion will be understood if we take
both these statements together.   It is not his intention that we should
regard the incarnation's embodiment and experience of pain and
pleasure as a false appearance and regard such things on our part
alone as real.   If we accept our own feelings and perceptions as
real, we must accept those of an incarnation also as real.   Therefore, what we have said before still stands.

12.   This will be clearly understood if we discuss it from another
standpoint.   The scriptures say that two distinct conceptions
of the world arise in us when we look at it from the two planes of
consciousness, the non-dual and the dual.   If we ascend to the
former plane and try to understand to what extent the thing we
call the universe is real, we get the immediate knowledge that it
does not exist and has never existed.   There is nothing but the
reality of Brahman, 'One only without a second'; while if we look
at it from the dual plane, the world, with the aggregate of
various names and forms, appears to be real and eternally existent,
even as it is now with us, ordinary human beings.   Although
possessed of bodies, the incarnations and the persons liberated
in life, devoid of body-consciousness as they are, dwell very often
in the non-dual plane of consciousness.   Therefore, they have
the conviction, even when they live in the plane of duality, that the
world is unreal like a dream.   Though, compared with the waking
state, a dream is known as unreal, the dream of a dreamer at the
time of dreaming cannot be called absolutely unreal.   Similarly,
compared with the state of their absorption in Brahman, the
semblance of the world in the minds of the incarnations and
persons liberated in life, is unreal; but when they are not in
Samadhi, it cannot be regarded as absolutely unreal.

13.   Just as the thing called the world is seen in two different
ways from the two above-mentioned planes, so also a particular
person in it is seen as two different beings from those two planes
of consciousness.   Seen from the plane of duality, he is known
as a man in worldly bondage; and seen from the infinite non-dual
plane, as Brahman, eternally free and eternally pure.   The infinite
non-dual plane is the highest region in the realm of ideas.   The

---

* See Sankara's commentary on Adhyasa in the *Brahma-sutra-bhashya*

human mind passes through higher and higher planes of consciousness before it reaches the non-dual plane, which is the goal. While
the mind of the aspirant ascends to those higher and higher regions,
both the universe and a particular individual in it assume for him
different forms, and his previous conceptions of them change in
various ways: for example, to him the world then seems to be made
of ideas only and a particular individual appears to be separate
from the body and endowed with extraordinary powers, or made
up of mind, or of the light celestial.

14. If an ordinary man approaches an incarnation of God
with devotion and reverence, he ascends unknowingly to the higher
and higher planes of consciousness spoken of before. Of course,
he gets that power of ascension owing to the incarnation's wonderful
powers. Viewing the incarnation from this newly acquired vantage-
ground, the devout aspirant recognises him only as pure Divinity
with wonderful powers, and he therefore interprets the human
element in the incarnation as mere feigning out of compassion for
the ordinary man. As his devotion grows deeper, the devout
aspirant is seen at first to have that conception about these devotees
of God and afterwards about the whole world, His creation.

15. It has already been stated that from their very childhood
these divine incarnations perceive the world of ideas with the same
intensity and vividness as they see the objects of the world of senses.
But as their power of higher perception develops in course of time,
they begin to attach more and more validity to the world of ideas.
Finally, attaining to non-duality and the knowledge of the One
without a second, the origin of all the worlds of name and form,
they reach perfection and the acme of their powers. These facts
are true also in the case of souls liberated in life (Jivan-mukta).
But there is the difference that they have to make a life-long effort
to attain to this realisation whereas the incarnations do so in a very
short time. Or even if they (Jivan-muktas) succeed early, they
manifest very little power of liberating others, as compared with
the divine incarnations. There is the Master's saying on this
point: "The difference between the Jiva and an incarnation
consists in the degree of manifestation of power only."

16. Enjoying the immediate knowledge of the cause of the
universe, the incarnations dwell for a while in the non-dual plane
and then descend to the lower planes of the mind. In the eyes
of the ordinary people they still appear as human beings, but in

8

reality they are not so: they have become super-men or god-men. After having the direct knowledge of both the universe and its cause, they feel the universe to be comparatively of a shadowy existence. The uncommonly high powers of their minds then continue to manifest of themselves for the good of humanity. They have, at that time, the knowledge of the beginning, the middle and the end of all things, and they attain omniscience. It is then only that we weak men, see their extraordinary character and action. Their ambrosial words infuse hope in us, and also indicate to us that the intuition of the Absolute, which brings about the immediate knowledge of the cause of the universe, is not possible until we have eliminated all the mental modifications caused by the perception of the external world and its objects.

17. The reader well versed in Western learning, will say, "Everything is spoilt now. You have only made your position weak by speaking like the frog-in-the-well of the fable. He who knows how far man's knowledge has progressed and is daily progressing as the result of investigations into the objects of the external world, living and non-living, can never accept what you say." To this we reply: We admit what you say about the progress of material sciences, but the ultimate truth can never be realized by you through them; for you are content to look upon the cause of the universe as insentient or as an entity inferior to, and less in consequence than, yourself. And with the progress of science, you have made the ever-increasing enjoyment of sights, tastes, etc., the only aim of your lives. Therefore, even if it can be proved in the future with the help of the scientific method that all the things in the world, sentient and insentient, owe their origin to one single insentient substance, the truths of the subjective realm will remain univestigated, unverified, and for ever hidden from you. Without the renunciation of desires and the consequent attainment of the inward-looking tendency of the mind (which is impossible if desires are multiplied), you can never know the transcendent and indivisible Truth and gain the strength of conviction and freedom resulting from it.

18. It has been said that all the incarnations were from time to time elevated to high states of spiritual awareness from their very childhood. For example, from time to time Krishna made his parents and friends realize his divinity in various ways even in his childhood. While strolling in the garden, Buddha entered

into ecstasy under the holy fig tree in his childhood and attracted the notice of gods and men. Jesus attracted sylvan birds in his childhood by the power of his love and fed them with his own hands. Sankara, while a boy, impressed and consoled his mother by his spiritual power, and renounced the world. In his early years Chaitanya became inspired with spiritual emotions and gave the indication that a lover of God sees the manifestation of God in all things, good or bad. There is no lack of such events in the Master's life also. We mention a few here as examples for the reader to understand the point. From these words, recounted by the Master himself, we understand that he had the experience of this mergence of his mind in the world of ideas even from very early in life. He said:

19. "In that part of the country (Kamarpukur) children are given parched rice to eat, in small baskets. Those who have no such baskets in their houses eat it from the folds of their cloth. While loitering about in the fields, some boys eat it from the baskets and others from the folds of their cloth. I was then six or seven years old. One morning I took the parched rice in a small basket and was eating it while walking on the narrow balks in the corn fields. It was the month of Jyaishtha or Ashadh. In one part of the sky there appeared a beautiful black rain cloud. I was looking at it while eating the rice. Very soon the cloud covered almost the whole sky, when a flock of milk-white cranes flew against the background of that black cloud. It looked so beautiful that I became very soon absorbed in an extraordinary mood. Such a state came on me that my external consciousness was lost. I fell down and the rice got scattered near the balk. People saw this and carried me home. This was the first time that I lost external consciousness in ecstasy."

20. The village called Anur is situated about two miles north of Kamarpukur, the birth-place of the Master. The Goddess Visalakshi of Anur is a living presence. The people of the surrounding villages, far and near, vow worship and offerings to the goddess for the fulfilment of various desires. And when they are fulfilled, they come to offer worship and sacrifices at the proper time. It needs no mention that women are comparatively more numerous amongst the visiting pilgrims than men. The majority of them go with votive offerings for recovery from illness. It is even now seen that groups of village ladies of high families, while coming to pay

obeisance to her, sing songs and tell stories about the first appearance and self-revelation of the goddess and travel across the fields without fear. Kamarpukur and the neighbouring villages were more populous and prosperous during the Master's childhood than now. This becomes evident to us when we find the deserted broken brick-built houses overgrown with jungles, dilapidated and decayed temples, the platforms for religious dances, and the like. Therefore, we infer, that the pilgrims to the goddess [1] at Anur were then very numerous.

The goddess resides in the field under the open sky. The cultivators build every year an ordinary covering of leaves to protect the place from rain and sun. There is an indication in the neighbouring heap of ruins that there was a brick-built temple at one time. Asked about it, the villagers say that the goddess broke it down of her own accord. They narrate a story:

"The cowherd boys of the village are the dear companions of the goddess. They come there in the morning, let loose the cows and sit there; they tell stories, sing songs, and play games. They pluck wild flowers and decorate her. They take the money and the sweets offered to the goddess by pilgrims and wayfarers and enjoy themselves. She cannot do without their sweet pranks. Once a rich man of a village, having had his desire fulfilled, built that temple and installed the goddess in it. The temple priest came as usual every morning and evening to perform the worship. But he now closed the door of the temple when he went away after the worship. Those who came to pay obeisance at times other than those of worship offered their respectful presents to the deity through the trellis of the door. Consequently, the cowherd boys could no longer collect the money, buy sweets, offer them to the goddess, eat them, and make merry. Grieved in their hearts, they prayed imploringly,

---

[1] It is difficult to ascertain whether the name of the goddess is Vishalakshmi or Visalakshi. Vishahari is another name of the goddess Manasa met with in ancient Bengali books. This word Vishahari may easily be transformed into Vishalakshmi. Again, in describing the form of Manasa, the word Visalakshmi is used in books like the *Manasamangala*. So, Manasa is perhaps Vishalakshmi or Visalakshi. The worship of the goddess is seen in many places. We saw a beautiful temple of that goddess on our way from Kamarpukur to Ghatal. We were convinced that there had been a very good arrangement for worship there, when we saw the music hall, the tank, the garden, etc., attached to the temple.

'Mother, you have deprived us of our feast. Your money enabled us to have sweets daily. Who will now give us these things to eat?'

"The goddess," the villagers add, "heard the complaint of the simple-hearted peasant boys, and the temple developed such a big crack the very night, that the next day the priest brought out the goddess hurriedly and placed her in the open lest the image should get buried under the debris of the temple. Since then, whoever has tried to build the temple again has been apprised in dreams or otherwise by the goddess that it is not to her liking." The villagers say that some of them were threatened and deterred from it by the goddess. She said to them in a dream, "I am all right here in the midst of the fields with the cowherd boys; if you confine me in a temple, I will ruin you. I will not keep any of your family alive."

The Master was eight years old. He had not yet been invested with the sacred thread. One day many ladies of respectable families of the village went through the fields in a group, in the aforesaid manner, to fulfil their promise of offerings to Visalakshi. Among them were one or two ladies of the Master's own family and also Prasanna, the widowed sister of Dharmadas Laha. The Master had a high opinion of her purity, amiability, simplicity, and spirituality. He told the Holy Mother many a time to follow her advice in all matters. He also spoke of Prasanna from time to time to his women devotees. Prasanna too had a genuine affection for the Master from his childhood. She looked upon him very often as God Himself. As a simple-hearted woman, she was charmed to hear the holy stories of gods and goddesses and devotional songs from him. She would now and again affectionately ask him, "Gadai, why is it that you often seem to me to be God Himself? Yes, truly I feel so." Gadai heard it and smiled sweetly but said nothing; or, he brought in various other topics and tried to evade the question. But Prasanna could not be evaded with those words. She said seriously with a nod, "Whatever you may say, you are not an ordinary mortal." Prasanna built a temple and installed in it the images of Radha and Krishna and used to do everything for their daily service herself. Dramatic performances with songs and dances were held in that temple on festive occasions. But Prasanna listened seldom to these songs. Asked about it, she would say, "I have heard songs sung by Gadai and no other songs sound so sweet. Gadai has spoilt my ears." Of course these events are of a much later date.

When he saw the ladies starting, the child Gadai said, "I too shall go with you." Although the ladies objected to his going on the ground that the distance was too long for him to walk, Gadai stuck to his decision and started with them. At this the ladies were happy rather than annoyed; for who is not charmed by a child who is always cheerful and merry? Besides, even at that young age, Gadai had got by heart all the songs and verses about gods and goddesses. On the way he would certainly repeat a few of them at their request. Moreover there would be no difficulty if he felt hungry while returning, for then there would be with them the offered articles of food, milk, etc. What could then be the objection? What was there to be annoyed at, if Gadai went with them? Thus the ladies thought over the matter and without hesitation started on their journey with Gadai. And Gadai also went cheerfully with them, and as they expected, told stories and sang songs about gods and goddesses.

But as he was singing the glory of Visalakshi, an unexpected event happened before they had crossed the field. The child stopped singing suddenly; his body and limbs became stiff and benumbed. Streams of tears flowed incessantly from his eyes and he did not even reply to their repeated and affectionate calls as to what ailed him. The ladies were apprehensive that the child, unaccustomed to walking distances, had a sunstroke. They brought water from a neighbouring pond and poured a little on his head and sprinkled some on his eyes. But he did not regain consciousness. They were anxious and felt very helpless. What was the way out? How was the promised offering to be given and the worship of the goddess performed? And how was another's darling, Gadai, to be taken home safe? There was not a single man anywhere in the neighbourhood to help them. What was to be done? The ladies were in a great fix and forgot all about gods and goddesses. They sat round the child and sometimes fanned him, sometimes sprinkled water on him, and again called him by his name.

A short time passed this way, when Prasanna felt suddenly in her heart: "Can't it be that an ecstatic influence of the goddess has come on the simple-hearted and devoted child? Have I not heard it said that the ecstatic influence of deities comes on men, women and children who are pure and simple-hearted like him?" Prasanna expressed this thought of hers to the other ladies, and asked them to repeat with concentrated minds the name of Visalakshi instead of calling 'Gadai' The ladies had reverence for Prasanna on account of her pure character. They readily believed her words and addressed the boy as the goddess, and said again and again, "O Mother. Visalakshi, be pleased! Save us, Mother! Please be compassionate to us! Take us to a safe haven, Mother!"

Wonder of wonders! No sooner had they called on the name of the goddess a few times than the face of Gadai brightened up with a sweet smile and signs of a slight external consciousness were seen. They felt reassured and were certain that an ecstatic influence of the goddess had come upon the child. They saluted him again and again, addressed him as Mother and prayed to him. [1]

The child regained external consciousness by degrees and was in his normal state again. But strange to say, no fatigue or weakness was observed in his body owing to the change which had come on him just a little while before. With overflowing devotion, the ladies then arrived at the place of the goddess with Gadai. They offered the worship duly, returned home and told everything to his mother. She was frightened, and offered that day a special worship to Raghuvir for the good of Gadai. She offered salutations to Visalakshi and vowed a special worship to her also.

Another event in the life of Sri Ramakrishna bears ample testimony to the fact that since childhood he ascended to high spiritual planes at times. It happened thus:

There lived a family of Suvarna-vanikas [2] a little to the south-west of the Master's ancestral house of Kamarpukur. That this family of Pynes was very prosperous then, can be known even now from their brick-built Siva temple decorated with artistic designs. One or two of the members of this family are still living; but the buildings are all in ruins. It is said by the people of the village that the Pynes were very rich then. The house was full of people. They were rich farmers also, having extensive lands and a large number of cattle and ploughs; they had also a decent income from their trade. But the Pynes were not rich like the landlords of the village. They belonged to the upper middle class of society.

The master of the Pyne family was a very religious man. He never tried to convert his dwelling house into a brick-built one,

---

[1] Some say the women, out of an intensity of devotion, offered the boy the articles they carried for the goddess.

[2] A trading class, originally traders (vanikas) in gold (suvarna). —Tr.

though he was in a position to do so.   He always lived in a two-storeyed house [1] of mud walls. But he got bricks burnt, employed a good mason and got the temple beautifully built.   His name was Rasiklal.   He had no sons but had many daughters.   We do not know why all the daughters, although married, always lived in their father's house.   We are told that the youngest of them reached her youth when the Master was ten or eleven years of age.   All the daughters were handsome and were devoted to the gods   and holy men.   They had much affection for the boy Gadai, their neighbour.   The Master spent much of his time in that religious family during his boyhood.   And even now one is told of many a *leela* (divine   "sport") of the Master in the house of the Pynes while in high planes of consciousness.   But we heard from the Master himself of the event which we now describe.

It seems that the devotees of Vishnu and those of Siva lived together at Kamarpukur without bearing any ill-will towards each other.   Even now the annual "seventy-two-hour singing of the glories of the names of Vishnu" is, like the "Gajan" of Siva, celebrated with great pomp.   The number of Siva temples, how-ever, was greater than that of Vishnu.   Many of the Suvarna-vanikas were bigoted Vaishnavas.   The Vaishnava faith prevailed to a great extent among the people of this class since Lord Nity-ananda initiated Uddaran Datta and delivered him from worldly bondage.   But the Pynes of Kamarpukur were devotees of both Siva and Vishnu.   The aged head of the Pyne family used to take the name of Hari thrice a day as prescribed, but at the same time he had installed Siva and used to observe the vow of Sivaratri every year. During Sivaratri a dramatic performance used to be arranged in that Siva temple so that it might help devotees keep vigil at night.

21.   Once on the occasion of a Sivaratri, the usual arrange-ments for the dramatic performance were made. The troupe belonged to the neighbouring village.   They were to play a few   scenes indicative of Siva's greatness.   The play was to begin about half an hour after dusk.   At dusk it was learnt that the boy of the troupe, who was to play Siva's role, was seriously ill.   No one else could be found to play that part.   The proprietor gave up all hopes and proposed with humility that the performance be postponed. What was to be done?   How could the vigil be kept during the

---

[1] Made of bamboo, wood, straw and earth, but no bricks.

night? The elderly people sat together for consultation. They sent word to the proprietor asking him whether he could conduct the drama that night if a person could be found to play the part of Siva. A reply came in the affirmative. The village council consulted again as to who might be asked to act as Siva. Although Gadai was young, he knew many songs on Siva and he had the appropriate looks for playing the part. So it was settled that he should be requested. As regards the speaking of a few words while playing that part, it would be managed by the proprietor somehow. Gadadhar was approached and when he saw that all were eager, he agreed. The play, as arranged, began about half an hour after nightfall.

Dharmadas Laha, the landlord of the village, was a great friend of the Master's father. So his eldest son Gayavishnu and the Master were friends. When Gayavishnu came to know that his friend would act as Siva, he and his companions began to dress him accordingly. The Master put on the dress of Siva, sat in the green-room and was thinking of Siva when he was called to appear on the stage. One of his friends came to lead him there. Called by his friend, the Master rose in a state of mental abstraction, and without looking in any direction, approached the stage with sedate and slow steps, and stood there motionless. The audience felt a vague indescribable divine emotion and were filled with joy and wonder when they saw the Master in that dress, bedecked with ashes and matted hair, calm and dignified in gait, and fixed and motionless in posture. They felt particularly charmed to witness that heavenly, indrawn and fixed gaze and that gentle smile on his lips. As the villagers are wont to do, they suddenly cried out the name of Hari. Some of the women uttered the auspicious sound of "ulu" and some blew conchshells. Afterwards, in order to restore order in the audience, the proprietor began reciting hymns to Siva even before the noise subsided. Although the audience became a little calm, they still gesticulated and nudged one another, whispering in low tones, "Bravo, how beautiful Gadai looks! We never thought the lad would act the part of Siva so well; it will be very good if we can secure the boy somehow and form a Yatra troupe of our own." But Gadadhar was all the while standing in that same posture. Moreover, incessant streams of tears were flowing down his cheeks. Some time passed this way, but Gadadhar did not speak or move. Then the proprietor and one or two elderly men of the village went to the boy and saw that his hands and feet were insensitive and that he had no external consciousness at all. The noise then doubled. Some cried out, "Water! Water! Sprinkle water over his eyes and face." Some said, "Fan him!" Some others, "An ecstatic influence of Śiva must have come on him; utter His name!"—and still others murmured, "The boy has spoilt the whole amusement; it is certain that the play cannot continue now." At last, the audience dispersed when the boy could not be brought to outer consciousness by any means. Some people carried Gadadhar home on their shoulders. That ecstasy, we are told, did not come to an end that night in spite of much effort, and there was much agitation in the house. He regained normal state the next day after sunrise. [1]

---

[1] Some say that he was in that ecstatic state continously for three days.

CHAPTER III

THE FIRST MANIFESTATION OF THE ATTITUDE OF A SADHAKA

(TOPICS: 1. Further examples of spiritual insight in childhood. 2. Six features of the Master's character. 3. His wonderful memory. 4. Strong determination. 5. Infinite course. 6. Love of merriment. 7. Natural constitution of the Master's mind. 8. His revulsion for bread-winning education. 9. The Master at the Jhamapukur Tol in Calcutta. 10. Ramkumar's ignorance of his brother's outlook. 11. The worldly condition of Ramkumar.)

1. Besides the events already mentioned, many other facts regarding the Master's absorption in spiritual moods in childhood are known. We get indications of that nature of his mind in connection with many small matters.

For example: The village potter was making images of Siva, Durga, and other deities. The Master went there with his friends in the course of a walk. He looked at the images for some time and suddenly said, "What is that? Do the eyes of a god look like that? They should be made thus." Saying so, he explained to the potter the manner in which the lines should be fashioned and the eyes portrayed, so that the expression of super-human power, compassion, inwardness, and bliss may be shown in the eyes, endowing the image with a living, divine look. All were amazed to think how the boy Gadadhar could understand and explain all this without being taught that art. But none could find out the reason.

To cite another occurrence: Desiring to worship some deity in boyish play with his friends, he made the image of that deity or delineated it on canvas so beautifully that people, seeing it, came to the conclusion that it was the handiwork of a skilful potter or painter.

Again, a voluntary and unexpected utterance of the Master to somebody removed a very long-standing doubt from his mind. That person got a clue to his spiritual path and the power to regulate his future life. Astonished at it, he was prone to think that it was his chosen Ideal in the person of Gadai that had shown him the path out of compassion.

Further the boy Gadai astonished all by solving with one word the problem which scholars, well versed in the scriptures, had failed to solve.

2. It is not true that every one of the unique incidents we heard about the early life of the Master were expressions of his divine powers from a higher plane of consciousness. Although some of them were of this nature, we may classify the others into six broad divisions, namely, those indicative of his wonderful memory, of his strong power of judgement, of his steadfastness and strong determination, of his infinite courage, of his love of merriment, and of his unlimited love and compassion. But purity, selflessness and unique faith formed a common factor in all of these, and it looked that these innate constituents of his nature were reacting from time to time to the impact of various worldly situations by setting up waves of memory, judgement, determination, courage, merriment, love and compassion. The reader will have a correct understanding of what we say when we give a few examples here.

3. Once a theatrical performance on the theme of Rama's or Krishna's life was held. Many people including Gadadhar had witnessed it. All of them forgot the songs and the sacred words of the Puranas the very next day, and were busy following their selfish ends. But there was no end to the waves of spiritual emotions produced by them in the mind of Gadai! The boy assembled his friends in the neighbouring mango grove in order to rehearse them and enjoy the bliss thereof. He made all his friends get by heart, as far as possible , the parts of the different characters of the play, and took upon himself the leading role and began to enact the drama. Simple-hearted cultivators, ploughing in the neighbouring fields, were charmed to see that play of the boys, and wondered how, after hearing them only once, they could get by heart almost all the words and songs of the play.

4. At the time of his investitutre with the sacred thread, the boy persisted, against the custom of his family and society, that he must have his first ceremonial alms from a blacksmith woman Dhani by name (cf. pp. 63). Charmed with her affection and devotion, and drawn by her intense prayer, the boy brushed aside the restrictions of society, snatched curry, sauce etc., cooked by

that woman of low caste and ate them. In great fear, Dhani forbade him to do it but could not make the boy desist.

5. The Naga Sannyasins, with their matted hair and ash-covered bodies, always generate fear in the minds of boys in towns and villages. There is a belief current everywhere in Bengal that these Fakirs entice young boys; or, when opportunity arises, they abduct them to distant places and add them to their own number. Groups of such Fakirs and Vairagis travelled daily in those days by the road to the south of Kamarpukur, leading to Puri, the abode of Jagannath. They would come to the village, beg their food, rest there for a day or two, and then start for their destination. Although Gadai's friends were afraid of these men owing to the prevailing beliefs about them, Gadai was above such fears. He mixed with the groups of these mendicants as soon as he saw them and pleased them by his service and sweet conversation. He used to spend much time with them in order to observe their conduct and behaviour. Sometimes, at their request he would partake of the food they offered to their Deity, and returning home, he would report to his mother about his having done so. Desirous of imitating them out of his admiration for their way of life, he one day appeared before his mother with his body smeared all over with holy ashes and wearing a loin cloth and *kaupina* made in their fashion from torn pieces of a new cloth presented to him by his parents.

6. Many of the people of the lower strata of society in the village did not know to read the *Ramayana* and the *Mahabharata*. When they wanted to hear those books read out, they generally invited a Brahmana or one of their own class who could explain the epics to them. When the reader arrived, he would be offered water to wash his feet, a smoke of tobacco, a good seat to sit on while reading, or lacking this, a new mat. Honoured thus, he would swell with pride and egotism. Fond of merriment as he was, Gada-dhar with his keen intelligence would closely observe and study the manners of the scriptural exponent—how he sat on an elevated platform before his village audience, how he gesticulated as he recited the verses of the texts in a peculiar affected tone, and how at every turn he made efforts to show off his learning and superiority over the people sitting before him. Gadai would after-wards mimic the mannerism and the voice of the man, causing peals of laughter and great merriment among the people.

7. By a study of these facts of the Master's early life, we realize the nature of the mind with which he was equipped to undertake spiritual discipline. We feel that such a mind could not but accomplish whatever it undertook, would never forget what it heard, and would at once throw away mercilessly whatever it came to know to be an obstacle in its path to the realization of its desired end. We realize that such a heart would perform all actions in the world placing firm reliance on God, on oneself and on the divine nature hidden within all human beings. No ideas having the slightest tinge of narrow-mindedness would be acceptable to it, let alone mean, impure ones; and love, purity, and compassion alone would regulate it all the time in all matters. It will also be realized that no idea, either within his own heart or within those of others, would be able to deceive him by disguising its nature. While proceeding to study his Sadhanas, it would help us understand their uniqueness if we closely remember what has been said about the constitution of his heart and mind.

8. We see the first definite manifestation of the attitude of an aspirant in the Master's life, when he was in his brother's school in Calcutta—on the day when Ramkumar, his eldest brother, admonished him to apply his mind to the acquisition of learning, to which he clearly replied, "I do not want to learn the art of 'bundling rice and plantain'. What I do want is an education which produces right knowledge and enables man truly to achieve the real aim of his life". He was then about seventeen years of age. Knowing that there was little chance of his education progressing in the villge school, his guardians, after mutual consultation, sent him to Calcutta. His religious-minded eldest brother, well versed in Astrology and Smriti, had started a Sanskrit school near the house of the late Digambar Mitra at Jhamapukur and was teaching some pupils. He also took charge of the daily service of the deities in the Mitra family as well as some other rich families of that quarter. Most of his time was spent in giving lessons to students and in performing his daily religious duties. Therefore, it proved very difficult for him in a short time to go twice every day to different houses and perform the temple service. Nor was he at the same time able to give it up so hastily; for the income from the school by way of farewell gifts was very small and was daily decreasing. How could the household affairs be managed if he gave up what he was receiving as fee for the service of the deities? After due

deliberation over all these aspects of the question, he had at last brought his youngest brother to Calcutta, placed him in charge of the service of the deities and applied himself to the work of teaching.

9.   On arriving at Calcutta, Gadadhar got his favourite work and performed it with pleasure.   Besides serving his eldest brother, he also studied a little.   Possessed of noble qualities, the pleasant-looking boy became dear to all the people in a short time.   The veiled ladies of the respectable families of this place, even like those of Kamarpukur, did not feel any hesitation in appearing before him when they became acquainted with his smartness, guileless behaviour, sweet conversation and devotion to the gods.   They were eager to get some odd jobs done by him and to listen to his devotional songs.   Here also, as in Kamarpukur, the boy became the centre of attraction of a group of loving people round him without any effort on his part.   Whenever he had leisure, the boy met those men and women and joyfully spent some time in their company.   The boy could therefore make no significant progress in his studies here also.

Although Ramkumar observed all this, he could not suddenly mention it to his brother; for it sat very heavily on his mind to think how he had already deprived his brother, their mother's youngest and dearest pet son, of the benefit of that maternal affection and brought him far away practically for his own convenience.   Should he, over and above this, put obstacles in the way of the boy's joy and satisfaction in life when, attracted by his noble qualities, people were lovingly inviting him to their houses?   And if he did so, would not the life of the boy in Calcutta be as unbearable as in a forest?   If there were no wants in the family, it would not have been necessary at all to take the boy away from his mother.   It would have been enough if he were sent to some village near Kamarpukur to study under a learned scholar.   In that case, the boy might have been with his mother and been educated at the same time.   Although Ramkumar did not complain for some time on account of these considerations, still, urged by a sense of duty, he admonished the boy mildly one day and asked him to apply his mind to studies.   For, it was clear to him that some day or other the simple-hearted and self forgetful boy would have to fend for himself.   If he did not now learn how to guide himself on the path leading to the improvement of his worldly affairs, could he do so in future? Therefore, it is clear that it was brotherly love and worldly wisdom that moved Ramkumar to act that way.

10. Although he had fallen into difficulties arising out of the selfish, harsh ways of the world and had acquired some experience, the affectionate Ramkumar did not know much of the extraordinary nature of the mind of his youngest brother. Although he was, no doubt, a man of considerable experience of the world and was well acquainted with the crooked workings of the minds of worldly-minded people, he had very little inkling of the unusual bent of Gadadhar's mind and its reaction to life's situations. He could hardly realise that in spite of his young age his brother had seen through the hollowness and the unedifying and ephemeral nature of the motives behind the life-long labours of worldly men, and had come to accept an entirely different ideal as the aim and goal of human life. When unmoved by the rebuke, the simple-hearted boy communicated his thoughts on the subject along the above mentioned lines, Ramkumar, could not comprehend him at all. He thought that the boy, a pet of his parents, was piqued or annoyed at being thus scolded for the first time in his life, and had, there-fore, answered him in that way. That day, the truthful boy tried his best to explain his reluctance to go in for what was a mere bread-winning education. But who would listen to the words of a boy? A boy is after all a boy! Lo! we are in a world which thinks that if a man is above selfish consideration in his efforts, he must be suspected to have a deranged brain!

That day Ramkumar did not understand those words of the boy. Moreover, just as, when we chastise an object of our love, we repent the next moment and try to regain our peace of mind by loving him a hundredfold more than before, so also did Ram-kumar behave with his brother for some time after this. But, when we examine Gadadhar's actions after this, we get a clear proof of the fact that since then, he was seeking an opportunity to fulfil the desire of his heart.

11. The current of events in the life of the Master and his eldest brother flowed a little fast during the next two years after this event. The pecuniary condition of his brother was daily deteriorating and although he tried in various ways, he could not improve it. He pondered much in his mind whether he should close his school and take to some other job. But he could not come

to any decision. He could clearly understand in his heart of hearts that if he spent his days that way, instead of soon adopting some other means for the management of his worldy affairs, he would be involved in debts and consequently suffer. But what means was he to adopt? He had learnt no other occupation than those of teaching, performing sacrifices and officiating at them. And had he the energy and perseverance at this period of his life to make an attempt to learn some lucrative profession suited to the times? Again, even if he did acquire an art of that nature and tried to earn money, it would surely be difficult for him to get time for his prayers and daily ritualistic observances. So, deciding to 'let Raghuvir shape his destiny according to His will', he turned his mind from these thoughts and continued to do, with a broken heart, what he had been so far doing. For, we think, Ramkumar, who had great faith in God, was content with the little he had, and being good-natured, was not very pushing in worldly life.

But there occurred now, by the will of God, an event which showed Ramkumar a way out of that uncertainty and relieved him of all his anxieties.

CHAPTER IV

THE KALI TEMPLE AT DAKSHINESWAR

(TOPICS: 1. Why Ramkumar started the Tol. 2. Rani Rasmani. 3. Her devotion to the Goddess. 4. Divine instruction about the temple. 5. Construction of the temple. 6. Problem of making cooked rice offerings. 7. Unhelpful opinions of Pundits on the question. 8. Ramkumar's favourable opinion. 9. The Rani's decision to consecrate the temple. 10. Ramkumar's catholicity. 11. The Rani's search for a suitable priest. 12. Mahesh Chandra offering to procure a priest. 13. Ramkumar invited to be the priest. 14. Installation of the Goddess. 15. The Master's behaviour on the installation day. 16. The Master on the founding of the temple. 17. His steadfastness regarding food. 18 His devotion to the Ganga. 19. His living on self-cooked food. 20. Difference between illiberality and religious steadfastness.)

1. Probably Ramkumar was forty-five when he started his Tol in Calcutta in A.D. 1850. Worldly wants, mishaps, etc. had caused him anxieties for some time past. His wife had died after giving birth to her only son Akshay. It is said that the Sadhaka Ramkumar had predicted the death of his wife and informed some members of the household that she would not survive the birth of her first son. The Master had now reached his fourteenth year. Many rich and middle class people lived in the wealthy city of Calcutta. Ramkumar could remain free from worldly anxieties if he could make the students of the school proficient in learning, as it would enhance his reputation as a scholar as well. He could perform religious worship and give written opinions on religious matters, which would surely fetch a few additional rupees. Some such thought perhaps brought Ramkumar to Calcutta after the death of his wife. Or it may be that at the death of his wife he felt a great change and void in his life, and the idea that he would be free from them to a certain extent if he were engaged in various works in a far-off place, made him take that course. We have told the reader earlier the purpose for which he brought the Master to Calcutta a few years after the starting of the school at Jhamapukur, and the manner in which the Master spent the first three year after his arrival there in A.D. 1852.

We must now turn our attention elsewhere, if we are to follow the subsequent events of the Master's life. The reader must now direct his mind to the series of events that were taking place by the will of God in a very well-known family in another quarter in Calcutta. At that time Ramkumar had enrolled himself in the party of Chhatu Babu in order to increase his income from farewell gifts and for improving the condition of his school.

2. A famous lady named Rani Rasmani lived in Janbazar in the south of Calcutta. She was the mother of four daughters and became a widow at forty-four. She inherited the enormous property of her husband Rajchandra Das. Since then she had managed it herself and improved it much, and had thus become well known to the people of Calcutta. She became famous and she endeared herself to all, not merely by her ability in managing the property, but also by her innumerable other virtues and good works, such as her faith in God, her energy[1], courage, intelligence, presence of mind, and above all, her sympathy for the poor[2]

---

[1] There was, it is said, a barrack of English soldiers situated near the Janbazar house of the Rani. Drunken and unrestrained, the soldiers one day overcame the gate-keepers by force, entered the house and began to plunder it. Mathur Babu, the son-in-law of the Rani, and other men folk were then out on business. Unopposed, the soldiers were almost ready to enter the inner apartment, when the Rani took up arms, ready to oppose them personally.

[2] It is said that the British Government imposed a tax on the fishermen for catching fish in the Ganga. Many of these fishermen dwelt in the estate of the Rani. Oppressed on account of the imposition of the tax, they narrated their tale of sorrow to her. The Rani heard it and told them not to be afraid. For a big sum of money she took on lease that part of the river for catching fish. The Government thought that the Rani would carry on a business in fish. But as soon as the said right was obtained, the Rani put chains across the river in many places. This made it almost impossible for ships and other vessels of the Government to enter the river. When the Government protested against that action of the Rani, she sent word, "I have purchased the right of catching fish in the river on payment of a large sum of money to you. What I have done is in accordance with that right. If ships and other vessels always pass through the river, the fish will flee elsewhere and I shall stand to lose much. How can I, therefore, remove the chains from the river? But, if you agree to abolish the new tax on the right to catch fish in the river, I, for my part, am ready to give up my right voluntarily. There will otherwise be litigation and the Government will have to pay damages to me." It is said that owing to that reasonable statement of the Rani and also knowing that she was doing so in order to protect the poor fisher-

expressed through her unceasing gifts and unstinted distribution
of food to all.   By her noble qualities and actions, she, although
born in a Kaivarta (fishermen's) family, proved herself worthy
of her appellation, "the Rani', and attracted the heart-felt love
and reverence of all groups of people irrespective of caste.   The
Rani's daughters were married and had children at the time we are
speaking of.   By then, the third daughter of the Rani had died and
had left behind only a son.   Thinking that the said event would
result in the gradual separation of debonair Mathuranath, her third
son-in-law, from the family, the Rani married her fourth daughter
Jagadamba Dasi to him and made him her own again.   The descendants of the four daughters of the Rani are living till this day. [1]

3.   Endowed with many virtues, Rani Rasmani had great
devotion to the holy feet of the Goddess Kali. 'Sri Rasmani
Dasi, longing for the Feet of Kali' were the words engraved in
the official seal of her estate. We have heard from the Master
himself that the Rani's devotion to the Goddess was expressed
in all her words and actions.

4.   The Rani, it is said, had cherished in her heart for a long
time a strong desire to go to Kasi and pay obeisance and offer

men, the Government abolished that tax in a short time.   The fishermen
then caught fish free of any tax and blessed the Rani.

The Rani evinced great interest in all matters conducive to the good
of the people. We find the proof of it in her building the markets at
Sonai, Beleghata and Bhawanipur; the Ghat and the house for the dying
at Kalighat ; the Ghat at Ganga at Halisahar ; the road to Puri for
some distance from the other side of Suvarnarekha; and many other virtuous acts. The Rani went on pilgrimage to Gangasagar,   Triveni,
Navadwip. Agradwip and Puri, and spent vast sums of money in the
names of gods. Moreover, she protected the tenants of the estate of
Makimpur against the oppression of the indigo planters. She spent ten
thousand rupees and got the Madhumati connected with the Navaganga
by the canal of Tona. These and various other acts of public utility stand
to her credit.

* For the information of the reader we quote here a genealogical table
of Rani Rasmani from the booklet *Sri Dakshineswar*;

Rani Rasmani—Rai Rajchandra Das

| Padmamani— | Kumari— | Karunamoyi ; Jagadamba— |
| Ramachandra Das | Pyari Chowdhury | Mathurmohan Biswas |

special worship to Visvesvara, the Lord of the universe, and Anna-purna, the Divine Mother.   It is also said that she had collected and set apart a vast sum of money for that purpose.   But, as her husband had died suddenly and she had had to shoulder the responsibility of managing the huge property, she was not able to carry out her intention so far.   Now that her sons-in-law had learned to help her in this matter, and particularly the youngest Mathuramohan had become her right-hand man, she was getting ready to start for Kasi. When everything was ready, she had the vision of the Goddess in a dream the night before her departure.*   The Goddess gave her this instruction: "There is no need to go to Kasi.   Install My stone image in a beautiful spot on the bank of the Bhagirathi and arrange for My daily worship and food offering. I shall manifest Myself in the image and accept your worship daily."   The devout Rani was highly delighted to receive this instruction.   She put off going to Kasi and made up her mind to spend the accumulated money on that holy undertaking.

5.   We cannot say how far that tradition is true, but it is certain that the Rani's long accumulated devotion to the Mother of the universe was about to assume a visible form in the shape of the temple and the image. She purchased a spacious piece of land on the bank of the Bhagirathi spending a large sum of money, and began to build on it a big temple with nine spires, besides some other small ones subsidiary to it.   There was provision also for a well-laid-out garden attached to them.   Though the work of construction was going on for seven or eight years, the whole edifice was not completed even by A.D. 1855.   So the Rani reflected within herself, "As life is uncertain, the desire of installing the Mother of the universe may not be fulfilled in my lifetime, if it takes such a long time to complete the temple."   Resolving in her mind thus, the Rani had the ceremony of the installation of the Mother performed on the 'Snanayatra' day on May 31, A.D. 1855.   As it is necessary for the reader to know a few events that took place before this, we narrate them below.

---

* Some say that Rani Rasmani started by boat and came to the village of Dakshineswar to the north of Calcutta.   She got that prohibitory commandment when she was passing the night there in the boat.

6. Either because of the divine commandment she received from the Goddess Herself or out of a natural hankering of her heart— for devotees always love to serve their chosen Ideals with things they consider best—there arose a great eagerness in the mind of the Rani to offer cooked food daily to the Mother. The Rani thought: "Temples and other buildings have been built to my liking. I am going to dedicate property sufficient for carrying on the service regularly. But, in spite of doing all this, if I cannot serve Her to my heart's content and offer Her cooked food daily, everything will be in vain. It will fetch me at the most a little reputation; people will say, 'How great Rani Rasmani was!' But of what avail are such words of the people to me?" "O Mother of the universe", she fervently prayed, "Thou hast given me much name and fame in other respects, but in this case do not befool me by giving me this trash. It does not matter whether fame accrues to me or not, but pray, remain always actually manifested here and fulfil the cherished desire of this servant of Thine by accepting daily service."

7. The Rani saw that her inferior status in the caste scale and the scriptural prohibitions connected with it, were what stood as the main obstacles in the way of her arranging for cooked food offerings. Her own heart, however, never doubted that the Mother of the universe would accept her offering of cooked food. In fact, her heart was always full of joy at that thought, and was never hesitant. Why was then that improper prohibition instituted? Who wrote the scriptures? Were the authors of the scriptures heartless men? Or, urged by self-interest, did they try to impose the distinction between the high and the low even before the Mother of the universe? If so, she had no use for such scriptures. She would rather follow the sacred longings of her heart. But what was the way out even then? If she were to act against the prevailing customs, the devout Brahmanas and good people would not come to the temple to take Prasada. What was then the solution? The Rani had the written opinions of Pandits brought from various places. But none of them was to her liking.

8. Although the construction of the temple and the making of the image had been completed, there was no sign of the fulfilment of the Rani's desire to serve Her to her heart's content. None of the views on scriptural injunctions expressed by scholars, big and small, proved helpful. When all her hopes were almost dashed to the ground, one day a ruling came from Ramkumar's Chatushpathi

at Jhamapukur, which read, "If the Rani makes a gift of the property
to a Brahmana and then installs the Goddess in the temple and
makes arrangements for the offering of cooked food, there will be
no violation of the injunctions of the scriptures. The Brahmanas
and other high castes will not then incur blemish if they take Prasada
in the temple."

9. Hopes revived in the Rani's heart. She decided to consecrate the temple in the name of her Guru and, with his permission,
take the position of an officer for superintending his property and the
service in his temple. Afterwards the Rani informed other Pandits
of her intention of following the scriptural prescription given by
Ramkumar. Although they did not dare to say plainly that it
would be an unscriptural action, they nevertheless said, "The
action is still against the prevailing custom of society. The Brahmanas and other good people cannot take Prasada there even though
it is done that way."

10. We can very well infer that the Rani's attention was
greatly attracted to Ramkumar by this event. When one ponders,
one finds that to issue such a prescription in those days was indicative
of not a little catholicity on the part of Ramkumar. The minds
of the Brahmana Pandits, the leaders of society, had got confined
to a narrow groove in those days. There were few amongst them
who could step out of it, read a liberal meaning in the injunctions
of the scriptures and give opinions according to the circumstances.
Consequently people felt an inclination to set at naught their
opinions.

11. The connection of the Rani with Ramkumar, however,
did not end there. Although she paid proper respect to the members
of the family of her spiritual teacher, the intelligent Rani observed
distinctly their ignorance of the scriptures and unfitness to perform
divine service according to them. Therefore, she made up her mind
to see that the whole charge of the service of the new temple was
permanently placed in the hands of Brahmanas of virtuous conduct,
well versed in the scriptures, taking care at the same time to see
that the just and proper gifts due to her Guru's family were not
affected. Here again, the prevailing custom of society stood in her
way. In those days, the Brahmanas born of good families and
devoted to religious traditions did not even salute the deities installed
by Sudras, let alone worshipping them. They regarded the
degraded Brahmanas, such as the family of the Rani's spiritual

teacher, virtually as Sudras. It was therefore no wonder that no Brahmana of virtuous conduct, able to perform the rituals and officiate as a priest, agreed to take charge of the worship in the Rani's temple. However, the Rani did not give up hope, and increasing the pay and other remunerations, continued to search for a priest at various places.

12. The home of Hemangini Devi, the Master's cousin, was in the village of Sihar, not far from Kamarpukur. Many Brahmanas lived there. One Maheshchandra Chattopadhyaya of that village served in the estate of the Rani. Thinking perhaps that he might be able to earn a little more money thereby, he came forward to procure Brahmanas for the Rani's temples to work as priests and cooks. Mahesh undertook to make that arrangement and selected his elder brother Kshetranath for the post of a priest in the temple of Radha-Govinda, either with a view to convincing the poor Brahmanas of the village that accepting employment in the Rani's temples was not reprehensible, or with a view to improving the pecuniary condition of his family, or both. As he appointed one of his own family to work for the Rani, it became easy to a great extent to procure other Brahmanas for service in the temples. But he became very anxious when, in spite of much effort, he could not procure a fit priest for the Kali temple.

13. Mahesh had been for a long time acquainted with Ramkumar. It seems, they had close acquaintance with each other from their friendly contacts in the village. It was not unknown to Mahesh that Ramkumar was a devout Sadhaka and had long ago got himself initiated in the Mantra of Sakti of his own accord. We infer that Mahesh knew also of the strained circumstances of Ramkumar and his family. So his attention was drawn to Ramkumar for solving the problem of finding a priest for the temple of Mother Kali. But the next moment he remembered that Ramkumar was a Brahmana who did not officiate in sacrifices performed by men of inferior caste. Although he sometimes accepted the post of a priest in the houses of Digambar Mitra and others in Calcutta, would he accept it in the temple of the Rani, who was a Kaivarta by birth? It was very doubtful. But the day for the installation of the Goddess was near at hand and a suitable priest was not available yet. Revolving all this in his mind, Mahesh thought it reasonable to make an effort once at least in that direction. However, he did not himself immediately

set about doing that.   He told the Rani everything and asked her
to invite and request Ramkumar to accept the office of the priest
for the day of the installation at least and perform all the rites on
that day.   The Rani had already a high opinion of Ramkumar's
fitness, as she had got the favourable scriptural prescription from
him.   So she was much delighted at the prospect of his officiating
as the priest and sent him an invitation with great humility.   "I
am now ready to install the Mother of the universe on the strength
of your prescription," wrote she, "and have also arranged everything
in order to perform that ceremony at an auspicious moment on the
day of the coming Snanayatra.   We have got a priest for Radha-
Govinda.   But no suitable Brahmana is coming forward to officiate
as the priest of the Mother Kali and help me in the act of Her
installation.   Therefore, please make any arrangement that may
seem possible to you and deliver me from this predicament.   As
you are a good scholar well-versed in the scripture, it is needless
for me to tell you that anyone and everyone cannot be appointed
to officiate as the priest."

Mahesh himself went to Ramkumar with the letter conveying
the request, explained the situation to him in various ways and
prevailed upon him to agree to officiate as the priest until a suitable
one was available.   It was without any pecuniary considerations
that devout Ramkumar at first came to Dakshineswar.   His only
idea was that the installation of the universal Mother should take
place without a hitch. [1]   Then at the humble request of the Rani
and Mathur Babu, he lived there for the rest of his life, as he saw
that there was no other suitable priest available.   All events of the
world, great or small, come to pass by the will of the Divine Mother.
Who can say whether or not Ramkumar, a devotee of the Goddess,
knew the will of that Source of all wills and accepted that office ?

---

[1] We heard from Hriday, the Master's nephew, the account mentioned above, of Ramkumar's coming to Dakshineswar, but Ramlal, the
Master's elder brother's son, gives a different account.   He says, "Ramdhan Ghosh of the village of Desra near Kamarpukur, was an officer of
Rani Rasmani.   The Rani held him in high regard for his efficiency and
he gradually rose to be her secretary.   As he was known to Ramkumar,
he sent him a letter of invitation to come to take his farewell gifts at
the time of the consecration ceremony of the Kali temple."   Ramkumar
came to the Janbazar house of the Rani and said to Ramdhan, "The
Rani is a Kaivarta by birth.   We are Brahmanas belonging to the Rarhi
class.   We shall be boycotted if we accept her invitation to take gifts."

14. Thus the Rani got Ramkumar to officiate as the priest in an unexpected way. She had the installation of the divine Mother performed with great pomp in this new temple on Thursday, May 31, A. D. 1855, the day of the Snanayatra. It is said that on that occasion the temple was continuously filled day and night with the noise and bustle of feasts and festivities. The Rani spent money unstintedly and did her best to make all the guests and others as happy as herself. Many professors of the Sastras and Brahmana Pandits came on that occasion from famous centres of learning— from such distant places as Kanyakubja, Kasi, Sylhet, Chittagong, Orissa, Navadvip, etc. Each of them got a silk cloth, a wrapper and gold coins as farewell presents. The Rani, it is said, spent nine hundred thousand rupees on the building and the consecration ceremony of the temple. She purchased from Trailokyanath Thakur for two hundred and twenty-six thousand rupees the Salbari Parganah in the sub-division of Thakurgaon in the district of Dinaj-pur and executed a deed of gift and dedicated the property to the service of the deities.

15. Some say that Ramkumar was given provisions, and he cooked them that day with his own hands on the bank of the Ganga, and after offering the cooked food to his own chosen Ideal, he took it as Prasada. But this sounds improbable. For Ramkumar was a devotee of the Goddess, and had himself given the prescription about the offering of cooked food according to his knowledge of the scriptures—and that without the expectation of any gain. It is quite unreasonable that he himself did not take that offered food and thus go against his own prescription and the injunction of the devotional scriptures. The Master also did not tell us so. Therefore, our impression is that at the end of the worship he took joyfully the

Ramdhan showed him a list and said, " Why? Just see how many Brah‑ manas of that class have been invited. They will all come and accept gifts from the Rani." Ramkumar agreed to accept gifts and came to Dakshineswar with the Master the day before the consecration. There flowed a current of bliss in the temple on that day on account of the performance of Yatra, the singing of the glory of Kali, the reading of the *Bhagavata* and of the *Ramayana*, and so on. There was no cessation of that current of bliss even during the night. Every nook and corner of the temple was as bright as day on account of innumerable lights. The Master used to say, 'Going round the temple, one felt that the Rani had brought the silver mountain and placed it there.' Ramkumar came to the Kali temple to see the festival the day before the installation."

cooked food offered to the Mother of the universe.   But, although
the Master joined the joyous festival whole-heartedly, he acted
according to his strict principle regarding food.   He bought from
the neighbouring market a pice worth of fried rice at the approach
of the evening and partook of it before he walked back to the school
at Jhamapukur for his rest at night.

16.   The Master himself told us on many occasions many
things about the founding by Rasmani of the Dakshineswar Kali
temple.   He used to say : "Rani Rasmani made ready to go
to Kasi, the abode of Visvanatha and Annapurna.   She fixed a
day for starting and had about a hundred small and big boats laden
with various articles at the Ghat.   She got a prohibitory instruction
from the Goddess on the night immediately before the day of starting
and gave up that resolve.   She then engaged herself in searching
for a fit plot of land to build the temple."

He said further: "Under the conviction that 'the western
bank of the Ganga is comparable to Varanasi', she at first searched
for a piece of land in villages like Bali and Uttarpara on the western
bank of the Ganga but failed to get one.[1]   For although the Rani
was ready to pay a vast sum of money, the famous landlords of
those places said that they would not come to the Ganga down a
Ghat constructed at the cost of anyone else at any place in their
possession.   Therefore, the Rani was compelled at last to buy this
spot on the eastern bank of the Ganga"

He used to say: "A part of the piece of land selected by the
Rani at Dakshineswar belonged to an Englishman.   In the other
part of the land there was a Muslim graveyard, associated with the
memory of a holy man.   The piece of land had the shape of the
back of a tortoise.   Such a graveyard according to the Tantras,
is very commendable for the installation of Sakti and for Her
Sadhana.   Therefore, as if guided by Providence, the Rani chose
this piece of land."

Again, he would raise the topic why the Rani installed the
Mother of the universe on the Snanayatra day, a day of the festival
connected with Vishnu, instead of any other day auspicious for
the installation of Sakti, and say: "The Rani practised severe
austerities according to the scriptures from the day on which the
making of the image began; she bathed three times a day, took

---

[1] The old people of these villages bear testimony to this fact even now.

simple food, lay on the floor and practised Japa, worship, etc.,
according to her capacity. After the temple was built and the
image made, there was delay in fixing an auspicious day for the
installation owing to the leisurely ways of people. In the meantime
the image was kept packed in a box lest it should be damaged. But
it suddenly perspired for some reason or other and the Rani got
the command in a dream, 'How long will you keep Me confined
this way? I feel suffocated; install Me as soon as possible.' No
sooner had she got that commandment than the Rani became
flurried and had the almanac consulted for an auspicious day.
But, as no such day could be found before the Snanayatra, she
resolved to perform the installation on that day."

Besides this, we heard from the Master many other things
including the consecration of the temple in the name of the Rani's
Guru so that cooked food might be offered to the Goddess. We
heard from Hriday two things only: first, that Ramkumar gave
the scriptural prescription to the Rani about the consecration of
the temple, and secondly, that he had recourse to the practice
of Dharmapatra [1] to convince the Master of the propriety of his
accepting the office of the temple priest.

---

[1] There is still the custom in villages, of people depending on Providence when there is no possibility of a decision being arrived at by reasoning on a particular matter, and of taking recourse to Dharmapatra,
the leaf of impartiality, to know the will of Providence. When they
ascertain it thus, they act accordingly, without further argument or reasoning. The leaf of impartiality is made use of in the following manner:

"Yes" and "No" are written on some fragments of paper or on
Vilva leaves, which are put into an empty water-pot, and a child is asked
to pick up one fragment or a leaf. If the child picks up a "Yes" fragment, the person who has recourse to this expedient knows that Providence
sanctions the contemplated course. If the other piece is picked up, he
takes it that the will of Providence forbids the course. The division of
property and other things also is sometimes made with the help of this
device. Take this for example ; Four brothers have been living in a
joint family ; they want to live separately now and divide the joint property, but cannot come to any decision as to the particular portion to
be owned by each. They then ask a few important people of the
village to give a decision. They divide the whole property, both movable
and immovable into four equal parts as far as possible. Then they
decide by means of the 'impartial leaf' which particular portion is to go
to which particular brother. Almost the same practice is followed here
also. The names of the owners of the property are written on small

We can know from the Master's behaviour at this time that Ramkumar had at first no mind to accept permanently the office of priest at the Dakshineswar Kali temple. On reflection also it would be clear that simple-hearted Ramkumar had no such idea at that time. He must have thought that he would give the prescription regarding the offering of cooked food to the Goddess and return to Jhamapukur after personally offering cooked food on the day of the installation.

From his behaviour towards his younger brother at this time we have reason to conclude that he was not at all hesitant about offering cooked food and that he did not consider there was anything wrong and unscriptural in doing so. We shall explain these things to the reader here.

Early next morning, the Master came to Dakshineswar either to enquire about his brother or to witness, out of curiosity, the ceremonies that were left over from the previous day. He remained there for some time, when he saw that there was no probability of his brother's returning to Jhamapukur that day. Therefore, although requested by his brother to stay there for the day, he did not obey him, but returned to Jhamapukur for taking his food. The Master did not go to Dakshineswar for about a week after that. He was staying at Jhamapukur thinking that his brother would return there in due course after finishing the ceremonies at Dakshineswar. But when Ramkumar did not return even after a week, he grew anxious and came to Dakshineswar again to get news of his brother. He then came to know that Ramkumar had agreed to assume permanent charge of the worship of the Divine Mother at the pressing request of the Rani. The Master could not approve of this, and was highly critical of his brother's conduct. He reminded his brother that their father neither officiated in the sacrifices of the Sudras nor accepted gifts from all and sundry, and tried to dissuade him from the course

---

pieces of paper. They are folded so that no one can read the names and then put into an empty water-pot. Each portion of the property divided into four parts is marked A, B, etc., and small pieces of paper similarly marked are placed, as before, in another pot. Two children are then called and one of them is asked to pick up one piece from one pot, and the other child, to pick up one from the other. The fragments of paper are then read and each brother is to accept the portion corresponding to his name.

he had taken. It is said that Ramkumar tried to vindicate his action to the Master in various ways with the help of reason and scripture, but nothing touched his heart. Therefore he had recourse to the simple expedient of Dharmapatra, the leaf of impartiality, at last. The leaf of impartiality, it is said, read, "Ramkumar has not incurred blame in accepting the office of the priest. It will prove beneficial to all."

17. Although the Master now became free from anxiety regarding his brother's decision, another thought occupied his mind. He thought over what he was to do, now that the Chatushpathi was abolished. The Master remained absorbed in that thought and did not return to Jhamapukur that day. But he could not be made to agree to take Prasada in the temple in spite of Ramkumar's loving persuasion. Ramkumar said, "It is a temple and the food is cooked with the water of the Ganga; besides, it has been offered to the Mother of the universe; it will not be reprehensible for you to take it." But these words did not appeal to the Master. So Ramkumar said, "Then take uncooked provisions from the temple store, cook them with your own hands on the sands of the Ganga under the Panchavati and have your meal. Don't you accept that the Ganga purifies everything on its banks and bed?" The Master's strict principle regarding food had now to yield to his devotion to the Ganga. His faith and devotion accomplished what Ramkumar, well-versed in the Sastras, could not do with the help of so much reasoning. The Master agreed, and continued to stay at Dakshineswar and take his daily meal prepared by himself in the way suggested by Ramkumar.

18. Ah, what a deep devotion to the Ganga the Master had all his life! He used to call the water of the Ganga, Brahmavari, i.e., Brahman in the form of water. He said, "Any person living on either bank of the Ganga has his heart changed into one like that of the gods, and virtues manifest therein of themselves. The wind filled with the sacred particles of the water of the Ganga purifies the land on both sides as far as it blows. By the grace of the Bhagirathi, the daughter of the great mountain, goodness, austerity, generosity, devotion to God and spiritual steadfastness are always manifest in the lives of the people living in those parts of the land." If anybody talked of worldly things for a long time or mixed with worldly people, the Master would ask him to drink a little of the water of the Ganga. If a man, averse to God and attached to

worldliness, sat in any part of the sacred abode of the Divine Mother and polluted it by worldly thoughts, he would sprinkle there the water of the Ganga. He felt much pained if he saw anybody cleaning himself with that water after answering calls of nature.

19. Within a few days the impact of many factors in his new environment brought about a transformation in the Master's mind. There was the situation of the temple on the banks of the imposing Ganga. There were those beautiful gardens filled with the chirping of birds. There was the divine service performed by devout Sadhakas in the spacious temple. There was the genuine affection of his elder brother who was verily like a father to him. And there was also the touch of the faith and devotion of Rani Rasmani and her son-in-law Mathur Babu on everything in the place. All these were experiences that conspired to endear Dakshineswar to him and make it a second Kamarpukur in his eyes. No doubt he continued to cook his daily food himself for some time more, but he lived there with a cheerful mind and discarded that attitude of uncertainty regarding his future duty.

20. On hearing of the firm principle of the Master regarding food, some may perhaps think, "Such narrow conservatism is generally seen in the minds of men like ourselves. By mentioning this example, do you mean to say that the ultimate goal of spirituality cannot be realized if one is not similarly conservative?" We say in reply "Illiberality and religious steadfastness are not the same thing. The former is born of egoism. When it prevails, a man sets the highest value on what he himself understands and does, and thus circumscribing himself, remains unconcerned. But the latter is born of the faith in the teachings of the scriptures and great souls; when it prevails, man curbs his egoism, makes progress in his spiritual life and gradually realizes the supreme truth. When that firm principle predominates, a person may, in the beginning, appear to be illiberal for some time; but he receives with its help, clearer and clearer light on the path of his life and the limiting narrowness vanishes of itself. Therefore, how can we deny that steadfastness is absolutely necessary on the path to spiritual progress? Acquainted with this quality in the Master's life in the manner mentioned above, we understand clearly that we too will be endowed with true liberality in time, and attain the ultimate peace, if we go forward to realize spiritual truths

with a single-minded devotion to the teachings of the scriptures, and not otherwise. We have 'to remove one thorn by another' as the Master used to say. We must have recourse to religious steadfastness in order to reach the liberality of truth—we must follow rules and regulations in order to reach the state beyond them."

Noticing this imperfection in the early days of the Master, some will perhaps say, "Why should he be then called an incarnation of God? Why not call him a man? But if you must make God of him, it is better to conceal such imperfections when you are writing his life." We say, "Brother, there was a time when we also never believed even in dream that God could assume a human body and incarnate Himself. When, however, out of his unlimited grace the Master made us understand that this was possible, he simultaneously gave us the insight to grasp the idea that the incarnation would assume mental imperfections also, just as he assumed the weaknesses of the body. The Master used to say, 'The shape of an ornament cannot be given to gold, if it does not contain some alloy.' He never made the slightest attempt to conceal those imperfections from us, yet he clearly told us over and over again, 'The One who became Rama and Krishna, has now come into this case (showing his body); but His coming down this time is *incognito*, just like a king going in disguise to see round the capital. It is like that'."

The image of Kali at Dakshineswar

KAMARPUKUR

Haldarpukur

School of Lahas, where Gadadhar studied

CHAPTER V

ASSUMPTION OF THE OFFICE OF THE PRIEST

(TOPICS: 1. Mathur's attraction for the Master from the first. 2. Hriday, the nephew of the Master. 3. The Master at the time of Hriday's arrival. 4. Hriday's love for the Master. 5. His inability to understand the Master's actions. 6. -Mathur praising the image of Siva. 7. The Master's opinion on service. 8. The Master hesitant to meet Mathur. 9. The Master accepting the office of priest. 10. The broken Govinda image. 11. The Master on the worship of a broken image. 12. His musical talent. 13. His first vision during worship. 14. Ramkumar instructing the Master in rituals. 15. Kenaram Bhattacharya initiating the Master in Sakti Mantra. 16. Ramkumar's death.)

1. The pleasing looks of the Master, his tender nature, his devoutness and his youth attracted the notice of Mathur Babu, the son-in-law of Rani Rasmani, within a few weeks of the consecration of the temple. It is often seen that where an intimate and lasting relationship of love is forged, the attraction leading to it is felt at first sight. The scriptures say that this arises from the impressions of the relationship we had had in previous lives. When we reflect on the profoundly loving relationship that developed later between the Master and Mathur, we are led to conclude that there arose an indefinable attraction in the mind of Mathur for the Master from the very early days of their acquaintance. For a month after the temple was consecrated, the Master lived at Dakshineswar without any particular work or plan for the future. In the meantime Mathur resolved to appoint him to dress up the Goddess, and discussed the matter with Ramkumar. Ramkumar told him the whole story about the mental attitude of his brother, and discouraged Mathur in his effort to carry out his plan. But Mathur was not a man to be easily deterred. Although his offer was thus discouraged, he waited for an opportunity to carry out his resolve.

2. Another person intimately connected with the Master's life came to Dakshineswar about this time. Hridayram Mukhopadhyaya, a son of the Master's cousin Hemangini Devi, came to Burdwan at that time in search of employment. He was then

10

sixteen. For sometime he stayed at Burdwan with an acquaintance from his own village then residing in that town, but could find no way to the accomplishment of his purpose. When he came to know that his maternal uncles were living in the new temple of Rani Rasmani and were held in great respect, he thought that there was every chance of his purpose being fulfilled if he could go there. So Hriday came to Dakshineswar temple without delay and began to spend his time joyfully there in the company of Sri Ramakrishna, his uncle. They were nearly of the same age and familiar with each other from childhood.

Hriday was tall, handsome and of a manly build. His physique was firm and strong, and his mind extremely active and free from fear. He could undergo hard labour and adapt himself easily to circumstances. He was resourceful and could surmount difficulties and adverse situations by inventing extraordinary means for the same. Moreover he had a very tender and genuine affection for his youngest uncle and spared no pains to make him happy even by undergoing endless troubles himself.

Always active, Hriday had not a trace of contemplativeness in him. Therefore, Hriday's mind, like those of all worldly people, could never be free from selfish urges. The more we discuss his relationship with the Master since the earliest days, the more shall we see that the little contemplativeness and selfless effort seen in his life, were all due to the constant company of the Master, who was in himself an embodiment of these virtues. Hriday was sometimes in the habit of imitating him in this respect. The help of a man of action, courageous, reverential, and amenable, was very necessary for the success of the contemplative life of one who was indifferent to eating, drinking, and all other bodily needs and who was altogether devoid of selfishness and ever absorbed in contemplation. Was this the reason why the Divine Mother brought a person like Hriday into the life of the Master at this initial stage of his Sadhana and established a bond of deep and meaningful relationship between them ? Who knows? It is, however, true that but for Hriday, it would have been impossible for him to keep body and soul together during that period. Therefore his name remains eternally connected with the life of Sri Ramakrishna ; and he deserves our heartfelt homage for ever.

3. The Master was twenty years and a few months old when Hriday came to Dakshineswar. We can easily infer that his life

now became easy to some extent when he got a companion in Hriday. Whatever he did from now on, bathing, walking, lying, sitting, etc., he did with his help. The doings of Sri Ramakrishna, who was always of the nature of a boy, appeared purposeless to the eyes of ordinary people; but Hriday, far from criticising them, approved of them heartily and sympathized with him. This endeared him to the Master.

4. Hriday himself said to us: "Many a time I felt an indescribable attraction towards the Master since then, and I always remained with him like his shadow. Even a minute's separation from him was painful to me. I bathed with him, walked with him, sat with him and lay down with him. We had to part for a while only at the time of taking our midday meals; for the Master took from the temple stores rice and uncooked provisions which he cooked with his own hands. He took his food under the Panchavati while I had Prasada in the temple. But I made all preparations for his cooking before I parted. His principle regarding food was so strict then that he felt uncomfortable even with self-cooked rice. At night, however, he used to take, like all of us, the Luchis offered to the Mother of the universe. I noticed on many occasions that his eyes became filled with tears when he took the Luchi and heard him complain sorrowfully to the Divine Mother about his predicament."

The Master himself also sometimes spoke to us about the events of those times: "I felt extremely afflicted to think that I should have to take food from a Kaivarta. Even many of the poor indigent people did not come to the Kali temple of Rasmani to take their food, for that reason. As sufficient number of people could not be procured to take the cooked food offered to the Deity, cows were fed with it, and the rest had to be thrown into the river." But we heard both from him and Hriday, that he had not to take food cooked by himself for long. Our impression is that he did so till he took charge as a priest of the Kali temple, which he did in two or three months after the consecration of the temple.

5. Hriday knew that the Master loved him dearly. There was only one thing regarding him which Hriday could by no means understand. It was this: when he went to assist his elder uncle Ramkumar or to take a little rest after his midday meal or to witness the evening service in the temple, the Master eluded him and disappeared for sometime, he did not know where. He could

not find him in spite of a great deal of search. Asked about it on his return after about a couple of hours, he did not give a clear reply but said, "I was just near about this place." At such times on some days, when Hriday went in search of him, he found him returning from the direction of the Panchavati, and he thought that he had gone there perhaps to answer calls of nature and did not ask him anything more.

6. This is what Hriday said: "Once at that time the Master had a mind to make an image of Siva for worship. We have already said that sometimes he did this in his childhood at Kamarpukur. As soon as there arose that desire in his mind, he took some earth from the bed of the river, made with his own hands an image of Siva, together with the bull, the tabor etc. and began to worship Him in the image. Mathur happened to come there in the course of a stroll and, eager to learn what deity the Master was worshipping intently, approached and saw that image. Though not big, the image was beautiful. Mathur was delighted to see it. He felt that images, so expressive of divine nature, were not available in the market. He then asked Hriday out of curiosity, "Where have you got this image from? Who has made it?" He was astonished to know from Hriday that the Master knew how to make images of deities and to set broken parts of images. He requested that the image might be given over to him after the worship. Hriday agreed and, with the permission of the Master, took the image when the worship was over and gave it to Mathur. When Mathur got the image, he looked at it very minutely and, being charmed with it, sent it on to the Rani to see. She too was highly pleased with it and expressed surprise like Mathur on knowing that the Master had made it.[1] Even shortly before this incident, the idea of appointing the Master for temple duties had dawned on the mind of Mathur. That idea became stronger when he became acquainted now with this rare accomplishment of the Master. The Master had already heard from his brother of that intention of Mathur, but ignored it, as he had made a firm resolve from childhood that he "would not serve anyone but God."

---

[1] Some say that this event happened after the Master had assumed the office of the priest and that Mathur showed the image to the Rani saying, "The Goddess will soon become 'awakened', as we have got such a competent priest."

7. We heard the Master express on many occasions this opinion about taking service. The Master did not hold in high regard anybody who served another without being hard-pressed by need. Once, when he came to know that one[1] of his boy devotees had taken service, he felt much pained; and was heard to say, "I feel more pained to hear that he has taken service than to hear he were dead." When the Master met him later and knew that he had taken service for the maintenance of his helpless old mother, he said, passing his hand affectionately over his head and body, "There is no harm in that; you are not to blame when you have taken service for that purpose; but had you done so without the compulsion of any such duty, but merely for acquiring money for selfish indulgences, I could not have touched you any more. So I say, my Niranjan has not the slightest ' anjan ' (stain) in him; why should he be so low?"

All the newcomers were surprised to hear those words of the Master to Nitya-Niranjan, for that was his full name, and one was cheeky enough to say, "Sir, you condemn service; but how can we maintain our families without taking to it?" The Master replied, "Let him take service who likes it; I don't forbid everyone to do that. I say this only to them (pointing to Niranjan and the other boy devotees). Their case is different." The Master was fashioning the lives of his boy devotees in a different manner; and he, it goes without saying, gave such advice, because taking service was not consistent with the attitude that an earnest spiritual aspirant had to develop.

8. When the Master knew of the intention of Mathur Babu from his brother, he tried to remain, as far as possible, out of his sight and avoid him. For just as he was no respecter of persons when such respect came into conflict with truth and religious principles, so was he reluctant to wound others by unnecessarily vaunting disrespect to them. Again, it was in the Master's nature to esteem the merits of a person of good qualities and honour a respectable man in a simple natural way, without any expectation of favours. If Mathur were to request him to accept the office of the priest in the temple before he had himself arrived at a conclusion about it, he would have to refuse it and thus pain him. We clearly see that this apprehension was at the root of the Master's conduct in avoiding

----

[1] Swami Niranjanananda.

Mathur Babu. Besides, he was then a young man of no importance, and Mathur, the Rani's right-hand man, was a very important
person. Under the circumstances it would not look well, and it
would be regarded as boyish wantonness on his part, if he were
to refuse Mathur's offer. Besides, the Master's mood too was
changing, as he himself was feeling through his power of introspection. With the passage of time he had begun to feel the charm
of the Dakshineswar temple garden, and life there seemed to him
quite pleasant and agreeable. He was no longer very anxious to
return to Kamarpukur, his birthplace. He had now no objection
to live at Dakshineswar itself, provided he was not burdened with
duties and responsibilities.

9. But what the Master apprehended came to pass very soon.
When Mathur Babu came to the temple one day to pay his obeisance,
he saw the Master at a distance and sent for him. The Master
was then walking with Hriday. Seeing Mathur at a distance, he
moved away from there, when Mathur's servant came and said to
him, "Babu wants you". Hriday saw the Master reluctant to go to
Mathur and asked him the reason. He said, "As soon as I go
there, he will ask me to remain here and take service." Hriday
said, "What is the harm in that? It is only good to be appointed
to work under a great man in such a place. Why are you then
reluctant?" The Master replied, "I have no mind to be tied down
to service for life. Besides, if I agree to perform the worship
here, I must be responsible for the ornaments on the person of the
Goddess; that is a difficult task; it will not be possible for me.
But if you take that responsibility and stay here, I have no objection to perform the worship."

It was really in search of employment that Hriday had come
there. Therefore he gladly agreed to what the Master said.
The Master then went to Mathur who, as anticipated, requested him
earnestly to take service in the temple. The Master expressed his
conditional assent, to which Mathur agreed. He appointed the
Master to dress the image in the Kali temple from that day and
asked Hriday to assist him and Ramkumar. Ramkumar became
free from anxiety to a great extent to see his brother agreeing to do
that duty at the request of Mathur.

10. All the events mentioned before came to pass within
three months after the temple was consecrated. It was the end
of A.D. 1855. The ceremonies in connection with 'The Eighth

Lunar Day,' the birthday of Sri Krishna, had been properly performed without let or hindrance in the temple. The next day was the day of the Nanda festival. The special mid-day worship of Radha-Govinda and food offerings to Him were over. The priest Kshetranath took Radharani to another room and put Her to bed there. As he was next taking the image of Govinda for the same purpose, the priest fell down, and as a result, one leg of the image got broken. There arose a great commotion in the temple over that event. Opinions of various Pandits were taken. In the end the broken leg of the image was set and the worship of the image was continued according to the Master's advice (vide III.6). Having seen the Master sometimes enter into ecstasy, Mathur became eager to seek his advice regarding the substitution of the broken image with a new one. Hriday stated that the Master was in an ecstatic mood before advising Mathur and that he said at the end of the ecstasy that substitution was not necessary. It was not unknown to Mathur that the Master could beautifully set broken parts of images. He, therefore, had to set right the leg of the image now, at Mathur's request. He did it so well that even now it cannot be known that the image ever got broken, even if one examines it very minutely.

11. After the image was broken, many people said many things about the fruitless worship of an image destitute of a limb; but Rani Rasmani and Mathur Babu had firm faith in the reasonable advice of the Master and did not give ear to those talks. Anyhow, the priest Kshetranath was dismissed from service for carelessness and the Master was placed in charge of the worship of Radha-Govinda since then. Hriday assisted Ramkumar in dressing the image of the Mother Kali at the time of Her worship.

Hriday mentioned to us another fact about the broken image on another occasion. There is the Ghat belonging to Ratan Roy, the well-known landlord of Naral, near Kutighat at Baranagar, a few miles north of Calcutta. There is a temple near that Ghat. The images of the ten Mahavidyas are installed there. Formerly there had been good arrangement for worship, offerings, etc., in that temple, but at the time we are speaking of, it was in a decaying condition. Some time after, when Mathur had come to have much devotion to, and reverence for, the Master, they both once went to see the temple. Finding the temple in straitened circumstances, the Master asked Mathur to make an arrangement for a monthly supply of two maunds of rice and a sum of two rupees, to which he readily agreed. One day while returning after paying one of his occasional visits to the temple, the Master saw Jaya-narayan Bandyopadhyaya, the well-known landlord of the place, standing with many people in the Ghat consecrated by himself. As he was known to Jayanarayan, he went to meet him. Jayanarayan saluted and welcomed him respectfully and introduced him to his companions. In the course of the conversation he raised the topic of the Kali temple of Rani Rasmani and asked the Master, "Sir, is Govinda of that temple broken?" The Master said to him, "Ah, what a fine understanding! Can the One, who is an indivisible Whole, be broken?" To avoid the possibility of various vain topics being raised on the question put by Jayanarayan, the Master changed the course of the talk. Introducing another topic, he advised him to give up the non-essential parts of everything and accept the essentials only. The intelligent Jayanarayan also took the hint from the Master and refrained from putting such vain questions.

12. We have heard from Hriday that the Master's way of worship was an act worth witnessing. Whosoever saw it became charmed. Oh, the songs sung by him in his sweet voice with his heart swelling with emotions! Whoever heard those songs could never forget them. There was in them nothing of the artificiality of the so-called masters of high-class music. Their only merits were the complete identification of himself with the emotion of the songs, an accurate expression of the same in a sweet voice touching the heart, and the correctness of time and cadence. Whoever had heard the Master singing would be convinced that emotion is the very life of music and that in the performance of most singers, this vital factor of music is thwarted on account of carelessness in the observance of time and cadence. Whenever the Rani came to Dakshineswar, she sent for him and listened to his songs. She was particularly fond of the following song:

"What is Thy idea, O Mother, that Thou standest with Thy foot on Hara's bosom?. Thou hast put out Thy tongue out of Thine own accord, as if Thou wert a very simple girl. I have understood it, O Saviour ; is it Thy hereditary trait? Did Thy mother stand on Thy father's bosom like this?"

There was another reason why the Master's songs were so sweet. He became so much absorbed in the emotion of the song at the time of singing that he forgot altogether that he was singing it to please

anyone. We have not seen in our life anyone else singing a song
and becoming so absorbed in the emotion as to lose himself
completely in it like the Master. Even devotional singers expect
a little at least of praise from their hearers. In the Master alone
we saw one who felt, when praised for his songs, that the praise
was for the emotion conveyed by the song and not for himself.

13.   Hriday used to say that while singing, copious tears flowed
from the Master's eyes. At the time of worship he got so absorbed
in it that he would be totally unaware of anyone approaching or
calling him. The Master said that while performing rituals like
Anganyasa,   Karanyasa, he actually saw the letters of the Mantras
in bright colours set in his body. He actually saw the Coiled
Power going up in the form of a snake through the Sushumna to
the Sahasrara (vide III. 2). He felt that the parts of his body left
behind by that Power, at once became still and insensitive and dead
to all appearance. Again, when according to the prescribed
method of worship, he uttered the Mantra "Rang",[1] sprinkled
water all round himself and imagined a wall of fire existing around
the place of worship, he actually saw an impassable wall of fire
with hundreds of tongues spread out, protecting the place of worship
from all obstacles. Hriday said that other Brahmanas, seeing
his mind quite absorbed and body shining all over with a resplendent
lustre, said to one another, " It is as if Vishnu Himself has assumed
a human body and has sat down to worship."

14.   Ramkumar, the devotee of the Goddess, was, to a great
extent, free from anxiety about the maintenance of his relatives after
he came to Dakshineswar. But he felt from time to time perturbed
over another matter; for he noticed in his young brother a fondness
for solitude and a queer mood of indifference to worldly affairs.
He found in him a complete lack of interest in everything. Ramkumar at first thought that the boy was perhaps anxious to return
to his mother at Kamarpukur and was always thinking of her.
He saw the boy always either sitting quiet under the Panchavati
or taking strolls on the bank of the Ganga away from the temple,
morning and evening. Or he saw him spending long hours in the
jungle that existed all round the Panchavati in those days, and then
coming out of it. Time passed but the boy expressed no desire

---

[1] Actual name of fire, or the sound produced by its Sakti, heard by
Yogins.—Tr.

to return home. Ramkumar sometimes asked him about it, and came to know that he felt no such desire. He thereupon gave up the idea of sending him home. He thought, "I am advanced in age and am daily becoming infirm. Who knows when my lease of life will come to an end?" Under the circumstances, he felt that some arrangement must be made to assure the future of his young brother. Before he passed away, it was his absolute duty to bring up the boy so that he might be able to stand on his own legs, earn a decent living and manage his worldly affairs. Therefore, Ramkumar was much pleased, when Mathur consulted him about appointing the boy to do the duties of the temple. He became free from anxiety to a great extent when, after a lapse of time, at the request of Mathur, the boy accepted at first the duty of dressing up the image and afterwards that of officiating as priest, and then began to perform those duties with ability. He now began teaching him the complete reading of the *Chandi* and the mode of worship of the Mother. He thought that the boy would thereby become proficient in worship and would be able to relieve him on occasions when he could not himself attend to the worship. The Master soon learnt them and, knowing that it is not proper to worship the Goddess without being initiated in Her Mantra, resolved to take the initiation.

15. A proficient Sadhaka of Sakti named Kenaram Bhatta-charya used, then, to live at Baithakkhana bazaar in Calcutta. He used to frequent the temple of Rani Rasmani at Dakshineswar, and it seems, he was acquainted with Mathur and all other members of the Rani's family. We were told by Hriday that those who knew him paid him great respect as a devout Sadhaka. He had been acquainted with the Master's brother Ramkumar for some time past. The Master resolved to be initiated by him. We are told that as soon as he was initiated, the Master entered into ecstasy. Kenaram became charmed to see his uncommon devotion and blessed him heartily so that he might realize his chosen Ideal.

16. Ramkumar himself generally performed the service of Radha-Govinda at that time and allowed the Master to worship the Mother Kali, either because of his physical inability at times or because he wanted to get the Master accustomed to the conduct of the worship. Mathur came to know of it in a short time, and with the permission of the Rani, requested Ramkumar permanently to perform the worship in the Vishnu temple thenceforward. So, the Master was now appointed to the office of the priest, and Hriday

to dress the image in the Kali temple. The reason why the arrangement of the worship was changed seems to be that Mathur thought that Ramkumar had become old and infirm and it was beyond his power to carry on the more difficult duties of the Kali temple. Ramkumar too was glad at this arrangement, and standing beside his brother in the Kali temple, taught him how to perform the worship and service of the Mother properly. He thus became free from anxiety. Shortly afterwards, he spoke to Mathur and had Hriday appointed to worship Radha-Govinda. He was now preparing to go home on leave for some time. But Ramkumar was never to go home again. He went on some business to a place called Syamnagar Mulajor, to the north of Calcutta, for a few days, and suddenly died there. Ramkumar lived and worshipped the Divine Mother for one year only, after the temple of Rani Rasmani was consecrated ; so, probably he passed away in the middle of A. D. 1856.

CHAPTER VI

THE SOUL'S ANGUISH AND THE FIRST VISION

(TOPICS: 1. The Master's behaviour at this time. 2. Hriday's anxiety at this. 3. The Panchavati at that time. 4. Hriday enquiring why he went to the jungle at night. 5. Hriday frightening the Master. 6. The Master on the need for being free from bondages before meditation. 7. Need of carrying out thoughts into action. 8. Thoroughness of the Master's renunciation. 9. Refutation of an objection to this. 10. The Master's mode of worship then. 11. Mathur's appreciation of the Master's worship. 12. Effects of God-love on his body. 13. The vision following the great yearning.)

1. The Master was very young when his father died. He was therefore brought up from his childhood under the affectionate care of his mother Chandradevi and his eldest brother Ramkumar. Ramkumar was about thirty-one years elder to him. Therefore the Master revered his eldest brother almost like a father. It is certain that the Master was very much grieved at the sudden death of his brother who in turn was as affectionate to him as a father. The renunciation of the world on the part of Lord Buddha, an incarnation of God, at the sight of illness, old age and death is well known. Who can say how far his brother's death contributed to the kindling up of the fire of renunciation in the Master's pure mind, by producing in him a firm conviction about the transitoriness of the world? Be that as it may, he applied his mind more closely to the worship of the Mother of the universe from this time on, and became anxious to know whether a man thirsting for Her vision can really become blessed with it. We are told that at this time he used to spend his days sitting with the Divine Mother in the temple at the end of the worship and becoming absorbed in Her. He became overwhelmed with, and lost himself in the love for the Mother while he was singing for Her the songs composed by devotees like Ramprasad and Kamalakanta. He was extremely reluctant to waste a single moment in vain talk now. And when the door of the temple was closed at midday or at night, he left all company,

entered the jungle round the Panchavati and spent his time in contemplation on the Mother of the universe.

2.   These actions of the Master were not agreeable to Hriday.
But what could he do?   It was not unknown to him that from his
childhood the Master accomplished whatever he set his heart upon,
and that nobody could prevent him from doing so.   It was therefore
of no avail to protest to him or hinder him.   But Hriday could not
help hinting to him his anxiety when he saw that mood growing
with alarming rapidity every day.   Hriday became very anxious on
noticing that, instead of sleeping at night, he left his bed and went
somewhere.   For, if he spent sleepless nights, he would not be able
to stand the hard labour involved in the divine service in the temple.
Beside, the Master did not take now as much food as he once used
to take.   It was probable that under the circumstances, his health
might break down if he did not sleep at night.   So Hriday resolved
to inquire about it and set things right as far as it lay in his power.

3.   In those days the land surrounding the Panchavati was not
as even as it is now. It was full of pits, ditches, lowlands, jungles,
etc.   There grew an Amalaki tree among the wild trees and plants.
It was a burial ground besides being a jungle.   Therefore people
hardly went there even in the day time. If they went that way at all,
they never entered the jungle.   So, going there at night was out of
the question.   No one ventured there for fear of ghosts.   We
have heard from Hriday that the tree grew on a low piece of land.
So, anyone sitting under that tree could not be seen from the high
land outside the jungle.   The Master used to sit under it for meditation at night.

4.   One night, when the Master started for that place, Hriday
followed him without his knowledge and saw him enter that jungle.
He did not go farther lest the Master should be annoyed.   But in
order to frighten him he threw stones and some gravel so that they
fell round about him for some time.   Seeing that this did not bring
the Master back, he could not do anything but return to his room.
He asked the Master during his leisure the next day, "What do
you do when you enter the jungle at night?"   "There is, " replied
the Master,   "an Amalaki tree there.   I sit under it and practise
meditation.   The scriptures say that anyone who meditates under
an Amalaki tree, with whatever desire in his mind, gets it fulfilled."

5.   As soon as the Master sat for meditation under that tree
after that event, there happened from time to time various kinds

of disturbances like stone-throwing for a few days. Although he knew that it was all Hriday's doing, the Master never mentioned it to him. But Hriday could not feel at ease when he found that he was not able to dissuade him by that means. One day he entered the jungle with silent steps shortly after the Master had gone to the tree and saw from a distance that he had put off his cloth and the sacred thread and was sitting at ease in meditation. When he saw this, he thought, "Has uncle gone mad? It is only mad people that would behave like this. If he wants to meditate, let him do it by all means; but why does he throw off the only cloth he has on?"

6. Thinking so, he immediately approached him and said, "What is this? How is it that you have put off the sacred thread and cloth and are sitting stark naked?" When thus shouted at a few times, the Master was roused to his normal consciousness from the state of inward absorption and heard Hriday put those questions to him. He said in reply, "What do you know? Thus freed from all ties, one should practise meditation. From his birth man labours under the eight bondages of hatred, fear, shame, aversion, egoism, vanity, pride of noble descent, and obsession with formal good conduct. The sacred thread also is a 'bondage,' for it is a sign of the sense of self-importance, 'I am a Brahmana and superior to all.' When one calls on the Mother, one should discard these bondages and call on Her with a concentrated mind. That is why I have put off these. I shall put them on again when I return at the end of the meditation." Hriday was aghast to hear these words, which seemed so unfamiliar to him, and unable to say anything in reply, left the place. A little while previously he had thought that he would convince his uncle of his mistake in various ways and scold him, but what happened was just the contrary.

7. It is good to state here one fact in connection with the event mentioned above; for if that is known, we shall be able to understand many of the events that followed in the Master's life. From the incident mentioned above, it would be seen that the Master could not rest content with the thought that by only mentally renouncing these eight bondages, he would be renouncing them in truth and in reality. He was satisfied only after renouncing them physically also. We see him behaving similarly with regard to all other matters in later life. Take for example the following facts:

In order to destroy the vanity born of noble descent and to acquire true humility thereby, he cleaned very carefully with his hands places which are absolutely shunned as unclean by others.

He had heard that the mind of a spiritual aspirant should regard alike a clod of earth, a precious stone, and a piece of gold—in other words, consider precious stones and metals as worthless like a clod of earth. Unless the mind could do this, it would not be possible for it to free itself from desire for bodily pleasures or to turn its flow completely Godward and practise Yoga. The Master, therefore, took in his hand a few coins and clods of earth and threw them into the Ganga, repeating over and over again, "rupee-earth, earth-rupee".

8. In order to make firm his knowledge that Siva (God) is in all Jivas (creatures), he ate and put on his head, as Prasada, a little of the leavings from the leaf-plates of the poor people after they had been fed at the Kali temple. Afterwards, he carried those leaves on his head to the bank of the Ganga, took a broom and swept and washed the place clean with his own hands. He felt happy to think that a little of the service of God had been performed with the help of that mortal body of his.

Many other similar events may be mentioned. It is seen in all these cases that he did not rest satisfied with mere mental renunciation of the obstacles on the path to the realization of God, but discarded them at first in their gross forms also. In other words, he kept his body and senses away from objects of temptation and compelled the former forcibly to act contrary to their natural inclinations. It is seen that acting thus, his mind had all its past impressions destroyed completely. The mind could thereafter grasp the new contrary inclinations so firmly that it could never go against them. He did not admit that the new ideas had properly been grasped and the contrary ones given up, till at least a little of the former had been converted into practice with his body and the senses.

9. Wholly averse to giving up past impressions, we think that there was no need for such actions on the part of the Master. In the course of discussion such actions of his, some have gone to the length of saying, "His actions such as cleaning dirty and abominable places, throwing into the Ganga the coins and the clods of earth repeating ' rupee-earth, earth-rupee', seem to be whims of his fancy. The mental development that he obtained through those extraordinary means could be obtained more quickly through far

easier ones." In reply we have to say: It all sounds very well. But how many people up till now have been able to become completely averse to sights, tastes and other worldly objects and have devoted their whole minds to God by adopting your so-called easier means of mentally giving up sensuous objects, without having recourse to external practices ? It can never be. One cannot succeed in any great undertaking, let alone the realization of God, when one's mind has one idea and moves in a particular direction, while the body acts contrary to that idea and moves in a different direction. But with his ingrained longing for the enjoyments of sight, taste, etc., man does not realize the truth of this statement. Dominated by past impressions, he does not try to give up the objects of the senses physically, even when he realizes that such renunciation is good, but goes on thinking, "Let the body do as it will, but let the mind soar high." Eager to have Yoga and Bhoga simultaneously, he decieves himself; for, like light and darkness, these two things can never co-exist. No one has so far been able to discover an easy method of spiritual advancement which combines simultaneously the service of God and of worldliness, which is only a synonym for lust and gold. [1] Therefore the scriptures repeatedly teach us, "Whatever ought to be given up, has to be given up with body, mind and speech, and whatever ought to be accepted, has to be accepted similarly. Then and then only will the aspirant be fit to realize God." That is why the sages say, "Man can never have the realization of the Self with the help of knowledge, unaided by practice and without putting on emblems, [2] which give rise to spiritual attitudes." It is also reasonable to believe that the human mind reaches the subtle state from the gross, and the causal from the subtle. "There is no other path to the realization of the supreme goal." [3]

10. We have said before that the Master was getting more and more engrossed in the worship of the Divine Mother after the death of his eldest brother. Prompted by a burning faith, he was now eagerly doing whatever he knew to be favourable to the attainment of Her vision. Singing the songs of Ramprasad and other great devotee-poets before the Goddess now became a regular auxiliary of his daily worship. His mind was filled with zeal

---

[1] Ye cannot serve God and   Mammon. *The Holy Bible. Matth.*VI 24
[2] *Tapasovāpyalingāt.—Mundaka Upanishad,* 3. 2. 4.
[3] *Svetasvatara Upanishad,* 6. 15.

when he sang those songs with his heart full of profound spiritual emotion. He thought, "Devotees like Ramprasad had the vision of the Mother. So it is certain that the Mother of the universe is realizable; why can I not then be blessed with Her vision?" He used to say with an eager heart, "Thou didst show Thyself to Ramprasad, Mother. Why then should Thou not reveal Thy self to me? I don't want wealth, friends, relatives, enjoyment of pleasure, and the like. Do show Thyself to me." He would pray and cry this way, while his bosom was flooded with streams of tears from his eyes. By this the heaviness of his heart lessened a little. Urged by a fond hope, he would be somewhat reassured like a child and become ready to please the Goddess by singing for Her again. He thus went on spending his days in worship, meditation, and the singing of devotional songs. His love and longing for Her increased daily.

Thus the wonderful worshipper's scheduled period of time for performing the worship and service of the Goddess went on increasing day by day. He sat for worship and, placing a flower on his head according to scriptural injunction, perhaps remained motionless like the trunk of a tree,, meditating for two long hours. After offering cooked food and other things to the Mother, he perhaps spent a long time thinking that She was taking them. Again, perhaps he spent a long time every morning in decorating the Goddess with garlands made of flowers plucked with his own hands. Or he remained engaged for a very long time in performing the evening Arati with a heart filled with loving devotion. Again, singing for the Mother of the universe in the afternoon, or at the end of the Arati, he sometimes became so much absorbed in, and overwhelmed with, spiritual emotions, that he could be made to perform the Arati, the evening services of food offering, etc., only when he had been reminded again and again that it was getting late for those services. The worship continued thus for a time.

11. It is clear that the attention of the people of the temple was drawn towards the Master when they saw such devotion, eagerness and spiritual steadfastness on his part. People at first deride and ridicule a person who is seen to give up the path generally followed by them and to conduct himself or do something in a novel way. But with the passage of time and the perseverance of that person in the path despite all criticism, their attitude changes and reverence takes its place. The Master's case was no exception

11

to this rule. Soon after he started his novel form of worship, he became the object of many people's derision. Sometime later some people began to revere him. It is said that Mathur saw the Master's worship at this time and said with great delight to Rani Rasmani, " We have got an extraordinary worshipper; the Goddess will be awakened very soon." The Master never deviated from his own course on account of the opinions of the people. Like a river flowing to the sea, his mind was from now on progressing incessantly towards the holy feet of the Divine Mother of the universe.

12. As days went by, the devotion and eagerness of the Master increased more and more. The continuous flow of his mind towards the spiritual goal had its effects on the body, too, giving rise to various physical symptoms. His need for food and sleep decreased. As 'the blood in his body was always moving speedily to his chest and brain, his chest appeared constantly reddish and his eyes became sometimes suddenly filled with tears. He felt a great eagerness for the realization of the Divine, and his mind was seized with an incessant anxiety as to what he should do and how he could have Her vision. Therefore there was in his body a state of restlessness and lack of tranquillity at all times except when he was meditating or worshipping.

We were told by the Master himself that one day at that time, he sang for the Divine Mother to hear, and then prayed to Her, weeping in his eagerness to have the vision, "Dost Thou not, O Mother, hear even a little of the many prayers I address to Thee? Thou didst show Thyself to Ramprasad. Why shouldst Thou not then reveal Thyself to me?"

13. He used to say, "There was then an intolerable anguish in my heart because I could not have Her vision. Just as a man wrings a towel forcibly to squeeze out all the water from it, I felt as if somebody caught hold of my heart and mind and was wringing them likewise. Greatly afflicted with the thought that I might never have Mother's vision, I was in great agony. I thought that there was no use in living such a life. My eyes suddenly fell upon the sword that was there in the Mother's temple. I made up my mind to put an end to my life with it that very moment. Like one mad, I ran and caught hold of it, when suddenly I had the wonderful vision of the Mother, and fell down unconscious. I did not know what happened then in the external world—how that day and the next slipped away. But, in my heart of hearts, there was flowing a current

of intense bliss, never experienced before, and I had the immediate knowledge of the Light that is Mother."

On another occasion the Master described to us in detail his wonderful vision mentioned above. He said, "It was as if the houses, doors, temples and all other things vanished altogether; as if there was nothing anywhere! And what I saw was a boundless infinite Conscious Sea of Light! However far and in whatever direction I looked, I found a continuous succession of Effulgent Waves coming forward, raging and storming from all sides with great speed. Very soon they fell on me and made me sink to the Abysmal Depths of Infinity. I panted and struggled, as it were, and lost all sense of external consciousness." The Master told us that at that time he saw a luminous sea of Consciousness. But what about the Divine Mother's form consisting of pure Consciousness only— the form of Hers with hands that give boons and freedom from fear? Did the Master then have the vision of that form also in that sea of Light? It appears that he had; for as soon as he had the slightest consciousness at the time of his first vision, he, we are told, uttered repeatedly the word "Mother" in a voice choked by emotion.

When that vision came to an end, there arose in the heart of the Master an eager, incessant urge and aspiration for a constant immediate vision of the Divine Mother's form, consisting of Consciousness only. Although it was not always manifested in external symptoms like weeping, etc., it always existed in his heart. Sometimes it increased so much that, unable to suppress it, he fell on the ground and struggled in pain. He wept so much saying, "Bestow Thy grace on me, Mother! and show Thyself to me," that people gathered all round him! Not even a shade of concern for what they would think of such restlessness arose in his mind at that time. He used to say, "Although people stood all round, they appeared unreal like shadows or pictures painted on canvas, and not even the slightest sense of shame or hesitation did cross my mind on that score. But immediately after, I lost consciousness on account of unbearable anguish, and then I saw that form of the Mother with hands that give boons and freedom from fear—the form that smiled, spoke and consoled and taught me in endless ways!"

CHAPTER VII

SADHANA AND DIVINE INEBRIATION

1. The Master became quite unfit for all work for some days as his mind was absorbed in the bliss arising from the vision of the Mother. It became impossible for him to perform regularly the worship and other duties of the temple. Hriday somehow managed them with the help of another Brahmana. He also thought of arranging for some treatment for his uncle, thinking that he .was afflicted with insanity. He had become somehow acquainted with a physician of the princely house of Bhukailas, under whose treatment he placed the Master now; and knowing that there was no possibility of a speedy recovery, he sent word to his mother and brother at Kamarpukur.

2. But the Master himself attempted to perform the worship on days when he was comparatively free from overpowering spiritual emotions and loss of outward consciousness from eagerness for God-vision. He told us sometimes a little of the thoughts and experiences at the time of his worship and meditation in those days. He said, "I used to show to my mind the image of the Bhairava in meditation pose on the parapet of the roof of the music hall and say to it, 'You must be firm and motionless like that and meditate on Mother's Lotus Feet.' No sooner had I sat down for meditation than I heard clattering sounds produced in the joints of my body and limbs from the direction of the legs upwards; and they got locked one after another as if some one

from within turned the keys. As long as I meditated, I had no power to move my body and change my posture even slightly or give up meditation and go elsewhere or do anything else at will. I was, as it were, forcibly made to sit in the same posture, as long as the joints did not make clattering sounds as before and were unlocked, this time from the direction of the head to the legs. When I sat and meditated, I had, in the beginning, the vision of particles of light like groups of fire-flies; I saw sometimes all quarters covered with masses of mist-like light; and at other times I perceived that all things were pervaded by bright waves of light like molten silver. I saw these things sometimes with my eyes shut and sometimes with my eyes open. I did not understand what I saw nor did I know whether it was good or bad to have such visions. I therefore prayed to Mother with a troubled heart, 'I don't understand, Mother, what is happening to me; I don't know Mantras etc., by which to call Thee; please teach me personally what may enable me to realize Thee. Mother! if Thou dost not teach me, who else will? For, there is no refuge for me except Thee.' I used to pray thus with a concentrated mind and weep piteously on account of the eagerness of my heart."

3. The Master's worship, meditation, etc., underwent novel changes. It is difficult to explain how whole-hearted and deep was his absorption in Her. It was characterised by a childlike simplicity, sweetness, faith and dependence on the Mother,— his sole stay and support. Free from the seriousness of an adult, he made no personal effort to observe the scriptural injunctions and prohibitions regarding time, place and person; nor did he care to conduct himself in a manner conforming to standards approved both by the worldly and the godly. Whenever one saw him, one thought that he had merged his little will and his little ego in the will of Her who was the source of all wills, and that he did everything as if he were completely an instrument in Her hand, praying in his heart of hearts, "O Mother, my only refuge! kindly make me, Thy boy, say and do what I should." It was natural that this marked variance of his conduct and behaviour from what worldly people considered proper, led to criticisms, at first in whispers and afterwards as loud gossip. But all these mattered little to him; for the boy of the Divine Mother that he was, he now moved about and did everything by Her direction. The vain clamour of the world did not reach his ears at all. For though

in the world, he was not of it. The external world was now transformed for him into a dream world. Now he could not attribute substantiality to it in spite of his efforts. The universal Mother's form, consisting of pure Consciousness and Bliss, was now to him the only reality.

4. Previously, on some occasions at the time of worship and meditation, the Master used to see a hand of the Divine Mother or a foot, bright and delicate, or Her sweet, affectionate and smiling face, supremely beautiful. Now he saw, even at times other than those of worship and meditation, the full figure of the effulgent Mother, smiling and speaking, guiding and accompanying him and saying, "Do this, don't do that."

Formerly when he offered cooked food etc., to the Mother, he used to see an extraordinary ray of light coming out, beaming from Her eyes. It touched all the offered articles, took their essential parts, and withdrew itself again into Her eyes. Now, he saw that even before the offering was made, the same Mother in Her very person, sat down to take the offerings, illumining the temple with the effulgence of Her holy presence. One day Hriday came suddenly at the time of the worship and saw that the Master had taken in his hands an Arghya consisting of china-roses and Vilva leaves, which he was going to offer at the Lotus Feet of the Divine Mother. He was absorbed in thinking of Her, when he cried out suddenly, saying, "Wait, wait. Let me utter the Mantra first; and then Thou wilt take it." He then offered the food ritually before finishing the worship.

Previously, at the time of worship and meditation, he saw a wonderful living Presence in the stone image before him. Now he did not see that image at all when he entered the temple; but saw instead, standing there, the living Mother Herself, all Consciousness, with hands that offered boons and freedom from fear. The Master said, "I put the palm of my hand near Her nostrils and felt that Mother was actually breathing. I observed very closely, but I could never see the shadow of the Mother's divine person on the temple wall in the light of the lamp at night. I heard from my room the jingling sounds of the Mother's anklets, as she went upstairs like a merry little girl. I came out to verify and found that She, with Her hair dishevelled, was actually standing on the verandah of the first floor of the temple and was now viewing Calcutta, and next the Ganga."

5. "One now felt awe-struck," said Hriday," when one entered
the Kali temple even when the Master was not there, let alone when
he was.   Yet I could not give up the temptation of seeing how the
Master behaved during the time of worship.   What I saw, when
I suddenly came there on many occasions, filled my heart with awe
and devotion.   But doubt arose when I came out.   I thought, 'Has
uncle really gone mad? Otherwise why does he do such forbidden
acts at the time of worship?' I felt apprehensive about what the Rani
and Mathur Babu would think and say when they came to know of it.
But such thoughts never crossed my uncle's mind, nor did he give
ear to what I told him about them.   Again, I could not venture now
to speak to him much; an indescribable fear and hesitation came and
pressed my mouth, I knew not why.   I felt an indefinable distance
between him and me for some unknown reason.   Having no other
alternative left, I served him silently as far as I could.   But
I felt apprehensive lest he should cause a scene some day."

Hriday gave us the following account of the Master's actions
which, when he enterd the temple suddenly at the time of worship,
filled his heart at once with awe, fear and devotion.   He said:
"I saw uncle prepare an Arghya consisting of china-roses and
Vilva leaves, touch with it his head, his bosom, all his limbs, and
even his own feet and at last offer it at the Lotus Feet of the
Mother of the universe. . . .

"I saw his bosom and eyes always reddish like those of a
drunkard.   Reeling in that condition, he left the worshipper's seat,
and ascending the altar caressed the Divine Mother by affectionately
touching Her chin and began singing, laughing, joking, and conversing with Her; or, sometimes, he caught hold of Her hands
and danced. . . . . .

"I sometimes saw that while offering cooked food etc., to the
Divine Mother, he got up suddenly, took in his hand some rice and
curry from the plate, touched the Divine Mother's mouth with it and
said, 'Mother! eat it, do eat it, Mother!' Afterwards perhaps he said,
'Dost Thou ask me to take it? Wilt Thou take it afterwards?
Very well, I am taking it now.' Saying this, he took a part of it
himself and putting the rest to Her mouth again, said, 'I have taken
it.   Thyself eat it now.'   One day I found that at the time of the
food-offering the Master saw a cat enter the temple mewing.   He
fed it with the food that was to be offered to the Divine Mother,
saying, 'Wilt Thou take it, Mother?'. . . .

"I saw him on some occasions at night put the Mother to bed and himself lie on Her silver bedstead for some time, saying, 'Dost Thou ask me to lie down?   All right, I am doing so.'....

"I saw again that when he sat to worship, he became so much absorbed in meditation that he had not the slightest consciousness of the external world for a long time....

"Uncle rose from his bed very early in the morning and collected flowers in order to make garlands for Mother Kali.   At that time too it seemed to me that there was some one there whom he caressed and with whom he spoke, laughed, joked and made merry and played the importunate child....

"I saw further that uncle had not a wink of sleep at night. Whenever I awoke, I found that, overwhelmed with spiritual emotions, he would be speaking or singing; or sometimes going to the Panchavati and getting merged in meditation."

6.   Hriday used to say that, although he was apprehensive regarding the Master's behaviour, he could not express his apprehensions to anybody for purposes of consultation.   For , that man might pass it on to the high officials of the temple and they might do harm to his uncle by poisoning the ears of the proprietors. But how could things be suppressed when every day, nay, every moment, such queer events were taking place?   Some worshippers who came to the Kali temple at the time of worship saw everything with their own eyes and complained to the cashier and other officers. The latter heard it, came to the Kali temple and saw it all.   But when they saw Sri Ramakrishna's excited, formidable visage, as of one possessed by a power, his unhesitating behaviour and his fearlessness and absent-mindedness, they shrank with an indefinable fear from mentioning anything to him or from forbidding him to do what he was doing.   They consulted one another when they returned to the office of the temple.   They concluded that the Bhattacharya had gone mad or was possessed by a ghost.   No one could otherwise behave in such an unscriptural way at the time of worship.   In any case, the worship, the food-offering and other services of the Goddess were, as a matter of fact, not being performed. The Bhattacharya had spoilt everthing.   They could not but send word to the proprietors.

Word was sent to Mathur at Janbazar.   He wrote back in reply that he would personally observe things soon and do what was proper.   He asked them to let the Bhattacharya perform worship and other services in his own way and not to obstruct him till he came. They received the letter from Mathur and were anxiously waiting for him to come. They were busy talking among themselves, "The Bhattacharya is sure to be dismissed this time. As soon as the Babu comes, he will expel him. Giving offence to the gods! How long will they put up with it?" and so on.

7. One day Mathur came suddenly at the time of worship, and without anyone's knowledge, entered the Kali temple and observed minutely the Master's actions for a long time. But being filled with spiritual emotions, the Master did not notice him at all. As on every day, his mind was absorbed in the Divine Presence and was oblivious of the coming or departure of anyone. This state was the first thing that Mathur noticed on entering the temple. He could also discern, when he saw later his importunate boyish requests to Her, that it was all born of his single-minded devotion to, and love of, the Divine Mother. What else could, he thought, bring about the realization of the Mother, if such sincere devotion could not? His heart became filled with an extraordinary bliss when he saw how streams of tears trickled down the Bhattacharya's eye as he performed worship, how he was filled with a genuine and unbounded joy, and how he sat motionless, devoid of external consciousness and oblivious of the surrounding objects. Mathur felt that the holy temple was actually filled with an intense manifestation of palpable divine presence. He had now the firm conviction that the Bhattacharya had really become blessed by having the grace of the universal Mother. With his eyes filled with tears and heart purified by devotion, he then saluted over and over agàin the Divine Mother and Her extraordinary worshipper from a distance, saying, "The installation of the Devi has answered its purpose at long last. It may be said that the Devi has truly been installed now and the real worship of the Mother has been performed." He returned home without telling the officers anything. The next day the chief officer of the temple got from him the order: "Do not obstruct the Bhattacharya in his worship, whatever might be the manner in which he performs it." (cf. III. 6.)

8. On hearing of the series of events mentioned above, a reader well-versed in the scriptures will easily understand the nature of the great change that had come over the Master's mind at this time. It passed beyond the limits of devotion based on the scriptural injunctions (Vaidhi Bhakti) and progressed fast

in the realm of pure devotional love (Ragatmika Bhakti). But this change came in such a simple natural way that even Sri Rama-krishna himself could not understand it clearly, let alone others. The only thing he understood was that, urged by his love for the Divine Mother, he could not but behave that way, as if he were being forced to do so. That is why we see him think sometimes, "What is happening to me? Am I on the right track?" He, therefore, eagerly said to the Divine Mother, "I don't know and don't understand, O Mother! what these things are that are happen-ing to me; please make me do what I should; teach me what Thou wantest me to learn and reveal Thyself to me! Continue always to hold me by the hand!" He addressed this imploring prayer to the Divine Mother from the bottom of his heart, completely eschewing from it all hankerings for worldly values like wealth, sex, honour, fame, pleasures and powers. The Mother of the universe, on Her part, held him by the hand, protected him under all circumstances and fulfilled his prayer. Unasked, She brought him, whenever necessary, all those things and all those persons that were required for the growth and perfection of his life as an aspirant and made him reach easily and naturally the ultimate goal of pure knowledge and pure devotion. The divine Lord has promised to His devotees through the Gita (IX. 22): "To those devotees of undivided mind who worship Me and always remain united with Me, and who place their whole mind in Me and do not think even of their food and movements necessary for life, I bring, even unasked, all the things they require." The more we study the life of the Master at this time, the more shall we be sur-prised and astounded to find how literally that promise in the Gita was fulfilled in his life. It became necessary to prove clearly again the truth of that promise of the divine Lord in this selfish modern age, which has lust and greed as its only motive forces in life. Although Sadhakas have been teaching men from age to age to "give up all in order to have the All", meaning that a Sadhaka will not suffer from the lack of anything if he renounces everything for the divine Lord, still, weak-minded men, entangled in worldly objects, could not believe in the promise without seeing it fulfilled in the modern age again. Therefore, the Mother of the universe enacted this wonderful play with the Master, who had a completely undivided mind, in order to show man the truth of that saying of the scripture. Listen to this, O man, with a pure heart, and advance on the path of renunciation according to your capacity.

9. The Master used to say that when the powerful flood of divine moods comes into human life unexpectedly, it cannot be suppressed or concealed by any effort. That is not all; the gross, material body fails to contain the spirit that is stirred by the powerful onrush of divine emotions, and very often gets completely shattered. Many Sadhakas meet with death that way. A fit body is necessary to contain the exuberant surge of emotions born of perfect knowledge or perfect devotion. It is only the bodies of great souls known as incarnations of God that have up till now been seen to bear its full force and continue to live in the world. This is why the devotional scriptures describe them again and again as possessed of bodies consisting of pure Sattva. The incarnations, they say, can bear the full impulse of spiritual emotions, only because they come down to the world with bodies made of the element of pure Sattva, devoid of all contact with Rajas or Tamas. Even in spite of their having such bodies, they, particularly the incarnations treading the path of devotion, are seen on many occasions, to be afflicted and overwhelmed with the powerful stress of divine moods. It is indubitable from the accounts we have received that the joints in the bodies of Lord Jesus and Sri Chaitanya relaxed and drops of blood oozed out like perspiration through every pore in their bodies owing to the powerful surge of spiritual emotions. No doubt, these physical changes were felt to be extremely painful, yet it was only through them that their bodies got adapted to contain those extraordinary upsurges of divine emotions. But in course of time, they became naturalised to these impulses, which therefore ceased to manifest in ways distressing to their bodies.

10. From now on, a series of extraordinary changes came ove the Master's body because of the surge of this devotional love. We have already made mention of the burning sensation in his body from the beginning of his Sadhana. He had to suffer on many occasions from its excess. The Master himself pointed out its cause to us on various occasions. "At the time of performing Sandhya and worship," said the Master, "I used to think, according to scriptural prescription, that the Papa-purusha within had been burnt up. Who knew then that there was actually a Papa-purusha within the body and that it could be actually burnt and destroyed?

A burning sensation came on the body from the beginning of the Sadhana. I thought, 'What is this disease?' It increased by degrees and became unbearable. Various kinds of oils prescribed by physicians were used; but it could by no means be alleviated. One day, while I was sitting under the Panchavati, I saw that a jet-black person with red eyes and a hideous appearance came reeling, as if drunk, out of this (showing his own body) and walked before me. I saw again another person of placid mien in ochre-coloured dress, with a trident in his hand similarly coming out of my body. He vehemently attacked the other and killed him. The burning sensation in the body decreased for a short time after I had that vision. I suffered from that burning sensation continually for six months before the Papa-purusha was burnt up."

We were told by the Master that a similar sensation came on him again, a short time after the burning up of the Papa-purusha. The Master had then gone beyond the limits of Vaidhi Bhakti or practice of devotional disciplines according to scriptural injunctions, and became engaged in the service of the Divine Mother with Ragatmika or loving devotion, in the manner spoken of before. That burning sensation gradually increased so much that he could not find relief even though he placed a wet towel on his head and kept his body immersed in the waters of the Ganga for three or four hours. We shall describe elsewhere (IV.1) the easy means by which the Brahmani, when she came later, cured it and pointed out that this sensation owed its origin to his longing for the full vision of the divine Lord and to his pang of separation from Him. The Master suffered again from that burning sensation in his body later at the time of practising the Madhura-bhava, the "sweet mood of the spouse of God." Hriday said, "The Master then suffered from a pain and a burning sensation similar to what one feels when a potful of live embers is placed on one's chest. He suffered long from that sensation, which came on him from time to time. A few years after his Sadhana came to an end, he became acquainted with Kanailal Ghosal, a lawyer of Barasat, who was an advanced Sadhaka of Sakti. He advised the Master to put on his person an amulet encasing the Mantra of his chosen Ideal. That sensation came to an end when the amulet was put on."

11. Mathur went back to Janbazar and told the Rani of the Master's extraordinary way of worship. The devout Rani was delighted to hear of it. She used to come to the Dakshineswar

temple and listen to the songs sung by the Bhattacharya, and had already grown affectionate towards him. On the occasion when the image of Govinda got broken she was astonished to know of his intelligence inspired by devotion (III. 5,6). It did not therefore take her long to understand that it was possible for one like the Master to have the grace of the universal Mother. But an event occurred shortly afterwards, which could have shaken the faith of the Rani and Mathur. One day the Rani went to the temple to worship the Divine Mother and pay her obeisance to the Goddess. But while she was externally engaged in worship, she was eagerly thinking of the possible success or failure of a pending law-suit instead of being absorbed in the divine service. The Master was then sitting there and singing songs for her at her request. He was in a state of ecstasy. Divining the state of the Rani's mind, he chastised and corrected her by striking her tender person and exclaiming, "Ah! That thought even here!" The Rani, a spiritual aspirant fit to have the grace of the universal Mother, realised the weakness of her mind and became repentant. Her devotion to the Master increased a great deal on account of this event. We shall mention all these things in detail elsewhere (III.5).

12.   Before long, the constant company of the Divine Mother brought him to such a state of blissful exaltation of the spirit that it was no longer possible for him to perform the daily and occasional services in the temple. The Master used to give an example of how, with the spiritual progress of an aspirant, the actions enjoined on him by the scriptures drop off by themselves. He said, "The mother-in-law allows her daughter-in-law to eat all kinds of food and do all manner of work till she conceives; but, as soon as she is with child a little discrimination about food and work begins. Later, as she is in an advanced stage, her work gets extremely limited. When gradually she approaches parturition, she is not given any work at all, lest harm should befall the embryo. And, when at last the baby is born, her days are spent only in nursing it." Similarly the Master's renunciation of the external worship and the services of the Divine Mother took place naturally. He was now no more conscious of the proper time for worship and other services. Always immersed in spiritual moods, he served the universal Mother whensoever and howsoever he liked. For instance, he sometimes offered food before performing the worship or, absorbed in meditation, he forgot completely the idea of his

separate existence from Her and decorated his own person with the flowers, sandal-paste, etc., brought for the worship of the Goddess. We were told by the Master himself that on many occasions his actions assumed this form because of his constant vision of the Divine Mother inside and outside. We were further told that any diminution in his constant experience of the Divine Mother's presence and absorption in Her, filled him with a poignant sense of separation which made him throw himself violently on the ground, rub his face against it, and fill the quarters with loud wailings. He would struggle for life and his breath would almost stop. He could take no notice of the fact that his whole body was getting cut and bruised and covered with blood. He was equally unaware whether he stumbled on fire or into water. Immediately afterwards, when he again got the vision of the Mother, that mental attitude of his vanished. His face then beamed with joy, and he became a different person altogether.

13. Mathur allowed the temple worship to be conducted somehow by the Master till the latter reached the state described above. But, finding that it was impossible to manage the worship that way any more, he resolved to make some other arrangement. Hriday said, "There was a special reason for that resolve of Mathur's. One day the Master suddenly got up from the worshipper's seat in a state of ecstasy and saw Mathur Babu and me in the temple. He then took hold of me by the hand, made me sit on that seat and said to Mathur, 'Hriday will perform the worship from today. Mother says, she will accept his worship in the same manner as mine.' The devout Mathur accepted those words of the Master as the command of the Mother." We cannot say how far Hriday's words are true; but Mathur knew well that it was impossible for the Master to perform the worship and other services daily, in that condition of his.

14. We have already said that Mathur's mind was attracted towards the Master from the day when he first saw him. Since then he had tried to remedy all his difficulties and keep him on at Dakshineswar. The more he became acquainted with the Master's extraordinary noble qualities, the more was he charmed by them; and he served him according to his needs, viewed him with an affectionate eye and always protected him against unreasonable oppression by others. Here is an instance: Mathur made arrangements for him to have a daily drink of the syrup of candy,

as he knew that the humour of wind was strong in his body. He protected him from all criticism and interference by unthinking people when his worship took that unusual turn under the influence of Ragatmika Bhakti. We have elsewhere (III. 6) mentioned a few other examples of this nature. But it seems to us probable that he had doubts in his mind about the Master's condition from the day he struck Rani Rasmani by way of teaching her. He concluded that the Master was suffering from insanity. Unable to realize the advanced state of the Master, the worldly-minded Mathur, it seems, inferred that there was in him a combination of spirituality and insanity; for he arranged at that time for the Master's treatment under Gangaprasad Sen, the well-known Ayurvedic physician of Calcutta.

Thinking that the Master had a physical disease, Mathur not only made all arrangements for his treatment, but also tried to comfort him by giving reasons and arguments, so that he might control his mind and proceed with his spiritual practices. We have described for the reader elsewhere (III. 6), how Mathur came to be convinced of the mistake of his estimate of the Master after the incident that led to his seeing two china-roses, one red and the other white, blossomed together on the same twig of a red china-rose plant.

Knowing that it was impossible for the Master to perform the fixed daily service of the Goddess in the temple, Mathur made another arrangement for it. Ramtarak Chattopadhyaya, a cousin of the Master, had come to the temple in search of a job. He was now appointed to worship the Goddess until the Master came round. These events came to pass in the year 1858.

15. The Master used to call Ramtarak, Haladhari. The Master told us many things about him on many occasions. Haladhari was a good scholar and Sadhaka, who was devoted to the practice of scripture-ordained rituals. He had proficiency in the *Bhagavata,* the *Adhyatma-Ramayana* and other sacred texts, and read them daily. Although he had a greater love for Vishnu than for the Devi, he had no aversion to the latter. Therefore, though a devotee of Vishnu, he did not feel any hesitation in taking charge of the worship of the Divine Mother at the request of Mathur. But before Haladhari took that charge, Mathur made an arrangement, at his request, for supplying him with raw foodstuffs, so that he might cook for himself. We are told that Mathur at first objected

to it and asked, "Why? Do not Ramakrishna, your cousin, and Hriday, your nephew, take Prasada in the temple?" The intelligent Haladhari replied, "My cousin is in an exalted spiritual state. Blemishes will not accrue to him in any way. I am not in that state; it will therefore be reprehensible for me to break my principle regarding food." Mathur was pleased to hear his words. Haladhari took raw provisions and daily cooked them for himself under the Panchavati.

Although Haladhari had no aversion to Sakti, he was not in favour of offering animal sacrifice to the Goddess. As it was the rule in the temple to offer animal sacrifice to the Divine Mother at the time of the festivals, he could not perform the worship at those times with joy and zeal. He performed the worship for about a month when, it is said, while performing his Sandhya one day, he saw the Goddess assume a terrible form and hear Her telling him, "Get up and go away from here. You shall not perform the worship. Your son shall die on account of the offence of your irreverent worship." It is said that he received the news of his son's death a few days after this event. He informed the Master of all these happenings and from then ceased to worship the Goddess. Therefore, Hriday took up the worship of Kali, and Haladhari, that of Radha-Govinda. We heard of this event from Hriday's brother, Rajaram.

CHAPTER VIII

THE LAST PART OF THE STORY OF THE FIRST FOUR YEARS OF SADHANA

(TOPICS: 1. Chronology of the Sadhana period. 2. Its main divisions. 3. A recapitulation of the experiences of the first four years of Sadhana. 4. Meaning of the Master's Sadhanas: checking of one's experience with the scriptures. 5. Analogy of Suka. 6. The Master practised Sadhana for others. 7. Realisation follows true eagerness. 8. The Master's Sadhana of the Dasya-bhava impersonating Mahavir. 9. The vision of Sri Sita. 10. Planting the Panchavati. 11. Practice of Hatha-yoga. 12. Curse by Haladhari. 13. Changing views of Haladhari on the Master. 14. Haladhari's pride in his scholarship. 15. Haladhari and the Kali conception. 16. Haladhari scolding the Master for breach of caste rules. 17. Haladhari's criticism and the Divine command-ment to remain in Bhavamukha. 18. Length of Haladhari's stay. 19. A discussion on the divine inebriation of the Master. 20. The fallacy of regarding it as a disease. 21. The Master's behaviour disproves such a conclusion. 22. Vaishnavacharan's first meeting with the Master. 23. The Master undergoing other kinds of Sadhana. 24. His mind functioning as the Guru. 25. The lesson from his visions. 26. His visions never proved untrue. 27. An example. 28. Mistaken notions of Rani Rasmani and Mathur.)

1. When we study the period of the Master's Sadhana, we must first of all remember what he himself told us about it. It will not then be difficult to ascertain its dates. The reader has already been told that we had heard from him that he was engaged in the disciplines of various faiths and doctrines for twelve long years continually. It is ascertained from Rani Rasmani's deed of gift regarding the temple endowment, that the Kali temple at Dakshineswar was consecrated on Thursday, May 31, 1855. At the end of the same year the Master assumed the office of the priest. It is therefore perfectly certain that the period of his Sadhana extends practically from 1856 to 1867. But, although this period is clearly ascertained as the period of his Sadhana, we shall see that he went on a pilgrimage to some holy places towards the end of this period and engaged himself in Sadhana there and again at Dakshineswar after his return.

2. We proceed to divide this period of twelve years into three divisions, each of which we are to study separately. First there are the four years from 1856 to 1859, the main events of which we have already studied. Next, an equal number of years from 1860 to 1863 were spent under the instruction of the Brahmani in the practice of all the disciplines of the sixty-four main Tantras, observing all the scriptural injunctions. Thirdly, he spent a period of equal length lasting from 1864 to 1867 in the practice of the following Sadhanas. He was initiated in the Mantra of Rama by a monk of the Ramawat denomination, named Jatadhari, and got the image of Ramalala; he was engaged in Sadhana in a woman's apparel during this period for six months in order to realize the spiritual attitude of a female friend of God, spoken of in the Vaishnava books; he also received the Vedic Mahavakya from Totapuri and attained to the Nirvikalpa plane of consciousness; and lastly he was taught the religion of Islam by Govinda (II.16).   During the period of these twelve years, he practised the discipline of the Sakhya-Bhava according to the Vaishnava scriptures and came in contact with the secondary Vaishnava denominations of Kartabhaja, Navarasika, etc. That he was closely acquainted with these denominations is very clear from the fact that Vaishnavacharan Goswami and other Sadhakas following these faiths came to the Master for spiritual help. If we divide the period of his Sadhana into the three divisions mentioned above and consider the matter deeply, we shall find that there is a clear difference in the nature of the Sadhanas of the first division from those of the other two.

3. We see that the only external help he got at the beginning of his Sadhana was the initiation he had from Sri Kenaram Bhattacharya. He straightway proceeded to practise that discipline. The extreme eagerness of his heart for the realization of God was his main support during that period. This eagerness became gradually stronger and stronger, shattered his body and mind in a short time and recast them into an unexpected new mould. Besides, it produced in him a great love for his chosen Ideal which took him beyond the firm steel-frame of the rules and regulations of ritualistic devotion to the spontaneity and freedom of the Ragatmika form of divine love, culminating in the immediate realisation of the Divine Mother as also the attainment of Yogic powers.

4. The reader may perhaps say, "Where was the need for any further Sadhana for him if he attained to the highest spiritual

realisation even in this first phase of Sadhana? What was then left
for him further to attain to?" We should like to say in reply
that although this is true in a way, Sadhana was necessary even
afterwards. The Master used to say, "Trees and creepers flower
first and bear fruit next, according to the usual law of nature; but
there are a few among them whose fruits come out first and flowers
next." The development of the Master's mind in the field of
Sadhana took place exactly like that of the latter class of trees and
creepers. Therefore, that objection of the reader is true in a way.
But although the Master had such visions etc., at the beginning of
his Sadhana, he could not become perfectly sure whether they were
real and whether he had reached the ultimate goal. He could
do this only on comparing the spontaneous experiences of his with
the recorded experiences of the Sadhakas of the past, and also
further by reproducing in himself, by following the practices prescribed in the scriptures, those identical experiences which he had
without their aid. Therefore Sadhana was afterwards necessary
for him. It became necessary for him to realize again, by following
the path and procedure described in the scriptures, what he had
experienced before by the incomprehensible grace of the Divine
Mother, with the eagerness of his heart as his only help. The
scriptures maintain that three conditions are to be fulfilled if an
aspirant is to have absolute conviction. He must have personal
experience. He has to compare his own visions and extraordinary
experiences with the truths taught by the Guru. He has also got to
compare them with the experiences of the past Sadhakas as recorded
in the scriptures. His doubts are absolutely dispelled when the
identity of the experience is established by this threefold comparison,
and his mind thenceforth rests in perfect peace.

5. As an example of what has been said above, we may point
to an event in the life of Sukadeva, the foremost of the Paramahamsas, the son of Vyasa. Sukadeva, untouched by Maya, used
to have various divine visions and extraordinary experiences in his
life from his birth. For the purpose of ascertaining whether they
were real and whether he had reached the goal, he studied the Vedas,
the six branches of study[1] auxiliary to them and other Sastras with

---

[1] (1) Siksha, the science which teaches the proper pronounciation of
words and laws of euphony; (2) Kalpa, that which lays down the ritual
and prescribes rules for ceremonial and sacrificial acts ; (3) Grammar ;

his father, Vyasa, who was a knower of all the scriptures.   When his studies came to an end, he said to his father, "I have been experiencing from my birth, all the spiritual states recorded in the scriptures; but I cannot be perfectly sure that these states and experiences are the ultimate truth.   So please tell me now what you yourself have experienced regarding those things."   Vyasa, of supreme knowledge, reflected within himself, "I have always been teaching Suka the goal of spirituality and the ultimate truth, telling him the experiences of my own life born of spiritual practices; but doubts have not yet been removed from his mind.   He thinks that although he has been desirous of knowing the truth, I, being over-powered by fatherly affection,   have not given him the whole truth lest he should leave the worldly life on being enlightened.   This, he thinks, is the reason why all his doubts have not been removed.   Therefore it is good for him to hear these things from some other wise man."   Thinking so, Vyasa said, "I am unable to remove your doubt; it is not unknown to you that Janaka, the king of Mithila, is truly a man of knowledge; go to him and have all your problems solved."   So directed by his father, Suka, it is written in the *Mahabharata,* went immediately to Mithila.   Taught by Janaka, a sage among kings, about the experience that knowers of Brahman have, Suka found a complete identity between the instruction of the Guru, the words of the scriptures and the experiences of his own life.

6.   Besides the above-mentioned reasons, there was another profound reason why the Master practised Sadhana later.   We shall merely mention it here.   The aim of the Master's Sadhana was not the attainment of peace only in his own life.   The Divine Mother made him assume a body for the good of the world.   He had, therefore, to be acquainted with the Sadhanas of all religions and their ultimate goal, so that he might be in a position to become a true spiritual teacher.   Therefore an extraordinary effort is seen on the Master's part to ascertain, by actual practice, the truth or falsity of all the religious doctrines.   That is not all.   By placing before mankind an almost unlettered person who could, by his spiritual practices, attain in a natural way the experiences recorded in all the scriptures, the Divine Mother has proved to the modern age the truth of the Vedas, the Puranas, the Bible, the Koran and

(4) Nirukta, the etymological explanations of difficult Vedic words; (5) The science of prosody and (6) Astronomy. They are collectively called the Vedangas.—Tr.

all other religious scriptures. That was why there was no cessation of his Sadhana even after he had personally attained peace. The more we proceed to study this extraordinary life, the more clearly shall we see how, with a view to accomplishing the specific end mentioned above, the universal Mother brought to the Master, at the proper time, perfected men and scholars of every denomination. By putting him directly under their instruction, She made him acquainted with the teachings and disciplines of various religions, which, with his rare spiritual genius, he could master very quickly and remember always, thanks to his wonderfully retentive memory.

7. We have said before that during the first four years of his Sadhana the Master depended for God-realization mainly on his intense eagerness. No one came to him at that time to help him in his spiritual progress by guiding him along the path prescribed by the scriptures. Therefore, the only means he had recourse to was the intense longing, which is the common requisite of all Sadhanas. As the Master had the vision of the Divine Mother with the help of this longing only, it is also proved that an aspirant may have God-vision similarly, even without any external aid. But we forget very often to reflect how great must be the degree of intensity of this eagerness in order that one may reach one's end that way. This becomes clear to us if we study the Master's life at this time. We have seen how under the intensity of this longing, firmly established habits of life and modes of thought, together with the mental impressions at their back, disappeared from him altogether. He paid no attention even to the preservation of his life, let alone physical health. The Master said, "As no attention was bestowed on the cleaning of the body, the hairs on the head became long and got matted owing to dirt and dust adhering to them. At the time of meditation the body used to become motionless like the trunk of a tree. Thinking it to be an inert thing, birds came and remained sitting on the head without any hesitation and stirred up the dust in the hair in search of particles of rice! Again, impatient on account of the separation from the divine Lord, I rubbed my face against the ground so vehemently that it got cut and bruised and bled in many places. I had no consciousness of how the whole day slipped away in prayer, meditation, devotional exercises, offering of the self, and so on. When afterwards at the approach of the evening, conch-shells

were blown and bells rung, I remembered that the day was at an end. Another day passed in vain; and I had not yet seen the Mother. Intense sorrow seized me and made the heart so restless that I could no longer remain calm. I threw myself violently on the ground, saying, 'Mother, Thou hast not shown Thyself to me even yet!' I filled the quarters with wailing and struggled on account of pain. People said, 'He has got colic pain and that is why he is crying so much'."

When we were with the Master, he used to tell us again and again those events of the time of his Sadhana in order to bring home to us the necessity for intense longing of the heart for the realization of God. He would add regretfully, "People shed floods of tears at the death of their wives, children, and the like, or at the loss of worldly possessions; but who will do so because they have not realized God? Yet they say, 'We called on Him so much and still He did not show Himself.' Let them but once weep for God with such intensity of feeling and let me see whether He keeps Himself back without revealing Himself." These words used to sting us to the quick. When we heard them, it became clear to us that he could speak so assuredly, only because he had found them true early in his life.

8. The Master did not rest satisfied with having only the vision of the Divine Mother during the first four years of his Sadhana. His mind was naturally attracted towards Raghuvir, his family Deity, after he had had the vision of the Divine Mother when he was in the Bhavamukha (III. 1 & 3.). Knowing that with the help of devotion it was possible to have, like Mahavir, the vision of Ramachandra, he engaged himself in Sadhana, assuming Mahavir's attitude, for the purpose of attaining perfection in the Dasya-bhava. The Master said that, thinking of Mahavir incessantly at that time, he became so much absorbed that he forgot altogether for some time his separate existence and individuality. "At that time," said the Master, "I had to walk, take my food and do all other actions like Mahavir. I did not do so of my own accord, but the actions so happened of themselves. I tied my cloth round my waist so that it might look like a tail and moved about jumping; I ate nothing but fruits and roots, which again I did not feel inclined to eat when skinned. I spent much of my time on trees and always cried, 'Raghuvir, Raghuvir!' with a deep voice. Both my eyes assumed a restless expression

like those of the animals of that species, and strange to say, the lower end of the backbone (coccyx) lengthened at that time by nearly an inch." When we heard the last-mentioned fact, we asked, "Sir, does that part of your body continue to be so even now?" He said, "No, in course of time it assumed slowly its previous natural size when the mastery of that mood over the mind had ceased."

9.　An extraordinary vision and experience came to pass in the life of the Master when he practised the Dasya-bhakti. That vision and experience was so novel, so different from his previous ones, that it was deeply imprinted on his mind and was always fresh in his memory. He said, "One day at that time I was sitting under the Panchavati—not meditating, merely sitting—when an incomparable, effulgent female figure appeared before me illumining the whole place. It was not that figure alone that I saw then, but also the trees and plants of the Panchavati, the Ganga and all other objects. I saw that the figure was that of a woman; for, there were in her no signs of a goddess, such as the possession of three eyes, etc. But the extraordinary, spirited and solemn expression of that face, manifesting love, sorrow, compassion, and endurance, was not generally seen even in the figures of goddesses. Looking graciously at me, that goddess-woman was advancing from north to south towards me with a slow, grave gait. I wondered who she might be, when a black-faced monkey came suddenly, nobody knew whence, and fell prostrate at her feet and someone within my mind exclaimed, 'Sita, Sita who was all sorrow all her life, Sita the daughter of King Janaka, Sita to whom Rama was her very life!' Saying 'Mother' repeatedly, I was then going to fling myself at her feet, when she came quickly and entered this (showing his own body). Overwhelmed with joy and wonder, I lost all consciousness and fell down. Before that, I had had no other vision in that manner without meditating or thinking. That was the first vision of its kind. I have been suffering like Sita all my life, perhaps because my first vision with the naked eye was of her—Sita whose life from the start was a bundle of sufferings." [1]

---

[1] Sri Sita, the author said to some, including the translator, made a gift of her smile to the Master. So, those who saw the Master smile, knew how she smiled—Tr.

10. Feeling the need for a suitable sacred place for practising austerities, the Master expressed to Hriday a desire to plant a new Panchavati, a cluster of five holy trees. Explaining the reason for it, Hriday said, "The small pond called the Duck Pond near the Panchavati was then re-excavated and the piece of land near the old Panchavati was filled up with the mud from that pond and made level. Also the Amalaki tree, under which the Master used to meditate before, was destroyed." The Master then planted with his own hands a holy fig tree to the west of the place where the Sadhana-hut now stands and made Hriday plant the saplings of a Banian tree, an Asoka tree, a Vilva tree and an Amalaki tree.[1]   And planting saplings of the holy basil and Aparajita creepers, he had the whole place hedged with the help of a temple gardener named Bhartabhari, in the wonderful way described elsewhere (III. 2).   The holy basil plants and the Aparajita creepers grew up so high and dense in a short time on account of the Master's regular watering and care that no one from outside could see him when he sat for meditation within the enclosure.

11.   After Rani Rasmani consecrated the Kali temple, pilgrims such as monks desirous of visiting Puri and Gangasagar began to accept the hospitality afforded by the devout Rani, and rest for a few days at the Dakshineswar temple when going to, and returning from, those two places of pilgrimage (IV. 2.). The Master said that many perfected souls and great Sadhakas used to come there from that time. Instructed by one of them, he seems to have practised at this time Pranayama and other exercises of Hathayoga. One day while he was describing to us the following incident regarding Haladhari, he hinted at it. He forbade us later to practise the Hathayoga exercises, because he himself practised them and knew their results. Approached by some of us for instruction on it, he said to us, "These practices are not for this age. Living beings are shortlived and their lives depend on food in the Kaliyuga;

---

[1] " The holy fig tree, the Vilva tree, the Amalaki tree, the banian tree and the Asoka tree, collectively called the Panchavati, should be planted in five directions for the purpose of practising austerities. The holy fig tree should be planted to the east, the Vilva to the north, the banian to the west, the Amalaki to the south and the Asoka to the south-east and a beautiful altar four cubits square and attractive to the mind should be made in the middle."—*Skanda Purana.*

where is the time in this age to practise Rajayoga, in other words, to call on God, after making the body firm by the practice of Hathayoga? Again, if one wants to practise those exercises, one has to live constantly with a teacher perfect in that Yoga and follow for a long time very hard rules regarding food, rest, exercises etc., according to his instructions. The slightest deviation from those rules produces diseases in the Sadhaka's body and, on many occasions, causes even his death. Therefore, it is not necessary to practise these things. Besides, is it not for the purpose of restraining the mind that one has to restrain the vital air by practising Pranayama, etc.? You will see that both mind and vital forces will themselves be gradually restrained by meditation and devotion to God. Human beings have short lives and possess little capacity in the Kaliyuga; that is why the divine Lord has graciously made their path to realization so easy to tread. In this age if the feelings of anguish and void, like those felt at the death of one's wife or son, are felt for God, and these persist even for twenty-four hours in one's mind, He is bound to reveal Himself to that person."

12. We have told the reader elsewhere that the devout Sadhakas who are the followers of the Smritis, very often have recourse to the Tantras also in practice. Such persons, belonging to the Vaishnava denomination, pursue the path of Sadhana of Parakiya love (II. 13 & IV.1). We have also told the readers that Haladhari was a very learned Vaishnava and a faithful observer of the scriptural rites and practices; but he also pursued secretly the Parakiya path of Sadhana some time after he was appointed for the worship of Radha and Govinda. People came to know this in time and started whispering; but there was a belief prevalent, that whatever Haladhari said of anybody, came true; so, nobody was bold enough to discuss or cut jokes on his ways in his presence lest he should incur his displeasure. The Master too came to know of the undesirable practices of his elder cousin. Finding that people were talking of it and calumniating him behind his back, the Master, outspoken and fearless as he was, told Haladhari everything plainly. Thereupon the latter became very angry and said, "Dare you, who are younger to me, despise me thus? Blood shall gush out of your mouth." The Master tried to appease him in various ways by explaining the reason for his speaking so to him but he did not give ear to whatever the Master said.

One day, shortly after this event, at about 8 or 9 p.m. the Master felt a creeping sensation in his palate and actually blood began to gush out of his mouth. The Master said, "The colour of that blood was like that of the juice of kidney-bean leaves. It was so thick that a portion of it fell away from the mouth while a portion coagulated within and hung like the aerial roots of a banian tree from the lips near the front teeth. I tried to stop the bleeding by pressing a piece of cloth against the palate but the bleeding could not be stopped. I was much afraid to see it. All came running when they heard of it. Haladhari was performing the service in the temple then. He also was apprehensive and came quickly when he heard of it. When I saw him, I said to him with tears in my eyes, 'Cousin, just see the condition you have brought on me by your curse!' He also wept to see that sorrowful condition of mine.

"A good Sadhu had come that day to the temple. He also came there when he heard the noise, and examining the colour of the blood and the spot within the mouth through which it was coming out, said, 'There is no reason to fear; it is very good that the blood has come out. I find you were practising Yoga. At the end of the practice of Hathayoga, one attains Jada Samadhi (ending in the death of the body). You were also getting to that stage. The Sushumna had opened, and there was great rush of blood to the head. It is very good that, instead of flowing that way, it has automatically made a channel leading to the mouth and come out. Had this blood reached your head, you would have been in Jada Samadhi which would have never broken. The Mother of the universe has some especial purpose to accomplish with your body. That is why, I think, She has saved it.' Hearing these words of the holy man, I was, as it were, brought back to life." Haladhari's curse was thus transformed into a boon by an accidental coincidence.

13. There was an element of sweet mystery in the Master's behaviour towards Haladhari. We have said before that he was the Master's uncle's son, and was older than him. He came to Dakshineswar probably in 1858 and was appointed priest to worship Sri Radha-Govinda. He held that post till some time in the year 1865. Therefore, he lived at Dakshineswar for the second four years of the Master's Sadhana period and for more than two years after that, and had the opportunity of knowing him intimately. But he could not form a definite opinion of the Master's high

spiritual state. Haladhari was a man devoted to the rites and practices ordained in the scriptures; he, therefore, did not like the Master's lack of regard for his dress and sacred thread at the time of ecstasy. He thought that his younger cousin had become mad or a non-conformist in ritualistic conduct. He sometimes went to the length of telling Hriday. "Hriday, he gives up his wearing-cloth and the sacred thread; that is very bad. It is due to a great accumulation of the merits accruing from the Karmas of previous births that one is born in a Brahmana family. Yet he considers the state of a Brahmana to be a trifling thing and wants to give it up. Has he realized a state high enough to do this with impunity? Hriday, he has some faith in your words. So you should keep an eye on him and see that he does not behave in this way. It will be proper to restrain him from doing all this even by keeping him bound."

Again, he was charmed to see the flood of tears flowing from the Master's eyes at the time of worship, his wonderful joy on hearing songs praising the glory of the Divine, and his extraordinary eagerness for the realization of God. He thought all those states of his younger cousin were certainly due to an infusion of the divine Spirit; they could not be seen in human beings otherwise. Haladhari was surprised to see and hear all these things, and sometimes said to 'Hriday, "Hriday, you must have felt some extraordinary power in him; you would not otherwise have served him so faithfully."

14. Always assailed by doubts, Haladhari's mind could not come to any assured conclusion about the Master's real state and kept oscillating between regard and pity. The Master said, "Haladhari became charmed to see me at the time of worship in the temple and said on many occasions, 'Ramakrishna, I have recognized your real nature.' To that I often replied jokingly, 'Beware lest you should get confused again.' He said. 'You can by no means throw dust in my eyes any more; there is surely a charge of Divinity in you; I have understood it thoroughly this time.' I heard his words and said, 'Very well, let me see how long the conviction lasts.' When, however, Haladhari, after finishing the service in the temple, took a pinch of snuff and started a discussion on the *Bhagavata,* the *Gita,* the *Adhyatma Ramayana* or some other book, he became immediately a different man on account of his egoism. I then went there and said, 'I have realized

all the states of which you read in the scriptures; I can understand all these.' No sooner had he heard it than he said, 'Indeed! You are a big fool. Is it for you to understand all these things?' I said, 'I say in truth, the One who is within 'this' (showing his own body) explains everything regarding the One of whom you spoke just now.' Hearing this, Haladhari got irritated and said, 'Away with you, you big fool! Which is the scripture that speaks of an incarnation of God except Kalki in the Kaliyuga? You have become insane and so you think like this.' I laughed and said, 'Did you not say just now that there would be no confusion again?' But who would give ear to all that then? This happened not once or twice but on many occasions. One day he saw me sitting naked on a branch of the banian tree of the Panchavati and passing water. He became thenceforward absolutely certain that I was possessed by a ghost."

15. We have spoken of the death of the son of Haladhari, under the peculiar circumstances explained earlier. Being a narrow-minded follower of the cult of Vishnu he had the conviction that Kali consisted of Tamoguna. One day he went to the extent of saying to the Master, "Can there be any spiritual progress from the worship of a deity consisting of Tamas? Why do you worship that Goddess with so much care?" The Master heard this, but did not then give him a reply. But pained to hear his chosen Ideal slandered, he went to the Kali temple and asked the Mother of the universe with tears in his eyes, "Mother, Haladhari, a scholar well-versed in the scriptures, says Thou consistest of Tamoguna; art Thou truly such?" When he was told the real truth about it by the Divine Mother, he was filled with joy and ran immediately to Haladhari. Jumping then straight on his shoulders, he said again and again in an excited voice, "You say Mother consists of Tamas! Is it so? Mother is all—She has become the three Gunas and again She is the pure Sattvaguna." Haladhari then had his inner eye opened, as it were, by the words and touch of the Master in that ecstatic condition. Seated then in the worshipper's seat, Haladhari accepted heartily what the Master had said. And having seen the manifestation of the Divine Mother Herself in him, he took a handful of flowers mixed with sandal paste and offered it with devotion at his lotus feet. Shortly after, Hriday came and asked him, "Do you not say, uncle, that Ramakrishna is possessed by a ghost? Why then did you worship

him?" "I don't know why," replied Haladhari, "he came back from the Kali temple and astonished me in such a way that I forgot everything and saw the light of God in him! Whenever I go to Ramakrishna at the Kali temple, he produces such feelings in me! Oh, that bewildering incident! I cannot understand anything."

Although Haladhari saw divine light in the Master over and over again, when he took his pinch of snuff and sat for scriptural discussion, he got intoxicated with the egoism arising from his scholarship and became his former self again, like the rat of the story "Punarmushika" (*Vide* Glossary).

16. It is clear from the behaviour of Haladhari narrated above that until the attachment to lust and gold vanishes, the practice of external cleanliness and the knowledge of the scriptures are not of much avail and cannot produce in man the knowledge of the ultimate truth. Looking upon the poor people who came to take Prasada at the Dakshineswar temple as Narayana, God Himself, the Master, as we said before, ate a little of the remains of the food left in their plates. Annoyed at this, Haladhari said to him, "I shall see how you marry your children!" Intensely irritated by those words of Haladhari, going contrary to his professed admiration for Vedantic knowledge, the Master said, "You rascal! Don't you yourself say that the Sastras enjoin us to look upon all beings as Brahman and the world as unreal? Do you think I shall say like you that the world is unreal and at the same time beget children? Fie on your Sastric knowledge!"

17. The childlike Master, confused sometimes by Haladhari's scholarship, ran to the universal Mother for Her opinion on what should be done. One day, we were told, Haladhari proceeded to prove that the divine experiences of the master in ecstasy were all untrue and pointed out, with the help of the scriptures, that God was beyond existence and non-existence. Great was the Master's perturbation. Narrating this incident, he said later, "I thought that the divine forms I saw and the divine words I heard during Bhavasamadhi were then all a delusion. Had the Mother indeed deceived me? Extremely anxious, I cried with the feeling of wounded love and said to Mother, 'Shouldst Thou, O Mother, deceive me so, because I am unlettered and ignorant?' That cry of agony would not stop. I sat and wept in the 'mansion'. Some time afterwards I saw a fog-like smoke rising suddenly from

the floor and filling some space in front of me. I saw later in that
smoke a beautiful living face of golden complexion, with beard
reaching to the breast! That figure looked steadfastly at me and
said with a profound voice, 'My child, remain in Bhavamukha.'
That figure repeated those words thrice and immediately dissolved
in the fog, and the fog-like smoke also vanished into the void.
When I had that vision, I got back my peace of mind." One day
the Master himself described this event to Swami Premananda.
The Master said that the same doubt had arisen in his mind once
again when he happened to remember those words of Haladhari.
"Sitting for worship," said our Master, "I cried and pressed Mother
importunately for a solution of the problem. Mother then appeared
near the worship-jar in the guise of a woman named 'Rati's mother'
and said, 'Do remain in Bhavamukha'." Again when Tota Puri,
the travelling teacher, left Dakshineswar after imparting to him
the Vedantic knowledge and the Master dwelt in the Nirvikalpa
plane of consciousness continually for six months, he heard in his
heart of hearts at the end of that period the incorporeal voice of
the Divine Mother, "Remain in Bhavamukha."

18. Haladhari lived for about seven years in the Dakshineswar
temple. Therefore he was a witness to all the events that had taken
place at Dakshineswar—the coming of the Sadhu of perfect knowledge behaving like a ghoul, of the Brahmani, of the holy man
of the Ramawat denomination named Jatadhari, and of Sri Tota
Puri, one after another. We were told by the Master himself
that Haladhari and Tota Puri sat occasionally together and read the
Adhyatma Ramayana and other scriptures. The above-mentioned
events concerning Haladhari occurred at different times while he
was at the Dakshineswar temple. But we have told the reader all
of them together here for the sake of convenience.

19. From the discussion of the Master's life of Sadhana so
far, it is clear beyond doubt that, although he was then considered
mad by the ordinary people, he was in fact not so; neither did he
suffer from any disease or derangement of the brain. An intense
longing for the realization of God arose in his heart. He could
not then control himself, on account of the intensity of that
longing. People therefore said that he had gone mad; for, with
the intense eagerness for the realization of God incessantly con-
suming his heart, he could not mix with them or spend his time
laughing and weeping over ordinary matters. And who can do so?

When the anguish of the heart transcends the normal power of endurance, no one can control himself and keep pace with a world running amuck for lust and gold and having its mind and speech and action at variance at every step.   But the limit of the power of endurance, one might say, is not the same for all; some become overwhelmed with a little misery or happiness; others, again, remain firm and steady like a rock in spite of there being a profound agitation in their hearts arising from either of them.   Therefore, how can one know the limit of the Master's endurance? In reply we can say that his power of endurance was extraordinary. This will be very clearly understood if we reflect on the other events of his life.   But is it not superfluous to speak of the extraordinary power of endurance of the body and mind of a person like our Great Master —a person who could remain calm in spite of being half-fed or unfed and sleepless for twelve long years; who rejected the offers of immense wealth as many times as they came, because they were obstacles in the path of the realization of God?   There are innumerable other instances; but we desist from mentioning them here. The careful reader will meet with them at every turn, as he goes on with this life.

20.   Again, the above mentioned state of the Master appeared to be a disease only in the eyes of those people who were extremely attached to worldly objects.   No one except Mathur, it is clear, was then present at the Kali temple at Dakshineswar, who could, with the help of reason and imagination, ascertain partially at least the mental state of the Master. We cannot say where Kenaram Bhattacharya vanished immediately after initiating the Master; for, nothing was heard of him from Hriday or any one else after that event. Therefore, the ignorant, covetous officers of the Kali temple were the only persons left to judge the actions and mental states of the Master at that time. What they said cannot at all be regarded as proof. It is, therefore, certain that the words of the holy men who came to Dakshineswar at that time are the only reliable proofs of it. From what has been heard from the Master and others, it is known that those Sadhakas and perfected men, far from deeming him a victim of insanity, had always a very high opinion of him.

21. When we study the events following this period, we see that he readily followed any advice given by well-wishers for the preservation of his health. But when the intense eagerness for the

realization of God made him oblivious of his body and the external world, he lost all regard for his own life. He was never seen to persist in his own resolve unreasonably. When people said, "Let him be under treatment," he agreed. When they said that he should be taken to his mother at Kamarpukur, he readily consented; again, when his marriage was proposed, he did not dissent. Considering all these, how can we take his actions and behaviour to have been caused by insanity?

Moreover, though he tried indeed to keep himself aloof from worldly people and worldly affairs, he raised no objection to mixing with people. On the other hand he eagerly sought and joined them, whenever they came together to worship God and sing His glory. This is clearly seen when we find that he used to visit the temple of the ten Mahavidyas at Baranagar, went sometimes to pay his obeisance to the universal Mother at Kalighat, and joined the great annual festival at Panihati. In those places also, he sometimes met and had conversations with Sadhakas well versed in the scriptures. We have understood from the little we know of these things, that those Sadhakas held him in great veneration.

22. We may mention, for example, the fact of the Master's visit to Panihati during the great festival in A.D. 1859. There, on that day, he saw Vaishnavacharan, the son of Sri Utsavananda Goswami, for the first time. Some of us have heard from Hriday and also from the Master himself that he went to Panihati and sat for some time in Manimohan Sen's temple, when Vaishnavacharan came and saw him. He immediately came to the definite conclusion that the Master was in a high state of spirituality and that he was one of the rarest of great souls. On that day Vaishnavacharan spent the greater part of his time with the Master on the festival ground, and purchasing at his own expense, mangoes, fried rice, curds and sweets, offered to the Lord a delicious mixture of them in earthen plates, and made merry, partaking of the Prasada along with the Master and the devotees. Again, while returning to Calcutta after the festival, Vaishnavacharan got down at Rani Rasmani's Kali temple for the purpose of having the privilege of seeing him again. When he was told that the Master had not returned from the festival, he felt disappointed. We have described elsewhere (IV. 1) how Vaishnavacharan met the Master again three or four years later and how an intimate relationship grew up between them.

23. During this period of four years, the Master often took in his hands a few coins and clods of earth and used them to practise discrimination between the real and the unreal, with a view to completely removing from his mind the attachment to gold. He came, with the help of reasoning, to the sure conclusion, that the person who had made the realization of Brahman, Existence-Knowledge-Bliss Absolute, the only goal of his life, could not derive any more help whatsoever from gold, than from a lump of earth. Therefore, repeating again and again, "rupee-earth, earth-rupee",[1] he threw them both into the Ganga, in order to make that conclusion firmly fixed in his mind. With a view to having the firm conviction that all things and persons without exception, from Brahma down to a blade of grass, are the manifestations and parts of the Divine Mother, the Master partook of the leavings from the plates of the poor and cleaned the place where they had taken their food. For the purpose of completely removing pride and egoism from the mind and of having the conviction that he was not superior in any way even to the object of universal aversion, he cleaned, like a sweeper, the abominably dirty places with his own hands. Again in order to overcome the sense of aversion for objects generally considered despicable, he adopted the practical step of looking upon ordure and sandalpaste as the same in so far as both of them are the products of the five elements. To reinforce this conviction on his mind, he touched the faeces of others with his own tongue with perfect equanimity of mind. All these and many more extraordinary and unheard of disciplines were performed by the Master during this period. When we ponder over those practices and the divine visions of the Master during the first four years, it becomes clear what a unique and intense longing for the realization of God had seized him, and with what an extraordinary faith he had plunged himself into Sadhana. Such features of his life make us convinced that even without any external aid, he was, by the sheer intensity of his yearning, able to attain the perfect vision of the Divine Mother and thus have the only ambition of his life fulfilled. And having thus

---

[1] That is: This is a rupee, this is a clod of earth. Both of them are useless, so far as God-realization is concerned. Some think "rupee-earth, earth-rupee" means "rupee is earth and earth is rupee", which is absurd, though it is conceded that both are modifications of earth. As effects, they are surely different, having different pragmatic values; but as means to that ultimate end, both are equally worthless.—Tr.

13

initially achieved the fruits of all the spiritual disciplines, he proceeded to compare them with the teachings of the Guru and the Sastras.

24. According to the Master's teachings, an aspirant's mind, when purified by self-control and renunciation, can play the part of his own Guru. The thought and ideas arising in such a mind can never lead him astray. On the contrary, they show him the right path and bring him quickly to the goal of his life. Such was the case with the Master himself. During these first four years of his Sadhana, his pure and holy mind became his Guru and taught him what was to be done and what was to be rejected. This was not all. On many occasions, assuming a form, as it were, of a different person, it emerged from his body and appeared before him and encouraged him to go forward with his Sadhana. Sometimes it threatened him with punishment if he did not dive deep in a particular discipline. It explained to him why a particular Sadhana should be performed and what would result from it. That is why the Master saw at the time of meditation a Sannyasin with a sharp trident in his hand come out of his body and say, "If you do not fully give up all other thoughts and meditate wholeheartedly on your chosen Ideal, I'll pierce your heart with this trident." On another occasion he saw that, when the Papa-purusha, the embodiment of the lower or animal nature in man, emerged from his body, a young Sannyasin too simultaneously came out and killed that evil being. Whenever a desire arose in the Master's mind to worship a divine image at a distant place or attend the chanting of the Lord's glories at functions held in places far away he found this same young Sannyasin coming out of his body in an effulgent form similar to his own and travelling to those places along a luminous path and returning along the same path to his gross body. We have been told by the Master himself of many such visions.

The Master began to have the vision of this young Sannyasin. within his body, like the image in a mirror, almost from the commencement of his Sadhana. He became gradually accustomed to be guided by his advice in the performance or non-performance of all actions. In the course of a conversation on the extraordinary visions and experiences of his life during his Sadhana, the Master said to us one day, "The figure of a young Sannyasin looking like me used to come out again and again from within me and instruct me on all matters; when he emerged, sometimes I had a little outer consciousness and, at other times, lost it altogether and lay inert, only seeing and hearing his actions and words, I regained full external consciousness only when he entered the gross body again. The Brahmani, Tota Puri and others came and taught me afterwards what I had heard from him previously—they taught me what I had already known.   It seems from this that they came as Gurus in my life in order that the authority of the scriptures, such as the Vedas, might be maintained by my honouring their injunctions. No other reason can be found for accepting the 'naked one' and others as Gurus."

When the Master went to Kamarpukur during the latter part of this period of his Sadhana, another extraordinary vision occurred. This vision took place while he was going in a palanquin from Kamar pukur to Hriday's house in the village of Sihar. Witnessing under the deep blue sky a vast expanse of open fields covered with paddy, green and dark-blue in hue and with rows of trees such as the fig, the banian and others affording cool shade along the path, he was proceeding with a heart full of joy, when two beautiful boyish figures of tender age suddenly came out of his body.   Now advancing with slow steps, now running playfully hither and thither, sometimes going far in to the fields in search of wild flowers, and at others walking beside the palanquin, they laughed and joked, conversed and made merry as boys do.   They thus proceeded happily for a long time, and then they came back and entered his body.   The learned Brahmani came to the Kali temple at Dakshineswar for the first time about a year and a half after this vision had taken place.   She heard of this vision from the Master and without being at all surprised, said, "My child, what you have seen is all true; Chaitanya is manifest this time in Nityananda's sheath (body)—Nityananda and Chaitanya have come together this time and are both residing in you, in one and the same receptacle."   Hriday said, "Saying so, the Brahmani recited the following lines from the *Chaitanya Bhagavata*: 'Throwing his arms round Advaita's neck, Sri Chaitanya says again and again: I will manifest my wonderful play once more.   My form will be that of bliss during the singing of the glory of God.' The Brahmani quoted again, 'Gora acts his play even today.   It is persons of the rarest good fortune that are privileged to witness it.'"

25.   When we were visiting him one day, the Master said to us in connection with the topic of this vision, "It is true that I had that

vision and it is also true that the Brahmani said so when she heard of it. But how can I say what the real meaning of it is?" From these words of the Master regarding that vision of his, we think that at this time the Master got some clear indication that, identified with his body and mind, some ancient Being known to the world for incalculable ages, was dwelling in him with a view to accomplish some important purpose. It seems that the extraordinary indication that he had about his individuality with the help of these visions and experiences, clearly convinced him in course of time, that "the One, who had manifested Himself in Ayodhya as Sri Rama-chandra, dear to Janaki, and at Vrindavana as Sri Krishnachandra, the beloved of Radha, for the purpose of establishing religion in past ages, has incarnated Himself once more as Sri Ramakrishna in a human body in order to impart a new ideal of religion to India and the world." For, when we were with him, we heard him say again and again, both when he was in full enjoyment of health and when the body was stricken down by agonising ailment, "The One who became Rama and Krishna is now within this case (showing his body). But His advent this time is like a king visiting his kingdom *incognito*."

26. If we want to test the truth of the vision mentioned above, there is no other means for it than believing what the Master him-self spoke about it at other times to his devotees of the inner circle. Leaving aside this vision, we can be sure of the truth of all the other visions of his; for, visions of this nature occurred daily in the Master's life when we were visiting him. And his sceptical English-educated disciples were defeated when they tried to test the truths of these visions and experiences. Though we have given a few such examples elsewhere (IV. 4), we shall record here one more, for the satisfaction of the reader.

27. It was the end of 1885 when the people of Calcutta—men, women and children—were all filled with joy and enthusiasm, as usual, on the occasion of the great autumnal worship and festival. Although the current of that bliss was being particularly felt in the hearts of the Master's devotees, there was a great obstacle standing in the way of its manifestation; for he, in whose company they felt the surge of delight, was seriously ill—the Master was suffering from cancer of the throat. The devotees had hired a two-storeyed house at Shyampukur in Calcutta and had brought the Master there about a month previously. Mahendralal Sarkar, the well-known doctor,

was treating him and doing his best to cure him. But the disease had shown no signs of abatement so far; on the contrary it was worsening by degrees. The householder devotees would come to that house, morning and evening, and supervise and make all necessary arrangements. Many of the young student devotees were engaged in the service of the Master at all times except when they went home to have their meal. Some again would, whenever necessary, spend all the twenty-four hours there, without going home even for this.

If the Master spoke much or went into ecstasy again and again, the blood in his body would flow upward and delay the cure by constantly irritating the sore in the throat. Therefore the doctor advised the Master to check himself in both these respects. The Master too was trying to follow the prescription, but in spite of his best co-operation in the matter, he could not help talking and falling into ecstasies again and again. For unlike ordinary men he did not regard the body as precious. All his life he was accustomed to look upon it with contempt, as a trifling cage of flesh and bone from which he had withdrawn his mind completely. As soon as a devotional topic was raised, he would forget all about his body and everything about maintaining it. Joining the discussion of the topic with the same enthusiasm as in the past, he would repeatedly go into ecstasy. There were many souls who came thirsting for spirituality. Unable to remain indifferent to the eagerness of their hearts, the Master taught them Sadhana in a low voice. Seeing his joy and enthusiasm in the work of spiritual ministration, many of the devotees thought that the Master's disease was simple and could be easily cured, and became free from anxiety. Strangely enough, some again opined that the Master had purposely assumed this disease in order to bestow his grace on the large circle of devotees who were being drawn to him.

The doctor was visiting him almost every day in the morning or in the afternoon. While he was examining the patient, writing the prescription and advising the attendants, he would be so absorbed in listening to the Master's conversation on God that he could not take his leave even after the lapse of two or three hours. Again, putting question after question and listening for a long time to the wonderful solutions of these, he would sometimes say regretfully, "I made you talk so much; it has been unwise, but don't talk with anybody else for the rest of the day, and then it won't do you any harm.. Don't you see, your words have such attraction that, whenever I come to you, I can't leave this place for two or three hours, and I have to neglect my profession. I don't even know how time flies. Anyway, don't talk so long with anyone else; (partly as a joke and partly with love and joy, he said) talk thus with me only when I come, that will not do any harm." At this the doctor and all others would laugh.

Surendranath Mitra, whom the Master sometimes called Suresh Mitra, was celebrating the Durga Puja that year in his residence at Simla. Formerly his family used to celebrate it every year, but there had once been a mishap and the worship had been discontinued since then. No one of his household was bold enough to perform it after that; and if any one tried to celebrate it, all others dissuaded him vehemently. Strengthened, however, by his faith in the power of the Master, Surendranath was absolutely free from fear of any mishap due to the interference of demigods etc. He did not care at all for anybody's objections or obstructions when he had once resolved to accomplish anything. Therefore, although all the members of the household raised objections, they could not make him refrain from carrying out his resolve that year. He got the Master's approval and arranged for the image of the Mother to be brought to his house, bearing all the expenses himself to the exclusion of other members of the joint family. The only element of sadness in Surendra's joy was that the Master would not be able to join the celebrations on account of his illness. Again as a few relatives fell seriously ill a few days before the commencement of the worship, he was held responsible for all that and had to incur the displeasure of all the household. But unperturbed, Surendra devoutly began the worship of the Divine Mother with great care and attention and invited all his fellow-disciples.

The worship pertaining to the seventh day of the lunar month had been finished the day before. It was the auspicious eighth day. Many devotees gathered together at the temporary residence of the Master at Shyampukur and were enjoying his blissful company, in the midst of inspiring talks and songs on the Divine. Narendranath began singing devotional songs immediately after the doctor's arrival at four in the afternoon. All were charmed by those exceedinglymelodious vibrations of tunes coupled with remarkable spiritual fervour, and lost themselves completely in them. The Master was sometimes having ecstasy, at the end of which he would explain briefly in a low voice the import of the songs to the doctor who sat beside him.   Some of the devotees lost consciousness in deep spiritual emotions.   There flowed in the room a strong current of bliss, which was almost palpable.   Time passed unnoticed.   It was now 7-30 p.m. The doctor was startled at this. He embraced Narendranath with paternal affection, took leave of the Master and stood up, when the Master also rose from his seat smiling, and entered immediately into deep Samadhi.   The devotees began whispering, "Is it not the time for the Sandhi Puja?   That is why the Master has entered into Samadhi.   Is it a matter of little surprise that he has entered suddenly into it without knowing the time!" About half an hour after, the Master's Samadhi came to an end and the doctor bade them good night.

The Master now said to the devotees about his Samadhi: "I saw that there opened a luminous path from 'here' to Surendra's house. I saw, further, that, attracted by Surendra's devotion, the Mother had appeared in the image and that rays of light were coming out from Her third eye. I also saw that rows of lamps were lighted in the front verandah and Surendra was sitting and weeping piteously in the courtyard in front of the Mother. You all go to his house now.   He will feel much comforted to see you."

All, including Narendranath, then saluted the Master and went to Surendra's place. They questioned him and came to know that rows of lamps were actually lighted in that verandah, and unable to check his surge of emotion, Surendra sat in the courtyard before the image and wept loudly like a boy, crying 'Mother', 'Mother', for about an hour at the time of the Master's Samadhi.   Finding the vision during the Master's Samadhi correspond to the external events in every detail, the devotees were filled with joy and amazement.

28.   At one time, during the first four years of his Sadhana, Rani Rasmani and Mathur Babu, her son-in-law, thought that the Master's perfect continence was responsible for what they considered to be his mental derangement and consequent restlessness. Imagining that he might regain his health if his continence were broken, they, with the best of intentions, tried to tempt him through Lachmi Bai and some other beautiful harlots with their amorous gestures, first at Dakshineswar and afterwards in a house at Mechua-bazar in Calcutta. The Master used to say that he saw the Divine Mother in those women, and that repeating, 'Mother', a few times,

he lost consciousness. His sex-organ became contracted and entered completely into his body like the limb of a tortoise. There arose, we were told, a feeling of maternal affection in the hearts of those fallen women and they were charmed by the childlike behaviour of the Master. Thinking that they had committed a great sin by trying to tempt him to break his continence, they begged his pardon with tears in their eyes, saluted him again and again and bade him goodbye with apprehensive minds.

CHAPTER IX

MARRIAGE AND RETURN TO DAKSHINESWAR

(TOPICS: 1. The Master at Kamarpukur. 2. Theory of possession by a ghost. 3. An exorcist invokes a Chanda. 4. The opinion of the Master's relatives. 5. An instance of the Master's Yogic powers. 6. Relatives decide on the Master's marriage. 7. Why the Master consented to marry. 8. The Master selects his bride. 9. The marriage. 10. The conduct of Chandramani and of the Master after marriage. 11. The Master's return to Calcutta. 12. The Master's divine inebriation for the second time. 13. Chandradevi's Prayopavesa before Siva. 14. The Master's state then. 15. Mathur seeing the Master as Siva and Kali.)

1. At Kamarpukur the Master's mother and brother were very much worried on hearing the news that he had given up priestly duties. Scarcely had two years elapsed since Ramkumar's passing away when Chandramani Devi, the Master's mother, and his second brother Rameswar came to know to their utter dismay that he was suffering from 'insanity'. Misfortunes never come single. One after another, mishaps come from all sides and darken a man's life completely. This was exactly what happened to them. Gadadhar, whom Chandradevi had borne in her advanced age, was naturally very dear to her. Overwhelmed, therefore, with sorrow, she made arrangements for bringing him back home. When he was with her, she noticed his indifference to the external world and his anxious longing, expressing itself in repeated and piteous cries of 'Mother!', 'Mother!' She tried various means to remedy them like administration of medicines and performance of rites for propitiating several gods and demigods. This was at the end of the year 1858.

2. Although after his return home the Master generally lived his normal life, he became sometimes overwhelmed with spiritual emotions, when his deportment and behaviour became quite contrary to the normal. Again, he felt a great pain on account of the burning sensation in his body. Thus, on the one hand, he displayed

his usual simple and amiable behaviour towards all, his devotion to God and his mother and his love for his friends; and on the other, there were evident in him from time to time an extraordinary or uncommon behaviour pattern—an indifference to everything; an absence of shame, aversion and fear; an exuberant eagerness for attaining a vague unknown object; and an obstinate effort to clear all obstacles from the path of his desired goal. These produced in the minds of the people a strange belief that he was possessed by a ghost.

3. That thought had crossed the mind of the simple-hearted Chandradevi also. Now when she heard others talking in the same strain, she resolved to call an exorcist for the good of her son. The Master used to say, "One day an exorcist came, bunt a wick sanctified by Mantras, and made me smell it; he said, 'If it is a ghost, it will flee'; but it was of no avail. Afterwards worship and other ceremonies were performed with the help of a few famous exorcists and a 'Chanda' was invoked. The Chanda accepted the worship and offerings, became pleased and said to the exorcists, 'Neither has he been possessed by a ghost nor is he suffering from any disease.' The Chanda then addressed me in the presence of all and said, 'O Gadai, you want to be a Sadhu. Why then do you take so much of betel-nut? Don't you know that it increases lust?' Indeed I liked betel-nut very much and used to take it very often; however, I gave it up at the Chanda's word."

4. Then the Master was about to complete his twenty-third year. To a great extent, he regained the normal state of his health during his stay at Kamarpukur. There must have been some particular reason for his regaining his normal health and the ceasing of his piteous crying. That he could now be at peace, was surely due to the repeated visions of the Divine Mother. We are firmly convinced of it from what we have heard about his state at that time from his relatives. We shall now narrate their accounts.

All alone, he spent a good part of his time in the two awe-inspiring solitary crematoria named Bhutirkhal and Budhuimoral, on the western and the north-eastern borders of Kamarpukur, respectively. Now his relatives came to know of the occasional manifestations of extraordinary powers in him. The Master, we were told, went out from home with a new pot full of sweets and other eatables in order to offer them to the jackals and the demigods that lived in the crematorium. When those eatables were offered as oblation to them, the pot, the Master told them, would go up in the air and vanish into the void and he could sometimes see those demigods with his own eyes. When his second brother Rameswar found that he did not return home even after midnight, he would go towards those places and loudly call his brother by name. The Master would hear him and reply in a loud voice, "Yes, brother. I am coming. Don't proceed any farther this side, the demigods might harm you." During this period the Master planted a seedling of a Vilva tree with his own hand in the Bhutirkhal crematorium. He used to sit under the old peepul tree that was there and meditate and perform Japa for long periods of time. From what the relatives of the Master told us, it appears that the painful want that he had been experiencing, the want of the vision of the Divine Mother, was now removed by some extraordinary spiritual visions and experiences. When we study this period of his life, it seems to us that he was now having constant visions of the Divine Mother's form, constituted of pure consciousness and extremely gracious to the Sadhaka—holding in two of Her hands a sword and a severed head, and stretching out the other two hands in the gesture of offering boons and absolute fearlessness. He was now moulding his life according to Her directions received in response to his questions. He had, it seems, the firm conviction since then, that he would soon have the unique fortune of having the Divine Mother's beatific vision constantly.

5. We have heard not only of the Master's being engaged in such rites and ceremonies as feeding jackals and demigods but also of his practising Yoga as a result of which he developed prophetic powers. Hriday and many people of Kamarpukur and Jayaramvati attested to it, and we heard the same from the Master himself.

6. By now the Master's mother and other members of the household had learnt that, by the grace of Providence, the disease which they thought he was suffering from had abated to a great extent. For, they noticed that he did not now cry piteously as before, and took food at the proper time, and that all his other actions and behaviour were just like those of ordinary persons. But the fact that he used to go very often to the cremation grounds and sit for worship and meditation, putting off his cloth without any sense of shame, that he would get annoyed at the interference with his prayer and meditation, and that he spent most of his time with gods and goddesses to the utter disregard of others' words—all

these were regarded as his natural inclinations from his childhood, and not as something unusual due to insanity.

Still they saw with great apprehension that the Master was completely indifferent to worldly affairs and that there was an uninterrupted inwardness about his personality. They had the anxious apprehension that so long as these characteristics persisted, there was always the danger of a relapse into his old mental abnormalities. The Master's affectionate mother and elder brother were now very often busy in inventing various means of saving him from such a relapse. At last after a good deal of thinking and consultation, the mother and the son decided to get the Master married; and, therefore, an urgent search began for a suitable bride. For, they thought that the Master's mind would be held back from its adventures into high spiritual moods if his love came to be fixed on a good-natured wife coming of a noble family. Although he was now in the prime of his youth, he was dependent in all respects on his mother and brother, and was the same guileless boy as ever. The slightest desire or endeavour for improving his own worldly conditions was not perceptible in him. How could it be forthcoming unless the responsibility of maintaining his wife and children rested on his shoulders?

The bride had to be brought into the bridegroom's family only after paying an amount as bridal money to the girl's party according to the custom of that part of the country. Had they the means to pay the high amounts that would be required to secure a girl of ten or eleven years? They hesitated. They had postponed Gadadhar's marriage till then, only because they could not raise the required amount on account of various mishaps in the family. Had he been married long before to a girl of five, she would have grown up by his time to attract her husband's mind and could have taken upon herself much of the management of the family. In any case what was destined to happen had happened; there should be no more delay. So they sought for a bride all around.

7. However secretly the consultation between the mother and the elder son took place, the shrewd Master came to know of it very soon. But he did not raise any objection when the proposal of marriage was made; rather, he behaved like a child who makes merry and feels happy on festive occasions in the family. Was it because he got an affirmative reply to this question from the Mother Universal that he was in such a mood of merriment?

Or was it due to his boyish lack of thinking and foresight? No doubt, people in general would point out the latter as the reason, but we have discussed the topic elsewhere (III. 4) and expressed our dissent from this view.

8. People were sent to the surrounding villages in quest of a suitable bride, but none could be found. Rameswar, the elder brother of the Master, did not venture to settle the marriage with any one of the few available girls, because their parents demanded amounts too high for him to pay. His friends of the village also advised him not to settle the marriage by paying such large sums. Chandradevi, however, became very anxious. For she was arranging this marriage for what she considered necessary for the future of her beloved Gadadhar, for his well-being and stability in years to come, and not for the mere personal excitement of a marriage celebration to brighten the gloom that had befallen her after the demise of her god-like husband and her eldest son Ramkumar. Therefore she could not rest satisfied with the thought that a bride was not available. A vigorous search was made again. As no suitable bride could be found in spite of their search, the Master's mother and brother became extremely worried, when one day the Master suddenly went into Bhavasamadhi and said, "It is useless to search here and there; go and search in the family of Ram Mukhopadhyaya of the village of Jayaramvati; the bride has been 'marked with a straw' (III. 4) and kept reserved there."

9. Although they could not place much faith in those words of the Master, still his mother and brother sent a man there to make an enquiry. He brought the news that, other things apart, the bride-to-be was too young, just a little more than five years. As no other bride was available anywhere else, and as this girl was identified in such an unexpected way, the Master's mother had no alternative but to agree to Gadadhar's marriage with that girl. Everything was settled within a few days of negotiations. Afterwards an auspicious day and an auspicious moment were fixed by consulting the almanac. Then Rameswar went with his brother to the village of Jayaramvati four miles west of Kamarpukur, and got performed the marriage ceremony of Gadadhar with that five year old girl, the only daughter of Ramachandra Mukhopadhyaya. They then returned home. A marriage portion of three hundred rupees had to be paid to the bride's party. It was the month of May, 1859, and the Master had reached his twenty-fourth year then.

10. Chandramani, it is evident, felt relieved to a great extent after Gadadhar's marriage. When she found that her son obeyed all her instructions regarding the marriage as in other matters, she thought that, after all, Providence was now propitious to her. For, would all things have come to pass so well, had He not been favourable? The listless son had returned home; a bride of noble descent had graced her family; want of money had been overcome providentially; and Gadai had entered the life of the world! So, how could it be said that Providence was not favourable? Therefore the virtuous, simple-hearted Chandradevi became somewhat happy now. But this happiness was short-lived. For she was reminded of the distressing poverty of her family. In order to please the bride's father and to keep up appearances, the bridal ornaments had been borrowed from the Lahas, their landlord friends, to adorn the bride on the day of the wedding. From the marriage day, Chandradevi, by lavishing her love on the bride, had made her new daughter-in-law her very own. Now that the time for returning those ornaments had come, the eyes of the old lady were filled with tears to think of taking off the ornaments from the girl's person. She, however, did not express the anguish of her heart to anyone, but it did not take long for Gadadhar to understand it. He pacified his mother with a few words and took off the ornaments from the person of his sleeping wife so deftly that she could not know it at all. The ornaments were immediately sent back to the Lahas. But the matter did not end there. The intelligent girl, when she woke up, said, "Where are those ornaments I had on?" With tears, Chandradevi took the girl on her lap and said by way of consoling her, "My child, Gadadhar will give you afterwards many ornaments better than those." The bride's uncle came that day to see her, and when he came to know of this, he expressed great displeasure and took her away. Chandradevi was once more rudely shocked. But very soon the Master removed that pain of hers by his playfulness and his jocular remark, "Let them say or do whatever they like; the marriage cannot be annulled now."

11. After his marriage, the Master spent about one year and seven months at Kamarpukur. His mother had him with her after a very long time and did not easily give him permission to return to Calcutta. She had also the apprehension that there might be a relapse of insanity if he returned. Anyway he stayed

on, and according to the custom of the family, went to his father-in-law's house for a few days and returned on an auspicious day to Kamarpukur together with his wife, who, by now, had reached her seventh year.

He resolved to return to Calcutta shortly after his "coming in a pair", as the above-mentioned ceremony is called. But for his poverty, he would not have had to go to Calcutta. Although his mother and brother asked him to remain at home for some time more, the poverty of the family was not unknown to him. How then could the affectionate and loving heart of the Master remain free from anxiety, fully knowing these conditions as he did? He did not comply with their wishes but returned to Calcutta, to the Kali temple, and took over the charge of the Divine Mother's service.

12. Scarcely had he performed the worship for a few days when he became so much absorbed in it that everything about Kamarpukur—mother, brother, wife, worldly affairs, poverty etc.—disappeared from his consciousness. The only idea that occupied the whole of his mind was how he could see the Divine Mother in all beings at all times. His chest became reddish again on account of continuous Japa, remembrance of God, and reflection and meditation on Him. The world and all talks thereof appeared to him as deadly poison; that terrible burning sensation came on him again; and sleep vanished as it were into the air. But as he had already experienced such physical and mental states once, he was not completely overwhelmed by them as before.

We were told by Hriday that directed by Mathur Babu, Ganga-prasad, the reputed Ayurvedic physician of Calcutta, prescribed for the Master medicines like Chaturmukha pills and Madhya-manarayana and other oils one after another for the cure of his sleeplessness, excess of the humour of wind, the burning sensation in his body and other symptoms. Although no immediate result was produced by the treatment, Hriday did not lose hope, and occasionally went with the Master to the Calcutta house of the physician for consultation. One day, the Master said, that when he went there with Hriday, Gangaprasad examined him carefully and prescribed new medicines. Then there was with him another physician of East Bengal. Attracted by the Master's looks and thinking deeply over his disease, he said, "It appears from the symptoms that he is in a state of divine inebriation. It is not curable by medicine."[1]   The Master used to say that this physician was the first person to ascertain the real cause of his physical changes which appeared as a disease.   But nobody then believed in his words.   Time passed on thus.   Mathur Babu and the other friends and well-wishers of the Master grew more anxious and went on trying various treatments for his extraordinary disease.   But the disease was on the increase and showed no signs of abatement.

13.   Gradually the news reached Kamarpukur.   Having no other alternative, Chandradevi undertook a complete fast unto death before Siva for the recovery of her son.   Knowing that the "ancient" Siva of Kamarpukur was an "awakened" deity, she went to His temple and lay prostrate without food or drink.   Here she got the instruction from the "ancient" Siva that she would have her desire fulfilled if she undertook that vow in the temple of the Siva of Mukundapur, where she went and undertook the fast again.   Although she knew that nobody used to undertake such fast in that temple before, the old lady had full faith in the divine instruction and undertook the fast.   Hardly had two or three days passed when she dreamt that Siva, the great God, more silvery in complexion than silver itself, bedecked with glowing matted hair and clad in a tiger skin, appeared before her and consoled her saying,   "Don't be afraid; your son is not mad; he is in that state on account of a tremendous awakening of the divine spirit in him."   Thus assured through divine intimation, the virtuous old lady offered worship to the great God with her heart purified by devotion, and returning home, began to serve Sitala and Raghuvir with undivided attention for her son's mental peace.   Many men and women, we were told, have since then been undertaking fasts in the temple of the Siva at Mukundapur and getting their desires fulfilled.

14.   Reminiscing about his experience of divine inebriation of those days, the Master used to tell us now and then, "Such a state is never produced in ordinary people.   For even a fourth of its intensity would have destroyed their body and minds.   I remained occupied with some vision or other of the Mother during the greater part of the day and night; that saved the situation; otherwise it would have been impossible for this sheath (showing his body) to survive.   I had no sleep at all for six long years.   The

---

[1] Some say, it was Gangaprasad's brother Durgaprasad, who saw the Master and said so.

eyes lost the power of winking; I could not close the eyes in spite
of all my efforts. I had no idea of the passing of time and was
not at all conscious of the body. When the attention turned from
the Mother to the body even a little, I felt apprehensive, and thought
'Am I on the verge of insanity?' I stood before a mirror and put
my finger into my eyes to see whether the eyelids closed; I found
the eyelids were even then equally incapable of winking; I became
alarmed and wept complaining to the Mother, 'Mother, is this
the result of calling on Thee? Is it the result of my absolute reliance
on Thee that Thou hast given this terrible disease to this body?'
And the next moment I said, 'Let anything happen to this. Let
the body go, if need be, but see that Thou dost not forsake me.
Do reveal Thyself to me and bestow Thy grace on me; for, Mother,
I have utterly taken refuge at Thy lotus feet and have absolutely
no support except Thee.' I used to weep thus for some time,
when my mind would again be filled with an extraordinary ecstasy.
The body appeared to be a trifling thing—something unworthy
of attention. Then I was blessed with Her vision and consoled
by Her words, assuring me freedom from fear."

15. Again it was during this time that one day Mathur was
astonished and dumbfounded on having an unexpected vision of
a wonderful divine manifestation in the Master by the inscrutable
decree of the Mother of the universe. We have described elsewhere (III. 6) how he had that vision of the forms of Siva and Kali
in the Master and offered his heartfelt worship to him as the veritable God. He was compelled to view the Master with a different
eye since that day and to look upon him with faith and devotion.
When we see such an impossible event happening, it is brought home
to us that the divine Mother, the Will of all wills, thus bound up
both of them inseparably with the cord of love, because Mathur's
help and service during the following period of the Master's life of
Sadhana were indispensable. One is wonder-struck to find from
such events, the proofs of how much care the Divine Mother took,
and what wonderful means She employed, in order to make the
Master's body and mind fit instruments for stemming the decline
of religion and infusing a new spiritual vigour into the modern
world overpowered by agnosticism, atheism and materialism.

CHAPTER X

THE COMING OF THE BHAIRAVI BRAHMANI

(TOPICS: 1. Severe illness of Rani Rasmani. 2. Rani's execution of a Devottara Deed and her death. 3. Her vision at the time of passing away. 4. The Rani's last apprehensions prove true. 5. Mathur's arrangement for service at the temple. 6. Mathur's resources meant for helping the Master. 7. The ideas of Mathur and others about the Master. 8. Arrival of the Bhairavi Brahmani. 9. Her first meeting with the Master. 10. Conversation between them. 11. Her vision under the Panchavati. 12. The discussion on the Sastras under the Panchavati. 13. Why the Bhairavi went to reside at the Deva-mandal-ghat. 14. The reasons for her conviction regarding the Master's incarnationhood. 15. Pandit Vaishnavacharan's visit to Dakshineswar.)

1. The Master after his marriage returned from Kamarpukur to Dakshineswar. After this, in 1861, two important events took place, which, because of their profound influence on his future life, require detailed treatment here.

The first is the death of Rani Rasmani. She had an attack of dysentery shortly after the Master's arrival at Dakshineswar. Some of us were told by him that one day the Rani had a sudden fall, which gave rise to fever, pain in the body, indigestion, and other complications, gradually leading to dysentery. The disease by degrees took a fatal turn.

2. The Rani, of innumerable noble qualities, had consecrated the Kali temple on Thursday, May 31, 1855; and for the perpetual continuation of the service of the deities, she had purchased on August 29 of the same year, three estates in the district of Dinajpur for two hundred and twenty-six thousand rupees.[1] Although she had resolved in her mind to make an endowment of the property, she had not so far executed a deed of endowment formally. Seeing that the hour of death was fast approaching, she

---

[1] Plaint in High Court Suit No. 308 of 1872 Puddomoni Dasee vs. Jagadamba Dasee, recites the following from the Deed of Endowment executed by Rani Rasmani: "According to my late husband's desire . . . . I on the 18th Jaistha 1262 B.S. (31st May 1855) established and consecrated the Thakurs . . . and for purpose of carrying on the seva purchased three lots of Zamindaries in District Dinajpur on 14th Bhadra 1262 B.S. (29th August 1855) for Rs. 2,26,000."

became very anxious to do it. Of the four daughters of the Rani, the second and the third, Kumari and Karunamayi, had died before the consecration of the Kali temple. Therefore, her two other daughters, the eldest Padmamani and the youngest Jagadamba, were present at her sick-bed. We were told that when the draft of the deed of endowment of the Kali temple, written according to the Rani's desire, came, she asked her two daughters to sign it giving their assent to the terms of the deed, thereby precluding all possibilities of future quarrels among her descendants regarding the object of the deed. Jagadamba signed that bond; but Padmamani did not, in spite of the repeated requests of the Rani at the time of her death. Therefore the Rani had no peace on her death-bed. As there was no other alternative left, the Rani signed[1] the deed of endowment herself on February 18, 1861, thinking, "The Divine Mother's will be done," and passed away to "the sphere of the Devi" the following night.

3. The Master said that Rani Rasmani came to her house on the Adiganga at Kalighat a few days before she passed away. Just before her passing away, she saw many lamps lighted before her and exclaimed suddenly, "Do move away all these; I relish them no more. My Mother, the Mother of the Universe is come now; all quarters have become illumined by the effulgence of Her holy person. (A little later) Mother, art Thou come? But Padma has not affixed her signature; what will happen, Mother?" Saying so, the virtuous Rani assumed a calm and tranquil mood and immediately slept on the Mother's lap, the sleep that knows no awakening. She had already been brought to the sands of the Ganga and the loud howling[2] of jackals was audible on all sides near by.

4. The Rani was very apprehensive at the time of her death about the future of the temple which was dearer to her than her life,

---

[1] The deed of Endowment dated 18th February 1861 was executed by Rani Rasmani; she acknowledged her execution of the same before J. F. Watkins, Solicitor, Calcutta. This dedication was accepted as valid by all parties in Alipore Suit No. 47 of 1867, Jadu Nath Chowdhury *vs.* Puddomoni, and in the High Court Suit No. 308 of 1872, Puddomoni *vs.* Jagadamba and also when that suit *(No. 308)* was revived after contest on 19th July 1888.

[2] The Devi is represented as being surrounded by jackals. So the howling of jackals is considered a good omen.—Tr.

and her anguish on account of this was more acute than the physical pain caused by her fatal disease. The subsequent history of quarrels and litigations among her grandchildren justified these fears of the farsighted Rani. It is seen from the official documents that the temple property is now mortgaged for a little less than one lakh of rupees[3] for defraying the heavy expenses of litigation. Who can say anything about the future of the temple estate—whether anything of it will remain as a result of these quarrels beyond the mere memory of it as an example of the unique and laudable piety of the Rani?

5. Since the foundation of the Kali temple at Dakshineswar, Mathuranath Biswas, the youngest son-in-law of the Rani, rose to be her right-hand man in managing the estate. He was already acquainted with the financial condition of the temple endowment, and from the very day of the consecration of the temple, he was actively engaged in planning the temple services and executing them in accordance with the wishes of the Rani. Therefore, it was he who continued managing it after the Rani's death. As the elevating influence of Sri Ramakrishna had gained a complete hold over the mind of Mathur some time previously, the service of the Mother at Dakshineswar did not evidently slacken in any department after the Rani's death.

6. We have told the reader many times of the unique relation of Mathur with the Master. Therefore, it is needless to mention it again. Suffice it to say that Mathur's position as the sole authority in the management of the temple after the sudden demise of the Rani, gave him a great opportunity to help the Master in his Tantric Sadhanas extending over a long period. Who can say whether this authority of Mathur over the management of the property was not brought about by the will of the Divine Mother for helping Her son, the Master? For, we find that from that time on till his death, Mathur engaged himself whole-heartedly in the service of the Master. To have that firm faith in one person for more than eleven long years and to spend one's life in an exalted spiritual mood are possible by the grace of God alone. One is convinced of the great good fortune of Mathur from the fact that he was daily growing in his faith in the Master, instead of giving

---

3 Debt due on mortgage by the Estate is Rs. 50,000; interest payable quarterly is Rs. 876-0-0; cost of the Referee already stated amounts to Rs. 20,000, as yet untaxed.

free rein to passions and losing his head on the acquisition of almost the sole mastery over the vast property of the Rani.

7. So far none but the Sadhakas of God could form any idea about the high spiritual state of the Master. The generality of people thought he was demented. For he, they said, did not at all distinguish what was good for himself from what was evil; he was not attracted by objects of enjoyment; he never tried to do harm to anybody but lived contented within himself, spending his days repeating the names of God—Hari, Rama, or Kali by turn. They also saw that he could not at all improve his worldly condition, nor would ever be able to do so, even though he was a favourite of the Rani and Mathur Babu—the persons whose favour was enough to make many people improve their fortunes in every respect. But one thing they all understood, namely, that although this mad man was hopelessly good-for-nothing, still his bright eyes, his extraordinary deportment, his sweet voice, his graceful speech and wonderful presence of mind had such an attraction and charm for all that he could unhesitatingly approach and endear himself to even those rich and respectable persons, whom others would not venture to approach. Although the people in general, and the officers of the Kali temple in particular, formed rather a queer idea of the Master, Mathur had quite a different view of him. Hriday told us that Mathur had said, " The reason why he looks like a mad man is that he has had the grace of the Mother of all."

8. Shortly after the passing away of the Rani, there came to pass another important event in the Master's life. There was a beautiful flower garden on the spacious embankment on the Ganga, to the west of the Kali temple. As the garden received very good attention, its trees and creepers grew luxuriantly, adding wonderfully to the beauty of the place and filling the quarters with the fragrance of the flowers. Though the Master did not perform the worship of the Divine Mother at that time, he used to pluck flowers daily in that garden, make garlands with them and decorate Her with his own hands. Even today there exists in the middle of the garden, a wide flight of steps leading from the Ganga to the temple, through a beautiful open portico, and a brick-built Ghat for the use of women at the northern end of the embankment, besides a Nahabat to the north of the Kali temple. People used to call that Ghat the Bakul-ghat on account of a big spreading Bakul tree close to it.

One day the Master was plucking flowers in that garden when a boat came to the Bakul-ghat and anchored. A beautiful lady in the dress of a Bhairavi, with ochre-coloured cloth and loose and flowing hair, got down with a bundle of books in her hand and proceeded towards the portico on the wide Ghat to the south. Although the Bhairavi was past her youth, nobody could take her to be advanced in age, because youthful grace and beauty still lingered on her person. We were told by the Master himself that the Bhairavi was then almost forty. We cannot say how far the Master foresaw at first sight his close future relation with her. But it is true that he felt that great attraction towards her, which people feel when they see one whose life is bound up with their own. For, as soon as the Master saw the Bhairavi from a distance, he returned to his room, called Hriday and asked him to fetch the Sannyasini to him. Hriday hesitated and said, " The lady is a stranger. Why should she come at all?" The Master said, "Request her in my name and she will come readily." Hriday said that he felt not a little surprised to see the eagerness of the Master to speak with a lady who was entirely unknown to him; for he had never before seen him acting thus.

However, Hriday knew that he could not but obey his mad uncle. So he went to the portico, saw the Bhairavi sitting there, and said to her that his maternal uncle, who was a devotee of God, requested her to meet him. Hriday was still more amazed when he saw the Bhairavi unhesitatingly standing up to accompany him without putting any question to him.

9. When the Bhairavi came to the Master's room and saw him, she became overwhelmed with delight and astonishment, shed tears of joy and said, "Ah, my child, you are here! I knew you were living somewhere on the bank of the Ganga, and I have been searching for you ever so long; at long last I have met you now." The Master said to her, "How could you know of me, mother?" The Bhairavi answered, "I knew long ago by the grace of the universal Mother that I would have to meet three of you. I have already met two in East Bengal and today I meet you here."

10. The Master then sat beside the Bhairavi, and like a child describing everything delightedly and with an open heart to its mother, went on narrating his extraordinary visions—the loss of his consciousness of the external world while talking on God,

the burning sensation in his body, his sleeplessness, and other peculiar bodily changes, because of which he was taken to be mad. He repeatedly asked her, "Mother, what are these things happening to me? Have I actually become mad? Have I been seized with a fell disease for calling on the Mother whole-heartedly?" Listening to these words of the Master, she, like a mother, became now excited, now delighted, and with her heart melting with compassion, consoled him, saying over and over again, " Who calls you mad, my child? It is not madness; you are in the state of Mahabhava and that is why all these things are happening to you. Is it given to ordinary people to understand the state you are in?   In their ignorance they say all sorts of things. All this happened to Sri Radharani and to Sri Chaitanya, the Great Lord. All these things are recorded in the devotional scriptures. I have got these books with me. I'll read them out to you and prove that these states came on those who truly called on God in the past and do so at the present time too." Hriday was simply flabbergasted to see the Bhairavi Brahmani and his uncle behave and converse with each other like close relatives or familiar friends of long acquaintance.

When afterwards the Master found that the day was far advanced, he gave the Bhairavi Brahmani for her breakfast, fruits, roots, butter, candy, etc., all Prasada of the Devi; and knowing that the Brahmani, inspired by a spiritual and motherly love towards him, would not take anything whatever without first feeding him, he first partook a little of all these things. After paying her obeisance to the deities and having her breakfast, she took from the temple stores some flour, rice, etc., as Bhiksha in order to make offering cooked to the stone symbol of Raghuvir that she wore on her neck, and engaged herself in cooking under the Panchavati.

11. Afterwards, when the cooking was finished, she placed food, drink, etc., before Raghuvir and offered them to Him. Then she meditated on her chosen Ideal. Her concentration becoming very deep, she entered into Samadhi and had an extraordinary vision. From both her eyes flowed profuse tears of love and she was completely oblivious of the world. Feeling an irresistible attraction to go to the Panchavati at that time, the Master came there in a state of ecstasy, and not knowing clearly what he was doing, started like one hypnotized, eating the food offered by the Brahmani to her chosen Ideal. The Brahmani regained her normal consciousness after some time and opened her eyes to see

that charming behaviour of the Master, who was then in Bhavasa-madhi and was devoid of consciousness of the world. Finding all this correspond to her vision, she was filled with bliss and astonishment, the hairs of her body standing on end. Coming down to normal consciousness, the Master felt uneasy at what he had done, and said to the Brahmani, "Who knows, mother, why I lose control over myself and do such things?" The Brahmani then reassured him like a mother and said, "You have done very well, my child. It is not you who have done this but the One within you. He has done what He does always. From what I experienced during my meditation, I have come to the certain conclusion as to who has done it, and I feel I need not perform ceremonial worship any more; my worship at long last has answered its purpose." So saying, the Brahmani unhesitatingly partook of the remnant of the food offering left over by the Master as the sacred Prasada of her chosen Ideal. And having obtained the concrete and abiding presence of Raghuvir in the body and mind of the Master, she now very carefully immersed in Ganga the emblem of Raghuvir, so endearingly worshipped by her all these days, shedding tears of love and joy as she did so in a semi-conscious state of spiritual absorption.

12. The mutual affection and attraction experienced at first sight by the Master and the Brahmani increased day by day. With her heart overcome by a spiritual and maternal affection, the Sannyasini stayed on at Dakshineswar. The Master and the Brahmani engaged themselves every day in conversation on spiritual matters under the Panchavati, and they used to be so absorbed in these that neither of them was aware of the passing of time. The Master told the Brahmani frankly about all his spiritual visions and states, now and then putting various questions to her. And the Bhairavi Brahmani solved all those problems with the help of books on Tantra. Some-times, again, she would read verses from the *Chaitanya Bhagavata*, the *Chaitanya Charitamrita* and other devotional books showing what signs were produced by the strong surge of divine love in the bodies and minds of incarnations of God, and in this way dispelled the doubts of the Master. Thus there flowed a current of divine bliss under the Panchavati.

13. Six or seven days passed this way, when it became evident to the keen intelligence of the Master that it did not look well to keep the Brahmani there, though there was nothing really

objectionable in it.   Unable to understand their holy relationship
worldly men, given to lust and gold, might start talking ill about
the character of the pure lady.   As soon as this thought crossed
his mind, he gave a hint about it to the Brahmani.   The Brahmani
also felt the reasonableness of the point and left the Kali temple,
deciding to live somewhere nearby and come daily for some time
to see the Master.

To the north of the temple in the village of Dakshineswar,
on the Ganga, is situated the Devamandal Ghat.   Here the
Brahmani went and dwelt.[1]   She roamed about in the village and
became dear to the ladies there by virtue of her noble qualities.
Therefore, she had no inconvenience whatever about her board
and lodge, and could meet the Master daily without any fear of
public criticism.   She used to visit the Kali temple every day for
some time and have conversation with him as before.   She gathered
by begging various kinds of provisions from the women of the village
acquainted with her, and brought cooked items to the temple
to offer them to the Master   (III. 8).

14.   From what she heard of the spiritual experiences, visions
and states of the Master, the Brahmani gained the firm conviction
that all those conditions were produced by his extraordinary love
of God.   When she saw that he felt supreme bliss during the singing
of the Lord's glory and often lost consciousness in Bhavasamadhi
during conversations on God, she became certain that he was not
an ordinary Sadhaka.   When she saw all these, she was reminded
time and again of the hints spread over the pages of the *Chaitanya
Charitamrita*, the *Chaitanya Bhagavata* and other books of Bengal
Vaishnavism, about the fact that Chaitanya, the Great Lord, would
again assume a body and come down on earth for the deliverance
of man.   The Brahmani, the great scholar that she was, compared
minutely the conduct and behaviour of the Master with those of
Chaitanya recorded in those books and found a great similarity
between them.   She found manifested in the Master, as in Chaitanya, the power of awakening spirituality in others by a touch
during Bhavasamadhi.   Again, garlands, sandal-paste, etc., recorded

---

[1] Hriday said, "The Master himself advised the Brahmani to live
at the Devamandal Ghat.   He sent her to the Mandal's house.   As soon
as she went there, she was received respectfully by the virtuous wife
of the late Navinchandra Niyogi.   This pious lady not only allowed her
to live in the room at the Ghat as long as she liked but also gave her
a bedstead, a maund of rice, pulses, ghee and other articles of food."

to have cured the constant burning sensation in the body
of Chaitanya suffering from the pangs of separation from God,
were applied by her to the Master also for the same purpose and
with the same result (IV. 1). Therefore, the memory of the divine
vision regarding Sri Ramakrishna which the Brahmani had under
the Panchavati on the first day of her arrival, as well as the few
facts just mentioned above, deeply convinced her that both Chaitanya
and Nityananda had come again in the present age, and were
dwelling in the Master's body and mind with a view to disseminating
love of God for the deliverance of Jivas. While going to the
village of Sihar, the Master, we have already told the reader, saw
two boys of tender age come out of his body. The Brahmani now
heard of that vision from the Master himself and became all the
more convinced of her own conclusion regarding him and said,
"Chaitanya is manifesting this time in the 'sheath' of Nityananda."

The Sannyasini Brahmani did not expect any favour from anybody in the world; she was not afraid of the likelihood of being
condemned or ridiculed if her own conclusion regarding Sri Ramakrishna were spoken out to others. Therefore, when asked about it,
she had no hesitation in fully expressing her view first to the Master
and then to all others. On a certain day the Master was sitting under
the Panchavati with Mathur and Hriday. In the course of conversation, the Master told Mathur about the Brahmani's faith regarding
himself and said, "She says the signs that were manifest in the
incarnations of God are there in this body and mind. She has
read many scriptures and has also many books with her." When
Mathur heard this, he laughed out and said, "Father, let her say
whatever she likes; the incarnations of God cannot be more than
ten. Therefore, how can her words be true? But it is true that
Mother Kali has bestowed Her grace on you."

They were talking thus when they saw a Sannyasini coming
towards them. Mathur asked the Master, "Is it she?" The
Master replied, " Yes". They saw that she had procured a plateful
of sweets from somewhere and was coming with that in hand in a
rare spiritual mood characterised by inwardness and forgetfulness
of the external surroundings. With a heart overflowing with love,
like Yasoda, Krishna's mother, all eagerness to feed her Gopala,
she was advancing towards the Master with the plate of sweets
in her hand. When she approached them, she saw Mathur Babu,
and so carefully restrained herself and handed over the plate to

Hriday to be given to the Master to eat from.   Pointing to Mathur, the Master then said to her, "Mother, I was telling him what you had said about me, to which he replied that the incarnations of God could not be more than ten."   Mathur saluted the Sannyasini in the meantime and admitted that he had actually raised the objection. The Brahmani gave her blessings to him and replied, "Why? Does not the *Bhagavata* speak at first of twenty-four principal incarnations and, afterwards, of innumerable ones?   Besides, the re-advent of the Great Lord Sri Chaitanya is distinctly mentioned in the Vaishnava books, and between him and Sri Chaitanya one can observe great similarities in respect of their experiences and character".   The Brahmani thus supported her own position and said if a good scholar of the *Bhagavata* and books of the Bengal Vaishnava teachers be consulted, he could not but admit the truth of what she said.   She was ready, she said, to support her position in the presence of a scholar.   Not knowing what he should say, Mathur remained silent.

15.   All people, big and small, at the Kali temple came gradually to know of the extraordinary conviction of the Brahmani regarding the Master.   This caused a great flutter among them. We have recorded elsewhere the result of this sensational development in detail (III. 5, 6; IV. 1)   Therefore, it will suffice here to mention that although the Brahmani raised the Master suddenly to the position of God and paid him the reverence due to God in the presence of all, he remained the same simple child of the Divine Mother untouched by egotism and the resulting changes.   But he wanted to know the opinions of persons well versed in the Sastras on the Brahmani's conclusion and insisted like a boy that Mathur should invite the Pandits to Dakshineswar.   As a result of this request, Pandit Vaishnavacharan came to the Kali temple. We have described elsewhere (IV.1) how the Brahmani, when she met Vishnavacharan, not only upheld her own position before him but also brought him round to hers.

CHAPTER XI

TANTRIC SADHANA

1. The Brahmani did not arrive at the above conclusion about the uncommon nature of the Master through reason and inference only. The reader may remember that she told the Master during the first meeting with him that she was to meet three persons, Sri Ramakrishna and two others, and help them in developing their spiritual life. She had that command from the Mother of the universe long before she had the privilege of meeting the Master. It is therefore clear that it was her divine insight produced by spiritual practices that brought her to Dakshineswar and helped her in understanding the Master. With the passing of days, as the Brahmani's association with the Master became more and more intimate, she came to have an exact appraisal of the part she was to play in his Sadhana and the nature of the assistance she was called upon to give him. Therefore she did not now spend her

time in merely removing the erroneous conception of the people about him, but engaged the Master in performing various disciplines according to the strict injunctions of the scriptures, so that he might have the perfect vision of the universal Mother, and endowed with Her infinite grace and favour, become firmly established in his own divine power, that is, his real nature.

2. When the Brahmani, herself an advanced aspirant, saw the Master and talked with him, it did not take her long to understand that the Master could not free himself from doubts regarding his own condition, because he had proceeded so far to attain the Divine Mother's vision with the help of his extraordinary devotion only, instead of strictly following the traditional paths of spiritual teachers. Therefore, the doubt was crossing his mind now and then whether his visions of the Divine Mother were the result of a derangement of the brain and whether his extraordinary physical and mental changes were the symptoms of a virulent disease. The Brahmani reflected on the problem, and induced the Master to follow the path of discipline prescribed in the Tantras. She knew that as soon as the Master followed the path of discipline trod by previous Sadhakas, and had experiences of the spiritual states similar to those experienced by them, he would understand that those states of his were not produced by any disease. When he saw it already recorded in the Tantras that particular results were produced by the performance of particular rites, and when he himself obtained those results through the practice of those rites, he would gain a firm conviction that, through discipline, man gets uncommon experiences by ascending to higher and higher planes of consciousness in the internal realm, and that his own physical and mental states had been produced in that way only. The result would be that, whatever uncommon experiences he might be having in future, he would know them all as true, and proceed towards his goal without being at all troubled by them. The Brahmani knew that the scriptures, therefore, advised the aspirant always to compare the experiences of his own life with the words of the Guru and the Sastras and see whether they tallied or not.

3. Why did the Brahmani, it may be asked, engage herself in making the Master practise these disciplines, though she knew that he was an incarnation of God? Does not one who understands the glory of the incarnations of God accept the conclusion

that they are perfect, and that disciplines are altogether unnecessary for them ? The answer is that this would have been true, if the Brahmani were always conscious only of the Master's transcendent greatness and devoid of the intimacy of personal affection for him. But that was not the case. We have already said that the Brahmani felt from the very first meeting a maternal affection for the Master. There is nothing on earth more powerful than love to obliterate in one, the consciousness of power in the object of one's love, and to impel one to do what one considers good for him. There is no doubt, therefore, that it was this genuine affection for him that moved the Brahmani to induce the Master to undertake these spiritual practices in spite of her awareness of his greatness. We come across the same situation in the lives of all the incarnations. Although the persons intimately related to such personages are sometimes overawed by their knowledge of the extraordinary spiritual powers in them, they, it is seen, forget all about it the next moment, and charmed with the attraction of their love, feel content with merely offering their hearts' love to them and seeking their welfare. Similarly, the Brahmani, amazed though she was at the frequent and extraordinary ecstasies and the manifestation of powers in the Master, forgot their import immediately, being blinded by maternal love. It is needless to say that the Master's genuine filial affection for her and his absolute dependence on, and faith in her played no small part in raising waves of tender, though austere, maternal affection in the Sannyasini's heart. It was this maternal affection that made her oblivious of his powers, and impelled her to undergo endless troubles for making the Master happy in every way, protecting him from others' tyrannies and helping him in his Sadhana during this phase of his life.

4. When there is an opportunity of teaching an exceptionally brilliant pupil, there naturally arises in a Guru's heart a supreme contentment and self-satisfaction. The Brahmani had never even dreamt that in the spiritual world such an excellent and very competent person as the Master could be born at the present time. Therefore we can very well infer what great joy must have filled her heart when she got the opportunity of teaching the Master. It was no wonder, therefore, that she was eager to make the Master experience in a very short time all the results of her studies and austerities.

5. We sometimes heard from the Master himself that he had asked the Divine Mother about the propriety and necessity of the disciplines according to the Tantras before he began to practise them, and that he undertook them with Her permission. It was, therefore, not merely the eagerness and inducement of the Brahmani that made him undergo those spiritual exercises, but also his divine insight born of Sadhana. That insight made him feel in his heart of hearts that the opportunity of attaining the immediate knowledge of the Divine Mother by resorting to scriptural methods had arrived. Therefore, the concentrated mind of the Master now advanced fast, driven by the power of aspiration, along the path of Sadhana taught by the Brahmani. It is not possible for us, ordinary mortals, to feel the measure and intensity of that eagerness. For, where is that tranquillity, and where, that one-pointedness in our minds, distracted as we are by many things from many directions? Where is that unbounded courage in us to jump headlong into the sea of deep consciousness and touch the very bottom of it, instead of being deluded by the wantonness of its surface waves represented by the objects of normal consciousness? Where is the power in us to eradicate the attachment to all the things of the world including our own bodies and plunge with utter abandon into the depths of spiritual inwardness, to realize which the Master urged us over and over again, saying, "Dive deep, dive to the depths of yourself." Overwhelmed with the anguish of his heart, the Master, we were told, rubbed his face against the sandy bank of the Ganga under the Panchavati, saying, "Mother, reveal Thyself," and was it a matter of a day or two? It went on unabated, and days passed by. Those words only enter our ears, but do not rouse corresponding echoes in our hearts at all. And how can it be otherwise ? Have we got that childlike all-consuming faith of the Master in the existence of the Divine Mother and in the possibility of attaining Her vision by renouncing everything and calling on Her with utter eagerness of heart?

6. One day while living at Cossipur, the Master astonished us by giving us a little indication of the measure and the intensity of his spiritual urge at the time of his Sadhana. We cannot say whether we shall be able to give the reader even a faint picture of what we then felt. We shall, however, try.

We were witnessing with our own eyes the intense eagerness of Swami Vivekananda for the realization of God—how spiritual awakening came on him when he was going to deposit the fee for his Law examination; how, goaded by intense zeal and oblivious of the world, he ran along the city road like one mad, bare-footed and covered with but a single piece of cloth, to the place where the Master was, and obtained his grace on laying bare to him the anguish of his heart; how, since then, he spent his time night and day in Japa, meditation, devotional songs and spiritual study; how on account of his boundless enthusiasm for Sadhana, his usually tender heart turned adamant and remained quite indifferent to the sufferings of his mother and brothers; and how, advancing with single-minded devotion on the path of Sadhana pointed out by his preceptor, he was having vision after vision, culminating at last in his first enjoyment of the bliss of the Nirvikalpa Samadhi in a short period of three or four months. All these things took place before our very eyes and completely struck us dumb. Greatly delighted, the Master used to praise highly the Swami's extra-ordinary devotion, eagerness and enthusiasm for spiritual practices. One day at that time the Master compared the Swami's love and enthusiasm for Sadhana with those of his own, and said, "Narendra's devotion and enthusiasm are extraordinary indeed, but compared with the urge that came here (pointing to himself) at the time of Sadhana, his is most ordinary. It is not even one fourth of that." Can you imagine, O reader, the overwhelming surprise we felt at those words of the Master ?

Thus the Master took the hint from the universal Mother, forgot everything else and merged himself in Sadhana. And the learned and masterly Brahmani took endless pains to collect from various parts of the country, things specifically necessary for particular rites, and gave the Master instructions regarding their application at the time of Sadhana.

7. The skulls[1] of five dead beings, including that of a man, were brought from somewhere far away from the Ganga; and

---

[1] 'Now hear, O queen of the Devas, of the best Sadhana with the help of skulls, by the performance of which the Sadhaka attains the supreme goal, which is the great Devi Herself. O one of excellent face, "the three skulls" are those of a man, a buffalo and a cat, or they are "three skulls" of men alone; and the heads of a jackal, a snake, a dog, and a bull and, in the midst of these, the head of a man— otherwise the five skulls of men alone, are called, O powerful one, "the five skulls" collectively . . . And on it an altar, a span square, should be made.

two altars[2] propitious for Tantric Sadhanas were constructed, one under the Vilva tree situated at the northern boundary of the temple garden, and the other, under the Panchavati planted by the Master himself. Sitting on either of these 'skull-seats,' according to need, the Master spent his time in Japa, meditation, etc. This extraordinary Sadhaka and his guide were not conscious, for a few months, how days and nights slipped by. The Master used to say[3], "In the day-time the Brahmani went to various places far away from the temple-garden and collected and brought various rare articles prescribed by the Tantras. Placing them under the Vilva tree or under the Panchavati at night, she called me, taught me how to make use of those things, and helped me in the performance of the worship of the Divine Mother according to the prescribed rules with their aid, asking me at last to merge in Japa and meditation. I acted accordingly. But I had to perform almost no Japa; for, hardly did I turn the rosary once when I merged completely in Samadhi and realized the results proper to those rites. There was thus no limit to my visions and experiences, all very extraordinary. The Brahmani made me undertake, one by one, all the disciplines prescribed in the sixty-four main Tantras, all difficult to accomplish, in trying to practise which most of the Sadhakas go astray. But I got through them all successfully by the Mother's grace.

Or an altar, four cubits square, O Devi, should be built.' *The fifth Patala—Yogini-Tantra.*

[2]The Sadhakas generally make one altar on the five heads interred, and sitting on it, practise Japa, meditation, etc. But the Master told us of two 'skull-seats'. Three human skulls were interred below the altar under the Vilva tree and five skulls of five species of dead beings were interred below that under the Panchavati. Shortly after he became perfect in his Sadhanas, he threw those skulls into the Ganga and broke down both the altars. Two 'seats' were made, because the seat of 'three-skulls' was favourable to Sadhana or because the spot under the Vilva tree was at that time wholly solitary, and therefore, more convenient for Sadhanas. Or it may be that no fire for Homa could be kindled under the Vilva tree on account of its proximity to the "Company's" (Government of India's) magazine.

[3]What we heard from the Master at different times is given here in a connected way.

15

8. "On one occasion, I saw that the Brahmani had brought at night—nobody knew whence—a beautiful woman in the prime of her youth, and said to me, 'My child, worship her as the Devi.' When the worship was finished, she said, 'Sit on her lap, my child, and perform Japa.' I was seized with fear, wept piteously and said to the Mother, 'O Mother! Mother of the universe! What is this command Thou givest to one who has taken absolute refuge in Thee ?   Has Thy weak child the power to be so impudently daring?' But as soon as I said so, I felt as if I was possessed by some unknown power, and an extraordinary strength filled my heart. And no sooner had I, uttering the Mantras, sat on the lap of the woman, like one hypnotized, unaware of what I was doing, than I merged completely in Samadhi.   When I regained consciousness, I saw the Brahmani waiting on me and assiduously trying to bring me back to normal consciousness.   She said, 'The rite is completed, my child; others restrain themselves with very great difficulty under such circumstances and then finish the rite with nominal Japa for a very short time only; but you lost all consciousness and were in deep Samadhi.'   When I heard this, I became reassured and began to salute the Mother again and again with a grateful heart for enabling me to pass that ordeal unscathed.

"On another occasion, I saw that the Brahmani cooked fish in the skull of a dead body and performed Tarpana.   She also made me do so and asked me to take that fish.   I did as I was asked and felt no aversion whatever.

9. "But, on the day when the Brahmani brought a piece of rotten human flesh and asked me to touch it with my tongue after Tarpana, I was shaken by aversion and said, 'Can it be done?' So questioned, she said, 'What's there in it, my child? Just see how I do it.'   Saying so, she put a portion of it into her mouth and said, 'Aversion should not be entertained', and placed again a little of it before me.   When I saw her do so, the idea of the terrible Chandika form of the Mother Universal was inspired in my mind; and repeatedly uttering 'Mother' I entered into Bhavasamadhi. There was then no aversion felt when the Brahmani put it into my mouth.

10. "Having initiated me thus in Purnabhisheka, the Brahmani made me perform daily Tantric rites too numerous to mention. I now don't remember all the details.   But I remember the day when I was able, by the grace of the Mother, to view with perfect

equanimity, the supreme pleasure of a pair of lovers, seeing nothing in it but the blissful sport of the Divine. The mind instead of descending even to the neighbourhood of ordinary human feelings, soared higher and higher, merging at last in deep Samadhi. After regaining normal consciousness, I heard the Brahmani say, 'You have reached the desired end of a very difficult Tantric Sadhana and become established in the divine mood. This is the ultimate Sadhana of the 'heroic' mode of worship.'

"Shortly afterwards, when I performed the worship of the female figure according to the Tantra rites, I did it with the help of another Bhairavi in the open music hall of the temple in the presence of all, during the day-time. When it was over, I saluted her according to Sastric prescription. This was the last rite connected with the heroic mode of worship, which I completed in that manner. Even as my mental attitude towards all women, namely, that of a child towards its mother, remained intact during the long period of the Tantric Sadhana, so also I could never take a drop of wine at that time. The mere mention of the name of Karana[1] (wine) would inspire in me the immediate experience of the universal Cause and I lost myself in it completely. Similarly, as soon as I heard other words of that kind, the Cause of the universe would present Itself before me and I would be in Samadhi."

11. One day while living at Dakshineswar, the Master made mention of his lifelong filial attitude towards all women and told us a story from the Puranas. The story describes how firmly the knowledge of filial relation with all women without any exception was established in the heart of Ganesha, the chief of the illumined ones. Before we were told that story, we did not have much of devotion to, and reverence for, this pot-bellied, elephant-faced god with the exudation flowing from his temples. But, since we heard the story from the Master's holy mouth, we have the conviction that Ganesha was truly fit to be worshipped before all the gods, as indeed he is worshipped. The story is this:

One day, in his tender age, Ganesha, while playing, saw a cat. which he, in his boyish playfulness beat, wounded and tortured in various ways. The cat escaped somehow with life and limb.

---

[1] In Bengali the word 'Karana' means both 'cause' and 'wine'; so by the law of association the mention of the one gave rise to the thought of the other, of wine to the universal Cause.

When Ganesha became quiet and came to his mother, he saw to his surprise marks of injury on various parts of the holy person of the Devi. Very much pained to see that condition of his mother, the boy asked her the reason of it. The Devi answered in a melancholy mood, "You yourself are the cause of this sad condition of mine!" More pained than surprised at it, the devoted Ganesha said with tears in his eyes, "How strange! Mother, when did I beat you? And I don't remember that this child of yours, ignorant as he is, has done any wicked action for which you have to suffer such insults at the hands of anyone."

Parvati Devi, whose gross external form the universe is, said, "Try to remember if you have beaten any living creature today." "Yes," said Ganesha. "I did so; I beat a cat a short time ago." Ganesha thought that the person to whom the cat belonged, beat his mother that way. Ganesha's mother took the repentant boy to her bosom and consoled him, saying, "It is not so, my child; nobody beat this body of mine; but it is I who have assumed the form of the cat; that is why you see the marks of your beating on my person. You have done so without knowing it; so, don't be sorry for it; but remember henceforward that all the Jivas of the world having female forms are parts of me and those having male forms are parts of your father. There are no persons or things in the world other than Siva and Sakti." Ganesha had faith in those words and enshrined them in his heart. When he reached the marriageable age, he did not consent to marry lest he should have to marry his mother. Ganesha thus remained a Brahmacharin all his life and became foremost among the illumined ones, inasmuch as he always had the conviction in his heart that the universe was of the nature of Siva and Sakti, Brahman and its Power.

12. After narrating this, the Master told us the following anecdote, also indicative of the greatness of Ganesha's knowledge: Showing once the precious necklace of gems hanging from her neck to Ganesha and Kartika, Parvati Devi said to them, "I shall give this necklace to the one who will circumambulate the universe comprising the fourteen worlds and come back to me first." Kartika, the commander of the celestial army, having for his vehicle a peacock, smiled with a touch of derision, thinking of his elder brother's fat and heavy body and pot-belly, and of the small power and slow movement of the mouse, his vehicle, and became cocksure

that the garland had already become his, and started immediately on the circumambulation of the universe. Long after Kartika had started, the sedate Ganesha left his seat calmly, and seeing with the eye of knowledge the universe consisting of Siva and Sakti situated in the body of Hara and Parvati, went round them with a gentle gait, worshipped them and took his seat. Long after this, Kartika returned when, pleased with the knowledge and devotion of Ganesha, Parvati Devi placed the garland of gems affectionately round his neck as a token of her grace.

Thus mentioning the greatness of Ganesha's knowledge and his filial relation with all women without exception, the Master said, "My attitude to women is also the same; that is why I had the vision of the maternal form of the universal Cause in my wedded wife and worshipped her and bowed down at her feet."

13. We have not heard of any other Sadhaka in any age, who, keeping intact that filial attitude towards all women, had resorted to the Tantric disciplines according to the prescribed rules of the heroic mode of worship. Following this heroic mode, the aspirants have all along been taking a woman companion at the time of Sadhana. As they do not see any aspirant of the heroic mode deviate from that practice, people have got a firm conviction that the realization of the desired end of the discipline, that is, the attainment of the grace of the Divine Mother, is quite impossible if that practice is not followed. This notion has brought these scriptures known as the Tantras into disrepute.

14. It is only the Master, the incarnation for this epoch, who set a new tradition in this respect by not keeping the company of a woman even in a dream. Through the Master's practice of the heroic mode of worship, in spite of his maintaining the filial attitude towards women all through , a hidden purpose of the Divine Mother is revealed.

15. The Master said, "It did not take me more than three days to succeed in any of the disciplines. When I took up a particular discipline and asked the Divine Mother importunately with a glowing eagerness of heart for the realization of its result, She benignly crowned me with success within a short period of three days. It is clearly proved that the company of a woman is not an indispensable auxiliary of those practices, inasmuch as the Master became successful in those disciplines in a very short time without taking a woman. If Sadhakas have been doing so, it is only the result of

their weakness and lack of self-control. The promise of the Tantras that, through the continued practice of their rites with a woman companion, a Sadhaka will eventually attain to the divine state or Divya-bhava (a state above sex nature), is only a concession made to weak man and an example of their catholicity and solicitude to make their discipline available to all. It should never be interpreted as an obligatory injunction on their part.

16. The common aim of all the Tantric practices, it is inferred, is to establish the aspirant, through self-control and repeated practice and perseverance, in the conviction that those very objects—sights, tastes and other sense experiences, which tempt human beings, involve them in repeated births and deaths, and prevent them from attaining self-knowledge by realizing God—are none other than veritable forms of God. Taking into account the differences in the capacity for self-control and the degree of conviction attained by aspirants, the Tantras have dealt with three different modes of worship, namely, the "animal" or the Pasu, the "heroic" or the Vira, and the "divine" or the Divya[1]; and have advised them to worship God adopting the first, the second or the third mode according to their fitness. In course of time people almost completely forgot that the Tantric practices would fructify only if the aspirants observed austere self-control as the basis of those disciplines. Instead, they indulged in gross sensuality due to their own weakness; but without proper understanding, critics, however, began to put all the blame on the Tantras for the abuses their followers indulged in. The success of the Master,

----

[1]The following is the significance of the classification. Pasu or the animal-minded man is the one without much of self-control. He is very likely to succumb to sense objects if exposed to them. He has therefore got to follow strictly the practice of 'cloistured virtue' i.e. of avoiding exposure to tempting sense objects. The Sadhanas for him are based on this principle. The Vira or the heroic Sadhaka is one whose power of self-control is highly developed and whose conviction in the teaching of the Tantras, that all manifestations of Nature—ennobling, beautiful and sublime as also degrading, tempting, terrifying and causing revulsion—are all alike the expressions of the Divine Mother, is developed enough to stand unmoved even when exposed to them. He is put in such situations as test of his strength and not for succumbing to them under the guise of piety. The Divya or the divine personage is one who has proved his strength and insight, and whose sense nature has been completely divinised. He sees God in everything.—*Translator*.

even while fully maintaining the filial attitude towards all women
throughout those practices, has been of immense benefit to both
the true aspirants and the Tantric scriptures—to the former, by
pointing out to them the right way to the goal of their lives, to the
latter, by bringing out their real glory and firmly establishing their
authenticity.

17. Although the Master practised the disciplines according
to the Tantric mysteries for three or four years, he, it seems, did not
tell any of us their consecutive order or give any one of us a detailed
account of them. But in order to encourage us on the path of
Sadhana, he told many of us of these facts on many occasions,
and according to individual needs, made a rare few of us perform
some of those practices. The Mother of the universe, it appears,
made the Master fully acquainted with this path at that time,
because if he had not himself had the uncommon experiences
resulting from the Tantric practices, he would not have been able
to detect the mental states of the devotees of different nature who
came to him in his later life, and to lead them forward on the path of
Sadhana. We have elsewhere (III. 1,2) given a little indication
of how the Master guided, along various paths of disciplines,
the devotees who came to him and took refuge at his feet. A
study of that section will show the reasonableness of what we have
said above.

18. Besides telling us, in this manner, of the Tantric practices,
the Master sometimes spoke to us about many of his visions and
experiences. We shall now describe a few of them. A root-and-
branch change came over his former nature at the time of the
Tantric Sadhana.

19. When he was told that the Divine Mother sometimes
assumed the form of a jackal, and that the dogs were the carriers
of Bhairava, he regarded the remnants of food taken by those
animals as pure and sacred, and partook of them as Prasada without feeling the slightest hesitation.

20. Offering heartily, as oblations to the lotus feet of the
Divine Mother, his body, mind, life and all, the Master saw
himself incessantly pervaded, inwardly and outwardly, by the fire
of knowledge.

21. The Master saw during this period the awakened Kundalini proceeding upwards to the head. All the lotuses from the
Muladhara, the basic centre, to the thousand-petalled Sahasrara

in the head, turned upwards and opened fully. As soon as they did so one after another, he got strange and wonderful experiences (III. 2). He saw for example that a luminous celestial went through the Sushumna, the Canal Centralis, to those lotuses, now turning upwards, and made them blossom, touching them with his tongue.

22. At one time, when Swami Vivekananda sat for meditation, there appeared before him a very large, wonderful triangle of light which, he felt, was living. One day he came to Dakshineswar and told the Master about this, when the latter said, "Very good; you have seen the Brahmayoni; while practising Sadhana under the Vilva tree, I also saw it. What was more, I observed it giving birth to innumerable worlds every moment."

23. At that time the Master heard, arising naturally and unceasingly everywhere in the universe, the Anahata Dhvani, the great Pranava sound, which is the aggregate of all the different sounds of the universe. Some of us heard from the Master himself that he could at that time understand the meanings of the cries of all animals.

24. During that period, the Master saw the Divine Mother Herself dwelling in the female form. In the latter part of this period the Master felt in himself the presence of the miraculous powers like the one of becoming as small as an atom. One day he went, at the instance of Hriday, to the universal Mother to know the propriety and utility of applying them and saw that they were to be shunned and discarded like excreta. The Master said that since then it appeared loathsome to him to hear the term 'miraculous power.'

25. We are reminded of one thing about the Master's possession of the 'eight miraculous powers'. One day he called Swami Vivekananda privately to the Panchavati and said, "Look here. I have got the well-known 'eight miraculous powers'. But I decided long ago that I will never make use of them; nor do I see any need for applying them. You will have to do many things like preaching religion; I have made up my mind to give them to you; here they are." The Swami said to him in reply, "Sir, will these help me in any way in realizing God?" The Master replied that they would not, but that in such works as preaching religion, they could prove useful. The Swami thereupon refused to accept them, to the immense joy of the Master.

26. There arose in the Master's mind during this period a desire to see the deluding power of the Mother of the universe. Accordingly he saw a female figure of extraordinary beauty rise from the waters of the Ganga and come with a dignified gait to the Panchavati. Presently he saw that the said figure was in an advanced stage of pregnancy. A few minutes later she gave birth to a beautiful baby in his very presence and suckled the baby very affectionately; the next moment he saw that the same figure assumed a very cruel and frightful appearance, and taking the baby into her mouth, masticated it and swallowed it! She then entered the waters of the river whence she had appeared.

27. Besides the visions mentioned above, there was no limit to the number of the Devi's forms, ranging from the two-armed to the ten-armed, that he saw during this period. Again, some of them engaged themselves in conversing with him and gave him various instructions. Although all those forms of Hers were of extraordinary beauty, we were told by him that they were not worth comparison in that respect with that of Sri Rajarajeswari, otherwise called Shodasi. The Master said, "I saw in a vision the beauty of the person of Shodasi which melted and spread all around illumining the quarters." At that time the Master had the visions of various male figures like Bhairava and also visions of celestial beings. From the time of his Tantric Sadhana, there were so many extraordinary visions and experiences in the Master's life day after day that it is beyond the power of man to mention all of them. It is therefore needless to spend any more time in making that attempt.

28. We heard from the Master himself that from the time of his Tantric Sadhana, the orifice of his Sushumna was fully opened and his nature was permanently converted into that of a boy. From the latter part of that period, he could not, in spite of his efforts, retain his cloth, sacred thread, etc., on his person for any length of time. He did not feel where and when all these things slipped off. It is needless to mention that this condition was caused by the absence in him of body-consciousness, on account of his mind remaining always absorbed in the lotus feet of the Divine Mother. We have it from the Master himself that, unlike the ordinary Paramahamsas, he never practised wandering or remaining naked—it naturally came to him with his gradual loss of body-consciousness. The Master said that at the end of those disciplines

his knowledge of non-duality with regard to all things increased so much, that he felt that those things which he considered to be trifling and worth discarding from his childhood now appeared to be as pure as the purest. He asserted, "The leaves of the holy basil (Tulasi) and those of Sajina (drumstick)[1] were felt by me to be equally holy."

29. Again, the splendour of the Master's person increased so much for a few years from that time, that he became the cynosure of all eyes at all times. As he was devoid of egoism, he was so much annoyed at it that he prayed on many occasions to the Divine Mother to be rid of that celestial beauty, and imploringly said, "Mother, I have not the slightest need of this external beauty; please take it away and give me instead the inward spiritual beauty." We have told the reader elsewhere (III. 7,8.) that this prayer of his was fulfilled afterwards.

30. Just as the Brahmani helped the Master in his Tantric Sadhanas, so did the Master help the Brahmani later in developing her spiritual life. We have already given an indication of the fact that but for the Master's help, she could not have established herself in the divine mood. The name of the Brahmani was Yogeswari who, the Master said, was a part of Yogamaya (the mystic power of the Lord).

Attaining divine powers on account of his Tantric Sadhana, the Master came to know another thing. He came to know by the grace of the Divine Mother that many persons would come in later days to him for the fulfilment of their life's purpose, namely, the attainment of spiritual enlightenment. He told this to Hriday, and also to Mathur who was greatly devoted to him. Mathur replied, "Fine, Father! We shall all make merry in your company."

---

[1] Hyperanthena moranga.

CHAPTER XII

THE SADHU WITH MATTED HAIR AND THE MASTER'S SADHANA OF THE VATSALYA BHAVA

(TOPICS; 1. Mathur's experiences and behaviour. 2. Gift of a 'mountain of food'. 3. Meeting with Padmalochan. 4. Why the Master undertook the Vaishnava Sadhanas. 5. Arising of feminine moods in the Master during certain Sadhanas. 6. The constitution of the Master's mind. 7. Absence of past impressions in him. 8. The noble qualities of the Master. 9. Some illustrations. 10. Mathur's services to holy men. 11. Jatadhari's arrival at Dakshineswar. 12. Intimacy between the Master and Jatadhari. 13. The mood of a female companion. 14. Vatsalya Sadhana practised during the prevalence of feminine mood. 15. His extremism in Sadhana. 16. Controlling of desires by confirmed Sadhakas. 17. They are unperturbed. 18. They are free from selfishness. 19. All their mentations correspond to facts. 20. The Master and Jatadhari. 21. Jatadhari gifting Ramlal's image to the Master. 22. Bhairavi Brahmani's help in Vatsalya Sadhana.)

1. Sri Yogeswari, the Bhairavi, came to the Kali temple at Dakshineswar after the noble Rani Rasmani had passed away in the latter part of 1861. The Master applied himself particularly to the Tantric disciplines from that time to 1863. Mathur Babu had the rare privilege and blessedness of serving the Master during the days when he plunged himself into the practice of those disciplines. Before that period Mathur had become firmly convinced, by repeatedly testing him, of his extraordinary love of God, his wonderful self-control, and his glowing renunciation and detachment. In the same way his experiences with the Master during this period of Tantric Sadhana established him in the conviction that the Devi, his chosen Ideal, had become pleased to manifest Herself to him in the person of the Master and accept his services (III. 6), and also to protect him in all respects, to accompany him everywhere, to maintain his influence and authority over the estate, and to shower on him honours and recognition as the time passed. He thought so because, during this time, he succeeded in whatever

he undertook, and felt the protecting hand of the Divine in the
friendly company of the Master. It was, therefore, no wonder
that Mathur spent unstintingly large sums of money in supplying
the articles needed for the Master's Sadhana and in serving God
and performing other virtuous deeds according to his wishes.

As the manifestation of the spiritual powers of the Master
increased day by day through the Tantric practices, Mathur, who
had taken refuge at his holy feet, also found his ardour, courage
and strength correspondingly increasing. His experience at this
time was exactly that of a devotee, who moved by a faith that God's
grace and protection are on him, feels an influx of extraordinary
strength and enthusiasm in his heart. But worldly-minded, as
Mathur was, with a predominance of Rajas in him, he remained
quite satisfied with rendering service to the Master and performing
virtuous acts. He never wished to advance far into the spiritual
realm. In spite of this limitation, Mathur was perfectly convinced
that the Master was the only source of his strength, his intelligence,
and his hope, that he alone was his prop and support in this world
and in the next, and that he was at the root of his worldly prosperity
and exalted position.

2. The undertakings that Mathur carried out at that time
prove that he now considered himself fully secure in his worldly
affairs through the grace of the Master. We read in the book
entitled "A story of the life of Rani Rasmani" that Mathuranath
performed the very expensive religious ceremony called the Annameru, consisting in the gift of a "mountain of food" and other
necessaries of life, in 1864 at Dakshineswar. Hriday said that
besides plentiful gold, silver, etc., he gave away to the Pandits
a thousand maunds of rice and an equal amount of sesame, and
appointed Sahachari, the well-known songstress, to sing the glory
of God, and Rajnarayan to sing the songs of Chandi, thus converting
the Kali temple into a festival ground for some time. Hriday
said further that Mathur saw the Master enter repeatedly into
ecstasy, listening to the highly devotional songs rendered by those
singers. In fact, he took the varying degrees of the Master's
appreciative reaction to be the measure of their talents and accordingly gave them as reward precious shawls, silks and hundreds
of rupees on that basis.

3. Attracted by the humility and the other virtues of Padmalochan, the then principal court-pandit of the Maharaja of Burdwan,

the Master had gone to see him some time before the gift of the "mountain of food" was made by Mathur. We were told by the Master that Mathur had a great desire to have that famous scholar brought to the meeting of the Pandits, convened at the time of that religious ceremony, and make him accept gifts. Knowing that the Pandit was greatly devoted to the Master, Mathur sent him an invitation through Hriday. But Padmalochan could not accept at that time the respectful invitation of Mathur. We have narrated in detail the story of Padmalochan elsewhere (III. 2).

4. The Master became attracted towards the disciplines of the Vaishnava doctrines after he had finished the Tantric ones. We find, as the result of our inquiries, some obvious reasons leading to that. First, the devout Bhairavi Brahmani was an expert in the disciplines of the Panchabhavas (the five spiritual moods) spoken of in the Vaishnava scriptures, and spent long periods of time in mastering one or other of them.   We have mentioned before that she fed the Master in the same affectionate spiritual attitude in which Yasoda used to feed her boy Gopala.   Therefore it is not improbable that she encouraged the Master to undertake the disciplines of the Vaishnava scriptures. Secondly, it was but natural for the Master, born as he was in a Vaishnava family, to have love for the disciplines and the spiritual moods of the Vaishnavas. He had had great opportunities for cultivating reverence for those Sadhanas which were prevalent at and around Kamarpukur. The third and the most important of those reasons, however, was that there was in the Master an extraordinary blend of the natures of both man and woman. Under the influence of one of them, he appeared to be the best of austere, valorous men, fearless like a lion, who would not rest satisfied without probing everything to the very bottom.   Under the influence of the other, he became possessed of a wonderful feminine nature, tender yet severe, applying himself to seeing and weighing things and persons in the world through his own heart.   He became by nature deeply attached to or detached from certain things and could bear with ease endless troubles when the heart responded, but unlike ordinary people he could do nothing when it did not do so.

5. During the first four years of the Master's spiritual practices when he did not accept any external help, he undertook the disciplines of the moods of Santa (peacefulness) and Dasya (servitude), and sometimes also of Sakhya (comradeship) like that of Sridama,

Sudama and other friends of Sri Krishna at Vraja, and attained success in all of them. The reader perhaps remembers that the Master had recourse to Dasya Bhava and passed some time in the mood of Mahavir to whom Ramachandra was as dear as life, and that he had the vision of Sita, Janaka's daughter, who suffered misery all her life. He, therefore, now applied his mind to the disciplines of the two principal devotional attitudes of Vatsalya (parental affection) and Madhura (conjugal love) practised by the Vaishnava teachers. During that period he looked upon himself as a woman friend of the Divine Mother, and engaged himself in fanning Her with a Chamara. Dressed in a woman's apparel and surrounded by ladies, he paid obeisance to the Devi during Her autumnal worship at the Calcutta house of Mathuranath, and on account of the absorption in feminine feelings, often forgot that he had a male body (III. 7). When we began to visit the holy feet of the Master at Dakshineswar, we sometimes saw this female nature manifested in him. But it did not then last so long as at the time we are speaking of. And there was no need of it; for, it then became easy for him, by the grace of the Divine Mother, to dwell at will in any mood whatsoever, of a man or a woman, or of non-duality, the source of all moods. He then stayed, for the good of the visiting devotees, in any of these particular moods as long as the spirit impelled him to do.

6. To form an adequate estimate of the great significance of the Sadhana period of his life, one has to take into account the great qualities inherent in him by birth, the way he reacted to the daily experiences as he moved about in life, and the nature of the change brought on him by the spiritual storm that raged in him during the past eight years of Sadhanas. We were told by him that he sincerely believed until he came to the Kali temple at Dakshineswar in the year 1855 and for some time afterwards, that he would lead, like his forefathers, the life of a strict and virtuous householder. As he was free from egoism from his birth, it never crossed his mind that he was superior to anyone in the world in any respect, or possessed nobler qualities than anyone. But his extraordinary speciality began to manifest itself when he stepped into the field of action. He felt as if an unknown, divine Power accompanied him every moment, painting in lurid colours the transitoriness and worthlessness of sights, tastes etc., before his eyes, and forcing him to orient his life in an opposite direction. A selfless seeker after

unalloyed truth, the Master very soon accustomed himself to move about in the world at the promptings of that Power. It is clear that it would have been difficult for him to do so, if he had a strong desire for attaining any objects of enjoyment in the world.

7. What we have said will become clear if one remembers the Master's lifelong behaviour on all matters. He discontinued his studies when he understood that the aim of the Brahmanas in acquiring this learning was only "bundling of rice and plantain", in other words, earning money. He accepted the post of a priest, thinking it would be of help in managing worldly affairs; but he soon realized that the aim of worshipping God was something quite different, viz., to see Him and live in Him; and at once he became mad after it. He knew that the realization of God depended on perfect self-control, and although married, he refrained from having any sexual relations with his wife through body, mind or speech. He understood that no man could have perfect reliance on God if he stored anything for future use, and at once he eradicated completely from his mind the idea of laying up even trifling things, not to speak of hoarding gold and other precious materials. Instances like these could easily be multiplied from his life. When one thinks of these facts, it becomes clear how little his mind was influenced by ingrained adverse tendencies that produce delusions in people's minds. The Master's power of grasping ideas and making them practical was so strong that no adverse tendency could stand against it and make him deviate from his path.

8. Besides, the Master was from his childhood a Srutidhara, a person of wonderful retentive memory, one who could repeat word for word in due order what he had heard but once and could retain it for ever. The reader already knows how in his childhood he, along with his friends, used to rehearse, in the fields and pastures of Kamarpukur, the songs, Yatras, and stories of the *Ramayana,* the *Mahabharata* and other texts, having listened to them but once. So we find that the Master entered on his life as a Sadhaka with three rare qualities—a memory with extraordinary powers, love of truth, and sincerity of purpose that would not stop without putting into practice an idea or principle that had been accepted as true and desirable by the mind. It is difficult for ordinary aspirants to acquire these qualities to any significant extent even after a whole life's effort. It was, therefore, no wonder that the Master attained in a short time to great success in his spiritual life.

The reason why we were amazed to hear that he succeeded in each of his disciplines even in three days, was that we did not then understand an iota of his uncommon mental constitution.

9. The reader will understand this better when we mention a few events of the Master's life. In the beginning of his spiritual practice, as soon as the Master discriminated between the real and the unreal and threw into the Ganga a few coins along with lumps of earth, repeating "rupee-earth, earth-rupee", the attachment to gold, which spreads its influence down to the very bottom of the human heart, became eradicated for ever from his mind. No sooner had he cleaned with his own hands those abominably filthy places, contacting which people ordinarily would not feel clean and purified without a bath, than his mind gave up the egoism arising from the consciousness of being a Brahmana by birth, and he became convinced for ever that he was in no way superior to those persons who were regarded in society as untouchables. As soon as he was convinced that he was a child of the Divine Mother and that "all the women of the world were parts of Her",[1] it became impossible for him to look upon any woman as other than an expression of the Divine Mother Herself, nor could he think of having conjugal relationship with any of them. When one ponders over these instances, one clearly feels that the Master could not have achieved those results if he had not had an extraordinary power of grasping ideas and making them practical. The reason why we cannot fully believe in these events of the Master's life, or feel astonished to hear of them, is the conspicuous absence of these qualities in ourselves. For example, if we look into our own hearts, we find that our attachment to gold will not vanish if we throw into water coins and lumps of earth a thousand times; that the egoism of our mind will not be washed off even if we clean dirty places innumerable times; and that the filial attitude towards every woman will not arise in our minds at the critical moment even if we are told all our lives of the truth of woman being a special manifestation of the Divine Mother. We cannot attain the results as the Master could in these matters in spite of our efforts, because our power of understanding ideas and making them practical is limited and obstructed by the impressions of our past Karmas. We enter the realm of Sadhana with minds devoid of self-control

---

[1] *Chandi*, 11.6.

and retentive power and containing all kinds of adverse traits.   And the results obtained too are correspondingly poor.

It is doubtful whether even in the course of four or five centuries there will come into the world one with a mind of such extraordinary powers as the Master's.   It is impossible for minds like ours even to imagine how unique his mind was—how by nature it was endowed with full self-control and perfect retentive power, how it was devoid of all evil traits, and how its extraordinary longing for the Divine Mother's vision, which displaced even the need for such vital concerns like food and sleep, heightened its natural power and insight.

10.   We have already said that the service of the Divine Mother in the temple at Dakshineswar was not in any way adversely affected by the death of Rani Rasmani.   Her successor Mathur, to whom Sri Ramakrishna was as dear as life, was not only not averse to spending the stipulated amount in Her service, but generously spent unusually large sums of money in addition at the Master's behest. Besides performing the services of deities, he was greatly fond of serving holy men.   For, owing to the teaching of the Master, Mathur, who had taken refuge at his feet, looked upon devout holy men as the veritable images of God.   Therefore, when the Master asked him to make arrangements for offering to the Sadhus articles of daily use like clothes, blankets, water-pots and other necessaries besides food, Mathur purchased and stored all of them in a room to its full capacity, so that they might be available for distribution to holy men at any time and in any quantity to their full satisfaction.   He told his officers that the articles in the new store should be distributed according to the Master's orders.   Again, when he came to know soon afterwards that a desire had arisen in the Master's mind to serve the devout holy men of all denominations by giving them articles useful to their spiritual practices, Mathur made due arrangements about it too (III. 2).   All these gifts were probably made in the year 1862-63, when the wonderful hospitality at the Kali temple of Rani Rasmani became widely known everywhere among the Sadhus.   Although, even during the Rani's lifetime, the Kali temple had been regarded by the travelling holy pilgrims as a resting place on their way to their destinations, its reputation now spread to a wider region, and devout monks, the foremost of all denominations, came there in large numbers. Pleased with the hospitality accorded to them, they went their

16

way blessing the manager for the services so devotedly rendered. We have recorded elsewhere, all that we were told by
the Master himself of the eminent holy men who came there in this
way. We mention it here again, only because we want to tell the
reader about the time of the arrival at Dakshineswar of the holy
man of the Ramawat denomination named "Jatadhari", by whom
the Master was initiated in the Mantra of Rama and from whom
he got the image of the child Rama called "Ramalala". It was
probably in the year 1864 that he came to the Master.

11. On many occasions we have heard from the Master
himself of Jatadhari's extraordinary love and attachment to Ramachandra. The image of the child Ramachandra was very dear to
him. Even before he came to Dakshineswar, long and devoted
worship of that image had brought him to a state of divine love
and inwardness which enabled him actually to see Rama as a
luminious child accepting all his services sanctified by intense
devotion. At first that vision appeared before him for a moment,
now and then, and overwhelmed him with bliss. But the more
he advanced in Sadhana with the passing of time, the more did the
vision become intense and continue for long periods, till at last it
became as vivid and continuous as ordinary objects of sight are.
Thus established in loving spiritual contemplativeness, he had the
child Rama for a constant companion almost. Engaging himself
daily in the services of that image of Ramalala, by means of which
he had come to realize that divine vision in his life, Jatadhari
travelled at pleasure to the various places of pilgrimage in India
and came to the Kali temple at Dakshineswar in the course of it.

12. Jatadhari, though applying himself wholeheartedly to
the service of Ramalala as a living presence, did not divulge to anyone the secret that he had the privilege of having every now and then
the vision of the form of the child Rama, the embodiment of love.
People could only see that he always served a metal image of a
child with extraordinary steadfastness every day. They knew
that much and nothing more. But the insight of the Master, the
matchless lord of the realm of spiritual moods, pierced the gross
external curtain at his very first meeting with Jatadhari and ascertained the hidden inward mystery. Therefore he had a great
respect for that monk and joyfully supplied him with all the articles
necessary for his service of Ramalala. Besides, the Master spent
long hours with him every day and devoutly witnessed his service

of Ramalala. The Master did so only because he, as we have said elsewhere (IV. 2), had the divine vision of Rama's celestial form, the embodiment of spiritual love, which Jatadhari also used to have. Accordingly the relation of the Master with Jatadhari gradually became intimate and respectful.

13. We have already mentioned that the Master spent some time in the mood of a woman to satisfy an urge to develop this aspect of his dual personality. Looking upon himself as the eternal female companion of the universal Mother, he applied himself wholly for a pretty long time to Her service. He would adorn and decorate Her with flower garlands prepared with his own hands and with new gold ornaments got ready by Mathur at his request, fan Her with a Chamara to cool Her person, and sing and dance before Her in a woman's dress to please Her. It is needless to say that the Master undertook to perform all these, because a strong urge to do so arose in his mind of its own accord.

14. The Master's love and devotion to Rama revived in the company of Jatadhari. The form that he now saw in the image under the revived impulse, was that of child Rama, the embodiment of spiritual love. Therefore, it is no wonder that his mind was now filled with maternal affection for that divine Child. The Master began to feel towards the divine Child that wonderful love and attraction which a mother feels towards her young child. That love and attraction alone, doubtless, made the Master now sit beside the child-image of Ramalala, and look at it so intently that he did not know how time slipped away. For, by means of various sweet childish pranks, the Master said, the extraordinary effulgent Child made him forget everything else, tried to detain him daily by His side, kept on watching him expectantly when he moved away, and accompanied him everywhere in spite of his request not to do so.

15. The active mind of the Master could not leave any work half done. This was true of him in regard to matters of the external world as also to the ideal realm of the spirit. It was seen that if any idea arose of its own accord in his heart, he could not rest satisfied without reaching its ultimate limits. On studying that nature of his, some readers may think, " But is it good ? Is it beneficial to a man to run in pursuit of any and every idea that may arise in his mind at any time and become a tool in its hands?" Although that nature of the Master did not lead him astray, it

should not be imitated by people in general inasmuch as all ideas, good and bad, arise in the minds of weak humanity. Man should never have such a faith in himself as to believe that only good ideas will arise in his mind. Therefore it should be the aim of man to rein in his desires. This is no doubt a reasonable argument, but there is another side to it on which we have something more to say.

16. We can by no means deny that the mind of a man, excessively desirous of enjoying sex and gold and completely fettered by them, should not repose so much faith in itself. Therefore, it is only the ignorant and the short-sighted who would question the need for people in general to control their desires. But with some rare Sadhakas, the Vedas and the other scriptures say, self-control becomes, by the grace of God, as normal a function as breathing. Therefore, completely freed from the attraction of lust and gold, their minds get converted into repositories of good and healthy ideas alone. The Master also said that no evil desire can, by the grace of the Divine Mother, raise its head and have mastery over the mind of a man who has taken perfect refuge in Her. He said, " Mother prevents him from taking a wrong step." A man who has reached such a state can perfectly trust each and every impulse of his; then it not only does him no harm but becomes a source of immense good to others. For, it becomes absolutely impossible for that man to seek his self-interest in that state, inasmuch as the little "I", which is born of the identification with the body, which produces selfishness and which remains ever unsatiated with worldly enjoyments, is merged for ever in the all-pervading "I" of God. Therefore the will of God, whose nature it is to do good to all, then manifests itself as various desires in the mind of that man for universal welfare. Or the Sadhaka, in that state, always feels in his heart of hearts, "I am the machine, Thou art the machinist"; and being sure that what appear as desires in his own mind are sprung from the will of God, the all-pervading Person, he does not at all hesitate to act according to their urge. The test of such inspired actions is that they always bring forth great benefits to others. Such a state comes very early in the lives of uncommonly great souls like the Master. Therefore these great souls, as we read in their biographies, trust completely the inclinations of their minds and very often undertake actions based on them without stopping to reflect and find reason therefor,

Keeping their little wills identified with the universal Will, they can always detect and understand things beyond the minds and intellects of ordinary people, inasmuch as the ideas that come up in their minds are eternal verities existing in a subtle state in the universal Mind.

17. Again, these great souls, although one with normal humanity, distinguish themselves from others by their absolute dependence on the universal Will and their freedom from fear and from pursuit of self-interest. So, unlike ordinary men, they are often seen to co-operate with circumstances and activities that cause their own destruction, in spite of their awareness of the ruinous consequences of such co-operation in advance. Not only do they show no aversion to them, but extend a joyous welcome. The reader will understand what we mean if we give a few examples. Conscious of the inevitability of Sita's banishment, Rama sent her away to the forest, though he knew that she was innocent. Though he knew that the forsaking of Lakshmana , who was dearer than his life, would inevitably bring his Lila as a human being to an end, he carried it out. Knowing beforehand that the race of Yadus, to which he belonged, would be destroyed, Krishna did not make the slightest attempt to prevent it.   On the contrary, he acted in such a way as to bring it about at the proper time. Again, knowing it for certain that he would meet with his death at the hands of the hunter, he concealed his whole body carefully behind the leaves of a tree and kept the two reddish feet dangling in such a way that, as soon as the hunter saw them, he mistook them for a bird and shot at them with his arrow. He then blessed and consoled the hunter, who was repenting of his mistake, and gave up his body.

Although he already knew that he would attain Parinirvana or bodilessness in the final beatitude if he accepted the hospitality of the Chandala, Buddha accepted it and ascended to that state having protected the Chandala by his blessing and consolation from others' hatred and reproach. Again, conscious that the religion preached by him would soon be polluted if he gave his approval to women's initiation into Sannyasa, he permitted the venerable Gautami, his aunt, to be so initiated.

In spite of knowing that Judas, his disciple, would betray him into the hands of the enemy who would put an end to his life, Jesus, another incarnation of God, remained uniformly affectionate to him.

18. We meet, on investigation, with many such events even in the lives of persons perfected and liberated in life, not to speak of the incarnations of God. If we try to find a rational reconciliation between such unusual expressions of personal effort so often seen in the lives of great men, with the theory of their absolute dependence on the universal will, we are inevitably led to the conclusion that their personal efforts are but the manifestations of the same all-pervading Will. Therefore it is clear that all the selfish impressions in the minds of these persons who depend absolutely on God's will, are destroyed once for all; their minds ascend to a holy plane of consciousness where pure desires alone, absolutely untarnished by selfishness, arise in them. So, freely reposing their faith in the desires of their minds and acting under their impulse, these Sadhakas, in that state, do not incur any blame. Such actions of the Master, it goes without saying, should not be imitated by ordinary people. But the Sadhakas, in the unique state mentioned above, will no doubt, be much enlightened by them in guiding their lives. The scriptures have compared their desires for eating, drinking, etc. which are necessary for the preservation of life, to fried seeds. Just as the roasted seeds of trees, creepers, etc., lose their vital power and cannot germinate, so the worldly desires of those persons, roasted over the fire of self-control and divine knowledge, can no more draw them towards enjoyment and lead them astray. The Master also has commented on this point thus, "Coming in contact with the philosopher's stone, a steel sword becomes golden; it retains unchanged its formidable form, but it can inflict no injury."

19. The seers of the Upanishads say that all the mental processes of the Sadhakas in that state correspond to facts. In other words, all the ideas arising naturally in their minds always prove to be objectively true and never otherwise. We could never have believed the above-mentioned words of the seers if we had not repeatedly tested the ideas of the Master established in Bhava-mukha and found them to be true. If he felt hesitation about taking any food, it was found on enquiry to have been polluted before. If he felt his power of speech failing him suddenly when he was about to give an advice on spiritual matters to anybody, it was proved that the said person was, in truth, completely unfit for it. If he felt that a certain person would not realize religious truths, or would realize but a few in this life, it actually came to happen

so. If any particular mood, or a particular form of a deity appeared in his mind when he saw a certain person, it was known that the said person was a Sadhaka of that mood, or worshipped that deity. If he suddenly said anything to any person under the influence of an inward mood, that person got much light by it and his life became altogether changed. Innumerable incidents of this type can be cited.

20. Urged by that irresistible inward devotional mood, the Master, as he used to do on many other occasions, now regarded himself as a woman both in body and mind and acted accordingly. So when he had the vision of Rama as a sweet child, he assumed the attitude of maternal affection towards Him. He had been, no doubt, initiated in the Mantra of Rama long ago in order to perform properly the worship and service of his family deity Raghuvir ; but he was not then attracted towards Him in any mood except that of a servant towards his Master. Having the above-mentioned new mood towards the deity, he now became anxious to be initiated by a Guru according to the scriptures in a Mantra befitting the new mood and to reach the ultimate limit of realization in that discipline. Perfected in the Mantra of the divine Child, Jatadhari came to know the eagerness of the Master and gladly initiated him in the Mantra of his own chosen Ideal. Merged in the Sadhana of that Mantra in the manner taught by him, the Master succeeded in the course of only a few days in having the divine vision of the child Rama constantly. Absorbed in the meditation of that divine form in the mood of maternal affection towards Him, he soon came to the realisation: "Rama, who is the son of Dasaratha, is in every being; the same Rama is immanent in the universe and yet transcends it." That is to say, Rama is not only Dasaratha's son but also exists as a Jiva in each body. Again, entering the universe and eternally manifesting Himself as it, He is ever existent in His own attributeless nature devoid of Maya and beyond everything in the universe. We heard the Master reciting on many occasions the Hindi couplet referred to above.

21. Besides initiating the Master in the Mantra, Jatadhari, before he went away, made a gift to the Master of the image of Ramalala, which he had served so long with a single-minded devotion. For, that living image expressed his desire to Jatadhari that he would henceforward live with the Master. We have described elsewhere (IV. 2) in detail the extraordinary Lila of that image

with the Master and Jatadhari. Therefore it is unnecessary to deal with that topic here.

22. When the Master applied his mind, in the aforesaid manner, to perfecting his Vatsalya devotion and experienced its ultimate result, the Bhairavi Brahmani was staying at Dakshineswar. We were told by the Master himself that she was as highly experienced in the disciplines of the Panchabhavas spoken of in the Vaishnava books, as she was in those of the Tantras. Did the Master receive any particular help from her while practising the Vatsalya and Madhura Bhavas? We have not clearly heard anything about it from him. But we were told by the Master and Hriday that established in the mood of maternal affection towards God, the Brahmani treated the Master as Gopala, the child Krishna. Therefore it is inferred that the Master got at least some help from her, both at the time when he assumed the mood of maternal affection towards the child Rama and had the ultimate experience in that mood, and when he practised Madhura Bhava, the sweet mood, in which he adopted the attitude of a woman towards her lover. One might doubt whether he actually got any particular help from her; but this much is admitted without doubt, that a strong desire to practise the disciplines of those moods arose in his mind when he saw the Brahmani engaged in them and heard her eulogize them.

CHAPTER XIII

THE ESSENCE OF THE MADHURA BHAVA
(SWEET MOOD)

(TOPICS; 1. The inward struggle of the aspirant. 2. Nirvikalpa Samadhi and extraordinary Sadhakas. 3. Sunya and
Purna, the same. 4. Nature of Non-duality. 5. The five moods
and God-realisation. 6. How the moods help man to progress.
7. Love and the personality of God. 8. Love and eradication
of power-consciousness. 9. Self-sufficiency of each mood.
10. Attainment of Non-duality through the moods. 11. Sadhanas
of different moods in different ages. 12. Development
of the five moods in India and abroad. 13. Indications of
the depth of the moods. 14. Uniqueness of the Master's
success in all the moods. 15. Lack of records on the spiritual
practices of the spiritual giants of the past. 16. Proof of this.
17. Madhura Bhava and Vaishnava teachers. 18. On the historicity of the Lila at Vrindavan. 19. What the Master said
about this. 20. Chaitanya and Madhura Bhava. 21. Chaitanya and contemporary spiritual conditions. 22. Main point
of the Madhura Bhava. 23. Love for God as for a paramour.
24. Madhura Bhava as more than the aggregate of all other
moods. 25. Chaitanya's service through Madhura Bhava.
26. Vedantins and Madhura Bhava. 27. Madhura Bhava and
the loving mood of Radha.)

1. It is well-nigh impossible for one who is not a Sadhaka to
enter into the spirit of the actions and experiences of Sadhakas and
arrive at a proper understanding of the same, for it is a matter
of the spirit, outside the field of the gross and deluding sense objects.
There the time sequence, which has reference to events and objects
of sense life, cease to have any significance. Thus the frantic
efforts of competitive life, which are born of man's lower nature
but wrongly interpreted as greatness and heroism by worldly people,
have no relevance. The only significant entities there are the
aspirant's mind and the endless currents of impressions stored up
in it from experiences of past lives. Attraction for high ideals
and an ultimate goal, born of dissatisfaction generated by the
conflicts of external life, is the guiding factor there. There is also

the consequent presence of the struggle against adverse impressions of the past — struggles which derive an added power from these very efforts of theirs to overcome them. Next, the life of a Sadhaka is characterised by a resolute attempt at continually diving deeper and deeper into one's own personality by turning the mind inward and away from the senses. Mining, as it were, into the deeper and deeper strata of the inner world, the Sadhaka experiences subtler and subtler realms of ideas until at last he strikes the Ground of his existence and remains one with it — the immutable reality without a second, which is devoid of sound, touch and form, and from which all ideas including his I-sense spring and have their being. This is the experience of Samadhi. If the subtle impressions of the mind have not been completely eradicated, a trace of ignorance is still left, and consequently the Sadhaka comes down from Samadhi, to experience the external world again by reversing the process through which it attained the immediate knowledge of the non-dual Reality. Thus does the mind of the aspirant continue to descend from the superconscious to the normal consciousness and again ascend from it to the superconscious, over and over again.

2. But the history of the spiritual world from the most ancient times to the present day has also on record the description of a few minds whose natural state appeared to be the plane of superconsciousness, but who somehow kept themselves forcibly confined for some time to the plane of the external world for the good of humanity. The more we study the history of Sri Ramakrishna's spiritual strivings, the more shall we understand that his mind belonged to this class. If that conviction is not produced in the minds of the readers from a study of this book, the shortcomings of the author should be held responsible for it; for the Master said to us repeatedly, "I hold forcibly to one or two trifling desires, with the help of which I keep the mind weighted down for you all; otherwise its natural inclination is to remain united and identified with the indivisible One."

3. Some of the ancient seers have described the indivisible non-dual Reality experienced in Samadhi as the ' Void' (Sunya, the great Emptiness of Being) and others as the 'Full' (Purna, the Plenitude of Being). As a matter of fact, both of them imply the same experience. For they have described It as the One from which all things come into being and in which they merge. The

Reality that has been called by the Buddha as the "Void" (the Sunya), in which all beings get extinguished, has been described by Sankara as the "Full", (the Purna), which constitutes the unmodified substratum of them all. If we leave aside the opinions of the later Buddhist teachers and study Buddha and Sankara, we irresistibly come to this conclusion.

4. The plane of the non-dual consciousness implied in the concepts of the "Void" and the "Full" has been described in the Upanishads or the Vedanta, as the state beyond all ideation. For, perfectly established in it, the mind of the aspirant transcends the limits of all other planes of consciousness produced by God's play of creation, preservation and dissolution, and merges in homogeneity. Therefore, the non-dual state of consciousness is something non-relational, different from the five moods, such as the Santa, Dasya, etc., with the aid of which the limited human mind enters the spiritual realm and becomes bound up with God in an eternal relation. Only when man becomes absolutely indifferent to all kinds of enjoyment, whether of this world or of the next, and attains on the strength of purity, a position higher than that of the gods, he comes to the non-dual mood. With the help of this he realizes the attributeless Brahman, in which the whole universe together with God, its creator, preserver and destroyer, has its eternal being and on the attainment of which the acme of life is reached.

5. Leaving aside the non-dual mood and the attributeless Brahman attainable with its help, we find the aspirants of Bhakti cults speaking of the manifestation of the "five moods" (Panchabhava)—namely, Santa (placid attitude), Dasya (a servant's attitude), Sakhya (comradely attitude), Vatsalya (parental attitude), and Madhura (conjugal attitude). The object attainable through each of these is Brahman with attributes, or Isvara, who is all-controlling, all-powerful and by nature eternally pure, awakened and free. The aspirant tries to know Him in the relation corresponding to one or the other of these moods he assumes himself. And He, the Lord, who is the inner controller of all beings and the repository of all moods, sees the single-minded devotion of the aspirant, and in order to help him in developing the mood, reveals Himself to him in the form appropriate to it and thus blesses him. It is thus that God, who is pure consciousness, assumes in different ages various forms that are the embodiments of these different

moods. He, we read in the scriptures, incarnates Himself even as a man to fulfil the desires of the devotees.

6. The five moods are the subtle and purified forms of those mundane relations by which human beings are bound to one another in their daily lives. We are conscious of particular relations with father, mother, husband, wife, male friend, female friend, master, servant, son, daughter, king, subject, teacher, disciple and so on, and we feel also that, with the exception of enemies, we should behave towards all others in a calm and respectful attitude of mind. The teachers of Bhakti have classified those relations into five divisions of the Santa and the rest mentioned above, and advised people to take up one or another of these moods for practice and establish themselves in a loving relationship with the Divine. For, it is easy for Jivas to try to know God with the help of these five moods, the nature of which is already known to them in their worldly relationships. That is not all. Those moods, which, while based on the worldly relations rooted in desires produce only aversion, attachment and other similar modifications that impel men to commit various evil actions, will now, when oriented towards God, help the aspirants advance towards the realization of God by their irresistible original impetus without their worldly corruption. Take for example, lust, which is a disease, so to say, of the heart and the cause of all misery,—when directed to God, it will manifest as desire for God-vision. The aspirant's anger will now be directed against the things and persons that are obstacles on the path to that vision. They will now become mad after, and infatuated with, the enjoyment of the wonderful beauty and love of God. Noticing the unique splendour of spirituality in persons who have succeeded in attaining the holy vision of God, the culmination of blessedness, they will now become anxious to have it themselves.

7. We cannot say with any certainty that the teachings on these five moods of loving relation to God were promulgated by any particular teacher at any particular time. But many great souls appeared in India, this great hermitage of the world, at different times and engaged themselves in practices for the realization of God through one, two or more of these moods, and having made the Lord their own by means of their extraordinary love, taught men to do likewise. When we study the unique lives of these teachers, it becomes clear that only the love for God is at the root of the Sadhanas of those moods and that the said love has always for

its object one or other of the numerous expressions of the personal aspect of God; for, as long as man does not experience the non-dual Reality, so long is he bound to have the conception and experience of God only as Person.

8. When we study the progress of love between two lovers, we find how it obliterates the distance and difference created by their respective positions and powers in their worldly situation. Similarly, love removes by degrees from the mind of the spiritual aspirant engaged in the Sadhana of any of these moods, his consciousness of God's unlimited powers, and teaches him to regard God as but his beloved according to his particular mood. Therefore the aspirant treading this path makes Him entirely his own by means of love, and does not at all hesitate to request, importune, or even scold Him out of his sense of loving intimacy with Him. The more the practice of one of these five moods enables the aspirant to forget the powers of God and experience nothing else but His love and sweetness, the more exalted is it regarded in this Sadhana of moods. It is only from this point of view that the teachers of Bhakti have ascribed superiority or inferiority to each of these five moods, and have assigned the highest place to the Madhura Bhava; otherwise each one of them is, as those teachers have unanimously admitted, capable of making the aspirant realize God.

9. It is known from the study of the history of religions that, with the ultimate development of any of the five moods, the aspirant forgets himself and feels happy when the object of his love is happy. Absorbed in the thought of Him during the time of separation from Him, he sometimes loses even the consciousness of his own existence. From the study of devotional books like the *Bhagavata*, it is seen that not only did the Gopis of Vraja forget in this way their own existence but actually felt on occasions identified with their beloved Krishna. It is well known from the devotional books of the Christians that, absorbed in the thought of the Passion of Christ, some mystics bore the stigmata and bled from those marks on their bodies.[1] Therefore we find that with the final development of each one of the five moods, the aspirant becomes absorbed in the thought of his or her object of love, and united and identified with Him under the strong impulse of love, realizes the non-dual

---

[1] *Vide* Life of St. Francis of Assisi, and of St. Catherine of Sienna.

state of consciousness. Sri Ramakrishna's unique life of spiritual striving has thrown wonderful light on this matter. He practised each of the five moods of spiritual love, and in each of them he became merged in the object of his love, and absolutely forgetting his own existence realized the non-dual Reality.

How, it may be asked, can the human mind experience, with the help of these moods, the reality of Non-duality, which is beyond all moods? For no mood can ever rise, exist or develop in the human mind without the consciousness of two persons.

10. Quite true. But the more a mood develops, the more does it spread its own influence and remove gradually from the aspirant's mind all contrary ideas. Again, when it is fully developed, the concentrated mind of the aspirant sometimes in meditation forgets 'I' (the servant) and 'Thou' (the Master) as also the relation between them, and remains perfectly identified through love with the Reality denoted by the word Thou. The human mind, the eminent teachers of India say, is not simultaneously conscious of I and Thou and the loving relation between them. It knows the entity denoted by the word 'Thou' one moment and that denoted by the word 'I' the next moment; but as the mind oscillates quickly between the ideas of these two entities, there develops in it an idea of a relation between them. It then seems to be simultaneously conscious of these two entities and the relation between them. But when the restlessness of the mind is destroyed by the influence of the matured mood of love, it gradually becomes able to detect what has been said above. The more the functioning of the mind is stilled at the time of meditation, the more does it understand by degrees that it saw the one non-dual Reality from two angles of vision and mistook it for two independent entities.

11. One is simply amazed to think what vast periods of time and what superhuman efforts of numberless aspirants were necessary for the full development of each of the moods through which the human mind was enabled to realize the non-dual Reality. When we study the history of religions as embodied in the scriptures, it becomes clear that a particular mood became the principal prop of the human mind during meditation in a particular age; and with the help of it many eminent aspirants of that age realized God and a rare few gained the immediate knowledge of the non-dual reality of Brahman. In the Vedic and the Buddhistic ages we find the ascendency of the Santa mood culminating in the experience

of Non-duality. The Dasya and the Apatya[1] moods are found to prevail in the Upanishadic age. The Santa and the Dasya moods mixed with motiveless action is the special feature of the epic period. A blend of the Apatya with partial Madhura is witnessed in the Tantric age. And the moods of Sakhya, Vatsalya and Madhura are seen to flourish in all their exuberance in the Vaishnava age.

12. In the religious history of India we find all these five moods fully developed and flourishing side by side with the experience of non-dual consciousness. But this is not so among the religious communities in other parts of the world. Among them, only the Santa, Dasya and Apatya moods are found to have flourished. Though the songs of King Solomon, the royal sage, expressing the friendly and sweet moods in relation to God are intact in the Jewish, Christian and Muslim communities, the members of these communities are unable to understand the import of those songs, and attribute a different meaning to them. The moods of Sakhya and Madhura are, it goes without saying, extant to a great extent in the Sufi community professing Islam, yet the generality of the Muslims regard such worship of God as contrary to the precepts of the Koran. Again although the Catholic Christian community pays homage to Mary, the mother of Christ, it is far from the recognition of the Motherhood of God. It has, therefore, not been as fruitful as the worship of the universal Mother extant in India; for it has not enabled the aspirant to realize the indivisible Existence-Knowledge-Bliss Absolute and to experience the divine manifestation in all women without exception. The current of the idea of the Motherhood of God has disappeared midway like the river Phalgu.[2]

13. When the mind of the aspirant is attracted to God with the aid of some loving mood, it becomes, as we have said before, gradually absorbed in that mood, turns away from the external world and merges itself in the Self. At the time of the mind's merging, its past impressions stand in its way and try to make it swim on the surface, pushing it upwards again and again. Therefore ordinary human minds, with a load of powerful past impressions, cannot generally become absorbed even in one mood in spite

---

[1] Apatya, i.e., the mood of looking upon God as father or mother, here as father.—Tr.

semi-mythical river.—Tr.

of striving for a whole life. When that happens, they at first become discouraged and give up the effort and at last, losing faith in the gospel of spiritual realisation itself, come to regard the enjoyment of sights, tastes, etc., of the external world to be the only thing worth having, and pursue the same with avidity. Aversion for outward things, absorption in the meditation of the object of devotional love, and the ecstasy produced by one's spiritual mood are, therefore, regarded in the sphere of this form of Sadhana as the measure of the aspirant's progress towards the goal.

14. It is difficult for one who has not attempted to cultivate any of these moods to understand the enormity of the inward struggle that an aspirant has to undergo in facing the strong obstacles caused by the manifestation of past impressions buried in the layers of the mind. Only one who has had the experience of these difficulties and sufferings involved, will feel astonished at the rapidity with which Sri Ramakrishna was able to get his mind absorbed in mood after mood. Also, he alone can appreciate the idea that the Master's mind must have been something more than human to have done so.

15. Is it because of the incapacity of the ordinary human mind to understand the subtle truths of the spiritual realm that the history of the Sadhanas of these spiritual heroes, who are known as the incarnations of God, has not been adequately recorded? For, all we get in recorded histories about them is concerned with their impressive acts of renunciation before they embark on the life of Sadhana, and with the wonderful powers they manifest after their Sadhanas in redeeming man from ignorance and worldly entanglements. We find in them very little record of the extraordinary inward struggle they must have engaged themselves in during the period of their Sadhanas for destroying and uprooting the deep impressions of their minds and for securing mastery over themselves. Or, that struggle has been described in such histories with the help of metaphors and hyperboles in such a way that it has now become quite impossible for us to separate the grain of truth from the chaff of descriptive extravagances.

16. The reader will understand what we mean when we give a few examples. Sri Krishna was engaged on many occasions in performing austerities with a view to acquiring particular powers for the purpose of doing good to humanity. But no description of the succession of the moods of his mind is found except that he

remained for some time standing on one leg, living on water or air alone.

We do not get as detailed an account of Buddha's Sadhanas as of his detachment from the world, of his leaving home for the purpose of becoming an anchorite and, afterwards, of his establishing the Dharmachakra, the wheel of religion. However, a little of the history of his spiritual moods is available, unlike in the case of other spiritual heroes. It is recorded that abstaining from food and drink and taking a firm resolve to succeed, he was engaged in practising austerity and meditation for six long years without leaving his seat, and that controlling the internal vital forces and practising meditation, he entered into Samadhi. His biographer has also tried to vivify his struggle against the latent impressions of the mind by introducing the story of his fight with Mara (the Buddhistic Satan).

The history of the striving of Jesus is also not available. After recording a few events of Jesus' life till he was twelve, his biographer has described how, in his thirtieth year, Jesus was baptised by John, a perfect holy man, and entered alone a lonely desert where he practised austerity and meditation for forty days; how, though tempted by Satan, he came out victorious and returned from there; and how at last he engaged himself in doing good to humanity. He continued to be in the gross body for three years only after that event. There are, therefore, no records whatever of how he spent his time from the twelfth to the thirtieth year of his life.

Although a good deal of the sequence of events in Sankara's life is found, one has very often only to infer the history of the moods of his mind.

Many events of the Sadhana of Chaitanya are found recorded; the story of his exalted love of God, devoid of the slightest tinge of desire, has been described in a way unintelligible to the ordinary minds, in the form of metaphors with the help of the stories of the love between Radha and Krishna and their separation from each other. And it has to be admitted that Chaitanya and his chief companions have recorded in some detail, though in metaphorical language, the changes that came upon the mind of the aspirant from the inception to almost the ultimate perfected state of each of the spiritual moods of Sakhya, Vatsalya and Madhura, with especial emphasis on the last. But they have not given out the ultimate truth that when the aspirant's mind becomes completely

17

absorbed in any of the aforesaid three moods, it experiences its oneness with the object of its love and merges in the non-dual Reality.
The unique life of Sri Ramakrishna and the extraordinary history
of his Sadhana have taught us that ultimate truth very clearly in the
modern age and enabled us to understand that all the religious
moods of all the religious communities of the world bring the mind
of the aspirant to one and the same goal. Leaving aside all the
other things that may be learnt from his life, it may be said here
that the whole world is undoubtedly indebted to him for all time
for the all-inclusive catholicity of his spiritual vision establishing
the truth of all religions.

17. The Madhura Bhava is said to be the greatest contribu-
tion of the Vaishnava teachers like Chaitanya to the spiritual world.
Had they not preached it, many people would have been without a
means to God-realization and the peace and bliss resulting from it.
They were the first to understand that the Vrindavan Lila of Sri
Krishna was not acted in vain, and also to make efforts to explain
it to others. But for the advent of Chaitanya, Vrindavan would
have been regarded as an ordinary forest.

18. Endeavouring, in imitation of the West, to record only
outward events, the historians of the modern age will say, "But
there is no evidence that the play of Vrindavan actually took place
as you say. Therefore, don't you see that so much of your joy
and sorrow, and the moods including the Mahabhava, are all without a basis?" The Vaishnava teachers would say in reply, "Can you,
on your part, produce sure evidence that these incidents mentioned
in the Puranas did not take place? Until we are convinced that
your historians have explored the history of these ancient ages
thoroughly, we would maintain that your doubts in regard to these
incidents mentioned in the Puranas are unjustified and invalid.
Moreover, even if you should ever produce such proof, our faith
will be unaffected. It will not affect at all the eternal play of the
Lord in the eternal Vrindavan. That mystic divine play will
remain eternally in the ideal spiritual realm. If you want to witness
the truth of this play of love between Radha and Krishna, you can
do so in the realm of spiritual consciousness; but before that, you
will have to make yourself fit for the same, first of all by eliminating
every vestige of lust from your body, mind and speech, and learn
to perform selfless service by following in the footsteps of any one
of the female friends of Srimati Radha. You will then see that

Sri Vrindavan, the playground of Sri Hari, is eternally there in your heart and that the said play is being enacted within you every day."

19.   He who has not learnt how to be independent of the external events and how to study with a pure heart the history of the devotional moods by a thorough acceptance of the ideal world as real, will never be able to enjoy the beauty and sweetness of His play at Vrindavan.   While Sri Ramakrishna was describing that play of the Divine with great enthusiasm to the English-educated young men who were with him, he found that they did not relish it, whereupon he said, "Why don't you mark and grasp the attraction of Srimati's heart for Krishna in that divine play?   When one has that kind of attraction for God, one realizes Him.   Just see how mad the Gopis were for Krishna, renouncing their all—husbands, children, family and propriety of conduct, honour and dishonour, shame and aversion, fear of public opinion and of society and so on!   When one can be so, one realizes the divine Lord."   "If," continued he, "one is not free from the least tinge of lust, one cannot understand the spiritual mood of Radha, the embodiment of Mahabhava.   As soon as they saw Krishna, the embodiment of Existence-Knowledge-Bliss, the Gopis felt a joy in their hearts, tens of millions of times greater than sexual pleasure; they then lost their body-consciousness.   Ah, could the idea of the sex-enjoyment by the contemptible body cross their minds then? Divine light, coming out of Sri Krishna touched their bodies producing in every pore of their bodies, infinitely greater pleasure, than that of sexual enjoyment."

At one time Swami Vivekananda raised an objection in regard to the historicity of the play of Radha and Krishna at Vrindavan and made an attempt to disprove its authenticity.   The Master said in reply, "Very well, let us take for granted that there was never any one called Radha and that some loving Sadhaka had an imaginary conception of Radha's personality.   But while picturing that character, the Sadhaka, you must admit, had to lose himself completely in Radha's mood, and thus to become Radha.   It is thus true that the play at Vrindavan was thus enacted in the outer world also."

Indeed, though innumerable objections regarding the divine Lord's play of love at Vrindavan may be raised, the Madhura Bhava, first discovered by the Vaishnava teachers led by Chaitanya and others and manifested in their pure lives, will remain eternally true. At all times the aspirant qualified for it will attain the hallowed vision of the divine Lord, feel blessed by looking on Him as husband and himself as wife, and with the final development of that mood, be also established in the pure, non-dual Brahman Itself.

20. Although for women it is easy and natural to attribute the role of the husband to the divine Lord and undergo the discipline accordingly, it appears to be unnatural for those who have male bodies. The question, therefore, naturally arises in one's mind why Chaitanya introduced such an unbecoming discipline in the world. It has to be said in reply that all the actions of the incarnations of an age are done for the good of humanity. That path of Sadhana was introduced by Sri Chaitanya for the same purpose. He made the aspirants advance on the path of the Madhura Bhava, keeping in mind the spiritual ideal which the aspirants of those times were for long eager to realize. It cannot be that the eternally perfect Chaitanya, an incarnation of God, engaged himself in practising that mood for his own good and established it as a perfect ideal in society. Sri Ramakrishna said, "Just as the external teeth (tusks) of elephants are for attacking their enemies, and the internal ones for masticating food and maintaining their bodies, so two kinds of moods were manifested in Sri Chaitanya, the one inward and the other outward. He did good to humanity with the help of the outward mood of Madhura Bhava, and being himself established in Brahman, the fruition of the love for God, enjoyed personally the immense bliss in the inward mood of Non-duality."

21. Historians say that there arose in this country teachers of the Vajra-yana at the end of the Buddhistic Age. They preached that having attempted to realize Nirvana, the final beatitude, and having almost been freed from the clutches of desires, the human mind went forward to merge in the great Void with the help of meditation. But then "Niratma", the goddess of non-existence, appeared before it and, instead of allowing it to do so, kept it united with her own body. Thus, though the gross body in which the aspirant enjoyed worldly objects did not then exist, she made him daily enjoy the aggregate of the essences of sensuous pleasures, inasmuch as he was even then possessed of a subtle body. Therefore it was no wonder that the doctrine that this sect preached, namely, the attainment of the subtle enjoyment of the ideal world by the

renunciation of the enjoyment of gross objects, should have become distorted in later ages; that the attainment of the constant enjoyment of the gross objects should have been regarded as the goal of religion; and that it should have resulted in the wide prevalence of loose sex relationship in the country.   At the time of the advent of Chaitanya, the uneducated people of the country adopted that distorted Buddhistic doctrine and were divided into various secret sects.   The pure Vamachara, spoken of in the Tantras, became distorted even among most of the higher classes, and the quest for the miraculous powers and enjoyment of sensuous pleasure by the motivated worship of, and meditation on, the universal Mother came into vogue.   In the midst of these cults, aspirants who wanted to attain to divine bliss by following any of the pure spiritual moods, found themselves forlorn without guidance.   It was in this situation that Sri Chaitanya appeared.   He at first placed before those aspirants the ideals of extraordinary renunciation and detachment by practising them in his own life, and afterwards pointed out that if one became pure and holy and looked upon oneself as a woman and upon God as one's husband, one can truly realize the unlimited divine bliss in the subtle ideal world.   Moreover, he preached the glory of God's names to the people in general and induced them to repeat continually His names and sing aloud His praise.   Many Buddhistic sects that had not got corrupted and fallen from the ideal were thus placed by his grace on the true spiritual path again.   Though the groups of the followers of the distorted Vamachara at first opposed him openly, they felt the extraordinary attraction of the unique ideal of his life, became self-denying and tried to have the vision of the universal Mother through motiveless worship.   Therefore, while recording the events of the extraordinary life of Chaitanya, some writers wrote that the Buddhists, the upholders of the doctrine of the Void, also rejoiced at the time of his birth.[1]

22.   Sri Krishna, the supreme Self, the embodiment of Existence-Knowledge-Bliss, is the only Purusha,[2] the Male Principle, and

---

[1] *Chaitanya-mangala.*

[2] Purusha = Existence-Knowledge-Bliss as the subject, the knower, the enjoyer; Prakriti = Existence-Knowledge-Bliss as the object, the known, the enjoyed. Existence-Knowledge-Bliss Absolute means pure or absolute consciousness, when the will (which, being a mode of consciousness, is not anything other than consciousness), is not active or is

all the Jivas and creatures, both gross and subtle, are parts of Prakriti, the embodiment of supreme love, and are therefore, His
wives. So, if the Jivas become pure and holy and whole-heartedly
worship Him as their husband, they attain by His grace, liberation
and the state of unending and unalloyed Bliss, which is their goal
and their highest fulfilment. This is the long and short of the
Madhura Bhava preached by Chaitanya. All the other devotional
moods are included in the one great mood, the Mahabhava, of
which the chief Gopi, Radha, is the embodiment. Each of the
other Gopis is an embodiment of one, two or more moods comprising the great mood. The aspirant is thus enabled to master
the moods constituting the Mahabhava by engaging himself in
Sadhana in imitation of the Gopis of Vraja, and at last he becomes
blessed with a flash of the great Bliss arising from the great mood.
The ultimate aim of an aspirant on this path is to become happy
in all respects at the happiness of Krishna, by giving up all desires
for his or her own happiness once for all, through the contemplation of the mood of Radha, the embodiment of the Mahabhava.[3]

23. The love between a pair of lovers, married according
to the rules of society, flows restrained by external conditions such
as birth, family, virtuous conduct, fear of society and public opinion.
Such a pair live within the bounds of these rules and undergo
sacrifices for each other's happiness, keeping in mind various things

not cognized. When the will is active or is cognized, the same pure
consciousness appears, or is viewed as split in two, the subject and the
object, and is talked of in terms of love, with emphasis on the bliss-
aspect.—Tr.

[3] The state in which one fears lest any harm should befall Krishna,
even when he is happy, and hence cannot remain patient for even a
moment, is the Rudha stage of the Mahabhava, i.e., the stage in which
the Sattvika Vikaras have reached almost the highest point. The Adhi-
rudha stage of the Mahabhava is the highest point of the Rudha stage;
it is that stage of bliss and pain, arising respectively from the union
with, and separation from, Krishna, of which all the happiness existing
in crores of universes and also the pain produced by the biting of all
the snakes and the stinging of all the scorpions, are just a drop in the
ocean, so to say. The last mentioned state of the Mahabhava has two
characteristics; first, Modana i.e., gladness to be found in the friends
of Radha only. Secondly, Madana, 'inebriation' which is the most
complete efflorescence of all the Sattvika emotions and bodily changes
to be found only in Radha.)

—The *Bhakti-granthavali* of Sri Chakravarty.

that should or should not be done.   Desirous of properly observing
the hard and fast social rules, the married woman does not hesitate
on many occasions to check or limit her relation of love with her
husband.   But the loving behaviour of a paramour is different.
On account of the impulse of love, such a woman very often dis-
regards all social conventions and does not hesitate to unite with
her lover even at the cost of all social security.   The Vaishnava
teachers have advised the aspirants to assume for themselves that
all-devouring loving relation towards God.   Therefore, though
Radha, the supreme lady of Vrindavan, is the married wife of Ayan
Ghosh, she has been described as one who renounced her all for the
love of Krishna.

24.   The Vaishnava teachers have described the Madhura
Bhava as the aggregate of the essences of the other four moods and
something more.   For the loving woman serves her lover like a
slave, gives good counsel under all circumstances like a friend,
feels happy at his happiness and miserable at his afflictions, engages
herself like a mother in nourishing his body and mind, and thinks
of his welfare in all respects.   Thus wholly effacing her own personality, she occupies herself in entertaining her lover and in every
way bringing joy and comfort to him, thus keeping him flooded
with extraordinary peace and bliss.   The woman who forgets
herself under the influence of love and keeps a perfect eye on the
welfare and the happiness of her lover is described in the devotiona!
books as the Samartha "the excellent" and her love as the best.
All the other kinds of love, tarnished with a tinge of selfishness,
have been assigned to two other classes, viz. Samanjasa "the balanced" and Sadharani "the common".   The woman of the former
class minds her own happiness to the same extent as her lover's
and she of the latter class regards her lover as dear for the sake
of her own happiness only.

25.   Be that as it may, Chaitanya preached the glory of the
names of God and taught the aspirants to guide their lives according to the ideal of austere renunciation and place themselves, in
respect of love, in the position of the beloved of Krishna, and thus
tried to stem the tide of sensuality prevalent in the society at that
time.   His mode of devotion and instruction to the aspirants,
did endless good to humanity. It showed the right path to those
who went astray, brought into the bounds of a new society those
who were excommunicated and who were living outside the pal

of the castes, embracing them all within a new caste called the "devotees of God", and held the high and pure ideal of renunciation and detachment before all the communities. However, that is not all. He proved beyond doubt that all the mental and physical changes called the "eight Sattvika Vikaras"[1] (whose Tamasika counterparts are produced by the love and union of ordinary pairs of lovers) actually came on the aspirant of pure mind in virtue of the intense meditation and contemplation on the Divine Husband, the Lover of the Universe. This converted, at that time, the Alankara Sastra, the science of rhetoric, into a spiritual scripture, and giving the sensual poetic and dramatic literature the colour of spiritual love, made it palatable to spiritual aspirants and conducive to their progress. It thus made the path of Sadhana easy for them. It brought poetry and romance into the life of the aspirant, besides making it easy for him to love the Lord as one's 'own', as his nearest and dearest one. It enabled him to sublimate the baser passions like lust and anger by directing them towards the Lord, unlike in the practice of the Santa-bhava, the mood of calmness, in which the passions are merely avoided or shunned.

26. Although in the eyes of some modern critics, the Madhura Bhava appears to be unnatural and unbecoming for those who have male bodies, it does not take long for a Vedantin to ascertain its proper value. He knows that as the result of a very long habit, all thoughts are converted into Samskaras in the human mind, and that it is owing to these impressions that man perceives the diversities of the universe, which really is the one non-dual Brahman. If he can, by the grace of God, really look upon the universe as non-existent this very moment, he will experience its immediate disappearance into the Void. The universe exists for a man only because he thinks it exists. I am a man, only because I look upon myself as one, and another is a woman because she regards herself as a woman. Again, it is a matter of daily experience that, when one mood becomes predominant in the human mind, it veils and

---

[1]The Sattvika changes are those that produce an emotional convulsion in the body and the mind. They are eight in number, namely, motionlessness, perspiration, horripilation, indistinctness of utterance, tremor, paleness, tears, and loss of consciousness. They are arranged in five grades, according as they give greater and greater enjoyments, taking their nomenclature from the blazing of fire, viz., smoking, smouldering, flaming, glowing and being incandescent.

gradually destroys all the other contrary ones. Therefore, an aspirant's effort to veil and gradually destroy all the other moods of his mind through the dominance of Madhura Bhava, is looked upon by the Vedantin as similar to the effort of "removing the thorn in one's foot with another". The consciousness of "I am possessed of a body", which is the basis of all other impressions of the human mind, and the firm belief, "I am a man or a woman", on account of one's connection with that body, are the two most dominant tendencies in the mind of man. When the male aspirant is able to forget his male nature by attributing the nature of the husband to the divine Lord and that of the wife to himself, he, it is needless to say, can very easily throw off as well the mood "I am His wife" and reach the state beyond all moods. Therefore a Vedantin finds it quite reasonable that an aspirant, when perfect in the discipline of the Madhura Bhava, should arrive very near the plane transcending all moods.

27.   Is the aim of the aspirant, it may be asked, the realization of the devotional mood of Radha? The Vaishnava teachers, however, do not advocate the practice of it. They maintain that the mood of only a friend of Radha is attainable and not that of her own. Still it has to be inferred that the latter is the ultimate aim of the aspirant. For, the difference between the mood of Radha and that of her friends is only one of degree and not of kind. Like Radha, her friends also worshipped Krishna, the embodiment of Existence-Knowledge-Bliss, as their husband and tried to bring about the union between Radha and Krishna in order to make the latter happy, inasmuch as He, they saw, felt most happy when united with her. Again, we see that, although Rupa, Sanatana, Jiva and other early Vaishnava teachers spent their lives at Vrindavan in the service of the different images of Krishna, they did not install an image of Radha by the side of Krishna. It is inferred that they did not do so, only because they considered themselves to be in the position of Radha.

Those who want to study in detail the Madhura Bhava, spoken of in the Vaishnava books, should go through the writings of the early Vaishnava teachers like Rupa, Sanatana, and Jiva, and also the poems of the Vaishnava poets like Vidyapati and Chandidas on *Purvaraga* (the dawn of the divine love), *Dana* (offering or dedication), *Mana* (the affected rejection of the Beloved's endearment due to excess of emotion), *Abhimana* (the wounded feeling of love) and *Madhura*[1] (pangs of separation). We have discussed the essentials of the Madhura Bhava here, because it will make it easy to understand what a wonderful pinnacle of excellence the Master reached in the practice of that mood.

_____

[1]These songs on the pangs of separation are collectively named Mathur, or associated with the city Mathura, because the Gopis of Vrindavan experienced those intense pangs when Krishna left for Mathura, from where He never returned.—Tr.

CHAPTER XIV

THE MASTER'S SADHANA OF THE MADHURA BHAVA

(TOPICS; 1. The Master naturally inclined to spiritual moods. 2. Effects of Sadhana on him. 3. His earlier attitude to Madhura Bhava. 4. Scriptural sanction for the Master's Sadhanas. 5. The Master's adherence to scriptural commandments. 6. The Master wearing female dress during Madhura Bhava. 7. Feminine traits manifest in him. 8. The Master as a lady friend in Mathur's family. 9. His indistinguishability in women's dress. 10. Physical changes during Madhura Bhava. 11. The Master's transcendental love. 12. Srimati's transcendental love. 13. Sri Gauranga on transcendental love. 14. The Master's vision of Radha. 15. The Master's identification with Srimati. 16. Extraordinary physical changes in the Master during the mood of a woman. 17. Mind creates the body. 18. The Master's vision of Sri Krishna. 19. A youthful aspiration of his. 20. The three as the One and the One as the three.)

1. The Master was accustomed to remaining completely absorbed in any spiritual mood that happened to be taken up by his pure and one-pointed mind. That particular mood fully occupied his mind for the time being and wiped off all other moods and converted his body into a perfect instrument suited for its manifestation. When we study his life, we find this mental trait was present in him from his very childhood. We observed this nature of his almost daily, when we were visiting Dakshineswar. While merged in any particular spiritual mood as the result of listening to devotional music or for any other reason, he felt extreme pain if anyone sang or talked in a manner suited to any other mood. Evidently he experienced pain because the flow of his mind in a particular direction under the influence of one mood was suddenly obstructed by the introduction of another mood. Patanjali, the great thinker, has described the mental state having only one current of thought centring on one particular object, as Savikalpa-samadhi. The same has been described as Bhava-samadhi in devotional scriptures. This shows that the Master's mind was

accustomed to merging in that kind of ecstasy from his very childhood.

2. The above-mentioned characteristic of his mind took an extraordinarily new turn from the time he commenced his spiritual practices. For, whereas in his early days his mind was found to remain in one mood only for a short time and then to change into another, it was now noticed that a mood once inducted continued to persist till it progressed to its utmost limits and ended with a glimpse of the non-dual consciousness beyond. As examples of this fact it may be said that, until he reached the farthest limit of the Dasya mood, he did not try to practise the Apatya, or the mood in which one looked upon God as a parent (mother); again, he did not engage himself in the practices of the Vatsalya and the Madhura Bhavas before he had the final experience of the Apatya, as taught by the Tantras. Instances of this can be easily multiplied if we study the events of the period of his Sadhanas.

3. When the Brahmani came, the Master's mind was deeply engaged in the contemplation of the Motherhood of God. At that time he saw the actual manifestation of the Divine Mother in all creatures, sentient or insentient, but specially in those having the female form. Therefore, we clearly understand the reason why he addressed the Brahmani as "mother" as soon as he saw her, and fully believed himself to be her son, sat at times on her lap, and took food out of her hand. Inspired by the devotional mood of the Gopis of Vraja, the Brahmani happened at times to sing songs conveying the idea of the conjugal relationship with God, when the Master would say, as reported by Hriday, that he did not like that mood, and request her to stop them and sing instead songs expressive of the Motherhood of God. The Brahmani rightly understood the Master's mood and started immediately singing songs indicative of the mood of the female attendant of the Mother of the universe; or she introduced songs full of the outburst of affection of Yasoda for her Gopala. These are, of course, events that occurred long before he became engaged in the discipline of the Madhura Bhava. His transparent and unalloyed sincerity is evident from this. As he himself used to say, "There is no swindling in the abode of my mind."

4. We have already seen how the Master passed through the attitudes of a servant of God and also of a child of His. Now

let us describe the practices he undertook when he engaged himself in the discipline of the Madhura Bhava.   Although the Master
was almost "illiterate", as that word is ordinarily understood, a study of his life reveals how he maintained the authority
of the scriptures all his life.   Even his early spiritual Sadhanas,
undertaken without the help of any Guru and guided solely by the
pure impulses of his heart, were not in contradiction with the Sastras.
They only prove their universality—the truth that success will
attend the efforts of any one in this field, provided one's heart
is pure, holy and full of aspiration, 'without any swindling'.   And
there is nothing to wonder at in this; for, a little thinking will show
that the scriptures have been compiled out of such original experiences.   The texts included as the Sastras are nothing but the
records of the experiences of hearts like that of the Master.   They
are the results of their efforts for the realization of the Truth.
The Master, however, was unlettered and therefore without any
previous knowledge of these Sastras.   But yet he attained to the
realization of the very truths recorded in them by his independent
efforts.   This extraordinary life therefore goes only to prove
the universality of the experiences recorded in the scriptures.   It
is, therefore, only a confirmation and not a contradiction of the
scriptures.   Swami Vivekananda pointed this out when he said,
"The reason of the Master's incarnating this time as an unlettered
person is to prove the states and experiences recorded in the Sastras
to be true."

5.   As examples of the Master's instinctive adherence to
the authority of scriptures, we may mention here how he put on
different kinds of dress, one after another, under the impulse of
different moods.   The seers have said through the Upanishads
that one cannot attain perfection by Tapas only, if it is without
the adoption of external emblems also.[1]   It is seen in the life of the
Master that, impelled by his own heart, he put on the dress and
other external emblems favourable to the practices of whatever
spiritual mood he undertook at a time.   For instance, he wore
red cloth, ashes, vermilion and Rudraksha beads as laid down in the
Tantras while he was practising the filial attitude towards God
as the Mother.   At the time of his practice of the devotional moods

---

[1] *Mundaka Upanishad*, 3. 2. 4.   Self-realization is not possible by
knowledge only without putting on the signs of Sannyasa, *e.g.*, ochre
cloth etc.

of the Vaishnava books, he donned Bhek, the well-known traditional garb of the Vaishnava ascetics, consisting of white cloth, white sandal-paste, garlands of beads made of the holy basil, etc. Desiring to realize the non-dual mood taught by the Vedanta, he put on ochre dress and gave up his sacred thread and the tuft of hair on the crown of his head. Again, just as he assumed various male forms of dress at the time of practising the male moods, so did he not hesitate to adorn himself with the female forms of dress and ornaments while practising the female moods. The Master taught us many a time that one could not realize God till one gave up the eight ties of shame, hatred, fear and the egoism due to birth, family, good conduct, etc. which accompany one from life to life. How far he himself followed that teaching all his life in body, mind and speech, can clearly be understood by a careful study of all his actions including that of his wearing of special dress, ornaments and other appropriate emblems at the time of his different Sadhanas.

6. Engaged in the practices of the Madhura Bhava, the Master became anxious to use clothes and ornaments proper to a woman. Knowing that desire of his, the greatly devout Mathur had the pleasure of adorning him at times with a precious sari, and at others with a skirt, a gauze scarf and a bodice. Desirous of making his female mode of dress perfect in all respects, Mathur decked him with a wig of long hair and a set of gold ornaments. This gift of Mathur, we knew from a reliable source, gave evil-minded people an opportunity to calumniate the Master's austere renunciation. But he and Mathur did not pay any attention whatsoever to that censorious talk. Mathur was highly delighted at the satisfaction they gave to 'father', and that was sufficient justification for the gift in his eyes. Dressed in this way and adorned with such ornaments, the Master became so intensely identified with the mood of Krishna's lovelorn women votaries of Vraja, that his male consciousness totally disappeared from him. His thoughts, words and movements began to resemble a woman's in every respect. We have heard from the Master that he was in this woman's attire for six months, with his mind absorbed in the feeling that he was the spiritual consort of God.

7. We have mentioned elsewhere the extraordinary co-existence in the Master of both manly and womanly temperaments. Is it, therefore, to be wondered at that, under the influence of the

womanly dress, the temperament of the fair sex should be roused in him? But nobody could ever imagine that, under the urge of that mood, his movements, speech, smile, glance, gestures and other actions of the body and the mind would become completely womanly. That all this did take place, however impossible it may appear, was borne out both by Hriday and the Master himself. When frequenting Dakshineswar, we saw him mimicking women's manners at times. These mimicries used to be so highly natural and perfect that even ladies were astonished to see them.

8. At that time the Master sometimes went to the Janbazar house of Rani Rasmani and lived there with the ladies in the inner apartment. Acquainted very well with the purity of the Master's character and his freedom from every trace of lust, these ladies looked upon him as divine. Besides, they were now charmed with his womanly deportment and temperament so sympathetically attuned to theirs. They therefore got habituated to think of him as one among themselves and ceased to feel any womanly hesitation or bashfulness in his presence (III.7). When the husband of one of Mathur's daughters came to the Janbazar house at that time, the Master, we have heard it from himself, decorated her with choicest dress and ornaments, dressed her hair, instructed her in various ways of entertaining her husband, led her by the hand like a woman friend to her husband's room, and returned after seating her by his side. He said, "As they looked upon me as a woman friend of theirs, they did not feel uneasy at all."

9. "When he remained thus surrounded by ladies," Hriday said, "it was difficult even for his very close relatives to recognize him quickly. One day at that time Mathur Babu took me to the inner apartment and asked, 'Can you say which of these is your uncle?' Although I had lived with him for so long and had served him daily, I could not at once distinguish him from them. When during that period of his life at Dakshineswar, uncle used to pluck and collect flowers in the garden early in the morning every day with a flower basket in his hand, we carefully observed him, and we noticed that, every time he started walking, his left foot moved first, like that of a woman. The Bhairavi Brahmani used to say, 'I mistook him very often for Sri Radharani when I saw him plucking flowers in that manner.' Having plucked flowers and made variegated garlands of them, he used to adorn Radha-Govinda every day, and sometimes, having adorned the Mother

of the universe also that way, he would pray imploringly to Her, as did the Gopis of Vraja to Katyayani, to let him have Krishna for his 'Spiritual Husband'."

10. Desirous of having the vision of Krishna and of getting Him as his Spiritual Husband, the Master now performed the service and worship of the Divine Mother. He then engaged himself in the service of the holy feet of Krishna with an undivided mind, and spent his days in eager prayer and longing. That eager prayer in his heart never ceased at any time—neither during the day nor during the night. Days and months passed without success, but neither despair nor any flagging of faith obstructed his urge. His prayer expressed itself as copious tears from the eyes and as a longing of the soul which developed into a restlessness, an anxious pining for the beloved like one possessed, making him unmindful of food, sleep and other vital concerns of the body. And how shall we describe the pangs of separation—that unbounded yearning for the complete union for all time with one's darling of the heart, now cruelly obstructed by manifold barriers; that yearning which churns one's heart, plays havoc with one's mind and devastates one's body and sense-organs — how shall we describe the pangs produced by such a yearning? Further, these pangs of separation did not end by merely manifesting themselves as agonizing mental modes but also brought about again that unbearable burning pain and intense heat which he had felt all over his body during the early stages of his Sadhana. We have heard from the Master himself that drops of blood oozed out then at times from every pore of his body under the powerful sense of the separation from Krishna. All the joints of the body seemed loosened or almost dislocated, the senses completely desisted from functioning and the body lay motionless and unconscious sometimes like that of a dead man — all because of the extreme anguish of the heart.

11. We, men, eternally identified with a body and conscious of being that and that alone, understand by love the attraction of one body for another. Or if we go, as the result of strenuous effort, just a little beyond the consciousness of the gross body and regard love as the attraction towards the aggregate of the noble qualities manifested in a particular body, we call it by the name of transcendental love and sing hallelujah over it. But it does not take one long to understand that even this, our so called transcendental love,

eulogized by generations of poets, is not free from the consciousness of the gross body and subtle desires for enjoyment. Ah, how worthless, insignificant and hollow that love appears in contrast with the true transcendental love manifested in the Master's life !

12. Srimati Radharani alone, the devotional scriptures say, realized this transcendental love in its fulness. In her we have its perfect model. Nowhere in the whole range of devotional scriptures is to be found a peer to her. For, completely oblivious of her own bodily and mental satisfactions, she could give up shame, hatred and fear, without caring in the least for social or popular opinion; she could trample upon the prestige due to birth, family, good conduct and respectable position, in order to feel happy in Krishna's happiness alone. According to these Vaishnava scriptures no Jiva can attain to the fulness of this form of love; only a partial realisation of it can be had by a Sadhaka, and even that by the grace of Radha alone. For Krishna, the embodiment of Existence-Knowledge-Bliss, is eternally captivated by her love, devoid as it is of the slightest tinge of lust, and he fulfils the desire of devotees for his vision, at her intercession. The implication of these teachings is that, until one realizes the kind of love experienced by Srimati (Radha), the embodiment of transcendental love, one cannot have God as husband and feel the perfect sweetness of love, which is called Madhura Bhava.

13. Although the extraordinary glory of the love of Radharani for Krishna has been highly eulogized by Sukadeva, the chief of the Paramahamsas, and by other self-controlled sages free from the sway of Maya, the generality of the people of India did not know for a very long time how to realize it in life. In order to make people understand how to realize it, the divine Lord, the Vaishnava teachers say, had to incarnate Himself with Srimati in one and the same body, as Krishna inside and Radha outside, in that extraordinary embodiment of His which is known as Gauranga or Sri Chaitanya. Thus Gauranga came on the earth to do good to humanity by teaching the extra-marital relation of love in the spiritual domain, with God as the lover and the Jiva as the woman in love with Him. All the signs that were manifested in Radharani's body on account of her love for Krishna, also manifested themselves in Gauranga's body, though male, owing to the power of his love for God. This led to the assertion that Gauranga

18

was Srimati; for the physical and mental signs of Madhura Bhava which had manifested in Srimati alone in the past, were found in him too. So, Sri Gauranga is the second example of that ideal ·of transcendental love.

14. Thus understanding that the attainment of the vision of Krishna was impossible without Radha's grace, the Master now applied himself thoroughly to gaining her favour. Lost in the remembrance and reflection of her form, the very embodiment of love, he incessantly offered at her lotus feet the ardent emotions of his heart. Consequently, he was very soon blessed with the vision of the holy form of Radha, devoid of the slightest tinge of lust. He now saw that this form also disappeared into his own body like the forms of other deities when he had had their visions. "Is it ever possible," said the Master, "to describe the glory and sweetness of that incomparable, pure, bright form of Radha who renounced her all for the love of Krishna! The splendour of her body was bright yellow like the pollen of Nagakesara (*mesua ferrea*) flowers."

15. From now on, the Master began to realize himself as Srimati in ecstasy. He completely lost the consciousness of his separate existence, on account of his profound contemplation of the holy form and character of Radha and through his ceaseless feeling of identification with her. Therefore, it can certainly be said that his love for God, taking the form of conjugal relationship, developed into a state as deep and as profound as Radha's. For, in reality, all the signs of Mahabhava which constitutes the acme of the Madhura Bhava, were manifested in him after his realization of the above-mentioned vision, even as they were in Radha and Gauranga. The descriptions of the physical signs manifesting in the Mahabhava are recorded in the writings of the revered Vaishnava teachers. The Bhairavi Brahmani, and later Vaishnavacharan and other Sadhakas, all well-versed in the Vaishnava scriptures, were astonished to see the manifestation of those signs of the Mahabhava stage of conjugal relationship in the holy person of the Master, and they offered him their heart-felt worship and reverence. Speaking of the Mahabhava, the Master told us on many occasions, "It is written in the devotional scriptures that the group of nineteen kinds of emotions manifesting together in one receptacle is called the Mahabhava. The whole life of a man is required for the practice of even one of such emotions before he can attain perfection in it.

Nineteen such moods were fully manifested all together here (show-ing his own body) in one receptacle."[1]

16.　We have mentioned before that blood oozed out from every pore of the Master's body on account of the extreme anguish arising from the sense of separation from Krishna. It happened at this time, in the ultimate stage of the Mahabhava. He became so much absorbed in the constant thought of himself as a woman, that he could not look upon himself as one of the other sex even in a dream. His body and senses functioned naturally like those of a woman.

17.　The Vedanta teaches that it is the mind of man that has created his body in its present form, and that it is re-forming it every moment of his life by decomposing and re-composing it through the functioning of intense desires. Though we are told of the great mastery the mind has over the body, we do not really comprehend the full extent of it. This is because there is no object for the attainment of which we experience that kind of intense desire, under the influence of which the mind turns away from all other

---

[1] The divisions of the Ragatmika Bhakti according to the Vaishnava teachers like Jiva Goswami are given below:

Ragatmika Bhakti
(The spontaneous flow of desire or attachment towards its object)

Kamatmika (consisting of desire for erotic-mystic enjoyment inspired by exclusive effort to please Krishna)	Sambandhatmika (consisting of a sense of relationship with Krishna)		
Sneha (affection, causing melting of the heart), Mana (affected repulse of endearment due to excess of emotion), Pranaya (friendly confidence), Raga (erotic transmutation of sorrow into joy) and Anuraga (love as a constant freshness)	Vatsalya	Sakhya	Dasya　Santa
	Sneha Mana Pranaya Raga and Anuraga	Sneha Mana Pranaya Raga and Anuraga	Sneha Mana Pranaya and Raga and Anuraga

The aforesaid nineteen divisions (excluding calmness i.e., Santa) of the two kinds of love, viz., Kamatmika and Sambandhatmika, co-exist in one receptacle in the Mahabhava—this is what the Master said.

N.B.—We are indebted to Prof. S. K. De for the English trans-lation of some of the above terms.—Tr.

objects and concentrates itself on that particular one, and thereby manifests extraordinary powers. The aforesaid teaching of the Vedanta, it is needless to add, is clearly proved by the fact that the Master's body changed in a short time on account of his intense desire to experience a particular object. Hearing the details of the spiritual experiences of the Master and desiring to compare them with those of the perfected seers of past ages, Padmalochan and other eminent Pandits said to the Master, "Your experiences have gone far beyond those recorded in the Vedas and the Puranas." One is amazed to study the physical changes of the Master under the influence of his strong emotions and has to remark that his bodily changes have gone beyond the facts so far discovered by physiology and indicate the beginning of a wonderful revolution in it.

18. As the Master's awareness of God as husband became perfected and intensified, he experienced in the above-mentioned way the grace of Radharani, the supreme Lady of Vraja, and was finally blessed, shortly after, with the holy vision of Krishna, the embodiment of pure Existence-Knowledge-Bliss. This form of Krishna realised in the vision also united with his holy person like all the other forms seen before. Tota Puri, the Paramahamsa, came two or three months after the Master had had that vision and engaged him in the discipline of the non-dual spiritual mood well-known in the Vedanta. Perfect in the practices of the Madhura Bhava, the Master was, it is clear, enjoying divine bliss in that mood for a short period. We have heard from the Master himself that at that time he lost himself completely in the thought of Krishna, and sometimes regarded himself as Krishna, and regarded all beings, from Brahma down to a blade of grass, as forms of Krishna. When we were frequenting Dakshineswar and were in his company, one day he plucked a flower of grass, came to us with his face beaming with delight and said, "The complexion of Sri Krishna, whom I used to see then (at the time of practising the Madhura Bhava), was like this."

19. A desire under the impulse of the female mood used to arise in the Master's mind in his adolescence before he left Kamarpukur for Calcutta. Knowing that the Gopis of Vraja had Krishna, the embodiment of pure Existence-Knowledge-Bliss, as their spiritual husband through love, because they were born as women, he used to think that he too would have been blessed enough to love and

have Krishna as husband, had he been born in a female form. Considering his male body to be an obstacle to his attainment of Krishna, he then imagined that, were he to be born again, he would become a beautiful child-widow with long hair, in a Brahmana family, and would not know any one except Krishna as husband. There would be some means of bare subsistence of coarse food and clothes. Near the hut there would be a Katha[1] or two of land, wherein she would produce, with her own hands, some greens and vegetables for her own use. And there would be with her an elderly woman as her guardian, a cow which she would milk herself, and a spinning wheel. The imagination of the boy proceeded further. He went on thinking that in the day-time, after finishing the household duties, she would spin yarn with that wheel, singing songs about Krishna, and after dusk would be ardently weeping in secret from a longing to feed Krishna with her own hands, with the sweets made of the milk of that cow. Krishna also would be pleased, and coming dressed as a cowherd, would eat them. This visit and departure would be repeated daily without the knowledge of others. Although in a modified form, his desire in this respect came to pass in the aforesaid manner at the time of his practising the Madhura Bhava.

20. We shall conclude the present topic by recording another vision of the Master when he was enjoying the Madhura Bhava. One day during that period, while he was listening to the reading of the *Bhagavata* in front of the Vishnu temple, he went into ecstasy and had the vision of Sri Krishna's luminous form. He saw that a beam of light like a cord came out of His lotus feet and touched the book, whence it touched the Master's heart and remained simultaneously touching all the three of them for some time. There arose from that vision the firm conviction in his mind that, although the three, viz., the scripture, the devotee and the divine Lord, appear as different entities, they are one and the same thing; in other words, they are the manifestations of the same Reality "The three—the Bhagavata (the scripture), the Bhakta (the devotee) and the Bhagavan (the divine Lord)—are One and the One is the three," he used to say.

---

[1] i.e., .016 acre.—Tr.

CHAPTER XV

THE MASTER'S SADHANA OF THE VEDANTA

1. Perfected in the discipline of the Madhura Bhava, the Master now reached the zenith of the Sadhana of all the devotional moods. But before recording the history of the rest of his extraordinary spiritual striving, it is necessary to make a study of his mental state at that time.

If an aspirant wants to be successful in the discipline of any one of the devotional moods, he will, we have seen, have to do it by shunning sights, tastes, and other worldly objects of enjoyment. The saying of the perfected devotee Tulsidas, viz., "There is no selfish action where Rama is,"[1] is really true. The history of the extraordinary striving of the Master bears this out. He had stood on the solid basis of the renunciation of lust and gold before he began practising the devotional moods. He could master in a short period whatever mood he practised at any time, only because he never deviated in the least from that basis. Therefore, we are to keep it clear before our mind that he was now incessantly

---

[1] There is no selfish action, where Rama is, and there is no Rama where selfish action is. Like the sun and the night, the two do not co-exist.—Tulsidas.

dwelling in a region far beyond the bounds of the temptation of lust and gold.

As he was incessantly making efforts for God-realization for a period of nine years by renouncing the desire for the enjoyment of worldly objects, his mind now reached, through constant contemplation, such a state in which even the thought of anything unconnected with God appeared as poison to him. The more he understood and manifested in body, mind and speech that the reality of God was the essence of all essences and the ultimate of all ultimates, the more did he grow absolutely indifferent to, and free from, any desire for the attainment here or hereafter of anything except God.

Forgetting all worldly things and the pains and pleasures of his body, he was now so much accustomed to the one-pointed meditation on his Chosen Ideal that his mind could in a moment withdraw itself from external objects, get concentrated on that Ideal and enjoy divine bliss. Days, months and years rolled on in that way, yet his bliss, the divine enjoyment, would not leave him even for a moment, nor could he ever lend himself to believe that there was anything but God to be desired for in life.

And having unlimited devotion, faith and dependence on the Universal Mother, the Ultimate Cause, as "the goal, the supporter, the lord, the witness, the abode, the refuge and the friend."[1] the Master had not only bound himself to Her in eternal loving relation, but also accustomed himself thoroughly to perform all actions of his life, big and small, exclusively at the command or hint from the Divine Mother. For, he had had various proofs of the fact that, through absolute childlike dependence on the Divine Mother, the aspirant can realise Her constant presence by his side, experience always the blessedness of Her sweet words and the support of Her powerful arms, and be relieved thereby of all fear in treading the difficult paths of life.

2. Why did the Master, it may be asked, engage himself in discipline even after thus knowing the Cause of the universe as his own Mother ever present by his side? What is the relevancy of any further spiritual disciplines when one has already realised that She, for attaining whom all disciplines and austerities are practised by aspirants, is utterly your own? Although we discussed

---

[1] Gita, IX, 18

this question before from one point of view, we shall now say a few words on it from another. Sitting at the holy feet of the Master and listening to the history of his striving, we felt that doubt in our mind and we did not hesitate to express it to him. We shall now describe here what he told us in reply. "Look here," said the Master, "one who always lives at the sea coast sometimes feels a desire to see what a variety and number of precious things lie hidden at the bottom of the ocean, which is said to be the mine of all gems. Similarly although I had realized Her and felt Her presence always by my side, a strong desire arose in me to experience Her, who is of multifarious forms and relations, in as many of such forms and relations as She would be pleased to reveal to me. Therefore, whenever I desired to see or enjoy Her in any particular form or relation, I would pray persistently to Her to reveal Herself to me in that form or relation. The compassionate Mother on Her part made me personally do whatever was necessary, supplied me with everything required for that particular form of spiritual practice, and revealed Herself to me in that form and in that relation. It was thus that all the various disciplines were performed."

Perfected in the discipline of the Madhura Bhava, the Master, as we have seen, reached the ultimate plane of the Sadhanas of the devotional moods. He then felt the urge to perform the discipline of the non-dual mood, which is beyond all moods as is well-known in the Vedanta. We shall now tell the reader how that urge came on the Master at the instance of the Divine Mother and how he now realized Her formless, attributeless nature, which is the Turiya or the Absolute.

3. The Master's aged mother was living at the Dakshineswar Kali temple when he began practising the non-dual mood. At the passing away of her eldest son Ramkumar, the bereaved old lady consoled herself with difficulty, looking endearingly on her surviving two sons. But, soon after, when it was rumoured that her dearest and youngest son Gadadhar had turned mad, her sorrow and grief knew no bounds. She had her son brought home, and when his condition improved a little, through various kinds of treatment and performance of propitiatory rites, hope came to her again and the old lady had him married. But when Gadadhar returned to Dakshineswar after his marriage and his former state seized him again, the old lady could no longer control herself. Praying for the recovery of her son, she went first to the Siva temple

in her own village and, afterwards, to the old temple of Siva at Mukundapur and undertook a fast unto death. When the great God Mahadeva told her in a vision that her son was in divine inebriation, she was reassured a little. Nevertheless, the world lost all its attraction for her and she came to her son at Dakshineswar shortly afterwards, determined to spend the rest of her life on the bank of the Ganga. For, what purpose would it serve her, she thought, to remain attached to the world in that old age when those for whom and with whom she was in the world were one by one leaving her and the world behind? We have already told the reader of the festival connected with Mathur's gift of the "mountain of food". Resolved to pass the rest of her life at Dakshineswar on the Ganga, the Master's mother, we infer, came to the Kali temple during the time of that festival in 1864. That resolve of the old lady was fulfilled. She never returned to Kamarpukur but spent the remaining twelve years of her life near the temple until she passed away in 1876. Therefore there is no doubt that it was during his mother's stay at Dakshineswar, that the Master was initiated into the Mantra of Rama by Jatadhari, received the image of Ramalala from him, and practised the moods of Vatsalya, Madhura, and the Vedanta.

4. We should like to tell the reader an event showing the complete lack of avarice on the part of the Master's mother. That event took place shortly after she came to Dakshineswar. Mathur, as we have said earlier, was now in full charge of the management of the Kali temple and was performing various acts of merit including the free distribution of a huge quantity of food. As there was no limit to his love, regard and reverence for the Master, he was always endeavouring to make some arrangements for the efficient continuance of the service of the Master even after his own time. But he never ventured to speak it out on account of the glowing renunciation he saw in the Master. One day, he was landed in a great difficulty, when, to know the Master's mind, he was consulting Hriday within his hearing about transferring an estate to him; for, as soon as a little of the talk reached his ears, the Master ran like one mad to beat him, saying, "Ah, you rascal, you want to make a worldly man of me!" But this idea never left Mathur; it was always burning in his mind. However, he found no opportunity to fulfil it. In the arrival of the Master's mother at Dakshineswar he found this long-awaited opportunity to fulfil his intention in

this respect. He soon began to make himself a favourite of the old lady by visiting her every day, addressing her as granny, and spending some time with her in various talks. Later, one day, finding an opportune moment, he made an earnest request to her thus, "Granny, you have never taken any service from me. If you really consider me to be your own, please ask for anything you want." The simple-hearted old lady was in a great fix; for, even after a good deal of thinking, she could not make out what she needed. In this predicament, she had to say, "My child, God bless you! Through your affectionate care, I lack nothing at present. When I require anything. I shall ask you for it". So saying, the old lady opened her portmanteau and said to Mathur, "Look here, I have so many clothes and through your loving care I have no trouble about food and drink. You have arranged and are arranging everything; what then shall I ask you for?" But Mathur was not a person to drop the matter so easily. He repeatedly requested her. "Please ask for something." After a good deal of thinking, the Master's mother hit upon something she had need of. She said, "If you must give me something, please buy an anna worth of tobacco leaf, for I want tobacco ashes for my teeth." The worldly minded Mathur's eyes became wet, and he saluted her and said, "Can any mother other than you give birth to such a self-denying son?" Saying so, he had the tobacco leaves purchased for her.

5. During the time of the Master's practice of the Vedantic discipline, his paternal cousin Haladhari was doing the service of Radha-Govinda at the Dakshineswar temple. He was senior to the Master in age and had some grasp of scriptures like the *Bhagavata*. He felt proud on that account. We have told the reader how he ridiculed the Master, criticised his spiritual visions and states as due to derangement of the brain, how, pained at it. the Master would run up to the Divine Mother for consultation, how he was again and again consoled by Her, and how on one such occasion of Haladhari's ridicule the Master went into an ecstasy in which he had the vision of a beautiful figure who instructed him to "remain in Bhavamukha". These events, we infer, came to pass shortly before he began practising the Vedantic discipline. Seeing the Master wear clothes, ornaments, etc., meant for ladies and live in the mood of a woman at the time of practising the Madhura Bhava, Haladhari concluded that he was devoid of Self-

Knowledge. When Tota Puri, the itinerant Paramahamsa, came to Dakshineswar and lived there. Haladhari, we have heard from the Master himself, was living at the Kali temple and used to have discussions on the scriptures with him from time to time. One day when Tota and Haladhari were thus discussing the *Adhyatma-Ramayana,* the Master had the vision of Rama along with Sita and Lakshmana. Tota came to Dakshineswar probably by the end of 1865. A few months after, Haladhari retired from service as the priest of the Mother owing to ill-health and other reasons, and Akshay, Ramkumar's son and the Master's nephew, was appointed in his place.

6. It is the nature of a devotee that he never tries to realize the state of liberation described as Sayujya or identification with the divine Lord, and as Nirvana or bodilessness. He always tries to enjoy the glory of the various forms and noble qualities of God with the help of particular devotional moods. The saying of Ramprasad, the devotee of the Devi, "I don't like to become sugar, but want to taste it." is well known as the natural outburst of the heart-felt emotion of the devotees. Therefore, the Master's effort to attain the non-dual state of consciousness beyond all devotional moods may appear to be contradictory to many. But we should remember before arriving at such a conclusion that the Master was not now capable of taking the initiative in doing anything. The child of the Divine Mother that he was, the Master depended entirely on Her, placed full reliance upon Her and felt highly delighted in being moved about and guided by Her always and in every way. The Divine Mother, for Her part, took upon Herself all his responsibilities, and with a view to accomplishing a particular purpose of Hers, cast him, without his knowledge, into quite a new mould. Through a revelation that came on him due to the Mother's will, the Master came to know what that particular purpose of his life was, towards the end of all his Sadhanas. And it was because of this knowledge that he bore with delight the great responsibility of doing good to humanity, thus thrust upon him by the Divine Mother with whom he was fully one in love, through keeping himself just a little separate as an individual personality.

7. There is another point of view also, which reveals the rationale of his adopting the non-dual mood after gaining perfection in the disciplines of Madhura Bhava. The relation of the

realm of devotional moods to that beyond them is one of effect
to cause. For, the immense bliss of the realm of non-duality,
which is beyond all loving moods, limits itself and then manifests
as the enjoyment of the bliss of the sight, touch, etc., of the realm
of those moods. Where then, except to the plane of non-duality,
could his mind go, when he had reached the ultimate limit of the
Madhura Bhava, which is the final stage of the realm of devotional
moods ?

Although the above argument is quite reasonable, the following
event proves, however, that the Master launched on the practice
of the non-dual mood only after he received the hint from the
Divine Mother.

8.   Desirous of bathing in the confluence of the sea and the
Ganga, and of having the vision of Sri Jagannath at Puri, the itinerant
teacher Tota came, wandering at will, from Central India to Bengal.
He was merged in spiritual practices on the banks of the holy river
Narmada, where he lived alone for a very long time and attained
the immediate knowledge of Brahman by practising disciplines
leading to Nirvikalpa Samadhi. The old monks of that place
bear witness to this fact even now. When he realized Brahman
in this way, a desire to wander at will arose in his mind and under
the impulse of that urge, he now came to Eastern India and travelled
from one place of pilgrimage to another. A knower of Brahman
is ever content in the Self. When he is in Samadhi, he is merged
in Brahman. At other times he sees the whole universe as a manifestation of Brahman through Maya and engages himself in
visiting temples, holy men and places of pilgrimage, experiencing
Brahman in them. Following this practice, Tota, a knower of
Brahman, began visiting temples and holy men and places
of pilgrimage, experiencing Brahman in them. He came to
Dakshineswar on his way back to the north-western parts
of this country after visiting the two places of pilgrimage
mentioned above. It was not customary with him to spend
more than three days at one place. He, therefore, came to the
Kali temple to spend there three days only. He did not at
first understand that, in Her inscrutable sport, the Mother of
the universe brought him there in order to complete his own
knowledge and to make Her own child practise Vedantic discipline
with his help.

9. Arriving at the Kali temple, Tota Puri came first of all to the big open portico of the Ghat. Wearing only one piece of cloth, the Master was then sitting in an absent-minded mood looking like any ordinary person. As soon as Tota's eyes fell on the Master's face, radiant with austerity and beaming with the surge of devotion, he was attracted towards him and felt in his heart of hearts that he was not an ordinary person and that there were few who were so fit for Vedantic Sadhana. Filled with curiosity and astonishment, Tota stepped forward and came up to the Master, thinking, " Ah, can there be such a fit aspirant for Vedantic discipline in Bengal, which is saturated with Tantric practices?" Observing him carefully, he asked the Master of his own accord, "You seem to be a well qualified aspirant; do you like to practise Vedantic discipline?" The Master said in answer to the tall, naked mendicant with matted hair: "I know nothing of what I should do or not do; my Mother knows everything; I shall do as She commands." Tota replied, "Then go, ask your mother and come back; for I may not be staying here for long." Without saying anything in reply, the Master went slowly to the Divine Mother's temple. There in a state of ecstasy he heard the Divine Mother's words of advice, " Go and learn; it is in order to teach you that the monk has come here."

10. In a divine state of semi-consciousness, the Master then returned to Tota, his face beaming with joy, and informed him of his Mother's instruction. On knowing that what the Master meant by 'Mother' was not his earthly mother but the image of the Devi installed in the temple, Tota, though charmed with his childlike simplicity, thought that the attitude of his mind was due to ignorance and superstition. We can very well imagine how at this thought the corners of Tota's lips curved in a smile of pity and derision. For, his keen intellect did not permit him to have any great regard for deities. He accepted only the idea of an Isvara of God spoken of in the Vedanta as the distributor of the fruits of the Karmas of the Jivas. According to him, beyond entertaining a faith in Him, there was no need for worshipping and practising devotion to Him as far as an aspirant endowed with self-control and given to the practice of meditation on Brahman was concerned. If this was his conception of Isvara, we can well guess his idea about Maya, the power of Brahman, consisting of the three Gunas. That is why the learned monk looked upon Her as but a delusion

and did not feel any necessity for admitting the existence of Her personality, far less for worshipping or propitiating Her. He felt in his heart of hearts that the aspirant's personal effort alone was what was necessary to liberate himself from the bondage of ignorance, and there was not the least utility in prayer for the benign grace of Brahman united with Its power, otherwise called Isvara. Consequently, he considered such persons as offer prayers, to be labouring under the influence of impressions born of ignorance.

11. He, however, did not say anything about it to the Master and introduced other topics, thinking that the above-mentioned impressions of the Master's mind would very soon vanish when, initiated by him, he would begin practising the discipline of the path of knowledge. He said that the Master would have to give up his sacred thread and the tuft of hair on his head before the scriptural initiation into Sannyasa. The Master hesitated a little and said that he had not the least objection if it could be done privately. But he would by no means be able to do it publicly, as it would deal a terrible blow to the heart of his old grief-stricken mother. The itinerant teacher understood the reason why the Master wanted to be initiated privately and said, "Very well, I shall initiate you in private when the auspicious moment comes." Then with a view to spending a few days in a suitable place, he came to the beautiful Panchavati situated to the north of the temple garden and spread his seat there.

12. Later, when the auspicious day arrived, Tota asked the Master to perform the Sraddha and other ceremonies for the satisfaction of the souls of his forefathers, and when those rites were finished, Tota made him offer Pinda according to scriptural injunctions for the satisfaction of his own soul. For, from the time of being initiated into Sannyasa, the aspirant totally renounces the hope of, and the right to the attainment of, any of the worlds such as Bhuh, Bhuvah, and Swah. That is why the scriptures enjoin his offering Pinda to himself.

The Master submitted himself without reserve to any one whom he ever accepted as his spiritual teacher and did his bidding with absolute faith. Therefore, it is needless to say that he followed to the letter what Tota now asked him to do. He performed the Sraddha and other preliminary rites, kept the necessary fast, collected at the Sadhana Kutir (hut) near the Pancha-

vati all the articles, as instructed by his teacher, for the rites connected
with the initiation into Sannyasa, and waited for the arrival of the
auspicious time for the ceremony.

When, about two hours before day-break, the auspicious
moment of Brahma-muhurta arrived, the Guru and the disciple
met in the hut. The preliminaries finished, the Homa-fire was
lighted. And the woods and the gardens round the Panchavati
reverberated with the sound of the holy and profound Mantras
chanted before taking the vow of utter renunciation for God—
the vow that has come down in an unbroken line from the Guru
to the disciple from the beginning of time till today and has maintained India as the foremost country in the field of Brahman-
realisation. The sensitive and affectionate bosom of the Bhagirathi
of holy waters, vibrating with the delightful touch of that sound, felt
the extraordinary infusion of a new life. She flowed dancing with
joy, bearing, as it were, through her murmurs to all quarters the
message that, after the lapse of ages, a true Sadhaka of India was
once again undertaking the vow of total renunciation for the good
of the many of this country and of the world at large. The Guru
was now ready to recite the Mantras and the disciple to repeat them
carefully and to offer oblations in the lighted fire. The prayer-
mantras were first uttered:

13. "May the truth of the supreme Brahman reach me! May
the Reality having the characteristics of supreme bliss reach me!
May the indivisible, homogeneous, sweet reality of Brahman
manifest itself in me ! O supreme Self, who art eternally
co-existent with Thy power of revealing the Brahman-consciousness
of all Thy children — Devas, human beings and others — to Thee
may I, Thy child and servant, be an especial object of compassion!
O great Lord, the destroyer of the evil dream of the worlds, destroy
all my evil dreams, the perception of duality! O Supreme Self,
I offer as oblations my vital forces, and controlling my senses, I
set my mind on Thee alone. O Shining One, who directest every
being, remove from me all blemishes that are obstacles to right
knowledge and ordain that the knowledge of Reality, free from
absurdities and contraries, arise in me! May all the things of the
world — the sun, the air, the cool pure water of rivers, grains like
barley and wheat, trees etc., ordained by Thee, illumine and help
me to attain the knowledge of Truth! Thou art manifest in the
world, O Brahman, as various forms with especial potency. I

offer oblation to Thee who art fire, with a view to achieving, through the purity of body and mind, the capacity to retain the knowledge of Reality. Be Thou gracious to me!"[1]

14. Then began the Viraja Homa: "May the five elements of earth, water, fire, air and ether in me be purified. Freed from the blemishes produced by Rajoguna, may I, by virtue of offering oblation, attain the nature of the Light of Consciousness Itself— Swaha!

May the vital airs, Prana, Apana, Samana, Udana and Vyana in me, be purified! Freed from the blemishes produced by Rajoguna, may I, by virtue of offering oblation, attain the nature of the Light of Consciousness Itself — Swaha!

"May the five sheaths of gross body, vital air, mind, intellect and bliss be purified! Freed from the blemishes produced by Rajoguna, may I, by virtue of offering oblation, attain the nature of the Light of Consciousness Itself — Swaha!

"May the impressions produced in me by the objects, sound, touch, sight, taste, and smell be purified! Freed from the blemishes produced by Rajoguna, may I, by virtue of offering oblation, attain the nature of the Light of Consciousness Itself — Swaha!

"May my mind, speech, body, actions, be purified! Freed from the blemishes produced by Rajoguna, may I   by virtue of offering oblation, attain the nature of the Light of Consciousness Itself—Swaha!

"O person of red eyes, dwelling in the body of fire and capable of destroying the obstacles to the attainment of Knowledge, do thou wake up! O fulfiller of desires, ordain that all obstacles to my attainment of Knowledge be destroyed and the Knowledge heard from the lips of the Guru arise in my mind! May everything that is in me be completely purified! Freed from the blemishes produced by Rajoguna, may I, by virtue of offering oblation, attain the nature of the Light of Consciousness Itself—Swaha!

"A reflection of Consciousness, I, who am of the nature of Brahman Itself, offer as oblation in fire—all my desire for wife, son, wealth, honour, beauty and other objects! I renounce them all —Swaha!"

15. Many oblations were thus offered and the Homa was brought to an end by the disciple, saying, "I give up from this

---

[1] The purport of the *Trisuparna-mantra*

moment the desire of attaining the Bhuh and all other worlds; I assure all beings of the universe, of freedom from fear on account of me." He then offered as oblation his sacred thread and the tuft of hair on his head, according to scriptural injunctions. Then putting on a pair of Kaupinas and ochre cloth [1] given by the Guru according to the custom followed by successive generations of Sadhakas from the beginning of time, he sat beside Tota to receive instruction from him.

16. Tota, a knower of Brahman, now encouraged the Master to practise the contemplation of "Not this", "Not this", a well known discipline in the Vedanta, and remain identified with Brahman Itself. He said to the Master: "Brahman, the one substance which alone is eternally pure, eternally awakened, unlimited by time, space and causation, is absolutely real. Through the influence of Maya, which makes the impossible possible, it seems that It is divided into names and forms. Brahman is never really so divided. For, at the time of Samadhi, not even an iota, so to say, of time and space, and name and form produced by Maya, is perceived. Whatever, therefore, is within the bounds of name and form, can never be absolutely real. Give up this unreal world of name and form. Break the firm cage of name and form with the overpowering strength of a lion and come out of it. Dive deep into the reality of the Self existing in yourself. Be one with It with the help of Samadhi. You will then see the universe consisting of name and form vanish, as it were, into the Void; you will see the consciousness of the little 'I' merge in that of the immense 'I', where it ceases to function; and you will have the immediate knowledge of the indivisible Existence-Knowledge-Bliss as yourself. 'The consciousness, with the help of which a person sees another, knows another or hears another, is little or limited. Whatever is limited is worthless; for the supreme bliss is not there. But the knowledge, established in which a person becomes devoid of the consciousness that one is seeing another, knowing another, and hearing another, is 'Bhuma,' the immense or the unlimited. With the help of that knowledge,

---

[1] Some among us say that Tota Puri gave the name "Ramakrishna" to the Master when he initiated him into Sannyasa. Others say that Mathuranath, who was a great devotee of the Master and served him wholeheartedly, called him first by that name. The first opinion seems to us to be reasonable.

19

one gets identified with the supreme Bliss. That immense and unlimited consciousnes who is the Knower in all beings and whose light reveals everything,—how can It be known by the limited mind and intellect? How can the Knower at all be the known?¹"

17. Tota tried to make the Master attain Samadhi on that day with the help of various arguments and conclusive quotations from the scriptures. We were informed by the Master that Tota strove his best on that occasion to put him immediately into the state of non-dual consciousness to which he himself had attained through lifelong Sadhana. "After initiating me," said the Master, "the naked one taught me many dicta conveying the conclusions of the Vedanta, and asked me to make my mind free of function in all respects and merge it in the meditation of the Self. But, it so happened that when I sat for meditation, I could by no means make my mind go beyond the bounds of name and form and cease functioning. The mind withdrew itself easily from all other things, but, as soon as it did so, the intimately familiar form of the universal Mother consisting of the effulgence of pure consciousness, appeared before it as a living presence and made me quite oblivious of the renunciation of names and forms of all description. When I listened to the conclusive dicta and sat for meditation, this happened over and over again. Almost despairing of the attainment of the Nirvikalpa Samadhi, I then opened my eyes and said to the naked one, 'No, it cannot be done; I cannot make the mind free from functioning, and force it to dive into the Self.' Scolding me severely, the naked one said very excitedly, 'What! It can't be done! What nonsense!' He then looked about in the hut, and finding a broken piece of glass, took it in his hand and forcibly pierced my forehead with its needle-like pointed end between the eye-brows and said, 'Collect the mind here at this point.' With a firm determination I sat for meditation again, and as soon as the holy form of the Divine Mother appeared now before the mind as previously, I looked upon knowledge as a sword and cut the form mentally in two with that sword of knowledge. There remained then no function in the mind, which transcended quickly the realm of names and forms, making me merge in Samadhi."

---

¹ *Brihadaranyaka Upanishad,* 2.4.14.

18.   Tota remained sitting for a long time beside the Master who entered into Samadhi in the manner mentioned above.   Then coming out of the hut silently, he locked the door up lest some one should enter the hut without his knowledge and disturb him.   He took his seat under the Panchavati, not far from the hut, and was awaiting he Master's call to open the door.

The day passed into night.   Slowly and calmly days rolled on.   At the end of three days, when Tota did not still hear the Master's call, he was filled with curiosity and astonishment, and left his seat to open the door.   With a view to knowing the condition of his disciple, he entered the hut and saw that the Master was sitting in the same posture in which he had left him and that there was not the slightest function of the vital force in his body. His face, however, was calm and serene and full of effulgence.   He understood that the disciple was completely dead to the external world and that his mind, merged in Brahman, was calm and motionless like an unflickering lamp in a windless place.

Being versed in the mystery of Samadhi, Tota became astounded and exclaimed within himself,   "Oh, wonderful! How can I believe my eyes? Has this great soul actually realized in a day what I could experience only as the result of forty years of austere Sadhana?" Filled with doubt, Tota applied his mind to the examination of the state of the Master and scrutinized minutely all the signs manifested in the disciple's body.   He examined especially whether his heart was beating and whether there was the least sign of breath in him.   He touched repeatedly the disciple's body which was in a steady posture, like a piece of wood, firm and fixed. But there was no change or modification, no was there any return to normal consciousness.   Beside himself with joy and astonishment, Tota cried out, "Oh, the divine Maya! It is indeed Samadhi—the Nirvikalpa Samadhi, the ultimate result attained through the path of knowledge spoken of in the Vedanta!   Ah, how very strange is the Maya of the Divine!"

19.   Tota then undertook the process of bringing the disciple back to the consciousness of the external world.   Profound sounds of the Mantra, "Hari Aum", filled the land, water and sky of the Panchavati.

We have described in another place (III. 8) how, attracted by the love of his disciple and desirous of making him firmly established in the. Nirvikalpa plane of consciousness, Sri Tota spent here day after day and month after month, and how, with the help of the Master, he had his own spiritual life made complete in all respects. We refrain, therefore, from repeating all that here.

Having lived continuously at Dakshineswar for eleven months, Tota started for the north-western part of the country. There arose immediately after this event a strong determination in the Master's mind to remain in unbroken Samadhi in the non-dual plane of consciousness. We have told the reader elsewhere (III. 2), how he carried into practice that resolve, how he could remain continually for six months in that high plane of Non-duality where even the Adhikarikas who are only a little lower than the incarnations of God, cannot dwell for a long time, not to speak of the ordinary Sadhakas, the Jivakotis; and how, at that time, a monk arrived at the Kali temple, and how, coming to know that humanity was to be greatly benefited in the future through the Master's survival, lived there for six months taking care of his body and saved his life by various means.

20. Before bringing this chapter to a close, we shall describe an event in Mathur's life, which would have ended in great calamity to him had it not been for the special grace that the Master bestowed upon him. Mathur's devotion to, and faith in, the Master had already increased enormously as a result of his seeing various wonderful divine powers manifested in him. An event that took place at this time confirmed and stabilised that devotion of his, making Mathur take absolute refuge in the Master for his entire life.

We had heard from the Master that Mathur, though born in a poor family, was exceedingly good-looking, and that it was because of this that Rani Rasmani gave her third daughter Karunamayi in marriage to him, and after the latter's death, her youngest, Jagadamba Dasi also. Therefore, immediately after his marriage, a profound change took place in his circumstances and within a short time he rose to be the right-hand man of his mother-in-law on account of his ability and intelligence. We have already narrated how, after the death of Rani Rasmani, he acquired in a way the sole authority for the management of the Rani's property.

Mathur's second wife, Srimati Jagadamba Dasi, had now an attack of dysentery. The disease gradually worsened so much that the well-known doctors and physicians of Calcutta at first felt anxious for her life and then gave up all hope.

Not only was Mathur now going to lose his dearest wife Jagadamba Dasi, but he was on the point of being simultaneously deprived of the said authority over the management of his mother-in-law's property. It is, therefore, needless to say much about his mental condition when the doctors gave up the case as hopeless. He became extremely anxious and came to Dakshineswar, and after saluting the Mother of the Universe, went to the Panchavati in search of the Master. Seeing him in that bewildered condition, the Master asked him very affectionately to sit by him and made enquiries about the cause of his worry. Mathur fell at his feet, and in a voice choked with emotion and with tears filling his eyes, informed the Master of everything, saying piteously again and again, "The worst is about to happen but, that apart, what grieves me most, Father, is that I am going to be deprived of the privilege of serving you."

Filled with compassion on seeing the miserable plight of Mathur, the Master entered into an ecstasy and said to him, "Don't be afraid, your wife will come round." The devout Mathur considered the Master as God Himself, and so at the Master's assurance, he was, as it were, brought back to life and he took leave of him that day. On his return to Janbazar he found that there was a sudden change for the better in the condition of the patient. "Jagadamba Dasi," said the Master, "gradually came round from that day, but her sufferings from that disease had to be borne by this body (showing his own). As the consequence of bringing round Jagadamba Dasi, I had to suffer from dysentery and other diseases for six months."

Speaking of the wonderful loving service of Mathur to him, one day the Master referred to the aforesaid event and said to us, "Was it for nothing that Mathur served me for fourteen years? The Divine Mother had shown him various wonderful powers through this (showing his own body). That was why he served so devotedly."

CHAPTER XVI

EPILOGUE TO THE MASTER'S VEDANTA SADHANA AND HIS PRACTICE OF ISLAM

(TOPICS: 1. The Master badly ill 2. The Master's auditive experience about remaining in Bhavamukha 3. Remembrance of past lives and Brahman realisation 4. The state in which all resolves come true 5. Light on the Master's extraordinary realisations 6. Reasons for their not being simultaneous 7. Non-dual consciousness as the ultimate aim of all disciplines 8. The unique realization of the Master 9. The Master's practice of Islam. 10. The arrival of the Sufi Govinda Ray 11. The Master's resolve after talking with Govinda 12. His initiation by Govinda 13. The Master's behaviour during Islamic Sadhana 14. Its significance 15. How strong the memory of Non-duality was in the Master's awareness 16. A few examples.)

1. Now the Master's strong body was shattered and he suffered from illness for a few months, as a result either of his curing the fatal disease of Jagadamba Dasi, as mentioned above, or of his superhuman efforts for six long months to dwell continually in the plane of the non-dual consciousness. We were told by him that he had then a severe attack of dysentery. His nephew Hriday engaged himself in nursing him day and night. Mathur placed him under the treatment of Gangaprasad Sen, the famous physician, and made special arrangements for his diet etc. Although his body was badly ill, it is staggering to think how extraordinarily calm and blissful his mind was, freed as it was from body-conscious-ness. At the slightest suggestion, his mind would free itself from body-consciousness, and simultaneously from the hold of the disease and all other objects and experiences of the world, and get absorbed in the subtle plane of Nirvikalpa, which no modification of the changeful spheres can disturb. No sooner did he hear the words Brahman, Atman or Isvara, than he merged in its content, forgetting all other things and his own separate existence for some time. There fore, it is clear, that in spite of that severe pain in his body owing to the fury of the disease, he actually felt very little of it. But that pain due to the disease, we heard from the Master himself, brought down his mind at times from high planes of spiritual experience and made it conscious of his body. The Master said it was during

this period, that the foremost of the Paramahamsas, the followers of the Vedanta, used to come to him. His room was then always reverberating with the sounds of their discussions on Vedantic dictums like *Neti Neti* (not this, not this), *Sat-Chit-Ananda* (Existence-Knowledge-Bliss Absolute), *Ayam-atma Brahma* (this Self is verily Brahman) and so on. When, during the discussions of those high Vedantic teachings, they could not arrive at the right conclusion on any question, the Master had to become the umpire and decide it. It is needless to add that had he been always distracted like other people on account of his disease, it would never have been possible for him to have taken part constantly in those abstruse philosophical discussions.

2. It was towards the end of the six month period of his absorption in the Nirvikalpa plane, that the Master had, as described in detail elsewhere (II. 8), the wonderful auditive experience, commanding him for the third time "to remain in Bhavamukha." Though we call it an auditive experience, the reader should understand by it a realization in the heart of hearts. For, the Master did not hear it, unlike on the two former occasions, from the mouth of any visible figure. Now it came to him as an immediate awareness of the existence of this idea or expression of will in the cosmic mind of the omnipresent Brahman. For his mind was then for the most part in complete oneness with the Absolute Non-dual Being, and whenever for brief periods he felt a hazy sense of distinction from the Absolute, he was poised in an awareness of being a part of the all-pervading Brahman with attributes (Savisesha-Brahman), which is the same as the Mother of the universe. (III. 3). On account of this realization, the future purpose of his life stood completely revealed to him.

He had no need of the body, nor was there left in him any trace of 'will to live', yet came the command of the universal Mother to 'remain in Bhavamukha'. From this the Master understood that he should thenceforth live in the body in accordance with the will and purpose of the sportive Divine. For this his body had to survive, and this would not have been possible if he were to remain identified with Brahman eternally. Hence the divine command. He also came to know of his former lives through Jatismaratwa (the power of remembering past lives) as also of his being an Adhikarika-purusha (one with a special divine commission), or rather an incarnation of God, who is eternally pure in nature, but has now assumed a body and performed Sadhanas in order to arrest the decline of religion in the modern age and to bring about the well-being of humanity. He came to know, moreover, that, it was with a view to accomplishing some special purpose of Hers that the universal Mother had brought him down to the earth as the son of a poor Brahmana family and as one devoid of all grandeur of external powers. He came to know, further, that only a few people would be able to know and understand, during his lifetime, the mystery of that play of the Divine Mother and that as soon as the generality of people would begin to understand it, the Mother would absorb Her child into Her own Person; but that the spiritual waves, which his body and mind were to generate, would go on surging with even greater momentum after his disappearance, contributing immensely to the well-being of humanity.

3. We must remember some of the statements in the scriptures, if we are to understand how the Master could have those extraordinary experiences. The aspirant, say the scriptures, attains Jatismaratwa[1] before he becomes fully established in Pure Consciousness itself with the help of the non-dual mood. In other words, with the fullest development of this remembrance, his memory reaches such a mature state that the entire history of his transmigration—how, where, and how many times he had had to be encased in bodies and what actions, good or evil, he had performed—is revealed with great vividness. The experience drives home to his mind the lesson of the transitoriness of everything and the utter futility of the involvement in the repetitive cycle of births and deaths and the pursuit of worldly enjoyments attainable through it. The intense detachment which then arises in the aspirant's heart frees him from all desires whatsoever.

4. The Upanishad[2] says that the resolves of such persons always come true. And their minds can, through Samadhi, explore any sphere they like, whether of gods, or of forefathers, or of any other supra-mundane beings. Patanjali, the great sage, mentions in his *Yoga-sutras* that all kinds of Yogic powers are attained by such persons. Again, the author of the *Panchadasi,* reconciling the apparent contradictions involved in the co-existence of Yogic powers and desirelessness in the same person, maintains that,

---

[1] Previous lives are remembered on attaining the knowledge of the Samskaras, the past impressions. The *Patanjali Aphorisms.* 4.18.

[2] *Chhandogya Upanishad.* 8.2.

although they attain such wonderful powers, they never apply them to further their own interests for the simple reason that they do not have any desires. Absolutely dependent on the will of God, the Adhikarika persons alone amongst them apply at times those powers for the well-being of the many. That is why the author of the *Panchadasi* says that such a person has the power but not the urge, to change the worldly circumstances in which he attains the knowledge of Brahman, and spends his time in that state.

5. If one studies the Master's life related to this period in the light of the scriptural sayings quoted above, the 'how' and the 'why' of most of the extraordinary realizations, if not all of them, stand fully revealed. One can understand how as a result of his whole-hearted offering of himself at the lotus feet of the Lord, he could attain perfect desirelessness and how in so short a time he could ascend and firmly establish himself in the Nirvikalpa plane of knowledge of Brahman. One can understand how he attained Jatismaratwa, as a result of which he had the immediate knowledge that the One, who had manifested Himself as Rama and Krishna in past ages and did good to humanity, had again assumed a body and manifested Himself in the present age as "Ramakrishna" (II. 21). One can understand why he never applied the divine powers for the comforts of his own body and mind, though their manifestations for the good of humanity were matters of almot daily occurrence; why he could and did awaken in others the power of realizing spiritual truths by a mere glance or wish; and why his extraordinary influence is slowly but surely spreading into, and acquiring mastery over, all the countries of the world.

6. Thus did the Master know the past and the future of his life at the time of his coming down to the realm of ideas from the non-dual state, in which he had been finally and fully established. But all those experiences do not seem to have come to him on one day or all of a sudden. He, we infer, had the perfect knowledge of all these things in a year after his coming down to the realm of ideas. During this time the Mother of the universe was removing, as it were, veil after veil from before his eyes, explaining clearly those things to him day after day. If we are asked why all those experiences were not revealed simultaneously to the Master's mind, we reply that, established in the non-dual state of consciousness and completely lost in the bliss of Brahman, he had no time or inclination to know them, till the modification of his

mind took an outward direction. Thus was fulfilled the Master's earnest prayer to the Mother of the universe at the beginning of his Sadhana, "Mother, I do not know at all what I should do; I'll learn what Thou Thyself wilt teach me."

7. Firmly established in the plane of the non-dual consciousness, the Master had the realization of another fact also. He came to feel in his heart of hearts that the realization of non-duality was the ultimate aim of all kinds of disciplines. For, having performed Sadhanas according to the teachings of all the main religious denominations prevalent in India, he had already been convinced that they all took the aspirants towards the non-dual plane. Asked about the non-dual state, he, therefore, said to us over and over again, "It is the finale, my child, the acme, which comes of itself in the life of all aspirants as the ultimate development of their love of God. Know it to be the last word of all faiths, and the faiths are only paths (and not the goal)."

8. Having thus had the direct experience of Non-duality, the Master's mind was filled with unbounded catholicity. He had now an extraordinary sympathy for all the religious communities which taught that the aim of human life was the realization of God. But he did not realize at first that this catholicity and universal sympathy were his discoveries (IV. 4), and that no aspirant, not even the foremost of them, in the past could attain them as fully as he. He came to be acquainted with this fact only gradually in the course of his contact with the wise Sadhakas belonging to the various religious communities at the Kali temple at Dakshineswar and at other well-known places of pilgrimage. But, thenceforward, he could not stand intolerence and exclusiveness in religious matters, and he tried in all ways to correct that narrow outlook.

9. We can clearly understand from a contemporary event how the establishment in the non-dual consciousness had brought the Master's mind to a state of extreme liberality. The Master, we have seen, was ill for a few months after he had reached the zenith of his practice of the non-dual mood. The event under reference came to pass when he had just recovered. About that time an ardent spiritual aspirant named Govinda Ray, who must have been in search of God for a long time, arrived at Dakshineswar. Hriday told us that he was a Kshatriya by birth. He was perhaps learned in Persian and Arabic. Having studied various religious doctrines and come in contact with different religious

communities, he was at last attracted by the liberal doctrine of Islam and was formally initiated into it. Govinda, thirsting for truth, accepted the Islamic faith, but we cannot say how far he followed its social manners and customs. But since he became initiated, he we were told, engaged himself ardently in the reading of the Koran and in the religious practices prescribed by that scripture. Govinda was an ardent lover of God. The method of worshipping God according to the teaching and mental attitude prevalent amongst the Sufis, followers of a sect of Islam, seems to have captivated his mind; for he now became engaged day and night in practising devotional moods like the Dervishes, the devotees belonging to that sect.

10.   Somehow or other Govinda now came to the Kali temple at Dakshineswar and began to spend his time there with his "seat" spread under the peaceful shade of the Panchavati, which he thought, was a place favourable to religious practices. Just like Hindu Sannyasins, Muslim Fakirs too were welcome at Rasmani's Kali temple, and the hospitality of the temple was equally accorded to both of them. Therefore, while staying there, Govinda had not to go round for alms. He spent his days joyfully in spiritual practices according to the teaching of his religion.

11.   The Master was attracted towards the devout Govinda, and happening to converse with him, was charmed with Govinda's sincere faith and his love for God. Thus was the Master's mind now attracted towards the Islamic religion. "This also," thought he, "is a path to the realization of God, the sportive Mother, the source of infinite Lila, has been blessing many people with the attainment of Her lotus feet through this path also. I must see how people taking refuge in Her are led along this path to the fulfilment of their spiritual aspirations. I shall be initiated by Govinda and shall engage myself in the practice of that spiritual mood."

12.   Thought was immediately followed by action. The Master expressed his desire to Govinda, and became initiated. He engaged himself in practising Islam according to its prescribed rules. The Master said, "I then repeated the holy syllable 'Allah' with great devotion, wore cloth like the Muslims, said Namaz thrice daily, and felt disinclined even to see Hindu deities, not to speak of saluting them, inasmuch as the Hindu mode of thought vanished altogether from my mind. I spent three days in that mood, and

had the full realization of the result of the practices according to that faith." At the time of practising Islam, the Master at first had the vision of an effulgent, impressive personage with a long beard; afterwards he attained the knowledge of the all-pervading Brahman with attributes, and then merged finally in the attributeless Brahman, the Absolute.

13. At the time of practising Islam, the Master wanted, according to Hriday, to take Muslim type of food. It was Mathur's solicitous request alone that made him refrain from doing so. Knowing that the childike Master would not abstain from it if that desire of his were not at least partially fulfilled, Mathur had a cook brought, under whose instructions a Brahmin cook prepared food for the Master in the Muslim style. The Master did not even once enter the inner courtyard of the Kali temple while practising Islam, but remained in the mansion of Mathur situated outside.

14. From the event mentioned above, it becomes clear how sympathetic the Master's mind became towards other religious communities after he had attained perfection in the Vedantic discipline. It also becomes clear how, by having faith in the Vedantic knowledge alone, the Hindus and the Mohammedans of India may become sympathetic towards one another and develop a brotherly feeling, Otherwise, as the Master used to say, "There is, as it were, a mountain of difference between them. Their thoughts and faiths, actions and behaviour, have remained quite unintelligible to each other in spite of their living together for so long a time." Does the practice of Islam by the Master, the divine incarnation of the age, indicate that the said difference would some day disappear and both the Hindus and the Muslims would embrace one another in love?

15. As the result of his being established in the plane of Nirvikalpa consciousness, the memory of Non-duality used to be suddenly awakened in him, and his mind would get merged in the Absolute even at the slightest suggestion received from sights and persons coming strictly within the bounds of the plane of duality. We saw how that state was brought on him by the association of ideas, even without his desiring it. It is, therefore, superfluous to add that he could attain at any moment to that plane by a mere wish. It will be clear from the following incidents, small though they be, how deep and wide his non-dual mood was and how his mind had a natural attraction for it.

16. The gardeners found it inconvenient to sow kitchen vegetables in the spacious temple garden at Dakshineswar when it became covered with grass in the rainy season. Therefore, grass-cutters were allowed to cut and take away the grass from there. One day, having got permission to take away grass without paying any price for it, an old grass-cutter began to cut grass and bundle it, and was about to take it to the market for sale. The Master saw that the old man had cut so much grass out of avarice that it was beyond his power to carry or even lift up that load of grass. But the indigent grass-cutter refused to acknowledge it, and in spite of his repeated efforts in various ways to lift that big bundle upon his head, he failed miserably. While looking at it, the Master was inspired with spiritual emotion and thought, "Ah, the Self, the knowledge infinite, abides within, and yet so much foolishness and ignorance without!" Then exclaiming, "O Rama, inscrutable is Thy play!" he entered into ecstasy.

One day at Dakshineswar the Master saw a butterfly flying with a tiny stick stuck into its tail. He was at first pained to think that some naughty urchin had done it, but the next moment he was inspired and burst into laughter, saying, "O Rama, Thou hast brought Thyself to this plight!"

At one time a particular spot of the garden of the Kali temple was covered with newly grown Durva grass and was beautiful to look at. While he was looking at it, the Master transcended the normal consciousness and was feeling identified with that spot when a man just happened to walk across that field. At this the Master became very restless, feeling unbearable pain in his chest. Mentioning that event, he said to us later, "I then felt just that kind of pain which is felt when anybody tramples on one's chest. That state of Bhavasamadhi is very painful. Although I had it only for six hours, still it became quite unbearable."

One day the Master, while in Bhavasamadhi, was gazing towards the Ganga, standing at the spacious Ghat with an open portico. Two boats were at anchor at the Ghat and the boatmen were quarrelling over some matter. The quarrel became gradually bitter, and the stronger man gave a severe slap on the back of the weaker one. At that, the Master cried out suddenly in pain. Hriday heard it from the Kali temple, went there quickly, and saw that the Master's back had become red and swollen. Impatient with anger, Hriday said repeatedly, "Uncle, show me the man who has beaten you; I'll tear off his head." Afterwards, when the Master had calmed down a little, Hriday was astonished to hear of the event and thought, "Is it ever possible?" Girish Chandra Ghosh had heard of the event from the Master's lips and narrated it to us. Innumerable events of this nature regarding the Master may be mentioned, but we refrain from doing so to avoid superfluity.

CHAPTER XVII

THE MASTER'S VISIT TO HIS NATIVE VILLAGE

(TOPICS; 1. The Master's visit to Kamarpukur with Hriday and the Bhairavi 2. Amidst friends and relatives 3. The Holy Mother at Kamarpukur 4. The Master's behaviour with all 5. The Master on the spiritual progress of some of them 6. The Master's feeling at Kamarpukur 7. The Master's love for his home village 8. The Master doing his duty to his wife 9. The Master's success in it 10. The Brahmani's apprehension 11. The Brahmani in a mood of pride and egoism 12. The event illustrating this 13. Hriday's quarrel with the Brahmani 14. The Brahmani's recognition of her mistake and departure 15. The Master's return to Dakshineswar)

1. The Master suffered for six months as already stated, and when he was cured of his ailment towards the close of that period, it was noticed that his mind, in place of constantly tending towards Non-duality, had got habituated to dwell in the state of Bhavamukha wherein multiplicity and Non-duality (Dvaita and Advaita) are simultaneously apprehended. But his body was not as strong and healthy as before, and it was feared that his dysentery might recur for want of pure drinking water when the waters of the Ganga became saline during the rainy season. It was therefore settled that he should go to Kamarpukur, his birth-place, for a few months. Accordingly arrangements were made for this proposed change for the Master in 1867. The devout Jagadamba Dasi, wife of Mathur Babu, knew that the Master's household was ever poor like that of Siva. So she made arrangements with much care about all the necessary articles so that "father" might not have inconvenience of any kind (IV. 1). The Master then started at an auspicious moment. Hriday and the Bhairavi Brahmani accompanied him. But his aged mother stuck to her previous resolve of living near the Ganga and stayed back at Dakshineswar under Mathur's care.

2. The Master had not come to Kamarpukur for the past eight years. Therefore, his friends and relatives, it is needless to add, were eager to see him. And it needs no mention that there were special reasons for it; for many strange rumours about him had reached their ears from time to time. They had heard that

he was crying "Hari, Hari" in a woman's dress, that he had become a monk, that he was repeating "Allah, Allah" continually, and was thus behaving in many strange ways. But, as soon as the Master was in their midst, they all found how baseless were the rumours; for, they found that he was just his old self. The same amiability, the same loving merriment, the same austere truthfulness, the same profound religious sensibility, and the same surge of overwhelming emotion at the name of Hari—all these old qualities of his were seen in him in the fullest measure as before. The only change they found in him was that his body and mind were glowing with such an indescribable, heavenly effulgence that they felt a great hesitation to appear before him suddenly or to broach worldly topics when he did not start them himself. Again, they all felt that their worldly anxieties disappeared into thin air when they were in his presence, and that instead, there flowed in their hearts a serene and tranquil current of bliss and peace. Besides, when they were away from him, they experienced a strong inexpressible desire to go to him once more. Thus, there was an incessant flow of bliss in that poor family when they had him in their midst after so long a time. And in order to fill the cup of happiness to the brim, a messenger was sent under the instruction of the ladies to Jayrambati, the village of the Master's father-in-law, to bring his wife. The Master knew it, but did not express either approval or disapproval. Hitherto his wife had met him only once after their marriage. This was when, according to the custom of the family, the Master was taken to Jayrambati on one occasion when she was seven years of age. But she was then too young to understand what marriage meant. Therefore, the only thing regarding the event that was retained in her memory was that, when the Master came to her father's house with Hriday, the latter brought with him a good many lotus flowers from somewhere, sought her out from a secluded part of the house where she had hidden herself, and worshipped her feet with those flowers as she shrank into herself out of bashfulness. Six years after this event, she was taken to Kamarpukur in her thirteenth year. This time she spent a month there. But she had not the good fortune then to see either the Master or her mother-in-law, as both of them were away at Dakshineswar. She came again six months later to her father-in-law's house for a stay of one and a half months, but could not see either of them for the same reason.

3. It was three or four months after her return from this visit to her father-in-law's house that news arrived about the Master's coming to Kamarpukur and about her being summoned to join him there. She had reached her fourteenth year some six or seven months before this event. Therefore, this was practically her first real meeting with her husband after her marriage.

4. It seems that the Master stayed at Kamarpukur for six or seven months on this occasion. The friends of his early days and all the men and women of the village known to him mixed with him as before and tried to make him happy. The Master too was very much pleased to see them after such a long time. In mingling with men and women of Kamarpukur, who were taken up with the affairs of their circumscribed worldly lives, the Master felt a joy similar to what great thinkers and scholars feel when, during their leisure after hard toils, they join children in their aimless and meaningless amusements. He, however, strongly felt that they should become conscious of the transitoriness of this life, and although living in the world, should gradually attain self-control and learn to depend on God in all matters. We infer this from the manner in which he always taught us the very same things through play and fun, mirth and merriment.

On finding that, even while living in the little world of the little village, some had made unexpected progress in spiritual life, he was struck with wonder at the inconceivable glory of God. He told us many times of an event to illustrate this.

5. The Master said that one day during that period, he was resting in his room after his midday meal. Some ladies, his neighbours, came to see him, sat near him, and became engaged in spiritual conversation with him. The Master suddenly went into an ecstasy and felt that he was a fish joyfully swimming and sporting, sometimes coming to the surface, and sometimes sinking deep—all in the ocean of Existence-Knowledge-Bliss. The Master used to fall into such ecstasies very often while talking with others. Therefore, not at all mindful of it, the ladies expressed their own opinions, which created a lot of noise. One of the company forbade the others to do so and asked them to be quiet till his ecstasy came to an end. She said, "He has now become a fish and is swimming in the sea of Existence-Knowledge-Bliss. If you make noise, that Bliss of his will be interrupted." Although many of them did not then believe in her words, all remained quiet. When he came

20

down from that state and was asked about his experience, the Master said, "Yes, what she said is true. How strange! How could she know it?"

6. It seems to us that the daily rounds of the men and women of the village of Kamarpukur now appeared new to the Master to a great extent. He now felt like a man who had returned home from a far off place, to whom every person and object of the village appeared to be new. For although the Master had been away from the place of his birth for a short period of eight years only, a violent storm of spiritual strivings had raged in his heart during that period and produced a radical change in it; for during those eight years he had forgotten himself, forgotten the world and ascended far beyond the bounds of time and space. But while descending from there, he came transfigured with the knowledge that Brahman existed in all beings, and he found all persons and things mellowed by an extraordinary new light. It is well known in philosophy that our consciousness of time and the measurement of its duration arises from the succession of our mental events. Therefore, a short period during which a great many thoughts rise and sink in our minds appears to us to be very long. One is astonished to think what tumultuous waves of thoughts and emotions surged in the Master's mind during this period. Is it, therefore, surprising that the said period should appear to him to be an age?

7. One is astonished to think of the wonderful relation of affection which the Master had established with all the people of Kamarpukur. The men and women of all families including those of the Lahas, the Brahmanas, the blacksmiths, the carpenters, the gold-merchants and others were all bound to him in a relation of reverential love. We were charmed to hear the Master speak on many occasions with great pleasure about the devotion and affection of a large number of men and women for him. Among them were the simple-hearted and devout Prasanna, the widowed sister of Dharmadas Laha; the Master's friend Gayavishnu Laha, the son of Dharmadas; Srinivas Sankhari of sincere faith; the devout ladies of the Pyne family; and the Master's Bhikshamata Dhani, the blacksmith woman. All of them remained mostly with the Master during those days of his at Kamarpukur. Those who could not do so on account of their household duties or other business used to come in the morning, or midday, or evening, whenever they

had leisure.   When they came, the ladies brought with them various
sweets and delicious dishes and felt delighted in feeding the Master.
We have given the reader elsewhere (IV. 1) an indication of how
the Master, although living in the family at home, surrounded
by the people of the village who behaved so sweetly, always remained
divinely inspired.   It is, therefore, needless to repeat it here.

8. The Master paid attention to the performance of another
great duty when he came this time to Kamarpukur.   At first,
the Master had been indifferent to his wife's coming to Kamarpukur,
but now he was intent on giving her education and training for her
well-being.   Knowing that the Master was married, Tota Puri,
his teacher, who initiated him in Sannyasa, had said to him at one
time, "What does it matter?   He only may be regarded as really
established in Brahman whose renunciation, detachment, discrimination and knowledge remain intact in all respects in spite of his
wife being with him.   He alone may be regarded as having really
attained the knowledge of Brahman, who can always look equally
upon both man and woman as the Self and can behave accordingly.
Others who have a keen awareness of the distinction of sexes (and
keep away from the opposite sex as a protective measure), may
be good Sadhakas, but are still far away from the knowledge of
Brahman."   The above remark of Tota Puri came to the Master's
mind and induced him to test his knowledge attained by spiritual
practices extending over a long period, as well as to look to his
wife's well-being.

9. The Master could never neglect or leave half-finished
anything he considered to be a duty.   The same held good here
also.   He did not stop at partially educating his girl-wife who
depended entirely on him regarding everything connected with her
worldly and spiritual welfare.   He was, from now on especially
mindful that she should learn household duties, know people's
character, put money to good use, and above all, surrender her all
to God and be an expert in behaving correctly according to place,
time and circumstance (III. 2 & 4). We have, in many other
places, hinted how far-reaching was the result of that teaching which
the Master imparted to her, reinforcing it with the example of his
own life of unbroken continence.   Suffice it to say that the Holy
Mother, as she is called by the devotees of Sri Ramakrishna, was
extremely happy with all these experiences.   In every respect she
continued to receive the Master's loving attention, devoid however

of the slightest tinge of lust, and she on her part, offered him her life-long worship as her chosen Ideal, following his footsteps and moulding her life according to his teaching.

10. The Bhairavi Brahmani did not, on many occasions, understand the Master when he went forward to do his duty to his wife. We have seen that she tried to make the Master give up his resolve of being initiated into Sannyasa when he came in contact with Tota Puri (III. 2). For, she thought that love of God would be completely uprooted from the Master's mind if he were so initiated. Some such apprehension took possession of her heart even now. She, it seems, thought that it would be prejudicial to the Master's continence if he mixed so intimately with his wife. But the Master could not comply with the Brahmani's ideas, even as he could not when she had expressed misgivings about his associating with Tota Puri. The Brahmani felt very much wounded by this conduct of the Master. This gave rise to egoism, which was aggravated into pride and vanity, resulting often in loss of faith in the Master. We were told by Hriday that she openly expressed her feelings from time to time. For example, if any one raised a question before her on any spiritual matter and said that he would ask Sri Ramakrishna and have his opinion on it, she would flare up and say, "What can he say? It is I who opened his eyes." Or, she would scold the womenfolk of the family for trivial reasons or for no reason at all. But the Master remained calm in spite of such words and oppressive behaviour of hers, and did not cease having devotion or paying reverence to her now as before. Instructed by the Master, the Holy Mother too paid the Brahmani the respect due to her own mother-in-law and always engaged herself in her service with love and devotion; and considering herself to be an ignorant girl, she did not protest against any of her words or actions.

11. When pride and egoism are in the ascendant, the intelligence of even a thoughtful man gets clouded. Owing to his own perverse behaviour, he begins to experience bumps and knocks at every turn before long. Repeated frustration resulting from such experiences would, if he has still some good sense left, teach him his own mistake and bring him back to the path of normalcy. Such was the case with the learned Brahmani now. Unable under the influence of her inordinate pride to make proper assessment of persons and circumstances, she created a very awkward situation one day. The incident was as follows:

12. We have already mentioned the name of Srinivas Sankhari. Although not born in a high family, Srinivas was higher than many Brahmanas in respect of devotion to God. One day during this period, he came to the Master for the purpose of having Raghuvir's Prasada. It needs no mention that the Master and all the members of his family became very happy with Srinivas in their midst. The devout Brahmani also was pleased to see Srinivas's faith and devotion. They talked on various devotional topics till midday, when the offering of food to Raghuvir and other services were finished and Srinivas sat down to take his food. When he finished it and was ready, according to the prevalent custom, to clean the place where he had taken his food, the Brahmani forbade him to do so and said, "We'll do it ourselves." At the Brahmani's insistence Srinivas had no other aternatlive but to leave the matter there and go home.

13. In villages of those times, dominated as they were by caste rules and regulations, great quarrels and party feelings often used to spring up on account of the breaking of those rules. And such an event happened now. For, the Brahmana women who came to visit the Master raised great objection to the cleaning of the leavings of Srinivas by the Bhairavi, who was Brahmana by caste. The Bhairavi did not admit the validity of their objection. The quarrel gradually increased. Hriday, the Master's nephew, heard of it. Knowing that a great quarrel might arise over that trifling event, Hriday asked the Brahmani not to violate the prevailing custom, but she paid no heed to his words. Hriday got incensed, and a noisy quarrel ensued between him and the Brahmani. Hriday said, "If you do so, we won't allow you to remain inside the house." The Brahmani was not the sort of a person to yield to threats. She replied, "What harm, if you don't? Manasa[1] will go to bed in Sitala's room."[2] All the other members of the house mediated, entreating the Brahmani to refrain from cleaning the place. This brought the quarrel to an end.

14. Although she submitted to this, the Brahmani's pride was severely wounded that day. When her anger subsided, she thought calmly over the matter and understood her own mistake. She thought that when she was committing such blunders again

---

[1]Manasa—goddess of snakes. The Brahmani thus compared herself to the angry snake.

[2]The temple in which Sitala, a goddess, was installed.

and again, she should no longer continue to stay there. When the eyes of an aspirant possessed of keen insight fall somehow or other on his own heart, no impure ideas lurking there can conceal themselves from him. That was what happened with the Brahmani now. Introspection made her also aware of the perverse change in her attitude towards the Master, and she became repentant A few days passed, when one day she made garlands of various flowers with her own hands and smeared them with sandal paste, and having beautifully adorned the Master as Sri Gauranga, asked his forgiveness with all her heart. Afterwards, controlling herself carefully and offering her heart and soul to God, she left Kamarpukur and took the path to Kasi, the abode of the Lord of the universe. Thus did the Brahmani take her final leave of the Master after having spent six long years with him at a stretch.

15. The Master spent about seven months in various spiritual moods at Kamarpukur, and returned to Dakshineswar (probably at the end of 1867) when he had regained his health and was almost as strong and healthy as before. An important event happened in his life shortly after his return. We shall present it to the reader now.

CHAPTER XVIII

THE MASTER'S PILGRIMAGE AND THE STORY OF HRIDAYRAM

(TOPICS: 1. The Master's pilgrimage settled 2. The day of starting 3. Arrangement about the pilgrimage 4. Visit to Sri Vaidyanath and service to the poor. 5. A mishap on the way 6. Stay at Kedarghat 7. The Master and Trailanga Swami 8. The Master's behaviour at Prayag 9. The Master's visit to Nidhuvan etc. in Vrindavan 10. Return to Kasi 11. Meeting the Brahmani at Kasi 12. The Master going to Mahesh the Vina-player 13. Return to Dakshineswar and subsequent doings 14. Death of Hriday's wife 15. Hriday in Bhavasamadhi 16. Hriday's wonderful vision 17. Hriday's mind became dull 18. Obstacle to Hriday's Sadhana 19. Hriday celebrating the autumnal worship of Durga 20. Hriday's vision of the Master 21. The last occasion of the worship of Durga)

1. Mathuranath and his wife were now getting ready to visit the principal holy places of north-western India. A day for the commencement of the journey was fixed in the month of January, and it was settled that many persons, including Mathur's Guru's son and others, should go with him. Mathur and his wife made earnest requests to the Master to go with them. Consequently, he agreed to accompany them with his aged mother[1] and his nephew, Hriday.

2. Mathur started with the Master and others on the auspicious day of January 27, 1868. We have told the reader many things about the Master's pilgrimage elsewhere (IV. 3). We shall, therefore briefly mention here what we heard about it from Hriday.

3. About one hundred and twenty-five persons in all—Sri Ramakrishna, his mother, Mathur, his wife, his daughter-in-law, his Guru's son, Hriday, a Brahmin cook, a gatekeeper and men and women servants—were included in that pilgrim party. One second class and three third class carriages were reserved for them by the Railway Company, and it was so arranged that those four bogies could be detached at any place required between Calcutta and Kasi.

---

[1] Some say that the Master's mother did not go on pilgrimage with him. But Hriday told us she did.

4. Mathur and others visited Sri Vaidyanath at Deoghar on the way and rested for a few days there, during which period an important event occurred. The Master's heart became filled with compassion on seeing the miserable plight of the men and women of a poor village there. He requested Mathur to feed them one day and give a piece of cloth to each of them (III. 7). Mathur did accordingly.

5. From Deoghar, Mathur went direct to Kasi. Nothing of importance happened on the way, except that when Sri Ramakrishna and Hriday got down at a certain station near Kasi, the train started before they could get into it. Mathur became anxious and wired from Kasi that they should be sent by the next train. But they did not have to wait for the next train. Rajendralal Bandyopadhyaya, an important officer of the Railway Company, arrived there on supervision duty in a special train shortly afterwards, and seeing them in that plight, took them with him up to Kasi. Rajendralal Bandyopadhyaya was a resident of the Baghbazar quarter of Calcutta.

6. On reaching Kasi, Mathur Babu hired two houses side by side on the Kedarghat. He behaved there like a prince in all respects (IV. 3). Whenever he went out, a silver umbrella used to be held over his head, while servants carried silver maces and other paraphernalia before and after him.

While staying at Kasi, Sri Ramakrishna went in a palanquin to pay his obeisance to Viswanath, the principal deity of Kasi, almost every day. Hriday accompanied him on foot. Even on the way to the temple, the Master used to pass into ecstasy, not to speak of the time when he saw the deity. Though he entered into ecstasy in all the temples, he especially experienced it in the temple of Kedarnath.

7. Besides visiting the temples, the Master went to see the eminent holy men of Kasi. Hriday always accompanied him. The Master paid a few visits to the famous Trailanga Swami, one of the foremost of the Paramahamsas. The Swami was then observing a vow of silence and was staying at the Manikarnika Ghat. On their first meeting, the Swami placed his snuff-box before the Master for his use by way of giving a cordial reception to him. Examining the sense organs and the limbs of the holy man, the Master told Hriday that he bore the signs of a true Paramahamsa and that he was, so to say, the living image of Siva. The Swami

had resolved to have a Ghat built near Manikarnika.   At the request of the Master, Hriday participated in that work by placing a few spadefuls of earth there.   One of those days, the Master invited and brought Trailanga Swami to the residence of Mathur and fed him with Payasam, serving it with his own hands.

8.   The Master stayed at Kasi for five or six days and then went to Prayag with Mathur.   He bathed in the holy confluence and stayed there for three nights.   Mathur and all the others shaved their heads there according to scriptural injunction, but the Master did not do so, saying, "It is not necessary for me to do it."   From Prayag they returned to Kasi, where they stayed for a fortnight before proceeding to Vrindavan.

9.   Mathur stayed in a house near Nidhuvan at Vrindavan. He displayed his pomp and power there also, as in Kasi.   He would go with his wife to visit temples where he offered a few gold coins as a token of respect while saluting the deities.   Besides visiting Nidhuvan, the Master paid visits to Radhakunda, Shyamakunda and the Govardhan hill, ascending to the top of that hillock in an ecstatic mood.   He heard of the eminent holy men of the place and paid visits to them.   He was highly pleased to meet Gangamata at Nidhuvan.   He indicated to Hriday the signs on her person and said that she had attained to a very high state of spirituality.

10.   Having stayed at Vrindavan for about a fortnight, Mathur and the others returned to Kasi.   In order to see Viswanath, the Great Lord of the universe, adorned in special dress and ornaments, they stayed there till about the middle of 1868.   The Master saw the golden image of Annapurna during this period.

11.   The Master, Hriday said, met the Bhairavi Brahmani, Yogeswari, at Kasi.   He went several times to her house in the quarter called the "Sixty-four Yoginis."   The Brahmani was living there with a lady named Mokshada.   The Master was pleased to see the faith and devotion of that lady.   The Brahmani accompanied the Master to Vrindavan, where he asked her to live permanently.   She passed away there shortly after the Master returned from Vrindavan.

12.   During their stay at Vrindavan, the Master had a desire to listen to the playing of the stringed instrument known as the Vina. But his desire was not fulfilled, as no Vina-player was available there at that time.   That desire again arose in his mind when he returned to Kasi.   Accompanied by Hriday, he went to the

house of the expert Vina-player, Maheshchandra Sarkar, whom he requested to play on the Vina for him. Mahesh lived in the quarter called Madanpura in Kasi. At the request of the Master, he played that day for a long time on that instrument with great delight. As soon as he heard the sweet ringing sound of the Vina, the Master was in ecstasy. When he regained partial normal consciousness, he was heard to pray to the Divine Mother, saying, "Mother, give me normal consciousness; I want to listen attentively to the Vina." Immediately afterwards, he was able to stay in the external plane of consciousness and listen to the music with delight, now and then also singing to the accompaniment of the Vina. From 5 p.m. to 8 p.m. he spent his time delightfully there, when he was requested by Mahesh to take a little refreshment, which he did, and returned to Mathur. Mahesh used to come daily to see the Master thereafter. The Master said about him, "He completely lost himself when playing on the Vina."

13. Mathur expressed his desire to go to Gaya, the abode of Vishnu. But, as the Master had a strong objection to it, he gave up the idea and came back to Calcutta. After this pilgrimage to the principal places for about four months, the Master, according to Hriday, returned to Dakshineswar in the middle of 1868. The Master brought from Vrindavan some earth and dust of Radhakunda and Shyamakunda. When he came to Dakshineswar, he scattered, with the help of Hriday, a little of the earth and dust round the Panchavati and buried the remainder with his own hands in his Sadhana-cottage, saying, "This spot becomes from today a holy place like Vrindavan." He requested Mathur, shortly afterwards, to invite Vaishnava teachers and devotees from various places. They came and the Master celebrated a festival at the Panchavati. Mathur paid sixteen rupees to each Vaishnava teacher and one rupee to each devotee at the time of farewell, thus showing his respect for them.

14. Hriday's wife died a short time after he had returned from the pilgrimage. On account of that event his mind was filled with dispassion for some time. Hriday, we said before, was not a man of a contemplative temperament. His ideal of life was to improve his worldly condition and spend his life enjoying the pleasures of the world as far as possible. Though other moods came on him from time to time because of keeping the constant company of the Master, they could not last long. Whenever there

came an opportunity to satisfy his desire for enjoyment, he forgot everything else, pursued the thing longed for, and until it was achieved, no other thought could enter his mind. Therefore, though all the Master's Sadhanas were performed during Hriday's stay at Dakshineswar, he was very little moved or influenced by the devotional fervour he witnessed in his uncle. However, Hriday truly loved his uncle and did not fail to render whatever service was necessary for him at any time, and as a result of it he developed great courage, adroitness and intelligence. The more he heard from holy men about the superhuman nature of his uncle and the more he observed the manifestation of divine powers in him during his spiritual practices, the greater was his feeling of strength within himself—thanks to his nearness to his dear uncle. His sense of nearness to his Master on account of his great service to him—the feeling that the Master was his 'own' and himself his favourite—made him think that all the spiritual achievements of the Master were his too in a way. Should he ever make an effort to have them, his uncle, by his divine powers, would enable him to attain them. He, therefore, did not feel that he was under any obligation to think of the hereafter. He would at first enjoy this world a little and apply his mind to spiritual matters afterwards. Such was his attitude towards life till now. Grief-stricken at the death of his wife, he now thought that the proper time for a change in his outlook and mode of life had arrived. He applied his mind more steadfastly than before to the worship of the Mother of the universe, and began to practise meditation, putting off his cloth and sacred thread in imitation of the Master. He also requested the Master earnestly to help him to have spiritual experiences similar to his own. The Master assured him strongly that he had no need to do these things; for all the results would be his by just serving the Master. He told him that if both of them were filled with divine inspiration day and night and forgot everything concerning the body like eating and sleeping, neither of them would be able to look after the other. But Hriday did not give heed to those words. The Master at last had to yield, and said, "Let the Mother's will be done. Does anything happen by my will? It was the Mother who turned my mind away from the world and brought about those conditions in me and made me have strange experiences; if the Mother wills so, you also will have them."

15. A few days after this talk, Hriday began to have, while

worshipping, a few wonderful visions and states of divine ecstasy attended with semi-absorbed states of consciousness. One day Mathur Babu saw Hriday in that state and said to the Master, "What is this state Hriday is in, Father?" The Master explained it to him, saying, "It is no sham with him. He importuned the Mother for spiritual visions; that is why he is having it. The Mother will bring him back to his normal condition after giving him a taste of it." "Father, " said Mathur, " it is all your play; only you have brought about this state on Hriday. So please calm him again. Both of us should be with you like Nandi and Bhringi and serve you. Why should these unusual states be with us?"

16. Shortly after this conversation between the Master and Mathur, one night Hriday saw the Master going towards the Pancha-vati. Thinking that he might require his waterpot and towel, he took them and followed him. As he was going, Hriday had an extraordinary vision. He saw that the Master was not a human being, that he was not composed of flesh and blood, that the Pancha-vati was illumined by the light coming out of his body, and that while the Master was walking, neither of his feet, which were also of light, did touch the ground but carried him through the air. Taking all this to be an optical illusion, Hriday rubbed his eyes again and again, observed all the surrounding things in their natural state and looked at the Master once more. But to no purpose. Although he saw all other things — trees, creepers, the Ganga, the hut etc. — to be what they were, he repeatedly saw the Master in that luminous form. Extremely amazed at it, Hriday asked himself whether there was any change in his mind which made him have that experience. Thinking thus, he looked at his own body and saw that he too was an effulgent being made of light — an attendant and companion of God Himself serving Him eternally, a part and parcel of His divine person of solidified spiritual lumino-sity, now having a separate existence for the sole purpose of serving Him. When he had this experience and came to know the mystery of his own life, his heart was flooded with a strong current of bliss. He forgot himself, forgot the world, and forgot to consider whether the people of the world would speak well or ill of him. He was now in ecstasy with only partial normal consciousness and cried aloud repeatedly like one mad, " O Ramakrishna ! O Ramakrishna! We are not mortal beings. Why are we here? Come, let us go

from country to country and set souls free from bondage! I am also what you are."

The Master said to us, "Hearing him crying out thus, I said, 'Ah, stop, stop! Why on earth are you behaving like this? People will run up here thinking some calamity has befallen us.' But did he give ear to it at all? I then came hurriedly to him, touched his heart and said, 'Make the fellow dull and drab again, O Mother'."

17. Hriday said to us that no sooner had the Master said so than his bliss and vision vanished into the void and he was his former dull self once gain. Thus, fallen suddenly from that state of ecstasy, his mind was filled with dejection. "Uncle," sobbed he, " why did you do this ? Why did you say that I should become dull? I shall never again have such a blissful vision." "Did I say," replied the Master, "that you should for ever be dull? I said, 'Be calm now.' What a noise you made with such a small vision! That was why I had to say so. What a wealth of visions and experiences I have all the twenty-four hours! But do I make any noise? It is not yet time for you to have such visions. Now be at rest; when it is time, you will have various visions and experiences."

18. Although Hriday had to remain silent at the words cf the Master, he felt much wounded. Under the influence of egoism, he thought afterwards that he would try to have that vision again somehow. Reflecting thus, he increased the period of his Japa and meditation, and resolved that he should go at night to the Panchavati, and that sitting under the tree, where the Master formerly used to sit for Japa and meditation, he should call on the Mother of the universe. Thinking so, once, at dead of night, he left his bed, went to the Panchavati, and sat down on the Master's seat to meditate. Strangely enough, the Master too felt a desire to go to the Panchavati at that time. Scarcely had he reached the place when he, heard Hriday piteously calling out to him, "Save me, uncle, save me! I am being burnt to death." The Master stepped forward quickly, came up to him and asked him, "What is the matter Hriday?" Restless on account of pain, Hriday said, "Uncle, no sooner did I sit down here for meditation than I felt as if some one threw a plateful of live charcoal over my body. I am suffering from an unbearable burning pain." The Master passed his hand over his body and said, "Don't be afraid; it will cool. Why do you do all this? Have I not told you again and again that you will

achieve everything by serving me?" Hriday used to say that all
his pain was immediately removed by the touch of the Master's
hand. He never afterwards went again to the Panchavati to
practise meditation, and a conviction grew in his mind that it would
not be good for him to act contrary to his uncle's advice.

19. Hriday, no doubt, got some sort of peace from the words
of the Master, but the daily duties of the temple now appeared
distasteful to Him. His mind was in search of some novel action
from which he could derive some joy. Seeing the advent of the
autumn season of 1868, he resolved to perform the autumnal
worship of the Mother in his house. Ganganarayan, his elder
half-brother, had then passed away, and Raghav, another relative,
now appointed to collect rent in the estate of Mathur Babu,was
earning a decent income. With the change of time, when prosperity
dawned, a new worship hall was built. Ganganarayan had
expressed a wish that he should once invoke the Divine Mother
and worship Her there. But he did not get an opportunity of
fulfilling that wish. Hriday remembered that desire of his and
tried to fulfil it. Knowing that Hriday, a man of action, might
possibly get peace by celebrating the worship, the Master agreed
to it, while Mathur rendered pecuniary help to him. Hriday
desired very much to take the Master with him and have him at
his residence during the worship. But Mathur would have none
of it, as he wanted the Master to be with himself during that period.
Wounded at heart on account of his failure in this respect, Hriday
made ready to go home alone to perform the worship. Seeing him
thus dejected, the Master, as Hriday told us, consoled him saying,
"Why are you pained? In my subtle body I shall daily go to see
your worship; nobody except you will see me. Have as the
Tantradharaka a Brahmana to dictate the Mantras to you and
perform the worship yourself with devotion. Instead of keeping
a complete fast, at midday drink some milk, Ganga water, and the
syrup of candy. If you perform the worship in this way, the Mother
of the universe will certainly accept your worship." Hriday said
that the Master gave him detailed instructions as to who should be
ordered to make the image, who should be appointed Tantradharaka
and how all other things should be done. He then started home
with great delight to perform the worship.

20. Hriday reached home, and did everything according
to the advice of the Master. He performed the rites pertaining to the

sixth day of the bright fortnight such as the awakening of the Goddess, the preliminary consecration of the image and the invocation of
the Devi, and engaged himself in the worship. While the light waving
service (Arati) was in progress at the conclusion of the worship on
the Saptami day, Hriday saw the luminous form of the Master standing in an ecstatic mood by the side of the image. Hriday informed us
how he used to be filled with a great spiritual ardour to have this
vision of the Master on every day of worship at the light waving
service and also at the special rites of the Sandhi-puja or junction-
worship, so called because of its performance at the junction of the
Ashtami and the Navami days of worship. Hriday came back to
Dakshineswar shortly after the worship was finished and narrated
to the Master everything concerning the worship. "At the time
of the Arati and the 'junction worship'," said the Master to him,
"I used to feel a great desire to see your worship and so enter into
an ecstasy. I felt then that I went along a ' path of light' and
was present in your worship hall in a luminous body."

21. Hriday told us that once the Master predicted in an
ecstatic mood: "You will perform the yearly worship thrice."
And it actually happened so. Disregarding the Master's words,
he was making preparations for the worship for the fourth time,
when such a series of obstacles occurred that he had, at last, to give
it up. Hriday married again shortly after the worship of the first
year. Thenceforth he applied his mind to the service of the Master
and to the worship at the Dakshineswar temple as before.

CHAPTER XIX

THE DEATH OF THE MASTER'S RELATIONS

(TOPICS: 1. The story of Akshay 2. The beauty of Akshay
3. Akshay's devotion to Sadhana 4. Akshay's marriage 5.
Akshay's severe illness after his marriage 6. Akshay's second
illness 7. Hriday's apprehension and behaviour 8. Akshay's
death and the Master's behaviour 9. His agony at the death of
Akshay 10. The Master's brother Rameswar appointed as priest
11. The Master with Mathur at Ranaghat and the service of the
poor as Narayana 12. The Master at Mathur's ancestral home
13. The Master at the Hari Sabha of Kolutola and at Kalna,
Navadwip etc. 14. Mathur's selfless devotion 15. Their mutual
love and devotion 16. An anecdote 17. Another anecdote
18. The Sastras on such unselfish devotion 19. Mathur's passing
away 20. The Master seeing the event in Bhavasamadhi.)

1.   We have already acquainted the reader a little with Akshay,
the son of the Master's eldest brother Ramkumar. Akshay came
to Dakshineswar and was appointed priest in the Vishnu temple
in 1865, a short time after the reversed Tota Puri came there. Akshay
was then about seventeen years old. It is necessary to say a few
words here about him. As his mother had died at the time of his
birth, he became an object of special love to all his relatives. He
was only three or four years old when the Master came for the first
time to Calcutta in 1852. The Master, therefore, had had the
occasion to take Akshay on his lap and bring him up with loving
care for two or three years before he came to Calcutta. But his
father Ramkumar never took him on his lap. When asked for the
reason, he would say, "It will be love lost; the child will not live
long." Afterwards the Master forgot himself, the world and all
its concerns during the days of his absorption in spiritual practices.
Akshay was then passing through the tender years of his boyhood.
and had by this time grown up into a handsome youth.

2.   We were told by the Master and his relatives that Akshay
was indeed a very handsome person. They said that his complexion
was as bright as his features were graceful. He looked like a living
form of Siva.

3.   Akshay's mind was very much devoted from his childhood
to Sri Ramachandra. He spent a long time daily in the service of
Raghuvir, his family deity. Therefore his appointment as the

Siva Temple of th... ...gas

Anur:
The image of
Visālākshī

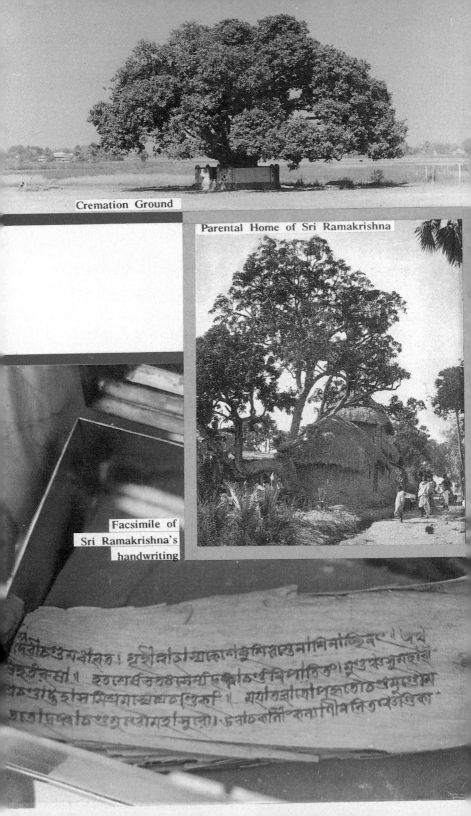

Cremation Ground

Parental Home of Sri Ramakrishna

Facsimile of Sri Ramakrishna's handwriting

priest of the Vishnu temple at Dakshineswar gave him a duty that was very much to his liking. The Master said, "While he was performing the worship of Radha-Govinda, he became so much absorbed in meditation that he had no idea of the crowds of people coming and going out of the temple, and would not regain his normal consciousness before the lapse of a couple of hours." Having finished the daily worship at the temple, he would go, we have been told by Hriday, to the Panchavati and spend a long time in worshipping Siva there. He would then cook his food with his own hands, and after taking his meal, apply his mind to the study of the *Bhagavata*. Besides, by a new urge of the love of God, he practised so much of Nyasa and Pranayama that his throat and palate bled and swelled now and again. Is it any wonder therefore, that such love and devotion on his part to God endeared him to the Master?

4. Years passed on one after another, till it was the end of B.E. 1275 (A.D. 1869). Akshay's uncle Rameswar came to know of this trend of his mind and began to search for a bride in order to check that trend. It was in the month of Chaitra that a suitable bride was found in the village of Kuchkol, not far from Kamarpukur, and Rameswar came to Dakshineswar to take Akshay home. Objections were raised against their starting on the ground that the month of Chaitra was held inauspicious for starting on a journey. Rameswar and Akshay did not pay any heed to it and said that the prohibition of the scriptures was not applicable in the case of homecoming from a temporary residence elsewhere. Akshay's marriage took place shortly after he returned home in the month of Vaisakh of B.E. 1276 (A.D. 1869).

5. Akshay fell seriously ill when he was in his father-in-law's house a few months after his marriage. Rameswar, on receiving news of this, had him brought to Kamarpukur, where he was placed under treatment and brought round. He was then sent to Dakshineswar. There his looks brightened and his health seemed to be improving, when suddenly he had an attack of fever one day. Doctors thought it was a simple fever and that he would be rid of it very soon.

6. When he heard that Akshay had fallen ill in his father-in-law's house shortly after his marriage, the Master, we were told by Hriday, had said, "Hridu, the omens are extremely bad; he has been married to a bride of Rakshasagana; the lad will die,

21

I am afraid." When the fever did not subside even after three or four days, he called Hriday to him, and said, "Hridu, doctors have not been able to diagnose the disease. Akshay has a complicated, high and continuous fever. Call a good doctor and administer good treatment to your satisfaction; but the boy, it is certain, will not survive."

7.   Hriday said, "When I heard him say so, I took him to task saying, 'Don't speak like that, uncle. Let not such words come out of your lips!' He said, 'Do I say so of my own accord? I say things involuntarily under the divine influence; I say what the Mother makes me know and say. Do I wish that Akshay should die?'"

8.   Hriday was very much alarmed to hear these words of the Master. He called in good physicians and tried in various ways to cure Akshay. But the disease went on worsening. Akshay suffered for about a month. When his last moment arrived, the Master went to his bedside and said, "Akshay, say, 'Ganga, Narayana, Om Rama'." Akshay repeated the Mantra once, twice, thrice, and passed away. We were told by Hriday that the more he wept at Akshay's death, the more did the Master laugh in ecstasy.

9.   Although the Master laughed that way, viewing from a high plane of spiritual consciousness the death of his dear nephew, Akshay of pleasant looks, it is not that he felt no great shock in his heart. Long afterwards he spoke to us of this event several times. He used to say that although during ecstasy he regarded death as but a change of state, he felt a great void at the death of Akshay when he came down to the normal state of consciousness (III.1). He could never again live in the mansion of the proprietors after Akshay's death, as it was there that he passed away.

10.   Rameswar, the Master's second elder brother, was appointed to worship Radha-Govinda at Dakshineswar after Akshay's death. But he could not always be at Dakshineswar as he was in charge of the whole management of the household at Kamarpukur. He used to place some suitable and reliable person in charge of his duty at Dakshinewar and occasionally go to his village to stay there. Ramachandra Chattopadhyaya and another person named Dinanath, we were told, officiated for him during his absence.

11.   It was during this period that Mathur, accompanied by the Master, went to his zamindari estate and to the house of his own Guru. He did this then perhaps to relieve the feeling of want produced by Akshay's death in the Master's heart. For, just as

on the one hand, the highly devout Mathur regarded the Master as God Himself and followed him implicitly in all spiritual matters, so, on the other, he looked upon him as but an ignorant child to be protected by him in all worldly matters. During this visit, the Master was very much moved to see the extremely miserable condition of the men and women in a certain village. He invited them all and made Mathur give each of them oil sufficient to cool the head, a full meal and a piece of new cloth. Hriday said that this event happened at a place called Kalaighat, near Ranaghat, when Mathur, accompanied by him and the Master, was on a boat trip in the Churni canal.

12. Hriday told us that Mathur had his own home in the village called Sonabere, near Satkshira. The villages round it were then included in Mathur's estate, to which he took the Master. The home of Mathur's Guru was not far from this place. There was a quarrel going on at the time among the members of the family of the Guru over the division of their property. They asked Mathur to intercede as a mediator. The village was called Tala-magro. On their way Mathur made the Master and Hriday ride on his elephant and himself went in a palanquin[1]. Pleased with the loving service of the sons of Mathur's preceptor, the Master spent a few weeks there before he returned to Dakshineswar.

13. Shortly after his return, there happened a remarkable event connected with the Master at Kolutola in Calcutta. A Hari Sabha, a meeting where Hari's name was sung, used to be in session in the house of Kalinath Datta, otherwise known as Kalinath Dhar. Being invited by the Sabha, the Master went there and in ecstasy sat on the seat reserved in the name and in honour of Sri Chaitanya, the great lord. We have given the reader a detailed description of the incident elsewhere (IV. 3). Not long afterwards, the Master had a desire to visit Navadwip, and Mathur took him to Kalna, Navadwip and some other places. We have told the reader elsewhere how he met the perfected devotee Bhagavan Das at Kalna and what a wonderful vision he had at Navadwip (IV. 3). It was perhaps in 1870 that he went to visit those holy places. He did not feel so deeply inspired while in Navadwip as

---

[1] Hriday said that, while he was going to the village, Mathur asked the Master to go in a palanquin as the road was uneven, and himself rode his elephant. Reaching the village, however, he satisfied the Master's curiosity by having him seated on the elephant.

when passing by the silted-up shoals in the bed of the Ganga near that place. Asked by Mathur and others for the reason of it, the Master said that the old Navadwip containing the spots of Chaitanya's divine sport, had been submerged in the river. They were situated where the shoals now stood. That was why he had deep ecstasy when he passed by them.

14. It will not be out of place to mention here, on Hriday's authority, an event illustrative of Mathur's selfless devotion, attained as the result of the whole-hearted service he had rendered to the Master continually for fourteen long years. Once Mathur Babu became bed-ridden on account of a boil in a joint of his body. Having come to know of Mathur's eagerness to see the Master at that time, Hriday told the Master of it. But the Master said, "What's the use of my going? Can I cure his boil?" When Mathur found that the Master did not come, he sent messenger after messenger and informed him of his eager desire. After this supplication, the Master had to yield. Mathur's happiness knew no bounds when the Master came to him. He got up with great difficulty, sat reclining against a bolster and said, "Father, give me a little of the dust of your feet."

The Master said, "Of what avail will it be to you to take the dust of my feet? Will it cure your boil?"

Mathur replied, "Father, am I so mean? Do I want the dust of your feet to cure my boil? Doctors are there for that purpose. I want the dust of your feet in order to cross the sea of the world."

As soon as Mathur said this, the Master was in ecstasy. Mathur placed his head on the Master's feet and regarded himself as blessed thereby. Tears of bliss streamed out from both his eyes. Mathur was cured of the disease in a short time after that.

15. Both Hriday and the Master had told us many things pertaining to those times, indicative of the great faith and devotion of Mathur for the Master. Mathur had the firm conviction that the Master was his only refuge and resort both here and hereafter. The Master's grace for him was also boundless. Although the independent-minded Master felt annoyed now and then at some of Mathur's actions, he forgot them immediately, granted all his requests, and tried to do what was conducive to his welfare both in this world and in the next. What a strong and profound loving relation subsisted between the Master and Mathur, is clearly seen from the following anecdote.

16. Once the Master said in ecstasy, "As long as you live, O Mathur, I too shall be here (at Dakshineswar)." Mathur was startled to hear it; for he knew that the Mother of the universe Herself in the person of the Master was always protecting him and his family. Therefore, when he heard it, Mathur thought that the Master would forsake his family after his passing away. He then said very humbly to the Master, "Why so, Father? My wife and son Dwaraka are also very much devoted to you." Seeing that Mathur was distressed, the Master said, "Very well; I shall be here as long as your wife and Dwari live." In fact, it actually turned out to be so. The Master left Dakshineswar for good, shortly after the death of Jagadamba Dasi and Dwarakanath. Jagadamba Dasi died in 1881[1] The Master was at Dakshineswar for a little more than three years after this event.

17. On another occasion Mathur said to the Master, "How is this, Father? You said your devotees would be coming, but where are they? I do not find them coming". The Master replied, "I don't know after how long the Mother will bring them. But truly the Mother Herself has revealed it to me. Whatever else She had made known to me, has proved to be true, one by one; who knows why this has not?" So saying, the Master was in a depressed mood and thought, "Was that vision of mine then a delusion?" Mathur felt sorry to see him depressed and thought within himself that it was foolish on his part to have raised that topic. In order to console the childlike Master, he then said to him, "Father, let them come or not. I am here, your devotee, always following you obediently. How then can it be said that your vision about devotees has not come true? For I am in myself a host of them. That is why the Mother said, 'Many devotees would come'." The Master replied, "What you say may be true; who knows?" Mathur did not proceed further with that topic, but raising another, diverted the Master's mind.

18. We have told the reader in the third part entitled "As the Spiritual Teacher" how great changes were produced in Mathur's ideas by keeping constant company with the Master. Those who render service to a liberated person become, say the scriptures, the recipients of the results of all the good actions done by him.

---

[1] "Jagadamaba died on or about 1st January, 1881, intestate, leaving defendant Trayluksha, then the only son of Mathura, heir surviving." Quoted from Plaintiff's statement in High Court Suit No. 203 of 1889.

So, is it a wonder that those who serve an incarnation of God should come to be endowed with many great excellences?

19. The ceaseless flow of time with its waves of adversity and prosperity, happiness and misery, union and separation, life and death, brought the world gradually to the year B.E. 1278 (A.D. 1871). The relationship of Mathur with the Master, deepening through the years, reached its fifteenth year. The months of Vaisakh and Jyaishtha had run their course, and Ashadh too had been half submerged into the abyss of the past, when Mathur became bed-ridden with fever. Rising rapidly, the fever turned into a complicated and continuous type, and in a week Mathur lost his power of speech. The Master knew beforehand that Mathur's vow of devotion was now at its end, and that the Mother was about to take Her devotee into Her bosom very soon. Therefore, although he used to send Hriday daily to see Mathur, he himself never went to see him even once. The last day came and Mathur was taken to Kalighat. The Master did not send even Hriday that day, but remained in deep ecstasy in the afternoon for two or three hours. His body lay at Dakshineswar while he went in a celestial body along a path of light to Mathur, his devotee, and helped him attain the goal, the fulfilment of his life. He personally made him attain to the sphere to which one is eligible only by a great accumulation of merits.

20. When the Master's ecstasy came to an end, it was past five in the evening. He called Hriday to him and said, "Mathur got into a celestial chariot into which companions of the Divine Mother lifted him affectionately and his spirit went to the sphere of the Devi." Hriday remained silent on hearing it. When the night was far advanced, the officers of the Kali temple returned and gave Hriday the news that Mathur had passed away at five in the evening. We heard from the Master on a different occasion—and have acquainted the reader with it elsewhere. (III.7)[1]—that the highly devout Mathuranath would have to return to this world, as his desire for enjoyment still remained unexhausted.

---

[1] "Mathura Mohan Biswas died in July, 1871, intestate, leaving surviving Jagadamba, sole widow, Bhupal since deceased, a son by his other wife who had predeceased him—and Dwarkanath Biswas since deceased, defendant Trayluksha Nath and Thakurdas alias Dhurmadas, three sons by the said Jagadamba."

Quoted from plaintiff's statement in High Court Suit No. 230 of 1889—Shyama Charan Biswas *vs.* Trayluksha Nath Biswas, Gurudas, Kalidas, Durgadas, and Kumudini.

CHAPTER XX

THE WORSHIP OF SHODASI

1. Mathur had passed away. But the tenor of the life at the Kali temple at Dakshineswar went on as before. Days and months passed and the year 1872 arrived. There happened a special event in the Master's life at that time. We must now turn our attention to the house of the Master's father-in-law in the village of Jayrambati in order to understand the series of events leading to it.

When the Master went with the Bhairavi Brahmani and Hriday to Kamarpukur, his native village, in 1867, the women relatives, as we mentioned before, had his wife brought there. That was, in reality, the first occasion when the Holy Mother met her husband, Anyone who has had the opportunity of comparing the young girls of towns like Calcutta with those of villages like Kamarpukur, will have noticed that the bodies and minds of town-bred girls become developed at an earlier age than those of village girls. In villges, girls of fourteen, and sometimes fifteen or sixteen, do not have the physical signs of their youth fully developed. Their minds also, like their bodies, develop late. This healthy feature in village-bred girls is perhaps because they have not got to live in small places, cribbed and cabined like birds confined in cages. They live in a natural environment breathing pure air and roaming about freely in their villages.

2. The Holy Mother, therefore, was very young when, at the age of fourteen, she met her husband in a real sense for the first time. Her powers of understanding the profound ideal and responsibility of married life, were just at the point of unfolding themselves. At that time the pure girl was delighted, experiencing an indescribable celestial bliss in having the divine company of the Master and in enjoying his selfless love and attention uncorrupted by corporeal considerations. On many occasions she used to describe that delight of hers to the women devotees of the Master, saying, "My heart was incessantly full of an indescribable bliss, and I felt always since then as if a jar of bliss, full to overflowing, was installed in my heart."

3. When, after a few months, the Master returned to Calcutta from Kamarpukur, the girl too went back to her father's home, feeling at heart that she was in possession of an infinite wealth of bliss. That feeling of delight produced a change in all her conduct, speech, movement and work. But it is doubtful whether people in general could notice it; for it made her calm and not fickle, thoughtful and not pert, selfless and not self-seeking. And above all, by removing from her heart the feeling of all kinds of want, it made her infinitely sympathetic to the sorrows and miseries of humanity, converting her by degrees into an embodiment of compassion itself. On account of the influence of this joy, even endless physical suffering now appeared to her to be of no consequence and she felt no pain at all even if her care and affection for others were not returned. Thus, content with the barest physical necessities and lost in herself, the girl lived then in her father's house only physically, her mind dwelling far away at Dakshineswar at the feet of the Master. Although a strong desire arose now and again in her mind to go to him and see him, she controlled it, and remained patient, thinking all the while that he who graciously loved her so much at her first meeting with him, could never forget her and would surely call her to him at the proper time. Thus passed days, one after another, and the girl, firm in her faith, awaited that auspicious day.

4. Four long years passed one after another. But the strong current of hope and longing kept on flowing uniformly in the girl's mind. Her body, however, did not continue in the same state as her mind, but, changing daily, shaped itself into that of a young woman of eighteen by the year 1872. Although the bliss due to

her first meeting with her godlike husband kept her high above
daily pain and pleasure, even that was not free from the intrusions
of a hostile and unsympathetic world. For in their gossip, the
menfolk of the village made cutting remarks, saying that her husband was mad, and that casting away even his wearing apparel,
he roamed about naked, repeating "Hari, Hari", and the women
of her age alluded to her as a mad man's wife and looked upon
her as an object of pity or contempt. She was much pained at
heart by all this, but said nothing. Though absorbed in the
thought of the Master, she sometimes yielded to doubts, "Is he
then not the same person as I saw before? Has such a change as
people say really come on him? If by the decree of Providence it
has actually happened, I must no longer be here; I must be by
his side and serve him." She reflected a great deal and came to the
conclusion that she should personally go to Dakshineswar and have
all her doubts cleared in the light of facts, and do as the circumstances demanded.

5. Sri Chaitanya was born on the full moon day of the month
of Phalgun, the day of the Dol-yatra, a day of festivity on which
Sri Krishna is rocked in a swing. Many people from the farthest
end of Bengal come every year to Calcutta to bathe on that occasion
in the holy waters of the Ganga. A few women distantly related
to the Holy Mother had decided that they would go there on that
occasion that year. She went to them and expressed her desire
to go for a bath in the Ganga. Thinking that it was not reasonable
to take her with them without her father's permission, the ladies
asked her father Ramchandra Mukhopadhyaya about it. As soon
as the intelligent father heard it, he understood why his daughter
wanted to go to Calcutta, and made all arrangements to take her
there himself.

Thanks to the railways, the distance between Calcutta and far
off Kasi or Vrindavan appear much reduced in terms of time
required to reach those places. But, not having that blessing in
those days, Kamarpukur, the birth-place of the Master, and Jayrambati, the birth-place of the Holy Mother, lay as far as ever from
Calcutta.

6. This is so even now,[1] not to speak of those times. In those

---

[1] One can now take a train from Howrah to Vishnupur or to Tarakeswar and then travel by bus to Jayrambati and Kamarpukur; or one can
travel directly by car or bus from Howrah to Kamarpukur.—Pub.

days the railway lines had not yet been laid either via Vishnupur or via Tarakeswar, nor was Ghatal connected with Calcutta by steamer. Therefore the people of those villages had no other course than to travel by palanquin or on foot. And all people, except the rich, such as the zamindars and others, used to have recourse to the latter only. So accompanied by his daughter and other companions, Ramchandra started on the long journey on foot. All of them walked with delight for the first two or three days. They saw one paddy field after another and ponds full of lotuses, and enjoyed the cool shades of trees like the peepul and the banian. But that delight did not continue up to their destination. Un- accustomed to the fatigue of journeys, Ramchandra's daughter got a severe attack of fever on the way, which made the father very anxious. Finding it impossible to proceed farther when his daughter was in that condition, he halted at an inn and stayed there.

7. What a terrible anguish the Holy Mother felt in her heart on account of the illness on the way, cannot be described. But she had a wonderful vision which consoled her. She sometimes used to give the following description of this vision to her women devotees: "I lost all consciousness on account of the high temper- ature and was lying unaware even about the state of my dress, when I saw a girl come and sit beside me. The girl was black in com- plexion, but I had never seen such a beauty before. She sat by me and began to pass her hand over my head and body. Her hand was so soft and cool that the heat and the burning sensation of my body began to subside. I asked her affectionately, 'May I know where you come from?' The girl said, 'I come from Dakshines- war.' Astonished to hear it, I said, 'From Dakshineswar! I thought of going there to see him and serve him (the Master); but as I have got this fever on the way, I shall not have the good fortune of fulfilling that desire.' 'Why not?' said the girl. 'You will surely go to Dakshineswar. Getting well, you will go there and see him. It is for you that I have detained him there.' I said. 'Is that so? Pray, tell me, are you related to us?' 'I am your sister,' said she. I said, 'Indeed! That is why you have come.' Conversing with her in this way. I fell asleep."

8. Ramchandra rose in the morning to see that his daughter's fever had subsided. He thought it better to continue the journey slowly with her, instead of helplessly waiting on the way. Encouraged by the vision of the previous night, the Holy Mother approved of

his idea eagerly. Scarcely had they walked a little distance when a palanquin became available. She had fever again. But, as it was not so severe as on the previous night, she did not lose control over herself. Neither did she mention it to anybody. They gradually reached the journey's end, and the Holy Mother came to the Master at Dakshineswar at 9 p.m.

The Master was somewhat worried to see her thus suffering from fever. He arranged for her a separate bed in his own room, lest her fever should increase on account of the cold, and said with a sigh, "You have come at long last. Alas! my Mathur is now no more. What care would he have bestowed on you!" On account of the good arrangements made for medicine, diet, etc., the Holy Mother came round in three or four days. The Master kept her in his own room for three or four days and personally supervised everything. He then made arrangements for her to live with his mother in the Nahabatkhana, the music room.

9. Thus were removed the worries caused by rumours. The dust of doubt, which was raised by rumours and was clouding her faith, now scattered in all directions and vanished. The loving care and the anxious attention that the Master bestowed on her confirmed her in her faith that he was just his former self and that it was only the worldly-minded with no power of discrimination, that had spread those false rumours. Her 'lord' was the same 'lord', thus mused the Holy Mother, and far from having forgotten her, he was as gracious to her as before. Therefore, she decided in no time what she should do. She lived in the Nahabat with a joyful heart and engaged herself in the service of the Master and his mother. Her father, happy in the happiness of his daughter, stayed there for a few days and then returned home joyfully.

10. We have told the reader about the Master's line of thinking on the situation he was confronted with by the arrival of the Holy Mother at Kamarpukur while he was staying there in 1867. Remembering the words of Tota Puri that a knower of Brahman overcomes the sense of distinction between man and woman based on body consciousness, he was prepared to utilise that situation both to test his own knowledge and to do his duty towards his wife. But he had to come back to Calcutta just when he had begun to accomplish those two purposes. Having her beside him now, he applied his mind again to those two objectives.

11. Why then, it may be asked, did he not bring his wife to Dakshineswar earlier and test his knowledge? It may be said in reply that an ordinary man, no doubt, would have done so. But the Master did not belong to the class of ordinary human beings and therefore his conduct was different. Those who are accustomed to do everything depending entirely on God at all times, do not previously draw up a plan of what they want to do. Instead of depending like us on the limited, little intellect in taking decisions on matters affecting the welfare of themselves and others, they look for help and direction from the all-pervading intellect of the Divine. They are, therefore, averse to courting any situation out of their own initiative. They go on behaving continually in full accord with the universal will, and if any testing time comes of itself without any initiative on their part, they proceed forward gladly to submit to it. The Master did not set himself wilfully to test the depth of his own divine knowledge. But when he saw that his wife had come to him at Kamarpukur and that, if he was to perform his duty by her, he must stand that test, then alone was he ready to submit to it. Again, when by the will of God the situation changed and he had to return to Calcutta and live away from his wife, he never sought to take her then on his own initiative. Until she herself came, he did not make the slightest effort to bring the Holy Mother to Dakshineswar. We can thus find even by means of our ordinary intellect, a congruity running through all the phases of the Master's behaviour towards her. Besides, we have to understand that with his Yogic vision he had the apprehension that such was the will of God.

12. Now when the Master saw that the time to submit to the test through the discharge of his duties to his wife had arrived once again, he was perfectly ready for it. Whenever an opportunity arose, he used to teach the Holy Mother everything about the aim and duties of human life. It is said that during this time he told the Holy Mother, "Just as 'uncle' moon is the uncle of all children, so, God is everybody's 'own'. It is every one's privilege to call on Him. Whoever calls on Him, will be blessed by His vision. If you call on Him, you also will see Him." The Master's method of teaching did not consist in merely giving instructions to a disciple. He would keep the disciple with him, make him in all respects his own through love and affection, and then give him instructions. Even at that, the Master would not stop. He would

keep a keen eye on how far the disciple carried the instructions into practice; and if the disciple inadvertently went contrary to his instructions, he would correct him by pointing out the deviations on his part. He now adopted the same method with respect to the Holy Mother also. How far he made her his own through love from the very first day, is clear from the fact that he asked her to live in his own room as soon as she came, and that, when she had recovered from illness, he gave her permission to share his own bed every night. We have told the reader elsewhere (III. 4) about the Master's pure and immaculate behaviour towards the Holy Mother at that time. We shall not therefore repeat it here. We shall only add a word or two to what is mentioned there.

13. One day during this period, while she was massaging the Master's feet, the Holy Mother asked him, "How do you look on me?" Out came the reply, "The Mother who is in the temple, the Mother who has given birth to this body and is now living in the Nahabat—the same Mother is now massaging my feet. Truly, I always look upon you as a form of the blissful Divine Mother."

14. On another occasion, seeing the Holy Mother asleep by his side, the Master addressed his own mind and started discriminating. "This is, O mind, a female body. People look upon it as an object of great enjoyment, a thing highly prized, and they die for enjoying it. But if one goes for it, one has to remain obsessed with the body consciousness. One cannot go beyond it and realize God who is Existence-Knowledge-Bliss. Do not, O mind, harbour one thought within and a contrary attitude without. Say in truth whether you want to have it or God. If you want, it is here before you; have it." He discriminated thus; but scarcely had he entertained in his mind the idea of touching the person of the Holy Mother, when his mind shrank and at once lost itself so deeply in Samadhi that it did not regain its normal consciousnes that night. He had to be brought back with great effort to normal consciousness the next morning by the repeated utterance of the name of God in his ears.

15. Incidents of this type, as narrated by the Master from the pages of his life in the company of the Holy Mother, depicting the utter non-attachment and absence of carnal desires in them both, even in the full bloom of their youth, are unknown in the life of any other incarnation of God in the spiritual history of the world. Charmed to hear these things, the human heart comes naturally

to believe in the divine nature of the couple and feels compelled to have heart-felt love and reverence for them. The Master, free from body-consciousness, passed whole nights in ecstasy at this time. And, even when he used to come down to the plane of normal consciousness at the end of his ecstasy, his mind dwelt in such an exalted state that body-consciousness like that of ordinary people never arose in it even for a moment.

16. Thus months rolled on, and more than a year passed away. Still, the self-control of the wonderful Master and of his equally wonderful holy spouse, did not give way. Not even for a moment by way of inadvertence did their minds consider physical union to be pleasing and desirable. Remembering what happened at that time, the Master said to us now and again, "Had she (the Holy Mother) not been so pure, had she, losing control over herself, assailed me, who knows if my self-control would not have broken down and body-consciousness arisen? I had implored the Divine Mother after my marriage to keep her mind absolutely free from lust. Having lived with her at that time, I knew that the Divine Mother had really heard and granted that prayer of mine."

17. One year's experiment convinced him that no corporeal passion could ever overcome his mind, and that his mental outlook on his wedded wife as part of the universal Mother or Brahman had become an abiding and unshakable proclivity of his consciousness. He felt assured that the Divine Mother had made him successfully stand that test, and that by Her grace, his mind was now established in the divine state in an easy and natural way. He now felt in his heart of hearts that his Sadhana, by the grace of the Mother, had been perfectly completed and that his mind was so much absorbed in Her lotus feet that there was no possibility of any desire contrary to Her will, arising in it knowingly or unknowingly. Ordained by the Divine Mother, an extraordinary desire arose in his heart now, which he carried out into practice without the slightest hesitation. We shall now tell the reader in a connected way what we heard about it now and then from the Master and the Holy Mother.

18. A little more than half of the month of Jyaishtha, B.E 1280 (Á.D. May 25, 1873) had elapsed. It was the new-moon day, the holy occasion for the worship of the Phalaharini Kalika Devi. It was the day of a special festival at the Dakshineswar temple. The Master had made special preparations on that day with a view to worshipping the Mother of the universe. These preparations,

however, had not been made in the temple, but, privately, in his own room at his desire. A wooden seat painted with Alimpana, the pigment of rice powder, for the Devi to sit on at the time of worship, had been placed to the right of the worshipper. The sun had set. The now-moon night, veiled in deep darkness, had alighted on the earth. Hriday, the Master's nephew, had to perform a special worship of the Devi in the temple. He had, therefore, helped as much as possible in the preparations for the Master's worship and had gone away to the temple. Having finished the nocturnal service and worship of Radha-Govinda, the first priest, Dinu, came to help the Master in the preparations. It was 9 p.m. when all the preparations for the mystery-worship of the Devi were completed. In the meantime, the Master had sent word to the Holy Mother to be present during the worship. She came to the room and the Master started the worship.

19. The articles of worship were purified by the Mantras and all the rites preliminary to the worship were finished. The Master beckoned to the Holy Mother to sit on the wooden seat decorated with the Alimpana. While witnessing the worship, the Holy Mother had already entered into a divine semi-conscious state. Not clearly conscious, therefore, of what she was doing, she like one charmed with Mantras, sat facing north to the right of the Master, who was seated with his face to the east. According to scriptural injunctions the Master sprinkled the Holy Mother repeatedly with the water purified by Mantras from the pitcher placed before him, then uttered the Mantra in her hearing and then recited the prayer:

"O Lady, O Mother Tripurasundari who art the controller of all powers, open the door to perfection! Purify her (the Holy Mother's) body and mind, manifest Thyself in her and be beneficent."

20. Afterwards the Master performed the Nyasa of the Mantras in the Holy Mother's person according to the injunctions of the Sastras, and worshipped her with the sixteen articles, as the Devi Herself. He then offered food and put a part of it into her mouth with his own hand. The Holy Mother lost normal consciousness and went into Samadhi. The Master too, uttering Mantras in the semi-conscious state, entered into complete Samadhi. The worshipper in Samadhi became perfectly identified and united with the Devi in Samadhi.

A long time passed. The second quarter of the night was over and the third had far advanced, when the Master, whose delight was only in the Self, showed a little sign of regaining normal consciousness. Returning to the semi-conscious state again, he offered himself to the Devi. He now gave away for ever at the lotus feet of the Devi his all — the results of his Sadhanas, his rosary etc., — along with his self, and saluted her, uttering the Mantras:

"O Thou, the auspiciousness of all auspicious things! O door of all actions! O refuge! O the three-eyed One ! O the fair-complexioned spouse of Siva! O Narayani! I bow down to Thee, I bow down to Thee!"

The worship was at an end.[1] The Master's Sadhana reached its culmination with the worship of the Ruler of the universe, the Divine Mother in the body of a woman, the embodiment of spiritual knowledge itself. The god-man attained perfection in all respects.

21. The Holy Mother stayed with the Master for about five months after the worship of Shodasi. She now, as before, engaged herself in the service of the Master and the Master's mother, spent the day-time in the Nahabat and shared the same bed with the Master at night. The Master had continual Bhava-Samadhi night and day. Sometime his mind suddenly merged in the Nirvikalpa Samadhi in such a way that signs of death were manifested in his body. Apprehensive of the sudden occurrence of such states at any part of the night, the Holy Mother could have no sleep. When on one occasion the Master did not come down to normal consciousness from Samadhi for a long time, she was alarmed, and not knowing what she should do, disturbed the sleep of Hriday and others. His Samadhi came to an end when Hriday came and uttered the names of God in his ears for a pretty long time. Coming to know of all this after his Samadhi broke, and also of the disturbance of the Holy Mother's sleep every night, the Master made arrangements for her taking her bed near his mother at the Nahabat. She lived thus for about a year and four months with the Master at Dakshineswar and returned to Kamarpukur probably sometime in October 1873.

---

[1] Regarding the exact date of the Shodasi Puja, there is another version that has come out after the publication of this work. It is contained in the Bengali work on the conversations of the Holy Mother, entitled *Mayer-Katha Vol. II*. There the Mother is recorded as saying that the Puja took place after a month and a half of her arrival at Dakshineswar. In that case it must have taken place on the Phalaharini-Kali puja of June, 1872, and not of May 1873.—Pub.

CHAPTER XXI

EPILOGUE TO THE STORY OF THE MASTER'S SADHANAS

(TOPICS: 1. The Master's desire for Sadhana abates with Shodasi-pooja. 2. Reason for this. 3. The practice of the religion of Lord Jesus 4. His vision of the true form of Jesus 5. His views about the Buddha 6. The Master's faith in the Jaina and the Sikh religions 7. Re-statement of the Master's extraordinary experiences. 8. Experiences about himself 9. Experiences about spiritual matters in general 10. Opinions of three scholarly Sadhakas on the Master 11. The time of the coming of these scholars 12. The Master's crying out to meet his devotees of the inner circle.)

1. The Master's vow of Sadhana was completed with the worship of Shodasi. The holy fire of passion for God inebriation was burning constantly in his heart for twelve long years, keeping him tirelessly engaged in the practices of various spiritual moods without allowing him any rest even after the completion of the Sadhanas of a particular mood. With the worship of Shodasi, it now ceased to burn, having received the Purnahuti or the completing and final oblation. And what else could it do? For, was there now anything left, which he might call his own and which he had not already offered as oblation to it? He had long ago sacrificed to it all the desirable things of the world — wealth, honour, name, fame, etc. He had offered as an oblation to its terrible flames, one after another, his heart, vital forces, mind, intellect, memory, egoism, etc. The only thing that had still remained with him was the desire to see the Mother of the universe in various relations and forms by travelling along different paths of Sadhana. That desire also he had now offered to the fire. What could it do now but subside?

2. Knowing the eagerness of the Master's heart, the Divine Mother had bestowed on him first the blessing of Her vision and afterwards brought him into contact with persons of extraordinarily noble qualities, with whose help he could tread along various scriptural paths, so that he could compare his first vision of Hers with the ultimate results of all the Sadhanas. So what could he ask of Her now? He also saw that the practices prescribed in the

22

sixty-four Tantras had all been practised by him one after another; that all the disciplines connected with the five moods of the Vaishnava faith prevalent in India had also been gone through by him according to scriptural injunctions; that, following the eternal Vedic path and being initiated into Sannyasa, he had had the vision of the formless and attributeless Divine Mother; and that, by Her inscrutable play, he had had the sure result of Sadhanas according to Islam, a religion which had come into existence outside India. So what could he now ask the Divine Mother to show or tell him?

3.   A year after, the mind of the Master again looked forward to the vision of the Divine Mother through another path. He had by that time become acquainted with Sambhucharan Mallick, who used to read the Bible to him. Thus he came to know of the pure life of Jesus and of the faith he had founded, and the desire to follow the Sadhanas of that path arose in his mind. Scarcely had that desire arisen in his mind when the Divine Mother fulfilled it in a marvellous way and blessed him. He had, therefore, no need to make any special effort for it. The event happened thus: The garden house of Jadunath Mallick is situated to the south of the Kali temple at Dakshineswar. The Master used to go there now and then for a walk. Jadunath and his mother had great devotion to the Master from the time they had seen him first. Therefore, even if they were not present in the garden at the time of the Master's walks there, the officers would open the door of the parlour and ask him to sit and rest there for some time. There were some good pictures hanging on the walls of that room. One of those pictures was that of the child Jesus in his mother's lap. The Master used to say that he sat one day in that parlour and was looking intently at that picture and thinking of the extraordinary life of Jesus, when he felt that the picture came to life, and that effulgent rays of light, coming out from the bodies of the mother and the Child, entered into his heart and changed radically all the ideas of his mind! On finding that all the inborn Hindu impressions were disappearing into a secluded corner of his mind and that different ones were arising, he tried in various ways to control himself and prayed earnestly to the Divine Mother, "What strange changes art Thou bringing about in me, Mother?" But nothing availed. Rising with a great force, the waves of those impressions completely submerged the Hindu ideas in his mind. His love and devotion to the Devas and Devis vanished, and in their stead, a great

faith in, and reverence for Jesus and his religion occupied his mind. He began to see Christian worshippers offering incense and light before the image of Jesus in the Church, and his mind entered into the spirit of their longing for the Lord as expressed through their earnest prayers. The Master came back to Dakshineswar temple and remained constantly absorbed in the meditation of those inner happenings. He forgot altogether to go to the temple of the Divine Mother and pay obeisance to Her. The waves of those ideas had a mastery over his mind in that manner for three days. At last, when the third day was about to close, the Master saw, while walking under the Panchavati, that a marvellous god-man of very fair complexion was coming towards him, looking steadfastly at him. As soon as the Master saw that person, he knew that he was a foreigner. He saw that his long eyes gave a wonderful beauty to his face, and that the tip of his nose, though a little flat, did not at all impair that beauty. The Master was charmed to see the extraordinary divine expression of that handsome face, and wondered who he was. Very soon the person approached him, and thereupon from the depth of the Master's pure heart came out with a ringing sound, the words, "Jesus the Christ! the great Yogi, the loving Son of God, one with the Father, who gave his heart's blood and put up with endless tortures in order to deliver man from sorrow and misery!" Jesus, the god-man, then embraced the Master and disappeared into his body and the Master entered into ecstasy, lost normal consciousness and remained identified for some time with the omnipresent Brahman with attributes. Having attained the vision of Jesus thus, the Master became free from the slightest doubt about Christ's having been an incarnation of God.

4. When we were visiting the Master long after this event, one day he raised the topic of Jesus and said, "Well, boys, you have read the Bible; can you tell me what is written in it about the physical features of Jesus? How did he look?" We said, "Sir, we have not seen this mentioned anywhere in the Bible; but as he was born a Jew, he must have been very fair in complexion, with long eyes and an aquiline nose, to be sure." When told so, the Master said, "But I saw that the tip of his nose was a little flat; I don't know why I saw him like that." Though we did not then say anything about what the Master said, we thought, "How could the form seen by him in ecstasy tally with the actual form

of Jesus? Like all the Jews he too must have had an aquiline nose." But we came to know, shortly after the Master passed away, that there were three different descriptions of Jesus' physical features; and according to one of them the tip of his nose was a little flat.

5. Knowing the Master to have been perfected according to all the main religions prevalent in the world, the reader may wonder within himself what his idea about the Buddha was. It is therefore but fair that we record here what is known to us about it. The Master regarded the Buddha as what the Hindus in general believe him to be. He always offered his loving worship and reverence to the Buddha as an Incarnation of God and believed that the Incarnation of Buddha continued even now to be manifest in the image at Puri of "the three gems" in the forms of Jagannath, Subhadra and Balaram. When he heard that the glory of the above-mentioned holy place was that, by the grace of Jagannath it obliterated all feelings of difference and thereby all distinctions due to caste, he felt an intense desire to visit it. But he gave up that idea (IV. 3), when he came to know that he would not survive a visit to that holy place. He understood, with the help of his spiritual insight, that the will of the Divine Mother was against his going there. We have already spoken of the Master's firm faith in the purifying power of the waters of the Ganga, which he looked upon as being Brahman Itself in the liquid form (Brahmavari). He had an equally firm faith that the mind of a man attached to worldly objects becomes immediately pure and gets fit to grasp spiritual ideas when he takes food offered to Jagannath. When compelled to be in the company of worldly people for some time, he took, immediately afterwards, a little water of the Ganga and the "Atke" Mahaprasad, the cooked rice offered to Jagannath, and asked his disciples also to do the same. Besides what has been said above about the Master's faith in the Buddha as an Incarnation of God, we came to know also of another fact in confirmation of it. When the great poet, Girish Chandra Ghosh, the highly devout follower of the Master, published his drama, *Buddhacharita*, depicting the divine play of the Buddha, the Master witnessed it staged and said, "It is certain that the Buddha was an incarnation of God. There is no difference between the faith founded by him and the Vedic path of knowledge." Our conviction is that the Master came to this conclusion through his spiritual insight.

6. The Master heard from the Jainas and the Sikhs, in the latter part of his life, many things about the Tirthankaras, the founders of the Jaina religion, and about the ten Gurus from Nanak to Govinda, the founders of the Sikh religion. He had much love and respect for them all. Besides the pictures of deities, there were a stone image of Mahavira the Tirthankara and a picture of Jesus on one side of his room. The Master adored them too every morning and evening, burning incense before them both, as he did before all the other pictures. But, although he thus showed great love and reverence for them, we did not hear him describing any of the Tirthankaras or any of the ten Gurus as an incarnation of God. About the ten Gurus of the Sikhs, he used to say, "They are all incarnations of the Rishi Janaka. The royal Rishi Janaka, I have been told by the Sikhs, had a desire in his mind on the eve of his liberation, to do good to the people. He, therefore, was born ten times as a Guru, from Nanak to Govinda, and having established religion among the Sikhs, became eternally united with the supreme Brahman. There is no reason why this saying of the Sikhs should not be true."

7. When he became perfect according to all Sadhanas, the Master had a few unique experiences. Of these experiences some were concerning himself, and some were about spiritual matters in general. Although we have already made mention of some of these experiences, we shall deal here only with the principal ones. While dwelling constantly in the divine state of Bhavamukha (the threshold of relative consciousness) at the end of the period of his Sadhanas, he seemed to have had a vivid consciousness of the meaning of those experiences. Although the Master had them with the help of his Yogic vision, we shall give here a rational explanation of them.

8. First, the Master had the conviction that he was an Incarnation of God, an Adhikarika Purusha, all of whose spiritual efforts were for the sake of others. Comparing the Sadhaka life of others with his, he could see a great difference between them with the help of his reason. He saw that an ordinary aspirant practised one spiritual mood all his life and that when he realized the vision of God according to that mood, he had complete satisfaction in his mind, and that marked the end of his Sadhana. But his own case was quite different. He could not remain content until he had practised disciplines according to all moods and faiths, and besides, it required

only a very short time for him to attain success in the practice of any of the moods and faiths he happened to adopt. An effect can never be produced but by a cause; a search on his part for the cause of the above-mentioned fact led him to profound meditation and showed him the reason given above. It showed him that his condition was unique because he was an especial incarnation of God the Almighty, who is ever free, ever pure and ever awakened. It made him realize further, that all his extraordinary spiritual practices had brought a new light to the spiritual world, and that he had to undertake them all not for the fulfilment of any personal want of his but for the good of others only.

He was convinced that, unlike the Jivas, he would not attain liberation. It does not take one long to understand this even with the help of ordinary reasoning. How can there be any talk of liberation for one who is eternally non-separate from God, being an especial part of Him, who is always free, pure and awakened and who has no want or limitation at all? As long as God's work of redeeming the Jivas continues, he will have to incarnate himself from age to age and do that work. So how can he have liberation? The Master used to say, "An administrator has to run to wherever there is any disorder in the estate." This was not the only thing about himself that the Master knew with the help of his Yogic vision. Pointing to the north-western direction, he told us over and over again that he would have to come in that region on the next occasion. Some[1] assert that he gave out the time of his next advent and said, "I shall have to come on that side (north-western direction) after two hundred years. Many will be liberated then. Those who do not get liberation at that time, will have to wait very long for it thereafter. "

The Master came to know in Bhavasamadhi the time of his passing away long before it happened. One day he said to the Holy Mother at Dakshineswar in an exalted spiritual mood: "When you will see me taking food out of the hands of anyone and everyone, passing nights in Calcutta, and taking the food a part of which has been already taken by someone else — know that the time of my passing away is near at hand." The aforesaid words of the Master proved to be literally true. On another occasion he told the Holy Mother in a mood of spiritual exal-

---

[1] The great poet Girish Chandra Ghosh and others.

tation, "I shall not take anything except porridge during my last days." We have elsewhere said how this came true (III.2).

9. We shall now record the second kind of his experiences, namely, those regarding spiritual matters in general. After attaining perfection according to all the faiths, the Master had the firm conviction that all religions are true — that all the faiths are but so many paths. It can be said that the Master realized it both by his Yogic powers and by reason. By performing Sadhanas according to all the faiths, he realized in his life the ultimate result of each kind of discipline. It does not take one long to understand that the purpose of the advent of the Master, the Incarnation of the present age, is to promulgate the truth mentioned above and stop the decline of faiths and end the quarrels among them. No other Incarnation of God had fully realized this truth in his life with the help of Sadhana and taught it to the world before. If the eminence of the Incarnations of God is to be determined on the basis of the liberality of the spiritual doctrines they held, the highest place must undoubtedly be accorded to the Master for preaching this doctrine.

Secondly, the doctrines of dualism, qualified non-dualism and non-dualism come of themselves to each man with his spiritual progress. The Master, therefore, said that they were not contradictory to one another but depended on particular stages of evolution of the human mind. A little thinking makes it clear what immense help man can derive in understanding the scriptures through this realization of the Master. Words cannot express adequately what an endless confusion has been produced, and how intricate the path to spirituality has been reduced to, by the three aforesaid doctrines discovered by the Rishis and recorded in the Vedas, Upanishads and other scriptures. Unable to find out their proper harmony with one another, the followers of each of these doctrines did their best to prove, even by torturing the scriptural texts, that what they preached, is the only correct interpretation of the scriptures. The result of this attempt of the commentators is that there arises a dread in the minds of the people at the very name of religious discussions for the determination of the Sastraic truths. And this fear has produced a lack of faith in the Sastras, leading to the spiritual degradation of India. It was, therefore, necessary for the Master, the Incarnation of the age, to realize all the three doctrines at different stages of his own life and propagate among all men their wonderful harmony. The only way that will lead us to the understanding of the Sastras is to remember always this conclusion of the Master. Remember what the Master said on this topic:

"Know that the non-dual state of consciousness is the ultimate one to be realized; it is a realization that is beyond mind and speech.

"Only the states up to qualified non-dualism can be understood by mind and intellect and expressed in words. In that state both the absolute and the relative are equally eternal. The Lord Himself, His name and His abode.— all are of Pure Consciousness.

"For ordinary human beings, in whom the attachment to worldly objects prevails, dualism is commendable. For them the loud singing of the Lord's name, His glory, His powers, etc., as directed in the *Narada Pancharatra*, is advisable."

The Master put limits to the performance of actions also for the spiritual development of man and said, "In a man with a predominance of Sattva, the tendency for action naturally drops off. He cannot perform them in spite of his efforts to do so. To put it in another way, God does not allow him to do so. Take, for example, a daughter-in-law in a home; the nearer she approaches confinement, the more do her household duties drop off, and, when the child is born, she has nothing more to do except nurse it. But, all other people should depend on God and perform all actions like the maid servant[1] in a rich man's family, in the parable. To perform actions in this way is what is called Karma-yoga. To repeat continuously God's name, together with meditation on Him, and to perform all actions in the aforesaid manner — this is the path."

---

[1]"A maid servant serves in a rich man's family, attends carefully to all her duties, takes care of all the articles of the house, brings up the children as her own, fondles and feeds them, behaves with other people and families in a manner befitting a member of the family and she serves and even quarrels with others for the sake of the family. But she knows all the while that she is not one of the family, that a word from the master or the mistress is enough to send her away from there, and that her real home and her own people are in a far-off village.

Similarly, O man of the world, live in the world, mix with the members of your family, and serve them as dutifully as you can, but know in your heart of hearts that they are none of yours and that your home and your real relatives are there in the kingdom of heaven, God being the very centre of them all, their life and their being."—*Gospel of Sri Ramakrishna*. (Collected from various parts of the book and adapted)—Tr.

The Master realized that, as an instrument in the hands of the Mother of the universe, he would have to found a new Communion especially fitted for the liberal faith revealed in his own life. The Master realized all this during the life-time of Mathur Babu. The Mother told him, he said to Mathur, that many devotees would come to him to attain spirituality. It is superfluous to add that it turned out to be literally true. Once at the Kasipur garden, the Master looked at his own photograph and said to us, "This is a picture showing a very high state of Yoga. It[1] will be worshipped hereafter from house to house."

Having known, with the help of his Yogic power, that those who were in their last birth would come to him to attain spirituality, he had quite a firm conviction about it. We have given the reader our own opinion about it elsewhere (IV.4). It is, therefore, needless to repeat it here.

10. Three eminent Sadhaka-pandits, well versed in the scriptures, came to the Master during three important periods of his Sadhana, saw with their own eyes his spiritual states and had the opportunity of having discussions on them. Pandit Padmalochan saw the Master after the latter had attained perfection in the Tantric practices. Pandit Vaishnavacharan met him after his success in the Vaishnava disciplines, and Pandit Gauri had the privilege of seeing the Master possessed of the divine splendour produced by the Sadhana when the latter had finished all his spiritual practices. Padmalochan saw the Master and said, "I see in you divine power and manifestation." Composing a hymn in Sanskrit, Vaishnavacharan sang it to the Master in ecstasy, describing him as an Incarnation of God. Similarly, Gauri, when he saw the Master, said to him, "I see tangibly realized in you all the high spiritual states recorded in the scriptures read by me. Besides, I see in you the manifestations of such exalted states as are not recorded in them. Your state has far transcended those mentioned in the Vedas, the Vedantas, and the other Sastras. You are not a mortal being. The Reality from which incarnations originate, is there in you." When we study the extraordinary story of the Master's life and his wonderful experiences mentioned before, we can clearly comprehend that those prominent Sadhaka-pandits did not speak

---

[1]This is the photograph in the sitting posture of the Master in Samadhi.

the aforesaid words by way of flattery. The dates of the coming of those scholars to Dakshineswar have been ascertained in the following way:

11. While she was staying at Dakshineswar for the first time, the Holy Mother saw Pandit Gauri there. Again, we were told by the Master that the Pandit came to Dakshineswar when Mathur Babu was alive. Therefore, he seems to have come to Dakshineswar some time in 1871 and stayed with the Master there till 1873. The Master always cherished a desire to see those Sadhaka-pandits who tried to carry into practice the scriptural knowledge acquired by them in their lives. As Bhattacharya Sri Gaurikanta Tarka-bhushan (for, that was his full name) belonged to this class of Sadhakas, the Master had the desire to see him, and had him brought to Dakshineswar through Mathur, who invited him to come there. The Pandit was an inhabitant of the village of Indesh near the Master's birthplace. Hriday's brother Ramratan went with Mathur's letter of invitation to Gaurikanta and brought him to the holy temple at Dakshineswar. We have elsewhere (III.1) told the reader about the wonderful power which came to him from his Sadhana and about the way in which he happened to renounce the world on account of the gradual development of intense detachment in him by his contact with the Master during his stay with him at Dakshineswar.

The date of the Annameru, the gift of a " mountain of food-stuff", has been ascertained to be 1864 in the book entitled " The Story of the Life of Rani Rasmani." We were told by the Master about the eagerness of Mathur to have Padmalochan brought to Dakshineswar by invitation and to make him accept gifts at that time. Therefore, the year 1864 may be said to be the time when Bhattacharya Sri Padmalochan Tarkalankar, the Vedantic scholar, came to the Master.

The time when Pandit Vaishnavacharan, the son of Utsavananda Goswami, came to Dakshineswar, can easily be ascertained. For, we have heard from the Master about his discussion at Dakshineswar on the question of the divinity of the Master, at first with Yogeswari, the Bhairavi Brahmani, and, afterwards, with Gaurikanta Tarka-bhushan. Like the Brahmani, Vaishnavacharan saw manifested in the Master's mind and body all the signs of the Mahabhava spoken of in the Vaishnava scriptures. He got lost in astonishment at this and agreed with the Bhairavi in her conclusion that the

Master was Gauranga Himself come in a new form. When one hears the above-mentioned words of the Master, it becomes clear to one that Vaishnavacharan came to the Master in 1865 after the latter had become perfected in the discipline of the Madhura Bhava. Vaishnavacharan frequented Dakshineswar now and again till 1873.

12. It was by divine inspiration that a new desire of great intensity arose in the mind of the Master after he had had the experiences mentioned before. He became very anxious to meet his devotees, previously seen in his Yogic visions, and to impart his own power of spirituality to them. "That anxiety," said the Master, "had no limit. With great difficulty I put up with that constant anxiety throughout the day-time. Hearing the vain talks of the worldly people, which verily seemed to be poison to me, I used to think that, when they all came, I would have pleasant conversations on God with them, which would pacify my mind and heart and refresh my ears. I would then tell them my own spiritual experiences and lighten the burden of my heart. The idea of their coming got associated with everything in and around me, and led me to think incessantly of them. I kept myself in readiness regarding what I should say or give to each one of them. When the day ended and the evening came, I could no longer control that surge of anxiety by any amount of patience; the thought arose that another day had passed away and none of them had come. When the temples rang with sounds of conchs, bells, etc., I got up to the roof of the 'mansion' of the proprietors. Being restless on account of the anguish of my heart, I called out at the top of my voice and with tears in my eyes, 'Where are you, my children? Do come, one and all. I cannot rest any more without seeing you'; and I filled the quarters with loud cries. So great were my anxiety and restlessness that it is doubtful whether a mother could desire so intensely to meet her child; nor had I ever heard of a pair of lovers or friends behaving that way in order to be united with each other. A few days after this, the devotees began to come one by one."

A few important events took place before the devotees came to Dakshineswar at that anxious call of the Master. As they are not directly connected with the present part of the book, we record them in the Appendix to Part II of the book.

THE PRINCIPAL EVENTS OF THE MASTER'S LIFE FROM THE WORSHIP OF THE SHODASI TO THE COMING OF HIS 'MARKED' DEVOTEES

(TOPICS; 1. Death of Rameswar 2. Rameswar's charitable nature 3. The Master's warning about Rameswar's death 4. The Master's solicitude for his mother's feelings 5. Rameswar's behaviour on the eve of his death 6. Rameswar's reappearance after death 7. Ramlal appointed priest 8. The story of Sambhu Mallick 9. Sambhu Babu building a room for the Holy Mother. 10. The Holy Mother's serious illness 11. Her Prayopavesa in Simhavahini's temple 12. Sambhu Babu's unperturbed behaviour at death 13. The last days of Chandramani 14. The Master attempting to perform Tarpana 15. The Master going to see Kesav Babu 16. Kesav in the garden at Belgharia 17. His first talk with Kesav 18. The intimate relation between the Master and Kesav 19. How Kesav behaved at Dakshineswar 20. The Master teaching Kesav 21. The Coochbehar marriage and after 22. Kesav honoured the Master but could not accept all his ideals 23. The New Dispensation and the Master's opinion on it 24. The Master and India's national problem 25. The Master's reaction to Kesav's death 26. The Master seeing Gauranga in Sankirtan.)

1. We have told the reader that the Holy Mother came back to Kamarpukur in the month of October, 1873, after the worship of Shodasi. Shortly after her arrival there, Rameswar, the second of the elder brothers of the Master, died of typhoid. Spirituality in some form or other was manifest in the life of each man and woman belonging to the Master's paternal lineage. We have heard many things illustrative of this in regard to Rameswar.

2. Rameswar was a man of a very liberal nature. He would give unhesitatingly to Sannyasins and Fakirs coming to his door, whatever they asked for, provided it was there in the house. We were told by his relatives that such religious mendicants used to come and want many things—one a cooking pot, another a water-pot, a third a blanket and so on,—and Rameswar brought them all out from the house and gave them away to them. If any member of the house raised an objection, he calmly said, "Let them take these. Don't raise any objections. Many such articles we shall

have again; why do you bother?" Rameswar had some knowledge of astrology too.

3. When Rameswar was going home from Dakshineswar for the last time, the Master knew that he would not return from there, and in an ecstasy, said to him, "You are going home, I see; go, but do not share the bed with your wife; if you do, it is doubtful whether you will survive." One of us[1] heard this from the Master himself later.

4. Shortly after Rameswar reached home, word came that he was ill. When the Master heard it, he said to Hriday, "He did not obey the prohibition; it is doubtful whether his life will be saved." After five or six days the news came that Rameswar had passed away. The Master was much afraid that the news of the death of her son would be a great shock to his aged mother. He went to the temple and prayed plaintively to the Mother of the universe to save her from grief. Then the Master went with tears in his eyes, we were told by himself, from the temple to the Nahabat to break the news and to console his mother. The Master said, "I was afraid that mother might completely lose her consciousness on hearing it and was doubtful about the chances of her survival. But, in fact, the contrary happened. Mother heard the news, expressed a little grief and started consoling me, saying, 'The world is transitory; die every one must, some day or other; it is, therefore, useless to grieve.' It seemed to me that the Divine Mother had tuned her mind to a high pitch like a Tanpura keyed up to a very high note, and that was why worldly grief and sorrow could not touch her. When I noticed this, I saluted the Divine Mother again and again and became free from anxiety."

5. Rameswar knew the time of his death five or six days before the event took place. He told his relatives of it and made all preparations for his obsequies and the Sraddha ceremony. Seeing a mango tree in front of the house being cut down for some reason, he said, "It is good; the wood will be of use in my funeral rites." He uttered the holy name of Sri Ramachandra till his last moments. He lay unconscious only for a short while before he passed away. Before his death Rameswar requested his relatives not to cremate his body in the burning ground but to bury it on the road nearby Asked the reason for it, he said, "I shall attain a high heaven by

---

[1] Swami Premananda.

virtue of the touch of the dust of many a Sadhu's feet treading the road." Rameswar died at dead of night.

6. Rameswar and an inhabitant of the village named Gopal, had been friends for a long time. Gopal said that after Rameswar's death—it must have been simultaneous with the incident—he heard a tap at the door of his home, and on enquiry, got the reply, "I am Rameswar, going to take a dip in the Ganga. There is Raghuvir there, in the house; please see that His worship does not suffer in any way". When Gopal was about to open the door at the call of his friend, he was told again, "I have no body; so you will not be able to see me even if you open the door." Gopal opened the door in spite of that but found no one there. He then went to Rameswar's house to know if what he had heard was true, and found that Rameswar had actually passed away.

7. Ramlal Chattopadhyaya says that his father, Rameswar, died in 1873 at the age of about forty-eight. He collected the ashes of his deceased father and came to Vaidyavati near Calcutta and immersed them in the Ganga. He then crossed the river there by boat for the purpose of coming to the Master at Dakshineswar. Looking at Barrackpur while crossing the river, he saw the temple of Devi Annapurna, which was being constructed on behalf of Jagadamba Dasi, the wife of Mathur Babu, in a half-built condition. The installation of the Devi took place afterwards in 1875. At Rameswar's death, his son Ramlal was appointed priest to perform the worship at Dakshineswar.

8. When Mathur died, Sambhucharan Mallick of Sinduriapati, Calcutta, came to be acquainted with the Master and developed a great love and reverence for him.[1] Sambhu had at this time a great attraction for the religion of the Brahmo Samaj. He became known to the people of Calcutta on account of his great munificence. His love and devotion to the Master became deeper day by day, and he had the privilege of serving him like Mathur. Sambhu was glad to supply his wants, whenever he came to know

---

[1] Some of the Master's devotees say that they heard him mention the fact that after the death of Mathur Babu, Manimohan Sen of Panihati took upon himself the loving duty of supplying all the Master's necessaries. Manimohan then had much respect for the Master and used to visit him very often. Sambhu took on that duty after Manimohan. But Sambhu, the Master himself pointed out, was the second supplier of his necessaries. So Mani Babu, it seems to us, could not continue to serve him long even though he had started to execute that self-imposed charge.

of any. He continued to serve him to the last of his days and felt
highly gratified. Sambhu addressed the Master as "Guruji",
honoured preceptor. Annoyed at it, the Master said, "Who
is the Guru and who is the disciple? You are my Guru." But,
instead of desisting, Sambhu called him so all his life. His addressing
the Master that way is a clear proof of the fact that the Master's
company had brought him much enlightenment and complete
success in his spiritual life. His wife also offered her heart-felt
worship to the Master as to God Himself. When the Holy Mother
stayed at Dakshineswar, she used to bring her to their house every
Tuesday[1] and worship her holy feet with the sixteen articles.

9. The Holy Mother came to Dakshineswar for the second
time, probably in the middle of 1874. She lived now as before
with the Master's mother at the Nahabat. Knowing this and infer-
ring that she was feeling it uncomfortable to live in that small room,
Sambhu purchased for two hundred and fifty rupees a plot of land
near the Dakshineswar temple, on which he wanted to build a
spacious thatched room for her. Captain Viswanath Upadhyaya,
an officer of the Nepal Government, was then paying visits to the
Master and had become greatly devoted to him. Knowing the
resolve of Sambhu to have the room built, Captain Viswanath
readily came forward with the offer of supplying all the timber
necessary for building it. For, the Sal wood business of the Government of Nepal was then in his hands, and therefore, it was not very
expensive for him to supply the timber. When the work of building
the room began, Viswanath sent three big logs of Sal wood from
his stock at the village of Belur across the Ganga. But, as there
was a strong flood tide in the river at night, one piece was carried
away. Hriday became annoyed at it and went to the length of
calling the Holy Mother "unfortunate". Hearing, however, that
one piece had been carried away, the Captain sent another and the
building was completed. The Holy Mother lived in that room for
about a year. A woman was then appointed to be with the Holy
Mother and to help her in the household work. The Holy Mother
cooked food there, brought it daily to the Master at the
Dakshineswar temple and came back after the Master had taken
it. The Master also used to come to that room to meet her, some

---

[1] Tuesday is regarded auspicious for the worship of the Devi—Tr.

time during the day, be with her for a short period and return to the temple. There was an exception to this routine only on one occasion. As soon as the Master came one afternoon, it began to rain so heavily and continuously till very late at night, that it was impossible for him to come back to the temple that night. He was, therefore, compelled to pass the night there. The Holy Mother cooked for him soup and rice; the Master partook of them and passed the night there.

10. The Holy Mother had a severe attack of dysentery after she had lived in that room for about a year. Sambhu Babu took much care to get her cured. He called Dr. Prasad and she was placed under his treatment. During her convalescence, she was sent to her native village Jayarambati, probably in 1876. Hardly had she reached the village when there was a relapse of the disease and she was again bed-ridden. It increased so much gradually that everyone doubted whether she would recover. Ramchandra, the revered father of the Holy Mother, had passed away by then. So, her mother and brothers served her as much as they could. Hearing of her severe illness the Master, we were told, said to Hriday, "So, Hriday, it looks as if her coming into the world and leaving it has been in vain! There is no point in assuming a human body, if its purpose of attaining God is not achieved."

11. Seeing that the disease was not alleviated by any means, the Holy Mother made a resolution to observe Prayopavesana (fasting unto death), before the Devi. Thinking that her mother and brothers might stand in her way if they knew of it, she went without their knowledge to Simhavahini's temple in the village and undertook Prayopavesana there. Scarcely had she been there in that condition for a few hours, when the Devi was pleased and prescribed the medicine for her recovery.

No sooner had she taken the medicine according to the bidding of the Devi than she came round and became strong as before. Since the Holy Mother undertook Prayopavesana and got the medicine, the Devi has become well known in the surrounding villages, as one especially "awakened"—that is, one with whom a votary can commune with and make offerings and pray with sure expectation of response.

12. Sambhu served the Master and the Holy Mother for about four years. He then fell ill. One day the Master went to see Sambu during his illness and said when he returned, "There is no

oil in Sambhu's lamp." The words of the Master came true, and soon after Sambhu died of diabetes with complications. Sambhu Babu was very liberal and he was an intrepid devotee of God. The cheerfulness of his mind was not impaired even for a single day during his illness. With a cheerful heart he said to Hriday a few days before he passed away, "I have no anxiety about death; I have packed up my bag and baggage and am quite ready to depart." Long before he was acquainted with Sambhu Babu, the Master, while in ecstasy, saw that the Mother of the universe had appointed Sambhu as his second supplier of necessaries, and he recognized him at first sight.

13. There happened an important event in the Master's life after the Holy Mother had gone to her father's house during her illness. The Master's mother Chandramani Devi passed away in her eighty-fifth year on his birthday in 1876. On account of senility the powers of her mind and senses were impaired to a great extent for a few years before her death. We record here the description of her death as it was given to us by Hriday.

Hriday was about to go home on leave, four days before she died. His mind became restless on account of a vague fear arising from unspecified forebodings, and he therefore felt great hesitation to go home, leaving the Master alone. Hriday apprised the Master of his apprehension, when the latter said, "Then don't go." Three days passed without anything untoward happening.

The Master used to go to his mother every day for some time and serve her with his own hands. Hriday also used to serve her, and Kali's mother, a woman servant, remained for almost the whole of the day-time with the old lady. She was not now well disposed towards Hriday. For, in her dotage she had a notion, from the time of Akshay's death, that it was Hriday who had killed him and that he was trying to kill the Master and his wife too. This was why she sometimes warned the Master and said, "Never comply with what Hriday says." Signs of her loss of understanding through age and infirmity were found in various other respects too. Take for example the following fact. The Alambazar jute mill was situated near the Dakshineswar garden. The workers of the mill were given leave for some time during midday. They were again called to work half an hour later by the sounding of a whistle. The old lady came to the conclusion that the sound of the whistle was the blowing of conchs in Vaikuntha. Therefore she would not sit to

23

take her food till that whistle was sounded. Requested to take food, she would say, "How can I eat just now? Food has not yet been offered to Lakshmi-Narayana. The conch in Vaikuntha has not yet been blown. Should one take one's food before that?" It was difficult to make her sit to take her food on mill holidays on which the whistle was not sounded. Hriday and the Master had to invent various means to make her take food.

The fourth day came. The old lady showed no signs of illness even then. The Master went to her after dark and filled her mind with joy by leading the conversation on to his early life and telling her accounts about it. She was sent to bed at midnight, when the Master returned to his room.

It was morning the next day. The clock struck eight. But the old lady did not open the door and come out. Kali's mother went up to the door of the room on the first floor of the Nahabat and called her repeatedly, but got no reply. She put her ears to the door and heard an unnatural sound coming out of the old lady's throat. She became alarmed and informed the Master and Hriday about it. Hriday went, opened skilfully the bar of the door from outside and found that she was lying unconscious. He then brought an Ayurvedic medicine and placed it on her tongue. He also began to make her drink milk and Ganga water drop by drop at short intervals. She continued in that condition for three days. Then came the last moments. She was taken to the sacred Ganga. The Master offered at her lotus feet flowers, sandal-paste and leaves of the holy basil. As it was forbidden for the Master, a Sannyasin, to perform the obsequies of his mother, his brother's son Ramlal was deputed by him to perform her funeral rites. When the period of defilement was over, Ramlal, at the request of the Master, set free a bull and performed the Sraddha ceremony according to the prescription of the scriptures.

14. Paying regard to the prestige and honour of Sannyasa and to the scriptural injunctions connected with it, the Master did not observe Asaucha or perform any other rites at the death of his mother. Feeling that he had thereby neglected the duties proper for a son, he was one day about to offer Tarpana. But no sooner did he take up an Anjali of water than a state of spiritual inspiration came on him; his fingers became insensible and separated from one another and all the water fell out between the fingers, in spite of his repeated efforts to perform the rite. Then with a heart laden with

sorrow, he sorely pleaded to his deceased mother his utter incapacity to do it.   He was told afterwards by a Pandit that this state comes to a man who has reached the state when actions drop off.   With his progress in spirituality he reaches a state when performance of all Vedic actions is naturally rendered impossible, and he incurs no sin on that account.

15.   An important event in the Master's life took place by the will of the Divine Mother a year before his mother passed away. In 1875 there arose a desire in the Master's mind to meet Kesav-chandra Sen, the leader of the Brahmo Samaj of India. While the Master was in ecstasy, he received the direction of the Divine Mother in this matter, and knowing that Kesav with his disciples was then engaged in spiritual practices at Jayagopal Sen's garden house in Belgharia, a few miles to the north of Calcutta, he went there with Hriday in Captain Viswanath's carriage and reached there at about 1 p.m.   The Master wore that day a piece of red-bordered cloth. The lower extremity of its front, tucked in folds, was thrown up over his left shoulder and it was swinging behind his back.

16.   Hriday got down from the carriage and saw Kesav and his followers sitting on the ghat of the garden pond. Coming up to him, he informed Kesav, "My maternal uncle is a great lover of God and likes to hear talks and songs on Hari. Listening to them, he gets inspired and enters into ecstasy. He has heard that you are a great devotee of God and has come here to listen to the talks on divine glory from you. If you kindly agree, I shall bring him here." Kesav gave his assent. Hriday helped the Master in alighting from the carriage and accompanied him. Kesav and the others were till then very anxious to see him, but when they saw him, their eagerness cooled down, as he looked quite an ordinary man.

17.   The Master came to Kesav and said, "Is it true, gentlemen, that you all have the vision of God? I have a desire to know the nature of that vision. That is why I have come to you."   In that way the topic of God was taken up. We cannot say what Kesav said in answer to the Master's words. But the Master, we were told by Hriday, sang the famous song of Ramprasad, "Who knows, O mind, how Kali is? She cannot be seen by the study of the six Darsanas," and immediately entered into Samadhi. When they saw that state of ecstasy of the Master, Kesav and the others did

not regard it as a high spiritual state. They thought that
it was mere feigning or was due to a derangement of the brain.
With a view to bringing him back to normal consciousness, Hriday
now began uttering the Pranava into his ears. At this his face brightened up with a sweet smile. Thus regaining partial consciousness,
the Master now went on explaining profound spiritual matters in so
simple a language with the help of common examples that all were
charmed and sat looking steadfastly at his face. Nobody noticed
that the time for bath and meal was long past and that imperceptibly
the hour for the next prayer was almost come. Seeing that mood
of theirs, the Master said, "If any other animal comes to a herd
of cattle, they go forward to gore it; but if a cow comes, they lick
one another's bodies. Our case is just like that today." He
then addressed Kesav and said, "Your tail has dropped off."
Unable to understand its meaning, the followers of Kesav looked
annoyed, when the Master charmed them all by explaining its
significance to them. "Look here," said he, "as long as the
tadpole has its tail, it lives only in water and cannot come up on
land; but, when the tail drops off, it can live on land as well as
in water. Even so, as long as a man has the tail of ignorance, he
can live in the water of the world only, but when that tail falls
off, he can as freely move about in the world as in Existence-
Knowledge-Bliss. Your mind, O Kesav, has now attained that
state in which you can live in the world as also in Existence-Knowledge-Bliss." The Master spent a long time discussing various
topics like this and came back to Dakshineswar that day.

18. Kesav's mind was so much attracted towards the Master
since he saw him first, that from now on till his passing away, he
deemed it an honour and a privilege to meet him and enjoy his
divine company. He would either come himself to the
Dakshineswar temple or take the Master now and then to his
"Kamal Kutir" residence in Calcutta. The relation between the
Master and Kesav deepened so much that both of them felt a great
want if they did not see each other even for a few days. At such
times the Master used to go to Kesav in Calcutta or the latter
would come to the former at Dakshineswar. Besides, Kesav
considered it to be a part of the annual festival of the Brahmo Samaj
to come with his companions to the Master or take him to them and
spend a day with him in conversations on the Divine. Many were
the occasions when he with his followers came to Dakshineswar in

a steamer singing the glory of God, had the Master brought into it, and took a trip with him on the Ganga, all the while listening to his ambrosial teachings.

19. Remembering the scriptural injunctions, Kesav never came empty-handed to Dakshineswar. Whenever he came, he brought with him some fruits and placed them before the Master, and like a devoted follower, sat at his feet and conversed with him. At one time the Master said to him by way of a joke, "Kesav, you charm so many people by your lectures. Why don't you speak something to me?" Kesav replied humbly, "Sir, should I come to a blacksmith's shop to sell needles? Please say something yourself and let me listen. People are charmed as soon as I tell them a few words of yours."

20. One day the Master explained to Kesav at Dakshineswar that if one accepted the existence of Brahman, one had similarly to accept the existence of the power of Brahman, and that Brahman and Its power were eternally one and the same. Kesav accepted it. The Master then told him that, like Brahman and Its power, the three entities,—namely, the divine words (the scriptures), the devotee, and the Divine Lord—are non-separate, in other words, eternally identical. The three, namely, the scriptures, the devotee and the Divine Lord are one, and the One is the three. Kesav understood and accepted this too. The Master went on to say that the three, namely, the Guru, Krishna (the Divine Lord) and the devotee are One, and the One is the three, which he was then going to explain to him. Kesav mused a little—we do not know what thoughts passed through his mind—and he said with humility, "Sir, I cannot accept now more than what you have already said. It is, therefore, needless to raise this topic at present." The Master said, "That's all right. Let us stop here." The mind of Kesav, which had been inspired with the Western ideas and ideals, thus received much light from the divine company of the Master. Day by day his understanding of the Vedic religion expanded and he got immersed in Sadhana. This is evident, because his religious views gradually underwent a change as he came into close contact with the Master.

21. The human mind, unless grievously wounded, does not feel like detaching itself from the world and realizing God as its all. Kesav got such a shock after he gave away his daughter in marriage to the prince of Coochbehar about three years after he

had become acquainted with the Master. This marriage produced a great commotion in the Brahmo Samaj of India, and split it into two. The party opposed to Kesav separated themselves from the society and formed a new one called the General Brahmo Samaj. The Master at Dakshineswar was much shocked to hear of that quarrel between the two parties over a petty matter. Hearing of the rule of the Brahmo Samaj about the marriageable age of girls, the Master, said, "Birth, death and marriage are things entirely under the will of God. They cannot be brought under hard and fast rules. Why did Kesav set about to fix that?" If any one raised the topic of the Coochbehar marriage and condemned Kesav in the presence of the Master, he used to say, "How is Kesav to blame for doing that? He is a man with a family. Why should he not do what is good for his sons and daughters? What is there to be condemned when a man, having the responsibility of a family on his shoulders, does this without deviating from the path of virtue? Kesav in no way acted contrary to religion or morality. He has, rather, discharged the duty of a father." Viewing it thus from the standpoint of the duties of a householder, the Master always supported Kesav's action as not in any way blameworthy. However, there is no doubt that this blow dealt by the incident of the Coochbehar marriage turned Kesav's mind more inward and led it more rapidly along the path of spirituality.

22. In spite of the Master's great love for him and the many opportunities he had to see the Master and listen to him, it is doubtful whether Kesav, inspired with Western ideas and ideals as he was, understood him perfectly. For, on the one hand, he looked upon the Master as a living embodiment of spirituality—he personally took him to his house, showed him round the places where he went to bed, where he ate, where he sat and where he reflected on the good of his Samaj, and asked him to bless him so that his mind might not forget God and think of worldly objects when engaged in any one of these places. Then leading him to the place where he meditated on God, Kesav offered flowers at his lotus feet.[1] When he came to Dakshineswar, he was seen by many of us to salute the Master uttering, "Victory to the (New) Dispensation!"

23. On the other hand, he was unable to accept fully the Master's saying, "All religions are true—as many faiths, so many

---

[1] We heard this from Vijaykrishna Goswami.

paths." Alternatively he tried to found a new faith called "The New Dispensation" by picking out what appeared to him to be the essentials of all religions and rejecting what seemed non-essentials in them. As this faith came into existence shortly after Kesav's acquaintance with the Master, it is probable that it was in partial acceptance and as propagation of the Master's final conclusion regarding the true nature of all religions.

24.   When the powerful waves of Western education and civilization came to India and began to bring about a radical change in people's spiritual and social outlook, every talented man of this country began to look for harmony between the culture and civilization of the East and those of the West. Just as in the province of Bengal, Rammohan Roy, Maharshi Devendranath, Brahmananda Kesav and others devoted their lives for that purpose, even so, in other parts of the country too, many great souls are known to have appeared and carried on the same work; but none of them could perfectly tackle it before the advent of the Master. The Master duly went through the disciplines of all the religions of India in his own life, and attaining to the results of the Sadhanas prescribed by each of them, showed that the religion of this country was not the cause of its degradation and that the cause must be sought elsewhere. He showed also that society, manners, customs, in short, the culture and civilization of India had their basis in religion, that it had brought glory and prosperity to this country in the past, that the same life-giving religion still exists undecayed, and that we could again successfully pilot our national ship, if only we could base all our efforts and endeavours on it and on nothing else. Living the ideal life himself, the Master showed further how religion could broaden the outlook of man. Next he transmitted the liberalizing power of that religion to his disciples— especially to Swami Vivekananda—who were till then inspired by Western ideas and ideals, taught them how to perform all actions in the world as ancillary to religion; and thus gave a wonderful solution for the above-mentioned intricate problem of India. Just as he established spiritual harmony among the religions of the world by demonstrating the truth of them all by actually following the spiritual practices advocated by them, he has stopped the wranglings between the various sects of Hinduism by following the orthodox practices of each of them and demonstrating their perfection in himself. He has thereby demonstrated to us the true

bases of our nationality in the past and what they should be in the future.

25. Even though Kesav failed to understand the full implication of the Master's ideals, the Master had a wonderful love for him, which we could understand from his reaction to Kesav's death in 1884. The Master said, "I could not leave my bed for three days when I got that news; it seemed as if a limb of mine was paralysed."

26. We shall bring this Appendix to a close by mentioning another event which happened when he met Kesav for the first time. The Master then had a desire to witness the all-bewitching ambulatory Sankirtan of Sri Chaitanya. The Divine Mother fulfilled that desire of his by showing it to him in the way described below: Standing outside his room he saw wonderful waves of Sankirtan coming towards him from the direction of the Panchavati, proceeding towards the main gate of the Dakshineswar garden and disappearing behind the trees. He witnessed that, absorbed in the love of God, Gauranga, the moon of Navadwip, was proceeding with a slow gait in the centre, with Nityananda and Advaita on either side, and surrounded by a dense multitude. They were all in a state of spiritual inebriation produced by God-love, some expressing the bliss of their hearts by losing control over themselves and others by wild ecstatic dances. The crowd was so great that it looked as if there was no end to the number of people there. A few faces in that wonderful Sankirtan got impressed on the canvas of the Master's memory in bright colours. When he saw them coming as his devotees shortly after he had had that vision, the Master arrived at the certain conclusion that they had been the companions of Chaitanya in a previous life.

Shortly after he had had that vision, the Master went to Kamarpukur and to Hriday's native village, Sihar. Phului-Shyambazar is situated a few miles away from the latter place. Hearing that there were many Vaishnavas there who filled the place with the bliss of Sankirtan everyday, he had a desire to go there and listen to it. The village of Belte stood near Shyambazar. Natavar Goswami of that village had met the Master before, and invited him to sanctify his home with the dust of his feet. Accompanied by Hriday, the Master went to his house, lived there for seven days and enjoyed the bliss of Sankirtan with the Vaishnavas of Shyambazar. Being acquainted with the Master, Ishanchandra Mallick of that place

invited him with great respect to his house to share the bliss of
Sankirtan there. The Vaishnavas were much attracted towards
him on seeing his wonderful moods during Sankirtan. The news
of his mystic moods spread all around—not only in Shyambazar but also to Ramjivanpur, Krishnaganj and other villages
far and near. Then came from those villages parties of Sankirtan
with a view to enjoying divine bliss with him. That made the
village very much crowded and Sankirtan went on night and day.
There was then a general talk that there had come a devotee of
God who died and revived many times a day. People forgot
food and sleep, and anxious to see him, climbed up trees and got on
the roofs of houses. Thus, for seven days and nights, there flowed
a tide of celestial bliss there. People became mad, as it were, to
see the Master and to touch his feet. The rush was so great that
the Master could not find time even for his bath or food. To save
him from the strain, Hriday fled with him secretly to Sihar and
that "mart of joy" thus came to an end. Ishan Choudhuri, Natavar
Goswami, Ihan Mallick, Srinath Mallick and others of the village
of Shyambazar and their descendants mention that event even
today and cherish great love and respect for him. The Master
also became acquainted with Raicharan Das, the famous Khol
(drum) player of Krishnaganj. As soon as he played on the
Khol, the Master would go into ecstasy. We were told of the
above-mentioned event partly by the Master and partly by Hriday.
We have been able to ascertain its date in the following way:

A great devotee of the Master, Mahendranath Pal, the physician
of Alambazar, met the Master after Kesav Babu had had the privilege
of meeting him in 1875. Mahendranath Pal had informed us that
his meeting with the Master took place just after the Master's
return from Sihar and that the Master spoke to him on that occasion about the happenings at Phului-Shyambazar. So these
events must have taken place only after 1879, the date from which
the chosen devotees of the Master began to come. Only Swami
Yogananda, whose house was situated in very close proximity to the
Dakshineswar temple, might have been to the Master earlier.

Swami Vivekananda came to him in 1881. The death of
Jagadamba Dasi took place in January, 1881. About six months after
this, Hriday foolishly worshipped the feet of Mathur Babu's grand
daughter of very tender age. Her father, apprehending that evil might
befall the child, became much annoyed and dismissed Hriday

from the service of the Kali temple. Hriday was still with the Master when his Phului-Shyambazar visit took place. So the event under discussion must have taken place some time in or before 1879.

Here ends the Sadhakabhava, the period of the Master's life as a spiritual aspirant practising Sadhanas.

Sri Ramakrishna The Great Master

PART THREE

AS THE SPIRITUAL TEACHER (1)

PREFACE

AS THE SPIRITUAL TEACHER

THIS is the Third Part of *Sri Ramakrishna The Great Master*. The events of the Master's life from the time he completed his Sadhanas to the time he became well known to the public have been in the main recorded here. We have not merely recorded them but have also discussed, as far as possible, the moods that prompted and the purpose that guided his actions. For, the human personality is a combination of the body and the spirit, and consequently the study of a man's life history is imperfect if it is only a study of the events of his external life, excluding the meanings and purposes that guide it. When writing a biography or a history, the materialistic West exhibits its ability mainly in recording events, while the spiritualistic Hindu applies his mind to a careful depiction of the mental functions only. It is our conviction that a true biography or history should be a combination of both and that the actions of the gross body should be recorded with a view to unfolding the history of the mind.

Moreover, we have discussed the extraordinary life of Sri Ramakrishna in the light of the scriptures in many places. We have been led to study the unique functioning of his mind, his experiences, and his activities in comparison with those of great souls like Krishna, Buddha, Sankara and Chaitanya of India and of Jesus and others of other countries. The Master said to us in unambiguous language again and again that " the one who, in the past, became Rama and Krishna is (showing his own body) in this sheath now," and that "the spiritual experiences of this (meaning himself) have gone beyond those recorded in the Vedas and the Vedantas." As a matter of fact, in discussing impartially, as far as possible, the life of Sri Ramakrishna establised in Bhavamukha, we have been constrained to confess that such an extraordinary life in the spiritual world has never been seen before.

Again, when we take into account the full implication of the new truth, viz. " As many faiths, so many paths ", discovered and proclaimed by him after actually following those faiths founded by the incarnations of the past, we are inevitably led to accept him as the summation of all the incarnations who have gone before. The more we have studied the unprecedented holy life Sri Ramakrishna, the greater has grown our conviction that he is the unique product of the universal and eternal spiritual ideas of the Vedas— the totality of their essence.

When the revered Swami Vivekananda had preached Sri Ramakrishna's ideas and the public became eager to know the facts of his life, many people published many accounts of him. But none of them pointed out clearly the hidden relation that existed between that unique life and the Vedic or eternal religion. Consequently, from a study of these books an impression has grown in the minds of people that Sri Ramakrishna was a man cut off from the tradition of the eternal Hindu religion and has left behind him a particular sectarian doctrine of his creation. Further, many of those stories contain errors regarding the life-history of the Master and lack appreciation of the real import of the events of his life and their relation with the historical past and the future trends. In order to meet to a certain extent that demand of the public and to correct mistaken notions, we have, following in the footsteps of Swami Vivekananda, attempted in this book a description of that unique life as it presented itself to us, with a view to depict that exalted state of the Master's mind (Bhava), the realization of a little of which has made Swami Vivekananda and others, including ourselves, dedicate their lives at the lotus feet of the Master. Let the reader know that if even a small part of the noble ideal of the Master's life, unintelligible to ordinary man, has been correctly portrayed in this book, it is due to his greatness; and whatever defect or incompleteness is observed, it is due to our lack of proper understanding and power of exposition. We intend to present to the reader later a description of the first and last part of the precious life of the Master.[1] Before we start, we intend to prefix the verses and the aphoristic article by Swami Vivekananda who has discussed therein the hidden relation of the eternal Vedic religion with the unfathomable life of Sri Ramakrishna abiding in Bhavamukha.

AUTHOR

---

[1] In writing this biography the author began with this part III first. Then he wrote in succession parts IV, II, I , and V.—Tr.

THE HINDU RELIGION AND
SRI RAMAKRISHNA

आचण्डालाप्रतिहतरयो यस्य प्रेमप्रवाहः
लोकातीतोऽप्यहह न जहौ लोककल्याणमार्गम् ।
त्रैलोक्येऽप्यप्रतिममहिमा जानकीप्राणबन्धो
भक्त्या ज्ञानं व्रतवरवपुः सीतया यो हि रामः ॥ १ ॥
स्तब्धीकृत्य प्रलयकलितं वाह्वोत्थं महान्तं
हित्वा रात्रिं प्रकृतिसहजामन्धतामिस्रमिश्राम् ।
गीतं शान्तं मधुरमपि यः सिंहनादं जगर्ज
सोऽयं जातः प्रथितपुरुषो रामकृष्णस्त्विदानीम् ॥ २ ॥

*THE One born as Rama of incomparable greatness in all the three
worlds; who was the very life of Janaka's daughter; who, though
himself beyond the world, lo, did not give up doing good to it; the
current of whose love ever flowed unchecked down even to a Chandala;
and whose body of supreme knowledge was enveloped by devotion
in the form of Sita; the One born as Krishna too, who sang the song
(the Gita) sweet and tranquil, yet deep as the roar of a lion, suppressing
the great cataclysmic tumult raised in the battle-field and destroying
the innate and deep-seated darkness of ignorance—that ever-renowned
Divine Personality is now born as Ramakrishna.*[1]

The word Sastra denotes the beginningless and endless "Veda".
It is this Veda only that is capable of teaching religion.

The Puranas and other books are denoted by the word Smriti.
They have authority only in so far as they have followed the Veda.

"Truth" is of two kinds: (1) that which is perceivable by the five
senses of human beings and is deducible therefrom by inference and
(2) that which is perceivable by the subtle powers arising from Yoga.

The knowledge acquired by the first means is called science
and that acquired by the second method is the Veda.

The beginningless and endless mass of infinite knowledge called
the "Veda" is eternally existent. The Creator Himself is creating,
maintaining and destroying this world with its help.

---

[1]The above is a translation of two Sanskrit stanzas composed by
Swami Vivekananda. vide. Complete Works VI pp. 181.—Tr.

The person in whom that power of intuition is manifested is called a Rishi, and the infinite knowledge that he comprehends through that power is called the "Veda".

The attainment of this Rishihood or seership, consisting in the immediate knowledge of the "Veda", is the true realization of religion. Until the aspirant's life opens out to it, religion for him is a "mere meaningless word", and he cannot be said to have set his foot on the threshold of religion.

The authority of the Veda holds good irrespective of time, place and person; that is, its authority is not confined to a particular time, country or person.

The Veda alone sets forth the Universal Religion. Although a little of that infinite knowledge is to be found in the Itihasas, Puranas, etc., of our country and in the religious books of foreign countries, yet as the first complete and unaltered collection of the entire body of the eternal knowledge, this mass of words compiled into four books called the Veda and well known to the Aryans, is worthy of occupying the highest place in all respects, — of being adored by the whole world and of being the ultimate proof of the truth of all scriptures, indigenous or alien.

Regarding the mass of words called the Veda, discovered by the Aryans, it must also be understood that that part alone of it, which is not Arthavada[1] (eulogy) or Aitihya[2] (tradition) or otherwise empirically known or knowable, is the Veda. This mass of words is divided into two parts, namely, that relating to knowledge and that relating to work. As the rituals of the Veda and their results described in the "work" portion exist for all time in the domain of Maya, they are subject to transformation according to the law of change with reference to time, place, person, circumstances etc. Yes, they have been and will be changed. As social manners and customs depend on this "work" portion, they also do and will undergo change. Similarly, popular customs and manners too have been and will be accepted from time to time, only in so far as they are not contrary to the scriptures and the conduct of the wise. One of the main causes of the downfall of the Aryans is their subjection to such popular customs and manners as are contrary to the Veda,

---

[1]Vide Glossary.—Tr.
[2]Vide Glossary.—Tr.

to the conduct of the wise and to the scriptures conformable to the Veda.

The "knowledge" portion of the Veda, otherwise known as the Vedanta, aided by selfless action, concentration of mind, devotion and self-knowledge, is eternally taking men across the ocean of Maya to the other shore of liberation. As it is not at all influenced by time, place and agency, it alone is the teacher of the universal religion —a religion that is meant for all peoples, all countries and all times.

It is on the basis of the "work" portion of the Veda that books on the social system like those of Manu and others have taught, in addition to other matters, those actions that are conducive to social welfare, varying with time, place and agency; while books like the Puranas have taken up the truths hidden in the Vedanta and have explained them in detail in their descriptions of the achievements and excellences of Divine Incarnations and other manifestations of one or another of the numerous aspects of the Divine.

But, in course of time, the descendants of the Aryans deviated from right conduct, and lacking dispassion, devoted themselves to the prevailing popular customs and grew feeble in intellect. They failed to understand the import of even the Puranas, which appeared as contradictory to one another on account of their teaching those different divine aspects and preaching the subtle truths of the Vedanta in gross and concrete forms in detail for the consumption of weak brains. Hence they split into numerous divisions the integral eternal religion, which is an aggregate of innumerable religious moods; and kindling the fire of sectarian hatred and jealousy, they endeavoured to throw one another into that fire. When they thus turned Bharata, the land of religion, almost into a hell, Bhagavan Sri Ramakrishna incarnated himself in order to show what the real religion of the Aryans was and where lay the unity amongst the numberless sects and denominations of the Hindu religion scattered pell-mell over a vast range of time and place— the religion that has become a source of delusion to the people of the land and an object of contempt to those of other countries, owing to its apparent division into innumerable ever- warring sects bristling with contradictory customs. This he did by holding aloft before the gaze of all his own life as a living example of that religion eternal by concentrating in himself its universality lost by the lapse of time.

The Divine, whose embodiment the Veda is, gave no facilities of literary education to this incarnation, in order to show how

24

the eternally existing Sastra — with the help of which Isvara evolves, maintains and dissolves the universe — reveals itself in the heart of a Rishi wherefrom all Samskaras have been erased, so that, when the truth of the Sastras is thus proved, religion would be re-discovered and re-promulgated.

It is well known from such books as the Smritis that the Divine incarnates Himself again and again for the protection of the Veda, the true religion, and of Brahmana, that is, the teacher of religion.

Even as a stream falling down a precipice gains in speed, and a wave rising after a fall swells higher, so after each downfall, as history demonstrates, did the Aryan society shed its morbidities and emerge more glorious and vigorous under the compassionate guidance of the Divine.

Rising again after each fall, our society reveals more of the eternal perfection hidden within; and the Divine, the internal controller of all beings, likewise manifests more and more of His real nature in successive incarnations.

Again and again did this land of Bharata faint away, and again and again did the divine Lord manifest Himself and re-awaken it.

But in the past no new-moon night of sorrow veiled this holy land with such a dense darkness as at present. That night is all but gone, it being now at the fag end of its last quarter. However, the last fall of the country has been, as it were, to the bottom of the ocean, whereas, by comparison, all previous falls have been but into the hoof-marks of a cow.

Therefore, compared with the splendour of this present awakening of the Aryan society, previous awakenings will appear as lacking in lustre, like stars before the effulgence of the sun. And compared with the great vigour of this re-awakening, similar occurrences of the past will appear as child's play.

On account of the lack of fit persons to prevent the calamity, the fragments of the various aspects of the eternal religion lay scattered in all directions during the present downfall, in the forms of petty sects. It was partially preserved in some places and utterly lost in others.

The most compassionate divine Lord has manifested Himself far more fully in this modern age, in the aforesaid form of the incarnation of the age, than He ever did in any other age, playing as He has done on the entire gamut of all the spiritual moods and experiences and utilizing to the utmost all arts and sciences.

In consequence of this fact, during this renaissance, the descendants of Manu, invigorated by this new strength, will be able not only to piece together the fragmented and scattered mass of spiritual knowledge, but also to re-discover the lost branches of arts and sciences, and to enrich their lives by the realization of those ideas and ideals through proper understanding.

Hence is being preached the harmony of all noble ideas and ideals at the dawn of this great age. And this infinite and eternal grand ideal that lay embeded and hidden in the ancient scripture and religion of India is being loudly proclaimed in society.

This new faith of the age is the fruitful source of all blessings to the world, especially to India (Bharata); and Sri Bhagavan Ramakrishna, the founder of this new religion of the age, is the reformed manifestation of the ancient holy founders of the religions of the past. Have faith in it, O man, and grasp it !

O man, a dead person never returns; a past night does not come back; an emotion, however passionate, never takes the same form over again; a Jiva, likewise, does not assume the same body twice. We, therefore, call you back from the worship of the past to that of the palpable present; from the useless expenditure of energy on regrets for the bygone to the grand endeavour of the living present; from the waste of energy in recovering lost pathways to the broad new-laid neighbouring highways. Wise one, take the hint!

Imagine and feel the fully developed state of the power, the mere opening sound of which is reverberating in all quarters to the very skies; give up all vain doubt, weakness, jealousy and malice common amongst a slave race and help in the work of turning forward the wheel of this great age. We are the servants of the divine Lord, His children, His playmates, assisting Him in His play. Have this faith firmly implanted in your heart and come up to the field of action.

VIVEKANANDA

CHAPTER I

SRI RAMAKRISHNA IN BHAVAMUKHA

(TOPICS: 1. Deep meaning of the Master's words 2. Similarity of the words of all incarnations of God 3. An example: Girish and the 'power of attorney' 4. The mental state of Girish 5. The state of Girish's mind after giving 'power of attorney' 6. Giving the power of attorney, a bondage of love 7. How Girish was taught henceforward 8. Girish understanding the deep significance of giving the power of attorney 9. The incarnations and the power of attorney 10. Examples 11. The Master's vision about this 12. The Master curing leucoderma 13. The difficulty of giving the power of attorney 14. The state of mind required for it. 15. Beware of the deception of the mind 16. Another point of veiw 17. The story of a Brahmin killing a cow 18. The profound meaning of the Master's words 19. Understanding will come at the right time 20. Necessity of sticking to Sadhana 21. Give up lukewarm devotion 22. Bodily changes with the change of moods 23. The Master's power of knowing all the moods in all persons 24. First example 25. Second example 26. Third example 27. Fourth example 28. The Master's power of knowing all mental states of women 29. Its cause 30. Why women felt free in his presence 31. First example 32. Second example 33. The Master bestowed equal grace on women 34. The Master mimicked the gestures of women 35. The moods of both men and women co-existed in the Master 36. Living in Bhavamukha, the cause of his universal understanding.)

THE mental states derived from Sattva, those from Rajas and those from Tamas verily proceed from Me. But I am not in them; they are in Me. Deluded by these three states, the modifications of the Gunas, all this world is ignorant of Me, who am beyond them and changeless.

— Gita VII. 12. & 13.

1. Many have now come to know that at the end of the extraordinary austerity practised continually for twelve years, the Master was bidden by the Mother of the universe to "Remain in Bhavamukha", which command he obeyed. But it is very difficult to understand and explain what it is to remain in Bhavamukha and how deep its meaning is. Twenty-eight years ago Swami Vivekananda once said to a friend (Harmohan Mitra), "Shelves of philosophical books can be written on each single sentence spoken by the Master." The friend was surprised to hear it and said, "Is that so?

We, however, do not find so deep a meaning in his words. Will you please explain to me any of his utterances in that manner?"

The Swami: "You would have understood it, had you the brains! Take any saying of the Master and I shall prove my statement."

Friend: "All right, please explain the story of the elephant-god and the mahout-god related by the Master to illustrate his instruction on seeing God in all beings."

The Swami at once took up the controversy over the doctrines of free will and of pre-destination, or personal effort and God's will, raging perpetually among the scholars of both the East and the West without their approaching any conclusion, and continued for three days to explain to the friend, in simple language, that this story of the Master was a wonderful solution to that controversy.

2. On reflection one is amazed to find such profundity of meaning in the ordinary daily conduct of the Master and in his teachings. This is true of every one of the Incarnations of God. One has to study their lives to be convinced of this truth. Leaving aside the instances of one or two great souls like Sankaracharya, who had to re-establish religion by tearing to shreds the whole fabric of the opponents' perverse arguments, we find in the lives of the other great souls that they said and explained the truths they had to teach in simple language and in short parables and in homely similes and allegories touching the heart. They kept themselves at a safe distance from grandiloquent bombast or elaborate rhetoric. But their simple words and plain similes have so much meaning and power in them for elevating ordinary people to high ideals, that even now we have not been able to comprehend their meanings in full or find a limit to their power, though we have been attempting to do so for thousands of years. The more we study them the more do we find deeper and deeper meanings; and the more we muse over them, the more does the mind renounce the transient, inauspicious realm of the world and ascend to higher and higher regions. And the farther one proceeds towards "the realization of the supreme goal", "the existence in Brahman", "liberation" or "the vision of God", as that state has been variously called by the great souls, the more does one comprehend in one's heart of hearts the deep significance of those simple words.

3. This is the law. We do not find any exception to the operation of this law in the Master's words and conduct. Oh, what a profound depth of content do the Master's words reveal and how little of it did they appear to possess at the first hearing ! It is enough to give here one example. After meeting the Master a few times, one day Girish offered himself completely to him and said, "What shall I do from now on?"

The Master: "Go on, be doing what you have been doing. Now keep to both sides, this (God) and that (the world). When one side (i.e., the world) drops off, whatever is ordained to happen will happen. But continue to remember and think of Him every morning and evening." Saying this, he looked at Girish, as if waiting for a reply.

At this, Girish was sad and thought, "The nature of my work is such that I cannot keep regular time even for satisfying my daily physical needs such as eating, drinking, sleeping, etc. I am certain to fail to remember God and to think of him morning and evening. Oh, what a calamity would it be to transgress Sri Guru's words! Evil will certainly befall me for it. So how can I agree? It is certainly wrong to fail to keep one's promise to any person in this world, much more so, a promise to a person whom one is going to accept as one's spiritual guide."

4. Girish was hesitating even to express his thoughts. He continued to think that surely the Master had not asked him to do a very difficult task. Had he said this to anyone else, he would have at once agreed. But what could Girish do? As he knew correctly the state of his mind, which was full of outgoing tendencies, he found that it was, as it were, beyond his power to practise even that little of religious duties every day. Again, looking at his own nature, he found that he felt suffocated even to think that he was to submit himself to an obligation binding him for ever to a vow or a rule. He felt that his mind would feel no peace till that vow or rule was broken. This was true all through his life. There was no difficulty in voluntarily doing anything good or bad, but his mind rebelled at the thought that he was bound to do such and such a thing. Realizing his very weak and helpless condition, he felt distressed and kept silent. He could neither say he would do it, nor could he say he could not. How could he be shameless as to say he could not do so easy a task ? And even if he said, so, what would the Master and others present there think ? They

would not perhaps realize his extremely helpless condition, and would think, even though they might not express it, that it was all a mere pretence.

Finding that Girish remained silent, the Master looked at him, and knowing his thoughts, said, "Very well, if you cannot do that, remember Him once before taking food and once before going to bed."

Girish continued to be silent. He asked himself if he could do even that. He took his food at 10 a.m. on some days and at 5 p.m. on others, and there was the same irregularity about his night meals. There were days on which although he might be taking his meal, he was not at all conscious of the fact, on account of the troubles and worries regarding the cases pending in the courts,—for example, for lack of information whether the fee sent by him to the barrister had reached him in time, and if not, how calamitous it would be if he did not appear in the court because of not being paid. If, however, such days repeated themselves — and this was not impossible — he would surely forget to remember and think of God on those occasions. Alas! the Master was asking him to do such an easy thing, and yet he could not say that he would do it. Girish was in a very sorry plight and remained motionless and speechless; but there raged, as it were, a storm of anxiety, fear and despair in his heart. The Master looked at Girish again and said smilingly, "You seem to say, 'I cannot do even that.' Very well, then give me the power of attorney."[1] The Master was then in a state of divine semi-consciousness.

5. This was to Girish's liking. His mind was now calm. And there swelled in his heart an infinite onrush of love for, and reliance on the Master and his infinite grace. He felt relieved that the bondage of rule, which was a terror to him, was now gone for ever. It was now sufficient to have the firm faith that whatever he might do, the Master would save him some way or other by his divine power.

6. Giving the power of attorney to the Master meant then to Girish nothing more than this : that he would not have to give

---

[1] i.e., transfer your responsibility. When one person transfers the power of managing one's worldly affairs to another person, the latter transacts all business, grants receipts, carries on correspondence and signs all documents on the principal's behalf.

up anything by means of personal efforts or to bother about spiritual practices, and that the Master would remove the last vestige of worldliness from his mind through his own powers.

But he did not then realize that he had put voluntarily round his neck a noose of love a hundred times stronger than the bondage of rule which, he thought, was so unbearable. He failed to dive sufficiently deep into the significance of what he had undertaken. He had not then the power to realize that it really meant that in any circumstance — favourable or adverse, leading to fame or infamy, to happiness or agonizing pain — he had nothing more to say or do, than to bear them all without a murmur. All other thoughts vanished from his mind and he was feeling the endless grace of Sri Ramakrishna — in fact, a new ego rooted in Sri Ramakrishna was born and was fast developing in him. A spirit of divine defiance of the world came upon him, and he thought that whatever the world might speak of him, even if it despised him, it was quite immaterial; for, the Master was un-doubtedly his in all circumstances and at all times. How could he then know that the constant feeling of this new egoism is regarded in devotional scriptures like Narada's *Bhaktisutras* as a kind of spiritual practice and a blessing that comes to human beings from an abundance of good fortune? Girish, however, was now free from anxiety. And while eating, drinking or being engaged in any other activity, he had but one thought, viz., Sri Ramakrishna had taken upon himself all his responsibility — a soothing thought, a balm to his mind, which, through its deepening impression, was gradually gaining mastery over his whole being and involuntarily making him meditate on the Master, thus bringing about a revolution in him, in all his thoughts and actions. He was happy, though he did not understand all that. For, he thought, was it not a fact, that he (Sri Ramakrishna) loved him and was more than his own ?

7. The Master always taught that "nobody's spiritual attitude of mind should be interfered with ", and he used to act accordingly in his daily dealings with the devotees. Knowing well Girish's spiritual mood, he began to give instructions thenceforth in accordance with that mood. One day when Girish said in the presence of the Master, "I will do it", in respect of a trifling matter, the Master remonstrated suddenly saying, "Look here! Why do you say 'I will do it'? Suppose you cannot do it. What then ? You should say, 'I shall do it if God so wills'." Girish on his part felt,

"This is quite right. I completely placed on God all my responsibility, and He has accepted it. I can do a thing only if He thinks it proper and good for me and allows me to do so. How can I do it by my own power?" Realizing this, he gradually gave up such words and ideas as " I will do it", "I will go", and so on.

8. Thus days rolled on, and at last the Master passed away. Girish met with various calamities, e.g., the death of his wife, son and others; but his mind began to assert every time, "He (Sri Ramakrishna) is allowing these events to happen, only because they are good for you (himself). You have transferred your responsibility to him and he has accepted it; but he has given you no assurance regarding the path along which he will take you. Knowing that this path is easy for you, he is leading you along it. You have no reason to say 'no' or grumble against it. Were they then empty words, that you gave him the power of attorney or transferred your responsibility to him?" Thus as days passed, the hidden meaning of 'giving the power of attorney became more and more clear to Girish. Was its meaning completely understood even at last ? Asked about it, Girish said, "Much remains to be understood even now. Did I know then that so much lay hidden in this simple giving of the power of attorney? I now find that at some time there is an end to the spiritual practices like Japa, austerities and other devotional practices, but there is no end to the work of a person who has given 'the power of attorney'." For he came to realize that he had to watch at every step and every breath whether in all his thoughts and deeds he was depending on Him and His power, or on this wretched 'I'.

9. Many thoughts occur to our mind in connection with this doctrine of acceptance of power of attorney. We find in the history of the world, that it is the great souls alone, such as Lord Jesus, Chaitanya and others, who could sometimes give assurance of this kind to some people. Ordinary teachers have no power to do so. They can at the most teach others the Mantras and particular practices with the help of which they themselves made spiritual progress; or they can attract people towards purity by living pure lives themselves. But when paralysed by various kinds of worldly bondages, man reaches the state of complete helplessness, and when asked to do even a trifling thing, he pleads his inability to do it and asks for help in utter despair, it is beyond the power of ordinary teachers to help him. It is beyond the power of any

man to say to another that he would take upon himself all the responsibilities for the latter's evil actions and that he himself would experience their results on the latter's behalf. It is when there is a very great decline of spirituality in the heart of man that the Lord out of His grace incarnates Himself and suffers the results of man's evil actions on his behalf and saves him from the constraint of that bondage. Although He does so, He does not absolve him altogether, but makes him put forth some little effort, so that he may learn. The Master used to say in this connection, "Man finishes the experiences of ten lives in one by their (the Incarnations') grace."

10. This is as true of an individual as of a nation. It is this which has been called in the *Gita* (XI. 8), "the attainment of the divine eye" by Arjuna for the purpose of having the vision of the universal form of Brahman; in the Puranas, "being blessed with the grace of God the Lord"; in the Bengal Vaishnava scriptures, "the saving of Jagai and Madhai or the crushing of the unbeliever in them"; and in the Christian scriptures, "the vicarious atonement" of Jesus through taking upon himself the sufferings of others. We could never have realized that there is truth in all this, if we did not get an indication of it in the life of SrijRamakrishna.

11. When the Master came and lived at Shyampukur in Calcutta for treatment, he had one day a vision that his subtle body came out of his gross one and was walking up and down. Regarding this vision the Master said, "I saw that it had sores all over its back. I was wondering why they were there, and the Mother showed that it was because people came and touched my body after committing all kinds of sins—because out of compassion for their sufferings, I had to take upon myself the results of the evil deeds. That is why this (showing his throat)[1] is there. Why, otherwise, should there be so much suffering, though this body never did any wrong?" We were dumb-founded and thought: "Is it a fact then that one can undergo the results of another's actions and make the latter free to make spiritual progress?" Hearing the Master's words, many thought, out of love for him, "Ah, why did we touch the Master after committing various evil acts like lying, cheating, etc? He is suffering so much, undergoing so much pain, because of us. We will never again touch his divine body."

---

[1] The Master was suffering from cancer in the throat when this conversation took place.—Tr.

12. We remember in this connection what the Master said on another occasion. Once, a man suffering from leucoderma came and pleaded persistently to the Master that if he would only pass his hand over it, he would be cured of the disease. The Master had compassion on him and said, "Well, I know nothing, but as you desire, I shall pass my hand. It will be cured if Mother wills." And he passed his hand over it. For the whole of that day, the Master felt so much pain in his hand that he became restless and said to the Mother of the universe, "I will never do such a thing again, Mother." The Master used to say later, "He was cured of the disease but the suffering was experienced here (showing his body)." These events of the Master's life clearly show us that in this age, the scriptures like the Vedas, the Bible, the Puranas, the Koran, the treatises on rituals, the sacred formulae, etc, can be easily understood, if studied in the light of Sri Ramakrishna's life. The Master also told us, "My children, coins current in the time of the Nawabs are not legal tender in that of the Badshas."

13. On a superficial view it may appear that the giving of 'the power of attorney' is a very easy affair, as if the power waits ready to be handed over to another. Man is a slave to his inclinations; he looks for advantages even while practising religion. He likes to keep both, the worldly pleasures and the bliss of God. He considers the worldly enjoyments to be so sweet, that without them he feels life to be meaningless and not worth living. It is for this reason that he is beside himself with joy when he comes to know that in the spiritual world 'the power of attorney' can be given. He thinks, "Well, how grand! Let me enjoy the pleasures of the world to my heart's content, be it by committing theft, cheating, robbery, etc., for that. And let Chaitanya, Jesus or Ramakrishna so arrange that I may be happy in the next world. I say 'the next world', because some day I have to die." He fails to see that it is nothing but a deception committed by his wily mind, that it is nothing but shutting his eyes to the terrible pictures of his own evil actions leading him headlong to destruction; and that some day he will be forced to open his eyes and see before him a shoreless ocean. He will then realize that no one accepts 'the power of attorney' given by a deceiver. Ah man! how many are the ways in which you are deceiving yourself, thinking that you have struck a splendid bargain! And hail Mahamaya! what a great delusion hast Thou created in

the human mind! What Ramprasad says in his song addressing
Thee is indeed perfectly true:

"Hail, O Mother Dakshina Kali!
Thou hast produced delusion in the world,
But hast made the magic wand of both Thy feet
That destroy delusion, fall to the lot of Siva.
Thou art the daughter of such a magician,
Thou hast kept the Father (of the universe) in the
    disguise of madness,
And assuming the three Gunas,
Thou hast transformed Thyself into Purusha and Prakriti.
I apprehend therefore, O Prasad,[1]
That you have become mad, as you hope to get
Those Feet, which could not be attained
By the destroyer of Tripura himself."

14. The power of attorney cannot be given for the mere
wish; man can rightly give it only when, as the result of much
effort and perseverance, the mind realizes a state in which that is
made possible. And it is only then that the divine Lord accepts it.
Even when running after the various things of the world to become
happy, man really feels that what he has attained is a shadow without
reality; even when performing spiritual practices, Japa and austerities, he feels in his heart of hearts that it can never be an adequate
price for the attainment of the infinite Lord; and even when employ-
ing unsparingly all means and methods with the hope and faith
of moving mountains by the sheer force of perseverance, he realizes
that he has no power to move even a straw—it is only then that he
begins to cry aloud in a plaintive voice, "O, Thou protector,
whoever and wherever Thou art, save me!" and then the Lord
accepts his power of attorney.

15. On the contrary, when the mind takes a perverse attitude
and says, "I do not find joy in performing spiritual exercises or
calling on the Lord but feel happy only in giving free reins to my
whims and fancies, and hence I shall follow them," and when
objection is taken to this attitude, it comes out with the prompt
reply, "Why, have I not given my power of attorney to God?
What shall I do when He is making me act thus? Why does he not
change my mind?"—then one should know that giving 'the

_____

[1]The composer of the song.—Tr.

power of attorney' in this manner is to deceive oneself as well as others, and to lose the here and the hereafter.

16.   This subject will be better understood, if discussed from another standpoint. Well, let it be granted that you have given the power of attorney and that you have no need to call on God or follow any kind of spiritual practice. If the power of attorney has been properly given, you cannot but constantly dwell upon His compassion in your heart. You will then feel that having fallen into this shoreless sea of the world and struggled in it helplessly for endless time, He has now saved you by His grace. Just imagine how much gratitude, love and devotion of your heart you will pour on Him when you feel like that. Will it be necessary to ask you always to think of Him and remember His name? Filled with grateful love for Him, won't your heart naturally do so? Even a vicious creature like a snake is said to feel grateful to the person who gives it shelter; it goes under the familiar name of a 'house snake' and does not harm any one in the household. Is your heart meaner even than that, not to be filled with grateful love for Him who has taken upon Himself your responsibility both in this world and in the next? So, if you find that after giving 'the power of attorney,' you do not feel any joy in calling on God, then know for certain that you have neither given properly 'the power of attorney' to Him, nor has He taken upon Himself your responsibility. Do not deceive yourself any more, thinking that you have given 'the power of attorney,' and do not attribute the stain of your own evil actions to the stainless divine Lord, eternally free from the touch of any evil whatever. To do so is most baneful and harmful to yourself. Remember the Master's story of a Brahmana killing a cow:

17.   A Brahmana succeeded, with much effort and great pains, in rearing a beautiful garden. He planted it with various kinds of fruit-and-flower-bearing trees and felt a great joy at their luxuriant growth. One day, finding the gate open, a cow entered the garden and was eating the plants. The Brahmana was away on business. He returned and found that the cow was even then feeding on his plants. He violently assaulted the cow and gave her such a blow with a stick on a vital part of the body, that she died on the spot. The Brahmana was seized with fear, and thought, "Alas! I, a Brahmana, have killed a cow—which is the greatest of sins." The Brahmana had read a little of the Vedanta and remembered

that each human sense organ derives its power of functioning from
a particular presiding deity. For example, the eye derives its sight
from the sun-god (Aditya); the ear its hearing from the wind-god
(Vayu); the hand its movements from Indra, and so on. The
Brahmana now recollected those words, and thought, "It is then
not I who killed the cow. The hand was moved by the power of
Indra; it is therefore Indra who killed the cow." The Brahmana
felt relieved at this conclusion.

18. Now, the sin of killing the cow (Go-hatya) came to enter
the body of the Brahmana, but he mentally warded it off with the
thought: "Go away, you have no place here. Indra has killed
her; go to him." So the sin went to seize Indra. Indra said to the
sin, "Wait a little, please; let me go and speak a word or two with
the Brahmana and come back. Seize me then if you like." Saying so, Indra assumed a human form, entered the Brahmana's
garden and saw him standing close by, looking after the plants
and trees. Indra began to praise the beauty of the garden in the
Brahmana's hearing, and slowly proceeding towards him, said,
"Oh, what a beautiful garden this is! With what good taste
have the plants and trees been planted, each in its proper
place!" Saying so, he approached the Brahmana and said, "Sir,
can you tell me whose garden this is? Who is it that has planted
the trees and plants so beautifully?" Hearing him praising the
garden, the Brahmana was beside himself with joy and said, "Sir,
this is my garden; it is I who have planted all these. Come, let
me show you round." While he was thus taking Indra round and
talking many things about the garden, praising himself all the time,
he came inadvertently to the place where the dead cow was lying.
Startled, as it were, Indra asked, "Who has killed the cow here?"
The Brahmana who was all the while speaking of everything in the
garden saying, "I have done this", "I have done that", was now
at a loss and did not know what to say. He remained silent. Indra
then assumed his own form and said, 'Ah, you hypocrite,
you have done whatever is good in the garden; it is the killing of
the cow alone that devolves on me! Is that so? Here is your
sin of cow-killing. Take it." Saying so, Indra disappeared and
the sin came and took possession of the Brahmana's body.

19. So much for the power of attorney. Let us now follow
the main topic[1]. Ask any devotee of the Master and he will un-

---

[1] Mentioned in Paras 1 and 2 of this chapter.

hesitatingly declare that with the passage of time, he finds through the Master's grace, deeper and deeper meanings in his words. Further, we are now amazed to find wonderful meanings and sentiments in many of the Master's words and actions, which at the time of our hearing or seeing them yielded no clear meaning, but were accepted because of the charm of his personality. For example, take the favourite saying of the Master: "Ah, my children, you will succeed at the right time; you will understand at the proper time. Can you get a fruit immediately after you sow the seed? First it becomes a sprout, then a sapling, and then a plant; next it produces flowers and at last it yields fruits. It is just like that. But one has to persevere and not give up the struggle. Listen to what is said in this song." Saying so, the Master would sing in his melodious voice:

"Oh brother, persist joyfully,
You will succeed gradually,
What went wrong will be set right.
Anka was saved, Banka was saved,
And the butcher Sujan was saved.
Teaching the parrot, the prostitute was saved,
So was saved Mira Bai.
Having the wealth and treasure of the world,
The trader still drives the bullock,
When misfortune overtakes him;
No trace (of all these) will be left.
Have such deep devotion in your mind;
Give up hypocrisy and craftiness.
The King of the line of Raghus will be attained easily,
By virtue of service, worship and surrender."

20. He would then say, "His service, worship and surrender, (humility)—everything will be achieved, if one has faith and adheres to these things; His direct vision is certain. But if one gives these up, all progress stops. There was a man who had a job, and with considerable difficulty he saved some money, little by little. One day, counting, he found that there was a saving of a thousand rupees. He was at once beside himself with joy and thought, 'Why should I be in service any more? There is already a saving of a thousand rupees. What more is necessary?' Saying so, he gave up the job. A puny man with a puny ambition! He was puffed up on account of this paltry sum and looked down upon others. But

how many days will it take to spend a thousand rupees? It got exhausted in no time. He then fell on evil days and had to dance attendance on office superintendents for a job. It will not do to act thus; one has to wait patiently at His door. If one is prepared to do that, then alone will one succeed."

21. Again while singing, "You will succeed gradually," the Master would suddenly say, "Ah, why gradually? One should not be lukewarm in devotion. One should have a burning faith in one's heart, and feel the urge: 'realization must come right now; I must see Him this very moment.' Can half-hearted devotion help one to realize Him?"

22. Whenever we looked at the Master, we felt that he was the very embodiment of spiritual moods. We felt that we saw his form because spiritual moods had, as it were, consolidated themselves into that form of his. We talk glibly of physical changes taking place simultaneously with the changes of mental moods, but come across only a little of such phenomena. But we could not imagine even in a dream that the surge of mental moods could bring about so much of change in the body, as in the case of the Master. In Nirvikalpa Samadhi, the Master's "I" consciousness disappeard totally, and along with it his pulse, heart-beat, etc., also stopped simultaneously. Mahendralal Sarkar and other doctors examined him with the help of instruments and found no sign of the functioning of his heart.[1] Not satisfied with that, his friend, another doctor, went further and touched with his finger the Master's eyeball, and found it insensitive to touch like that of a dead man. At the time of practising "Sakhi-bhava" the Master continually meditated on himself as a woman servant of Sri Krishna and became so much identified with that idea that womanly behaviour, woman's mode of standing, walking, sitting, talking, etc., became naturally manifested in his body, so much so that Mathuranath and others who were his constant companions, mistook him on many occasions for a woman guest.[2] We have heard so much from the Master and have ourselves seen so many similar phenom-

---

[1] This examination took place in our presence when the Master was staying in the house at Shyampukur (in Calcutta) for the treatment of the disease in his throat.

[2] It was in Mathuranath's house that the Master practised Sakhi-bhava.—Tr.

25

ena, that we feel the laws of modern psychology and physiology, so far considered to be conclusive, have to be re-enunciated. Will people believe these occurrences even if they are told?

23. But the most striking thing we have seen in him was his power of roaming everywhere in the realm of ideas—his power of understanding all ideas, great or small, of all persons, of a boy or an adult, of a monk or a householder, of a devotee or a Vedantin, of a man or a woman; his power of grasping the inner thoughts and sentiments of each spiritual aspirant, of knowing how far he had advanced in the realm of spirituality, what path he had adopted, what his current needs were for taking him further along his own line of progress; and what is most important, his wonderful power of prescribing just the course that was needed and suitable. When we deeply think of these things, it seems to us that the Master had previously experienced in his life the whole range of ideas past, present and future without exception; that he had stored his memory with the entire and detailed history of each of the states from the time of its appearance to that of its disappearance; and that it was owing to this fact that whenever anyone came and told him of his mental state, he could grasp and understand it by comparing it with what was stored up in his mind and give the appropriate prescription then and there. This was his rule in everything. When anyone came to him as a humble inquirer, confronted with, and inextricably involved in extremely trying situations like worldly attachment, worldly turmoil, or the persistence of some idea or emotion contrary to the pursuit of renunciation and other spiritual values, the Master would invariably give him the proper direction, and by way of encouragement, tell him of his own experiences under similar conditions. He would say, "My child, such and such events came to pass then, and I adopted such and such means." It is needless to add that a great hope filled the inquirer's heart when the Master said so, and with much faith and perseverance, he went forward along the path specified by the Master. That was not all; he felt how great the Master's love for him was when he saw him confiding his heart's secrets to him. One or two examples will make this clear.

24. A promising son of Manimohan Mallick of Sinduriapati, Calcutta, died. No sooner had he performed the ceremonies connected with the cremation, than Manimohan came to the Master. Saluting the Master, he sat with a heavy heart in a corner of the

room. He saw many inquiring devotees, seekers after truth, men and women, sitting in the room, and the Master was talking to them on various spiritual topics. He had sat for a short time when the Master's eyes happened to fall on him, and with a nod of his head, he asked him, "Well, why do you look so sad today?' In a choked voice, Manimohan answered, "So-and-so (naming his son) died today." Seeing his haggard appearance and hearing his choked voice, everyone in the room was dumbfounded and sat speechless. Everyone felt that any word of consolation could not assuage the deep pain and agony raging in his heart. Nevertheless they began to console him in words such as: "Such is the way of the world, everyone must die some day. Whatever has happened cannot be undone by shedding tears a thousand times. Therefore give up grief, have patience." From the beginning of creation we have been consoling men and women struck with grief in these words. But, alas, how few are the hearts that are thereby consoled! And how can they be? It is only when the three things viz., our minds, words, and actions are inspired by the same feeling, that our words can touch others' hearts and raise similar waves of feeling there. But with us this qualification is altogether wanting. We say, "The world is transitory," but every thought and action of ours is contrary to this idea. Though we advise others to consider this world to be transitory like a dream, we always regard it in our heart of hearts as eternal and make arrangements for living here for ever. How can our words acquire that power to carry conviction?

Although all the others poured forth the hackneyed phrases of consolation to Manimohan, the Master was all the time merely listening to his words of grief without speaking anything whatever. When they saw that indifferent mood of his, some were surprised and thought how hard, how devoid of compassion, his heart was.

As he was listening to the words of the old man, the Master gradually passed into ecstasy—a state of divine semi-consciousness. Suddenly with the stance and energy of a wrestler, he struck his left arm just below the shoulder with the palm of his right hand, stood up and began singing with an unprecedented vigour:

O man, prepare yourself for battle,.

There, see Death entering your house in battle array;

(Therefore) ride on the chariot of great virtue,

Harness to it the two horses of devotion and spiritual practice,

> Stretch the bow of knowledge,
> And set the unfailing arrow of the love of God.
> Listen, there is another plan of good strategy;
> All the enemies can be killed without a chariot or a
> charioteer,
> If Dasarathi[1] takes the field on the bank of the Bhagirathi.

The tune of the song, expressing great vigour and the appro-priate gesture coupled with the spirit of heroic renunciation and strength coursing from the Master's eyes, produced in the hearts of all a current of wonderful hope and energy. The heart of every one was raised from the realm of grief and delusion, and filled with a wonderful divine bliss which was beyond the senses and beyond the world. Manimohan too felt it in his heart, forgot the agonizing grief, and was now calm, grave and in perfect peace.

The song came to an end; but the few words constituting it, sung in the manner described above, generated waves of spir-ituality which filled the room for a long time and were palpably felt like a presence by all. All were still, being lost entirely in that spiritual mood, which seemed to declare: "It is God alone who is our own; we have to offer our heart and life to Him. May He bestow His compassion on us and reveal Himself to us!" When the Master's ecstasy came to an end a little later, he sat by the side of Manimohan and said, "Ah! What burning pain is there on earth which can compare with the grief at the death of a son? A son is born of this sheath (body); isn't he? So his relation with the body persists as long as it lasts." Saying so, the Master began to describe to him so touchingly about the death of Akshay as an example, that it seemed as if he was visualizing before his eyes the death of his relative. He said, "Akshay died. I felt nothing at the time. I was standing and was witnessing how man dies. I saw there was, as it were, a sword in a sheath, and the sword was being drawn out of it. The sword was not at all affected. It remained as it was, and the sheath lay there. I felt great joy to see it. I laughed and sang and danced. They then burnt the body and returned. The next day I was standing there (pointing to the verandah to the east of the room, near the courtyard of the

---

[1] The composer. According to the orthodox custom of that time com-posers mentioned their names in the last stanza, perhaps to indicate that the sentiments of the songs are directed towards themselves.—Tr.

Kali temple), and do you know what I felt? I felt as if my heart was being wrung in the way a wet towel is wrung. My heart was feeling for Akshay like that. I thought, 'Mother, this (his body) has no relation with (i.e. cannot retain) even the cloth it wears; what attachment can this (himself) have for a nephew! Still how bitterly I feel his demise! When it is so even here (with himself), how agonizing the pain must be to the householders! Thou art showing that, aren't you ?"

"But do you know?" continued the Master, a little later, "Those who take refuge in Him do not sink to the bottom even on account of this unbearable grief. They regain their balance after a few tossings. Persons of small capacity, like small vessels, lose their control, their balance, altogether and go down. Haven't you noticed the plight of the small fishing boats when steamers pass through the Ganga? It looks as if they are lost and are gone. Some are capsized altogether. The bigger vessels, carrying tons of load, regain their balance after a few tossings. But a toss or two must be felt by all."

After a short pause of serious gloom, the Master added again, "How few are the days during which the relationship among all these (sons, parents, etc.) in this world lasts! Desiring happiness a man enters the world; he marries. begets a son; the son grows; he gets his son married; thus a few days pass pleasantly. Then one gets ill, another dies, still another goes astray, and the man is beside himself with worries and anxieties. The more the frustration, the louder the lamentation! Haven't you noticed how the wet fuel burns in a sweetmaker's oven? It burns well at first. Then as it is burning, the sap begins to ooze out through its hinder part and assumes the form of froth which bubbles and bursts and produces various kinds of hissing sounds. It is just like that." He was thus consoling Manimohan by speaking to him on a variety of topics such as "the transitoriness and hollowness of the world", "taking refuge in the divine Lord, the only source of happiness" and so on. Manimohan felt consoled and said, "This was why, Sir, I came running to you. I knew that there was no one else who could assuage this fire of my grief."

We were amazed at this extraordinary behaviour of the Master and thought, "Is this the person whom we considered a short time ago to be hard-hearted and indifferent? One who is really great is not like the common run of people even in small matters. His greatness is discernible in every action, great or small. Is this the same person whose heart-beat stopped a little while ago as he was experiencing ecstasy or the nearness of God? Is he the same person, who, in sympathy with Manimohan's condition, is behaving like an ordinary man? He could have altogether dismissed the words of the old man, saying, "It is all a mere delusion, a trifling matter"; it is not that he could not have done so. Had he displayed his greatness that way, we would have felt that he might be a great spiritual teacher or anything else, but that he was certainly not of this world; we would have felt that he had not the power to enter into the feelings of ordinary mortals and would have said, "We wonder how he could have remained indifferent to the play of Maya if he had fallen but once into the helpless condition into which we, weak human beings, have fallen owing to our attachment to our wives and children!"

25. The very next moment, perhaps, a young man comes in a dejected mood and asks, "Sir, how can one be freed from lust? Passions and unhealthy emotions disturb the mind sometimes and make me restless in spite of me."

The Master: "Ah, lust does not vanish till God is realized. So long as the body lasts, a little of it continues even after that realization; but then it cannot raise its head. Do you think I myself am altogether free from it? At one time, I thought I had conquered lust. When I was sitting under the Panchavati such an onrush of lust came that it seemed to be beyond my power of control. I then wept rubbing my face against the dust on the ground and said to the Mother, 'I have done a great wrong, Mother. I shall never again harbour the idea that I have conquered lust.' It was then only that it vanished. Do you know, you people are now passing through a high tide of youth. This is why you cannot stop it. When a high tide comes, does it heed an embankment? It then swells up, breaks the embankment and rushes forward. Then water stands as high as a bamboo over the paddy fields. But it is said that a mental sin is no sin in the Kaliyuga. Again, even if an undesirable feeling happens to rise once or twice in the mind, why should you feel worried because of it? It is natural to the body; it sometimes comes and goes; pay no more heed to it than to the bodily functions like the calls of nature. Do people feel worried because of such functions? Similarly consider these feelings to be very trifling, unworthy of any attention, and do not think of them any more. Moreover, pray to Him heartily, repeat continually the name of Hari and meditate on Him. Do not take notice whether they come or go. They will slowly come under control." The Master had become, as it were, a youth speaking to a youth.

26. In this connection, we remember Swami Yogananda, who was amongst the very few whom we knew to have conquered lust. One day he asked the Master this very question at Dakshineswar. He was then young, about fourteen or fifteen years of age, and had been visiting the Master for a short time. A Hathayogi named Narayan was then living in a hut near the Panchavati and was attracting some people's curiosity by showing them the arts of Neti-Dhauti.[1] Yogen said that he was also one of those people. On seeing those performances, he thought that lust would not vanish and God could not be realized unless they were practised. He therefore hoped, when putting the question, that the Master would instruct him on some posture, advise him to take Haritaki or some other drug, or teach him some process of control of the vital force. "In answering my question," continued Yogen, "the Master said, 'Go on repeating the name of Hari and it will vanish, nothing more will be necessary.' The answer was not at all to my liking. I said to myself, 'I see, he does not know any process and that is why he has prescribed to me a useless something. Does lust vanish on repeating the name of Hari? Very many people are doing it; why does it not vanish in them?' Another day I came to the Kali temple and instead of going straight to the Master, was standing near the Hathayogi at the Panchavati, listening eagerly to his conversation, when I saw the Master himself coming suddenly there; and no sooner had he seen me than he called me, took me by the hand to his room and said, 'Why did you go there? Don't do that. Your mind will stick only to the body if you learn those processes of Hathayoga. It will not thirst after God.' I thought, 'He is thus speaking to me lest I should give up visiting him.' I

---

[1] To swallow gradually a wet piece of cloth ten or fifteen cubits long and about an inch broad and then to pull and bring it out, is what is called Neti. And to drink two or three seers of water and to vomit it out—that is what is known an Dhauti. To draw water through the anus and bring it out again is also called Dhauti. Hathayogis thus force out all the phlegmatic humour and such other things existing within the body. They say this prevents diseases and makes the body firm.

always had a high notion of my intelligence. What a free rein I gave to the intellect! It did not then occur to me that my visits mattered so little to him. Ah, what a roguish and suspicious mind I had! But there is no limit to the grace of the Master. In spite of my harbouring such improper thoughts, I was given refuge.[1] Then came the thought, 'Why don't I do what he told me to do and see what happens?' Thinking thus, I took the name of Hari with a concentrated mind. And as a matter of fact, I began directly to experience the result mentioned by the Master."

27. Many are the examples that can be cited of the Master's ability to grasp the mental condition and needs of all. We have already introduced Mani Mallick of Sinduriapati. A relative of his, a woman devotee, frequently visited the Master. One day, she came and said to him with great humility that when she sat down to meditate on God, worldly thoughts, the words of one, the face of another, etc., came into her mind, and she could not attain to restfulness. The Master at once understood the mood. He knew that she loved someone whose words and face came to her mind. He asked affectionately, 'Well, whose is the face that comes to your mind? Whom do you love?' She replied that she loved a young nephew of hers, whom she was bringing up. The Master said, "Very well, whatever you do for him—feeding, dressing, etc.—do with the idea that he is Gopala; have this attitude that God resides in him in the form of Gopala and that it is He whom you are feeding, dressing and serving. Why should you think that you are doing all this for a human being? As is your mood, so will be your gain." We are told that as the result of doing so, she made considerable spiritual progress in a short time, so much so that she attained even Bhavasamadhi.

28. It is explicable that the Master could comprehend and know the mental states of men because he had a man's body. But one's surprise is unbounded when one thinks how the Master could correctly know all the moods of women, upon whom God has bestowed an extra capacity for experiencing tenderness, affection for children, etc. "The Master," say his women devotees, "did not usually seem to us to be a man at all. It seemed to us that he was one of us. That is why we did not feel the slightest shyness or hesitation in his presence, as we usually do in the presence

---

[1] He was a disciple of the Master and renounced the world.

of men. Even if it came on rare occasions, we forgot it immediately and would express to him our feelings without any hesitation
whatever."

29. The Master had for long concentrated on Krishna with
the assertion 'I am a lady friend of Krishna, a maid attending
on the Divine Lord,' and had come to perfection in this attitude.
Was it because of this that whenever he willed, he could completely
forget the feeling of being a male and assume that of a female?
Patanjali says in his *Yoga Aphorisms,* "If the idea of doing injury
to others completely vanishes from your mind, no one in the world,
not even tigers and snakes, will injure you, not to speak of
human beings. The very idea of doing injury to you will not
cross their minds when they see you." This must be understood
to be equally true of all the other feelings of the mind such as lust,
anger, etc. Many examples of this fact are found in the Puranas.
One, however, will suffice here. The stainless young Suka, free
from Maya and always merged in God-consciousness, was passing
along, having renounced the world. And Vyasa, his old father,
blinded by affection for his son, was running after him, crying:
"Where are you going, my son, where are you going?" On their
way they passed the celestial damsels bathing in a lake after leaving
their clothes on the bank. They felt no bashfulness or qualms in
their minds when they saw Suka, and went on bathing as before.
But as soon as the old Vyasa arrived, all of them covered their
bodies in great haste. Vyasa thought, "Ah, this is very strange
indeed! My youthful son passed by before and they did not even
stir; but they feel very shy on seeing me, an old man!" Questioned about the reason for this strange behaviour, the ladies
answered, "Suka is so pure that the only thought he always has
in his mind is, 'I am the Self of the universe.' He is not at all
conscious whether he has a man's or a woman's body. This was
why shyness did not arise in our mind when we saw him. But
you are old, you have been much acquainted with the gestures,
postures and glances of women, and have extensively described
their grace and beauty. You do not, unlike Suka, look upon men
and women as the Self, and neither will you ever have the capacity
to do so. That is why the idea of a male arose in our minds on
seeing you; and simultaneously shyness also arose."

30. This very idea comes up in our mind in connection with
the Master. His illumining Self-knowledge and his vision of the

Self in all beings, both male and female, kept the minds of all near
him at such a high level of spiritual reltion that the ideas such as
"I am a man", "This is a woman" etc., would not usually cross
their minds as long as they were with him.   That is why, like men,
women also felt no shyness in his presence.   That is not all.   That
vision of the Self in them in the company of the Master became
so deep-rooted at that time that at his request they performed
easily and without any hesitation, those actions which they would
have ordinarily hesitated to do and which they would never perform
at the request of anyone else.   At the Master's request those ladies[1]
of very respectable families, who never travelled anywhere except
by carriage or palanquin, walked on foot through the main road
at day-time to the bank of the Ganga, took boats and travelled
to the Kali temple at Dakshineswar.   What was more, they would
perhaps go at the behest of the Master to the neighbouring market
and make purchases for him and would return on foot to Calcutta
at dusk.   An example or two will make the matter clear.

31.   It was towards the end of 1884.   The Holy Mother was
then at her father's house at Jayarambati.   Balaram Basu went to
Vrindavan with his father.   With them went Rakhal (Swami Brahmananda), Gopal (Swami Advaitananda) and several other devotees, men and women.   A lady of a respectable family of Baghbazar,
who had heard of the Master, had had a great desire to come and
see him.   She expressed this to a woman acquaintance of hers.
The latter was told of this because she had been frequently visiting
the Master for the past two years.   A plan was fixed; and in the
afternoon of the very next day the two arrived at Dakshineswar.
They saw the door of the Master's room closed.   They looked
through the peep-holes in the northern wall of the room and saw
the Master resting.   Therefore they went to the Nahabat where
the Holy Mother used to live and waited there.   The Master got
up a little later, and on opening the northern door, found that
they were sitting on the verandah of the first floor of the Nahabat.
He called out to them, "Hallo! come here."   When the women
devotees came and sat down, the Master got down from his wooden
cot and sat near the woman devotee who was known to him.   At
that she felt shy and was going to move away a little when the

---

[1]The reader should remember that in those days such ladies would
not come out in public.—Tr.

Master said, "Why this shyness? Realization of God is not possible as long as the three, viz., shyness, aversion and fear, are there. (Making a movement of his hand) I am verily what you are. But (pointing to the hairs of his chin) you feel shy because these are there. Is it not so?"

Saying so, he started immediately a conversation on God and gave them various instructions. The women devotees also forgot the distinction between man and woman. They put questions and listened to answers without any hesitation whatever. When they took leave after a long conversation, the Master said, "Come once a week. In the beginning visits should be more frequent." Again, finding that they were poor, though belonging to respectable families, and thinking they could not always get carriage hire, the Master added, "Three or four of you should join and take a boat while you come; and walk to Baranagore and share a carriage there while you return home." It is needless to say that the women devotees acted accordingly since then.

32. Another woman devotee said to us one day, "There was nice Sar (sweet cream) in the shop of Bhola, the famous sweet-maker. As we knew that the Master liked Sar, we purchased a big piece. Five of us together then hired a boat and arrived at Dakshineswar without prior notice. But we were informed that the Master had gone to Calcutta. We were at a loss to know what to do. There was brother Ramlal there. On being asked to which place in Calcutta the Master had gone, he said that he had gone to the house of the 'teacher'[1] at Kambuliatola. Hearing this, A-'s mother said, 'I know that house; it is near my father's; will you go? Come, let us go. What is the good of waiting here?' All agreed. We handed over the sweets to brother Ramlal and went away saying, 'Please give it to the Master when he comes.' We had already dismissed the boat. So we started on foot. But such was His will that hardly had we covered the short distance to Alambazar when an empty carriage returning to Calcutta was available. We hired the carriage and reached Shyampukur. There was fresh trouble awaiting us. A-'s mother could not find out the

---

[1] Mahendranath Gupta, the great devotee of the Master, to whom the public is indebted for his publication of *Sri Ramakrishna Kathamrita* translated into English as "*The Gospel of Sri Ramakrishna*" and published by Sri Ramakrishna Math, Mylapore, Madras.

house. After taking us from place to place, she stopped the carriage in front of her father's house and called a servant. He came with us and showed the house. Thus we succeeded after all in reaching the teacher's house. How can I blame A-'s mother either? She was three or four years younger than us—she was about twenty-six or twenty-seven then. A mere daughter-in-law, she had never walked on a road. Moreover the house was in a lane and how could she recognize it?

"We reached it with great difficulty. We were not then acquainted with the teacher's family. Entering the house, we saw the Master sitting on a small wooden cot in a small room. There was no one near him. As soon as he saw us, he laughed and said affectionately, 'Ah, how could you come here?' We saluted him and told him the whole story. He was very happy and asked us to sit in the room and began to talk on various subjects. Every one now says, he did not allow women to touch him or even to approach him. We laugh to hear it and think, 'Oh! we are not dead yet.' Who will know how kind he was? He had the same attitude towards men and women. But it is true that if women stayed near him long, he would say, 'Please go now and pay obeisance to the presiding deities of the temples.' We have heard him ask menfolk also to do likewise. However that may be, we were sitting and speaking with him. Those two of us who were elderly sat very near the door, and the rest, the three of us, in a corner within the room, when Pranakrishna Mukhopadhyaya, whom the Master called 'the fat Brahmana,' came quite unexpectedly. Should we have gone out? No, that was out of the question. For where were we to go? There was a window near the door. The two elderly ones took their seats there. And the rest, the three of us, made our way together under the cot on which the Master was sitting, and lay there. Each one of us had her whole body swollen on account of the mosquito bites. What could we do? There was no possibility of movement. We were lying still. 'The fat Brahmana' talked for about an hour with the Master and left. We then came out laughing.

"The Master was then taken to the inner apartment for light refreshments. We accompanied him there. The Master afterwards got into the carriage to go to Dakshineswar. We all then walked back home. It was about 9 p.m.

33. "The next day we went to Dakshineswar again. As soon as we were there, the Master came near and said, 'Ah! I took almost all your sweets; there is only a little left over. There was no illness or anything of the kind; only the stomach was just a little heavy' I was surprised to be told so. Nothing suited his delicate stomach, and fancy, he had taken a whole piece of Sar! Then I heard that he took it while in the state of divine semi-consciousness. I was told that the Master had taken his food at the house of the teacher and had come to Dakshineswar at 10-30 p.m. Shortly after his arrival he got into ecstasy and said to Ramlal, 'I am very hungry, give me whatever there is in the room.' Being so ordered, brother Ramlal brought the piece of Sar and placed it before the Master, who ate up almost the whole of it. Then we remembered what we had heard from the Holy Mother and sister Lakshmi of his taking abnormal quantities of food sometimes in the ecstatic mood and digesting them. Ah! so overwhelming was the grace he bestowed on us! It cannot be expressed in words what that compassion was· And what attraction! Even we ourselves do not know or under- stand how we all used to go to him and do all those things. Why, we cannot now go in that manner on foot anywhere to unknown people's houses without informing anybody, to see a holy man or to listen to spiritual talks. Such boldness has vanished with him by whose power we acted that way. We do not know why we have been living to this day after we lost him."

Many similar examples can be given. Those who never went out of their houses were asked to go and make purchases in the market and also to beg from door to door in order that their pride and egoism might vanish. They were taken by the Master to the religious fair of Panihati and brought back after they had witnessed it, and they also did all these and more, unhesitatingly and with great delight. It does not seem to be a small matter when we think deeply over it. The ideas which arise in the minds of all from the knowledge of difference of rank, sex, etc., and which restrain one's behaviour had been for the time being washed away by the waves of spiritual consciousness. Every one saw the perfect ideal of his or her own spiritual mood in the Master, who was an embodiment of different divine moods. Men bowed down their heads to the perfect manifestation of manliness in him; and women, finding in him the fullest manifestation of all the noble womanly moods,

regarded him as dearer than the dearest, and cast away all hesitation
in moving with him.

34. The Master would now and then mimic the gestures and
postures of women much to our merriment. We were surprised
to find the mimicry so exact. On one occasion a woman devotee
said to us in this connection, "One day the Master began to show
in our presence the gestures which women make when they see
men — that pulling of the veil, pushing back of the tresses near
the ear, pulling of the cloth over the breast, speaking various unnecessary and meaningless words. The imitation was perfectly
accurate. We saw it and began to laugh, but we felt shame and
pain, thinking that the Master was thus looking down upon women.
We thought, 'Why, are all women like that?' After all we were
women; we would naturally feel pained if anybody caricatured
women like that. Ah! the Master immediately understood and
said affectionately, 'Well, I don't mean you. You are not of the
demoniac nature. It is women of that nature only who behave
that way'."

35. Every one of the devotees of the Master has more or less
seen the co-existence in him of the moods of both men and women.
Girish had an experience of this nature one day and took the liberty
of asking the Master, "Sir, are you a man or a woman?" The
Master laughed and said in answer, " I do not know". Who
would now decide in which sense the Master made that remark,
whether in the sense of a man of self-knowledge who, identifying
himself with the Atman, maintains that he is neither male nor
female, or in the sense that he found in himself a harmonious blend-
ing of both?

36. Dwelling in Bhavamukha, the Master became an embodiment of all moods, and could therefore know exactly the mental
states of all, men and women, and appear to each as one of his or her
sex. He himself expressed this to some of us. A highly devoted
woman devotee[1] told us that the Master said to her one day, "I
know the nature of a man by a mere look; I know who is good and
who is bad; who is of noble descent and who is not; who is a man
of knowledge and who is one of devotion; who will realize God
and who will not. All these things I know, but I do not speak it
out lest they should feel pained." As he was all along dwelling in

---

[1]The mother of Swami Premananda.

Bhavamukha, the whole of the universe always, nay, every moment, appeared to him to be composed of nothing but ideas. He felt as if all things — men and women, cows and horses, wood and earth — were rising and merging as different aggregates of ideas in the Universal Mind, and through those coverings of ideas, the infinite indivisible ether of Existence-Consciousness was manifesting itself in varying degrees, here less, there more, while in some other places the veils seemed to be so dense that its manifestation appeared to be non-existent. Again, the immaculate son of the blissful Mother of the universe that he was, the Master found himself on the point of merging in Her for good, realizing through Samadhi the bodiless state of absolute Bliss after the voluntary offering of everything belonging to him — the body, mind, mental functions and all — at Her lotus feet ; but reaching that point, he came to know that the Divine Mother willed otherwise. In complete obedience to Her command, he forcibly covered his mind, which had got fully merged in the indescribable state devoid of duality and non-duality, with the veil of Vidya Maya, the force tending Godward, and engaged himself in carrying out Her behests. The Universal Mother, the embodiment of infinite power, on Her part, became pleased with the Master: and although She kept him encased in a body, She always kept his mind keyed to a lofty pitch, a high state of Oneness, from which all ideas rising in the infinite Universal Mind were always felt to be his own. The identification was so intimate and natural that whoever saw him felt that the Mother was the Son and the Son the Mother; both were Consciousness: "The abode is Consciousness, the name is Consciousness, and the Lord is Consciousness!"

We have said as much as we could. Now, O reader, reflect and know who this Master, this embodiment of infinite moods, is.

CHAPTER II

A FEW WORDS ON BHAVA, SAMADHI AND DARSANA

(THE SPIRITUAL MOODS, PROFOUND MEDITATIONS AND SPIRITUAL VISIONS)

(TOPICS: 1. Samadhi is not a disease of the brain 2. It is by Samadhi alone that one attains spirituality and eternal peace 3. Visions and spiritual progress 4. The real signs of spirituality 5. Adhikarika Purushas, Isvarakotis and Jivakotis 6. Difference in degree in non-dual consciousness 7. Savikalpa Samadhi and deepening of moods 8. Bodily changes inevitable with changing spiritual moods 9. How to ascertain higher and lower ecstasies 10. Incarnations alone can fully experience all spiritual moods 11. The Brahmani against the Master's discussing the Vedanta 12. The Master's determination to dwell always in the Nirvikalpa plane 13. The uniqueness of the Master's mind 14. The Master's devotion to truthfulness 15. First example 16. Second example 17. Third example 18. The universal Mother did not allow him to take a wrong step 19. The obstacle on his path to Nirvikalpa, Samadhi 20. Six months in Samadhi 21. The Captain on the Master's Samadhi 22. The Master himself on the same 23. Views on bodily changes produced by ideas 24. Kundalini, the Coiled Power 25. The relation between body and mind 26. The need of keeping holy company 27. Bodily change due to concentration of mind 28. Harmony of Bhakti and Yoga 29. The Coiled Power and its states 30. The progress of the awakened Coiled Power 31. The Master's experience regarding this 32. His attempts at describing the experience of Nirvikalpa Samadhi 33. The five movements of the Coiled Power on the path of Samadhi 34. The seven planes of the Vedanta 35. The Master's retentive power 36. His explanation of non-dual state in simple language 37. To Swami Turiyananda 38. The Vedantic dictum; 'Brahman is real, the universe is unreal' 39. God-realization not possible without His grace 40. The Master's answer to Pandit Sasadhar on curing his own disease 41. The same request by disciples 42. The depth of the Master's non-dual state of consciousness 43. The Master stood tests of every kind 44. The correspondence between the Master's inner experiences and external facts 45. Variations of his relations with different devotees 46. The two classes of devotees 47. The Master's knowledge of the inner nature of each devotee 48. How he led the devotees forward on the path of spirituality 49. The devotees and divine visions 50. A devotee getting the vision of Vaikuntha 51. Instruction to devotees of God with forms 52. Flush the mind before meditation 53. Which doctrine is higher; that of God with form or without form 54. The harmony between the two doctrines 55. Swami Vivekananda and blind faith 56. Instructions on meditation 57. The Master advising devotees to meditate on his own form 58. Need of relationship with God 59. Exerting loving pressure on Him 60. The example of a perverted woman 61. Resolution to realize 62. Desires must be given up one by one 63. Perseverance as in angling 64. The divine Lord is quick-eared 65. The Master's attention to details in spite of spiritual moods 66. First example 67. Second example 68. Third example; instruction to the Holy Mother 69. The last word on the topic 70. The Master a veritable king in the realm of ideas 71. Swami Vivekananda's remark on it.)

Listen again to My supreme word, the profoundest. You are dear to Me; therefore, I will tell you what is good for you.

—Gita, XVIII. 64.

It will not be an exaggeration to say that, before the Master became well known, the people of Calcutta, both the educated and the uneducated, were completely ignorant about Bhava, Samadhi or the extraordinary visions and experiences of the spiritual realm. The uneducated masses had a fantastic conception about these, sprung from fear and a sense of mystery; while the modern educated community, drifting on the currents of foreign ideologies introduced by a system of education that was devoid of the indigenous religious background, looked upon this kind of vision, ecstasy etc., as impossible or as derangement of the brain. The bodily changes due to ecstasy, belonging to the domain of spirituality, appeared in their eyes to be a fainting fit or a peculiar disease. Although conditions have changed to a great extent, very few people are, even now, really able to understand the inner meaning of Bhava and Samadhi. Again, it is necessary to have a fair knowledge of the nature of Samadhi in order to understand, even to a very small extent, the state of Bhavamukha, in which Sri Ramakrishna was always dwelling. Hence we shall now try to explain a little of these to the reader.

1. What the people in general do not experience is called by us "an abnormal state." But the subtle experiences of the spiritual world can never be the objects of knowledge for the ordinary human mind. Such experiences require instruction, training, constant practice etc. The extraordinary visions and experiences

26

fill the spiritual aspirant with purity and gradually make him fit for realizing eternal peace by filling him every day with new vigour and ideas. Is it then reasonable to call these visions, experiences etc., abnormal? Every one has to admit the fact that all abnormalities without exception make men weak and bring about a deterioration in their intellectual and other powers. As the effect of the visions and experiences of the spiritual world is quite the opposite of deterioration, it must be admitted that the cause of all these is also opposite; and therefore these cannot be called diseases or derangements of the brain.

2. It is through these visions etc., that especial spiritual experiences have always been gained. But a man cannot be fit to realize the eternal peace, till he has reached the Nirvikalpa state through the cessation of all mental modifications, and the non-dual state of consciousness has become natural to him. As an example of this, Sri Ramakrishna used to say, "When a thorn runs into the body, one has to take it out by means of another thorn and then throw away both." Forgetting the divine Lord, man has come into this abnormality, the world. The abnormalities of sights, tastes etc., gradually get attenuated by those visions and experiences, which ultimately lead man to the knowledge of Non-duality. He then feels blessed by knowing the truth of the Rishi's utterance, (Tai.Up.2.7): "He is verily Bliss itself." This is the process. All the doctrines, experiences, visions, etc. of the spiritual world, without exception, help man to go forward towards that goal. Swami Vivekananda often said that these visions, experiences etc., indicated how far the aspirant had gone forward towards the goal; he called them the " milestones on the way to progress". Therefore let not the reader think that when there is a little intensity of a particular spiritual mood or when one experiences the vision of the forms of one or two deities through meditation, spiritual realization has reached its culmination. In that case he will fall into a great error. Falling into this kind of error in the religious world, aspirants miss the goal; they get bogged in a single idea or mood and are filled with hatred and animosity towards others. If a man makes this error in cultivating devotion to God, he becomes "fanatical" and "bigoted." This defect forms a great thorn in the path of devotion; it arises out of the "mean, narrow mind."

3. Again taking such visions to be the whole of religion, many come to the wrong conclusion that any one who has not had

such experiences is not at all spiritual. Spirituality and aimless miracle-mongering seem to them to be the same thing. But this kind of hankering after miracles does not make man spiritual; on the contrary it makes him weaker daily in all respects. That which does not lead to steadfastness and strength of character, that which does not enable man to take his stand on the rock of purity and truth in defiance of the whole world, or that which entangles him more and more in various kinds of desires instead of setting him free from them, — is outside the realm of spirituality. If extra-ordinary visions have not produced such results in your life and nevertheless you are having those visions, know that you are still outside the realm of spirituality, and that the visions are due to a diseased brain and so are of no value. If, on the other hand, instead of having wonderful visions and experiences, you find yourself acquiring strength, know for certain that you are on the right path and that you will also have these visions and experiences at the proper time.

4. Finding that some of the devotees of Sri Ramakrishna were experiencing ecstasy while he, though he had been visiting the Master for a long time, had had no such experience, a friend[1] of ours felt much perturbed, and going to the Master with tears, laid bare to him the distress of his heart. Hearing it, Sri Ramakrishna consoled him and said, "Don't be silly, my child. Do you think everything is gained when that is attained? Is it something very big? Know for certain that true faith and renunciation are far greater. Why, Narender[2] (Swami Vivekananda) does not gene-rally have these ; but just see how great is his renunciation! — how great his faith, his strength and his steadfastness!"

5. When competency for living in oneness with the divine Lord arises in certain aspirants through the elimination of desires, helped by steadfastness, firm faith and single-minded devotion, there comes up in them sometimes on account of past impressions such pure desires as " I will do good to the people, I will act for the happiness of the many." Under the influence of such desires, they cannot then remain wholly in the non-dual state. They come down just a little from that high plane of consciousness to the realm of "I" and "mine" again. But that " I-ness" of

---

[1] Gopalchandra Ghosh.

[2] The Master used to pronounce it like that.—Tr.

theirs lives in constant unbroken consciousness of an intimate
relation with God, such as "I am a servant, a child or a part of
Him." That "I" can no more devote itself day and night to
lust and gold. Knowing that God is the quintessence of everything, that "I" does not any more hanker after the enjoyment
of worldly objects such as sight, taste, etc. It is interested in
them only to the extent they are conducive to the realization of
that end and no more. Those who were once in worldly bondage,
but have now attained perfection by means of Sadhana and are
living the rest of their lives in some loving relation with the
divine Lord, are known as the "liberated-in-life". It is those
who are endowed from their very birth with the consciousness
of such a special relation with God and have never in this life
fallen in bondage like ordinary men, that are termed in the scriptures as "Adhikarika-Purushas", "Isvarakotis", "ever-free ones"
and so on. Again, there are Sadhakas, who, after attaining
the non-dual state of consciousness, never come down from that
state even for the purpose of doing good to humanity; they are
spoken of as "Jivakotis". And we have heard from the Master
that most of the liberated ones belong to this category.

6. Even among the first category, namely the Iswarakotis,
who come down from the non-dual state of Samadhi to do
good to humanity, there is a difference in degree in their experience of oneness with the Cause of the universe. Some of them
have merely seen the sea of Consciousness from a distance, some
have gone near and touched it, and others have drunk but a few
drops. Sri Ramakrishna said by way of illustration, "Narada,
the celestial seer saw that sea from a distance and came back;
Sukadeva touched it but thrice, and Siva, the spiritual teacher of
the world, took three sips only and lay devoid of consciousness
of the external world. Becoming one with the non-dual consciousness even for a short time is what is called Nirvikalpa Samadhi."

7. Just as there are differences in the experiences of the non-
dual state, there are differences in the experiences of the devotional
moods, such as Santa, Dasya, Sakhya, Vatsalya, etc., — all belonging
to the lower strata of consciousness leading the aspirants ultimately
to the non-dual state. Some become blessed by fully experiencing
any one of these states; while others have just a glimpse of it.
The full experience of any of these devotional moods has been
termed in the scriptures on Yoga as Savikalpa Samadhi.

8. Wonderful bodily changes, spiritual visions, etc., come on the aspirants in all spiritual states of consciousness, in the higher non-dual state as well as in the lower Savikalpa states. Again, these visions and transformations are seen to be different in different individuals; these changes are observed in some people after only superficial experiences; while very little of these is observed in others even when they have profound experiences. In illustrating this, Sri Ramakrishna used to say, " If a couple of elephants get into the water of a small pool, the water is thrown into a violent agitation and it overflows; but the water in a vast lake remains as still as ever even when scores of them get into it." Nor is it a fact that mere bodily changes, visions etc., are inevitable signs of the depth of ecstasy.

9. If, however, the depth of spiritual experiences is to be measured, it must be done, as said before, from observing one's steadfastness, renunciation, strength of character, the attenuation of desires for enjoyment etc. It is by means of this touch-stone alone, and by no other means, that the amount of dross in ecstasy can be assessed. One thing, therefore, is very clear, namely, the complete picture of the fully developed stage of one or another of the moods of Santa, Dasya, Sakhya, Vatsalya and Madhura can be seen only in those persons who have realised their nature to be pure, awakened and free, by giving up all kinds of desires, and not in those who are entangled in the pursuit of lust and gold. One blinded by desires feels the attraction of desires only; how can such a one feel those sentiments towards God which could be experienced only by minds free from the slightest tinge of desire?

10. We have tried to explain the nature of ecstasy as we have heard it from the Master. It is necessary to say here a few words more in this connection, so that the reader may understand it clearly. From what we have said about the differences amongst the aspirants in their capacity to experience the moods of Santa, Dasya, etc., and of Non-duality, it is not to be inferred that even the Incarnations of God remain confined within any limits in the matter of experiencing those moods. They can at will manifest fully in themselves any of these devotional moods. Again, they can, by adopting the non-dual mood, proceed in the experience of oneness with God to an extent which is not in the power of any mortals—Jivanmuktas, the ever-free or Isvarakotis. For having once proceeded far in the experience of their oneness with Bliss Itself, ordinary mortals

cannot come down again to the realm of "I" and "mine" by separating themselves from that Bliss. This is possible in the case of the Incarnations of God alone, and it is by the recording of their wonderful experiences that the scriptures like the Vedas and the Bible have come into being. Is it, then, strange that the spiritual experiences of Incarnations should go beyond those recorded in the Vedas and other scriptures? Sri Ramakrishna used to say in corroboration of this point: "The state of this place (meaning his own experiences) has gone much beyond what is written in the Vedas and the Vedanta". It is because Sri Ramakrishna was the foremost amongst them that he could return to the realm of "I" and "mine" "for the good of the many" and "for teaching the people", even after remaining absorbed in the non-dual state of consciousness continually for six months. That is a wonderful story. It will not be out of place to say a few words about it here.

11. On the third day of his initiation into Sannyasa by Tota Puri, the Master attained the ultimate realization of Nirvikalpa Samadhi or complete oneness with God, spoken of in the Vedanta. By that time the Master had finished the disciplines according to the Tantras, and the learned Bhairavi Brahmani — the Master spoke of her as Bamni — who had collected necessary articles for these Sadhanas and taught their application, was living at Dakshineswar. We have heard from the Master that the Bhairavi forbade him to mix with Tota Puri and said , " My cjhld, do not mix so much with him. These people lack devotion. Your love and affection for God will then vanish". But the Master did not pay heed to her advice and used to be absorbed night and day in the discussion of the Vedanta and its realization.

12. Tota Puri stayed at Dakshineswar for eleven months and left. The Master then decided to dwell in the unbroken experience of oneness with God or the state of Non-duality, instead of remaining in the realm of "I" and "mine". His decision was immediately followed by the actualisation of it. This episode of his life is, indeed, a wonderful story. The Master was then not at all conscious that he had a body. Even ideas necessary for maintaining the body, like those of eating, sleeping, answering the calls of nature, etc., did not cross his mind, not to speak then of desires like "talking with others". No such ideas as "I" and "mine", "you" and " yours" have any existence in that state. The idea of "two" or of "one" also does not exist there, as that of " one" can be experienced only

when there is the memory of "two". In that state all the functions of the mind without a single exception are completely stilled. A perfect calm prevails. There exists only "an indescribable something of the nature of eternal Consciousness and Bliss, incomparable, transcending all limitations, eternally free, nameless, limitless like ether, without parts, devoid of all ideas, an infinite immensity, untouched by cause or effect, a mood beyond all moods which a man of self-knowledge is conscious of in his heart during the profound concentration of mind called Samadhi."[1] Bliss and bliss alone ! It has no direction, no space, no object, no form, no name. There abides alone the bodiless Self of the nature peculiar to Itself, indescribable and blissful ; it abides as a mood beyond all moods and ideas which exist only within the domain of the mind and the intellect—a state beyond all states, which the scriptures speak of as a sport of the Self with the Self. The Master was always experiencing such an indescribable state without any break.

13. The Master said that no worldly object or relation acted as an obstacle in the path leading to his experience of the Nirvikalpa Samadhi according to the Vedanta. For, he had verily renounced for Her sake all kinds of desires from his mind. While offering everything to the Mother, he had said, " Mother, here is Thy knowledge and here is Thy ignorance, here is Thy good and here is Thy evil, here is Thy vice and here is Thy virtue, here is Thy fame and here is Thy calumny. Grant me pure devotion to Thy lotus feet and show Thyself to me." Thus had he renounced all kinds of desires for enjoyment out of pure love for Her and in order to have a direct vision of Her holy feet. Can we ever dream even of doing this to a small extent ? Leave aside having a direct feeling of that divine love for love's sake. Even if we ever practise resignation to the Lord, saying, "Here, O Lord, are all my belongings ! They are verily Thine"—still when we feel their need for ourselves afterwards, we oust the Lord from their possession and calculate our own profit and loss out of our so-called act of resignation. When we do anything, we think of what people will say. We get agitated in many ways and restlessly run after many things ; thinking of the future, we alternate between the abyss of pain and the height of pleasure ; we have this deep-rooted egoism in us, making us feel that even if we cannot upset the whole world for the fulfilment

---

[1] *Viveka-Chudamani*, 408–9.

of our selfish purposes, we can at least give it a sufficient turn towards that end. But the Master's was not a cheat's mind like ours. So the moment he made a total offering of everything to the Divine Mother, saying, "Here, O Mother, is whatever Thou hast given me!" — he could never more cast a covetous glance at them. Never did he have such subtle regrets as: "Alas! I have given my word; what can I do now? It would have been better not to have done so." That is why the Master could never claim anything as "mine", if he had once made an offering of it to the Mother.

14. We would like to say another thing in this connection. The Master could not say to the Divine Mother, " Here is Thy truthfulness and here is Thy untruthfulness, O Mother!" though he made to Her an offering of everything belonging to his mind and body, merit and demerit, vice and virtue, good and evil, fame and calumny and the like. Once the Master himself told us the reason of it. "If I give up truthfulness in this way," said the Master, "how can I keep the truth that I have offered everything to the Mother of the universe?" And ah! what a great devotion to truth did we witness in the Master, who had surrendered everything else to the Mother! If he once said he would go to a place, he was there without fail at the proper time. If he once said he would accept a thing from a certain person, he could not take it from anyone else. When he happened to say that he would not eat a certain thing or do a certain action, he could not from that day on eat it or do it. "One who has devotion to truthfulness," said the Master, "realizes the God of truth. Mother prevents his words from turning untrue." Ah, how many illustrations of this point have we not seen in the Master's life! We would mention a few here.

15. One day it was arranged at Dakshineswar that the great devotee "Gopala's mother" should cook rice for the Master and feed him. Everything was ready ; the Master sat down to take his food. He found the rice hard, not properly boiled. The Master was annoyed and said, "Can I eat this rice? I shall not take rice out of her hands any more." When these words came out of the Master's mouth, everyone thought that the Master had only warned Gopala's mother in order to make her careful in future; it was impossible to imagine that he would not take rice any more out of her hand, seeing that he had so much love and

respect for her.   He would perhaps forgive her a little later, and there
the matter would end.   But the contrary happened; for the Master
had shortly afterwards a disease in his throat.   It became gradually
so acute that he could not take rice any more.   In this way circumstances conspired to make that casual remark of his come true.

16.   One day, while he was in a spiritual mood, the Master
said at Dakshineswar, "I shall not eat anything except porridge
henceforward."   The Holy Mother was bringing his food to him
at the time.   Hearing this and knowing that any word coming
out of the Master's mouth never proved untrue, she felt nervous
and said, "Why, I shall cook for you rice and soup.   Why porridge
then?"   "No, porridge, " were the words uttered by him in that
spiritual mood.   Soon after, he got the throat-disease, and it
turned out that none of the preparations that are generally
taken with rice could be taken by him; he lived on porridge, milk,
barley, and the like.

17.   The Master specified the well-known Sambhuchandra
Mallick of Calcutta, who was generous and wealthy, as the second
of the four ' suppliers of his provisions'.   He had a garden near
the Kali temple of Rani Rasmani.   There he used to spend much
time with the Master in discussing spiritual matters.   There
was in that garden his charitable dispensary.   Sri Ramakrishna
suffered often from stomach troubles.   Coming to know of this
one day, Sambhu advised him to use a small dose of opium everyday and asked him to take it from him before he returned to
Rasmani's garden.   The Master also agreed.   Afterwards, engaged
in conversation, both of them forgot about it.

18.   He bade good-bye to Sambhu and came to the road,
when he remembered about his agreeing to take the opium from him.
He came back to take it, but found that Sambhu had gone into the
inner apartment.   Instead of calling him, the Master asked his
manager for it, and having got a little, was returning to Rasmani's
garden.   But as soon as he came to the road, he felt a sort of reeling
and could not see the road. His legs were drawn,as it were,towards
the drain by the road.   He said to himself, "What is this?   This
is by no means the road."   At the same time, he could not find out
the cause. As a last resort, he thought that there might be a mistake as to the direction, and turning to Sambhu's garden, he saw that
the road leading that way was distinctly visible.   He thought a
little and came back to Sambhu's gate, and ascertaining the road

well from there, again proceeded with care towards Rasmani's garden. But no sooner did he advance a couple of steps than he found himself in the same plight — he could not see the road. His legs were being drawn in the opposite direction. When it happened thus a few times, it struck him that Sambhu had asked him to take the opium from him; but instead of doing that he had taken it from his manager and that too without Sambhu's knowledge. That was why the Mother had been preventing him from going. The manager should not have given it without Sambhu's orders, and he too should have taken it from Sambhu himself, as he had promised to do Hence, as it was, two wrongs, theft and lying, were being committed by him. That was why the Mother was preventing him from returning. Thinking thus, he came to Sambhu's dispensary and found that the manager also had gone. Therefore, he threw the packet of opium through the window and said in a loud voice, "Hullo, here is your opium". Saying so, he started towards Rasmani's garden. This time he did not have that reeling, and the road was clearly seen and he reached the garden without difficulty. "Have I not, " said the Master, "completely taken refuge in the Mother? That is why the Mother has taken hold of my hand. She prevents me from taking a single wrong step." There are many such examples in the Master's life, of which we have heard. Ah, what a wonderful thing! Can we even in our wildest imagination conceive of such devotion to truthfulness and such entire dependence on God? Is it about this kind of dependence on God that the Master spoke again and again to us in the following parable? "In that part of the country (Kamarpukur)," he said, "there are narrow ridges by the fields. People walk from one village to another along those ridges. It is a common sight to see a father walk along those ridges, carrying in one of his arms his younger child lest it should slip, while the elder one walks by his side holding the other hand of the father in his. As they go, the children see a white kite and clap their hands in joy. As the child in the father's arms knows that its father is holding it, it is free from fear and claps joyfully. But the other child, who is holding its father's hand, forgets all about the ridge, and claps its hands in astonishment after letting go its hold; when it immediately falls down and cries out. Even so, he whose hand the Mother clasps, is without fear, while he who clasps the Mother's hand is in fear; for, the moment he lets go his hold, he falls."

19. Thus no kind of worldly desires or impressions stood as obstacles to the Master on his path to Nirvikalpa Samadhi, because owing to the intensity of his love for God, he felt no restraining force from behind nor any attraction for any person or thing of the world. The only thing that stood as an obstacle was the form of the Divine Mother, "beautiful, more beautiful than the most beautiful," the only one that the Master was so long lovingly worshipping with devotion, knowing Her to be the Essence of all essences and the Cause of all causes. "No sooner," said the Master, "had I collected the mind and concentrated it on one point than the Mother's form appeared before me. I could not have the heart to leave that form behind and go beyond. It happened so, as often as I tried to make the mind objectless, driving away everything from it. At last after a great deal of thinking, I gathered much mental strength, regarded knowledge as a sword, and with that sword mentally cut that form in two. There was nothing left in the mind then; and it rushed quickly up to the complete Nirvikalpa state." These seem to us to be meaningless words, for we have never made any form of the universal Mother our own—never established any loving relation with Her, never learnt to love anyone with all our heart. Whole-hearted, intense love, we have only for this ego of ours and for this lump of flesh called the body. That is why we entertain in our mind so much fear of death or of any radical change. But the Master had indeed none of it. He knew the lotus feet of the Divine Mother in his heart of hearts to be the only essential thing in the world and was devoting his time to meditation on those feet and to the service of Her divine form day and night. Therefore what else could support his mind in the world when he somehow removed the Mother's form from it? It became completely objectless and devoid of all modifications and reached the Nirvikalpa state. Reader, try at least once to have an imaginative grasp of this stupendous feat even if you cannot fully comprehend it! You will then feel how far the Master made the Divine Mother his own and with what an intense eagerness he loved Her.

20. The Master was in that Nirvikalpa state continually for six months. "I was," said the Master, " for six months in that state from which ordinary mortals never return; for the body of one attaining to that state lives for twenty-one days only and then falls like a dry leaf from a tree. There was no consciousness at all

of time, of the coming of day or the passing of night. Just as flies enter into the nostrils and the mouth of a dead man, so they entered into mine; but there was no awareness of it. The hair became matted on account of the accumulation of dust. Calls of nature were perhaps answered unconsciously. It was a miracle how the bodily life was sustained. It should have succumbed then and there. But a holy man came there to save it. He had a small stick like a ruler in his hand. He recognized my state as soon as he saw it, and came to know that much of the Mother's work was yet to be done through this body, that much good would be done to many if only it could be saved. Therefore he would carry food in time, and by striking this body again and again, would try to bring it back to consciousness. The moment he saw signs of consciousness appearing, he would thrust some food into the mouth. Thus on some days a little food found its way into the stomach and on others it did not. Six months passed that way. Then the Mother's command was heard, 'Remain in Bhavamukha! For the spiritual enlightenment of man, remain in Bhavamukha!' This was followed by illness, blood-dysentery; there was a wringing pain in the intestines and it was excruciating. It was after continually suffering for about six months that the mind gradually came down to the normal body-consciousness; before that it used to be merged in the Nirvikalpa state always."

21. As a matter of fact, we are informed by those who had the good fortune to meet the Master some ten or twelve years before he passed away, that even then they rarely heard him speak; for he used to be in ecstasy continually all the twenty-four hours. Where is the question of speaking or hearing under these circumstances? We have been told by Visvanath Upadhyaya, an official of the Nepal Government, that he saw him absorbed in ecstasy continuously for three days and three nights. Moreover he said that on such occasions when deep Samadhi continued for a long time, cow's ghee used to be rubbed at intervals on the person of the Master from the neck to the lower end of the backbone, and from the knee to the soles of the feet, in a downward direction. When this was done, consciousness tended towards the realm of "I" and "mine" from high planes of Samadhi.

22. The Master himself said to us on many occasions: "The natural tendency of this mind is towards the Nirvikalpa plane. Once in Samadhi, it does not feel inclined to come down. It has

forcibly to be brought down for your sake. This force is not in itself sufficient for bringing me down; so I hold on to some trifling desires of the lower plane, as 'I shall smoke tobacco', 'I shall drink water', 'I shall take this', 'I shall see so-and-so', 'I shall talk', etc. These desires too have to be retained in the mind by effective repetition. It is only then that the mind gradually comes down to the state of body-consciousness. Again, when coming down, it flies off in that (upward) direction. It has to be brought down again by means of such desires." What a wonderful phenomenon! When we were told of all this, we sat astounded and thought, "If the meaning of his saying, 'Tie the knowledge of Non-duality in the corner of your cloth and then do whatever you like', is this, ah, what hope have we of realizing it in our lives!" We find that the only way for us is to take refuge in him and wait for his grace. But when we try to do so, we are faced with difficulties in a short time. The roguish mind sometimes would think, "Why should the Master not love me more than others? Why should he not love me as much as he loves Narendra? In what respect am I inferior to him?" and so on. So much for the Master's mental make-up; let us now follow the main topic. (III. 2.8)

23. We shall now try to touch on certain aspects of the spiritual consciousness of higher planes and on the nature of Samadhi, as far as we have understood them from the Master's teachings, and then pass on to explain the state of Bhavamukha. We have already mentioned that some bodily changes are sure to accompany any ideas, higher or lower, arising in the mind. This requires no explanation; it is a matter of daily experience. It is easily understood by observing the ordinary ideas experienced every day; for example there is one kind of change when anger comes and another kind when love is felt. Again, when there is a great preponderance of good or evil thoughts in a person's mind, so much change is produced in his body that one can know his nature as soon as one sees him. Looking at a man, we say among ourselves, "See, how angry he appears or how lustful or how honest?" These daily expressions are clear proofs of our contention. Again, many of us must have observed how the appearance and gestures of even a person of perverted nature and of hideous appearance become gentle and free if he spends continually, say, a period of six months, for some reason or other, in thinking holy thoughts

and living a good life. The Western physiologist too says, "Whatever may be the nature of an idea that comes to your mind, it will for ever leave a mark in your brain. Your character is built more or less of the aggregate of these two kinds of impressions, good and bad, and you pass for a good or a bad character accordingly."

24. But the Yogis and Rishis of the East, especially of India, say, "Those two kinds of ideas do not stop with merely impressing two kinds of marks in the brain, but they get transformed into subtle powers of impulsion and abide eternally in the sacral plexus called the basic centre (Muladhara) situated at the lower end of the vertebra, from where they urge you to do good or bad deeds again in the future. It is this centre that forms the repository of these powers of impulsion accumulated in the past lives. These are what are called 'impressions' or ' past impressions' ; and it is only by the direct realization of the divine Lord or the attainment of Nirvikalpa Samadhi that these can be destroyed. Otherwise, at the time of leaving one body for another, the Jiva carries with him this bundle of impressions, 'just as the wind carries smell from its receptacle.'[1]

25. This intimate relation, spoken of before, between the body and the mind continues to exist till the attainment of the knowledge of Non-duality or what may be called the direct realization of God. The body reacts on the mind and the mind on the body. Again, like the relation between the body and the mind of the individual, there exists a relation between the body and the mind of the whole of mankind — the aggregate of the individual bodies and minds. My body and mind react to the actions of your body and mind and *vice versa*. Thus do the external or gross world and the internal or the subtle world stand eternally related, and are continually acting and reacting on each other. It is therefore noticed that you feel grief when others are in grief; similarly a mood of devotion comes to you unnoticed in the company of devotees. This holds good everywhere.

26. It follows therefore that like physical disease and health, ideas or mental modifications are also infectious. They travel to persons of the requisite receptivity. That is why the scriptures have so much eulogized the company of holy men for infusing love of

---

[1] *Gita*, XV. 8.

God into human minds. For the same reason, the Master used to say to new visitors, "Frequent this place; in the beginning one should pay more frequent visits here."

27. The spiritual moods arising out of intense love of God similarly cause extraordinary physical changes. For example, when this kind of love grows in the mind, an aspirant ceases to feel attraction for sense-objects like sights, tastes etc., reduces food and sleep; develops a taste for certain kinds of food and distaste for others; and feels a desire to shun like poison his relations whose association deflects him from the divine Lord. The Master used to say in this connection, "I could not then bear the very atmosphere of worldly people, and felt when in the company of relatives, as if my breath would stop and the soul leave the body." And again he would say, "The Mahavayu (the flow of nervous energy due to deep spiritual concentration) in the body of a man, who calls on God sincerely, cannot but rush to his head."

28. It is therefore clear that the mental changes or impressions that are produced on account of the love of God have, each of them, a corresponding bodily manifestation. The Vaishnava scriptures, taking into consideration these mental changes, have called these spiritual moods (Bhavas) and divided them into five, namely, Santa, Dasya, Sakhya, Vatsalya and Madhura; while the scriptures on Yoga, in dealing with the bodily changes caused by those ideas or spiritual moods, have described them in terms of the coiled power (Kundalini) and the seven centres (Chakras) in the spine and the brain.

29. We have acquainted the reader to a certain extent with what is called the coiled power (Kundalini). The great seers who have written treatises on Yoga have given this name to that great power of impulsion generated by the mental modifications undergone by the individual in his past and present lives, and expressing itself through its physical counterpart (in the base of the spinal column). The Yogi says that it remains almost completely asleep or unmanifest in mortals who are in bondage. That is why it is called coiled up. It is in this sleeping state of the coiled power of impulsion that the mental modifications such as memory, imagination, etc., are rendered possible. If by some means or other it gets fully awakened or manifest, it leads a man to the realization of infinite knowledge, and through it, to the direct vision of God. If it is asked how memory, imagination, etc., can arise from the sleeping

coiled power, our answer is : although asleep, it gets a sort of
momentary awakening through the nervous vibrations communicated to the brain through the doors of sense-organs by external
objects like sights and tastes, just as the hand of a sleeping man
bitten by a mosquito automatically strikes it or rubs the bitten
part of the body.[1]

30. The Yogi says that the Supereme Self or the divine Lord
who is indivisible Existence-Knowledge-Bliss resides in His own
nature of Pure Consciousness in the space, or the ether, existing in
the aperture [2] in the crown of the head.   The coiled power has a
great attraction for It, or to put it in another way, the divine Lord
is continually attracting it. But as it is not awake, the coiled power
does not feel that attraction.   The moment it is awakened, it will
feel that attraction of the divine Lord and approach Him.   The
path leading the coiled power to the divine Lord also exists in the
body of each of us.   Starting from the brain this path comes straight
through the spine down to the lowest centre (Meru Chakra) called
the basic or Muladhara situated at the lower end of the vertebral
column.   This path has been spoken of in the scriptures on Yoga
as Sushumna-vartma (the spinal canal)[3].   The Western physiologist has described this as Canal Centralis, but has not so far
discovered its function or utility.   It is by this path that, separated
initially from the Supreme Self, the coiled power has come from the
brain down to the basic centre and has been lying there asleep.   It
is by this path again that this power arrives at last at the brain,
crossing one after another the six centres, situated one above the
other within the spine. [4]   As the awakened coiled power

---

[1] The fact is: almost the whole power lies dormant leaving an in-
finitesimal part of it active, which is sufficient to carry on the normal
work of the body and the brain. But as portions of it are roused through
Yoga, wonderful visions and experiences follow, ultimately leading to
the non-dual consciousness.—Tr.

[2] Ait. Up. II. 12.—Tr.

[3] Katha. Up. VI. 18.—Tr.

[4] Treatises on Yoga mention six centres and their places one above
the other thus; Muladhara, at the lowest part of the Canal Centralis;
Svadhishthana, at the root of the organ of generation; Manipura, in the
navel; Anahata, in the heart; Visuddha, in the throat; and Ajna, between
the eye-brows. It is to be understood that these centres are situate,
in the Canal Centralis of the spinal column, and that heart, throat, etc.
mean the spots opposite to them in the Canal.—Tr.

passes from one centre to another, the aspirant begins to have novel experiences; and as soon as it reaches the brain, he realizes the highest experience that spiritual awakening can give; in other words, he reaches the consciousness of Non-duality, the oneness of the self with the Supreme Self. It is then that the aspirant has the ultimate experience of his particular devotional mood. It is then that he becomes one with that great Idea from which all ideas are arising every moment in human minds—that Idea beyond all ideas.

31. Ah, how very simple were the words with which the Master explained to us these intricate facts of Yoga! "You see," said he, "something goes up creeping from the feet to the head. Consciousness continues to exist as long as this power does not reach the head; but as soon as it reaches the head, all consciousness is completely lost. There is no seeing or hearing any more, much less of speaking. Who can speak? The very idea of 'I' and 'You' vanishes. While it goes up, I feel a desire to tell you everything—how many visions I experience, of what nature they are, etc. Until it comes to this place (showing the heart) or at most this place (showing the throat) speaking is possible, and I do speak. But the moment it goes up beyond this place (showing the throat) some one forcibly presses the mouth, as it were, and I lose all consciousness. I cannot control it. Suppose I try to describe what kind of visions I experience when it goes beyond this place (showing the throat). As soon as I begin to think of them for the purpose of description, the mind rushes immediately up, and speaking becomes impossible."

32. Ah! How many times, the Master made fruitless attempts to control himself with great effort in order to reveal the nature of the visions, experiences, etc., that he had when his mind reached the centre above the throat! "One day," says one of our friends, "the Master said very emphatically, 'I'll tell you everything today and will not keep anything secret.' He described clearly the centres and the corresponding experiences up to the heart and the throat, and then pointing to the spot between the eye-brows, he said, 'The Supreme Self is directly known and the individual experiences Samadhi when the mind comes up here. There remains then but a thin transparent screen separating the Supreme Self and the individual self. The Sadhaka then experiences'.....saying this, the moment he started to describe in detail the realization of the Supreme Self, he was in Samadhi. When

27

the Samādhi came to an end he tried again to describe it; he was again in Samadhi. Finally after repeated attempts, he said to us with tears, 'Alas! I have indeed a desire to tell you everything without concealing anything whatsoever, but in spite of all my efforts, the Mother does not allow me to speak; She presses my mouth.' We were surprised and thought, 'Ah, how strange it is! We see he is trying so much to tell us, and we also realize that he is feeling much pained that he is unable to express himself. That Woman, the Mother, is surely very naughty. Ah! Why press the mouth when he is to speak of holy things, things about the realization of God?' Did we then understand that the mind, intellect and the like, with the help of which speaking becomes possible, have not a very long range? And again, did we then understand that the complete realization of the Supreme Self could not be attained if one did not go beyond this range? Did we then understand that the Master was trying to make the impossible possible on account of his love for us?"

33. The Master used to describe in detail the nature of the experiences he had when the coiled power went up through the Canal Centralis. "Look here," he would say, "the something that goes up to the head producing a tingling sensation does not always do it in the same manner. It has five kinds of motion as described in the scriptures.

1. The motion like that of ants :—There begins a creeping sensation at the feet, as if ants carrying food in their mouths were creeping along in a line. It then goes slowly up till it reaches the head, when there is Samadhi.

2. The motion like that of frogs: Just as frogs hop twice or thrice and then rest, and again do so twice or thrice and then rest, and thus proceed, a sensation is felt as moving in a similar way from the feet in the direction of the head; and as soon as it reaches the head, there is Samadhi.

3. The motion like that of snakes: A snake lies motionless in coils or at full length. But the moment it sees a prey or is frightened, it wriggles zigzag to the prey or to its place of hiding. A sensation like that is felt going upwards direct to the head. When it reaches there, one goes into Samadhi.

4. The motion like that of birds: A bird at the time of perching comes flying, sometimes a little high, sometimes a little low, and stops nowhere until it reaches its destination. A sensation

with similar movements is felt proceeding to the head, culminating in Samadhi.

5.   And the motion like that of monkeys: Just as a monkey, when it goes from one tree to another, jumps from branch to branch suddenly and reaches the destination in two or three leaps, so a sensation is felt to reach the head in two or three movements, and Samadhi follows.''

34.   About the visions in each centre while the coiled power goes up by the passage of the Sushumna, the Master used to say, "The Vedanta speaks of seven planes.   The experiences in these planes differ from one another.   The mind normally moves up and down in the three lowest planes. Its functioning is fixed to the anus, the organ of generation, and the navel—to eating, dressing, coition and the like.   If, however, it happens to transcend those three planes and reaches the heart, one has the vision of Light.   But although the mind rises sometimes to the heart, it comes down to the three lower planes again.   If anyone's mind goes up to the throat, he cannot speak on any mundane topics.   He will speak only of God.   In those days, I felt as if I was struck on the head with a stick when anyone spoke of worldly matters;   I would fly to the Panchavati where I would not have to hear the talks on those topics. I would feel frightened and would hide myself when I saw worldly people.   Relatives appeared to me to be enemies trying to push me down into deep pits, falling into which once, I felt I might not be able to get up again.   I felt suffocated;   it seemed I was at the point of death.   I could have peace only when I fled from them. The mind might come down again to the anus, the generating organ and the navel even though it had reached the throat;   one should even then be alert.   If, however, anybody's mind reaches the spot between the eyebrows, he has no more fear of a fall.   He then has the direct knowledge of the Supreme Self and remains continually in Samadhi.   There is only a screen, transparent like glass, separating this centre from the thousand-petalled lotus[1]   in the brain, the Sahasrara.   The Supreme Self is so near then that it seems as if one is merged in Him, identified with Him.   But the identification is yet to be.   If the mind comes down from here, it comes at the most down to the throat or the heart.   It cannot come lower down.   The Jivakotis never come down from this

---

[1] In each of the centres there is a "lotus" differing from one another in the number of petals, colour, etc.—Tr.

plane. After the experience of continuous Samadhi for twenty-one days, the screen is pierced and the oneness of the self with Him becomes complete. To be completely merged in the supreme Self in the Sahasrara is what is called reaching the seventh plane."

35. Hearing the Master speaking of the Veda, the Vedanta and the science of Yoga, some of us, however, would sometimes ask him, "Sir, although you never learnt even reading and writing, how did you know all these?" Unique as he was, the Master would not be annoyed even at that strange question. He would smile a little and say, "Ah, it is true I did not study myself but I have heard much. I remember all that. I have heard the Vedas, the Vedanta, the Darsanas and the Puranas from good and reliable scholars. After hearing them and knowing what they contained, I made a garland of them all (the books) in my mind and offered it at the lotus feet of the Mother, saying, ' Here are all Thy scriptures, Puranas and the like. Please grant me pure devotion.' "

36. He would say of the non-dual mood or the mood beyond all moods: "That is the last word. Do you know how? Suppose there is an old servant. His master is pleased with him on account of his good qualities, has faith in his words, and consults him on all matters. One day as an expression of his high appreciation, the master takes hold of his hand and tries to make him sit on his (the master's) own seat. The embarrassed servant quails. Still the master drags him, makes him sit there and says, ' Do sit down, you and I are one.' It is just like that."

37. A friend of ours (Hari alias Swami Turiyananda) paid much attention to the study of the Vedanta at one time. The Master loved him on account of his continence from childhood, devotion, steadfastness and other virtues. As he applied himself to the study of the Vedanta, meditation, devotional exercises and the like, the friend did not or could not visit the Master as usual for some time. This did not pass unnoticed. One day the Master saw a boy, who used to visit him along with our friend, come alone to Dakshineswar, and asked him, "Well, how is it that you come alone; hasn't he come?" The boy said in reply, "Sir, he is now applying his mind intensely to the study of the Vedanta. He spends night and day in study, discussion and argumentation. It is perhaps because he thinks that time will be wasted that he has not come." The Master heard this and said nothing more.

38. The person we are speaking of came to Dakshineswar

a few days after. As soon as he saw him, the Master said, "Well, I hear you are now given much to the discussion of the Vedanta. That is very good. But does it teach anything more than this— Brahman is real, the world is unreal? Is there anything more?" The friend: "Yes sir, what else can there be?" The friend said afterwards that the Master opened his eyes to the import of Vedanta in those few words. Hearing them, he was surprised and thought, "It is indeed true that everything of the Vedanta is understood when one is convinced of the truth of these few words in one's heart of hearts."

The Master: "Hearing, thinking and meditating. First hearing — you at first hear that Brahman is real, the universe unreal. Then thinking — by reason and discrimination you get that idea deeply and correctly imprinted in your mind. And after that, meditation — you apply your mind to Brahman, the Real entity, by renouncing the universe, the unreal entity. Of what avail will it be if one hears and understands this, but does not try to give up what is unreal? It is like the knowledge of the worldly people. One cannot attain Reality by means of that kind of knowledge. Conviction is necessary, renunciation is imperative. It is then alone that one can succeed. Otherwise you may repeat, 'There is no thorn, no pricking', but the moment you touch the thorn, you feel the prick and cry out in pain. You merely utter, 'There is no universe, it is unreal; it is Brahman alone that exists,' and so on, but as soon as the objects of the world — sights, tastes, etc., come before you, you take them to be real and you get entangled. There came a holy man to the Panchavati. He used to speak incessantly on the Vedanta to the people. Then one day I heard that he had contracted an illicit connection with a woman. I went in that direction in order to ease myself, when I saw him sitting there. I said, 'You talk so much about Vedanta, what is this talk about you then?' He replied, 'What does it matter? I can make it clear to you that there is no harm in that. When it is a fact that the world is unreal in the past, the present and the future, will my action alone be real? That is also unreal.' I was annoyed when I heard this and said, 'Fie on your knowledge of Vedanta! That is the kind of knowledge which the worldly people have of Vedanta. That knowledge is no knowledge at all."

There the conversation ended. The Master told him all this while he was walking with him under the Panchavati. Our friend had been labouring under the apprehension that the Vedanta could not be understood, and liberation would be a far cry, till difficult books like the *Upanishads*, *Panchadasi* and the like were studied and a clear understanding of the philosophical systems like Sankhya, Nyaya, etc., was attained. From the Master's talk that day, he came to understand that the only purpose of all Vedantic discussions was to have that conviction in one's heart. One might read shelves of books on philosophy and logic, but if one did not have the firm conviction, "Brahman alone is real, the world is unreal", it would make no difference whether one studied them or not. He bade good-bye to the Master and returned to Calcutta, deciding that he should thenceforward apply his mind more to the practice of spirituality than to the study of books. Determined to know God direct through the spiritual practices, he now applied himself wholeheartedly to them.

Whenever the Master came to the house of anyone in Calcutta, the news of his coming spread in a short time to the devotees of the inner circle. No one in particular took the responsibility of spreading it among all. But the hearts of the devotees were extremely eager to see him. So if business preoccupation prevented them from visiting him at Dakshineswar, they would very often visit one another's house and derive great joy in conversing about him. If anyone amongst them somehow came to know of the Master's arrival, the news would travel automatically from mouth to mouth and spread amongst them all. It is very difficult to explain to the reader how through the Master's grace the devotees were bound by an indescribable bond of love. It was in the quarters of Baghbazar, Simla and Ahiritola that many of the Master's devotees lived. For this reason the Master would come on most occasions to one or other of those three places. Of the three places again, it was to Baghbazar that he would come most often.

A short time after the event mentioned above, the Master came one day to the house of Balaram Basu at Baghbazar. Many of the devotees of that quarter came to know of this and assembled there. Our friend lived nearby. The Master made enquiries about him. A young acquaintance of his fetched him at once. As soon as the friend entered the spacious parlour on the first floor of the house of Balaram Babu, he saw the Master surrounded by the devotees, and saluting him, sat down near him on one side. The Master made loving enquiries about his health and welfare and went on with the subject of his conversation. From a word or two the friend understood the drift of the discourse. The Master was emphasising that nothing whatever, be it knowledge, devotion or direct spiritual experience, could be achieved without God's grace. As the friend was listening, it struck him that the Master had introduced the topic in order to remove a misconception of his mind and that the whole discourse was meant for him only.

39. He heard the Master say, "Well, is it a very easy matter to realize that lust and gold are really unreal and to have the firm conviction that the universe is eternally non-existent? Is it possible without His compassion? It is possible only if His grace produces the conviction in us. Can a man have that conviction by his own effort? Ah, how small is his power and how small is the effort he can put forth with that power!" Thus speaking of the grace of God, the Master went into ecstasy. After a while he was in divine semi-consciousness and said, "Man cannot have a clear idea of even one thing, and he wants another." Then the Master began in that state to sing the song:

> "Why are you proud, O Kusa, O Lava?
> Could you have captured me if I had not
> Allowed myself to be captured?"

As he was singing, streams of tears flowed down from the Master's eyes and a part of the sheet covering the carpet got wet. Caught up in the pathetic sentiment conveyed by the teaching, the friend also could not check himself and shed profuse tears. It was some time before both of them came to the normal state. The friend says, "That teaching has for ever been imprinted on my mind. I have known from that day that nothing can be achieved without the grace of God."

40. We cannot refrain from mentioning here another fact about the depth of the Master's non-dual knowledge. When there was a crisis in the Master's illness at Kasipur, Sri Sasadhar Tarkachudamani heard of it and came with a few others to see him. "Sir," said the Pandit to the Master in the course of conversation, "we have read in the scriptures that persons like you can at will cure bodily diseases completely. Diseases are fully cured if a strong desire is created in the mind that one should get cured, and the concentrated mind is directed once to the diseased part of the body for some time. May you not just try this once?"

The Master said, "Ah, how could you, a Pandit, speak like that? Can I feel an inclination to withdraw the mind from the

Existence-Knowledge-Bliss to whom I have offered it, and place it on this dilapidated cage of bones and flesh?"

41.   The Pandit was silent.   Swami Vivekananda and the other devotees, however, did not remain passive.   As soon as the Pandit left, they requested the Master persistently to act as the Pandit had suggested.   "You must," said they, "cure the disease; for our sake you must cure it."

The Master: "Ah, do I wish that I should suffer from a disease?   I wish I were cured, but do I get cured?   To be cured or not depends on the Mother."

Swami Vivekananda: "Then please ask the Mother to cure the disease.   She will surely grant your request."

The Master: "You say so, but such a request does not come out of my mouth."

Swamiji: "No, Sir, that will not do.   You must ask the Mother.   For our sake you must do it."

The Master: "All right, I shall see if I can ask Her."

After a few hours the Swami came again to the Master and asked him, "Sir, did you ask Her?   What did the Mother say?"

The · Master: "I said to the Mother, 'I cannot eat anything on account of this (showing the sore in his throat).   Please do something that I can eat a little.'   But the Mother said, 'Why? You are eating through all these mouths (showing all of you).'   I could speak no more for shame."

42.   Ah, how wonderful was his lack of body-consciousness! How extraordinary was the non-dual knowledge wherein he was established!   He was then for six months continually on a daily diet of about half a pound of barley-water only.   As soon as he heard the Mother of the universe telling him in that condition, "You are eating through so many mouths," the Master became silent and bent his head in shame thinking, "What an evil act have I committed!   I have called this limited body 'I'."   If only we could appreciate even a little of this exalted mood of the Master!

43.   Oh, what a wonderful Master we had the good fortune to meet!   What a marvellous harmony of all the paths of religion—of knowledge and devotion, of concentration and action, both ancient and modern—have we not seen in him!   The Rishis, the authors of the Upanishads, say that a person who is a true knower of Brahman knows everything and all his thoughts and desires come true—he becomes a Satya-sankalpa (truth-willed).

All objects and powers of the external world obey his desires implicitly and undergo corresponding changes. Is it any wonder if his own body and mind also did the same? It is not in the power of ordinary people to test the truth of these facts. But we can say confidently that, though we are men of small powers, the manner in which we used to test the Master left no ground for disbelief in his credentials. The Master stood the tests smilingly and used to tell us, as if in ridicule, "Ah, lack of faith even now! Have faith, firm faith. The very One who appeared as Rama and Krishna is now within this sheath (showing his own body), but this time the advent is incognito, like the supervision of his own kingdom by a king in disguise! As soon as there is publicity or whispering, he moves away from that place. It is just like that."

44. Many events of the Master's life open our eyes to the truth of the above-mentioned ideas of the Upanishad. All the ideas that arise in a man's mind are truly known to himself alone, that is, he alone can gauge their frequency, intensity, range, etc. Others merely infer them from external signs. The subjective nature of these ideas is within the direct experience of all. Like the ideas of ordinary persons, those of men who experience Samadhi are also mere modifications of the mind or manifestations of mental powers; they arise in the mind and merge in it. It is impossible to see or show their counterparts in the external world. But the reverse is the case in regard to many of the ideas of the Master. Take, for example, his desire to put up a fence around the Panchavati when he saw that the plants planted by him were cropped by cattle. Shortly after, there was a high tide in the Ganga and all the articles necessary to make that fence—some mangrove posts, coir-rope etc., with even a chopper came floating and ran aground just near the spot, and he put up the fence with the help of the gardener of the Kali temple named Bhartabhari. Take another example: his assertion in the course of an argument with Mathuranath, the son-in-law of Rasmani, that "anything can happen by the will of God, that a plant producing red flowers can yield a white flower too," and the latter's refusal to accept the proposition. The very next day the Master saw two flowers, one red and the other white, on two twigs of the same branch of a china rose in the garden. He broke the branch with the flowers and handed it over to Mathuranath. Take again another example: the arrival at the Kali temple

at Dakshineswar of a perfected person in each of the faiths of the Tantra, the Vedanta, the Vaishnava, Islam, etc., and the initiation of the Master by each in his particular faith, whenever a strong desire to practise any of those faiths arose in the Master's mind. Or, still another example: The Master yearned to meet his inner circle of devotees whom he had seen in visions long ago and called out for them in the intensity of his longing; and they came one after another, and he recognized and received them. Many such instances may be cited. On a close scrutiny of the subject, these facts make it clear that many of the ideas of the Master did not end like those of ordinary human minds in mere mental modifications, but produced corresponding changes in the events of the external world through the influence of an inscrutable power. These were the facts—let the reader ponder them critically and arrive at his own conclusions.

45. We have already said that the Master used to remain in Bhavamukha (III. 1.36) at all times except during the Nirvikalpa Samadhi. That is why we see that he used to have different spiritual relations of love with different devotees—a particular relation with a particular devotee—and he always kept that relation intact. His lifelong filial relationship with all women, who are the especial manifestations of the bliss-giving and nourishing aspects of the Mother of the universe, is now well known to all. But the fact that he had particular relationships with individual men devotees is perhaps not yet generally known. Therefore it will not be out of place here to say something in this connection. The Master divided his devotees into two broad categories—one born of an aspect of Siva and the other of Vishnu. He said that the devotees of these two groups differ in their nature, behaviour and in their preference and suitability for particular forms of spiritual discipline. He could clearly understand the difference, but it is beyond our power to explain what this difference is.

46. Therefore, let the reader know this much, that the characters of Siva and Vishnu are, as it were, two moulds or models, and the mental make-up of a devotee is cast in one or the other of these two moulds. The Master had all kinds of spiritual relationships of love, viz., Santa, Dasya, Sakhya, Vatsalya, etc., established with all those devotees—he having particular relations with particular persons. For example, he used to say of Narendranath, "Narendra is, as it were, my counterpart—the Principle that resides

within this (showing himself) is female and that which is within him (showing Narendranath) is male." He looked upon Swami Brahmananda as his very son. The Master had a particular relation of this nature with each of the intimate devotees, both lay and monastic. It is needless to say that he had the relation of calmness (Santa) with the ordinary devotees; for he had the firm conviction that they were all forms of Narayana Himself.

47. It is on knowing the internal nature of each of the devotees that the Master had a particular spiritual relationship established with him. For, he used to say, "I clearly see everything in a man's mind like articles in a glass case." One can never act contrary to one's nature; therefore it was not in the power of any of the devotees to act contrary to that spiritual relation of love in which the Master stood to him. If, however, any one, in imitation of another, acted contrarily, the Master felt much annoyed and would clearly point out his mistake. As an example, we cite the case of a devotee. The Master called Girish a Bhairava.[1] One day he saw during his ecstasy in the temple of Kali that Girish was a Bhairava. He would smilingly put up with Girish's importunities and rude language; for he saw that there was an extraordinary tender feeling and complete dependence hidden under the covering of the rudeness of his language. One day, another beloved devotee of the Master imitated Girish's rude language in his behaviour with him, at which the Master became extremely displeased with him and afterwards pointed out his mistake.

48. Established in Bhavamukha, the Master knew well the spiritual mood natural to each man or woman, and in accordance with that mood had a relation of love with him or her. We shall here present the reader with some of the numerous methods the Master would adopt in leading each devotee to the realization of God according to his spiritual mood. We have to remind the reader of the Master's first vision of the Divine Mother in the temple precincts after he threatened to kill himself due to the agony of separation, and of the experience of non-dual consciousness that followed the vision. It was after this experience that the Master practised the devotional moods of Sakhya, Vatsalya and Madhura,

---

[1] The Bhairavas are a kind of terrific demi-gods, addicted to strong drinks and meat-eating and noted for their extraordinary powers; they are devoted followers of Siva.—Tr.

and attained the highest stage in each of them.   Long afterwards, when the devotees of the inner circle came to him, a desire arose in the Master's mind one day that the devotees also might experience ecstasy, and he prayed to the Mother accordingly; and immediately some of them began to have such experiences.   In that mood o spirituality their consciousness of the external world including their own bodies grew dim to a certain extent, and an internal current of a particular spiritual mood, for example, the thought of a form of God, became so manifest that they saw that form come, stand before them, smile, speak and do things, as if it were vividly living. They mostly experienced that state while they listened to devotional songs.

49.   The Master had another class of devotees who did not have a similar experience when listening to devotional music, but had visions of forms of gods at the time of meditation.   To begin with, they had visions of mere forms, then with the deepening of meditation, they saw their movements and heard their words. Others, again, had various kinds of visions in the beginning, but did not have any when their meditation grew deeper.   But it is a matter of great surprise that immediately on hearing about the visions and experiences of each of them, Sri Ramakrishna knew the class to which each belonged, his current needs and his future visions and experiences.

50.   Let us mention here one devotee as an example. Instructed by Sri Ramakrishna, one of our friends (Swami Abhedananda) began practising meditation and other spiritual exercises, and in the beginning had clear experience of his Chosen Ideal in various forms at the time of meditation.   He used to go to the Master at Dakshineswar at short intervals and inform him of his experiences.   On hearing of them the Master would say, "Very good," "Practise this way", and so on.   Later, that friend saw at the time of meditation that all the forms of gods and goddesses merged in the body of one form.   When the Master came to know of it, he said, "Fine, you have had the vision of Vaikuntha. You will have no more visions." Our friend said, "As a matter of fact that was what exactly happened. I could not any longer see any form whatever during meditation.   Higher ideas such as the all-pervasiveness of the divine Lord arose in my mind and occupied it. I had then a great liking to have visions of forms and tried hard to have them again. But all to no purpose; no form could be seen any more."

51. "At the time of meditation," said the Master to the devotees who believed that God had forms, "think that you have tied
your mind with a silk thread to the lotus feet of your chosen form of
God, so that your mind may not stray away from there. Why do
I say 'silk thread'? Because, those lotus feet are indeed very
soft and delicate. They will be hurt if any other kind of string is
used." He would sometimes say, "Should one think of the Chosen
Ideal at the time of meditation only and then forget Him at other
times? You should always keep a part of the mind attached to
Him. You must surely have noticed that a sacrificial lamp has to
be lighted at the time of the worship of Durga. That light should
always be kept burning near the Deity, it should not be allowed to
go out. If it does, it augurs ill for the householder. Even so, after
the Chosen Ideal is brought and seated on the lotus of the heart,
the sacrificial lamp of meditation on Him should always be kept
burning. While one is engaged in worldly duties, one should
watch at intervals whether that lamp is burning within or not."

52. Sometimes he would say, "Ah! In those days before
beginning to meditate on the Chosen Ideal, I imagined that I was
thoroughly flushing out the inside of the mind. You see, there
exist various kinds of dirt and dust (bad thoughts and desires)
within the mind. I imagined that I was washing them off and was
then making the Chosen Ideal sit there. Do just like that."

53. The Master spoke to us at one time about the meditation
on the two aspects of the divine Lord, the one with forms and the
other without forms. He said, "Some reach the formless aspect
through that with forms, others attain that with forms through
the formless." At the house of the great devotee Girish, a friend
of ours, Devendra Nath Basu, one day asked him, "Sir, which is
higher—the conception of God with forms or that without forms?"
"There are," replied the Master, "two conceptions of the formless
aspect, the 'ripe' and the 'unripe'. The 'ripe' conception of
the formless aspect of God is very high indeed; one has to
reach that through the aspect with forms. As regards the
'unripe' conception of the formless aspect, it is all darkness as
soon as one shuts one's eyes, as is the case with the Brahmos.[1]

---

[1] Let no one think that the Master condemned the modern Brahmo
Samaj or the modern knowers of Brahman. We have mentioned it out of
regard for truth. We have again and again heard him utter the words
"Salutation to the modern knowers of Brahman" when he saluted all the

54. As the result of Western education there was also another circle of devotees of the Master, who were proceeding in Sadhana through the "unripe" conception of the formless aspect of God. He forbade them to imitate the Christian missionaries in condemning the meditation on the aspect of God with forms, in hating the devotees going forward in Sadhana with the help of images or other symbols of the divine Lord, and in calling them "idolaters", "blind believers", and so on. He said, "Ah! it is true that He is with forms and it is equally true that He is without forms. Who knows what else He is, besides these?" "Do you know how God with forms is like? It is just like ice formed in water. By freezing, water becomes ice; ice is water inside as well as outside. Ice is nothing but water. But look here ; water has no form. It has no particular shape; but ice has. Similarly the indivisible Existence-Knowledge-Bliss-Absolute gets condensed, as it were, through one's devotion, and assumes various forms like ice." This analogy used by the Master must have clarified the doubts of countless people and convinced them that these two apparently contradictory aspects can co-exist in the Supreme Being.

55. We cannot but make mention here of another fact. Swami Vivekananda was the foremost in the circle of the Master's devotees following the "unripe" doctrine of the formless aspect of the Divinity. The Master placed him above all—not only of this class of devotees but of all classes. Having come under the influence of Western education and the Brahmo Samaj, the Swami used sometimes to pass uncharitable remarks on the devotees. This mood was particularly noticeable in him at the time of argumentation. But the Master enjoyed the fun sometimes by bringing about a vehement discussion between him and some devotees of God with forms. During such discussions it often happened that none could stand his argument and some felt hurt when silenced by his keen intellect. The Master also described joyfully that fact to many persons on many an occasion and said, "The other day Naren 'cut to pieces' the arguments of so-and-so with utmost

devotees of all denominations at the conclusion of the singing of God's name. Every one knows that it was the great devotee Kesav, the well-known leader of the Brahmo Samaj, who first preached the Master to the public of Calcutta ; and Vivekananda and a few others of the monastic devotees of the Master freely admit that they are indebted for ever to the Brahmo Samaj.

ease. Ah, what a sharp intellect!" and so on. But the Swami was silenced on one occasion during a discussion with Girish, who followed the doctrine of God with forms. It seemed to us on that occasion that in order to make Girish's faith more firm and perfect, the Master was on his side. However, in the course of conversation with the Master on another occasion, Swami Vivekananda referred to the faith of the devotees of God with forms as 'blind faith'. The Master said in reply, "Well, can you explain to me what you mean by 'blind faith'? All faith is indeed blind. But then has faith any eye at all? Speak either of 'faith' or of 'knowledge'. But no, you will speak of some one's faith as blind and of some other's as having eyes; how is that?" Said the Swami later, "Indeed, I was in a fix in trying to explain to the Master that day the meaning of 'blind faith'. I could find no meaning for the expression. I have given up using that phrase since then, as I was convinced of the truth of the Master's contention."

56. The Master used to view the followers of the "unripe" doctrine of God without forms and the devotees of God with forms as being on a par. He told them also what form of meditation would be helpful. "Look here," said he, "in those days I used to imagine the divine Lord to be an ocean filling the whole universe, and me to be a fish, diving, floating, swimming in that vast sea of Existence-Knowledge-Bliss. And again, sometimes I considered myself to be a pitcher immersed in the water of that indivisible Existence-Knowledge-Bliss-Infinite, which pervaded me through and through."

57. He would again say, "Look here! Once think of 'this' (showing himself) while sitting down for meditation. Why do I say so? Because you have faith 'here'. Thinking of 'this' will remind you of that divine Lord. Just as when one sees a herd of cows, one remembers the cowherd, when one sees the son, one is reminded of the father, when one sees a pleader, one recalls the court, even so will the thought of 'this' help you to direct your mind to God. Do you understand? The mind is scatterd here, there and everywhere. Thinking of 'this', it will get collected in one place, and right meditation will follow when it is directed towards God."

58. Moreover, he would say, "Hold fast to some form of God or some mood, which is to your liking; it is only then that there will be steadfastness. 'He is realizable by means of spiritual mood (Bhava) alone. How can He be realized by one who lacks it?'

Spiritual moods are necessary. One should cultivate a particular
spiritual mood and then call on Him. 'As is one's mood, so is
one's gain; it is faith that is at the root. It is through a mood
that love sprouts.' Spiritual moods are an imperative necessity.
So is faith; it is necessary to hold fast, then only one succeeds.

"Do you know what a spiritual mood (*Bhava*) means? It is
to establish a relationship with God and to keep it bright before
our eyes at all times—at the time of eating, drinking, sitting,
sleeping.

59. "For example, 'I am His servant,' 'I am His child,'
'I am a part of Him'—this is what is called the 'ripe I', the 'I' of
knowledge. And 'I am a Brahmin', 'I am a Kayastha', 'I am
the son of so-and-so', 'I am the father of so-and-so'—all these
constitute the 'I' of spiritual ignorance. These should be given
up, should be renounced. They bring about bondage by strength-
ening egoism and pride. Constant remembrance is necessary.
A part of the mind should always be kept turned towards Him.
It is then only that success comes. One must make Him one's
own by holding fast to one particular loving relationship; it is in
that way alone that loving pressure can be exerted on Him. Just
see, when intimacy first starts or is about to start, we address
a person as 'Sir'; as it deepens, it gives place to 'you'; when it
reaches the culmination, 'you' also sounds flat; then 'thou' and
'thee' become necessary. He must be made more than one's
own. Then comes success.

60. "Take, for example a woman gone astray. She is just
beginning to love a paramour; how much of secrecy, fear, coyness
is there! Then when the love has grown intense, none of those
emotions remain. She then stands outside her family fold, going
to the extreme length of holding him by the hand in the presence
of all. If that man hesitates to take care of her and desires to
desert her, she puts a piece of cloth round his neck, and pulling
him says, 'Look here! I have left hearth and home and have
rendered myself helpless for your sake; and now you seek to desert
me! Maintain me, you must!' Similarly a person who has
renounced everything for God's sake and made Him his own, exerts
the pressure of love on Him and says, 'I have renounced everything
for Thy sake. Thou hast therefore got to reveal Thyself to me'!"

61. When he found that the love of God had decreased in
anyone, he used to ask, "Why do you say, 'I shall realize Him in

the next life, if not in this?' One should not have such lukewarm devotion. 'I will realize Him by His grace in this very life, this very moment.' Such strength, such faith, should be maintained. Can one succeed otherwise? In that part of the country, when cultivators go to buy oxen, they extend their hands to feel their tails. There are some oxen that do not get annoyed when people put their hands at the roots of their tails, but relax their bodies and lie on the ground. They know that such oxen are no good. Those that jump up and become frisky as soon as hands are put on their tails, are the promising ones. The man then selects his oxen out of them. Lukewarm devotion is no good.

62. "Have strength, have faith and say, 'I will surely realize Him, there is no doubt about it. I will realize Him this very moment.' It is then and then only that realization comes." "Give up," he would continue, "all the worldly desires one by one. Far from giving these up one by one, you are increasing them; how can you then expect to succeed?"

63. When devotees, conceiving God as either endowed with form or without it were stuck in the quagmire of despondency in practising meditation, devotional exercises, prayer and the like with no response, the Master encouraged them thus, "A bait must be thrown into the pond first, if one wants to angle for fish. You have perhaps been sitting long with the fishing rod in your hand; no sign of fish is seen and you think there are perhaps no fish in the pond. One day perhaps you notice the flouncing of a big fish and you immediately believe that there are fish in the pond. Another day the float on the line perhaps moves and you believe that evidently a fish has come near the hook. After some days, it may be, the float sinks and you lift the hook only to find that the fish has eaten the bait and fled. Again you put a bait on the hook and holding the fishing rod, sit very watchfully. One day at last as soon as a fish has taken the bait you pull the line, and the fish comes up on land."

64. He sometimes said, "Ah! He is very sharp-eared; He hears everything without exception. He has heard everything that you said to Him in your prayer. He will without doubt show Himself some day or other. He will show Himself at least at the time of death." He said to some, "If you cannot ascertain whether He is with form or without, pray to Him saying, 'I do not know, O Lord, whether Thou art with form or without; please reveal Thyself to me out of Thy grace, whatever be Thy nature'."

28

He said to some others, "Ah! verily God can be seen. Just as you and I are sitting together and speaking, so can He be seen and spoken with. I say this in truth, in very truth."

65. If a person remains in the contemplative mood, that is, in Bhava, for all the twenty-four hours, contemplativeness increases so much that no worldly duties can be performed by him. He cannot apply his mind to the small things of the world. This is what we see everywhere. Examples of this are found even among people devoted to science, politics etc., not to speak of those devoted to spirituality. Ordinarily such people are unable to attend to the cleanliness of their own bodies or to other small matters like keeping articles of daily use in their proper places. But we see in the Master's life that he was meticulous about even these small matters, in spite of his intense contemplativeness. It was only when he was devoid of all external consciousness as in Samadhi, that he was unmindful of outward punctiliousness. But when he was in normal consciousness, he was careful about everything. This is a matter of no little surprise. We shall cite here three instances.

66. One day the Master was going to the house of Balaram Babu from Dakshineswar, and with him were going Ramlal and Yogananda. All got into a carriage. The carriage started and came up to the gate when the Master asked Yogananda, "Well, have you brought the cloth and the towel?" It was morning then. Yogen answered, "No, Sir, I have brought the towel but have forgotten to bring the cloth. They (Balaram and others) will be glad to get you a new piece of cloth." The Master said, "What is it that you talk? They will say, 'What! A wretched, luckless fellow has come!' They will be put to trouble and will be in a fix. Stop the carriage, go and bring it."

The Master continued, "There is 'sufficiency' and no want when a good man, a lucky one, comes as a guest. But there arises difficulty in everything, when an unlucky, wretched fellow comes. He will come on the very day on which there is dearth of necessaries in the house, and the householder has to undergo much trouble to look after him."

67. One Pratap Hazra used to spend long periods at Dakshineswar when the Master was alive. All of us used to call him Hazra Mahasay.[1] He also sometimes accompanied the Master

---

[1] An honorific epithet added to surnames of gentlemen.—Tr.

when he went to see the devotees at Calcutta.   On one such occasion, while returning from Calcutta along with the Master, he forgot to bring back a towel.   At Dakshineswar, the Master came to know of it and said to him, "In the name of God I lose the consciousness even of my very wearing cloth, but never on a single occasion have I left my small bag or towel behind at Calcutta.   And you, doing only this little Japa, are so forgetful!"

68.   The Master taught the Holy Mother, "At the time of getting into a carriage or a boat, go and get into it first, and when leaving it, get down last after examining whether anything has been left behind."   The Master had such an eye even for very small details.

69.   Thus, though remaining incessantly in Bhavamukha, the Master was careful about all the necessary things.   He would keep a thing invariably at its proper place, take care of the articles of daily use such as clothes, the small bag of spices etc., belonging to himself, inquire whether any necessary thing had been forgotten or left behind at the time of going to, or returning from, any place. He would also bestow his thought on how the environment of devotees can be made favourable for their spiritual practice.   In this connection, he would make the same kind of searching enquiries into the worldly situation as into their spiritual problems.

70.   The Master appeared to us as a visible embodiment of the 'aggregate of all kinds of ideas'.   Such a great king in 'the world of ideas' was never seen before.   Constantly dwelling in Bhavamukha, the Master manifested in himself to the fullest degree all the spiritual states from the non-dual Nirvikalpa to the Savikalpa, acquainted devotees of all classes with the details of their particular paths and goals, and thus brought to them extraordinary light in the darkness of ignorance, unprecedented hope in despair, and incomparable peace amidst worldly trials and tribulations.   Words fail us to express what a safe haven of hope he was to all of us, what power he wielded in the entire realm of the spirit.

71.   "It is not a very difficult matter," said Swami Vivekananda, "to bring under control the material powers and to flaunt a miracle; but I do not find a more marvellous miracle than the way this 'mad Brahmin' (Sri Ramakrishna) used to handle human minds like lumps of clay, breaking, moulding and remoulding them at ease and filling them with new ideas by a mere touch."

CHAPTER III

SRI RAMAKRISHNA AS THE SPIRITUAL TEACHER

(TOPICS: 1. The Master's humility and his mood as spiritual teacher; their reconciliation 2. He was servant of all, because he saw God in all 3. The devotees' reaction to the daily manifestation of Teacher-power in him 4. Limitless nature of his moods 5. Grasping the significance of Bhavamukha is necessary to understand how the Master could be both a Bhakta and a Jnani 6. Savikalpa Samadhi, Nirvikalpa Samadhi, and deep sleep 7. Results of genuine Samadhi 8. The Master's Nirvikalpa Samadhi of six months 9. How his body survived the long period 10. A Yogi feeding him by force 11. The Mother's command "Remain in Bhavamukha" 12. Brahman, the Saguna-Nirguna, the Universal I, Iswara, and the Divine Mother 13. Universal "I-ness' is what is called Bhavamukha (the source of all ideas) 14. The Master's experience in the Nirvikalpa state and in the Savikalpa or Bhavamukha state 15. 'Remain in Bhavamukha'—its meaning 16. Dualism, qualified non-dualism and non-dualism according to spiritual progress 17. Hanuman on this topic 18. Necessity of accepting both the aspects of Brahman, the Absolute (Nitya) and the Relative (Lila). 19. A few illustrations given by the Master 20. The experience of Bhavamukha explained 21. Vidya Maya and the experience 'I am servant, devotee, child or part of God'. 22. The Master endowed with the universal 'ripe I': implications of this in Teacher-mood 23. His power of awakening spirituality: the event of January 1, 1886 A.D. as example 24. Experiences of devotees at the touch of the Master 25. Unpredictability of his mood of bestowal of grace 26. Teacher-mood manifests on the disappearance of 'unripe I' 27. Teacher-mood a manifestation of the Divine Mother 28. Why devotion to God and to the Guru is the same 29. Story of Vibhishana's devotion to the Guru 30. Stimulation of devotion through association of ideas: Chaitanya's example 31. Arjuna's devotion to the spiritual teacher 32. Place of devotion to one's own Guru in the light of this general Guru concept; Hanuman's example 33. The power of the spiritual teacher dormant in all men 34. The Master's words: 'The mind becomes the spiritual teacher at last' 35. The Guru compared to a woman-friend 36. The Guru merging in the Chosen Ideal.)

Some look upon It as strange,
Others speak of It as strange,
Others again hear of It as strange;
Though hearing (seeing and speaking), no one
Knows It fully.
                                        —Gita II. 29

1. Those who have seen the Master but a few times and have had only a superficial acquaintance with him, are often amazed to hear about his divine sport with the devotees as their spiritual teacher. They consider all such talks as downright falsehood. Again, when they find that a good many people are speaking in the same strain, they think, "These people have formed a group and hatched a plan to raise Ramakrishna into a Divinity. They are going to add one more to the already existing three hundred and thirty-three millions of deities! Why? Are not the existing deities sufficient for you? Why do you not select any one or more from amongst them? Why increase the number by another? Ah, how strange! These followers do not understand that when their falsehood is detected, people will lose all respect for such a pure soul. Have we not seen him? How humble he was, how meek, how patient, how devoid of egoism—lowlier than the lowliest! You say, you have also seen that he could not at all put up with being addressed as a spiritual teacher, a father or a patriarch. He would burst out, 'God is the only spiritual teacher, father and patriarch. I am the lowliest of the lowly, a servant of servants, equal to a hair on your body—a tiny hair at that, by no means a big one.' And saying so, he would immediately take the dust of your feet and place it on his own head! Has anyone witnessed a more humble attitude? And it is this very person whom they are making into a spiritual Teacher and God—which he was not!"

2. It is because of the possibility of such controversies being carried on for an indefinite period that we are prompted to put in a few words about the Master's mood as the spiritual teacher as we have seen and heard. For, as a matter of fact, the conviction that every being from the highest down to the lowest is God Himself, was so firmly ingrained in him that the attitude of a servant, not only of men but of all living beings, was normal to him. It is, no doubt, a fact that during his normal state of consciousness, he regarded himself as lowlier than the lowliest, humbler than the humblest, and took the dust of the feet of all; and that at that time he could not really endure being addressed as a spiritual teacher, a father or patriarch. Nevertheless we cannot deny the truth of the Master's extraordinary exploits when the mood of the spiritual teacher was on him. Then, under the influence of the divine Power manifested in him, he became Its instrument, and by a mere touch put

anyone in Samadhi or deep meditation or in the inebriation[1] of divine bliss never felt before.

3. Or when we found that, by the exercise of a mysterious Power, he could remove so much of the impurity of one's mind as to make one feel immediately an undreamt-of concentration of mind, purity and bliss, and to induce in one a sense of fulfilment in life and a mood of absolute self-surrender at his feet—then we could not but concede that the Master was not that lowliest of the lowly but a strange divine Power manifesting Itself through him in play (Lila) and making him behave that way. Then we felt that the Master, as the revealer of the supreme abode of the divine Lord, was indeed the spiritual teacher and the saviour of human beings, who, blinded "by the darkness of ignorance, scorched by the three kinds of misery,"[2] and suffering from the disease of worldliness, have been reduced to utter helplessness. Keeping this divine state of the Master in view, the devotees use the expressions "spiritual teacher", "the merciful one", "the Lord", and so on. In this age we have actually seen in Bhagavan Sri Ramakrishna this true humility of a devotee and this wonderful divine mood of the spiritual teacher, contradictory though they might appear, co-existing in one person. And because we have seen that, we are now trying to present to the reader what little we have understood about how they can exist together in the same mind.

4. We feel diffident to explain correctly even the little we have understood, and it goes without saying that it is beyond the power of both the writer and the reader to explain and understand it perfectly; for there was no limit to the moods of the Master who was established in Bhavamukha. The Master used to say, "There is no limit to the divine Lord." It is our personal experience that there was also no limit to the moods of this extraordinary personage.

---

[1] It was a fact that a sort of overpowering feeling like the intoxication produced by smoking too much hemp was felt at that time. We have seen some reeling. In the Master's case it was so much that it beggars description. Under the overpowering feeling of that intoxication he reeled so much that he had to take hold of some one of us in order to be able to walk at that time. People thought that he had taken too much of intoxicants.

[2] i.e., misery that pertains to the body, that caused by other animals and that due to the unusual effects of natural powers e.g., lightning, flood, storm, earthquake, etc.

5. As soon as people hear that the Master used to dwell incessantly in Bhavamukha, they generally jump to the wrong conclusion that he was not a man of Vedantic knowledge and that he always lived his life in the midst of the emotional surges of pain and pleasure arising from the separation from, and union with, the divine Lord. But a correct appreciation of the present subject would be possible, only if we have a clear grasp of what it is to be in Bhavamukha and under what conditions it is possible. Therefore let us here discuss briefly once again the state of being in Bhavamukha from a different standpoint (II. 1. 2-7). The reader will recall that the Master attained Nirvikalpa Samadhi in one day (II. 15.21) and remained in that state for three days and nights at a stretch.

Question: What is Nirvikalpa Samadhi?

Reply: To bring the mind to the state in which it is completely freed from all mentations.

Question: What are mentations?

Reply: They include all the mental modifications such as the perception of the objects of the external world consisting of sights, tastes, etc.; the feelings of pain, pleasure, etc.; the faculties like cogitation, imagination, inference, etc.; and the desires such as "I will do this", "I will understand that", "I will enjoy this " "I will renounce this" and so on.

Question: On what do these modifications depend for their existence?

Reply: On the awareness of "I", "I". If the consciousness of "I" vanishes|or is stopped altogether for some time, there can be no modification in the mind; nor can it grip the mind during that period.

6. *Question:* It is a fact that in the condition of swoon and deep sleep also the knowledge of "I" vanishes. Is Nirvikalpa Samadhi then something like that?

Reply: No, in swoon or deep sleep the consciousness of "I" continues inwardly; but the instrument called the brain, with the help of which the mind manifests self-consciousness, becomes inactive and ceases to function for some time; that is, all the modifications continue to crowd at the bottom of the mind. The Master gave the example of "pigeons sitting with inflated throats after eating peas and cooing; you think there is nothing within their throats; but if you feel them with your hand, you will find peas all crowding there."

7. *Question:* How am I to know that the I-consciousness continues in that way in swoon or deep sleep?

Reply: By observing the result. For example, on those occasions the heartbeat, the pulse, the circulation of blood etc., are not stopped. All these physical activities too take place centring on the I-consciousness. Moreover, although the external signs of swoon or deep sleep are somewhat similar to those of Samadhi, when man returns to the ordinary waking state, the amount of knowledge and bliss in respect of the former continues only as before; that is, there is not the least increase or decrease of it. For example, the lust of the lustful remains as it was; so does the anger of the angry, the greed of the greedy, and so on. But when the state of Nirvikalpa is attained, these modifications cannot raise their heads any more; extraordinary knowledge and infinite bliss fill the mind; and doubts, such as whether there is a next world or whether God exists, vanish for ever on account of the direct realization of God, the Cause of the universe.

Question: Yes, I see. Granted that the I-consciousness completely vanished for some time when the Master was in Nirvikalpa Samadhi; but what then?

Reply: Well, when the I-consciousness vanished this way, he had for some time the direct vision of the Divine Mother, the Cause of the universe. Not satisfied with that three-day vision, he tried to have it continuously.

8. *Question:* What was the state of the Master's mind as a result of that attempt and what were the signs manifested in his body indicating that state?

Reply: Sometimes, by the complete merging of I-consciousness, the symptoms of death appeared on the body externally, and the unobstructed vision of the Mother internally. Sometimes again, with the reappearance of a little of the I-consciousness, symptoms of life returned slightly and the vision of the Divine Mother continued, though a little obstructed because of the intervention of the screen of the mind, which was then pure, transparent and holy owing to the preponderance of Sattva. Thus, sometimes, there was the vanishing of the I-consciousness, the complete cessation of mental modifications and the full direct vision of the Divine Mother; again, sometimes, there was the resurgence of a little of I-consciousness, accompanied by slight modifications of the mind and a slightly obstructed vision of the Divine Mother. This recurred again and again.

Question: How long did he continue to make that attempt?

Reply: Continually for six months.

9. *Question:* Six months! How then did his body last? For a human body cannot last without food for six months. Besides, you also say that although the Master's I-consciousness revived now and then during that period, it never manifested itself in his body to such an extent as to make activities like the taking of food possible.

Reply: It is true that his body would not have lasted. He had not the slightest desire to prolong the life of the body. Yet his body survived because the Mother of the universe wanted to manifest Her wonderful spiritual powers through his body for the good of the many.

10. *Question:* That may be so; but did the Mother assume a form and come to feed the Master by force for those six months?

Reply: Yes, it was somewhat like that. For, a holy man arrived there of himself at that time, nobody knows from where. He clearly understood that the Master's state, which was almost like that of a dead man, was the result of his practice of Yoga and of his feeling of oneness with the divine Lord. The holy man stayed for those six months at the Kali temple and tried to bring the Master down to a little body-consciousness even by striking his body. And when he saw that a little consciousness was returning, he would immediately thrust a morsel or two of food into the Master's mouth. We do not know why the holy man felt this unusual eagerness and keen interest in keeping alive an altogether unknown person who was dead and inert to all appearances. Incidents like this have to be explained only as caused by the Divine will. Therefore, what else shall we say except that such an impossible event became possible by the direct will and power of the Divine Mother in order that the Master's body might be kept alive!

11. *Question:* Yes, I see; what happened afterwards?

Reply: Then the Mother of the universe—who is none but the divine Lord or the Cosmic Consciousness manifested as the universe, pervading in and through all beings, sentient and insentient and appearing as diverse names and forms—commanded the Master, "Remain in Bhavamukha!"

12. *Question:* What does it mean?

Reply: We shall presently explain it. But to comprehend what Bhavamukha is, it is necessary to understand the mental state of the Master at that time, as far as it is possible to do so with the help of our imaginative faculty. We have said that at that time his I-consciousness sometimes vanished altogether and sometimes reappeared just a little. Even when that little of I-consciousness returned, the universe did not appear to him as it appears to us. The world appeared to him as an "immense mind" in which innumerable waves of ideas were rising, surging and merging. His own body, mind, and I-consciousness, not to speak of those of others, seemed to be but a component wave in that immense mind. In that state the Master had the direct experience and vision of the real nature of that universal consciousness and power as the "One without a second"—as the one living and wide-awake Being, as the source of all will and action, as the Mother of infinite grace. It is the same Being whom the self-styled materialistic scholars of the West, looking through their clouded intellects and scientific instruments, view as inert and insentient, though admitting its unity. The Master saw further that the "One without a second" is Itself divided into its two aspects of Saguna (with attributes) and Nirguna (without attributes). It is this that is called Svagatabheda (difference-in-identity) in the scriptures — the idea that an immense I-ness pervades everything from Brahma down to the lowest created being. He saw that an infinnite number of waves of ideas was rising in that cosmic mind; that the limited I's of men perceived these waves of ideas in parts and mistook them as an external world of objects and spoke and dealt with them accordingly. He also saw that the limited I's had their being in, and performed their works with, the strength of that unlimited I; and that because of their inability to grasp and understand the unlimited I, the limited ones regard themselves as possessed of free will and power of action. It is this spiritual blindness that is called in the scriptures as Avidya or ignorance.

13. It is this universal I-ness existing between the aspects of Saguna and Nirguna that is called Bhavamukha; for, infinite ideas owe their manifestations to that all-pervading I-ness. This universal I is the I of Isvara (God) or the Divine Mother. In their attempt to describe the nature of this immense I, the Vaishnava teachers of Bengal have called It the divine Sri Krishna, the embodi-

ment of Pure Consciousness, which is of the nature of "inconceivable difference in non-difference" (Achintya-bhedabheda).

14. When the I-consciousness of the Master vanished altogether, he remained in oneness with the 'unqualified being of the Divine Mother' beyond the limits of this all-pervading I. And with the vanishing of this 'individual I' vanished also the last vestige of the infinite waves of ideas emerging from that 'immense I', which we call the universe. Again, when a little of the I-consciousness manifested itself in him, he saw both the Saguna immense I and all the ideas in It, united with (or in non-separation from) the Nirguna aspect of the Divine Mother. In other words, as soon as he attained the Nirguna state, the existence of the difference-in-identity in that "One without a second" vanished from the Master's consciousness. And when he was conscious of that Saguna immenseness, he felt that what is Brahman is verily Sakti, and what is called the Nirguna is verily the Saguna. Prakriti (Power in manifestation) is really that which is Purusha (Pure Consciousness). "The motionless snake is now moving" ; that is, that which is Nirguna in Its own nature is Saguna in sport. After he had the full direct vision of the nature of the Divine Mother in the combined aspects of Nirguna and Saguna, the Master got the command, "Remain in Bhavamukha", that is, "Do not remain in the Nirguna by the complete mergence of the I-ness, but live your life and do good to people, being in constant, complete and immediate knowledge of the fact that you are none other than that 'limitless I', from which all kinds of ideas as the universe spring, and that your desires and actions are verily Its desires and actions."

15. Thus, to have the direct experience and conviction or feeling in all respects, at all times and in all states, that I am that 'Immense I' — what is called the 'ripe I' — is the meaning of remaining in Bhavamukha. When one reaches the state of Bhavamukha, all the ideas such as "I am the son of so-and-so", " I am the father of so-and-so", "I am a Brahmana", "I am a Sudra", and so on, are completely washed off from the mind and no sign of them is left; and one always feels that one is that 'immense I' pervading the vast inconceivable universe. The Master, therefore, always taught us: "My children, all the I's, such as ' I am the son of so-and-so', ' I am the father of so-and-so', 'I am a Brahmana' ' I am a Sudra', ' I am a Pandit', ' I am rich', and so on, are 'unripe I's'; they bring about bondage. Give up these and think, 'I,

am His devotee', 'I am His son', or 'I am a part of Him'. Keep this mood firm in your mind." Or, he would say, "Tie the non-dual knowledge (Advaita-jnana) in the hem of your cloth and then do whatever you like" (III. 2.5).

16. The reader will perhaps say: " Was not then the Master a true follower of the doctrine of non-dualism'? Did he not accept the full implication of the non-dual doctrine founded by Sankaracharya, in which the very existence of the universe has been denied? For the Master, you say, upheld a difference in the Divine Mother Herself (Svagatabheda) and saw Her existence in the two different aspects of Nirguna as well as Saguna". No, it is not exactly that. The Master accepted all the three doctrines of non-dualism (Advaita), qualified non-dualism (Visishtadvaita) and dualism (Dvaita). But he used to say, "These three doctrines are accepted by the human mind according to the stage of its progress. In one stage of the mind dualism finds acceptance; the other two are then felt to be wrong. In a higher stage of spiritual progress the docrine of qualified non-dualism is regarded as true; one then feels that the Reality, which in Itself is eternally devoid of attributes exists in sport as always possessed of attributes. One then cannot but feel that not only is dualism wrong but there is no truth in non-dualism also. Finally, when man reaches the ultimate limit of spiritual progress with the help of Sadhana, he experiences the Nirguna nature of the Divine Mother and remains in oneness with Her. All the ideas, such as I and You, subject and object, bondage and libreation, vice and virtue, merit and demerit, are then all merged in the One."

17. In connection with this topic, the Master mentioned the experience of Hanuman, who was a bright example of the Dasya attitude of devotion. He said, "At one time Ramachandra asked Hanuman, his servant, 'What is your attitude towards Me? How do you look upon, think of and worship Me?' ' When, O Rama,' replied Hanuman, 'I am conscious of my body, in other words, when I feel I am this visible body, I have the conviction that Thou art the Lord and I am Thy servant, Thou art the One to be served and I am the one to serve, Thou art the One to be worshipped and I am the one to worship. When I am conscious of myself as the individual self, one with the mind, the intellect and the soul, I have the conviction that Thou art the Whole and I am a part. And when, again, I remain in Samadhi, in the mood that I am the pure

Self devoid of all qualifying adjuncts, I have the conviction that I am also verily that which Thou art, that Thou and I are one, there being no difference whatsoever. '''

18. The Master said, "One who has realized the non-dual state becomes silent! Non-dualism is not a matter to be described. As soon as one tries to speak or say anything, dualism becomes inevitable. As long as there are thought, imagination, etc., there is also dualism within the mind; non-dual knowledge has not yet been attained. It is only the reality of the Brahman, in other words, the Nirguna aspect of the Divine Mother alone, that has not been contacted by the mouth and thereby defiled'." That is, It has not been expressed by human speech. For this Truth is beyond human mind and intellect; how can It be spoken of or explained by words? This is why the Master said about the non-dual Truth, "My children, it is the ultimate Truth to be realized." The Master therefore used to say: "As long as the ideas of 'I', 'You', and the bodily functions like speaking, walking, etc., are there, one must accept in practice both the aspects, Nirguna and Saguna, or as they are otherwise called the Nitya (the absolute) and the Lila (the relative). You are then for all practical purposes a qualified non-dualist, though you may talk of non-dualism." Many were the examples that the Master gave to illustrate this.

19. He said, "Take, for example, the natural and the reverse orders of the musical scale. You raise the pitch of your voice in the natural order of ' do, re, mi, fa, sol, la, si, do' (sa ri ga ma pa dha ni sa) and lower it in the reverse order of 'do, si, la, sol, fa, mi, re, do'. Similarly you realize the knowledge of Non-duality in Samadhi, come down again and then remain in the I-con-sciousness.

"Again take a Vilva fruit in your hand and try to ascertain which of the three, the outer shell, seeds or the pulp, is the fruit. At first you discard the shell as not being the substance; and do the same with the seeds; and then, on isolating the pulp, say that that is the real Vilva fruit. Then comes the decision that the shell, like the seeds, belongs to what the pulp is made of — it is the shell, seeds and the pulp that together make the Vilva fruit. Similarly, after directly knowing the Absolute, comes the conclusion that that which is the Absolute is in sport the Relative.

"By removing the sheaths of the stem of a banana plant, you reach the pith and think that to be the essence. Then comes the realisation that it is to the sheaths that the pith belongs and it is to the pith that the sheaths belong — it is both these together that make the stem.

"And just as when one goes on removing the coats of an onion nothing is left over, so, in order to ascertain the self, when one goes on eliminating the body, the mind, the intellect etc., and makes sure that none of these is the self, one finds that there is nothing separate called 'I', but everything is He and nothing but He—it is like saying 'It is my Ganga' by putting a fence round a part of the water of the Ganga."

20.   Now to come back to our main topic again. It is needless to say that, when the Master was having the full knowledge of his 'universal I' in Bhavamukha, he dwelt in the realm of Vidya Maya (the Maya leading Godward), a few steps below the attributeless being of the Divine Mother, and was seeing the manifestation of the ' many' from the 'One'. But even while experiencing the many, the knowledge of that One was so clear that the Master felt quite fully that it was he who was doing, thinking and saying, whatever anyone in the world was doing, thinking and saying. Even a glimpse of this state is very wonderful. The Master said that when one day a man was walking upon a bed of grass, he was feeling very much hurt in his chest, as if it was on his chest that the man was walking. In fact, the blood in his chest coagulated to produce black marks, and he began to writhe in pain.

21.   The mood "I am the servant of the Divine Mother", "I am Her devotee", "I am Her child" or "I am a part of Her", was always there in the Master's mind when he came further down to the lower state of the realm of Maya. And still further down is the realm of the Avidya Maya (the Maya leading away from God) or that of lust, anger, worldly attachment. By constant practice, his mind never descended to this state, or, to put it in another way, the Divine Mother pervented its descent to that realm. The Master used to say, "The Mother prevents one who has taken complete refuge in Her from taking a wrong step.'

22.   Therefore, we find that after he attained the Nirvikalpa Samadhi, the limited or the unripe I in him vanished completely. And the little of the 'I' that was left over, was united for all eternity

with the immense or the ripe 'I'. That 'I' sometimes used to feel that it was a part or a limb of the universal I, and again approaching nearer and nearer to that all-pervading I, used to merge in it. It was through this process that he came to know all the ideas of all minds. For, it is this immense I that is the source from which all the ideas of all the minds in the world spring. The Master was able to know and understand all the waves of ideas rising in all the minds in the universe, only because he could remain identified with that all-pervading I. In that high state, the Master's mood, "I am a part of the divine Lord" also gradually vanished, and the universal I or what may be called the "I of the Divine Mother" manifested Itself through him as the spiritual teacher, possessing the power of bestowing grace and inflicting punishment. Therefore, the Master did not then appear to be the "humblest of the humble"; instead, all his actions, such as his movements, behaviour with others, etc., assumed a different form. He, like the mythical wish-fulfilling tree, then asked the devotee what he wanted. We saw the Master at Dakshineswar daily assume that mood in order to bestow his grace on especial devotees. And again we saw him in that mood on January 1, 1886. On that day he was in that mood and by his touch transmitted spirituality to, or awakened the dormant spiritual power in the devotees present there. That is a wonderful story. It will not be out of place to narrate it here.

23. It was the first day of January 1886. It was a little more than two weeks since the devotees had brought the Master, according to the advice of Dr. Mahendralal Sarkar, to a garden house at Kasipur in the north of Calcutta, belonging to Gopal Babu, the son-in-law of Rani Katyayani. The doctor had said that the air in the garden quarters was purer than in Calcutta proper and that it was possible that the Master's disease in the throat would be cured or alleviated if he could live in a place where he could breathe absolutely pure air. It was a few days after he had come to the garden that Dr. Rajendralal Datta came to see him and administered Lycopodium 200. After that it appeared that there was a little alleviation of the disease. But since his coming there, the Master had never got down from the first floor of the house to the ground floor or taken a walk in the garden. He felt much better that day and in the afternoon expressed a desire to have a walk. The devotees were therefore very happy on that day.

Swami Vivekananda was then feeling an intense detachment and had given up all desire for worldly prosperity. He was then living in the company of the Master, and in order to realize the divine Lord, was practising various spiritual exercises according to his instructions. He used to kindle a holy fire under a tree and pass nights in meditation, Japa, reading and other devotional exercises. A few other devotees also such as the junior Gopal, Kali and others brought the necessary articles for helping him in Sadhana, and they themselves also practised it according to their capacity. The lay devotees could not always remain with the Master on account of their various worldly affairs. But whenever they had an opportunity, they came to the Master, made all arrangements about the food and other necessaries for those who always remained busy in the service of the Master, and sometimes stayed there for a day or so. As it was the New Year's day, the offices were closed, and many devotees could come to the garden.

It was 3 p.m. Dressed in a red-bordered cloth, a shirt, a thick wrapper also with red border, a cap covering the ears and a pair of slippers, the Master came down slowly from the first floor with Swami Adbhutananda and entered the hall dowstairs. He observed it closely, and coming out of the western door, started for a walk in the garden. Some of the lay devotees saw him thus going for a walk and followed him with great joy. The young devotees like Narendra were then sleeping in the small room adjacent to the hall, as they were fatigued on account of keeping vigil the previous night. When he saw that the lay devotees were going with the Master, Adbhutananda thought it unnecessary for him to go any farther with him. So he returned on reaching the southern bank of the small pond in front of the hall. He took with him another young devotee, and both of them busied themselves in sweeping and cleaning the Master's room upstairs and in sunning his bedding and clothing.

Of all the lay devotees, Girish was then feeling the greatest attachment to God. At one time the Master highly praised his wonderful faith and said to the other devotees, "Girish has more than a hundred per cent faith. People will hereafter be surprised to see his spiritual progress." On account of the great surge of faith and devotion, Girish always looked upon the Master as the divine Lord Himself, incarnated through His grace to liberate souls from the bondage of the world. Although forbidden by the Master, he expressed publicly this conviction of his, to one and all.   Girish was also present in the garden on that day, and was sitting and conversing under a mango tree with Ram and a few other lay devotees.

Surrounded by the devotees, the Master was slowly proceeding by the broad path in the garden towards the gate and came to the middle of that path near the mango tree where he saw Ram and Girish sitting under its shade. He then addressed Girish and said, "Girish, what have you seen (in me), which makes you say so many things publicly in glorification of me before one and all?"

Although Girish was so abruptly questioned, his faith remained unshaken. Hurriedly and with overflowing adoration, he stood up, came to the path, knelt down at the feet of the Master, and with folded hands, said in a choked voice, "What more can I say about Him, even a fraction of whose glory Vyasa and Valmiki miserably failed to express in their immortal epics and Puranas!"

Hearing Girish's words charged with such wonderful faith, the Master had horripilation all over the body. His mind ascended to a high plane and he was in Samadhi. Then seeing the Master's face illumined with a divine halo, Girish cried out in great joy, "Glory unto Ramakrishna! Glory unto Ramakrishna!" and took the dust of his feet again and again.

Meanwhile in a state of divine semi-consciousness, the Master looked at all present and said smilingly, "What more shall I say to you? May all of you be spiritually awakened!" When the devotees heard those words of blessing and protection from fear, they raised repeated cries of joy, exclaiming, "Glory to Ramakrishna." Some of them saluted him, some showered flowers, some again came and touched his feet. No sooner had the first devotee touched his feet and stood up than the Master in that state of divine semi-consciousness touched the devotees chest, and passing his hand in the upward direction, said, "Awake". As soon as the second person came and saluted him and stood up, he did the same thing to him; so also to the third, to the fourth and so on. In this way he touched, one after another, all of those who approached him thus. And there arose by that marvellous touch a wonderful mood in the mind of each. Some of them began to laugh, some to weep, some to meditate, and some again to call aloud all others in order that they might also

29

be blessed by receiving the grace of the Master—the sea of uncon-
ditioned mercy—and be sharers in the bliss that was overflowing. The
noise and cries were so great that some of the devotees, who afterwards became monks, got up from their sleep and others gave up
the work they were engaged in. They came running and saw that
all the devotees stood surrounding the Master on the pathway
in the garden, and were behaving like madmen. At once they
understood that the Master was now in that same blessed divine
mood under the influence of which he had blessed his special
devotees at Dakshineswar. He was now enacting that same divine
play, the bestowal of his grace, on a wider circle of people that
had now gathered at his feet. Hardly had these devotees, who
were the monks-in-the-making, come, than that state of the Master
changed, and he was in his normal condition again.

24. It was known on enquiry that the devotees blessed by
the Master had wonderful experiences and visions. One felt bliss
and a sort of intoxication such as is produced by smoking hemp;
another, an unknown power creeping up within his body with
accompanying bliss. Others saw ecstatic visions the moment they
shut their eyes—one, of light, another, of the shining form of God
he had been meditating upon but had not been able to see—all
hitherto unseen, unheard-of and unfelt experiences! It was, however, clear that although each had a different vision and experience,
the feeling of being filled with an extraordinary divine bliss was
common to all. More than this, each felt that the extraordinary
mental change or experience was brought about by the trans-
mission of a superhuman power by the Master. There were only
two of the devotees present whom the Master did not touch, saying
"Not now". And it was those two only that considered themselves unfortunate and felt dejected on that happy occasion.[1]

25. Another fact stands out from this, that it was not at all
certain when that divine Power would graciously manifest Itself
through the Master and bless any one. It is also doubtful whether
the Master himself could have known or understood this, in his
normal consciousness.

26. But it is important to note that the Master could become
a great instrument of the Universal I or the Divine Mother in
manifesting power, only because he could give up completely the

---

1 Some days later the Master touched these two also that way.

unripe or limited I. And that wonderful manifestation through him of the aspect of the Divine Mother as the spiritual teacher of man became possible because he completely gave up that unripe I and converted himself into the humblest of the humble. The history of the religions of the world is an eternal witness to the fact that it was only by the merging of the limited I-ness in this way that the mood or the power of the spiritual teacher became manifest in the lives of all the incarnations of the world.

27. We have been hearing from time immemorial that one cannot realize spirituality or God if one held the belief that the spiritual teacher is a mere human being. We have always been repeating with or without faith the hymn, "The spiritual teacher is Brahma, the spiritual teacher is Vishnu, the spiritual teacher is the divine Maheswara" with reference to the teacher who initiates us in Mantras. Many, who are under the spell of a foreign system of education, and have given up their own national culture and education based on religion, regard it to be a great sin to use such words with reference to a particular human being, and are not slow to indulge in noisy controversy. For, who then knew that, though it manifested itself through the personalities of some human beings, the mood of the spiritual teacher was not anything rooted within the realm of human consciousness? Who then knew that, even as She manifested Herself as water, air, food and other materials for the maintenance of the bodies of all beings, it was the Divine Mother that revealed Herself in the mood of the teacher through the body and mind of the Master, rendered pure, awakened and free from the limited ego, for the purpose of removing the three kinds of miseries scorching man—for freeing him from the bondage, in which the tight chains of Maya have been holding him? And who then knew that one became the instrument for the manifestation of that mood or power in direct proportion to one's capacity to give up one's egoism of the unripe I? Ordinarily a very little, a drop or two, so to speak, of this divine power manifests in the minds of persons who are 'liberated in life' (Jivan-muktas). The manifestation is so slight that it eludes our understanding. But when, through an abundance of good fortune, one witnesses the wonderful Lila of that divine power in Krishna, Buddha, Chaitanya, Sankara, Jesus and other incarnations of the past, and in Ramakrishna in the present age, one feels in one's heart of hearts that

such manifestation of power does not belong to any mortal man but to God alone. Only then do the scales of dross and delusion fall off from the eyes of those who suffer from this world-disease and who consequently go in pursuit of false values. They cry out then in an outburst of joy, "O Master, Thou art not man—thou art He!" Therefore we see it is the universal Mother who manifests Herself as the exalted divine power and removes all kinds of impurities due to spiritual ignorance from the human mind. This is what is called the mood or power of the spiritual teacher (the Guru-bhava or the Guru-sakti). It is this divine power (Sakti) which the scriptures speak of as the spiritual teacher, and it is to this power that man is called upon to offer his heart's reverence and adoration with unflinching faith.

28. The human mind that is conversant with the gross world only and is just learning the first lesson in devotion and reverence, cannot of course love a bodiless intangible power; and it is for this reason that the scriptures advise us to look upon the person who initiates us into this life divine as the Guru and to have devotion to his personality, seeing the real divine Guru in and through him. Therefore, to those who say that they have reverence and adoration for the power manifesting as the spiritual teacher but cannot, on that account alone, bow their heads in reverence and devotion to the body through which that power manifests itself—to those who thus make a distinction between the power and the medium of its manifestation—, our reply is a grave warning that they should not fall a prey to self-deception by discriminating between the unseen power and its seen medium of manifestation, and pretend to pay homage to the unseen while neglecting to do so to its seen manifestation. The difference itself is as thin and indistinct as that between fire and its burning power; and as to the act of adoration of the unseen and the unknown, the least said the best. How can one of the two be adored and the other rejected? A man who loves or admires somebody feels special attachment for even a trifling thing used by his beloved. He considers even a flower touched by him or a piece of cloth worn or a small thing used by him as sacred. The very ground he treads is regarded by him to be very dear and precious. Does it then need to be explained that he will have a natural reverence for the body through which He accepts his worship and bestows grace on him? Those who disagree do not understand at all what is meant by the mood of

the spiritual teacher. For, one who has true devotion to that Power cannot but have devotion to the body, the receptacle of that Power.

29. The Master used to illustrate this point by citing the example of Vibhishana. He said, "At one time, long after Sri Ramachandra passed away, a boat sank and a man was thrown by the waves on the coast of Lanka. Vibhishana is immortal and has been ruling over Lanka through the three cycles of time, since Ravana's death. The news reached him. The mouths of many of the Rakshasas in the assembly began to water at the news of the coming of a dainty morsel, the human body. But this brought about an extraordinary mood in Vibhishana, the king. He began to say again and again with tears in his eyes, and voice choked with devotion, 'O what good luck! O what good fortune!' The Rakshasas could not understand his feeling and were dumb-founded. Vibhishana then explained, 'Is it not a rare good fortune that after a very long time I shall get today the opportunity of seeing a human body such as the one in which my Rama-chandra set His foot on Lanka and blessed me? It seems to me that Ramachandra Himself is coming in that manner.' Saying so, the king came to the coast with all his ministers, courtiers and other nobles and took the man to the palace with great love and reverence. Then the king seated him on the throne and together with his family began to serve and worship him like an obedient servant. He kept him there at Lanka for some time, made presents of jewels and other precious articles, bade him good-bye and sent him home escorted by his servants."

30. Finishing the story, the Master remarked, "This happens when there is true devotion. One then remembers God through the association of even a trifling thing and becomes filled with love and devotion. Haven't you heard that Sri Chaitanya was in ecstasy saying, 'Ah, drums are made of this earth!' One day, while he was passing through a certain place, he was told that the people of that village maintained themselves by making and selling the drums that were played at the time of singing the Lord's name. As soon as he heard it, he exclaimed, "Ah, drums are made of this earth!' and saying so he immediately passed into ecstasy and lost normal consciousness. For there was the association: of this earth drums are made; the drums are played at the time of singing

the name of Hari, that Hari is the life of life in all, more beautiful than the most beautiful.   All these thoughts at once passed through his mind, and it became completely concentrated on Hari.   A man who has such devotion to his Guru cannot but remember him through association, not only when he sees his relatives but also when he sees an ordinary man of the Guru's native village; and out of his respect for the Guru, he salutes the villager, takes the dust of his feet, feeds him, and serves him in every way.   When this state is reached, one does not see any shortcomings in one's spiritual teacher.   Then the truth of the proverb, 'My spiritual teacher is Nityananda (i.e. the divine Lord who is of the nature of eternal bliss) even if he frequents a tavern', applies to him; otherwise a human being cannot but have good and bad qualities.   But just as everything looks yellow to a jaundiced eye, so he, owing to his overflowing devotion to the Lord, sees God and not man in the Guru.   His devotion then shows him that it is God who has become the whole universe.   It is He alone who has become the spiritual teacher, father, mother, man, cattle—everything, sentient or insentient."

31.   One day at Dakshineswar, an arrogant but sincere young devotee (Vaikunthanath Sanyal) was raising objections against what the Master was telling him.   He continued arguing even when the Master had repeated his statement several times, at which he gave him a mild rebuke and said, "What sort of a man are you? I say it again and again, and still you don't accept it!"   The heart of the young man was touched and he said, "When you say it, I accept it of course.   It was for the sake of argument that I spoke thus."   On hearing this, the Master smilingly said with an expression of delight in his face, "Do you know what devotion to the spiritual teacher is like?   One endowed with it is certain to perceive immediately whatever the spiritual teacher mentions.   Arjuna had that devotion.   One day while driving with Arjuna in a chariot, Krishna looked at the sky and said, 'See, friend, how beautiful is the flock of pigeons flying there!'   Arjuna saw it and immediately said, 'Yes, friend, very beautiful pigeons, indeed!'   The very next moment Sri Krishna looked again and said, 'How strange, friend, they are by no means pigeons.'   Arjuna saw them and said, 'Quite so, friend, they are not pigeons at all.'   Now try to understand the matter; Arjuna's truthfulness was unquestionable. He could never have flattered Krishna when he said so.   But he had

such great devotion to him and faith in his words that he actually
saw with his eyes whatever Krishna described to him, real or fanci-
ful."

32. If, as the scriptures point out, the spiritual teacher's
power to remove the darkness of ignorance is understood to be
a special power of God Himself in the manner spoken of above,
then another fact also must simultaneously be admitted as true.
And that is this: the spiritual teacher is one and not many.
Although the receptacles of this power or the bodies through
which it is manifested are different, your spiritual teacher and mine
are not different but One only, that One being none other than
that Power. As an example of this may be quoted the story in the
Mahabharata of Ekalavya, who accepted as his teacher an earthen
statue of Dronacharya and worshipped him in it with devotion
and thereby acquired proficiency in archery. Reasonable as this
fact is, it requires a great deal of time and Sadhana for a man to
accept it whole-heartedly; and once he accepts it, he has no alternative but to worship the spiritual teacher in the body through
which that divine Power has bestowed grace on him. The Master
used to tell us, as an instance of this, what Hanuman, a bright
example of steadfast devotion, said. The Master said, "At one
time during the battle of Lanka, Ramachandra and Lakshmana
were bound with a noose made of snakes by the great hero Megh-
anada. Then they remembered Garuda, the eternal enemy
of the race of snakes, and invoked him there. As soon as the
snakes saw Garuda, they became frightened and fled in whatever
directions they could. Pleased with his devotee Garuda, Ramachandra appeared before him in the form of Vishnu, who was the
eternal object of worship of Garuda, and explained to him that
Vishnu had thus incarnated Himself as Rama. But Hanuman did
not like to see Ramachandra assume the form of Vishnu; and the
only thought he had in his mind was how soon he would re-assume
the form of Rama. Ramachandra did not take long to know that
sentiment of Hanuman. Immediately after bidding good-bye to
Garuda, he re-assumed the form of Rama and asked Hanuman,
'Why were you disturbed, my child, seeing me in the form of Vishnu?
You are possessed of the great knowledge, and it is of course not
beyond your understanding that the one who is Rama is Vishnu too.'
Hanuman replied humbly, 'It is true that the same supreme Self
has assumed both the forms and therefore there is no difference

between the consort of Sri (i.e., Vishnu) and that of Janaki (i.e., Rama); but my mind is always anxious to see the feet of the lotus-eyed consort of Janaki only; He is my all in all. It is through that form that I saw the manifestation of the divine Lord and had my life's aim fulfilled'."

33. Thus it is evident that the power of the spiritual teacher is a power of the universal Mother and that power is either lying dormant or is awake in all men. This is why an aspirant highly devoted to the spiritual teacher, reaches at last a spiritual state when that power, manifesting through the aspirant himself, goes on explaining to him the hidden complex truths of spirituality. The aspirant has then no more need to ask any outside agent to have any doubt removed. The divine Lord said to Arjuna in the Gita (ii. 52): "When your intellect is freed from the delusion due to ignorance, there will be no necessity on your part to have anything to do with the teachings of the scriptures, such as 'this should be heard', 'that is in the scriptures' and so on; you will go beyond all this and will be able to understand everything yourself." Such is the state the aspirant attains then.

34. The Master said with reference to this state: "It is the mind that becomes at last the spiritual teacher and acts as such. 'A human teacher imparts a Mantra in the ears; the divine Teacher imparts it in the soul.' " But there is a gulf of difference between the mind then and now. At that time the mind, by assuming the nature of pure Sattva, would get purified, and so becomes a conduit for manifesting the higher power of God. But now, in the state of ignorance, it wants to be engrossed in the enjoyment of pleasures, in lust, anger etc., and turns away from God.

35. The Master used to say, "The spiritual teacher is, as it were, a woman-friend; until Radha is united with Krishna, there is no end to her love-errands. Even so, as long as the Sadhaka is not united with the chosen Ideal, the work of the spiritual teacher does not come to an end." It is thus that the supremely glorious spiritual teacher takes hold of the hand of the disciple, who is burning to know the truth, ascends to higher and higher regions of spirituality, and bringing him at last before his chosen Ideal, says, 'Boy, look there!' and disappears at once."

36. Hearing the Master say so, one day a devotee thought, "Then some day the separation from the spiritual teacher is inevitable," and with a painful heart he asked, "Sir, where does

he go then?"   The Master said in reply, "The teacher then merges in the chosen Ideal.   The three viz., the teacher, Krishna (the chosen Ideal) and Vaishnava (the devotee) are One, and the One is the three."

CHAPTER IV

THE FIRST MANIFESTATION OF THE MOOD OF THE SPIRITUAL TEACHER

(TOPICS: 1. 'Fruits first, flowers next' is the law with all incarnations 2. The first manifestation of the Guru-mood in the Master 3. A similar event in the life of Jesus 4. The Jewish pilgrimage of those days 5. Jesus explaining the scriptures in the temple of Jehovah 6. Refutation of Max Muller's view 7. Why did the Master marry: discussion of various views on the question 8. The Hindu marriage and its ideal 9. Knowledge through experience and discrimination 10. The Master on how to overcome urge for pleasures. 11. Non-observance of continence and national degradation 12. The Master married for the revival of the great ideals connected with it. 13. The Holy Mother's remarks on this 14. The Master married to teach people 15. The need of pursuing the Master's ideal 16. A few objections to the Master's ideal answered 17. The Master's marriage and his Teacher-mood.)

Ignorant of My supreme nature as the great Lord of all beings, foolish people slight Me who am in a human body.

—*Gita,* IX. 11.

We find the mood of the spiritual teacher manifested in the Master from his very childhood, though it must be admitted that its full manifestation took place only in his youth after he had attained the Nirvikalpa Samadhi. Let no one think that the above statement is an exaggeration intended to extol the Master's greatness. If anybody critically studies the Master's life without any bias, he will never be tempted to entertain that error. Let anybody study, with all the critical power at his command, the events of this extraordinary life, and he will then find that it is his own power of judgement that gets baffled, bewildered and benumbed in making any such critical estimate of him. Our own minds were not a little suspicious at first. Many of us doubted, tested and examined the Master more critically than it will perhaps even occur to many in the present age. It is difficult to enumerate the occasions when most of us, doubting the Master, went to test him and got defeated and hung our heads in shame. We have given the reader a little indication

of this already in the second chapter, and more will be given
later. The reader will then be in a position to judge for
himself.

1. The Master always used to quote in connection with the
lives of the eternally free Isvarakotis the saying, "Fruits first,
flowers next, as is the case with the creepers called gourds." The
meaning of the saying is that in the case of Isvarakotis, whatever
practices they are seen to undertake for achieving perfection in
matters spiritual, are only for the purpose of showing people that
they will have to undertake similar practices in order to achieve
like results. From a critical study of the lives of these persons,
one fact stands out. It is this: that from their childhood they
always behave in a way which is possible only for those who are
already in full possession of spiritual enlightenment, but none
the less they are seen to work hard for its acquisition in their later
life. It is as if the knowledge is already theirs from the very commencement of their lives, but yet they seem to work for its attainment afterwards. When this holds good even in the case of
Isvarakotis, it is superfluous to say that it applies to the divine
incarnations also. The manifestation of such knowledge in them is
seen throughout their lives—such is the verdict of the scriptures.
And it is also seen that there is a great similarity between many
of the actions of the incarnations of different ages. We find,
for example, the power of transmitting spirituality to others
by a touch in the lives of every one of them—Jesus, Sri
Chaitanya and Sri Ramakrishna. Besides, in several other
respects too we find similarities in their lives. A few of these
may be listed as follows: some particularly holy men were
informed in a superhuman way of the advent of these incarnations. The mood of the spiritual teacher was manifest in them
from their childhood. They knew from their boyhood that they
had come down on earth, out of compassion, as incarnations
in order to show special paths to the people in general. There
are many other facts as well. Therefore, no one need be surprised to hear that the mood of the spiritual teacher was manifest
in the Master's life from his childhood. The incarnations are
a class by themselves. One will fall into a great error if one
thinks that, because such events cannot happen in the lives
of ordinary men, they cannot occur in the lives of incarnations
also.

2. We find a very clear instance of the first manifestation of the mood of the spiritual teacher in the life of the Master at Kamarpukur. He had then been already invested with the sacred thread, and must have been about nine or ten years of age. The well-known scholars of that part of the country were invited on the occasion of a Sraddha ceremony to the house of the Lahas, the landlords of the village. And as usual in such meetings of scholars, there started a heated controversy amongst them. When no decision on a particular disputed point in the scriptures could be arrived at, the boy Gadadhar said to a scholar known to him, "Can't the point at issue be decided this way?" Many boys of the village came to the meeting out of curiosity and they could not understand even a little of the meaning of the noisy controversy accompanied by the gesticulations of the scholars. Some of these boys took all this as a huge joke and indulged in boisterous laughter. Some others mimicked the gestures of the scholars, while still others remained completely indifferent to it and engaged themselves in play. Therefore, this scholar was not a little surprised to see how this wonderful boy had listened with patience to what they had said, how he had understood everything and arrived at the right conclusion by reflecting on the matter. He then told the others known to him about Gadadhar's conclusion. Finding that it was the only possible solution regarding the disputed point, they explained it to all others. All then admitted unanimously that it was the only rational solution regarding the point at dispute and looked for the person whose keen intellect was the first to arrive at that wonderful solution. When they came to know that it was the boy Gadadhar who had solved the problem, some of them became astounded, and thinking the boy to be possessed of divine powers, remained gazing steadfastly at him, while others, filled with joy, took him in their laps and blessed him.

3. It is necessary to discuss the subject a little more. There is an event recorded in the Bible (Luke: 2.42-48) exactly similar to this, in the life of Jesus, an incarnation of the divine Lord and the founder of the Christian religion. He was then twelve years of age. His poor, god-fearing father ' Joseph and mother Mary started that year on foot with him in the company of other pilgrims from his native village of Nazareth in the province of Galilee to offer worship at the famous temple at Jerusalem. This place of pilgrimage of the Jews was like the pilgrim centres of the Hindus.

Here the devout aspirant felt blessed by directly experiencing the manifestation of Jehovah in the gold casket and worshipped the Deity by burning incense on an altar before Him and by offering leaves and flowers, fruits and roots, and by sacrificing animals and birds like sheep and pigeons.   The sacrificing of pigeons and other birds in the Hindu places of pilgrimage like Kamakhya and Vindhya-vasini is in vogue even today.   Worship, offering and sacrifices being over, Joseph and Mary started with their companions on the return journey to their village.

4.   At that time the condition of the pilgrims coming from various quarters to visit Jerusalem was to a certain extent similar to that facing pilgrims proceeding on foot to Puri and other places of pilgrimage here, before the railways had been laid.   There was the same expression of man's simple faith in God and dependence on Him; the same conglomerations of humanity on the move organised into groups for protection against thieves and brigands; the same dusty tracks, long and narrow, rendered beautiful here and there with irrigation wells, ponds and clusters of trees; the same guide-priests functioning as companions and leaders of the pilgrims; the same inns, rest-houses and charitable guest centres providing food and shelter at nights; the same petty shops vending provisions and other necessaries; and above all those same swarms of mosquitoes rendering a friendly service to the pilgrims by making it impossible for them to forget their religious preoccupations in deep sleep.

5.   Now in the course of their travel the parents of Jesus found that he was not with them.   They thought that he was perhaps coming behind the party with some other pilgrim boys.   But even after travelling a long distance, when they found Jesus not coming up, they were greatly perturbed; and when a thorough search in the big party revealed that he was not with them, they anxiously turned their steps towards Jerusalem again.   They looked for him in various places there, but could get no information about him. At last they entered the temple in search of him and found that the boy Jesus was sitting and discussing the scriptures among the Sadhakas well versed in them and was charming all by his lucid and inspired explanations of the complicated points at issue which confounded even the scholars.

6.   The great scholar Max Muller has expressed a doubt in his *Life and Sayings of Ramakrishna* about the truth of the incident in the Master's life stated earlier on the ground of its great

similarity with the corresponding incident in the life of the Lord Jesus just mentioned.   He has not even shrunk from passing the uncharitable remark that the English-knowing disciples of Sri Ramakrishna have introduced the story of Jesus' childhood into the life of their Master in order to heighten the latter's greatness. In spite of the great savant's learning and intelligence, we feel unable to agree with him.   We do not want to dilate more on it beyond stating that we heard of that event of the Master's childhood from many old people of his birthplace at Kamarpukur and also from the Master himself on several occasions.

7.   When studying the Master's life, one is confronted with the question: why did he marry?   Why did a person who was never inclined to have any carnal relationship with his wife marry at all?   It is of course difficult to find the reason.   The following points may, however, be considered in this connection:

(a) To the suggestion that his relatives married him against his will, when on reaching youth he became almost mad owing to his constant thinking of God, we reply, it is silly to entertain such an idea.   From his childhood no one could make him do anything against his will, in however trivial a matter.   Again, whenever he wanted to do anything, he never failed to accomplish it by some means or other.   Take, for instance, his having for his Bhiksha-mata a blacksmith woman named Dhani at the time of his investiture with the sacred thread.   Social rules and regulations were not observed in the villages with as much laxity as in Calcutta; so no one could act according to his own sweet will in the villages. The Master's parents also were not a little orthodox, and it was the custom of the family too to assign the duty of the Bhiksha-mata to a Brahmana lady.   So all the elders of the family of the boy Gadadhar were against his receiving Bhiksha from a blacksmith woman.   In spite of all these, opposition melted away before Gadadhar's insistence, and Dhani became the Bhiksha-mata. This was a matter for no small surprise.   It was even so in all other matters.   The Master's will and words ever prevailed against the wills and desires of others.   How then can we say that in such an important event in his life he merely acquiesced because of the pressure of his relatives?

(b) It might again be said, "What is the necessity of admitting that the Master had the idea of renouncing everything out of love of God from his very childhood?   We can say instead that the

Master at first had the desire to marry and enjoy worldly pleasures like people in general, but that no sooner had he attained maturity than there came about a sudden revolutionary change in his mind, and that a violent storm of detachment from the world and attachment to God raged in his heart, overturning all his previous plans and desires. In that case all objections will be removed in a natural way. All objections are removed if it be said that the Master's marriage took place before that storm began to rage."

(c) We say that although this explanation is plausible, there are some irrefutable objections against this attitude. First, the Master was married at the age of twenty-four, and the storm of renunciation was then furiously raging in his heart. So it is quite unlikely that a person like him, who hesitated all his life to give the slightest trouble to anyone for his own sake, should have proceeded thoughtlessly to do an act which he knew full well would be the cause of lifelong suffering for a lady. Secondly, the more we think, the more can we understand that no act in the Master's life was done without a purpose. Thirdly, it is quite certain that he married willingly; for he told his nephew, Hriday and all the members of the family when they were in search of a bride, that it had already been divinely settled that he should be married to the daughter of Ramachandra Mukhopadhyaya of the village of Jayrambati. The reader will either be surprised to hear this, or will disbelieve it and say, "Fancy, speaking of such incredible things! Can these statements be accepted in the twentieth century?" We have to say in reply, "Whether you believe it or not, it was indeed a fact. There are many still living who will bear it out. Why don't you just investigate?" When in their search for a bride his relatives failed to get one, the Master himself said, "Go and see such and such a girl of such and such a village. She has been 'marked with a straw'[1] for the purpose." Therefore it is clear that the Master knew that he would be married. What was more, he knew also

---

[1] There is a custom among cultivators in Bengal villages, to attach, as a mark, a straw to fruits like cucumber which they consider the best in their garden, and offer them to the divine Lord. It is done to prevent the cultivator or any one else in the family from inadvertently plucking and selling them. The Master applied the simile to this case, meaning thereby that it was divinely ordained that he should be married to the daughter of such and such a person and that the girl had, as it were, been reserved by Providence to be his bride.

the place of marriage and the person to whose daughter he would be married. He did not also raise any objection to that. It was of course during his Bhavasamadhi that he had come to know of it. What then is the meaning of the Master's marriage?

(d) Some reader, well versed in the scriptures, will perhaps be annoyed and say, "How silly! You are raising a storm in a tea-cup. First consult some scriptures and other books, and then venture to record the events of the lives of great and pious souls. Scriptures say that actions accumulated in previous lives that are yet to bear fruit (Sanchita) and those that are done after the attaiment of the knowledge of Brahman (Agami) are all destroyed when God-vision or perfect Knowledge is attained. But the results of the works done in the previous births that are already bearing fruit (Prarabdha) have to be experienced in this life even if the knowledge of Brahman is attained. Suppose there are some arrows in a quiver tied to the back of a fowler. He has shot one arrow at a little bird on a tree, and has taken another in his hand, ready to shoot. Just at this moment there arises a sudden outburst of compassion in the mind of the fowler and he resolves he will no more injure any living being. He throws away the arrow in his hand and also the arrows on his back. But can he withdraw the arrow he has already shot at the bird? The arrows on his back are, as it were, his actions accumulated (Sanchita) in past lives; the arrow in his hand represents future (Agami) acts which he is yet to do in this life. These kinds of acts are destroyed on the acquisition of knowledge. But his Prarabdha acts, being in the process of fruition,are like the arrow that has already been discharged; their results he has to experience. So even great souls like Sri Ramakrishna have to experience the results of their Prarabdha actions so long as their present embodied state lasts. The experiencing of these results is inevitable; and they know and understand what kinds of events will happen in their lives according to their Prarabdha acts. Therefore, it was not extraordinary for Sri Ramakrishna to mention whom he would marry and where his marriage would take place."

(e) In reply to the above objection we say that we are not really learned so well in the scriptures. But so far as we know, we can say that a man of right knowledge has not got to experience even the results of his Prarabdha actions. For he has dedicated to God for ever the mind which feels pain and pleasure. Where

then is the possibility in his mind of experiencing pain and pleasure? But if you say that Prarabdha actions are experienced in his body, how is even that possible? If he by his own will keeps a little of I-ness for some reason or other, as for instance for doing good to others, it is only then that he will be conscious of his mind and body again and experience the results of his Prarabdha actions. Therefore, men of right knowledge can experience or abstain from experiencing at will the results of those actions; such is the power they attain. That is why they are called " the conquerors of the worlds", "the conquerors of death", "all-knowing" and so on.

(*f*) Again, if we are to believe the experience of Sri Ramakrishna himself, he cannot even be classed amongst the ordinary men of absolute knowledge. For, we have heard him say again and again, "One who was Rama and Krishna is now Ramakrishna" ; that is, He who incarnated Himself as Rama and Krishna in past ages is present in the form of Sri Ramakrishna and is manifesting a wonderful divine sport. If one is to believe this, one must admit that he is an incarnation of God, eternally pure, eternally awakened and eternally free. And when one admits that, one cannot say that he is under the control of Prarabdha. Therefore, we are to give a different interpretation of the Master's marriage. We give the same below:

(*g*) The Master talked to us on the topic of his marriage on several occasions and joked about it in a very charming manner. One day at Dakshineswar he sat down to take his food; and Balaram Basu and a few other devotees sat and conversed with him. That day the Holy Mother had started for Kamarpukur for a stay of a few months; for it was the occasion of the marriage of the Master's nephew Ramlal.

The Master (To Balaram): "Well, just tell me of what significance is marriage to one like me? What is the place of a wife in the life of one who does not even know whether his wearing cloth is on or off?" Balaram smiled and kept silent.

The Master: "Oh! I see (taking up a little vegetable from the plate and showing it to Balaram); it is for this that there was marriage; otherwise who would cook for me this way! (Balaram and the other devotees laughed). Really, who would have cared to see how I took my food? They went away today, — (the devotees did not understand who went) — Ramlal's aunt; do you understand? Ramlal is going to be married; so they have all

30

gone to Kamarpukur. I stood and looked on impassively. Really, it was as if just someone went. But afterwards there was some anxiety as to who would cook for me. Don't you see? All kinds of food do not agree with my stomach, and sometimes there is not consciousness enough to take food. She (the Holy Mother) knows what kind of food suits me; she makes this or that preparation; that's why the anxiety arose as to who would do it."

(h) Raising the topic of his marriage, one day at Dakshineswar the Master said, "Do you know why one has to marry? There are ten kinds of sanctifying ceremonies for a Brahmana's body, and marriage is one of them. It is only when one has performed all of them that one can become a religious teacher." He used to say again, "One who becomes a man of perfect knowledge (Paramahamsa) has finished experiencing all states, from those of the scavengers and sweepers to those of kings and emperors. Otherwise how could true dispassion come? The mind will feel eager to experience that which it has not experienced and will become restless; do you understand? A 'piece' has to move through all the squares before it reaches the 'home'. Have you not seen it at the time of the game of dice? It is similar to that."

8. Although the Master stated this as the reason for the marriage of an ordinary teacher of religion, we shall now explain the special reason for the Master's marriage, as we have understood it. The scriptures teach us at every step that the purpose of marriage is not enjoyment. To observe the rule of maintaining the creation of God by producing virtuous children and thereby doing good to society should be the purpose of the Hindu marriage. The scriptures tell us this again and again. Does it mean that the Hindu should have no self-interest in his marriage? Do the scriptures teach such absurd things? No, they do not. The authors of the scriptures had perfect insight into human nature. They knew that the average man, weak as he is, cared for nothing but self-interest and that he would undertake nothing unless it promoted the same. So when they laid the above rule about marriage, they took this feature of human character fully into account. They knew that the only way to help self-centred man is to help him connect his self-interest with some high ideals and motives. Men would otherwise be entangled in the bondage of births and deaths and suffer endless pain.

9. Man runs after the sensuous enjoyments of sight, taste, etc.,

and considers them to be very pleasing and attractive, only because he has forgotten his own nature, which is eternally free. But, ah! how few are the people who are intelligent enough to understand that all pleasure is connected for ever with pain, and that if one wants to enjoy pleasure, one will have to be simultaneously ready to suffer pain also! Swami Vivekananda used to say, "Pleasure comes to people with a crown of thorns on its head." People who are busy enjoying pleasure only have no leisure to think that it has this crown of thorns on its head and that they will have to be ready to hug pain also if they welcome pleasure as their own. Therefore the scriptures remind them of this fact and say, "Children, why do you consider the attainment of pleasure as the goal of your life? If pleasure is accepted, pain also has to be welcomed. Why do you not find your life's fulfilment in a higher value and look upon the pleasurable and painful experiences of life as your teachers? That higher value, the one worth-while aim of life, is to be delivered from both pleasure and pain for eternity." The aim of the authors of the scriptures is evidently to introduce an element of discrimination between good and evil, the permanent and the impermanent, into the enjoyments of the married life. Through the inevitable round of pleasurable and painful experiences, they seek to lead man on to a thorough dispassion for the seeming, momentary pleasures of the world, so that he may thereafter be filled with a genuine love of God and go forward with great eagerness to be blessed with His vision, taking Him to be the essence of all essences.

10. There is no doubt about the fact that the mind will give up what it enjoys with discrimination — that is, with proper assessment of advantages and disadvantages. That is why the Master said, " Children! the discrimination between the real and the unreal is very necessary. One should always have discrimination and say to one's mind, 'You, mind, are eager to enjoy many things—to eat this, to put on that and so on. But discriminate and see that the five elements out of which potatoes, rice, pulses, etc., are made, are also the ingredients of Sandesh, Rasagolla and other delicious sweets. Again, the bodies of yourself and of all other men, as also of animals such as cows, goats, or sheep, are made of the very bones, flesh, blood and marrow derived from the same five elements of which the body of a beautiful woman too is made. Why then do you crave and die for it ? By

no means will it lead you to the realization of God, the Existence-Knowledge-Bliss.' If the mind cannot desist from them still, then they should be enjoyed once or twice with due discrimination, and then finally renounced. Take this example: the mind is persisting in the desire to eat Rasagolla and would by no means obey the reins of restraint; all your efforts at discrimination are being set at naught. Then bring some Rasagollas, put them into your mouth, and say to the mind while masticating them, 'Mind, this is what is called Rasagolla ; this is also made of a combination of the five elements of which potatoes and Patols are made. This also, when eaten, will be converted into blood, flesh, faeces and urine within the body; it is sweet as long as it is in the mouth;you will not feel the taste when it goes below the throat; again, if you eat too much of it, you will fall ill. And still you are so intensely hankering after such a thing! Fie upon you! Now that you have taken it, don't want to eat it again.' (Looking at the devotees who were to renounce the world)—it is only with regard to small matters that their renunciation is possible after their enjoyment with discrimination; but with regard to big things, this is not possible. One gets entangled as soon as one begins to indulge in their enjoyment. That is why such desires should be driven away from the mind by becoming aware of their defect through discrimination."

11. Oh! how few are the people who entertain such a high idea in their minds at the present time, though the scriptures speak of it in glowing terms! How few are those who make themselves and the society blessed by observing continence in married life according to capacity! How few are the wives who stand by the side of their husbands, urging them to undertake this high vow so beneficent to the world at large, let alone its relevancy to the realization of God! How few are the husbands, again, who accept that the aim of life is renunciation and teach it to their wives! Alas, India, just try to think and see into what a spineless beast you have been converted by the doctrine of Western materialism, which regards worldly enjoyments as the be-all and end-all of life, and which has entered into your very marrow! Was it without any reason that Sri Ramakrishna said to his world-renouncing devotees, pointing out to them the defect in modern married life, "Ah! if it is wrong to make the enjoyment of worldly objects the *summum bonum* of life, then do you think simply throwing a few

flowers[1] at the time of marriage will make it pure or free from all blemishes?" It is, indeed, doubtful whether the indulgence in sensual pleasure in married life was ever so excessive as it is now in India. At the present time we have almost forgotten that, besides the satisfaction of the senses, there is a very sacred and high purpose in marriage, and forgetting this is the reason why we are being reduced to a state worse than that of beasts. It is only in order to destroy this beastliness of men and women of modern India that the Master, the teacher of the people, was married. Like all the other acts of his life, the act of marriage also was performed for the good of all.

12. "Whatever is done here (meaning himself)," said the Master, "is done for you all. Ah! if I do all the sixteen parts [2] (the whole), you may possible do one. Again, if I piss standing, [3] you rascals will do it turning round and round." It is for this reason only that the Master took upon his shoulders the duties and responsibilities of married life and followed in practice that very high ideal before the eyes of all, by actually discharging them to the farthest limit. If the Master had not been himself married, the lay disciples would have said, "It is only because he is not married, that he is able to talk glibly on continence. It is only because he has not made his wife his own and has never lived together with her that it is possible for him to give us long sermons." It was only to forestall all such senseless assessment that the Master not only married but had his wedded wife in the days of her youth by his side at Dakshineswar. When the state of divine madness in him became normal after he had had the holy vision of the Divine Mother, he lived together with his wife, directly feeling the manifestation of the Divine Mother in her, worshipped her as the Mahavidya, the divine Shodasi, and then offered himself to her as the Divine. He lived together with her continually for eight months, sharing even the same bed. He himself went sometimes to Kamarpukur, and sometimes to Jayrambati, to visit the house of his father-in-law, and spent there a month or two for the training of his wife and for her mental peace and happiness.

---

[1] The ceremony of marriage requires the use of flowers among other things.—Tr.

[2] The metaphor is from the sixteen annas that make a rupee, the Indian coin.—Tr.

[3] This is regarded opprobrious amongst the Hindus.—Tr.

13. Remembering the events of the time when the Master lived with her at Dakshineswar, the Holy Mother says even now to women devotees, "It cannot be expressed in words in what wonderful divine moods he passed his days and nights then. In that state of divine semi-consciousness what strange and wonderful words he spoke and with what flow! Sometimes he laughed, sometimes he wept, and sometimes was quite motionless in ecstasy. That was how he passed whole nights. What a wonderul presence and what an ecstasy! The whole of my body would tremble to see that, and I would wish the night might soon come to an end. I did not then understand anything of ecstasy. One night when I saw that his ecstasy did not come to an end, I was frightened, and wept and sent for Hriday. He came and went on repeating the Lord's name in his ears, when, after a long time, he regained normal consciousness. Then, when he came to know of my suffering, anxiety and fear, he himself taught me how, in particular kinds of ecstasy, particular names and Mantras of God were to be repeated into his ears. After that I did not feel so much frightened; he would return to normal consciousness when those names and Mantras were uttered into his ears. A long time passed that way, when one day he asked me to go to bed separately in the music room, as he had come to know that I had no sleep in the nights and remained in suspense, watching when and what kinds of ecstasy he might have." The supremely revered Holy Mother says that the Master taught her then all domestic matters such as how to place the wick in the lamp, how to assess the nature of each member of the household, how to behave with each of them, and how to behave when she went to the house of someone else. He taught her also devotional exercises, the reciting of the names and glories of God, meditation, Samadhi and even the knowledge of Brahman. O men rearing families! How many of you teach your own wives this way? How many of you can have devotion to your wives, respect and love for them all your lives this way, even if for some reason or other the very contemptible physical relationship comes to an end forthwith?

14. We, therefore, say that it was for you. alone that this wonderful incarnation of the age married, lived a life with no physical relationship for even a single day with his wife, and at the same time maintained a sweet and loving attitude towards her all through life. He did all this, so that you might learn that

it was not for indulgence in sensual pleasure that the institution of marriage had come into being, but that it carried with it the very high moral purpose: that both of you, wife and husband, might keep your aim fixed at this high ideal and be blessed by observing continence (Brahmacharya) according to your capacity in married life, and that you might prove a blessing to the modern society- a society that has become devoid of vigour, devoid of grace and devoid of power—by producing heroic and virtuous offspring of wonderful intelligence and memory. In the ages past there was no necessity to demonstrate this ideal, as it was more or less accepted by the people. But it is not so today. So unlike any of the great spiritual teachers of the past—Rama, Krishna, Buddha, Jesus, Sankara, Chaitanya and others—Ramakrishna has set an example in this respect for the benefit of you, me and all. Thus a sacred mould (ideal) of married life, unseen and unheard of in the past, has been cast for the first time in the world as a result of the severe and life-long austerities and Sadhana of the Master. Now, as the Master used to say, "Cast your own lives into that 'ideal-mould' and get them shaped after it."

15. "But—" says the married householder. Yes, we see your difficulty. We, therefore, reply, quoting what Swami Vivekananda said in speaking of spiritual practices in general, "Do you think that each of you can become a Paramahamsa Ramakrishna? That is not to be; for, 'neither will nine maunds of oil burn nor will Radha dance'. [1] Only one Paramahamsa Ramakrishna is born in the world; ' only one lion lives in a forest'." O rearers of families! We also similarly say in reply to your 'But — ': the Master knew very well that it is beyond your power to observe absolute continence (Brahmacharya) living with your wife like him. He knew it, and yet he set the exacting example to you because you might then be encouraged to do at least ' one-sixteenth ' of it. But know it for certain that if you do not follow that high ideal, if you do not try to look upon women as the direct representations of the Mother of the universe, and to offer according to your capacity, the selfless love of your heart to them; if, on the other hand, you always look upon women, who are the mothers of the

---

[1] A dancing girl of that name stipulated that she would dance only when the stage was illuminated by lights burning nine maunds of oil. It means a thing beyond the range of possibility.—Tr.

world, with beastly eyes, as your dependent slaves and objects for providing enjoyments for you,—then know that your destruction is certain and near at hand.   And remember what happened to the race of Yadus for neglecting the advice of Krishna as also the sad plight of the Jews who disregarded the instructions of Jesus. Treating the incarnations of the age with indifference has been the cause of the destruction of nations at all times.

16.   After replying to one more query, we shall conclude speaking about the unprecedented manifestation of the mood of the spiritual teacher through the married life of the Master and then take up other topics for discussion.   Slaves, as men in general are, to the objects of the senses and to the numerous attachments for persons and things surrounding them, they are likely to feel the following type of objection to the Master's example of a married life. Having after all entered into the married state, it would have been better if he had begotten at least one child and then given up physical relationship with his wife. If he had done that, perhaps it would have been proved that all men without exception have for their duty the maintenance of the divine Lord's creation, and at the same time the authority of the scriptures would not have been violated. For the scriptures say that a householder should leave behind at least one son, if he were to be freed from the debt he owes to his forefathers. To this objection we reply:

First, is creation really nothing more than what little is perceptible to our senses and our mind ? It is the law of creation that there should be diversity in it. It will not be very long before creation is destroyed, if from this moment we all begin to think and act alike in all matters. We then ask you, "Have you known all the laws governing creation? And is it really true that it is only with a view to perpetuate God's creation that you flout the ideal of continence today? Be sincere in your reply, and don't try to deceive yourself and others. Or as the Master would say, 'Don't commit perjury in the shrine of sentiment.'' Well, let us assume for argument's sake that you are obeying that law of the maintenance of creation. What right have you to ask others to do the same? Is it not also a legitimate rule of life coming within the sphere of creative living, that energies should not be wasted on small and counter-productive indulgences ? Is it not a fact that then only can these energies be helped to manifest as the higher powers of the mind? Who would have manifested the higher spiritual powers, if, like you, every one were to waste the energies in lower pursuits? Spiritual development would then have become an impossibility.

17. Secondly, it is our habit to select from the scriptures passages that are to our liking. The injunction regarding the begetting of an offspring is also similarly quoted. For the scriptures again say to persons of adequate fitness: "*Yadahareva virajet tadahareva pravrajet*,"[1] that is, "As soon as one's love for God increases and produces detachment from the world, one shall renounce it." Therefore, who would have maintained the authority of this saying of the scriptures, if the Master had followed your opinion? The same thing applies to the paying off of the debt to one's forefathers. The scriptures say that a true Sannyasin liberates, by virtue of his spiritual merits, seven generations of his family. Therefore, we have no reason to be worried on the score that the debt of the Master to his forefathers was not paid off.

It was in order to teach us this truth that the Master tied himself down to matrimony. We can know a little of what a high and sacred ideal he has left behind for us from the fact of the Holy Mother's worshipping the Master all her life as the Mother of the universe. It is generally seen that a man cannot hide his weaknesses from his wife, though he can do it from others. The Master used sometimes to say to us about it, "All the bigwigs — Babus, judges, magistrates, etc., however big they may talk — are all, as it were, earth worms, slaves to their wives. When orders, even though unjustifiable, come from the 'inner apartment', they have no power to over-rule them." Therefore, if anybody's wife offers sincere, heartfelt devotion to him and worships him all her life as God Himself, it becomes indubitably clear that there is no dross in the ideal which he preaches. This is what we cannot say so definitely about any person other than the Master. This is not the place to describe the story of the Master's wonderful Lila of love with his wife, though there is much to say about it. We introduced this topic only as an illustration of the Master's mood as a spiritual teacher.

---

[1] *Jabala Upaniṣhad.*4

CHAPTER V

THE MOOD OF THE SPIRITUAL TEACHER IN YOUTH

(TOPICS: 1. The making of a spiritual teacher 2. The unlimited "I-ness", and the spiritual teacher 3. Its natural manifestation in the Master 4.Teacher-mood at the time of his Sadhana 5. The strange nature of the Master 6. Difficulty of the wealthy and the learned to recognize him 7. Mathur's attraction towards him and others' opinion of him 8. The Master punishing Rasmani in Teacher-mood 9. Its result 10. Similar events in the lives of Chaitanya, Jesus and Sri Krishna 11. The good fortune of Rani Rasmani 12.Characteristics of the mind merged in God 13. The why of such behaviour of these religious teachers is enigmatic.)

Veiled by My Maya consisting of the three Gunas, I am not manifest to any (except to some of My devotees). The deluded world does not know Me, the unborn and the immutable.

—*Gita*, VII. 25.

1. A special manifestation of the mood of the spiritual teacher in the Master's life began on the day he engaged himself to perform the sacred daily worship of the Divine Mother at Dakshineswar. It was the starting of the period of his Sadhanas. He was then in a state of 'divine madness' on account of love of God. In spite of all that, one who is a spiritual teacher is always so; for one who is a leader is so from childhood. It is not as if people form a committee, consult one another and accord him the position of the spiritual teacher or the leader. As soon as he appears before society, the minds of people are filled with respect for him, and bowing their heads before him, they immediately begin to learn from him and obey his commands. This is the law. Swami Vivekananda said, "A leader is always born and never made." It is therefore seen that the acts which call forth irrevocable punishment from an angry society when they are committed by ordinary people, make the same society follow them fondly, when they are performed by the teachers of men. Bhagavan Sri Krishna says in the Gita (III.21), "People follow whatever he (a teacher of

the people) sets as the standard by his own action." Strange as it may appear, it has all along been a' fact and will continue to be so. "Let the worship of Indra," said Sri Krishna, "be stopped from today and that of Mt. Govardhana commenced," and people began to do so. "From today," said Buddha, "let animal sacrifice be stopped," and immediately society discarded the injunction *Yajnarthe pasavah srishtah*—animals have been created (to be killed) for the purpose of sacrifices. Jesus gave permission to his disciples to have their meals on the Sabbath day. That became the rule. Mohammad married many wives, and still people respect and follow him as a religious hero and a selfless teacher. In all things, great or small, that is the case—whatever they say and do, become the standard of moral conduct.

2. We have already said (III. 3.11.15) why that happens. The limited self, the "I" of the world teachers, is completely destroyed for all time and its place is occupied by the universal "I", which is the origin of all thoughts and beings. It is the nature of that "I" to seek the good of the many. And just as the bees come to know of the blossoming of flowers, and desirous of getting honey, gather eagerly round them, though the flowers do not send them a loving invitation, so also, as soon as the universal "I" manifests itself in any person, the afflicted people of the world come to know of it somehow or other and run uninvited to him for peace and bliss. It is only with great difficulty and after a good deal of austerities, that a little drop or two, so to speak, of the manifestation of that unlimited "I" takes place in the ordinary perfected man, whereas, in the lives of the world teachers, there is some manifestation of it from the very beginning of their lives. In their youth there is a greater degree of manifestation than in childhood; and at last its fullest manifestation is found in the wonderful acts and deeds of their mature years, witnessing which men, in awe and amazement, look upon them as one with God. For, the manifestation of that superhuman mood then becomes as natural to them as their common daily actions like breathing, eating, drinking and walking. What can, therefore, an ordinary man do except adore them? Unable to fathom the depth of their divine nature with his plumb-line of selfishness, what can man, poor and perplexed as he is, do but look upon them as God Himself, and with absolute reliance and devotion, take refuge in them?

3. When we study the Master's life, we find in him also the gradual unfoldment of this mood daily when he was in the state of a Sadhaka in his youth. At the end of his austere spiritual practices for twelve years, it became fully manifested and became natural to him. At that time the ordinary human intellect was at a loss to know in which "I-consciousness" the Master was at any particular moment—whether he was his usual self, or the mood of the spiritual teacher was manifesting in him through identification with the universal "I". But when this mood attained its fullest development, is a distant story, and it will be told at its proper place. Now, it is necessary to tell the reader here a little of how he behaved on many occasions in his youth at the time of his Sadhana when he was beside himself with this divine mood.

4. We find the first manifestation of the mood of the spiritual teacher in him as a youth in his relations with Rani Rasmani, the founders of the Kali temple at Dakshineswar, and her son-in-law Mathuranath. None of us have had the good fortune of seeing either of the two. But, from what we have heard from the Master himself, it is very clear that at the very first sight, they felt attracted to the Master and this attraction gradually assumed unusual depth. It will perhaps appear to our minds to be a fairy tale instead of a fact, to be told that persons of their status in life could love an ordinary man so much and have so much reliance on, and devotion to him; for, on a superficial observation the Master was then an ordinary, insignificant priest, while they were the leaders of society, great in wealth, position, learning and intelligence, though low in the scale of caste.

5. Now, the Master had a strange nature from his childhood. Wealth, respect, learning, intelligence, big titles and appellations at the end of one's name—in short all those considerations that make a person great in the estimation of people generally— had no importance in his eyes. He used to say, "When one ascends the Monument[1], the three or four-storeyed buildings, the tall trees and the grass growing low on the ground—all look alike". We also find that from his childhood the Master's mind generally dwelt on such a high plane, that to his view from that summit of the spiritual elevation of Truth and God-love, these differences in wealth, status, learning, etc.—on account of which we get puffed

---

[1] The Ochterloney Monument at the Calcutta maidan.—Tr.

up and feel that "the vast earth appears to be but a saucer"—, all that paled into absolute insignificance and ceased to be noticed even. It was also found that before the Master undertook anything, he would always discriminate and arrive at a definite conclusion by deep thinking as to why a thing should be done, where the relation with a particular person would ultimately lead him, and where it had led others under similar conditions. So false appearances could, never deceive him by their glittering show and deflect him from the right course. The reader may argue, "But this kind of discriminating intellect will bring first of all the defects of all things before the eyes and paralyse all urge for activity and make all undertakings impossible." It is exactly so. If the intellect were not purified before and freed from desires, and if it were not turned to the high ideal of the realization of God, the attitude of extreme caution and calculation would undoubtedly render man aimless and inactive and sometimes self-willed and reckless even. If, on the contrary, the intellect has attained to the required degree of refinement in outlook and aspiration, it can do this probing and assessment of defects without any detriment to its capacity for energetic action and quick progress along the path to realisation of God. Therefore Sri Krishna in the Gita (XIII. 9) has asked only men of such faith and devotion to find out the painful evils inherent in birth, death, decrepitude and disease, and there by attain dispassion. Let us observe how well-developed was that faculty of finding the hollowness of worldly things in the Master's character from his childhood. When put to school, he was quick in understanding the hollowness of the so-called education. He felt no attraction for such titles as Tarkalankara or Vidyavagisa, as he found out that these big Tarkavagisas and Nyayachanchus were dancing attendance at the doors of the rich, parading their learning by long quotations from Nyaya and Vedanta for the "bundling of rice and plantain"—that is, for their mere livelihood. Even though married, he was not at all attracted by worldly pleasures and amusements, but found out instead, the evils in committing oneself once for all to the worldly life, characterised by the pursuit of ephemeral and ignoble values and of wealth for meeting one's ever-increasing wants. The experience of how money could secure all desirable things of life did not induce him to devote himself heart and soul to the earning of it, but on the contrary made him only aware of its limitation—namely, its utter futility in helping one attain to God-realisation in spite of its usefulness in securing rice, pulses, cloth, bricks, land, timber and other objects of daily utility. Again, he was not attracted towards acquiring name and fame as a man of charity or a philanthropist,[1] as he had the clear perception that though as a result of life-long effort a few free schools and centres of medical relief might be established, ultimately when death intervenes, the philanthropist would have to pass away, leaving the world in as much want and suffering as at the start of his benevolent activities. In this way in all matters his spirit went to the very depth of things.

6. Therefore, it was very difficult for ordinary men, especially for the people proud of their learning and wealth, to rightly recognize and understand the Master who had such a peculiar nature. For, such persons are never accustomed to hear plain and straight-forward talk on questions, as most of those who surrounded them are psychophants who want only to please them. So situated, they gradually lose the very capacity to withstand such flattery, surfeited, as they are with wealth and public honour. No wonder that such people, unable to recognize him, should take him to be vulgar, mad or proud. It is therefore, all the more surprising that contrary to this attitude, Rani Rasmani and Mathur, who were among the wealthy and important persons of those days, should look upon him with love and reverence in spite of his peculiarities. It seems to us that it was only by the grace of God that they not only retained their attitude of love for him but surrendered themselves entirely at his holy feet, accepting his peculiarities only as manifestations of his divine mood as a spiritual teacher. Otherwise, it would not have been easy for Rani Rasmani and Mathur Babu to give up egoism and pride of wealth, and contract a love for the Master at first sight and maintain and develop it to the last to a surprising degree in spite of his queer behaviour and conservative habits. For example, he went without food on the day of the dedication ceremony of the Kali temple at Dakshineswar, and later, when he had to stay in the temple, he would day after day rather do his own cooking on the river bank with the provisions supplied from the temple-stores, than partake of the food offered to the Deity and sanctified by Her—all because

---

[1]That the author does not hereby mean to discourage selfless work leading to liberation will be evident from II. 21. 13.—Tr.

the cooked food belonged to a person of a low caste and would, as he thought, pollute him, though his own brother had performed the worship, offered the food and partaken of it as Prasada. Mathur's love and vague admiration for the Master led him to seek an opportunity to appoint him as a priest of the Mother Kali, but the eccentric Master avoided talking with the worldly Mathur, the latter's repeated attempts notwithstanding. Is it not extraordinary that under such circumstances the love and admiration of Mathur and the Rani went steadily increasing?

7. The Master had by now got married. He was in the hey-day of his youth. He had returned to Dakshineswar after his marriage and had taken charge of the worship of Kali, the Divine Mother. And as soon as he had done so, the divine madness was again upon him (II. 7). In his agony at not having realized God, he rolled on the ground restlessly and rubbed his face mercilessly against it, crying piteously all the while, "Mother! Mother!" People would gather round him in multitudes and in sympathy would say, "Ah! the poor man must be suffering from a terrible colic. Nothing else can make one so restless."

Sometimes he became motionless at the time of worship, placing all the flowers for worship on his own head; and again, sometimes, like one mad, he went on singing for a long time the songs composed by Sadhakas. At other times, however, when he was somewhat in the normal mood, he behaved with all as he should. But when meditating on the Divine Mother, such ecstasies would manifest in him, not once or twice but very often, not in mild forms but with such overwhelming intensity, that he would have no consciousness of the surroundings, nor hear anybody's words, nor reply to anybody. But even during those times people felt very often the exquisite beauty of his divine nature; for, even then if anybody requested him to sing a song or two on the Mother, he would begin immediately to sing in his exquisitely sweet voice, and filled with the spirit of the song, lose himself in it.

Now, not only the lower officers but also the cashier, the chief officer of the temple, brought many tales of the Master's improper and unceremonious actions to the ears of Rani Rasmani and Mathur Babu. It was reported: "The junior[1] Bhattacharya is

---

1The Master's elder brother was called the senior Bhattacharya; the Master was therefore known as the junior Bhattacharya.

ruining everything. The Mother's worship and food offering are
not done properly. Can the Mother accept anything that is done
so improperly?" They complained like this, but it did not produce
the desired results. For Mathur Babu, who used now and then
to come suddenly to the temple without informing anybody, noticed
unobserved the longing devotional behaviour of the Master,
his affectionate and childlike importunities to the Divine Mother
during the worship, and his profuse shedding of tears out of the
joy of devotion. Subsequently he ordered the officers of the temple:
"You shall not obstruct the junior Bhattacharya or find fault with
him in anything he might do. You shall inform me first and then
act as I order."

Rani Rasmani also, whenever she came from time to time to
the temple, became charmed with the floral decoration of the
Mother and with the songs about Her name and Her glory sung by
the Master in his exquisitely sweet voice. So on such occasions
she would call the junior Bhattacharya to her and request him to
sing her a few songs. The Master also would completely forget
that he was singing for any mortal, and filled with the spirit of the
songs, go on singing as if he were doing it for the Divine Mother
Herself. Thus days were rolling on. As in the big household of
the world, so in the small one of the temple too all were busy with
their own affairs, relieving the humdrum monotony of their lives
by indulging in such piquant subjects as speaking ill of others,
carrying tales and inventing new ones during the little leisure they
could snatch from their pre-occupation with the various concerns for the promotion of their own worldly interests. Therefore, who was there to notice what changes were being brought
about in the mind of the junior Bhattacharya on account of his
love of God? "He is a mad fellow. The Babus (the proprietors)
have somehow taken a fancy to him, and that is why he still retain-
the job. But how long can he retain it? He is sure to commit
some strange act some day and will be sacked. Is there any certainty about the temper of these big folk? It takes very little
time to please them and to displease them too." This was the kind
of talk that sometimes went on among the officers. The Master's
nephew and attendant Hriday had joined him there by that time.

8. One day Rani Rasmani had come to the temple. All
the officers were very busy. Even the shirkers were that day
attending to their duties very carefully. After taking her bath in

the Ganga, the Rani went to the Kali temple. The worship and
the decoration of the divine Kali were by then finished. The Rani
saluted the Mother and sat down on a seat near the holy image
within the temple to perform her daily worship. She saw the
junior Bhattacharya near and requested him to sing the "Mother's
name." The Master also sat down near the Rani, and filled with
devotional emotions, began to sing the songs of Ramprasad,
Kamalakanta and other mystics. She was listening to these songs
while performing worship and Japa. This went on for some time,
when the Master suddenly got annoyed and stopped singing and
sharply exclaimed in a harsh tone, "That thought alone! That
thought even here!" Saying so, he immediately struck the tender
person of the Rani with the palm of his hand. The Master was
in that very mood now in which a father becomes angry and punishes
his child on seeing something wrong in its conduct. But who
could understand that?

9.   All the officers of the temple and the women attendants
of the Rani raised a hue and cry. The gatekeeper ran hastily to
catch hold of the Master. Wondering what the noise within the
temple was due to, the officers came there out of curiosity. But
those who were the main cause of this noise—the Master and Rani
Rasmani—were both calm and tranquil, without taking any notice
of the noise and of the officers running hither and thither. The Master
was calm, quiet and serenely poised in the Self, with a charming
smile playing on his lips. As for the Rani, finding on self-analysis
that she had been thinking about the result of a particular case
pending in a law court at that time instead of meditating on the
universal Mother, she was at first a little embarrassed, and next
repentant and serious. Again, wondering how the Master could
know her thought, the Rani felt also an element of surprise in her mind.
Brought suddenly to her senses by the noise made by the officers,
she apprehended that there was a possibility of some great injury
being inflicted on the innocent Master by the mean-minded people.
She therefore commanded them in a serious mood: "Bhattacharya
is not at all to blame. Do not find fault with him." Later, Mathur
heard the whole story from the Rani and approved of her order.
Some of the officers became very much disappointed; but what
could they do? They thought, "What business have we with the
affairs of big people!" and remained quiet. While perusing this
account, the reader will perhaps think, "What a strange mood of

31

the spiritual teacher is this! What a queer manifestation, if it should end in assaulting people!"

10. We reply: "Read the religious history of the world, and you will see such events recorded in the lives of the great religious teachers of the world. Remember the event in the life of Sri Chaitanya, of his bringing the Kazi to his senses and of his transmitting devotion to Acharya Advaita by beating them. Think, and you will find that such incidents were not lacking in the life of Jesus also. Surrounded by his disciples, Jesus came to visit the temple of Jehovah at Jerusalem and to offer worship, sacrifices etc., there. The Jewish mind undoubtedly felt the same pure and wonderful devotion at the time of visiting the temple at Jerusalem as the Hindus do in visiting the holy places like Varanasi, Vrindavan and other centres of pilgrimage. Over and above that, the mind of Jesus was then in Bhavamukha.[1] Completely filled with love of God, he ran to have the direct vision of the Deity as soon as he saw the temple from a distance. Many people were there outside the temple, at the gate and in the courtyard, variously busy in worldly affairs such as earning money, deceiving others etc., regardless of whether the pilgrims had the vision of the Deity or not. The temple priests were attentive only to their pursuit of extracting a little money out of them and the shopkeepers and others were all much given to considering how they could gain a little more than usual by selling animals, flowers, and other accessories of worship. Who felt the necessity of thinking that he was in the presence of God in the temple? While he was entering the temple, nothing of these things, however, attracted the attention of Jesus, who was filled with spiritual emotions. Going straight into the temple and having the vision of the Deity, he was beside himself with joy to see that He was within oneself as the Life of one's life and the Self of one's self. He began to feel that the temple and all the persons and things in it were more than his own; for it was on coming here that he was blessed with the vision of the source and solace of his life. When, however, on coming down again to the ordinary level of consciousness, the mind was looking for the manifestation of that inner mood in the persons and things outside, he found that everything was the very opposite

---

[1]III.3.11-15 and III.1.34-35.—Tr.

of it,—that no one was engaged in the service of God, the solace of one's life, but on the contrary all were given to the enjoyment of lust and gold. His heart was then filled with despair and sorrow. He thought: "What is this? Why don't you do whatever you like in the world outside? Why attend to all these worldly affairs here, where there is a special manifestation of God? Instead of thinking of Him while you are here and doing away with your worldly anguish, why have you brought in worldliness here too?" Thinking thus, he was seized with divine anger, and he assumed a terrible appearance, and with a cane in hand, drove off all the shopkeepers and others out of the temple by force. Having got a momentary awakening of the spirit from his words, they also went out without offering any resistance whatsoever, thinking that they had been indeed committing misdeeds. The men, who were steeped in worldliness and could not be awakened by words, got the awakening on being flogged and went out. Neither were they angry, nor did they dare harm him in any way.

In the life of Sri Krishna also many events of this nature are found. Many an evil-minded person who came to confront him with bad intentions was elevated to spiritual heights on being punished by Him. They then sang hymns of praise to Him as the divine Lord Himself. Again extremely earth-bound souls who went to harm him, got perplexed and stupefied by his words and laughter. Enough now of these incidents from the Puranas.

11. This event of the Master chastising Rani Rasmani described above is a bright example of the way in which he, under the impulsion of the divine power manifested as the spiritual teacher, used to lose his individuality and teach and behave towards others. If we probe to find out the deep implications of the event, we shall find it is not an insignificant affair. What a gulf of difference existed between the two persons involved in it—on the one hand the insignificant temple-priest receiving a very small salary, and on the other, Rasmani, the Rani whose wealth, status, wisdom, fortitude, courage and strength of character astounded the cream of the Calcutta citizenry of those times. One is led to believe that such a poor Brahmana would find it difficult even to approach her; or, if he could somehow do so, he would seek an opportunity to please her by flattery and such other methods, and would consider himself blessed if he succeeded. But what actually happened was quite the contrary. The poor Brahmana did not merely protest

against her wrong action but inflicted public punishment on her person! Looking at the incident from the Master's side, it seems to be a matter for no little surprise; from the Rani's too, it is equally surprising that anger, egoism and the idea of punishment did not cross her mind in spite of the apparent objectionable behaviour of the Master. But as we have seen, when face to face with a great soul, who is impelled by the mood of the teacher which is born of identification with the universal 'I', ordinary men are automatically impelled to bow down before them. Much more so in the case of persons of Sattvika nature like the Rani who was a true devotee. For by virtue of the grace bestowed on them by the Teacher, they are able to understand automatically that the words and actions of the latter are in their spiritual self-interest, and so they feel no hesitation to act in accordance with his directions. Again, as the Master used to say, "A man cannot become great in anything, nor can he digest fame, power, position etc., if he has not a special part of God in him." It was only because the Rani, who was thoroughly Sattvika in nature, possessed some divine traits in her that she could show the required calmness and receptivity to stand and absorb that rather strange and apparently offensive expression of Divine grace that was bestowed on her through the Master. "Rani Rasmani," said the Master, "was one of the eight Nayikas (attendant goddesses) of the Divine Mother. She came down to the world to spread the worship of the Divine Mother. 'Sri Rasmani Dasi desirous of realizing the feet of Kali'— were the words engraved on her office seal. A steadfast devotion to the Divine Mother was manifested in every action of the Rani."

12. There is another thing to be mentioned. It is recorded in the scriptures that a mind completely merged in God manifests various moods. Sri Sankara has described it beautifully in his book the *Viveka-chudamani* (v. 540): "Persons who have had their life's purpose fulfilled by the realization of the Self, roam about in the world in strange attires—some with ordinary clothes on, ome clad in barks of trees, still others with the points of the compass as their dress (i.e., stark naked), some like madmen, some like boys free from the slightest tinge of lust and greed, and still others like ghouls."

13. Ordinary people find this element of strangeness and abnormality in them, only because the latter are poised in the universal 'I', unlike the matter-of-fact man. It is by virtue of this

fact, that these extraordinary persons alone become the channels
for the manifestation of the Divine Power as the spiritual teachers
removing the darkness of ignorance in men. For, as we have
already said, it is only where the elimination of the little self-centred 'I' has taken place that the immense all-pervading 'I' of the
Divine Power as Teacher would find manifestation. While looking
like ordinary men, these enlightened ones on whom the role of a
teacher falls—the Rishis—have to *assume* (or manifest) for the
purpose of teaching, all the highly coveted excellences like good
conduct, steadfastness, self-restraint, intelligence, benevolence,
scriptural knowledge and the like—in short to adhere to all that is
morally and spiritually uplifting and eschew all that is degrading
in this respect. We have used the word *assume* (or manifest)
because their natural state is that of the absolute and non-dual
Brahman in which there is no place for dualities and for opposing
values like good and bad, moral and immoral, pious and impious—
all of which belong only to the relative world of Maya. Under the
circumstances, the manifestation of the relative values of the world
in them can only be spoken of as an assumption for the purpose
of teaching. When to be clothed in such an *assumed* humanity is
the way of even ordinary enlightened teachers, it is all the more so
with the world teachers, whom we call incarnations for their
being basically one with the Divinity. It is indeed this presence of
utter humanity in them that makes it difficult for ordinary men to
understand and gauge their nature.   It is especially so in the case of
Bhagavan[1] Sri Ramakrishna, the incarnation for the modern age.
For, the greatness, power, splendour, etc., recorded in the scriptures as manifesting in the incarnations of God, were hidden in such
a way in him that no one could get an inkling of these things by
seeing him superficially a few times.   Only those who were intimately
connected with him as genuine seekers of truth and had received his
grace, could understand him. Consider: What is the external quality
in him by which you could feel attracted? By knowledge?—he
was, so to say, practically illiterate. But do you know that
the Veda, the Vedanta and all other scriptures had been read
out to him and he had completely mastered them all by virtue

1The person in whom all the six auspicious qualities—lordliness,
dharma, fame, splendour, knowledge and dispassion—are manifested
in the fullest measure is known as Bhagavan.—Tr.

of his prodigious memory?   Will you gauge him by his intellect?
What counsel would you seek from one, from whose lips are always
heard words like, "I am nothing, I don't know anything, my Mother
knows everything"—one who, on being approached for guidance,
would say, "Ask Mother, and She will tell you"?   Can you keep
your faith steady and act according to his words?   You will consider
them commonplace and think.   "Ah, what a piece of advice he
has given us! We have all been hearing since we read the primers
like *Kathamala* and *Bodhodaya*[1] that God is all-knowing, all-powerful,
formless and of the nature of pure consciousness; that He can , if
He wills, give us the knowledge and understanding of everything.
But do we really act up to this teaching?"   Will you make an
estimate of him by wealth, name and fame? Ah, the Master himself
had indeed plenty of all these!   And he would again advise you
from the very beginning to renounce them.   Such was the case with
everything around him.   The only means by which to gauge him
was by seeing his purity, love of God and goodwill.   If you are
attracted by these, well and good; if not, it is beyond your reach
to gauge and understand him.   We, therefore, say that it was
not a matter of small fortune for Rani Rasmani, that she, instead
of rejecting, through egotism and pride, the grace bestowed on
her—because of the crude way in which it was bestowed—could
understand and profit by the Master's mood as the spiritual teacher
and treasure it up in the innermost chamber of her heart.

---

[1]These were two children's text books in Bengali.—Tr.

CHAPTER VI

THE MOOD OF THE SPIRITUAL TEACHER AND MATHURANATH

(TOPICS: 1. It takes a long time for a big flower to blossom 2. The strange relation of the Master with Mathur 3. Both friends and enemies only help the incarnation. 4. Play of the Divine in the lives of all 5. Though a devotee, Mathur was not foolish 6. His attraction towards the Master 7. Effect of infectious power of devotion on him 8. Alteration in Nature's law; China-rose incident 9. Mathur's solicitude for the Master's health 10. Incident of the recital of Mahimna-stotra 11. Quickening of spiritual progress in the Master's company 12. Mathur's vision of Siva and Sakti in him 13. The result of the vision 14. Mathur's great good fortune 15. Spiritual experiences of the Master: Mathur's test of them confirms his faith 16. Jealousy of priest Haldar 17. Incident concerning Varanasi shawls 18. The Master's non-attachment 19. Priest Haldar's wicked conduct 20. The Master's relation with Mathur's family 21. Contrary moods co-existing in the Master 22. The Pandits' convention at Dakshineswar concerning broken image 23. The Master's decision.)

I shall now declare to you, O best of the Kurus, My principal manifestations of power unknown to men; the details (of this aspect of Mine) are, however, endless.

—*Gita*, X. 19

1. We have already said that the gradual manifestation of the mood of the spiritual teacher in the life of the Master took place to a great extent before the eyes of Rani Rasmani and Mathur Babu. "A large flower," said the Master, "takes a long time to blossom. Trees having pith take a longer time to grow." It took not a little time and discipline for the unprecedented mood of the spiritual teacher to manifest itself in the Master's life also. It required twelve years of continued and austere discipline. This is not the place to give a description of those Sadhanas. Here we are specially concerned with the Master's mood as the spiritual teacher,—the flower that blossomed in its full beauty and glory under the rays of the sun of Consciousness universal. But certain other topics will of course come in by the way, as we describe from the beginning to the end the manifestation of that mood. A description of those devotees connected with the unfoldment of this mood of the Master will also inevitably come in.

2. The relation of the Master with Mathur Babu was a strange one. Mathur was wealthy and magnanimous; though a man of the world, he was a devotee; though a man of discrimination who knew the distinction between the permanent and the impermanent, he liked the things of the world; and though prone to anger and rashness, he had patience and strong determination. Mathur was not unacquainted with the knowledge and the view of life that the English had brought to the land. He was given to much argumentation and yet was open to correction. Though a devotee having faith in God, he was not the man to accept anything without exercising his reason, even if the speaker be his spiritual teacher himself. Though of a liberal nature, he was not the man to be deceived like a fool in worldly affairs; rather the shrewd intellect of a crafty politician, and the unscrupulousness of landlords in the means they adopt for extending their possessions, were sometimes seen in him. As a matter of fact, Mathur Babu, the youngest of her sons-in-law, was the right-hand man of the Rani, who was without male issue, in managing all her worldly affairs, though she had other sons-in-law living. And it was only because of this combination of the talents of both, the mother-in-law and the youngest son-in-law, that the name of Rani Rasmani became so very well known then.

3. The reader will perhaps say, " Why this 'song of Siva while husking paddy? ' [1] Why bring in Mathur while you are speaking of the Master?" In answer, it may be said that it was Mathur who caught just a little glimpse of the future glory that was to manifest, and came forward to protect and assist it in its development, in the days when the Master's mood as a spiritual teacher was only just cutting open the cocoon but had not yet come out. Under a very pure, sacred urge, Rani Rasmani built a fit place where this unique character could unfold itself freely; and under a similar noble urge Mathur helped its further development by supplying whatever else was necessary. It is of course only now, after the lapse of many years, that we can understand it all. But although both of them got a little inkling of it from time to time, it does not seem that either of them ever could have had a full understanding as to why they were doing all this This

---

[1] A proverb current in Bengal meaning introducing something irrelevant to the subject under discussion.—Tr.

fact is borne out by the study of the lives of all great souls of all
ages. There is an unknown Power functioning, in ways unseen
and mysterious, in and through the lives of these great ones—
clearing their paths of all obstructions, protecting them, drawing
others into the sphere of their influence and making them offer
their allegiance to them. The persons thus involved in their lives,
whether as friends or apparently as foes, do not often have the
least inkling that they are but tools, the means employed by that
great unknown Power, to assist in bringing out the latent power
of these great ones, in clearing their way of obstructions, and in
promoting the work they have come to accomplish. These happenings and their significance are so unobtrusive and unrecognised
at the time, that people are amazed long afterwards when their
discovery is made. See the result of Kaikeyi's sending away Sri
Ramachandra to the forest; see the ultimate result of the lifelong
efforts of Kamsa in keeping Vasudeva and Devaki imprisoned;
see the result of the building up of the pleasure-garden by King
Suddhodhana lest Siddhartha should be overcome by dispassion; see
the result of the cruel Kapalika Bauddha's effort at killing Acharya
Sankara by means of incantations; see the result of the acts of
enmity done against Sri Chaitanya with the help of government
officials for preaching the religion of love; and see the result of
killing the supremely glorious Jesus on a false charge of having
committed a crime. In every one of these cases the results turned
out to be the opposite of what had been intended, as in the story[1] of

---

[1]This current proverb (in Northern India) has for its source the
following story: There was a holy man of the Vairagi denomination
who travelled from one place of pilgrimage to another for a long time.
He himself carried the bundle of his paraphernalia of necessary articles
like the metal cooking-pot and water-pot. One day the holy man thought
that he might be free from the trouble of carrying the bundle if he could
get a horse. As soon as the thought occurred to him, he began to go
round to secure a horse on charity, crying out, "O Rama, please let me
have a horse." An army of the king of the country happened then to
pass that way. On the way a mare was foaled. "Whew!" thought the
rider of the mare, "the army will march from here immediately; the
mare can walk, but how can I take the young one that is just born?"
After a little deliberation, as soon as he went out in search of a man
to carry the foal, he met with the holy man, crying out, "O Rama, please
let me have a horse." And finding him strong, the officer without any
other consideration, forced him to carry the young one. At this turn
of events, the holy man was perplexed and began to repeat again and

"Rama took it contrariwise". Yet both the very powerful and intelligent adversaries and the affectionate friends always thought "otherwise" and acted from their own motives — and will do so in future — applying the whole stock of their subtle policy and worldly wisdom.   But, as recorded in the *Bhagavata* and other books, one acting as an enemy has to remain completely ignorant of the actions and purposes of that divine Power, while others can sometimes have a little knowledge of this Power if they follow it with faith and devotion.   And with the help of that knowledge they can become fit to attain liberation and eternal peace by becoming gradually free from desires.   Mathur's conduct towards the Master was of the latter type.

4.   It is not that the play of the divine Power is seen only in the lives of great souls like the incarnations.   The truth is that in the lives of these incarnations the play of that divine force is most conspicuously noticed, causing wonder in our minds.   But indications of it are seen even in our ordinary daily life and in all the affairs of the practical world.   A careful study of the lives of several men would convincingly show that man is but a puppet in the hands of that divine force.   There is necessarily a great resemblance between the lives of incarnations and ordinary men, as the former is meant to be a pattern and a model for the latter to shape their lives on.   Hence the relevance of these incarnations in the lives of ordinary men.   Do you not see that a few great souls like Rama, Krishna, Chaitanya and others have retained a hold on the lives of the people of India, the vast meeting ground of the cultures of various people?   Again, see how quickly the ideal of the life of Sri Ramakrishna, the incarnation of the present age, the unique mould formed by the combination of the ideals of all the previous great souls, is spreading its own influence and in a very short time getting a hold on the lives of the men and women of this country and abroad.   How far this influence will spread in course of time, O reader, you may guess, if you can.   We are, however, unable to conjecture and express this.

5.   Another point in Mathur's character needs explanation. It is said he had more than hundred per cent of love and reverence for the Master.   Our minds, clouded with doubts, react at the very

---

again, "Rama took it contrariwise.   Far from the horse carrying me and my bundle, I am now to carry this foal!"

outset: "This Mathur must have been an absolute fool. Otherwise, can a man have such love and reverence for another? Had we been in his position, we would have challenged this Ramakrishna at every step to prove his worth and character in place of blindly reposing our trust and affection in him in this way." Ah! as if it were guilty to love and revere another! When all that we heard about Mathur from the Master is stated, it will be seen that Mathur was not that naive and simple as it is assumed. He was not in any way less intelligent or critical than we. He too was suspicious of the strange and unintelligible aspects of the Master's character and actions and did not spare him from tests at every step in the beginning. But of what avail was it? How could the elephant of Mathur's scepticism withstand the force of the strong and furious current of the very powerful Mandakini (Ganga) of the Master's unprecedented and unheard-of spiritual mood, with knowledge for its roar and divine love for its eddies? The animal shook, slipped, was crushed and defeated, turned over and carried off, to an unknown destination. So was Mathur's scepticism rendered ineffective. Completely defeated, Mathur had to take refuge at his holy feet wholeheartedly. That being so, it would be easily perceived that in dealing with this topic, we are only describing the Master's mood as the spiritual teacher, though we may apparently be speaking of Mathur.

6. Mathur was attracted towards the Master at the very first sight on account of the latter's straightforwardness like that of a boy, his sweet nature and good looks. Afterwards, during the first stage of Sadhana, the state of the divine madness began to come on the Master, and he sometimes lost control over himself. While he was worshipping the universal Mother, he was beside himself with joy at the vision of Her within his heart. Thereafter he often began to offer all the ingredients of worship on himself with a sense of identification with the Divine Mother perceived within. Thus on account of the force of the strong current of the love of God, he overstepped the limits of ceremonial devotion, and consequently became an object of opprobrium and criticism among the temple servants. For though he was motivated by the highest expression of devotion, he was doing things in a way contrary to scriptural injunctions, and this was something meaningless, nay, reprehensible in the public eye. But Mathur, though a man of the world, reacted differently to these criticisms

owing to his keen intelligence and sense of justice. "Nothing shall be done against him," he suggested to himself, "until I have seen things with my own eyes; for I had seen him so fine and straightforward on my very first meeting with him." That was why Mathur came secretly to the Kali temple, observed all his actions minutely and as a result came to the conclusion, "Young Gadadhar is a living embodiment of divine love and straight-forwardness; all his strange behaviour is due to an excess of devotion and faith." So the intelligent man of the world that he was, what Mathur did subsequently was to correct and persuade the Master thus: "It is good to do things according to one's mood if only it can last. It is good to have faith and devotion, but will it do to be completely overwhelmed? You will be an object of public criticism for this. Moreover, there is a chance of your losing your wits and becoming mad, if you behave as you like without paying heed to what people say." But although he tried to persuade the Master in this way, the feeling of devotion lying dormant within Mathur became awakened by the power of the holy company he was fortunate enough to have, and he would therefore sometimes recall all of a sudden: "In Ramprasad and other earlier Sadhakas, this kind of behaviour verging on madness had been noticed. It was due to the intensity of their devotion that they behaved like that. Can't this be the case with Gadadhar also?" Therefore, instead of placing any obstacles in the way of the Master, Mathur decided to go on observing how all these would take shape and to take the proper step at the proper time. Such behaviour on the part of an employer of Mathur's status and worldly experience towards a petty employee, is an indication of not a little patience and respectful regard.

7. Devotion has a contagious influence. We see daily that, like physical states, mental moods also are contagious. For, it is no longer necessary to refer to the experiences of the Vedic seers to prove—for modern science has all but proved it now — that the entire universe, both gross and subtle, is made up of modi-fications of one substance and is governed by the same laws. Is it therefore surprising that the modification called devotion, when awakened in one person, will awaken a similar mood lying dormant in another? That is why the scriptures have declared so earnestly that the company of spiritual men is a great help to the awakening of spirituality. It can very well be inferred that owing to his good

luck, it happened so in the case of Mathur also. The more he began to observe day after day the actions and behaviour of the Master, the more did the mood of devotion awaken in him without himself being aware of it. We find clear signs of this in his successive actions. But it is certain that Mathur's mind, like that of all worldly people, was for a long time oscillating between doubt and devotion, before faith in the Master was firmly fixed in his heart. So while in the beginning Mathur was ready to view the Master's unusual mental state as due to excessive devotion, he later changed his mind, and began to doubt if the Master was really out of his wits. This doubt only stimulated his loving kindness towards the Master. He thought of engaging a good physician to treat him and improve the health of his body and mind.

8. Mathur had a fair knowledge of English. He had also acquired that peculiar attitude of self-importance and independence of outlook which the Western style of education generally produced in the temperament and thinking of people. Therefore we find him trying to dissuade the Master from going too far in cultivating exuberant love of God, which he thought was the cause of his mental derangement. A conversation between the Master and Mathur on whether God has to obey His own laws as regards natural phenomena may be mentioned as an example of it. The Master said, "Mathur was of the opinion that God had also to obey His own laws. Even He had not the power to overrule the laws He has once made. I said, 'What do you mean? He who makes a law can as well unmake it if He so desires, or replace it by another.' He would by no means accept this. He said, 'A plant producing red flowers invariably produces red ones and never white ones; for it is His law. Well, let Him, if He can, produce a white flower in a plant bearing red ones.' I said, 'He can, if He wills, do everything—even that.' But he did not accept the proposition. The next day when I went to answer the calls of nature towards the cluster of tamarisk trees, I found that, on two twigs of one and the same branch of a red china rose plant, there were two flowers, one red and the other brilliantly white, without the tiniest red spot in it. No sooner had I seen them than I broke the branch together with the flowers, brought it and placed it before Mathur and said, 'Here you are!' Mathur then said, 'Yes, father, I am defeated'." Mathur sometimes believed that it was physical illness that produced in the Master

a sort of mental derangement which manifested itself as an excess of devotional feelings, and tried, by reasons and argument, to dispel that mood of the Master.

9. Thus the worldly-minded Mathur would spend a long time with him, reflecting and discussing a great deal about his condition, partly out of curiosity and partly out of kindness, as he mistook that he was genuinely ill. But at the same time he had also a feeling that all that he saw in the Master was caused by true love of God. Every day instances were coming to his notice of the Master's strange behaviour under the influence of this fresh outburst of divine love,—instances which deepened his anxiety and perplexity regarding his health and mental condition. For example, one day the Master saw a vision of the Divine Mother within himself, and seating himself on the seat for worship, offered all the articles of worship to himself; the previous day he had performed Arati of the universal Mother continuously for three long hours, making the officers of the temple restless and agitated; the day before he had rolled on the ground, rubbing his face against the dusty earth for not having realized God, and wept so piteously that people gathered round him. Ah, how many indeed are such incidents of his life that we heard from the Master!

10. One day the Master entered a Siva temple[1] and began to recite a hymn on the glory of Siva called the *Mahimna-stotra*. In the course of his recital, he was beside himself with an ecstatic mood when he came to the following verse: "O Lord, if the blue mountain be the ink; the ocean the ink-pot; the biggest branch of the heavenly tree the pen; the earth the writing leaf; and if, taking these, the goddess of learning herself were to write for eternity—even then the limit of Thy excellences cannot be reached."

Reciting the above verse, the Master lost himself in the intense experience of the glory of Siva, forgot the hymn, the language of the hymn, the order of the verses and all other things, and began to cry out loudly, saying again and again, "O great God, how can I express Thy glory!" And tears flowed profusely from his eyes down his cheeks, breast and clothes to the floor until it got wet. The servants and officers of the temple came there running from all sides, attracted by his strange behaviour and by the

---

[1] There are twelve Siva temples facing the courtyard of the Kali temple at Dakshineswar.

noise produced by his weeping and the half-uttered exclamations
in a choked voice as that of a mad man. When they saw him
in that state, some were surprised and waited to see what would
happen next, saying, "Oh! It is all the madness of the junior
Bhattacharya!" Said one, "I took it to be something else. I see,
it is very much in excess today!" "Will he not, " said another,
"ride on the shoulder of Siva? What do you say? It is better
to pull him away by the hand." Such comments went on. It is
needless to add that there was also much merriment over it.

But the Master had no consciousness of the external world
at all. Merged in the feeling of the glory of Siva, his mind had
then gone up very high beyond the external world, where the
tainted ideas and words of the world never reach. How then
could the words of these temple servants, expressing derision or
fun, reach his ears?

At that time Mathur Babu was at the Kali temple. Hearing
that uproar in connection with the Bhattacharya's behaviour, he
came to the spot immediately. The officers hastened respectfully
to make way for him. Mathur Babu came and saw the Master
in that mood and was charmed at the sight. When some one of
the officers suggested that the Master should forcibly be removed
from the Siva temple, where he was then seated, Mathur was
infuriated and exclaimed, "Leave him alone! He who interferes
with the Bhattacharya will do so at the risk of his own head!"
The officers were, therefore, frightened and dared not say or do
anything. A little afterwards the Master regained consciousness of the outer world, and seeing Mathur Babu standing there
with the officers of the temple, looked frightened like a boy and
asked him, "Did I happen to do anything wrong when I had no
control over myself?" Mahur saluted him and said, "No, Father,
you were reciting a hymn; I stood here lest some one should disturb
you unthinkingly."

11. Recalling his condition at the time of his Sadhana, the
Master said to us one day, "Those who used to come here at that
time had the godly tendency kindled very soon in the company 'here'
(i.e., himself). Two youths used to come from Baranagar. They
were low by birth, may be Kaivarta or Tamli. They were very
good-natured. They had great love and reverence for 'here' and
used to come very often. One day I was sitting with them under the
Panchavati when a certain state came on one of them. I saw that

his breast grew red and eyes deep red; streams of tears were rolling down; he could neither speak nor stand; he was just like one who had drunk two bottles of wine. That mood of his was in no way coming to an end. I was then afraid and said to the Mother, 'What have you done to him, Mother? People will say I have done something and brought about that condition in him. He has his father and others; he will have to go home just now.' I passed my hand over his chest while I was saying so to the Mother. He then became somewhat calm and went home a little afterwards."

12. We have heard from the holy mouth of the Master that at one time, Mathur, too, caught up in the 'infectious' spiritual fervour emanating from his company, got into a wonderful state, and his reverence and devotion increased a thousandfold. Indrawn and oblivious of the surroundings due to absorption in a spiritual mood, the Master was one day pacing up and down the verandah extending east to west, to the north-east of his room. Mathur was then sitting by himself in one of the rooms of the separate house which stood between the temple and the Panchavati and which is even now called the "Babus' mansion". The place where the Master was pacing was within easy range of vision from where Mathur was sitting. Therefore Mathur, as he sat speculating on the future trend of his own worldly affairs, was also occasionally observing and thinking about the Master whom he saw walking up and down in an indrawn mood. The Master was not at all conscious of the fact that Mathur was sitting in the parlour observing him that way from time to time. And what would it have mattered even if he were conscious of it? The disparity between the domestic, social and other conditions of the two was so great that there was no cause for either of them feeling any concern for the other. Rather it would have been reasonable for the Master to feel hesitant and move away from the place, had he known of Mathur's presence there, which he could not, due to his inattentiveness to external events brought on by his divine mood. For how could the Master, who was an ordinary, insignificant, poor temple-priest, whom people knew to be foolish and mad for not paying heed to ritualistic formalities, and who was therefore the butt of ridicule for them all, help feeling hesitant in the presence of Mathur, who was a wealthy, respectable, learned and intelligent Babu (gentleman), and who might well be regarded

as the proprietor of the temple and the whole estate of the Rani? That he happened to view the Master with a benevolent eye, was the only reason why the latter had not so far been driven away from the temple. But the event that now transpired turned out to be something unthinkable and incomprehensible. For. Mathur himself came all of a sudden, running in a great flurry to the Master, bowed down to him, clasped with his hands both the feet of the Master and started weeping.

The Master said: "I asked him, 'What is this you are doing? You are a Babu, the son-in-law of the Rani. What will people think if they see you act like this? Please be calm and get up.' But who would give ear to it! Afterwards when he became collected, he narrated everything without any reserve. He had had a strange vision. He said, 'Father, as you came forward walking in this direction, I saw you distinctly as my Mother installed and worshipped in the temple, and immediately you turned about in the opposite direction, I saw you as Mahadeva Himself. I thought at first that it was an optical illusion. I rubbed my eyes well and looked, but saw the same thing. This happened as often as I looked.' He repeatedly said this and wept. I said, 'Why, as a matter of fact, I know nothing of this affair!' But who would listen! I was afraid lest some one should come to know of this and report it to the Rani. What would she think? She might perhaps say that I have cast a spell on him. He became calm when I consoled him in various ways. Was it for nothing that Mathur did so much for me and loved me so much? Mother gave him many visions and experiences about 'here'. It was in fact written in Mathur's horoscope that his chosen Ideal, the Divine Mother, would be so very compassionate to him that She would assume a body, accompany and protect him wherever he went."

13. Thenceforward Mathur's faith became very firm; for this was the first time he got an indication that the Master was surely not an ordinary man. He, towards whom he felt attracted at first sight and whose mental attitudes he could very often detect and understand though others condemned them—Mathur now came to understand him to be no one other than the Divine Mother of the universe Herself, who, out of compassion for him, was residing in the Master's body. It was from this time on that he believed that the One present in the stone image in the temple had perhaps assumed a body and was accompanying him wherever

32

he went, as was written in his horoscope. From now on, Mathur's relation with the Master became especially intimate.

14. Indeed, a great good fortune smiled on Mathur. The scriptures say that not only ordinary people but even those who have become liberated in life cannot but experience the result of actions of both kinds, good and bad, as long as their bodies last. Ordinary men experience the results of their good and bad actions themselves. Now, who experiences the results of the good and bad actions done through the body of the liberated? For, the liberated one cannot be that experiencer, as his ego has been burnt up by knowledge, and without an ego, there is no liability to enjoyments and sufferings springing from action. Who then can possibly be the experiencer? The results of actions are inevitable. Even the liberated ones cannot but do some actions, good and bad, till their bodies fall like a dry leaf. The scriptures say that those unliberated persons who serve and love the liberated ones enjoy the results of the good actions of the latter, and those who hate them suffer the results of the bad actions done through their bodies.[1] Who can say how great is the result of the loving and devoted service rendered to the incarnations of God, seeing that great results are attained through the service of even ordinary liberated persons?

15. As days passed, Mathur's vision of the spiritual mood in the Master became clearer and his devotion to him firmer. Meanwhile there happened many events: the appearance of an extremely painful burning sensation in the Master's body on account of the separation from God and the treatment thereof; the Bhairavi Brahmani's advent at Dakshineswar and the demonstration with the aid of evidence from Vaishnava scriptures, in the presence of a circle of Pandits invited by Mathur, that the Master was an incarnation of God; the arrival of Tota Puri, the great Vedantin, and the Master's initiation into Sannyasa; the coming of the aged mother of the Master to Dakshineswar and her stay there; and so on.

---

[1]"Similarly there is the reading in the Satyayani recension, 'His sons come by the patrimony; friends, the results of his good actions; and foes, those of his bad actions." Again similarly the Kaushitakins read, "He (the man of knowledge when dead) shakes off the results of his good and bad actions by that (by the strength of his knowledge); his dear *Jnatis*, or relatives enjoy the results of his good actions, and his haters, those of his bad actions."

Commentary of Sankara on the *VedantaAphorisms*. III.3.26

Since the day on which the strange vision mentioned above took place, Mathur became closely connected with almost all the events that happened daily in the Master's life. Mathur made arrangements for the Master's treatment by Gangaprasad Sen, the famous physician of Calcutta, and by Dr. Mahendralal Sarkar. The Master felt a strong loving desire to adorn the Mother with anklets and other ornaments of the same pattern as are used by ladies of Uttar Pradesh; and Mathur had them made at once. Again at the time of practising the attitude of a female friend of the Divine Mother as prescribed in Vaishnava books, he had a mind to put on the dress and ornaments such as those used by women, and Mathuranath had a suit of diamond-set ornaments, a Varanasi Sari, a wrapper and such other things brought immediately. When he came to know that the Master had a desire to go and see the festival at Panihati, Mathur immediately made arrangements for that visit. That was not all; he himself went in disguise with a body-guard with him in order to protect the person of the Master lest he should be put to inconvenience on account of the big crowd. Just as, on the one hand, we have heard of Mathur's wonderful service, so, on the other, we have also heard from the Master that he set dissolute women on him to see whether there arose in the Master's mind any impure feeling; that he proposed to transfer in writing all the trust property of the temple to the Master, at which, in a state of divine anger, the latter was about to beat him saying, 'Do you want to make me a worldly man?'; and that Mathur was once saved by him from the danger of being very severely punished by the court on a charge of homicide in connection with a riot on his estate, whereupon in order to escape from that danger, he confessed to the Master everything and took refuge in him. We see from these facts that devotion to the Master was gradually taking firm root in Mathur's mind. And how could it be otherwise? Just as the Master's wonderful character, unintelligible to human beings and rare even among the gods, stood all the tests of Mathur and appeared brighter as days passed, so, correspondingly, his never-failing selfless love completely captivated Mathur's heart. Mathur saw that he could not be deflected from the path of renunciation even by an inch by an offer of a property worth lakhs of rupees; that one could not produce a change in his mind with the lure of beautiful women; that he could not be led astray or made egotistic by any offer of worldly respect and reverence (for no greater respect can a man offer to another than to worship him as God); and that he did not want anything in the world for himself. Mathur also knew that the Master did not look down upon him in spite of knowing all the weaknesses of his character, but loved him as more than his own and saved him from dangers again and again, and was always thinking of his welfare in all respects. Mathur put this question to himself, "What do these signify?" And he felt that though human in body, the Master was a person of 'the country where there is no night', that his renunciation was wonderful, his self-control, knowledge, devotion and actions were all wonderful, and, above all, his love and grace for a weak but vain mortal like himself too was very wonderful.

Another thing that Mathur felt simultaneously in his heart of hearts was the sweetness of that unique character. The Master remained a simple boy, though there was that unprecedented manifestation of divine power in him. There was not the slightest egotism in him! How strange! Like a boy of five, he did not conceal even a little of whatever thoughts arose in his mind. There was always the same mood within and without. Whatever was in the mind was wholly manifest in words and deeds in all sincerity. Yet he never expressed anything which might be harmful to anybody, even if he had to suffer bodily pain. Is it possible to find such sweetness in man?

16. Jealousy broke the heart of Haldar, the Kalighat priest of Mathur Babu, when he saw the latter's firm devotion to the Master. He thought that this man (the Master) must have charmed the Babu by means of incantations. "Ah," he thought, "Is this rogue of a fellow going to spoil my long attempt at getting the Babu under my control? He again feigns the mood of a simple child! If he were so simple, let him tell me the incantation for 'putting a man under a spell'. I had exhausted all my spells on this Babu and he was almost on the point of succumbing to my influences; but now this interloper of a fellow has come between us."

Now with the increase in his devotion and reverence, Mathur began to have a strong desire for keeping the Master's company constantly and for serving him more and more. Therefore by extending pressing invitations, he often brought him to his house at Janbazar in Calcutta and enjoyed his company from time to time. In the afternoon he would take him for a drive to the Eden

Garden and other places of interest in Calcutta. He thought, "Can any and every plate, cup etc., be considered fit for Father to eat and drink from?" Thinking so, he had a new set of gold and silver things made in which he offered him food and drink. He dressed him in excellent clothes and said, "It is you, Father, who are the owner of all these (his estate and other property). I am nothing but the steward. For, see how you eat and drink from these gold plates and silver cups and glasses and then leave them behind without even looking at them, and it is I who get them cleaned and kept in a safe place, so that you may use them again. Then again, I have the duty of taking care of them and seeing that they are not broken or stolen."

17. We heard from the Master of the sorry fate of a pair of Varanasi shawls which Mathur purchased for a thousand rupees at that time. To whom but the Master should he make a gift of them? Thinking thus, Mathur wrapped them around his holy person and was filled with great joy. The pair of shawls was indeed very valuable; for, their price even at that time was so high, and now perhaps their like is not available at all. With the shawl on, the Master was at first going about very happily like a boy. He was looking at it again and again, calling others, showing it to them and telling them that Mathur had bought it for him at such a high price. But the next moment the Master was like a boy in a different mood. He thought, "What is there in it? It contains nothing but a quantity of 'animal hair'. It is also a modification of the five elements of which all things are made. And as regards prevention of cold—why, quilts and blankets are equally adequate. Like all other things, it is also not at all helpful for the realization of God. Rather, when one puts it on, one thinks oneself superior to others, and one's mind turns away from God, since it increases pride and egotism. Ah, so many are its defects!" Thinking so and throwing the shawl on the ground, he said, "It does not help one in realizing Existence-Knowledge-Bliss. I spit on it." Saying so, he actually started spitting on it and then rubbed it against the dust on the ground. He was at last ready to set fire to it when some one happened to come there and recover it from his hands. When Mathur Babu came to know of the fate of the shawl he did not at all feel sorry; on the contrary, he said, "Father did very well."

18. It is very clear from the events recorded above, on what

a high plane the Master's mind always dwelt, in spite of Mathur's best endeavour to keep him in the midst of comforts and enjoyments. But wheresoever it might dwell, it was always filled with ecstasy. That mind saw Light only—the Light that casts no shade, that is not liable to waxing and waning, and before which "the brightness of the sun, moon, and stars and the flash of lightning, let alone fire, are very dim, nay, almost dark".[1] While others saw and lived in masses of darkness, his mind dwelt in that realm of Light. This other realm of darkness—the world filled with malice, hatred and crookedness, and a permanent abode of lust and anger—why, it was just a place to which he had come on a flying visit out of compassion. So although he was living at Janbazar in Mathur Babu's house abounding in all kinds of luxuries and worldly enjoyments, the Master was the same Master, unattached, devoid of egoism and beside himself night and day with his own divine mood.

19. One day, just before dusk, the Master was lying in a divine semi-conscious state in Mathur's Janbazar house. There was no one near him. The Master's ecstasy was coming to an end and he was gradually having a little consciousness of the outer world, when Haldar, the Kalighat priest of Mathur mentioned earlier, happened to come in. When he saw the Master alone in that state, he thought it to be just the opportunity he was looking for. He approached him, looked around and said again and again while pushing his holy person about, "O man! Tell me how you have made the Babu subservient to you? Why do you keep mum, feigning ignorance? How did you captivate him? Speak out." Although he repeated the questions again and again, the Master did not or could not say anything; for he had not then the power to speak at all. Haldar then became angry, kicked him violently, saying, "Damn you, rascal! You want to hide your secret from me!" and went away. Devoid of egotism, the Master made no mention of the incident, since he knew that Mathur Babu was sure to be furiously angry and inflict very severe punishment on the priest, should he come to know of it. A short time after, the priest incurred Mathur's anger by committing some other offence and was dismissed. Afterwards one day, in the course of a conversation, the Master happened to mention this incident to Mathur. Hearing of it, Mathur said in anger and anguish,

---

[1] *Katha Upanishad* 2.2.15 and *Mundaka Upanishad* 2.2.10.

"Had I known it before, Father, that fellow would indeed have lost his head!"

20.   Mathur and his wife did experience in their heart of hearts, the infinite grace emanating from the Master as the divine teacher, and they had as a consequence surrendered themselves to him as to the very Deity Himself.   A convincing proof of this attitude of theirs was the fact that they never concealed anything about themselves from the Master. Both of them knew and said, "Father is not a man (but God Himself)!   Of what avail is it to conceal anything from him?   He knows everything, the inmost secret of anybody's heart." These were not just empty words;   they acted up to them.   How many were the occasions on which they did everything—eating, drinking, walking etc.,together with Father! What did it matter if Father freely visited the inner apartment of their house?   What mattered it again if he did not do so ? For, on many occasions they got proof of the fact that he knew every kind of thought passing through the minds of all.   And Father might very well be considered as good as a wall or some other insentient thing as regards the chief evil, the feeling of mental impurity arising from the free mixing of men and women.   Was it not a fact that none of the ladies in the inner apartment had felt that kind of shyness and hesitation, as they did in the presence of other men?   Did they not feel that he was but one of them or a boy of five?   We were surprised to hear many stories from the Master's own lips about the wonderful loving relation that existed between Mathur's family, including the members of the inner apartment, and the Master, who had converted himself thoroughly in thought and feeling into a female companion of the Divine Mother by constant and prolonged meditation on his own identity with such a character.   Sometimes, he said, he would come out dressed as a woman in the company of the ladies of the family, with a Chamara in his hand, to the place in the outer apartment where Mother Durga was being worshipped, and would fan Her holy image.   Sometimes again, when the husband of a young lady of the family arrived, he would adorn her with beautiful dress and ornaments. Just as, on account of his mood of the spiritual teacher, these ladies were firmly convinced of the Master's divine nature and revered him as such, even so were they thoroughly acquainted with his immaculate selfless love for them and poured out their heart's love to

him and acted and behaved with him with a freedom hardly imaginable.

21. How strange it is to contemplate! Here on the one hand we find the Master like a female friend in the midst of the ladies of Mathur's inner apartments (family), dealing with them with a love and intimacy devoid of any sexual tinge in it! Next, on the other, we find the same strange Master in the company of learned scholars and men in general behaving towards them with incomparable intelligence and divine insight! Who could this mysterious Master be with such a multi-form personality and a harmony of conflicting moods!

22. In those days it was the practice at the Dakshineswar temple, to bring the two images of Radha and Govinda from the adjacent bedroom and seat them on the throne in the main room of the temple, and to take them back to that bedroom for rest when the midday worship, food-offering etc., were over. They were again brought to the throne from there after four in the afternoon and were taken back in the night after Arati at dusk and offering of food. One day the marble floor of the temple had become slippery because of water spilt on it, and as the priest was taking the image of Govinda to the bedroom, he fell down and a leg of the image got broken. There arose a great stir; the priest himself got hurt and was also trembling with fear. The news reached the proprietors. They were faced with an insoluble difficulty. The worship could not be performed with a broken image. What was the way out now? Rani Rasmani and Mathur Babu invited all the famous scholars of the city for a meeting to ascertain the procedure to be adopted. The opinions of those scholars who were unable to be present owing to some business or other were also collected. The occasion was very sensational. It was also very expensive, as all the Pandits invited had to be given rich farewell presents according to their status. The Pandits opened their books, applied snuff to their nostrils, as if they were going to stimulate the source of their intelligence and delivered their dictum "Let the broken image be immersed in the water of the Ganga and a new one installed in its stead." And a sculptor was accordingly given orders to make a new image.

23. At the close of the meeting, Mathur Babu said to the Rani, "But Father has not been consulted on the matter ; what he thinks must be ascertained." Saying so, he asked Father for

his opinion. "If," said the Master in an ecstatic mood, "any one of the sons-in-law of the Rani had broken his leg owing to a fall, would he have been forsaken and another person placed in his stead, or would proper arrangement have been made for his treatment? Let that procedure be followed here also; let the broken parts of the leg of the image be joined and the worship continued. Why should the image be thrown away?" All were surprised to hear of the prescription. Ah, nobody had sufficient brains for this very plain reasoning! If is to be admitted that the image is living on account of the divine manifestation of Govinda, that manifestation must surely depend on the deep love and devotion in the heart of the devotee and His grace or compassion for him. So, why is that manifestation not possible in a broken image as well, if there were love, reverence and devotion in the heart? And the merit or demerit of the broken image can by no means touch that manifestation. Moreover, can the reverence for the image, in which the worship of the divine Lord has been performed and to which one's heart-felt love has been offered so long, vanish from the heart of a true devotee simultaneously with the breaking of a particular limb of that image? The Vaishnava teachers again teach that devotees should serve the divine Lord in the same way in which they themselves like to be served. They think that the divine Lord loves what one oneself likes in any particular condition, and inculcate upon us that kind of service. The prescription to give up the image is not proper from that standpoint too. Therefore, the ban on worshipping the Deity in a broken image which is found in the Smritis, is surely meant for the novice who is devoid of love for God and has just begun to tread the path of devotion. Some of the proud scholars, however, differed from the Master's decision ; some others did not clearly express their views lest their farewell gifts should suffer reduction ; and some others again who had acquired a little of true knowledge and devotion through learning, very highly praised the solution offered by the Master when they came to know of it. The Master, with his own hands, joined the broken leg of the image afterwards and the worship of it went on as before. When the sculptor made a new image and brought it, it was merely placed on one side of the temple of Govinda but was never duly installed. After the passing away of the Rani and Mathur Babu. their descendants made preparations from time to time for the installation of that

new image, but were compelled to put it off on account of some
worldly mishap or other on each such occasion. The new image
of Govinda is therefore preserved in that condition even now.[1]

_____

[1] Afterwards the new image was installed.—Tr.

CHAPTER VII

GRACE BESTOWED ON MATHUR IN THE MOOD OF THE SPIRITUAL TEACHER

I am the Self residing in the hearts of all creatures; I am the beginning, the middle and the end of beings.

—Gita X, 20.

1. There was great rejoicing that year on the occasion of the worship of Mother Durga at the Janbazar house of Mathur For, year after year the same indescribable bliss was shared by all — the old and the young, the ladies and the gentlemen —

there was something special at this year's worship of the Divine
Mother of the universe. Father was gracing the occasion with
his holy presence, and this had enhanced that bliss a thousandfold. There was, therefore, no limit to the rejoicings. Just as
a child, beside itself with joy and free from fear, makes importunate requests to its mother, and without any cause laughs,
dances and exclaims before her, so did Father, the unique child
of the Divine Mother, behave under the influence of his divine
mood, incessantly experiencing the direct manifestation of the
Mother in the image. And the image appeared to be living and
smiling and to be made of light. Again, the manifestation of the
Mother in that image and the manifestation of the same Mother
in the Master's divine body and mind combined together to fill the
atmosphere of the worship hall with an indescribable and indefinable Divine Presence, felt even by the dullest minds. This
evident Presence in the worship hall appeared to have illumined
not only the hall, but the hearts of every member and every
nook and corner of the entire house, and lent a unique beauty
everywhere.

And it could not but be so. For the Rajasika devotion
of the wealthy Mathur had left nothing to be desired in
the collection and arrangement of the materials required
for the worship. The collection of adequate quantities of
flowers, fruits, roots and sweets; the adorning of the
image with valuable clothes and ornaments; the decoration
of the walls, doors and floors of the house with green
leaves, flowers, flags and buntings; the provision of musical
instruments such as flutes and the like—all these had been attended
to with meticulous and exhaustive care. Besides, the presence of
the Divine Master at the house had, as it were, penetrated these
inert material substances and infilled them with the joyous sub-
limity of the spirit. The elevating beauty suggested by the ochre
cloth of many austere monks in the sublime setting of clumps of
evergreen deodars on snow-covered Himalayas; the tender inno-
cence emanating from a beautiful suckling at the breast of a handsome mother; and the unique glow that pure thoughts and
sentiments produce in a beautiful face — the charm of all these had,
as it were combined together to produce a wonderful atmosphere in
the house of Mathur Babu. Need it be said that all these indicated
the dawn of an era of unique good fortune on Mathur? Need it be

said that the master of the house and his wife, in spite of their being busy in making proper arrangements for worship and reception, were constantly being filled with an indescribable bliss and were feeling in their heart of hearts the grace and beauty of the holy atmosphere ?

2. The ceremonies of the day came to an end. The worshippers snatched a little time somehow to offer flowers with great delight at the holy feet of Father and of the Divine Mother.

It was dusk. Now the Arati of the Mother of the universe would begin. Father was then in the inner apartment and had completely forgotten his male body under the influence of a maddening spiritual mood. The only thought that expressed itself through his words and actions was, that he had, all his lives throughout the ages, been a woman companion of the Divine Mother. The Divine Mother was his life, his mind, his all in all; it was for the service of the Mother alone that he had assumed a body and was living in the way he had adopted. The Master's face was brightened with a spiritual emotion and love of the Mother, and his lips were beautified with a unique smile; his looks, the movements of his hands and feet, and his gestures resembled those of a woman. The Master was dressed in the beautiful silken cloth given by Mathur Babu and he had put it on in the manner of a sari. Who would say that he belonged to the male sex? The beauty and complexion of the Master at that time were so charming that they overflowed, as it were, all around. That complexion assumed a bright hue when there was a spiritual emotion, as if a light came out of his body. People could not turn their eyes away when they saw that beauty in wonder. We have heard from the Holy Mother that the colour of his body and that of the golden amulet (symbolizing his chosen Ideal) which he used to put on his holy person, mingled together, as it were, and became one. We have also heard from the Master himself, "Ah! There was such beauty then that people used to stare at me; the chest and the face used always to be red, as if a light emanated from the body. As people used to stare, I always kept the body covered with a thick wrapper and asked the Divine Mother importunately; 'Here is your external beauty, Mother, please take it back and give me internal beauty.' I used to pass my hand over the body, slapping it again and again, and say, 'Go in, go in'. As the result of this, the exterior became pale, as you see it."

3. We remember another event in the Master's life in connection with his personal beauty. At that time the Master used to go every year to Kamarpukur and spend there three or four months in the rainy season and then return to Calcutta. He went sometimes to the house of his nephew Hriday at the village of Sihar. The path leading to Sihar lay through Jayrambati, the village of his father-in-law. The people of that village made importunate requests to him to stay there for a few days, to which he agreed. Hriday, who was highly devoted to him, used to be always with him serving him in every way.

During the period of the Master's stay at Kamarpukur, there used to be crowds of people there continually from morning till evening in order to see him and hear a few words from his lips. The women of the neighbourhood finished sweeping and cleaning their houses very early in the morning and came with pitchers on their hips to take water home after their bath. And placing the pitchers on the bank of the Haldar pond near the Master's house, they would come to the Chatujyes' house[1] and sit there. They would spend an hour or so in talks with the Master and the women of his house, and then go to bathe. That happened every day. And if sweetmeats or other special preparations had been made the previous night in their houses, they would keep portions of them for him before using them themselves and take that opportunity to bring and give them to him. Fond of merry-making, he sometimes said to them on seeing them come when it was scarcely dawn: "The Gopis met Sri Krishna at Vrindavan at various times in various ways; we are told that they had their 'pasture meeting' at the time of going to the bank of the Yamuna to bring water, the 'sunset meeting' when the divine Lord returned with the cows after grazing them, then the 'dance meeting' at night and so on. So may I ask if it is your 'bath-time meeting'?" The women would roll with laughter to hear it. The men of the village came to the Master after the women had gone home to do their day-time cooking and other duties. They sat and talked with him as long as they liked. The women came again in the afternoon and some of the men-folk also came in the night. Again men and women from distant places came very often in the afternoon and returned before sunset.

----

[1]The house of the Master was so called because of their family surname, Chatropadhyaya or Chattarya or colloquially Chatterji or Chatujye.—Tr.

Thus there used to be gatherings of people like those during the
Car Festival (Ratha) and the ' swing' festival (Dol).

4. Once while the Master was staying at Kamarpukur,
arrangements were made for him to visit Sihar from Kamarpukur.
As the Master used constantly to be in ecstasy, his body became
very soft like that of a boy or a woman. He could not travel
even a small distance without a palanquin or a carriage. This
was why a palanquin was brought for him to go to Sihar via
Jayrambati. Hriday made ready to accompany him. In a red
silken cloth and with the gold amulet symbolizing his chosen Ideal
on his arm, he came chewing betel after his noon-day meal to get
into the palanquin; he saw there was a big crowd on the road
near the palanquin. Men and women were standing all around.
Surprised to see it, he asked Hriday. "Why has such a big crowd
gathered, Hriday?"

Hriday: "For what else? You will go there today; they
(showing the people) will not have an opportunity of seeing you
for some time; this is why they all have come to see you."

The Master: " But they see me every day; is there
anything new for them to see today?"

Hriday: "You look very handsome when you appear dressed
in silk cloth, chewing betel, which makes your lips shine with a
ruddy hue. That is why they want to see you. What else can the
reason be?"

The Master's mind was filled with an unprecedented feeling.
He thought, "Alas! They are all occupied with this ephemeral
external beauty only and do not want to see Him who is residing
within!" He had all along a sincere repugnance to physical
beauty. It increased a thousandfold by this incident. He said,
"What? Men to crowd thus to see a man! Cancel all programmes.
I will not go anywhere; for people will crowd thus wherever I
go." At once he went direct to his room in the inner apartment
of the house, took off his dress and sat down, worried and afflicted.
Filled with humility, the Master did not go to Jayrambati and
Sihar that day. Hriday and all the others of the household
exhorted him in various ways, but all their efforts were of no avail.
Just imagine, O reader, what a mean and contemptuous idea
this divine personage had of his own body! And think of ourselves
—how mad after beauty we are! What rubbing and massaging!
What an array of cosmetics — mirrors, combs, razors, brushes,

powdered pulse, soap, essences and pomades! And, again, in imitation of the West, what an excessive indulgence in the delusion that this " cage of bones and flesh " is our self, and what an inordinate scramble for plunging ourselves headlong into utter ruination through that! To be neat and clean in order to have a pure and holy mind on the one hand, and this excessive concern with physical appearance on the other — can you, O reader, take them to be the same! Let us, however, resume our topic.

5. The Arati of the Divine Mother was about to begin, but that ecstasy of the Master did not come to an end. Srimati Jagadamba Dasi thought she would somehow or other bring the Master to normal consciousness and go to witness the Arati with the other ladies of the house; but she was at a loss to know what she should do when she found that the Master's ecstasy did not end. She did not think it proper to leave him alone there and herself go to attend the Arati. She deliberated, " What shall I do? Once the Arati music begins, any one whom I might leave here to look after him would surely run to the worship hall there as fast as her legs could carry her. And Father also cannot take care of himself when he is in the grip of spiritual emotions. Thus devoid of normal consciousness, he once fell on a live charcoal and was not conscious of it. It was only after a great deal of care and treatment that the sore could be healed. If I leave him alone, some similar disaster might happen on this happy occasion. What shall I do now? And what will my husband think?" She was thinking thus when a plan suggested itself to her. Taking out hurriedly all her precious ornaments and putting them on his person, she began to whisper again and again into his ears, "Let us go Father. The Mother's Arati is to begin soon. Will you not fan the Mother with the Chamara?"

6. It was always observed that however deep the Master's absorption might be in a spiritual mood, however distant his thought had traversed into the subtle realm of ideas from the persons, thoughts, words or objects inciting that inward concentration, his mind was always open to those inciting words or thoughts, and the utterance of them a few times in his ear was sufficient to bring him back to normal consciousness. That such is the behaviour of a concentrated mind, is recorded briefly, if not at length, in the Yoga scriptures of Patanjali and others. The reader well versed in the scriptures, therefore, will not take long to

understand such a behaviour of the Master's mind. And those who have as a result of many virtuous actions attained a little of mental concentration in their lives will more easily understand it. Let us, therefore, follow the subject of which we were speaking.

7. The words of Jagadamba Dasi entered the Master's ears. And immediately on regaining his normal consciousness to a great extent, he accompanied her, partially conscious and brimming with joy. No sooner had they arrived at the worship hall than the Arati commenced. Surrounded by the ladies, the Master began to fan the image with a Chamara. The ladies stood on one side of the hall and the gentlemen, including Mathur Babu, on the other, to witness the Arati of the Divine Mother. As soon as Mathur Babu's eyes fell on the ladies, he saw that a new lady stood near his wife and was fanning the Mother with a Chamara, radiating wonderful beauty from her person, dress, and ornaments. Although he looked again and again, he could not know who she was. He thought at last that she might be a friend of Jagadamba, some rich man's wife who had perhaps come by invitation.

The Arati was over. The ladies saluted the Divine Mother, went back to the inner apartments and were busy doing their duties. In that state of partial consciousness, the Master went into the inner apartment with Mathur Babu's wife and came gradually to normal consciousness. He then took off the dress and the ornaments, came out and sat with the men-folk, and raising various religious topics, charmed all by his lucid explanation and apt illustrations.

8. A little afterwards, Mathur Babu went to the inner apartment on some business and asked his wife, in the course of the conversation, about the lady who had been standing near her and fanning the Mother with a Chamara at the time of the Arati. Mathur Babu's wife smiled and said in reply, "Could you not know who she was? Father in an ecstasy was fanning the Divine Mother thus; that is quite possible; for one cannot know Father to be a man when he puts on the dress and ornaments of a woman." Saying so, she told Mathur Babu everything from the beginning to the end. He was very much surprised and said, "This is why I say, 'Who can recognize Father even in trifling matters if he does not allow himself to be recognized?' Don't you see! I could not recognize him today, though I see him and am with him for all the twenty-four hours."

33

9. The seventh, eighth and ninth days of the fortnight passed in great joy. It was the morning of the tenth day (Vijaya Dasami). The priest was hastily finishing the Mother's brief worship for the day; for the looking-glass had to be immersed[1] at the moment prescribed in the almanac. The image itself was to be immersed after sunset. There descended, as it were, a shadow of sadness over the minds of all the household of Mathur Babu, and there was a feeling of an indescribable, an undefined fear of an inevitable and immediate separation from a very dear person. A penumbra of such sadness is always attached to even the purest bliss of this world! It is perhaps according to this law that the pain due to the separation from God is felt from time to time even in the life of the greatest lovers of God. And even the hearts of the strong among us melt into tears when we go to immerse the image on the Vijaya day. The case of Mathur's wife needs no mention. Since the morning she had often been rubbing the tears away from her eyes with the end of her cloth, while she was engaged in her duties.

10. In the outer apartment, however, Mathur had yet no idea of the approaching moment. His heart was swelling with joy as before. Having brought the Mother of the universe to his house and enjoyed the blessed company and grace of Father, Mathur was experiencing a fullness of joy within himself and was forgetful of the outer world. Who was interested in what was to happen in the world? And where was the need? His days would undoubtedly pass in that way in the company of the Divine Mother and Father. Just at that time word came from the priest, that the "immersion ceremony" of the Mother was about to take place. He wanted to know whether the Babu would be pleased to go to the worship hall and pay his obeisance to the Divine Mother before that ceremony.

11. Mathur could not even understand at first what was said to him. When he came to understand it after questioning those about him, he became conscious of the fact that it was the tenth day, the Vijaya. And as soon as this knowledge dawned on him he was stunned, as if he had received a severe blow on his head. Filled with grief and pain, he began to think, "The Mother to be

---

[1] A pot, full of water, is kept in front of the image and a looking glass is held over it in such a way as to catch the reflection of the image. Then it is immersed in the water. This is what is known as the "looking-glass immersion" of the Mother.—Tr.

immersed today! Why? By the grace of Father and the Divine Mother I stand in need of nothing. Unlike before, my mind too has been filled with bliss by the holy advent of the Mother to my house. Why should I then court dejection by immersing the Mother? No, I cannot break up this 'fair of bliss'. Oh! The immersion of the Mother! I feel suffocation even to think of it." Mathur was himself immersed in such thoughts and began shedding tears.

In the meanwhile, time was nearly up. The priest was sending word every now and then, "Babu, please do come once and stand. The Mother's immersion has to take place." Mathur felt much annoyed and sent word, "I will never allow anyone to immerse the Mother. The worship will continue as it is going on now. If anybody immerses the Mother without my approval, a grievous disaster is sure to happen. There may even be bloodshed and murder!" Saying so, Mathur sat in a very stern mood. Seeing his master in this strange mood, the terrified servant moved away, and going to the worship hall, told the priest everything. All held their breath!

12. All of them consulted together and sent those members of the household who were held in respect by Mathur to persuade him to agree to the immersion. They also went and tried, but failed to change his mind. The Babu said, "Why? I shall perform the daily worship of the Mother. As I have the means for that by Her grace, why should I bid good-bye to Her?" What could they do under the circumstances? They too came back, and every one concluded that Mathur's brain must have got deranged. That conclusion apart, what was now the way out? Everyone of the household knew how rash Mathur was. Everyone knew that when angry, he bade good-bye to his faculty of reason and understanding. Who was going to incur his displeasure by ordering the immersion ceremony of the Deity without his approval? Nobody came forward to do that. Exaggerated news reached the mistress of the house. Overwhelmed with apprehension and alarm, she requested the Master to try to persuade him. For who but Father was there to save them from danger? Who knew if the Babu's brain had not really been deranged?

13. The Master came and saw Mathur deeply absorbed in thought and pacing up and down the room with his face sombre and eyes red. As soon as he saw the Master, Mathur came up

to him and said, "Let them say whatever they like, Father, I cannot bid good-bye to Mother before I breathe my last. I have told them that I shall perform Her daily worship. How can I do without Mother?"

Passing his hand over Mathur's heart, the Master said, "Oh! Is this your fear? But who says that you will have to be without Mother? Moreover, where will She go even if the ceremony of immersion be gone through? Can a mother afford to be away from her child? Sitting in the outer hall She accepted your worship these three days. She will now be nearer to you. Sitting in your heart, She will hereafter accept your worship."

14. It is difficult to explain what a marvellous and charming power these words and the touch of the Master had! It was seen on many occasions that a visitor was engaged in a heated discussion with the Master and was by no means inclined to accept his conclusion, when the latter would cleverly touch the other's person, and immediately the strong tendencies of his mind due to which he had held contrary views would vanish, leading him to wind up the arguments with the acceptance of the Master's view unreservedly. He said to some of us on this matter: "Do you know why I touch people that way when I speak? I do it, so that the power by virtue of which that obstinacy is persisting in them might lose its force and they might realize the truth rightly and accurately." We have seen and heard many instances of how, by a mere touch, he used to diminish, and sometimes even destroy for ever, the strength of the powers standing as obstacles in others' path to the realization of truth. By touching he could draw those obstructing forces into himself. We have often noticed how the very words, spoken by others without making any emotional impact on the listener's mind, made very deep impression on them, even instantly changed the course of their lives, when they came from the Master's mouth. We shall acquaint the reader with these incidents on some other occasion. Now let us go on with Mathur Babu's story.

15. By the touch and words of the Master, Mathur gradually regained his normal consciousness. We do not know whether this was effected by any kind of vision produced by the Master's will and touch. We think this probable. But it seems to us that his eagerness to retain the image must have disappeared only because he began to experience the thrill of joy produced by a

keen sense of the Divine Mother's presence within, illumining the dark cavern of his heart with an effulgence unknown to him before. When a true spiritual teacher draws the attention of the disciple to the splendour of a higher ideal, the spiritual moods and planes pertaining to the lower levels naturally disappear from his consciousness.

16. There is no doubt that Mathur's devotion to, and reliance upon, the Master were also the result of his variously testing him, strange though it might appear to us. He tested the Master in every manner, by offering him wealth, beautiful women and unlimited mastery over himself and all his household, as also by freely spending money on his relatives, such as Hriday and others. But he found that, unlike others, he was above all temptations. He saw also that before the Master's discerning eye, the cloak of insincere love and devotion could not conceal its real nature for long. On the contrary, if even after committing misdeeds like homicide and other heinous offences, anybody sincerely and openheartedly took refuge in him, he pardoned him all his offences and cordially accepted him, granting him the power of gradually recognizing and comprehending higher ideals. He would find to his surprise that what had been impossible became possible for him now by virtue of a wonderful and unknown power, which was none but the Master.

17. Keeping the company of the Master and observing his experience of unlimited bliss, Mathur, though a worldly man, once had a desire to directly understand for himself what that experience was. He then had the firm conviction that Father could make all persons experience it at his mere will. For was he not himself all the Deities — Siva, Kali, Krishna, Rama? Where was then any difficulty in his granting divine visions? And how would it then be strange if he could reveal to anyone by his grace — what was nothing but his own other forms? This conviction was, in truth, a matter of no small wonder. All those who mixed with him intimately had gradually the conviction that the Master could by his will make the impossible possible — that by his mere wish he could make anyone realise the Truths of the spiritual realm. By virtue of his own spiritual power and the strength of a pure character, an ordinary teacher finds it difficult to produce such a realisation even in one person —what to speak of being able to do so in the hearts of many? It is given to a divine incarnation

alone to be able to do so. In fact it is one of the especial proofs of one being an incarnation. And knowing that many will try to deceive people in this world of falsehood and fraud in their holy names, the incarnations have proclaimed: "When I shall go beyond the ken of mortal eyes, many hypocrites will appear before you and say, 'I am an incarnation of God, I am the refuge and saviour of weak mortals.' Beware of them all."[1]

18. As soon as Mathur felt that desire, he went to the Master and said importunately, " Father, you must do something that I may have ecstasy." We can with certainty imagine that the Master said to him what he used to say to all others on similar occasions: "Oh, it will surely come at the right time. Does a seed sprout into a tree as soon as it is sown and yield fruits to be eaten immediately? Why? You are all right. You are keeping a fine balance between God and the world. If you have those things (ecstasy and the like), your mind will give up the world. Who will be there then to take care of your estate and other properties? Sure as anything, they will then be plundered away and enjoyed by all and sundry. What will you do then?"

19. But who would give ear to those words? Mathur was importunity itself; Father must make him attain ecstasy. When he found that such dissuasion produced no result, the Master raised the topic to a higher pitch. "Ah," said he, " do devotees want to see Him? They only want the privilege of serving Him. Direct experiences produce fear through the knowledge of the powers of God, and consequently love for Him gets suppressed. Krishna went away to Mathura and the Gopis were overwhelmed with the pangs of separation, and he sent Uddhava to console them. Uddhava was a person of Vedantic knowledge. He could not appreciate the spiritual attitude of the Vrindavan people, viz., shedding tears, feeding and dressing Krishna, and the like. He looked down upon the pure love of the Gopis as something inferior and within Maya. Uddhava was destined to change his views and learn by experience — that was also another consideration in sending him. Uddhava came and began to console the Gopis, 'Why do you behave this way and call on Krishna repeatedly? Do you not know that He is the divine Lord and is all-pervading? It cannot be that He is at Mathura and not at Vrindavan. Instead

---

[1] Matthew, XXIV—11.23-26.

of giving yourselves up to sorrow and despair, just once shut your
eyes and see that the One, having a dark-blue complexion like a
newly-formed cloud, wearing a garland of wild flowers and playing
on the flute, is always there within your heart.' 'Uddhava,' said
the Gopis, when they heard this, 'you are a friend of Krishna
and a man of knowledge. Still how do you speak like this! Are
we persons given to meditation or persons of knowledge? Or
have we got Him by practising Japa, austerities and so on, like
the Rishis and Munis? We actually adorned and beautified Him,
fed and dressed Him. Are we now to do these acts in meditation?
Can we do so at all? Have we that mind with which we can
meditate and perform Japa? It was long ago dedicated at the
lotus feet of Krishna. Have we got anything to call our 'own ',
even a self, to which we may attribute the 'I-consciousness' necessary to enable us to do the act of Japa?' Uddhava was surprised
to hear all this. He then understood the depth and the nature of the
love of the Gopis for Krishna, saluted them as his spiritual teachers
and returned. Consider — do true devotees want to see Him?
They feel the highest bliss in His service only. Beyond that they
do not want anything, visions and the like. These hamper their
spiritual relation of love with Him."

When Mathur could not be dissuaded even by this, the Master
said, "I know nothing, my friend. However, I shall tell Mother
and she will do whatever She likes."

• 20.   Mathur then had ecstasy after a few days. The Master
told us: "He sent for me. When I went I found that he was,
as it were, a different man. His eyes were red and tears were flowing.
Speaking of God, he was shedding floods of tears. And his heart
was trembling with quick pulsation. When he saw me, he clasped
both my feet and said, 'Excuse me, Father, I admit my defeat.
I have been in this condition for the last three days. I cannot at
all apply my mind to the affairs of my estate in spite of all my
efforts; consequently everything is going wrong. Please take back
the ecstasy conferred by you. I don't want it.' 'Why,' said I,
'did you not pray for ecstasy?' He then said, 'Yes, I did so
and there is also bliss in it; but of what avail is it? Everything
on this side is going to ruins. This ecstasy of yours, Father, befits
you only. We don't want all these things. Please take it back.'
I then laughed and said, 'I told you so previously.' 'Yes, Father,
said he, 'but could I understand then so clearly that something like

a ghost would possess me, and that I should have to take every step according to its whim all the twenty-four hours, and could do nothing even if I had a mind to?' I then passed my hand on his chest."

21. It will not do simply to have Bhavasamadhi. How many are the people who can bear the power of its upsurge; how many can retain it? It is impossible to do so, as long as there is the slightest worldly desire. That is why the scriptures ask the pilgrim on the path to the realization of God to be free from desires even at the outset. "It is by detachment and renunciation that some attained immortality," so goes the teaching of the Upanishads.[1] A Samadhi of a lower plane may be had by the momentary exuberance of emotions, but it cannot be maintained in a man in whom masses of desires for wealth, name, fame and the like abound. Acharya Sankara says (in *Vivekachudamani*, 79): "The crocodile of desire clutches by the neck those who proceed to cross the sea of the world without taking with them the antidote of detachment for their journey, makes them turn round and forcibly drowns them in the unfathomable waters of that sea."

22. We add below one of the many instances of this truth we had observed while we were with the Master. He was then staying at the Kasipur garden. One day a few Vaishnava devotees came with an absent-minded young man. We never saw them come before. The reason why they came was that they wanted to show the young man to the Master and know the Master's opinion about the strange spiritual state that had suddenly come upon him. Word was sent to the Master and he saw the young man. The face and chest of the young man were red: and he was seen taking the dust of the feet of all with humility. As he was repeating God's names, he was having frequent tremors and horripilations, and both his eyes were reddish and a little swollen owing to an incessant flow of tears. He was of a dark-blue complexion, was neither fat nor thin, and had a tuft of hair on his head. His face and limbs were graceful and well-built. He wore a rather unclean white cloth without borders. He had neither a wrapper for his upper garment nor a pair of shoes for his feet. He seemed quite indifferent to the cleanliness or preservation of his body. We were told the high-strung state had come on him

---

[1] *Kaivalya Upanishad*—1.2; *Mahanarayana Upanishad*—12.14.

suddenly when one day he was singing the praises of Hari. Since
then he had been virtually taking no food and having no sleep;
he was weeping day and night and rolling on the ground in his
longing to realize the Lord. He had been in that state during
the last few days.

23. We have seen in nobody but the Master such a power
of noticing and diagnosing physical changes produced in man by
the prevalence of spiritual emotions. The spiritual teacher has
been described in the *Guru-gita* and other books as "the physician
of the world-disease."   We did not at all understand that so much
hidden meaning was there in it before we had the blessing of
meeting the Master. We had no notion of the fact that the Guru
was indeed the physician of mental diseases and could diagnose
at first sight the modifications of the human mind due to the
influence of spiritual emotions. What is more, if from the reading
of the external signs, the Guru finds them favourable, he prescribes
methods following which the aspirant can scale higher altitudes of
spirituality. And if he finds them unfavourable, he devises means
which slowly remove them without harming the aspirant. It is
only because we saw the Master doing this every day that we have
a firm conviction on this matter in our minds. When Swami
Vivekananda attained the Nirvikalpa Samadhi for the first time,
we saw the Master prescribe immediately, "Do not take food out
of anybody's hands now for some days; cook your own food.
In this state one can at the most take food out of one's own
mother's hands; this state gets destroyed if one takes food out of
anyone else's hands. But there is no such fear when afterwards
it becomes natural." When he saw Gopala's mother suffering
physically, due to the increase of the affection of the 'humour of
wind' in her body, he said, "That windy humour of yours is nothing
but the 'humour of Hari'; what will you occupy yourself with if it
goes? It must continue. But when you feel the pain unbearable,
eat something." When he saw that a certain devotee's mind could
not merge in God forgetting the body, owing to a firm habit of
observing external purification and attachment thereto, he prescribed privately, "Call on God once by making a mark on your
forehead with the clay of the place where people answer nature's
calls." Seeing that an unrestrained bodily agitation during
Sankirtan was adverse to the progress of some one, he scolded
him and said, "Ah, you rogue, you have come to show off your

spiritual emotions to me! Do spiritual emotions ever produce these agitations ? One then merges completely and becomes motionless. Why this agitation? Be calm and tranquil. (To the others): Do you know what kind of spiritual emotions these are? They resemble a Chhatak (about 2 ozs.) of milk being boiled in a cauldron over the fire. One thinks it to be a large quantity, a cauldronful. You then take it down to find not a single drop there; the very little that was there has stuck to the sides of the cauldron." Perceiving the mental inclination of some one else, he said, " Enjoy to your heart's content, you rascal; but don't think that you do all these as religious duties."

24. The moment the Master saw the above-mentioned young man, he said, "Ah! It is, I find, the commencement of the Madhurabhava.¹ But this state will not last; he cannot retain it. It is very difficult to retain this state. As soon as a woman is touched (lustfully), this spiritual mood will vanish." Be that as it may, the devotees who came felt a little consoled when they knew from the Master's words that the young man's brain was not deranged, and went back. A little afterwards news reached us that the Master's prediction came true; the young man had been overcome by the fateful calamity. He had ascended fortunately to a very high plane indeed owing to the momentary excitement of Sankirtan, but alas! he came down to as low a plane as the heights to which he had risen. For he lacked the fitness to sustain the reaction of that mood which he had haphazardly obtained without the necessary previous preparations. Swami Vivekananda therefore always favoured devotion with discrimination and taught people to practise that kind of devotion lest they should otherwise fall victims to dangers of this type.

---

¹The Vaishnava literature has called that ecstatic mood of spiritual love "the Madhurabhava", which was seen in Radharani at Vrindavan in its fully developed stage with all the nineteen modifications, classified into eight groups and named as the "eight Sattvika modifications"— e.g., laughing, weeping, tears, tremor, horripilation, sweating, fainting, etc. The culmination of this Madhurabhava is known as the Mahabhava or the "great mood". It is in this stage that all the nineteen physical modifications mentioned above, are manifest fully—all owing to a superabundance of love for the Lord. It is said that ordinary mortals, even when perfected, cannot reach that dizzy height—it is possible for the divine Incarnations only.

25. Just as there was nothing to be concealed by Mathur from Father, so also Father always had, except at the time of ecstasy, the attitude of a child towards its mother or of a friend towards his friend in respect of Mathur. He spoke out to Mathur everything, took his counsel, accepted his advice, and sought his loving care. We have already told the reader the scriptural statement that when a person ascends to the highest stage of supreme knowledge, he appears at the best child-like, or at the worst mad, in the eyes of the ordinary people. What is more, Sankara, the teacher adored of the world, has stated clearly in his writings that such a person never loses his poise, whether he happens to be enjoying incomparable kingly wealth, or to be subsisting merely on alms dressed only with a Kaupina,—whether he is in a state of happiness or a state of misery according to popular estimation. Always dwelling in the bliss of the Self, he is absolutely content in the Self alone. Says Sankara:

"A liberated person roams in the world sometimes like an ignorant man, sometimes like a learned one, and at other times again like one having the opulence of a king. He sometimes appears to be like one mad, and sometimes like one calm, quiet and intelligent. At other times again he is seen to be living like a boa, without asking even for the means to meet his daily needs such as food. Sometimes he is very much respected, in some places he is insulted, and again in some other places he lives entirely unknown. He remains thus filled with supreme bliss, steady under all circumstances." When this is the case even with ordinary liberated persons, it is no wonder that the supremely glorious incarnations of God remain steady under all circumstances and behave like children. Such behaviour, therefore, of the Master with Mathur is not at all surprising. But it was no small good fortune for Mathur to have been so intimately connected with the Master for such a long time.

26. Ah, how sweet was the relation existing between Mathur and the Master! During the time of his Sadhana and even afterwards, if the Master required anything, he immediately asked Mathur for it. About the visions or the spiritual moods that were experienced by him at the time of ecstasy or at other times, he used to ask Mathur, "Will you please tell me why such a thing happened? Please say what you think of that." The Master kept an eye on Mathur's welfare, so that his money might be properly

utilized — so that the money, meant for the service of the Deity, might be spent for that purpose, and thereby guests, poor people, holy men and others be maintained and great merit, conducive to his good, be acquired by him. We have often heard of such conduct on the part of the Master even when we were living with him long after the virtuous Rani Rasmani and Mathur had passed away. It will not be out of place here to give one example:

27. From the time of Mathur, it had been arranged that daily after the food offering and other services in the temples of Kali and Radha-Govinda had been completed, one big plateful of cooked rice with some other dishes of offered preparations and another plateful of fruits, sweets, and other eatables should be sent to the Master's room, so that the Master himself and others with him might partake of that consecrated food. Besides that, a part of the special offerings made to Mother Kali and Radha Govinda on festive occasions also used to be sent to the Master.

It was the rainy season — the day of the worship of Phala-harini. It was customary to celebrate the occasion on a small scale in the temple every year. There used to be a special worship of Kalika, the Mother of the universe, and various kinds of fruits and roots were offered to her. On this occasion also the same celebration was gone through. Flutes and other musical instruments were being played in the Nahabat. Swami Yogananda and some other devotees were there with the Master that day.

28. Particular characteristics of particular deities used to be manifested in the Master's body and mind on particular ceremonial occasions. On Vaishnava festivals the characteristics of Vishnu, and on Sakta days those of Sakti, would manifest in him. For example, on the occasion of the worship of Sri Durga, especially at the time of the " junction worship[1]", or during the worship of the Mother Kali, the Master used to feel identified with the Mother of the universe. He would be motionless, and sometimes his hands would assume the gestures, like those of Kali, offering a boon with one hand and protection against all fears with the other. Similarly, on ceremonial occasions like Janmashtami, the eight Sattvika Vaishnava signs like trembling, horripilation, etc., were

---

[1] Sandhi Pooja done at the confluence or junction of Ashtami and Navami days in the Navaratri worship.

seen in him, and he would be completely absorbed in the thoughts
of Radha and Krishna on those days. Again those spiritual moods
used to come on him naturally without any effort whatever. For
on many such occasions, if he were engaged in conversation with
devotees on various matters without any awareness of the day
being auspicious to a special manifestation of the Divine, it was
observed that, as if by the pull of some extraneous power, his
mind would be suddenly drawn away from the conversation and
be completely absorbed in identification with the particular aspect
of the Divine. At Shyampukur in Calcutta, we have seen many
similar instances. Once, engrossed in conversation with a large
number of men including Dr. Mahendralal Sarkar, the Master
suddenly entered into such an ecstasy at the time of the "junction
worship" of Sri Durga. Having then seen his luminous face
beaming with that splendorous smile, who would say that he had
any illness or even that he was the same person with the pale face,
indicative of the sufferings of illness, seen a moment ago?

There was a similar manifestation of a mood in the Master's
body and mind that day—the day of the worship of Phalaharini.
Sometimes filled with bliss, he like a boy of five, danced and sang
the Mother's name. All were charmed, gazing at the unprecedented beauty of his face. They were, moreover, experiencing in
their hearts, various wonderful divine emotions by virtue of the
company of the god-man. The night came almost to an end when
the Mother's worship was finished. So nobody could take any
rest. It was dawn.

The next morning, at about eight or nine, the Master saw
that the portion of the special offerings of the day, which was to be
sent to him according to the usual practice, had not yet arrived.
He called his nephew Ramlal, the priest of the Kali temple, and
asked him the reason; but he could not say anything. "All the
offered articles," said he, "have, as usual, been sent to the chief
temple officer. They are being distributed from there and every
one is getting the share he is entitled to, according to the established
custom; but I cannot say why it has not reached here even now."
The Master was uneasy, nay, troubled, about it. He asked many
persons one after another, "Why has Prasada not yet come from
the office?" and went on talking about it. He waited a little but
when he found that it had not reached him even then, he put on
his slippers and himself went to the chief officer. He asked the

officer, "Hallo, how is it that the Prasada due to that room
(showing his room) has not yet been sent as usual? Has there
been a mistake? It is wrong that such a long-standing arrangement
should be upset through a mistake." The officer looked small
and said, "Has it not yet reached there? That is very bad. I shall
just now send it."

29. Swami Yogananda was then a boy. He was of course
a little proud, as he was born in the ancient and respectable family
of Savarna Chaudhuris. The chief official, other officers, priests
and others of the temple did not count at all in his estimation.
But he had completely surrendered himself at the holy feet of the
Master on account of the latter's disinterested grace and love.
His home being adjacent to Rasmani's garden, it was convenient
for him to visit the Master daily. And how could he refrain from
visiting? For the strange attraction of the Master took him there
by force, as it were, at the fixed time every day. Though thus
respectful towards the Master, he had not cultivated any familiarity
with the temple officers. So on finding the Master anxious over
his portion of the temple offerings, he, instead of going to make
enquiries about it, blurted out, "What does it matter if they don't
come? Ah, how precious the articles are! These things again
never suit your stomach; you take none of these things; under
such circumstances is there any harm if they are not sent at all?"
But apparently without even hearing his objections, the Master
went in a hurry to ask the chief officer for the reason. Yogin then
thought, "How strange! Why is he so anxious today about those
trifling fruits, roots and sweets? Why is he in this state of mind
today? I never saw him thus agitated under any circumstances."
When after a good deal of reflection he could not find out any
special reason whatever for it, he came at last to the conclusion,
"Oh, I see it now; it is the family tradition that tells, whether he
be the Divine Lord Himself or any other great personality. He
is born in a family of priests accustomed generation after generation
to 'bundle rice and plantain'. Won't that family tradition cling
to him a little at least? How else could this be accounted for?
He never feels uneasy even over important matters; but he has
become so restles about this trifling affair. If that were not the
fact, why is he so anxious for those food offerings which he cannot eat or use otherwise? It cannot but be the habit inherited from
his ancestors."

30. Cogitating thus in his mind, Yogin (or as he was after-wards known, Swami Yogananda) arrived finally at that conclusion and was waiting in the room. The Master now returned and said to him, "Do you know why I did so? Rasmani has bequeathed so much property so that holy men and devotees may get Prasada after the articles of food have been offered to the Deity. The food offerings sent here are invariably eaten by the devotees and the spiritual aspirants visiting this place. That fulfils the purpose of Rasmani's gift. But do you know how they (the priests of the temple) utilize these things? They sell the rice for money. Some of them again keep prostitutes; they take these fruits etc., to feed them. I fight so much in order that a little at least of Rasmani's intentions is fulfilled." Swami Yogananda was surprised to hear it and thought, "Ah me! Such is the hidden meaning even of this act of the Master!"

31. Ah, what a sweet relation the Master thus established with Mathur! It is very clear that by virtue of the motiveless grace of the Master, Mathur's love was so intensified that Father became his very life. Besides that, it was his behaviour like that of a boy, which attracted Mathur in no small measure. Is there a man, whose mind will not be attracted towards a boy innocent of all worldly ways? Is there any one who, being near him will not keep an eye of concern on his sweet motiveless movements and go forward to protect him lest he should be harmed in the excitement of play? And, again, there was not the slightest artificiality in the boy-like behaviour of the Master. When he was in that mood, he looked just a boy in every sense, genuinely incapable of pro-tecting himself. Is it, therefore, strange that there arose in the powerful, vigorous and intelligent Mathur a spontaneous inclina-tion to protect him in all circumstances? Therefore, just as on the one hand, he depended on the Master's divine power, so, on the other hand, he always kept himself ready to protect Father, whom he knew to be like an inexperienced boy. When Mathur saw that there was thus a strange juxtaposition in Father of the all-knowing nature of the spiritual teacher and the little-knowing nature of a boy, he perhaps came to some such conclusion as this, that he would have to protect Father as regards all worldly matters, including his personal safety, while Father would protect him in all matters pertaining to the subtle realm of the spirit that lay beyond human vision and power. We, therefore, see clearly

that Mathur's love for Father assumed an unintelligible nature that was in keeping with the strange and mysterious personality of Father who was a wonderful meeting ground of a very complex aggregate of contrary attributes such as Godhood and manhood, all-knowingness and little-knowingness. Although the Father, established in Bhavamukha and having his hands in the posture[1] symbolic of bestowing boons and protection from fear, was the chosen Ideal of Mathur, the latter had, however, sometimes to divert himself from the attitude of worshipful reverence towards him and console that very august Father who looked the living embodiment of simplicity and dependence in his child-like moods.

32. The love of Mathur for him endowed him with the power of providing plausible explanations for all the queries and doubts of Father. One day Father went out suddenly when he was talking with Mathur and returned with a sad face. He then asked Mathur, "Will you please tell me what this disease is? I saw a worm going out from my body with the urine. Nobody, I am sure, has such worms within his body. What is it that has happened to me?" The very Father, who perhaps a little while ago was charming everybody with wonderful explanations of the hidden spiritual truths, was now beside himself like a boy with causeless anxiety, depending wholly on Mathur's intelligence and words of assurance. No sooner had Mathur heard this than he said, "It is very good, Father, that it has happened so. Every one has a worm that generates lust in his body. It is this lust-worm, that produces various bad thoughts in him and makes him commit evil actions. That lust-worm has left your body by the grace of the Mother. Why are you so uneasy about it?" As soon as Father heard this, he was consoled and said, "Ah! You are right; how lucky it was that I asked you!" Saying so, he expressed his joy like a boy.

33. "You see," he said one day in the course of conversation to Mathur, "The Mother has shown and convinced me that there are many devotees of mine who are to form an inner circle. They will all come and hear and know of God from 'here' and will have direct knowledge of Him, realize Him, and be blessed with divine love and knowledge. The Mother will sport in various ways

---

1As he was then feeling himself identified with the Kali form of the Divine Mother.—Tr.

with this 'case' (that is, his body), and will do good to many. That is why She has not broken the 'case' but has kept it on. What do you say? Are all these mere hallucinations of the brain or real and true perceptions? Please tell me that."

"Why should they be hallucinations, Father?" said Mathur, "When the Mother has not shown you anything deceptive up to this time, why should this only be wrong? This also will prove to be true. But why is there delay in their coming? Let them by all means come soon; we shall then be together and be happy with them."

Father was thereupon convinced that what the Divine Mother had shown was true. He then said, "I don't know when they will come. But the Mother has said so. She has shown me that whatever is to happen by the Mother's will, will happen."

34. Rani Rasmani had no son, but had four daughters. Mathur Babu married the third, and after her death, the youngest daughter. The intelligent Rani fixed and marked in her life-time the share of the estate for each of the sons-in-law, lest there should arise a dispute among themselves over the estate. One day after the estate had been thus divided, Mathur Babu's wife, or as she was known in the family, the "third mistress," went to bathe in a pond in another's share of the estate, saw a luxuriant growth of the green Susni there, plucked some and brought it away with her. It was the Master only who saw her do it. As soon as he saw her doing that, he was extremely worried. "The 'third mistress'," thought the Master, "has taken another's porperty without asking her for it. It is immoral. She did not think it an act of theft to take another's property without her knowledge. And, again, why should she covet another's property?" He was thinking thus when he met that daughter of the Rani to whose share the said pond had fallen. The Master narrated to her immediately the whole incident. She could not control her laughter on hearing it and on seeing that serious mood of the Master, as if the 'third mistress' had acted very wrongly. She said humorously, "Ah, the 'third mistress' acted very wrongly, Father!" Just at that time the 'third mistress' also happened to come there. She also said jokingly when she knew the reason of her sister's laughter, "Father, is it proper for you to expose me like this? I stole the greens and secretly took it away lest she should see it! You have thus put me out of countenance!" Saying so, the two sisters burst into a roar

34

of laughter. The Master then said, "I don't know your worldly ways. But when the property has been divided, it is not good to take anything without the knowledge of the owner. This is why I told her all this, so that she might know it and settle matters as she liked." The daughters of the Rani began to laugh all the more at his words, and thought how frank and naive Father was.

35. On the one hand, Father had such a childlike nature that made him depend on Mathur. On the other, there were occasions when the position was reversed, and Mathur became the suppliant needing protection from the Master. There were sometimes quarrels between Mathur and other landlords, leading to free fights between their followers. On one such occasion a murder was committed at Mathur's orders, and Mathur was in great danger of criminal proceedings. He therefore came imploring to the Master: "Father, save me!" The Father grew angry at first and scolded Mathur much. "You rascal!" said he, "you will create an affray every day and come and say, 'Save me!' What can I do? Go and suffer the consequences. What do I know?" Then on account of his importunities the Master said, granting his prayer, "Well, whatever is to happen by the Mother's will, will happen." And as a matter of fact that danger passed away.

36. Many are the examples that reveal these two aspects of the Master's personality. Having had such experiences, Mathur was firmly convinced that it was by the grace of the Father of many-sided personality that he possessed whatever he had, namely, wealth, respect, power and everything. Therefore, there is nothing to be surprised at in the royal honour that Mathur paid to the Master as an incarnation of God and at the unflinching devotion and steadfast faith he evinced in respect of him. The extent of worldly men's devotion can be gauged by the amount of money they are prepared to spend for the objects of their devotion. Especially it is so in the case of a person like Mathur, who, like most clever men of the world, was somewhat miserly in spending money. It was therefore due to the intensity of Mathur's faith in the Master and devotion for him that he spent money unstintedly on him. Mathur once dressed him in beautiful attire and seated him to witness a Yatra performance, placing before him one hundred rupees or more in stacks of ten rupees each for him to give as rewards to the singers and actors. Father went on listening to the Yatra and when he experienced deep spiritual

emotions or was charmed with some captivating song or speech of an actor, he immediately pushed the entire sum of money with his hand towards the person concerned and rewarded him with that. Mathur was not at all annoyed at it. He expressed his joy saying, "A reward just befitting the high mind of Father." He placed stacks of coins over again in similar rows before him. How long could that money last with Father, who had become established in Bhavamukha and had always been absolutely free from covetousness owing to his conviction, 'money is earth, earth is money'? Beside himself with the overwhelming inebriation of the divine emotions, he would give away once more the whole amount at once. Afterwards finding no money near him, he took off the shawl and the precious cloth with which Mathur had adorned his own person, and gave them away as presents, remaining motionless in Samadhi with the divine consciousness alone as his garment! Mathur, filled with bliss, thought that his money had been put to its proper use, and began to fan him.

37. Many are the examples of the liberality of the miserly Mathur for pleasing the Master. He took the Master with him when he made his pilgrimage to Kasi, Vrindavan and other holy places. At Kasi he obeyed his words, and like a wish-fulfilling tree, made liberal gifts; he gave to everyone whatever articles they asked for. He requested the Master also to ask for something at that time but the latter could find nothing of which he was in need. He said, "Give me a water-pot (Kamandalu)." Mathur's eyes were wet with tears to see his spirit of detachment.

38. The Master's heart was filled with compassion to see the poverty and misery of the village people when going through a village near Vaidyanath at the time of his pilgrimage to Kasi, Vrindavan and other holy places with Mathur. "You are," said he to Mathur, "but a manager of the Mother's estate. Give these people sufficient oil to cool their heads and each a piece of cloth to wear and feed them to their fill once." At first Mathur was a little hesitant and said, "Father, the pilgrimage will require much money, and the poor are too many. I may later be in want of money if I begin to do all that. What do you advise under these circumstances?" But the Master was not satisfied with this reply. There was an incessant flow of tears from his eyes to see the misery of the villagers and his heart was filled with an unprecedented compassion. "You rascal, I will not go to your Kasi. I will

remain here with them; they have none to call their own; I will
not leave them behind and go." Saying so, he became obstinate
like a boy and went and sat down amongst the poor people. Seeing
such compassion in the Master, Mathur had bundles of cloth
brought from Calcutta and did as Father had asked him to do.
Beside himself with joy to see the villagers happy, Father also
bade goodbye to them and started gladly with Mathur on his
journey to Kasi. We are told that the Master went on another
occasion with Mathur to a certain village in his estate near Ranaghat
where he was seized with a similar compassion to see the miserable
plight of the villagers, and he made Mathur do likewise once again.

39. Identified with the Supreme Divinity as the spiritual
teacher, the Master bound Mathur to himself for ever in a sweet
relationship. Such unprecedented relation with Mathuranath was
the mature result of the Master's prayer to the Divine Mother at
one time during his Sadhana under the influence of a sudden
strange mood. He had prayed, "Mother, do not make me a dry
Sadhu; keep me appreciative of your creative Bliss." For, as the
result of that prayer, the Divine Mother showed him four persons
(the suppliers of provisions) who had been sent with him into the
world for the maintenance of his body by providing him with the
necessities of his life, and Mathuranath was the first and the foremost of them. Could this relation have remained unimpaired for so
long a time if it had not been determined by Providence? Alas! O
world, how many such pure and sweet relations have you seen so
far! And alas! O desire for enjoyment, with what an adamantine
chain have you bound man! Although we have seen and established our relationship with such a wonderful Master—a being so
pure, illumined and untrammelled, a veritable image of selfless
love—our minds even now cast a longing, lingering look at lower
objects. While one day a friend was listening attentively and with
amazement to the story of Mathuranath from the Master himself,
he asked the Master, in great admiration for Mathur for his unprecedented good fortune, "What happened to him, Sir, after death?
It is certain, he will not have to be born again!" Questioned so,
the Master answered, "He must have taken birth as a king somewhere; for he had the desire for enjoyment." Saying so, he immediately started another topic.

CHAPTER VIII

THE RELATION OF THE MASTER AS THE SPIRITUAL TEACHER WITH HIS OWN TEACHERS

(TOPICS: 1. Incarnations are born spiritual teachers. 2. The Master initiated by several teachers 3. The Bhairavi Brahmani 4. The Brahmani's assistance to the Master in Sadhana 5. The Vaishnava scriptures on the Brahmani's experiences 6. Mathur's suspicions 7. The Brahmani's antecedents 8. The Brahmani, a spiritual aspirant of a high order 9. The Brahmani's Yogic vision 10. The story of Chandra 11. Miraculous powers lead to spiritual downfall 12. Chandra's fate 13. The story of Girija 14. Girija's miraculous power 15. Chandra's and Girija's powers 16. Miraculous powers are obstacles 17. They increase egoism: parable of the elephant. 18. The Brahmani's ignorance of non-dual consciousness 19. The "animal mode","hero mode", and "divine mode" of the Tantras 20. Brahmani not qualified yet for the "divine mode" of worship 21. The proof of it 22. The Brahmani's recognition of her limitation 23. The story of Tota Puri 24. The Master's contacts with saint Puri 25. Fearlessness and freedom of the knowers of Brahman 26. High state of Tota Puri 27. Fearlessness of Tota Puri 28. Tota Puri's teacher 29. Tota Puri on his Order 30. Antecedents of Tota Puri 31. Tota Puri's mind 32. Tota Puri's ignorance of the path of devotion 33. Proof thereof 34. Incident leading to Tota's giving up anger 35. God-realisation possible only on Maya clearing the path 36. An example thereof 37. Tota ignorant of the Divine Mother 38. Tota Puri's illness 39. Tota disregarded the indication of his mind 40. His desire to depart and the aggravation of his illness 41. Tota's attempt at drowning and the Mother's vision 42. Tota giving up his determination to die 43. His understanding that Brahman and His Power are one 44. Tota accepted the Divine Mother and left 45. Tota's knowledge of alchemy 46. Conclusion.)

I reside in the hearts of all. From Me come memory and knowledge and also their loss. It is I alone who am demonstrated by all the Vedas. I am the founder of the institutions for the handing down of the meaning of the Vedanta and am the knower of the Vedas.

—*Gita*. XV. 15

1. We have already said (III. 5-1) that in those who are born to be world teachers, indications of their capacity in this respect are

seen from their very childhood. In the case of the great souls known as the incarnations of God, this fact needs no mention. Born, as they are, to establish certain doctrines among men, they are seen as embodiments of these doctrines from their very childhood. No doubt the slow growth of their body and mind, as also the influence of time and favourable circumstances, may seem to help the development of their thought and their special capacity, but these are never the cause of the truths they proclaim or the capacity they express as world teachers. The capacity is born with them, and all efforts to trace it to some other source are futile. This analysis is found to tally exactly with the development of the spiritual power of the Master as the world teacher. One is surprised to discover the manifestation more or less of this power during his childhood, youth, the time of his Sadhana and all other periods of his life. And however much one may ponder over it, one can by no means ascertain how this power first originated in his life. We have no desire to increase the volume of our book by mentioning here the events of his childhood. But it will not be out of place to state what yet remains to be told about the Master's youth and the period of his Sadhana, during which time manifestations of spiritual powers as world-teacher are to be seen in his relation with several others besides Mathur Babu.

2. The Master tried on many occasions to explain to us, by adverting to the story of the world-renouncing Avadhuta spoken of in the *Bhagavata*, that though there should be one teacher only to initiate one in the Mantra of one's Chosen Ideal, there may be more than one subsidiary teacher or, in other words, instructor, teaching religious matters in general. It is written in the *Bhagavata* that, being taught particular spiritual matters by twenty-four subsidiary teachers, one after another, the said Avadhuta attained success. In the Master's life too we do not find any lack of instructors for acquainting him with particular ways of spiritual practice for realizing the Truth as presented by particular spiritual traditions. We, however, heard him often mention only the names of three such teachers—the Bhairavi Brahmani, the "naked" Tota Puri and the Muslim Govinda. The Master mentioned but rarely the names of other teachers, though he learnt from them the methods of spiritual practice according to other Hindu denominations. The only thing he mentioned was that he learnt from

other teachers the processes of spiritual practice according to their sects and attained perfection in each discipline within three days. He abstained from mentioning their names. But it is difficult to say now whether he forgot their names or they were not worth mentioning. But it is clear that he had contacts with them for very short periods only. That is why they do not deserve special mention.

3. Of all these teachers, the Bhairavi Brahmani stayed with the Master the longest, but it is hard to tell how long. For, before we took refuge at the holy feet of the Master, she had left Dakshineswar for good. The Master afterwards met her at Kasi where she was practising austerities.

4. We have heard from the Master that the Bhairavi Brahmani lived for a very long time at the Dakshineswar temple and other places like Devamandal-ghat on the bank of the Ganga in the neighbourhood. She made the Master practise one after another the disciplines recorded in the sixty-four principal Tantras. She was well versed in the Vaishnava scriptures also, and she helped the Master in certain matters at the time when he practised Sakhibhava and other devotional moods. Honoured by all, she lived at Dakshineswar for a period of about twelve years, extending even beyond his Sadhana period when her help was needed. She went with the Master and Hriday for some time during that period even to Kamarpukur and lived there among the Master's relatives. From that time on, the Holy Mother respected her like her own mother-in-law and called her "mother".

5. The Brahmani followed the Sadhana according to the Vaishnavas and experienced a little of the bliss arising from the loving attitudes towards God such as Sakhya and Vatsalya. Overwhelmed with Vatsalya towards the Master, with butter in hand and with her clothes wet with tears, she used to cry out loudly "Gopala", "Gopala", while she was staying at Devamandal-ghat in Ariadaha; and simultaneously the Master's mind at Dakshineswar felt a sudden yearning to see the Brahmani. We are told that he would cover that distance of two miles at a run, go to her like a child running to its mother, sit down near her and eat that butter. Besides, wearing red Varanasi silk cloth and ornaments collected by her from somewhere, carrying various kinds of eatables in her hand and singing songs, she sometimes used to come with the ladies of the neighbourhood to the Master at Dakshineswar, feed

him and then return. The Master said that she, with her dishevelled hair, and her agitated mood due to spiritual emotions, was taken to be none other than Yasoda herself, the queen of Nanda, grieving on account of her separation from Gopala.

6. The Brahmani possessed unusual beauty and accomplishments. We have heard from the Master that Mathur Babu had some doubts about her character, and became suspicious when he saw her grace and beauty and heard of her unrestricted travelling everywhere alone, without any companion. One day, it is said, he went to the length of speaking out in derision, "Where is your Bhairava, O Bhairavi?"[1] The Brahmani was then coming out of the temple of Kali after paying her obeisance to the Deity. Although suddenly questioned thus, she did not feel at all embarrassed or angry, but calmly looked at Mathur and pointed her finger at the Great God lying as a dead body under the feet of the Mother's image and showed Him to Mathur. The suspicious and worldly Mathur was also not a man to let the matter drop easily. He said, "But that Bhairava does not move!" "Why have I become a Bhairavi," retorted the Brahmani in a calm and serious voice, "if I cannot make the immovable move?" Ashamed and perplexed, Mathur stood speechless at the serious mood and answer of the Brahmani. Later on, his mind became free from that vicious suspicion, as he began to be acquainted day after day with her noble and innumerable good qualities.

7. We have known from the Master that the Brahmani was born somewhere in East Bengal and everyone who saw her was impressed with the idea that she must undoubtedly have been a lady of a very respectable family. She was indeed such. But we never heard from the Master whose house she had illumined as a daughter and in what village she was born; nor do we know whether she ever shed lustre on any one's house as a wife, or the reason why she felt detachment from the world and travelled from place to place as a Sannyasini in her middle age. And none of us knows in the least where she acquired so much learning nor where or when she made so much progress in Sadhana.

8. It needs no mention that the Brahmani was far advanced in Sadhana. This is very evident from the fact that she was

---

[1] 'Bhairava' is masculine gender, while 'Bhairavi' is feminine; the insinuation was that she might have a paramour.—Tr.

selected by Providence to be a spiritual teacher of the Master. We heard from the Master himself that even before she came to him she could know by the power of Yoga that in her lifetime she would have to help three men in their Sadhana, these being the Master himself and two others, and that as soon as she saw them in different places at different times, she did recognize them and help them. This is convincing proof that she was an aspirant of a very high order.

9. She spoke to the Master of Chandra and Girija, the two others mentioned above, at her very first meeting with him. "My child," she said, "I have already met both of them. And today I meet you whom I have been seeking all the time. I shall afterwards introduce them to you." And as a matter of fact the Brahmani brought them afterwards to Dakshineswar and introduced them to him. We were told by the Master himself that they were both aspirants of a high order. But though they were far advanced on the path of Sadhana, their desire for realizing God remained unfulfilled. They attained some special powers of working miracles and were, on account of that, doomed to lose their way in the woods of occultism.

10. The Master told us that Chandra was of a contemplative nature and a lover of God. He attained success in working a miracle with a Gutika or tiny ball. With that ball, sanctified by a Mantra, on his person, he could vanish from the vision of ordinary eyes and could easily get in and get out unseen even from carefully protected and unapproachable places. But the weak human mind becomes egoistic if it acquires such miraculous powers before the realization of God. And it is needless to say that it is the increase of egoism that entangles man in the net of desires, prevents him from going forward towards higher ideals and at last becomes the cause of his fall. Ah, how many and various are the ways in which the Master explained this to us over and over again: "It is the increase of egoism that leads to the increase of sin, and its decrease conduces to the attainment of virtue. The increase of egoism is accompanied with the decrease of virtue, and the destruction of egoism results in the realization of God. Selfishness is sin and selflessness is virtue. When the 'I' dies, all troubles are over." "Ah!" he continued, "it is egoism only that is called in the scriptures, 'the knot that attaches Spirit to matter'. Spirit or Consciousness means the Self which is of the nature of pure

knowledge, and matter means the body, the senses and the like. This egoism has tied these two together and has created in the human mind the firm delusion, 'I am a Jiva possessed of the body, senses, etc.' One cannot make any progress if one cannot cut this difficult knot asunder. It has to be given up. Again, Mother has shown me that miraculous powers are to be shunned like faeces. Attention should not be paid to them. They sometimes come spontaneously to one when one applies oneself to spiritual practices; but one who pays attention to them has to stop short there and cannot go forward towards God."

11. With Swami Vivekananda, meditation was, as it were, his life. He kept his mind meditating on God at all times, even while he was eating, lying, sitting and doing other necessary physical acts. The Master used to say that he had 'attained perfection in meditation'. While he was meditating one day, there suddenly came to him clairvoyance and clairaudience i.e., the power of seeing and hearing from a distance. As soon as he sat down to meditate and the meditation became just a little deep, his mind ascended to a plane from where he could see persons and hear their talks. No sooner had he such experiences than there arose a desire in his mind to go and see whether the vision was true or not. And he gave up his meditation immediately, went to those places and found that whatever he had seen during his meditation was entirely true. When he told the Master about it a few days after the occurrence, the latter said, "All these are obstacles on the path to the realization of God. Don't meditate for a few days now."

12. Egoism grew in Chandra when he attained success in the Mantra. We were told by the Master that the attachment to lust and gold grew gradually in Chandra's mind. He became enamoured of the daughter of a respectable well-to-do man and began to frequent his house by means of that miraculous power. Thus on account of the increase of his egoism and selfishness, Chandra lost the power and met with various kinds of humiliation.

13. The Master told us also of the strange power of Girija. He said that he went one day with him for a walk to the garden of Sambhu Mallick in the neighbourhood of the Kali temple. Sambhu Mallick loved the Master very much and considered himself blessed if he could be of any service to him. He acquired on lease a piece of land near the Kali temple at a cost of rupees two hundred and fifty and built on it a room for the Holy Mother

to live in. In those days she used to live in that room, and from there went to have a bath in the Ganga and visited the Master. Once, while she was staying there, she had an attack of severe blood dysentery. Sambhu Babu then made all arrangements for her treatment and diet. His wife was also a devotee who worshipped the Master and the Holy Mother as God incarnate. She took the Holy Mother home on "auspicious"[1] Tuesdays and worshipped her as the Divine Mother of the universe. Moreover, Sambhu Babu provided whatever was necessary for the Master, such as food and carriage hire for going to, and from, Calcutta. It was of course after the passing away of Mathur Babu that he got the privilege of serving the Master that way. The Master described him as his second "supplier of provisions", and in those days he used very often to go to his garden for a walk, spend a few hours in religious conversation with him and then return.

14. On one occasion he went with Girija for a walk to Sambhu Babu's garden and a long time passed in conversation with him. "Devotees," said the Master, "are like hemp-smokers in some respects. A hemp-smoker first has a strong pull at the bowl, hands it over to another and then puffs out the smoke slowly. He does not enjoy the intoxication till he passes the bowl to another. Similarly when devotees come together, one devotee, absorbed in the divine mood, speaks on God and, filled with bliss, becomes silent; he then gives another devotee an opportunity to speak on Him and enjoys the bliss as a listener." As Sambhu Babu, Girija and the Master came together that day, none of them was conscious how time flew. It was gradually dusk, and the first quarter of the night passed away imperceptibly, when the Master realised that they had to return. Bidding good night to Sambhu, he came to the road with Girija and began to proceed towards the Kali temple. But it was pitch dark. Unable to see anything of the road, he was slipping at every step and mistaking the direction. That it was dark, did not occur to the Master and, being deeply absorbed in divine talks, he forgot to ask Sambhu for a lantern. What was he to do now? He caught hold of Girija's hand and began somehow to feel his way. But he was experiencing great

---

[1] Every Tuesday is regarded as auspicious for the worship of the Divine Mother. Hence all Tuesdays have got the qualification, "auspicious".—Tr.

difficulty. Seeing him suffering thus, Girija said, "Wait a little, brother; I shall show you light." Saying so. he turned about, stood and illumined the road with a long stream of effulgent light emanating from his back. The Master said, "The whole of the road up to the gate of the Kali temple was very clearly seen in that bright light, and I had light all the way I went."

15. The Master then smiled and immediately added. "But those powers of theirs did not continue long. They disappeared when Chandra and Girija lived for some time in this (my) company" Asked by us for the reason, the Master said, "Mother withdrew their powers into this (his own body) for their good. And when that happened, they gave up all those vain things and their minds went towards God."

16. Saying so, he continued, "What is there in these powers? Entangled in them the mind travels far away from Existence-Knowledge-Bliss. Listen to a story: A man had two sons. Dispassion came on the elder in his youth. He left home as a monk, while the younger got his education and became learned and virtuous. He then married and applied his mind to the performance of the duties of a householder. Now, there is a tradition among monks that if they like, they may go to see the place of their birth once after the expiry of twelve years. The said monk also came thus to see his birthplace. Surveying the land, the cultivation, the wealth and other possessions of his younger brother, he came to his gate, stood there and called him by name. On hearing the call, the younger brother came out and saw his elder brother. As he was meeting him after a long time, the younger brother was beside himself with joy. He saluted him, brought him in, and sitting by his side, began to serve him in various ways. The two brothers conversed on various topics after taking their meal. The younger brother then asked the elder, 'Brother, you gave up all these worldly pleasures and wandered as a monk for so long a time. Please tell me what you have gained by it.' As soon as the elder brother heard this, he said, 'Do you want to see it? Then come with me.' Saying so, he went with his younger brother to the bank of the river in the neighbourhood, and said, 'Just see,' and immediately stepped on the waters of the river and walked to the other bank and called out to him, 'Have you seen it?' The younger brother paid half a penny to the ferry man, crossed the river by boat, went up to his brother and said, 'What have I

seen?' The elder brother said, 'Why? Have you not seen my crossing of the river on foot?' The younger brother then laughed and said, 'Brother, have you not seen that I also have crossed the river by paying half a penny? But is this all you have got in return for putting up with so much suffering for twelve long years? You have got only what I accomplish so easily for just half a penny!' The elder brother was awakened by these words of the younger one and applied his mind to the realization of God."

17. Thus, through stories, the Master explained to us in many ways that the attainment of such small powers, compared with things in the spiritual world, was very trifling and quite purposeless and was to be avoided by all means. We cannot abstain from narrating here another similar story of the Master: "A Yogi attained the power of bringing about whatever he mentioned. Whatever he said to anybody came to pass immediately. Even if he said to anybody, 'Die', he would die immediately: if he said to him again, 'Live', he would come to life at once. One day, while on a journey, that Yogi met a devout holy man. The Yogi found that he was always repeating the name of God and meditating on Him. He was told that the devotee had been practising such austerities there for many years. On seeing and after hearing all these things, the egoistic Yogi went up to that holy man and said condescendingly, 'Well, you have indeed been repeating the name of God for so long a time; tell me if you have gained anything?' The holy man replied humbly, 'What do I expect to get? I have no desire of getting anything except realizing Him; and one cannot realize Him without His grace. That is why I have been lying here and calling on Him that He may some day have compassion on me, knowing that I am so humble and lowly.' The Yogi retorted, 'If you have not gained anything, then what is the utility of this useless effort? Direct your effort so as to get something!' So advised, the devotee remained silent. But a little later, he asked the Yogi, 'Well, sir, may I hear what you yourself have got?' The Yogi said, 'Well, do you want to hear? Just see.' Saying so, he said to an elephant tied under a tree close by, 'Elephant, die.' And the elephant dropped down dead at once. The Yogi said proudly, 'Do you see? Now see again.' With this he said to the dead elephant, 'Elephant, live.' And the elephant came back to life at once, shook the dust off his body and stood there as before. The Yogi now said triumphantly, 'Well, have you now seen?' The

devotee had kept silent so long; but now he said, 'Well, what more have I observed than seeing the elephant die and come back to life again! But will you please tell me what you have gained thereby? Have you become free from repeated births and deaths by attaining that power? Have you got deliverance from old age and disease? Or have you realized the indivisible Existence-Knowledge-Bliss Itself?' The Yogi then remained speechless and was awakened."

Though Chandra[1] and Girija proceeded far on the path to the realization of God with the help of the Brahmani, they were far from being perfect. When they obtained the sanctifying company of

---

[1] Swami Vivekananda started for the second time for England and America in the month of June 1899. A short time after this, one day, a man came to the monastery at Belur, introduced himself as Chandra and stayed there for about a month. Swami Brahmananda always used to live in the monastery at that time. We have seen this person having much private talk with him. We have been told that he asked the Swami again and again, "Are you aware of anything here?" He meant whether the Swami felt the living presence of the Master there.

Chandra used to say that whatever the Master had said about him had turned out to be true. The only thing that even then remained unverified as true was the Master's promise to appear before him at the time of his death. He used to go to the shrine-room at the monastery every day and perform Japa and meditation with great devotion for a long time. Tears of love for God would flow out of his eyes at that time. When asked by anybody anything about the Master, he used to say with great delight what he knew of him. He appeared to us to be a man of a quiet nature. Seeing that he always sat quiet in one place and remained with his eyes shut, some one asked him derisively one day, "Are you, sir, in the habit of taking opium?" "What offence have I given you," said he humbly, "that you speak so?"

When he went to the temple and made salutations, for the first time, he addressed the Master's holy image as "elder brother," and filled with ardent affection and intense love, shed profuse tears. At first sight, he appeared to be an ordinary man, having no external insignias of religion like ochre cloth or sandal-paste marks on the forehead. He had a very ordinary cloth and an upper garment on, with an umbrella and a canvas bag in his hands. He had another cloth, a towel, and perhaps a pot used for drinking water, in the bag. He said that he travelled very often from one place of pilgrimage to another that way. Swami Brahmananda requested him very courteously and respectfully to live at the monastery for all his life. He also agreed and said, "I shall come and live here after making some arrangement of the landed property at home." But he never turned up at the monastery again. The person spoken of as Chandra in the text was perhaps the same man.

the Master, their power of performing such miracles, with its roots in egoism, was destroyed, it being absorbed into him. Thus they got an awakening and advanced with redoubled energy along the path leading to God-vision.

18. We have convincing proof of the fact that, though the Bhairavi Brahmani herself had proceeded very far along the path of Sadhana, she had not had the full realization of the indivisible Existence-Knowledge-Bliss Absolute. It was after the Master had attained perfection in the disciplines prescribed in the Tantras with the help of the Brahmani, that Tota Puri, who had realised the Nirvikalpa state of consciousness, the ultimate plane spoken of in the Vedanta, came for the first time, in the course of his travels, to the Kali temple at Dakshineswar. No sooner had Tota Puri seen the Master than he recognized him to be one of the fittest persons to enter the path of the Vedanta and taught him the Sadhana leading to the Nirvikalpa Samadhi by initiating him into Sannyasa. The Brahmani then made great efforts to make him desist from proceeding along that path. "My child," said she, "don't visit him often; don't mix much with him. His path is dry and austere. All your ardent affection and intense love for God will vanish if you mix with him." It is evident from this that although the learned Brahmani was an extraordinary person in respect of devotion to the Divine Lord, she never knew nor even dreamt that the unqualified state of Consciousness spoken of in the Vedanta, described and regarded by her as a dry and austere path, was the first step to the realization of the true, supreme devotion. She did not know that those persons alone who were pure, awakened and absolutely content in the Self could have selfless and ardent affection and intense love for God and that "the two, pure devotion and pure knowledge, are one and the same," as the Master used to say. Our inference is that the Brahmani did not understand it; and, because she could not understand it, the Master concealed from her as well as from his mother the fact that he practised Nirvikalpa Samadhi, shaving his head, putting on ochre-dyed cloth and taking initiation from Swami Tota Puri into the mystery of Sannyasa. We are told that the old mother of the Master used to live then on the first floor of the music room to the north of the Dakshineswar temple grounds. Confining himself to a room, the Master kept out of her sight, as also of others during the three days he practised the Vedanta. It was the revered Puri alone who used to go to him

from time to time. It is needless to say that the Master did not even give ear to the Brahmani's words.

19. As far as we have been told by the Master, it seems that the Brahmani was an expert in the 'hero-mode' of worship of the Tantras. In the Tantras three modes of practice for the realization of God, namely, those of the 'animal', the 'hero' and the 'divine' are indicated. Those aspirants in whom the animal feelings of lust, anger etc., prevail are aspirants of the animal mode of worship. They are enjoined to keep away from all objects of temptation, to keep a special eye on external purity and conduct, to engage themselves in the repetition of the Mother's name, Purascharana and the like. The love of God prevails over the animal feelings such as lust, anger etc., in aspirants following the hero-mode. The attractions of lust and gold and objects of sight, taste etc., intensify the love of God in them. They therefore should try to devote their whole mind to the Divine Mother, living in the midst of the temptation of lust and gold and other things, but remaining unperturbed under their action and reaction. They alone can become aspirants of the divine mode of worship in whom lust, anger etc., have for ever been washed away by the strong current of the love of the Divine Mother, and the practice of the good qualities[1] of forgiveness, rectitude of conduct, kindness, contentment, truthfulness, etc., has become natural like inhaling and exhaling. These, in short, are the rough definitions of these three modes of worship. The best, mediocre and lowest aspirants spoken of in the Vedanta are respectively those following the divine, heroic and animal modes described in the Tantras.

20. Although she was the foremost amongst the aspirants following the hero-mode, the Brahmani had not developed even the qualifications for following the divine mode. Having seen the living example of the Master and having got assistance from him, there arose in the Brahmani a strong desire for achieving the qualifications to follow the divine mode. She saw in the Master the following unique characteristics of one established in that mode. As soon as he heard of Siddhi (hemp) or Karana[2], let alone taking either, he became intoxicated with the feeling of his oneness with God, the cause of the universe. As soon as he saw a woman,

---

[1] *The Ashtavakra Samhita.*

[2] The word Karana means; (1) wine, (2) cause, i.e., the cause of the universe; and the word Siddhi means; (1) hemp, (2) perfection, i.e.,

whether chaste or unchaste, he was powerfully drawn to the bliss-giving and nourishing aspects of the Mother of the universe, evoking in his mind the attitude of the child of the Divine Mother. At the touch of gold and other metals, his hands and other limbs got contracted even during deep sleep. In the company of one like the Master—a blazing fire of divine love—who on earth would not have that fire kindled in his own heart? Who would not develop aversion for ephemeral values like wealth and power? Who would not discern that God is our eternal relation, one 'more than our own'? That is why the Brahmani turned a new leaf in her life, devoting the rest of it to the practice of intense austerities.

21.   We have also heard from the Master that the Brahmani felt jealous if he mixed much with anyone else or showed great respect to any other aspirant or devotee of God. Her attitude in this respect was like that of a grandmother in a family who feels distressed on finding that a child whom she had brought up turns his attention in later years to serve some one else in the family. But it was not proper for an aspirant of so high an order as the Brahmani to have such a feeling in her heart. She had had the opportunity of observing the Master day and night for so long a time in all his actions, and she ought to have known from this long and intimate experience with him that the love, respect, etc., of the Master were not momentary and fleeting like those of others. She ought to have known that the love and respect he reposed in her, were reposed for ever and there was no ebb and flow in them. But alas, O worldly love! and O mind of a woman! You always want to bind the object of your love for ever and make him your posses-sion. You do not like to give him the slightest liberty. You think that as soon as the object of your love gets a little liberty, he will not be yours and is sure to love some one else more than you. You do not understand that it is the weakness of your mind that prompts you to think so. You do not understand that the love that does not allow freedom to the object of love and cannot or does not learn to forget itself and feel happy in what that object of love wants, very often evaporates in a short time. So, if you have reposed your heart-felt love in anybody, know

oneness with God. Hence by the law of association of ideas, the Master used to be reminded of the second meanings when the words were uttered, and merged into Samadhi.—Tr.

35

for certain that the object of your love will remain yours only, and that pure love, free from the slightest tinge of selfishness, will, in the end, bring for the object of your love as well as for yourself even the direct vision of God and absolute freedom from all bondage.

22. It is very surprising that although she was an aspirant of a high order, loving God intensely, the Brahmani did not understand this simple matter, or was incapable of assimilating it even if she had understood it. For there was indeed a lack of that conviction in her. Placed fortunately in the position of the spiritual teacher of Sri Ramakrishna, she was developing slowly in her mind such ideas as, 'I am superior to all; they should always obey me; otherwise they will meet with harm.' We are told that she did not even like the Master's teaching the Holy Mother, which he used to do from time to time. We are also told that the Holy Mother used to be always hesitant and afraid of her and would shrink within herself when confronted with such attitudes of the Brahmani. At last, by the grace of the Master, the Brahmani came to realize this weakness of her mind. She realized that if under the circumstances she kept away from him, she would be able to conquer her growing weakness, and that, though the attraction of hers towards the Master was like the tie of a golden chain, she had nevertheless got to break it and go forward along her chosen path. We understand very well that this was why the Brahmani at last left Dakshineswar and the holy company of the Master, and knowing that 'an itinerant Sadhu and flowing water never become polluted'[1], she spent her time in travelling alone from one place of pilgrimage to another and practising austerities. It is needless to say that it was only through the Master's mood of the spiritual teacher that the Brahmani got this awakening.

23. Next let us take the example of Tota Puri, the great Sannyasin who taught the Advaita Vedanta to the Master. Tota Puri was a tall and stalwart figure. He was able to make his mind still and devoid of any functions whatever, in Nirvikalpa Samadhi, as a result of practising mental abstraction and meditation for forty long years in solitude as an all-renouncing ascetic. He

---

[1] This is a saying current among holy men who have renounced the world. The meaning of the saying is that the mind of a holy man wandering incessantly does not get attached to any thing or person.

nevertheless, spent much time daily in practising meditation and Samadhi. The Master referred to him as the 'naked one', as he used always to remain nude, like a boy. Or the Master did so, more probably because one should not always speak the name of one's spiritual teacher or call him by name. The Master said that the 'naked one' never lived in a house and always worshipped fire inasmuch as he belonged to the denomination of the Nagas. The holy men of the Naga denomination look upon fire as very sacred, and that is why they collect wood and keep a fire lighted near them wherever they live. This fire is usually called the Dhuni. Naga holy men offer Arati to the Dhuni every morning and evening and also offer all food obtained as Bhiksha to the fire in the form of the Dhuni, and then eat that offered food. That is why at Dakshineswar, the 'naked one' had his seat under the Panchavati where he resided and kept a Dhuni lighted near him. His Dhuni burnt uniformly in rain or sunshine. It was near the Dhuni that the 'naked one' took his food and rest. When again, forgetting all worries and anxieties, the whole of the external world lay happily at the dead of night in the arms of the rest-giving sleep like a child in its mother's lap, the 'naked one' would get up and make the Dhuni brighter. He would then sit down in a posture steady and firm like Mount Sumeru and merge his mind in Samadhi, restful like the motionless flame of a lamp in a windless place. In daytime also Sri Tota meditated most of the time; but he did it in such a way that people could not know of it. That is why he was very often seen to be lying at full length like a corpse, with his body covered from head to foot with his wearing wrapper. People thought he was sleeping.

24. The 'naked one' kept near him a water-pot and a pair of long tongs only. He had a piece of skin to sit cross-legged on, and he always kept his body covered with a thick wrapper. He polished daily the water-pot and the tongs and kept them glittering. Seeing him practise meditation every day, the Master one day asked him direct, "You have realized Brahman and become perfect; why do you then practise meditation daily?" At this he looked at the Master calmly and pointing with his finger to the water-pot, said, "Don't you see how bright it looks? But what will happen if I don't polish it daily? Will it not lose its lustre? Know that the mind also is like that. The mind also accumulates dirt if it be not polished daily by the practice of meditation." Possessed of a keen

36

insight, the Master accepted the opinion of his 'naked' teacher but queried, "What will be the case if the water-pot be one of gold? Surely it will not then become dirty even if it be not polished every day." Tota smiled and assented, saying, "O yes, it is true indeed!" The Master remembered all his life the words of the 'naked one' regarding the utility of the practice of daily meditation; he quoted him to us on many occasions. And it is our impression that the words of the Mastr, viz., "a golden water-pot never becomes tarnished", were also imprinted for ever in Tota's mind. He was convinced that the mind of the Master was indeed bright like a golden water-pot. Thus from the very beginning a kind of interchange of ideas between the teacher and the disciple used to take place.

25. It is stated in the Vedantic scriptures, that man becomes completely free from fear immediately on the attainment of the knowledge of Brahman, and that it is the only way to be absolutely free from fear. Truly so. For how can a person who has known that he himself is the Self, the indivisible Existence-Knowledge-Bliss Itself, ever pure, ever awakened, all-pervading and devoid of old age and death—how can such a person have in his mind the fear of any thing or person? For whom and how can a person have fear, when in truth he always sees and feels in his heart of hearts that except the One, there is no second thing or person in the world? He feels himself to be the indivisible Existence-Knowledge-Bliss Itself, at all times and in all circumstances, whether eating or drinking, sitting or lying, sleeping or waking. He always feels his eternal and all-pervading existence everywhere and in every being. He feels that he does not eat or drink, walk or rest. dream or sleep. He is always awake. He has no want or abundance, no idleness or activity, no grief or joy, no birth or death, no past or future—in fact he has nothing whatever which a man sees, hears, thinks or imagines with the help of the five senses, the mind and the intellect. It is this experience that the scriptures have described as the last stage in the progress of the discriminative process of 'Not this', 'Not this', beyond which is that infinite Self intuited directly in Samadhi. To have this Self-knowledge always and at every moment of one's life is what is known as being established in the state of identification with the absolute pure Consciousness; and as soon as one is so established , there arises the experience of freedom from all bondage whatsoever. The Master used to say: "When a Jiva realizes this state of being

completely one with that Consciousnes, his body continues for
twenty-one days only, when it falls off like a dry leaf, or in other
words, gets destroyed. And as he never again has this 'I' consciousness, he does not return to this world any more. Again in
contrast to this are the Jivas, described as 'liberated-in-life', who
continue to have at intervals of short periods, this direct realization
of the Self—this experience of being one with pure Consciousness—
until it culminates in the end in their full and final establishment in
the Self. The 'ever free' Iswarakotis, however, born as they are in
this world only to do good to others by establishing some particular
aspect of the Truth, get this experience of being one with pure Consciousness for short periods at intervals even from their very childhood. At last when they have accomplished the work for which
they have come, they merge completely and finally in that absolute
Consciousness. Again, those persons of extraordinary spiritual
powers, about whom the world has so far failed to ascertain whether
they are human beings with exceptional powers or God Himself
embodied and come down on earth to do good to humanity—
those persons, the incarnations of God, can from their every childhood reach at will up to the perfect state of knowledge, stay there as
long as they like, and of their own accord come down again to the
consciousness of this world of ours—the meeting ground of birth
and old age, of joy and sorrow—in order to help Jivas caught up
in the cycle of birth and death."

26. The revered Tota Puri attained the state of being 'liberated
in life' mentioned above as a result of austere spiritual practices
of forty years, and this was why no action of his like eating, resting,
sleeping, wandering, etc., was like that of the common run of human
beings. Like the eternally free wind without any restraint, he used
to roam about freely from place to place. Like the wind, again,
he was untouched by the good or evil of the world, and like the
very wind he could not remain confined in any place; for, we have
heard from the Master that Tota would not stay more than three
days in one place. On account of the Master's wonderful attraction,
Tota, however, lived continuously for eleven months at Dakshineswar. Ah, what a charm the Master had!

27. The Master said many things to us about Tota's fearlessness. Amongst them there was a strange event concerning a
spirit. On one occasion at the dead of night Tota made the Dhuni
bright and was ready to sit for meditation. The surroundings

were calm, without the slightest noise. No sound reached the ear except the chirping of crickets and sometimes the deep hooting of the owls living in the holes of the pinnacles of the temples. There was also no stir in the wind. The branches of the trees of the Panchavati suddenly shook and a tall human form came down from the tree to the ground, and looking steadfastly at Tota, came with slow steps to the place of the Dhuni and sat down there. Surprised to see that personage, naked like himself, Tota asked him who he was. The person replied, "I am a Bhairava (a demigod). I reside here upon the tree for the purpose of protecting this holy place." Tota was not at all afraid and said, "Very well, you and I are the same being, you are one manifestation of Brahman, and I am another. Come, sit down and meditate." The person laughed out and vanished, as it were, into the air. The 'naked one' also was not at all perturbed by this event; he applied his mind to meditation. The next morning Tota related the incident to the Master. The Master replied, "Yes, it is true, he lives here. I have also met him many times. He sometimes predicted certain future events to me. At one time the Company (Government of India) tried to acquire the whole plot of the Panchavati for the purpose of building a powder magazine. Hearing of the proposal, I was much worried lest I should lose the opportunity of sitting and calling on the Mother in this place away from the noise and turmoil of the world. Mathur instituted a case against the Company on behalf of Rani Rasmani to prevent the acquisition of the piece of land. At that time, one day I saw the Bhairava sitting on the tree. He said to me, by a sign, that the Company would not be able to acquire the land; they would be defeated in the case. It actually came to pass."

28. We have not heard anything from the Master about the exact place of Tota's birth in the north-west part of the country. The Master also perhaps did not think it necessary to ask him about it. Generally, if questioned about the details of their pre-Sannyasin life—their names, birthplaces, etc.,—monks do not mention them. They say, "To put these questions to monks and for monks to answer them are both forbidden by the scriptures." This is why, perhaps, the Master never asked the 'naked one' that question. But, while travelling in the north-western part of India after the Master had passed away, the Master's Sannyasin disciples of the monastery at Belur made enquiries of old Paramahamsas

and came to know that the said Puri was born at some place in
or near the Punjab. The monastery of his spiritual teacher was
at Ludhiana, a place near Kurukshetra. His teacher also was a
famous Yogi and a monastery was established there. It is not
clearly known whether that monastery was founded by him or
by any one of his predecessors. But the old monks told the disciples of the Master that Tota Puri's teacher was the Mohanta
the head of that monastery, and that even then there used to be
held an annual fair there, where the people of the neighbouring
villages assembled in his honour. As he used to smoke tobacco,
the villagers even now bring tobacco during the fair and make a
present of it to his 'community'. It was Tota Puri who was installed
as the head of that Math after the passing away of his teacher.

29. It seems from the words of Tota Puri himself that he
was taught the Vedanta even in his boyhood by his own teacher,
the head of the community of monks. He lived with him for a
long time, studying the scriptures and practising Sadhanas. He
told the Master that there lived in their community seven hundred
monks and they daily practised, according to their teacher's instruction, meditation and other spiritual exercises in order to realize in
their lives the truths that are hidden in the Vedanta. Tota Puri
gave the Master some indication of the very odd method of
teaching meditation and other spiritual exercises in that community.
The Master spoke about it on many occasions for our instruction.
He said, "The 'naked one' used to say that there were seven hundred
such spiritual aspirants in their community. Those who were
beginning to learn meditation were asked to do so on cushions;
for, they might feel an ache in their legs if they were to sit and
meditate on hard seats and their unaccustomed minds might come
to think of their bodies instead of God. Then afterwards, the
deeper their meditation became the harder were the seats on which
they had to sit. And at last they had to sit on a piece of skin
only or on the bare ground to practise meditation. They were
also made to observe strict rules in all matters concerning their
daily life. As regards their dress, the disciples were also made
to practise gradually how to remain naked. As man is bound by
the eight fetters of shame, hatred, fear, egoism regarding one's
birth, lineage, custom, status and so on, they were taught to give
them up one by one. Afterwards, when they developed deep
concentration of mind, they had to go out and travel from one

place of pilgrimage to another, at first with other monks, and later alone, and then return. The 'naked monks' had such rules." The Master was told by Sri Puri of the practice of electing their President (Mohanta). The Master said to us one day in the course of conversation: "That one alone, who was found amongst the naked monks to have attained the true state of a Paramahamsa, was elected by all to the seat of the Mohanta of the community when it fell vacant. Otherwise, how could the elected person remain true to his vows when he would command so much money, respect and power? He would then surely have his headturned. That is why they placed on the Mohant's seat only a person who had no attraction for gold. He had to take charge of large amounts of money and other valuable property. It was such a person alone that could be trusted to spend that wealth rightly in the service of God and holy men."

30. From these words it becomes very clear that Tota Puri was from his childhood brought up under the affectionate care of his teacher as if in a heavenly realm, far from worldly attachments, delusion, jealousy, hatred and the like. In the north-western parts of this country there is a custom of couples without issue vowing that they would make a Sannyasin of their child if one were born, and thus offer him for the service of God. They actually carried out their promise always. Was the revered Puri offered to his teacher that way? It is inferred to be so, as he never mentioned anything about his parents, brothers, sisters and others of his pre-monastic life.

31. As a result of the impressions arising out of virtuous actions done in the past, the mind of the saint was endowed with a simple and sincere faith. Acharya Sankara has written in the very beginning of his *Viveka-chudamani* (1.2) that the attainment of all the three things together, namely, a human birth, a yearning for the realization of God, and the refuge in a teacher who is a knower of Brahman, is very rare in the world. It is not possible to attain them without the grace of the Divine Lord. Not only did the saintly Puri fortunately get all those three opportunities together, but he could put them to proper use and attain liberation, the ultimate aim of human life. His mind assimilated his teacher's instructions and used always to carry them out in practice exactly according to his teaching. He does not seem to have suffered

much from the deception and hypocrisy of the mind.   There is a saying amongst the Vaishnavas, "The three, namely, the spiritual teacher, the chosen Ideal and the devotees may indeed be kind to man, but if he has not the kindness of 'one', he is sent to rack and ruin."   Here 'one' means one's own mind.   If the mind is not kind, man is ruined. We do not think that the saint Puri had to suffer at the hands of such a 'rascally' type of mind.   His simple mind reposed its trust in God sincerely and was going forward slowly along the path pointed out by his teacher. While it was going forward, it never cast behind a single covetous glance, prompted by any ungratified wish, towards the sins and temptations of the world.   That was why the saint came to the conviction that his individual effort, perseverance, self-reliance and self-confidence were all in all.   Ah! The saint did not know that when the mind became self-willed or refractory, its effort was washed away like a bundle of straw before a strong current of water.   He did not know that in the place of that self-reliance and self-confidence, there would come a terrible diffidence regarding one's own power, making one weaker than a worm.   The circumstances of his life being naturally favourable to spiritual development, he could never believe that it was by God's grace alone that such an advantage was possible, and that without that, all the efforts of man would only produce contrary results, involving him in bondages of greater complication.   And why should he not think so?   All his life he was able to do whatever he undertook.   He was able at all times to carry into practice in his own life whatever he thought to be good for man.   Therefore, it is doubtful if the saint could even imagine that man could ever be in the state where his "intellect understands but the heart does not yield".   He had never the occasion to experience the conflicting situation in which the heart incessantly felt the stings of a hundred scorpions, as it were, for failing to make "words (and actions) correspond to one's thought".   Nor did he ever experience the sufferings arising from a thousand lurking tendencies of the mind urging one to carry out their vicious whims, or from every one of the senses being in revolt against one's conscience or higher understanding, driving one to a state of terrible despondency.   Or even if he knew it, still there was a great difference between 'learning by hearing, learning by seeing, and learning by actual bitter experience'.   There was therefore a world of difference between the imaginative mental picture of suffering that the saint might have had in his mind and what a man in the throes of actual protracted suffering felt. That is why the saint Puri was quite ignorant of the influence of the beginningless Avidya Maya, the power of Brahman, that was difficult to overcome. For this reason he was capable only of a hard-hearted aversion for man's failings instead of any sympathy for him in his helpless predicament in life. He was corrected in this respect only after his contact with the Master in his divine mood as the teacher of men. In his company experience convinced him of the dominating power of Maya over men, as also of the identity of Brahman and Brahma Sakti (Power of Brahman). Having learnt this lesson, he bowed down his head in devotion to the Divine Mother and bade good-bye to Dakshineswar. We shall now begin to describe these events.

32. An austere man of renunciation, observing continence from his childhood, Tota had indeed the impression, as already remarked by the Brahmani, that the path of devotion to God was a fantastic one. He did not realize that love and devotion could teach man gradually to renounce everything, including his own happiness, for the sake of his beloved, and lead him on ultimately to the realization of God; that in the ultimate development of his devotion, a true devotee and Sadhaka acquired the capacity of attaining the knowledge of perfect non-duality; and that Japa, glorifying the excellences of the Lord in songs and praises, chanting His name and practising other auxiliaries of devotional Sadhana were not therefore to be scoffed at. It is for this reason that the saint sometimes ridiculed the devotional acts performed under the influence of great spiritual fervour. The reader, however, must not understand from this that the revered Puri was a sort of an atheist or that he had no love for God. Possessed of the control of the internal and external senses and other virtues auxiliary to his Sadhana, the revered saint himself had a calm nature and his devotion to God belonged to the Santa or calm mood. He could understand in others only that kind of devotion to God. But it never entered the mind of Sri Puri that one could attain to the Supreme Being directly and with equal speed by loving Him, the Maker of the universe, through the personal form of love as one's own master, friend, son, or husband. The devotee's compelling appeals to God under the influence of his loving mood, his feeling of separation, his great yearning, his pique and egoism, all centring

on God, as also the physical expression of this in laughing, weeping, etc., under the influence of unrestrained divine sentiments—all these Sri Puri could not but regard as the incoherent talks or whims and antics of mad people. Nor could he ever imagine that an aspirant of this nature might quickly attain the desired result with the help of these love-inspired sentiments. Therefore, there used to take place on many occasions a loving conflict of views between the Master and Tota Puri regarding men's heart-felt devotion to the Mother of the universe, the Power of Brahman, and the unrestrained emotionalism resulting from it.

33. It was a habit with the Master from his childhood to clap his hands morning and evening for a short time and sometimes to dance under the influence of devotional moods, as he went on chanting loudly the excellences of the Lord such as these: "Call on Hari, call on Hari. Hari is the Teacher, the Teacher is Hari. Ah! Govinda , my vital force, my life! The mind is Krishna, the vital force is Krishna, knowledge is Krishna, meditation is Krishna, consciousness is Krishna, the intellect is Krishna. Thou art the universe, the universe is in Thee. I am a machine, Thou art the operator." He used to do so daily even after the attainment of Nirvikalpa Samadhi and the acquisition of the knowledge of Non-duality. One afternoon, sitting near Sri Puri, he was engaged in conversation with him till it was dusk. Seeing it was dusk, the Master stopped all conversation and started chanting the names and excellences of the Lord accompanied with clapping of hands. Seeing him do so, Tota Puri became surprised and wondered why a person, whose exceptional fitness for Vedantic discipline brought him Nirvikalpa Samadhi in such a short time, should practise such Bhakti disciplines meant, as he thought, for men at the lowest rung of spiritual development. And he sarcastically remarked, "Are you fashioning Chapatis by clapping your hands!" He was just ridiculing this type of Bhakti discipline by the allusion to the way in which Chapatis are made, discarding the use of rolling pin and plank, by people in North-Western India, who shape the dough with the pressure of their two palms, producing a clapping sound in the process. In response, the Master laughed and said, "What foolishness! I am taking the names of God, and you say I am fashioning Chapatis!" At this straight and simple answer of the Master without any sting, Sri Puri also laughed, realizing that such an act of the Master might

not be meaningless, though its hidden meaning was not clear to him. It was better not to pass a remark on what he did not understand.

34. On another occasion the Master was sitting after dusk near Sri Puri's Dhuni. In the course of conversation about God the minds of both the Master and the saint ascended to a very high plane and were about to merge in the non-dual knowledge. As the flames in the Dhuni blazed, it looked as if it was throbbing with the sense of its self being one with theirs, and sending up its numerous tongues as a blissful smile in appreciation of this fact! Just at that time a servant of the garden wanted to have a smoke, and preparing tobacco in his bowl, came up there for some charcoal fire and started taking it by putting a piece of burning wood from the Dhuni into his bowl. Merged in conversation with the Master and enjoying the bliss of the non-dual Brahman within, the saint had not so long been aware of his coming and taking charcoal fire from the Dhuni. Now all of a sudden he noticed that, and extremely annoyed and angry, began to call him names and shook the pair of tongs at him threateningly. For, as we have already said, the holy men of the Naga denominations worship and show great respect to the Element Fire in the form of Dhuni.

Bursting into a roar of laughter in a semi-conscious mood, the Master exclaimed at this behaviour of Sri Puri, "Ah, wretchedness! Ah, forgetfulness!" He said it over and over again, laughed and rolled on the ground. Tota was surprised to see that mood of the Master and said, "Why are you doing like that? Don't you see how wrong it was on the part of the man?" The Master laughed and said, "Yes that is true; but I see at the same time the depth of your knowledge of Brahman! Just now you were saying, 'There is nothing except Brahman and all things and persons in the universe are merely Its manifestations.' But forgetting everything the very next moment, you are ready to beat a man! This is why I laugh, thinking of the omnipotence of Maya." Hearing this, Tota became serious and silent for a short time and then said, "You are quite right. Under the influence of anger I forgot everything indeed! Anger is surely very reprehensible. I give it up this very moment." As a matter of fact, since that day the saint was never seen to be angry again.

35. The Master used to say, 'Caught in the net of the five elements, Brahman weeps.' You may shut your eyes and try to persuade yourself that there is no thorn and no prick, but as soon

as the hand touches the thorn, it hurts and you cry out in pain. Similarly, you may do your best to persuade your mind that you have no birth or death, no vice or virtue, no pain or pleasure, no hunger or thirst—that you are the immutable Self, Existence-Knowledge-Bliss Absolute Itself. But as soon as your body falls a prey to some disease, you forget all about your immutable Self; or if your mind is attracted by the pull of lust for objects of enjoyment and of greed for gold, you are forced to do evil, unable to resist the temptations that confront you. Delusion, anguish, pain and the like crop up and harass you very much, making you forget all your discrimination and carefully-drawn conclusions. Therefore, know it for certain, my child, that no one can have Self-knowledge and be freed from the misery of the world till the grace of God descends on him and Maya opens the door to liberation and moves away. Have you not read in the *Chandi*,[1] 'When She becomes gracious, She confers the boon of liberation on people'? Nothing is possible if Mother does not bestow Her grace and move away from the path.

36. "Rama, Sita and Lakshmana were going through the forest. The path in the forest was narrow—not even two could go abreast. Rama walked in front with bow in hand; Sita followed; and Lakshmana came after her with bow and arrows. Lakshmana had so much devotion to, and love for, Rama that he had a desire in his mind always to see his form, blue in complexion, like, a newly formed cloud. But as Sita was between them, he could not see Rama as they were walking, and so became anxious to see him. The intelligent Sita understood it, and sympathizing with Lakshmana in his sorrow, moved a little to one side and said to him, 'There—see!' It was then that Lakshmana saw to his heart's content the form of Rama, his Chosen Ideal. Similarly, Maya, represented by Sita, stands between the Jiva and Isvara. Know it for certain that the Jiva who is represented by Lakshmana cannot see God till, feeling sympathy with him, She moves to one side. The moment She bestows Her grace, the Jiva is blessed with a vision of Narayana, represented by Rama in the example, and he is relieved from all the trials and tribulations of the world. Otherwise, however much you may discriminate and draw logical conclusions, it would be of no avail. It is said that one grain of ptychotis digests

---

[1] 1.56.

one hundred grains of rice; but when there is a disorder in the stomach even one hundred grains of ptychotis cannot digest a single grain of rice. This is a good analogy."

37. Swami Tota Puri was a recipient of the grace of the Mother of the universe from his birth. He was in possession, from his childhood, of good impressions, a sincere mind, the company of a great Yogi, and a firm and strong body. Maya, the power of the Lord, did not show him her dreadful and all-devouring form, horrible as the shadow of death; nor did she draw him into the snares of Her bewitching forms of spiritual ignorance. Therefore, it became an easy affair for him to go forward with the help of his individual effort and perseverance, attain Nirvikalpa Samadhi, realize God, and acquire Self-knowledge. How could he understand that the Divine Mother Herself had removed all obstacles and impediments with Her own hands from the path of his progress and Herself moved away from it? Now, after so long a time, the Mother was pleased to explain it to Swami Puri. He now got the opportunity of detecting that mistake of his mind.

38. The revered Puri had the robust physique found in the north-western parts of India. He never knew what illness, indigestion and a hundred other kinds of bodily indispositions were. Whatever he ate he digested. He was never in want of deep sleep wherever he was. And mental bliss and peace arising from the knowledge and direct realization of God flowed in his mind in incessant streams in a hundred channels. Attracted by the love and respect of the Master, he had stayed with him for a few months; but the water of Bengal, and its warm and dense air full of humidity told upon his health, and his firm body fell an easy prey to illness. He had a severe attack of blood dysentery. On account of the wringing pain in the intestines day and night, his mind, although calm and tranquil and accustomed to Samadhi, moved away from its abidance in Brahman and came down to body-consciousness. "Brahman has been caught in the net of the five elements"; what was the way out now except the grace of the Divine Mother, the ruler over all!

39. For some time, before he fell ill, his watchful mind poised in Brahman had made it known to him that inasmuch as the body was not keeping well, it was not reasonable that he should

remain any longer there.   But should he go away out of love for his body, leaving behind the wonderful company of the Master? The body was a "cage made of bones and flesh", full of blood and other filthy fluids and abounding in various kinds of germs and worms.   Its very existence has been asserted in the Vedanta Sastra to be a delusion.   And looking upon such a body as "mine", should he go away hurriedly forsaking the company of that divine man, the source of infinite bliss?   And what was the good of going elsewhere—was it not possible that the diseases of the body and other kinds of trouble could occur anywhere?   And what fear had he, even if diseases and other troubles came upon him?   It was the body that would suffer, become emaciated, or at the most get destroyed.   But what was that to him?   He had, without the shadow of a doubt, seen and felt clearly that he was the Self unattached and immutable, and he had never any relation with the body; what should he then be afraid of? These and other similar thoughts saved the revered Puri from being restless.

40. Gradually, as the pain increased a little, the strong Swami Puri felt a desire to leave the place.   He went to the Master from time to time to take leave of him, but absorbed in talks on divine topics, he forgot completely to mention that.   And when he happened to remember to take leave of the Master, some one from within, he felt, stopped his mouth for the time being. Feeling hesitant to speak out, the Swami thought that he would better talk of it on the morrow and not on that day.   After taking such a decision and having had a conversation on the Vedanta with the Master, the Swami Tota would return to his seat under the Panchavati. Time passed.   The Swami's body became weaker and the disease grew more acute.   Seeing that the Swami's body was thus daily becoming emaciated, the Master had in the mean-time made arrangements for his special diet and a little medicine and other remedies.   But, in spite of all that, the illness went on worsening. The Master began to take care of him and serve him to the best of his power.   He asked Mathur to make a special arrangement for medicine and diet for him.   Up till now it was only in the body that the Swami felt much pain.   He had perfect peace of mind. He could forget all physical pains by merging the mind at will in Samadhi; for, up till then, he retained full control over his mind.

41. It was night.   The pain in the intestines had very much increased.   That pain did not allow the Swami even to lie quiet.

He tried to lie down a little but could not, and sat up immediately. There was no relief even then. He thought, "Let me merge the mind in meditation and let anything happen to the body." But scarcely had he brought the mind to rest by its withdrawal from the body, when it turned sharply towards the pain in the intestines. He tried again and again, but with little success. Hardly had the mind reached the plane of Samadhi where the body was forgotten, when it came down on account of the pain. He failed as many times as he attempted. The Swami then became terribly annoyed with his own body. He thought, "Even my mind is not under my control today on account of the trouble from this 'cage of bones and flesh'. Away with this nuisance of a body! I have undoubtedly known that I am not the body; why do I then remain in this rotten body and suffer pain? What is the utility of preserving it any more? I will put an end to all suffering by immersing it in the Ganga at this dead of night." Thinking so and fixing the mind with great care on the thought of Brahman, the 'naked one' slowly got down into the water and gradually waded farther into deeper water. But was the deep Bhagirathi in truth dry that night? Or was it only the external projection of his mental picture? Who could say? Tota almost reached the other bank but could not get water deep enough for drowning himself in. When, gradually, at last the trees and houses on the other bank began to be visible like shadows in the deep darkness of the night, Tota was surprised and thought, "What strange Divine Maya is this? Tonight there is not sufficient water in the river even to drown oneself in! What a strange unheard-of play of God?" And immediately some one, as it were from within, pulled off the veil over his intellect. Tota's mind was dazzled by a bright light and he saw, "Mother, Mother, Mother, Mother, the origin of the universe! Mother, the unthinkable Power! Mother in land and Mother in water! The body is Mother and the mind is Mother; illness is Mother, and health is Mother; knowledge is Mother and ignorance is Mother; life is Mother and death is Mother; everything I see, hear, think or imagine is Mother. She makes 'nay' of 'yea' and 'yea' of 'nay'! As long as one is in the body one has no power to be free from Her influence, no, not even to die, till She wills! It is that Mother again who is also beyond body, mind and intellect—the Mother, the supreme 'Fourth', devoid of all attributes! That One whom Tota has so long been realising as Brahman, to whom he has been offering his heart-felt love and devotion, is this very Mother! Siva and Sakti are One, ever existing in the form of Hara-Gauri!—Brahman and Brahma-Sakti are one and the same!"

42.   Wading his way through the water in the same manner in which he had gone, Tota now started back to the shore. His heart was now full of devotion. He felt that all the quarters were reverberating with cries—Mother! Mother! At the dead of night he had directly realised the Mother of the universe in Her all-pervading form, beyond the ken of the senses and the sense-bound intellect. He had offered himself completely as an oblation at Her feet. Though there was pain in the body, there was now no feeling of it. His heart was now beside itself with an unprecedented bliss arising from the memory of Samadhi. The Swami came slowly to the Dhuni under the Panchavati, sat there, and spent the rest of the night in meditation and repetition of the name of the Divine Mother.

43.   As soon as it was morning, the Master came to enquire about his health and found him a different person altogether. His face was beaming with bliss, lips blooming with a smile, and his body, free from all illness whatever. Tota asked the Master by a sign to sit near him and described slowly all the events of the night. "It is the disease," he said, "that has acted as a friend to me. I had the vision of the Mother of the universe last night and am freed from the disease by Her grace. Ah, how ignorant I was so long! Well, please persuade your Mother now to allow me to leave this place. I am now convinced that it was She who kept me confined here somehow or other in order to teach me this Truth. It cannot be otherwise; for I thought long ago of going away from this place, and went to you over and over again to take leave of you. But some one, as it were, diverted my mind to other topics and prevented me every time from mentioning it to you." The Master said smilingly, "Well, you did not accept the Mother before and argued with me saying that Sakti was unreal! But you have now seen Her yourself, and direct experience has now got the better of your arguments. She has convinced me already of the fact that just as fire and its burning power are not different, so, Brahman and the power of Brahman are not different, but one and the same."

44.   When they heard the morning tunes from the Nahabat,

both the great souls, bound to each other in the relation of teacher
and disciple like Siva and Rama, stood up, went to the temple of
the Divine Mother, and prostrated themselves before Her holy
image.   Both of them felt in their heart of hearts that the Mother
was pleased and had graciously given Tota permission to leave
that place.   A few days later, he took leave of the Master, left
the Dakshineswar Kali temple and started westward.   This was
his first and last visit to that temple.   He never again went there.

45.   One word more, and we shall have said everything we
heard from the Master himself about Tota Puri.   Puri believed
in alchemy.   Not only did he have a belief but said to the Master
that he, by virtue of that knowledge, had converted on several
occasions copper and other baser metals into gold.   Tota used to
say that the ancient Paramahamsas of his community knew the
art and he inherited the knowledge from them lineally.   He said
besides, "It is completely forbidden to serve one's selfish interest
or enjoy luxury with the help of this art.   There is the curse of
the teachers on such use.   But there live in the community many
holy men, and the head of the community has sometimes to go
with them from one place of pilgrimage to another.   At that time
arrangements have to be made for their food and other necessaries
of life.   The teachers have, however, allowed us to make use of
this knowledge for that purpose, if we are ever in need of money."[1]

1More information on Tota Puri and his monastery is given in an
article on the subject in the 1977 November issue of the *Prabuddha
Bharata* by Swami Alokananda.   The following facts are gleaned from
the results of his research (1962) published therein: Tota Puri's Math
is not at Ludhiana near Kurukshetra, but in the village Ladhana in
Karnal Dist., about 56 miles from Ambala.   It is called Baba Rajpuri
Math after its founder.   Though once a prosperous institution, it is now
in a dilapidated and poverty-striken condition.   It has only three inmates,
and they take only one meal a day for want of funds.   Situated at a very
lonely spot, the campus has a large number of Samadhis of dead monks.
There are five temples there, one for keeping the Dhuni, and the others
as memorials on the Samadhis of some important Gurus.   One of these
is on Tota Puri's Samadhi.   The present head is a very old man, named
Badri Puri.   The exact name of Tota Puri's Guru could not be ascertained,
although the Guru-cum-disciple line is given thus, as if in descending order:
Marhi Bhagawan Puri, Jagmohan Puri, Janged Puri, Hardwar Puri,
Mansa Puri, Saraswati Puri, Raj Puri, Siddha Puri, Bhandar Puri, Dalel
Puri, Aan Puri, Tota Puri, Chaitanya Puri, Hazari Puri, Gopal Puri,

46. It is thus that the Bhairavi Brahmani and the Brahman-knower Tota Puri were blessed, having reached perfection in their particular paths with the help of the Master as the spiritual teacher. We can also very well infer from this that the other subsidiary spiritual teachers of the Master were also similarly imbued with spiritual catholicity with his help.

Kedar Puri, Badri Puri, and Shyam Puri. Beyond this, nothing more could be known about the sacred Ashrama where once Srimat Tota Puri lived.—*Publisher.*

46.   It is thus that the Bharavi Brahmana and the Brahmana-known Tota Puri were blessed, having reached perfection in their particular paths with the help of the Master as the spiritual teacher. We can also very well infer from this that the other subsidiary spiritual teachers of the Master were also similarly blessed with spiritual enfoldment with his help.

Kedar Puri, Baba Puri, and Swami Puri. Beyond this, nothing more could be known about the sacred Ashrama where once Srimat Tota Puri lived. — Prabhakar.